Publisher
Jim Scheikofer
The Family Handyman®

Director, Publication Services
Sue Pohlman
Home Design Alternatives, Inc.

Editor
Kim Karsanbhai
Home Design Alternatives, Inc.

Newsstand Sales
David Algire
Reader's Digest Association, Inc.

John Crouse
Reader's Digest Association, Inc.

Marketing Manager
Andrea Vecchio
The Family Handyman

Production Manager
Judy Rodriguez
The Family Handyman

Plans Administrator
Curtis Cadenhead
Home Design Alternatives, Inc.

The Family Handyman®

Vol. 17, No. 6

MW00908177

Contents

Featured Homes

Plan #702-0141 is featured on page 90.
Photo courtesy of Home Design Alternatives, Inc., St. Louis, MO

Plan #702-CHP-3054-B-3 is featured on page 201.
Photo courtesy of Chatham Home Plans, Mobile, AL

Sections

Home Plans	**2-299**
Our Blueprint Packages Include...	**16**
What Kind of Plan Package Do You Need? Other Helpful Building Aids	**17**
Home Plans Index	**18**
To Order Home Plans	**19**
Quick & Easy Customizing	**20**
Shed and Garage Project Plans	**300-319**
Shed and Garage Project Order Form	**320**

The Family Handyman magazine and Home Design Alternatives (HDA, Inc.) are pleased to join together to bring you this collection of home plans with Southern Accents from some of the nation's leading designers and architects.

Technical Specifications - At the time the construction drawings were prepared, every effort was made to ensure that these plan and specifications meet nationally recognized building codes (BOCA, Southern Building Code Congress and others). Because national building codes change or vary from area to area some drawing modifications and/or the assistance of a professional designer or architect may be necessary to comply with your local codes or to accommodate specific building conditions. We advise you to consult with your local building official for information regarding codes governing your area.

On The Cover . . .

Kitchen

Foyer/Dining Room

Living Room

Study

Master Bedroom

Plan #702-CHP-4156-A-1 is featured on page 263.
Photos by Chatham Home Plans; Mobile, AL Steve Gorum, photographer

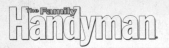

Plan #702-0174

Quaint Exterior, Full Front Porch

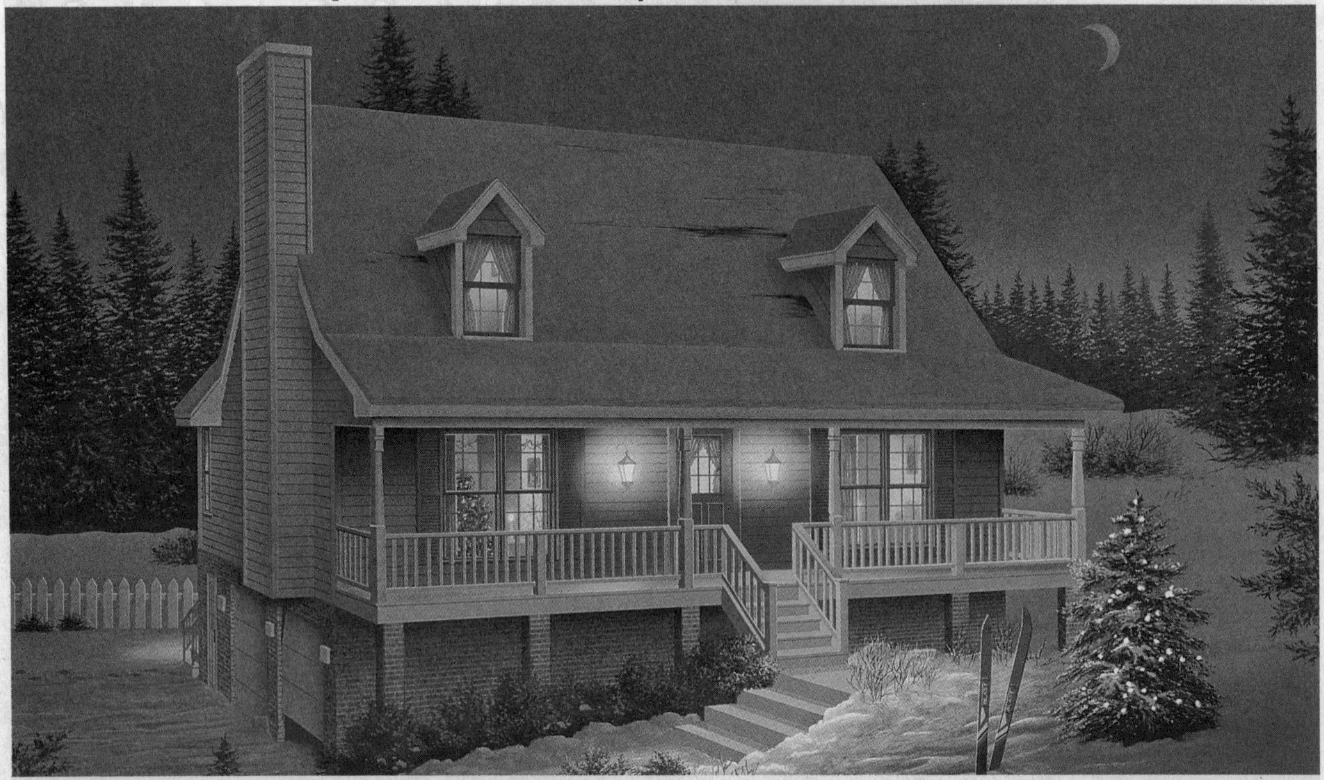

1,657 total square feet of living area **Price Code B**

Special features

- Stylish pass-through between living and dining areas
- Master bedroom is secluded from living area for privacy
- Large windows in breakfast and dining areas
- 3 bedrooms, 2 1/2 baths, 2-car drive under garage
- Basement foundation

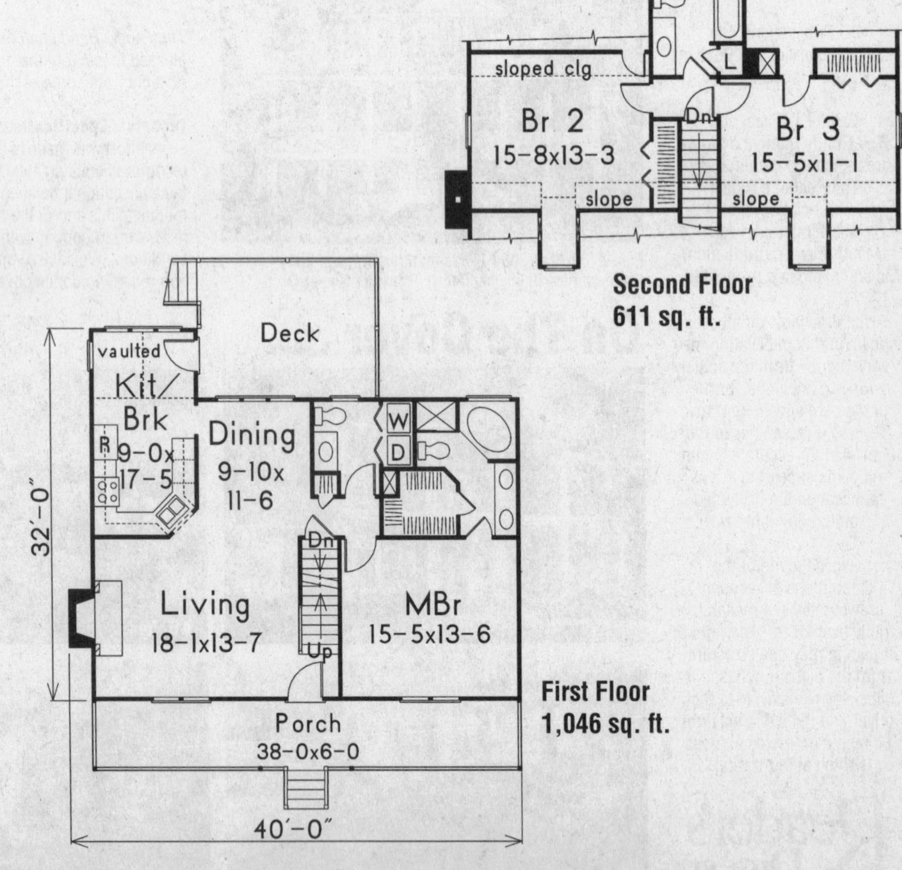
sloped clg
L
Dn
Br 2
15-8x13-3
Br 3
15-5x11-1
slope
slope
Second Floor
611 sq. ft.
Deck
vaulted
Kit
Brk
9-0x
17-5
R
Dining
9-10x
11-6
W
D
Dn
Living
18-1x13-7
Up
MBr
15-5x13-6
Porch
38-0x6-0
32'-0"
40'-0"
First Floor
1,046 sq. ft.

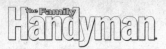

Plan #702-0138

Impressive Victorian Blends Charm And Efficiency

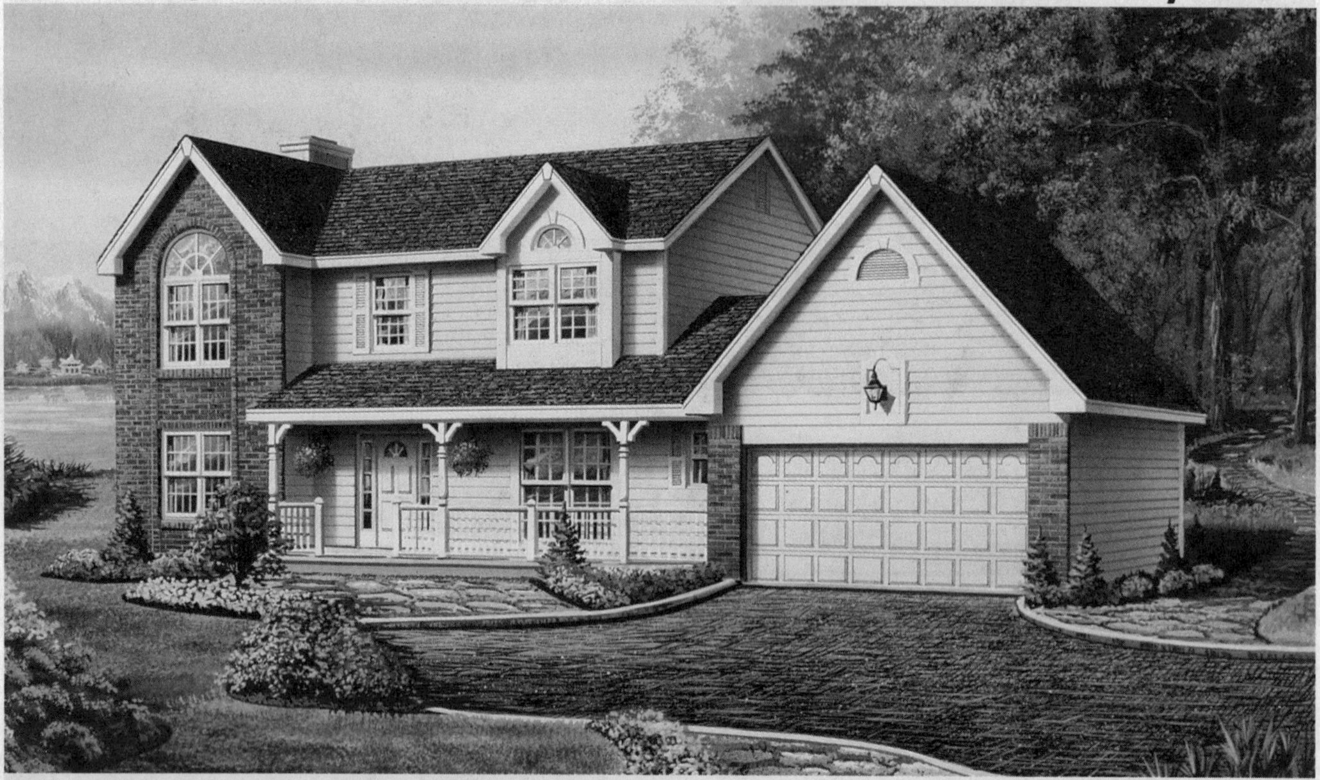

2,286 total square feet of living area

Price Code E

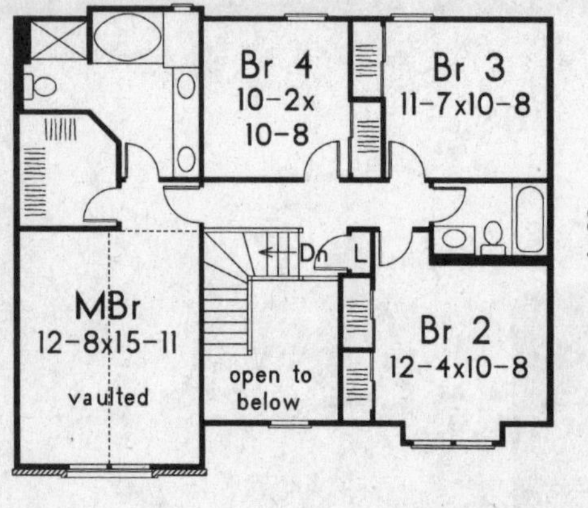
Br 4
10-2x
10-8
Br 3
11-7x10-8
Dn
L
MBr
12-8x15-11
vaulted
open to
below
Br 2
12-4x10-8

Second Floor
1,003 sq. ft.

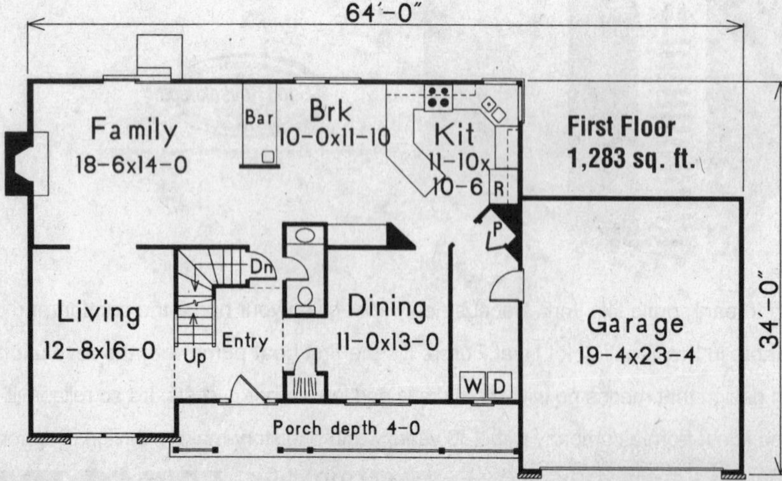
64'-0"
Family
18-6x14-0
Bar
Brk
10-0x11-10
Kit
11-10x
10-6
R
P
Dn
Living
12-8x16-0
Up
Entry
Dining
11-0x13-0
W
D
Garage
19-4x23-4
34'-0"
Porch depth 4-0

First Floor
1,283 sq. ft.

Special features

- Fine architectural detail makes this home a showplace with its large windows, intricate brick-work and fine woodwork and trim
- Stunning two-story entry with attractive wood railing and balustrades in foyer
- Convenient wrap-around kitchen with window view, planning center and pantry
- Oversized master suite with walk-in closet and master bath
- 4 bedrooms, 2 1/2 baths, 2-car garage
- Basement foundation, drawings also include crawl space and slab foundations

Plan #702-1305

Extra Amenities Enhance Living

2,009 total square feet of living area

Price Code C

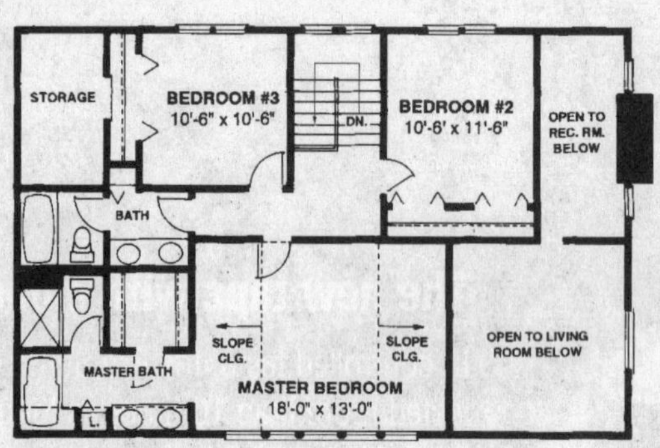
STORAGE
BEDROOM #3
10'-6" x 10'-6"
DN.
BEDROOM #2
10'-6' x 11'-6"
OPEN TO
REC. RM.
BELOW
BATH
SLOPE
CLG.
SLOPE
CLG.
OPEN TO LIVING
ROOM BELOW
MASTER BATH
MASTER BEDROOM
18'-0" x 13'-0"

Second Floor
847 sq. ft.

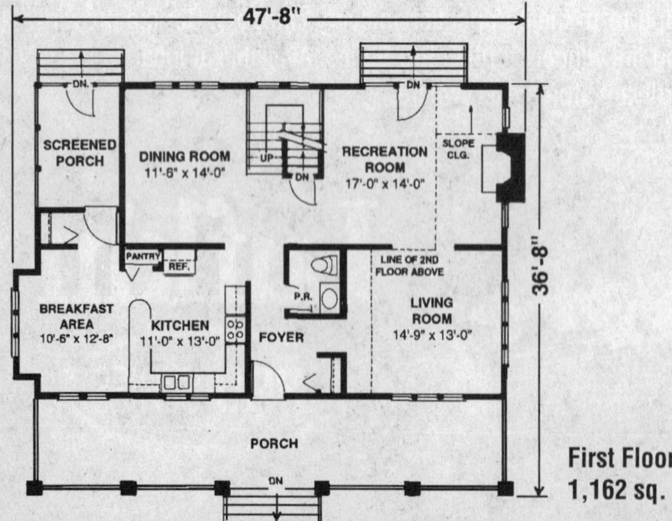
47'-8"
DN.
DN
SCREENED
PORCH
DINING ROOM
11'-6" x 14'-0"
UP
DN
RECREATION
ROOM
17'-0" x 14'-0"
SLOPE
CLG.
PANTRY
REF.
LINE OF 2ND
FLOOR ABOVE
36'-8"
P.R.
BREAKFAST
AREA
10'-6" x 12'-8"
KITCHEN
11'-0" x 13'-0"
FOYER
LIVING
ROOM
14'-9" x 13'-0"
PORCH
DN

First Floor
1,162 sq. ft.

Special features

- Spacious master bedroom has dramatic sloped ceiling and private bath with double sinks and walk-in closet
- Bedroom #3 has extra storage inside closet
- Versatile screened porch is ideal for entertaining year-round
- Sunny breakfast area located near kitchen and screened porch for convenience
- 3 bedrooms, 2 1/2 baths
- Basement foundation

TO ORDER BLUEPRINTS USE THE FORM ON PAGE 19 OR CALL TOLL-FREE 1-877-671-6036

View thousands more home plans online at www.familyhandyman.com/homeplans

Rubbermaid
TOUGH TOOLS™
Introducing Rubbermaid Tough Tools
and the handy new Picture Hanging Kit.
So convenient and tough it makes hanging pictures
possibly too easy. You'll find this new assortment of
Rubbermaid Tough Tools at your local Wal-Mart.®
There you can Feel The Difference.™
GUARANTEED FOR
LIFE

Incredible Designs to
Master Your Dreams.

The Family
Handyman

Plan #702-0298

Columns And Dormers Grace Stylish Exterior

3,216 total square feet of living area

Price Code F

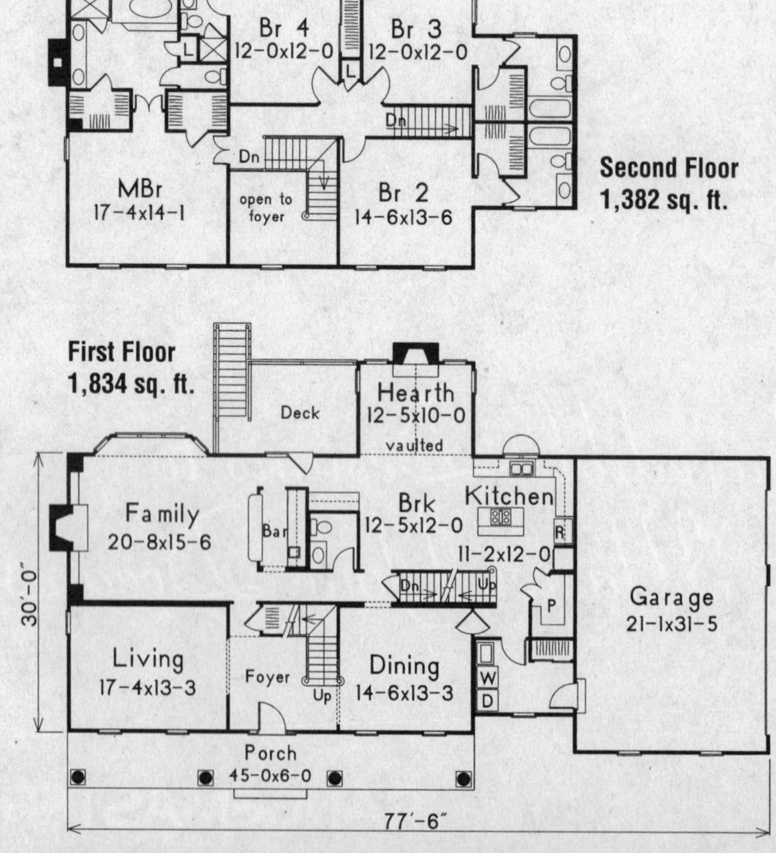
Br 4
12-0x12-0
Br 3
12-0x12-0
L
L
Dn
Dn
MBr
17-4x14-1
open to
foyer
Br 2
14-6x13-6
Second Floor
1,382 sq. ft.
First Floor
1,834 sq. ft.
Deck
Hearth
12-5x10-0
vaulted
Family
20-8x15-6
Bar
Brk
12-5x12-0
Kitchen
11-2x12-0
R
Dn
Up
P
Garage
21-1x31-5
30'-0"
Living
17-4x13-3
Foyer
Up
Dining
14-6x13-3
W
D
Porch
45-0x6-0
77'-6"

Special features

- All bedrooms include private full baths
- Hearth room and combination kitchen/breakfast area create large informal gathering area
- Oversized family room boasts fireplace, wet bar and bay window
- Master bath with double walk-in closets and luxurious bath
- 4 bedrooms, 4 1/2 baths, 3-car side entry garage
- Basement foundation

Plan #702-0417

Five Bedroom Home Embraces Large Family

2,828 total square feet of living area

Price Code E

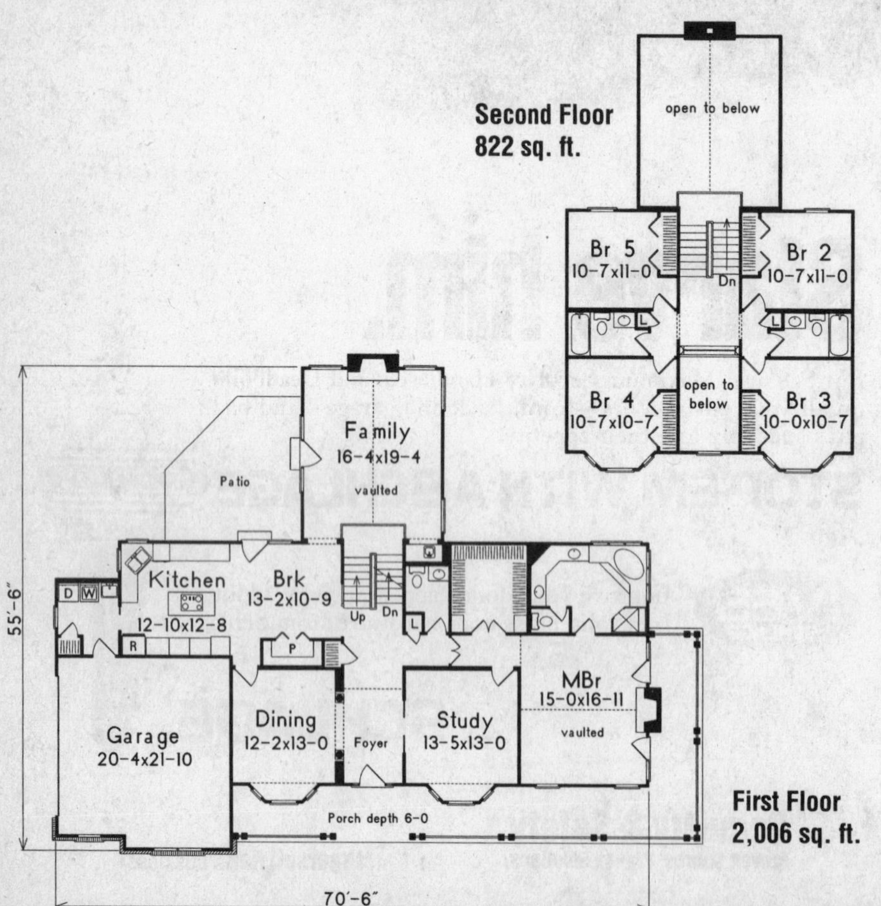
Second Floor
822 sq. ft.
open to below
Br 5
10-7x11-0
Br 2
10-7x11-0
Dn
open to below
Br 4
10-7x10-7
Br 3
10-0x10-7
Family
16-4x19-4
vaulted
Patio
Kitchen
12-10x12-8
Brk
13-2x10-9
Up
Dn
D
W
R
P
Garage
20-4x21-10
Dining
12-2x13-0
Foyer
Study
13-5x13-0
MBr
15-0x16-11
vaulted
Porch depth 6-0
55'-6"
70'-6"
First Floor
2,006 sq. ft.

Special features

- Popular wrap-around porch gives home country charm
- Secluded, oversized family room with vaulted ceiling and wet bar features many windows
- Any chef would be delighted to cook in this smartly designed kitchen with island and corner windows
- Spectacular master suite
- 5 bedrooms, 3 1/2 baths, 2-car side entry garage
- Basement foundation, drawings also include crawl space and slab foundations

TO ORDER BLUEPRINTS USE THE FORM ON PAGE 19 OR CALL TOLL-FREE 1-877-671-6036

View thousands more home plans online at www.familyhandyman.com/homeplans

The Family
Handyman

Plan #702-0448

Country-Style With Wrap-Around Porch

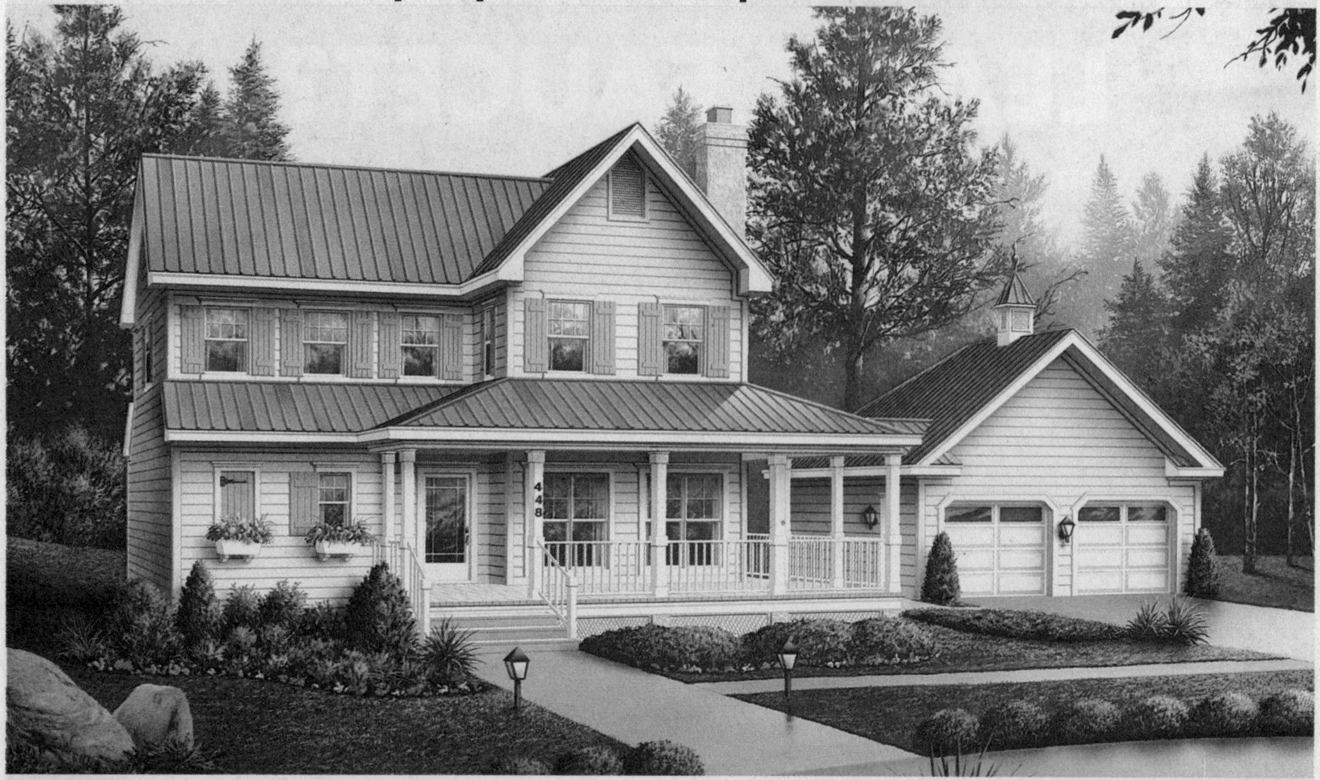

1,597 total square feet of living area

Price Code C

Special features

- Spacious family room includes fireplace and coat closet
- Open kitchen and dining room provides breakfast bar and access to the outdoors
- Convenient laundry area located near kitchen
- Secluded master suite with walk-in closet and private bath
- 4 bedrooms, 2 1/2 baths, 2-car detached garage
- Basement foundation

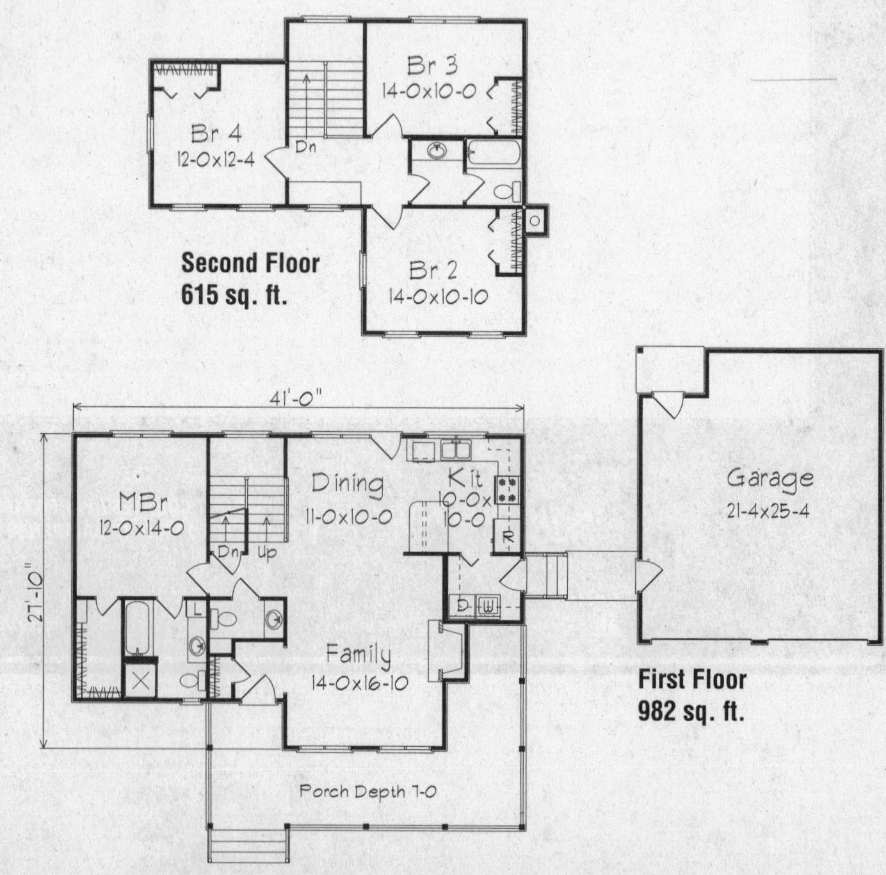
Br 3
14-0x10-0
Br 4
12-0x12-4
Dn
Br 2
14-0x10-10
41'-0"
27'-10"
MBr
12-0x14-0
Dn
Up
Dining
11-0x10-0
Kit
10-0x
10-0
R
D
W
Family
14-0x16-10
Porch Depth 7-0
Garage
21-4x25-4

Second Floor
615 sq. ft.

First Floor
982 sq. ft.

Our Blueprint Packages Offer...

Quality plans for building your future, with extras that provide unsurpassed value, ensure good construction and long-term enjoyment.

A quality home - one that looks good, functions well, and provides years of enjoyment - is a product of many things - design, materials, craftsmanship.

But it's also the result of outstanding blueprints - the actual plans and specifications that tell the builder exactly how to build your home.

And with our BLUEPRINT PACKAGES you get the absolute best. A complete set of blueprints is available for every design in this book. These "working drawings", are highly detailed, resulting in two key benefits:

- Better understanding by the contractor of how to build your home and...
- More accurate construction estimates.

When you purchase one of our designs, you'll receive all of the BLUEPRINT components shown here - elevations, foundation plan, floor plans, sections, and/or details. Other helpful building aids are also available to help make your dream home a reality.

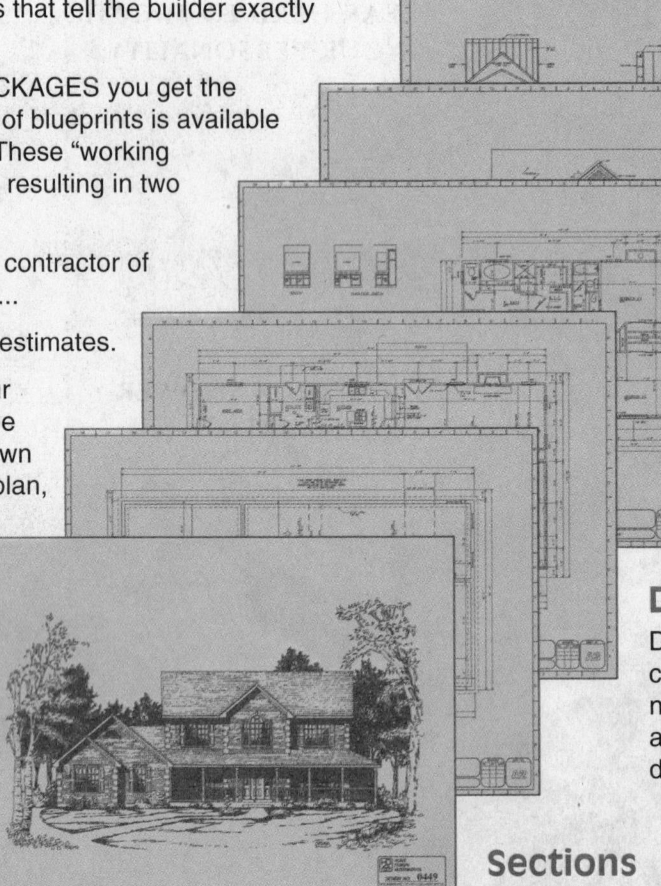

Cover Sheet

The cover sheet is the artist's rendering of the exterior of the home. It will give you an idea of how your home will look when completed and landscaped.

Interior Elevations

Interior elevations provide views of special interior elements such as fireplaces, kitchen cabinets, built-in units and other features of the home.

Foundation Plan

The foundation plan shows the layout of the basement, crawl space, slab or pier foundation. All necessary notations and dimensions are included. See plan page for the foundation types included. If the home plan you choose does not have your desired foundation type, our Customer Service Representatives can advise you on how to customize your foundation to suit your specific needs or site conditions.

Details

Details show how to construct certain components of your home, such as the roof system, stairs, deck, etc.

Sections

Sections show detail views of the home or portions of the home as if it were sliced from the roof to the foundation. This sheet shows important areas such as load-bearing walls, stairs, joists, trusses and other structural elements, which are critical for proper construction.

Floor Plans

The floor plans show the placement of walls, doors, closets, plumbing fixtures, electrical outlets, columns, and beams for each level of the home.

Exterior Elevations

Exterior elevations illustrate the front, rear and both sides of the house, with all details of exterior materials and the required dimensions.

What Kind Of Plan Package Do You Need?

Now that you've found the home you've been looking for, here are some suggestions on how to make your Dream Home a reality. To get started, order the type of plans that fit your particular situation.

YOUR CHOICES

- **THE 1-SET PACKAGE** - We offer a 1-set plan package so you can study your home in detail. This one set is considered a study set and is marked "not for construction". It is a copyright violation to reproduce blueprints.
- **THE MINIMUM 5-SET PACKAGE** - If you're ready to start the construction process, this 5-set package is the minimum number of blueprint sets you will need. It will require keeping close track of each set so they can be used by multiple subcontractors and tradespeople.
- **THE STANDARD 8-SET PACKAGE** - For best results in terms of cost, schedule and quality of construction, we recommend you order eight (or more) sets of blueprints. Besides one set for yourself, additional sets of blueprints will be required by your mortgage lender, local building department, general contractor and all subcontractors working on foundation, electrical, plumbing, heating/air conditioning, carpentry work, etc.
- **REPRODUCIBLE MASTERS** - If you wish to make some minor design changes, you'll want to order reproducible masters. These drawings contain the same information as the blueprints but are printed on erasable and reproducible paper. This will allow your builder or a local design professional to make the necessary drawing changes without the major expense of redrawing the plans. This package also allows you to print as many copies of the modified plans as you need.
- **MIRROR REVERSE SETS** - Plans can be printed in mirror reverse. These plans are useful when the house would fit your site better if all the rooms were on the opposite side than shown. They are simply a mirror image of the original drawings causing the lettering and dimensions to read backwards. Therefore, when ordering mirror reverse drawings, you must purchase at least one set of right reading plans.

PLAN #702-0449 Pg. 73

Other Helpful Building Aids...

Your Blueprint Package will contain the necessary construction information to build your home. We also offer the following products and services to save you time and money in the building process.

- **MATERIAL LIST** - Material lists are available for many of the plans in this book. Each list gives you the quantity, dimensions and description of the building materials necessary to construct your home. You'll get faster and more accurate bids from your contractor while saving money by paying for only the materials you need. See the Home Plans Index on page 18 for availability. Refer to the order form on page 19 for pricing.
- **DETAIL PLAN PACKAGES:** Framing, Plumbing & Electrical Plan Packages - Three separate packages offer homebuilders details for constructing various foundations; numerous floor, wall and roof framing techniques; simple to complex residential wiring; sump and water softener hookups; plumbing connection methods; installation of septic systems and more. Each package includes three-dimensional illustrations and a glossary of terms. Purchase one or all three. Cost: $20.00 each or all three for $40.00. Note: These drawings do not pertain to a specific home plan.
- **THE LEGAL KIT™** - Our Legal Kit provides contracts and legal forms to help protect you from the potential pitfalls inherent in the building process. The Kit supplies commonly used forms and contracts suitable for homeowners and builders. It can save you a considerable amount of time and help protect you and your assets during and after construction. Cost: $35.00
- **EXPRESS DELIVERY** - Most orders are processed within 24 hours of receipt. Please allow 7 working days for delivery. If you need to place a rush order, please call us by 11:00 a.m. CST and ask for express service (allow 1-2 business days).
- **TECHNICAL ASSISTANCE**- If you have questions, call our technical support line at 1-314-770-2228 between 8:00 a.m. and 5:00 p.m. CST. Whether it involves design modifications or field assistance, our designers are extremely familiar with all of our designs and will be happy to help you. We want your home to be everything you expect it to be.

HOME DESIGN ALTERNATIVES, INC.

Home Plans Index

Plan Number	Sq. Ft.	Price Code	Page	Mat. List
702-0106	1,443	A	63	X
702-0111	1,582	B	34	X
702-0112	1,668	C	36	X
702-0113	1,992	C	165	X
702-0122	1,922	C	23	X
702-0127	1,996	D	77	X
702-0133	2,214	D	83	X
702-0134	2,216	D	55	X
702-0138	2,286	E	4	X
702-0141	2,826	E	90	X
702-0143	2,449	E	27	X
702-0151	2,874	E	35	X
702-0152	2,935	E	32	X
702-0156	3,050	E	159	X
702-0163	1,772	C	212	X
702-0167	2,282	D	135	X
702-0168	2,940	E	271	X
702-0171	2,058	C	258	X
702-0174	1,657	B	2	X
702-0177	2,562	D	217	X
702-0183	2,847	E	54	X
702-0187	3,035	E	230	X
702-0188	1,800	C	114	X
702-0190	1,600	C	30	X
702-0201	1,814	D	22	X
702-0203	1,475	B	30	X
702-0207	1,550	B	169	X
702-0210	2,361	D	145	X
702-0213	2,059	C	267	X
702-0217	1,360	A	52	X
702-0220	3,391	F	229	X
702-0221	1,619	B	39	X
702-0224	2,461	D	289	X
702-0229	1,676	B	249	X
702-0231	2,213	E	234	X
702-0232	2,932	F	270	X
702-0233	2,772	E	279	X
702-0234	2,066	C	182	X
702-0239	1,496	A	256	X
702-0247	2,988	E	246	X
702-0249	1,501	B	99	X
702-0252	1,364	A	86	X
702-0254	1,732	B	43	X
702-0263	3,003	E	88	X
702-0264	1,689	B	50	X
702-0284	1,672	C	219	X
702-0285	2,648	E	151	X
702-0287	2,718	E	140	X
702-0289	2,513	D	274	X
702-0290	1,700	B	269	X
702-0293	1,595	B	114	X
702-0294	1,655	B	86	X
702-0298	3,216	F	10	X
702-0303	2,024	C	276	X
702-0305	2,605	E	123	X
702-0306	2,360	D	113	X
702-0307	3,153	E	192	X
702-0312	1,921	D	44	X
702-0322	2,135	D	197	X
702-0348	2,003	D	85	X
702-0350	2,452	D	214	X
702-0359	2,659	E	68	X
702-0360	2,327	D	278	X
702-0379	1,711	B	209	X
702-0386	2,186	C	167	X
702-0387	1,958	C	174	X
702-0388	1,695	B	226	X
702-0389	1,777	B	161	X
702-0390	2,351	D	282	X
702-0391	2,685	E	176	X
702-0394	1,558	B	183	X
702-0396	1,880	C	162	X
702-0408	2,498	D	47	X
702-0413	2,182	C	104	X
702-0417	2,828	E	12	X

Plan Number	Sq. Ft.	Price Code	Page	Mat. List
702-0429	3,149	E	118	X
702-0434	2,357	D	75	X
702-0436	2,801	E	72	X
702-0437	2,333	D	175	X
702-0439	2,665	E	272	X
702-0448	1,597	C	14	X
702-0449	2,505	D	73	X
702-0488	2,059	C	290	X
702-0489	1,543	B	237	X
702-0491	1,808	C	149	X
702-0521	2,050	C	100	X
702-0522	1,818	C	264	X
702-0523	1,875	C	273	X
702-0526	2,262	D	154	X
702-0528	2,511	D	59	X
702-0529	1,285	B	255	X
702-0537	1,664	B	131	X
702-0540	2,352	D	250	X
702-0542	1,832	C	240	X
702-0598	1,818	C	95	X
702-0600	3,025	E	191	X
702-0651	962	AA	240	X
702-0657	914	AA	257	X
702-0672	2,043	C	93	X
702-0674	1,476	A	143	X
702-0676	1,367	A	79	X
702-0677	3,006	E	133	X
702-0678	1,567	B	239	X
702-0686	1,609	B	128	X
702-0688	1,556	B	219	X
702-0690	1,400	A	152	X
702-0692	1,339	A	236	X
702-0698	1,143	AA	238	X
702-0705	2,758	E	193	X
702-0706	1,791	B	111	X
702-0709	2,521	D	247	X
702-0712	2,029	C	71	X
702-0713	3,199	E	97	X
702-0714	2,808	E	297	X
702-0722	2,266	D	157	X
702-0723	1,784	B	153	X
702-0724	1,969	C	242	X
702-0726	1,428	A	152	X
702-0728	2,967	E	245	X
702-0732	1,384	A	102	X
702-0736	2,900	E	125	X
702-0739	1,684	B	69	X
702-0742	1,883	C	243	X
702-0747	1,977	C	203	X
702-0748	2,514	D	136	X
702-0749	2,727	E	108	X
702-0755	1,787	B	110	X
702-0765	1,000	AA	228	X
702-0766	990	AA	287	X
702-0767	990	AA	222	X
702-0768	1,879	C	171	X
702-0774	1,680	B	233	X
702-0777	2,458	D	260	X
702-0784	3,556	F	31	X
702-0795	1,399	A	215	X
702-0797	2,651	E	186	X
702-0799	1,849	C	189	X
702-0801	2,544	D	121	X
702-0802	2,645	E	223	X
702-0804	2,795	E	57	X
702-0805	2,750	E	221	X
702-0809	1,084	AA	174	X
702-1101	1,643	B	168	
702-1213	2,554	D	261	
702-1300	2,253	D	198	
702-1305	2,009	C	6	
702-1307	2,420	D	164	
702-1308	2,280	D	207	
702-1309	2,562	D	148	
702-1311	2,112	C	187	

Plan Number	Sq. Ft.	Price Code	Page	Mat. List
702-1336	1,364	A	235	
702-1396	1,820	C	296	
702-AMD-2163	1,978	C	116	X
702-AMD-2229	2,287	D	127	X
702-AP-1612	1,643	B	155	
702-AP-1717	1,787	B	275	
702-AP-1914	1,992	C	139	X
702-AP-2020	2,097	C	94	
702-AP-2416	2,484	D	268	
702-AX-5380	1,480	A	265	X
702-AX-7944	1,648	B	37	X
702-AX-91316	1,097	AA	53	X
702-AX-93308	1,793	B	89	X
702-AX-96355	1,699	B	283	X
702-BF-1901	1,925	C	252	X
702-BF-2107	2,123	E	288	X
702-BF-2108	2,194	C	25	X
702-BF-3007	3,012	E	80	X
702-CHD-18-53	2,310	D	74	
702-CHD-20-51	2,084	C	76	
702-CHD-27-35	2,743	E	248	
702-CHD-29-58	3,369	F	213	
702-CHP-1633-A-18	1,618	C	205	
702-CHP-1833-A-13	1,819	C	295	
702-CHP-2343-A-30	2,356	E	294	
702-CHP-3054-B-3	3,266	H	201	
702-CHP-3244-B-18	3,444	G	158	
702-CHP-3444-A-16	3,493	H	293	
702-CHP-4156-A-1	4,187	H	263	
702-CHP-4355-A-2	4,380	H	291	
702-DBI-2285	2,115	C	49	X
702-DBI-2408	2,270	D	210	X
702-DBI-4642	1,712	B	190	X
702-DBI-5498	2,188	C	78	X
702-DBI-5520	2,615	E	180	X
702-DBI-24038-9P	2,126	C	124	X
702-DBI-24045-9P	1,263	A	262	X
702-DDI-95-234	1,649	B	92	
702-DDI-98-203	2,504	D	132	
702-DDI-100-215	1,757	B	227	
702-DDI-100-219	2,646	E	166	
702-DDI-101-205	2,487	D	67	
702-DDI-100213	2,202	D	60	
702-DDI-100214	2,104	C	253	
702-DH-1786	1,785	B	130	
702-DH-1854	1,856	C	298	
702-DH-2313J	2,123	C	109	
702-DH-2352	2,352	D	196	
702-DH-2600	2,669	E	220	
702-DH-2775A	2,775	E	208	
702-DH-3329	3,029	E	204	
702-DL-17353L1	1,735	B	216	
702-DL-21644L1	2,164	C	26	
702-DL-25454L1	2,545	D	119	
702-DR-2290	1,124	AA	222	X
702-DR-2590	1,700	B	142	X
702-DR-2615	2,889	E	206	X
702-DR-2884	2,135	C	87	X
702-DR-2937	1,288	A	259	X
702-DR-2939	1,480	A	225	X
702-DR-3406	1,754	B	292	X
702-DR-3812	2,129	C	106	X
702-DR-3814	2,590	D	101	X
702-FB-582	1,497	A	134	
702-FB-676	1,373	A	41	
702-FB-902	1,856	C	117	X
702-FB-1043	1,692	B	281	
702-FB-1148	1,491	A	62	
702-FB-1158	2,072	C	232	
702-FDG-7963-L	1,830	C	170	
702-FDG-8701-L	2,578	D	115	
702-FDG-8729-L	2,529	D	66	
702-FDG-8753-L	2,674	E	284	
702-GH-24706	1,470	A	202	X
702-GH-24713	2,269	D	277	X

Plan Number	Sq. Ft.	Price Code	Page	Mat. List
702-GH-24724	1,982	C	51	X
702-GH-24736	2,044	C	126	X
702-GH-34043	1,583	B	254	X
702-GH-34603	1,560	B	218	X
702-GH-34901	1,763	C	65	X
702-GH-35002	1,712	B	138	X
702-GM-1253	1,253	A	28	X
702-GM-1550	1,550	B	266	X
702-GM-1815	1,815	C	141	X
702-GM-1966	1,966	C	82	X
702-GSD-1748	1,496	A	42	
702-GSD-2107	2,422	D	184	
702-HDG-97006	1,042	AA	173	
702-HDG-99004	1,231	A	173	
702-HDS-1558-2	1,885	C	56	
702-HDS-1571	1,571	B	181	
702-HDS-1627	1,627	B	24	
702-HDS-1668	1,668	B	29	X
702-HDS-1963	1,963	C	172	
702-HDS-1993	1,993	C	244	
702-HDS-2802-2	2,802	E	105	
702-HP-C316	1,997	C	21	X
702-HP-C460	1,389	A	146	X
702-HP-C619	1,771	B	147	X
702-HP-C659	1,118	AA	61	X
702-HP-C662	1,937	C	163	X
702-HP-C675	1,673	B	241	X
702-HP-C681	1,669	B	177	X
702-HP-C689	1,295	A	251	X
702-JA-65996	1,962	C	38	
702-JFD-20-1868-1	1,868	C	280	
702-JFD-20-1887-1	1,887	C	84	
702-JFD-20-2097-1	2,097	C	70	
702-JFD-20-2643-2	2,643	E	188	
702-JV-1325-B	1,325	A	58	
702-JV-1735A	1,735	B	120	X
702-JV-1870-A	1,870	C	286	
702-JV-2008-B	2,008	C	91	X
702-JV-2091-A	2,475	D	150	
702-LBD-17-14A	1,725	B	144	
702-LBD-19-15A	1,955	C	64	
702-LBD-19-16A	1,993	C	224	
702-MG-96132	2,450	D	40	
702-MG-97099	1,093	AA	146	
702-NDG-111	2,698	E	199	X
702-NDG-619	3,060	E	107	X
702-NDG-649	1,458	A	299	X
702-NDG-794	1,120	AA	194	X
702-NDG-795	1,462	A	112	X
702-RDD-1753-9	1,753	B	129	
702-RDD-1815-8	1,815	C	137	
702-RDD-1895-9	1,895	C	160	
702-RJ-A1387	1,382	A	33	
702-RJ-B123	1,270	A	122	
702-RJ-B1416	1,455	A	96	
702-SH-SEA-023	1,358	A	52	X
702-SH-SEA-058	2,170	C	165	X
702-SH-SEA-061	2,493	D	200	X
702-SH-SEA-078	2,389	D	211	X
702-SH-SEA-100	2,582	D	178	X
702-SH-SEA-208	2,516	D	81	X
702-SH-SEA-212	2,632	E	98	X
702-SH-SEA-242	1,408	A	156	X
702-SH-SEA-245	1,578	B	185	X
702-SH-SEA-303	1,583	B	179	X
702-SH-SEA-307	2,462	D	231	X
702-SH-SEA-310	1,108	AA	103	X
702-SH-SEA-400	1,568	B	195	X
702-SH-SEA-405	2,693	E	45	X
702-VL947	947	AA	61	
702-VL2069	2,069	C	46	X
702-VL2888	2,888	E	285	X
702-VL3011	3,011	E	48	X

IMPORTANT INFORMATION TO KNOW BEFORE YOUR ORDER

- **Exchange Policies -** Since blueprints are printed in response to your order, we cannot honor requests for refunds. However, if for some reason you find that the plan you have purchased does not meet your requirements, you may exchange that plan for another plan in our collection. At the time of the exchange, you will be charged a processing fee of 25% of your original plan package price, plus the difference in price between the plan packages (if applicable) and the cost to ship the new plans to you.
- **Building Codes & Requirements -** At the time the construction drawings were prepared, every effort was made to ensure that these plans and specifications meet nationally recognized codes. Our plans conform to most national building codes. Because building codes vary from area to area, some drawing modifications and/or the assistance of a professional designer or architect may be necessary to comply with your local codes or to accommodate specific building site conditions. We advise you to consult with your local building official for information regarding codes governing your area.

Please note: Reproducible drawings can only be exchanged if the package is unopened, and exchanges are allowed only within 90 days of purchase.

Questions? Call Our Customer Service Number 1-877-671-6036

BLUEPRINT PRICE SCHEDULE

BEST VALUE

Price Code	1-Set	SAVE $110 5-Sets	SAVE $200 8-Sets	Material List*	Reproducible Masters
AAA	$225	$295	$340	$50	$440
AA	$275	$345	$390	$55	$490
A	$325	$395	$440	$60	$540
B	$375	$445	$490	$60	$590
C	$425	$495	$540	$65	$640
D	$475	$545	$590	$65	$690
E	$525	$595	$640	$70	$740
F	$575	$645	$690	$70	$790
G	$650	$720	$765	$75	$865
H	$755	$825	$870	$80	$970

Plan prices guaranteed through June 30, 2004.
Please note that plans are not refundable.

- **Additional Sets* -** Additional sets of the plan ordered are available for $45.00 each. Five-set, eight-set, and reproducible packages offer considerable savings.
- **Mirror Reverse Plans* -** Available for an additional $5.00 per set, these plans are simply a mirror image of the original drawings causing the dimensions & lettering to read backwards. Therefore, when ordering mirror reverse plans, you must purchase at least one set of right reading plans.
- **One-Set Study Package -** We offer a one-set plan package so you can study your home in detail. This one set is considered a study set and is marked "not for construction". It is a copyright violation to reproduce blueprints.

***Available only within 90 days after purchase of plan package or reproducible masters of same plan.**

SHIPPING & HANDLING CHARGES

U.S. SHIPPING	1-4 Sets	5-7 Sets	8 Sets or Reproducibles
Regular *(allow 7-10 business days)*	$15.00	$17.50	$25.00
Priority *(allow 3-5 business days)*	$25.00	$30.00	$35.00
Express* *(allow 1-2 business days)*	$35.00	$40.00	$45.00

CANADA SHIPPING (to/from) - Plans with suffix DR & SH	1-4 Sets	5-7 Sets	8 Sets or Reproducibles
Standard *(allow 8-12 business days)*	$25.00	$30.00	$35.00
Express* *(allow 3-5 business days)*	$40.00	$40.00	$45.00

Overseas Shipping/International - Call, fax, or e-mail (plans@hdainc.com) for shipping costs.

* For express delivery please call us by 11:00 a.m. CST

How To Order

For fastest service, Call Toll-Free
1-877-671-6036
24 HOURS A DAY

Three Easy Ways To Order

1. CALL toll-free 1-877-671-6036 for credit card orders. MasterCard, Visa, Discover and American Express are accepted.
2. FAX your order to 1-314-770-2226.
3. MAIL the Order Form to:

HDA, Inc.
4390 Green Ash Drive
St. Louis, MO 63045

ORDER FORM

Please send me -

PLAN NUMBER 702BT - ______________

PRICE CODE ______ (see Plan Index)

Specify Foundation Type - see plan page for availability
☐ Slab ☐ Crawl space
☐ Basement ☐ Walk-out basement

☐ Reproducible Masters $ ______
☐ Eight-Set Plan Package $ ______
☐ Five-Set Plan Package $ ______
☐ One-Set Study Package (no mirror reverse) $ ______
☐ Additional Plan Sets
______ (Qty.) at $45.00 each $ ______
☐ Print in Mirror Reverse
______ (Qty.) add $5.00 per set $ ______
☐ Material List $ ______
☐ Legal Kit (see page 17) $ ______
Detail Plan Packages: (see page 17)
☐ Framing ☐ Electrical ☐ Plumbing $ ______
SUBTOTAL $ ______
SALES TAX (MO residents add 7%) $ ______
☐ Shipping / Handling (see chart at left) $ ______
TOTAL ENCLOSED (US funds only) $ ______
(Sorry no CODs)

I hereby authorize HDA, Inc. to charge this purchase to my credit card account (check one):

☐ MasterCard ☐ VISA ☐ DISCOVER NOVUS ☐ AMERICAN EXPRESS Cards

Credit Card number ______________

Expiration date ______________

Signature ______________

Name ______________
(Please print or type)

Street Address ______________
(Please **do not** use PO Box)

City ______________

State ________ Zip ______________

Daytime phone number (_____) - ______________

I'm a ☐ Builder/Contractor
☐ Homeowner
☐ Renter

I ☐ have
☐ have not
selected my general contractor

Thank you for your order!

QUICK AND EASY CUSTOMIZING

MAKE CHANGES TO YOUR HOME PLAN IN 4 STEPS

HERE'S AN **AFFORDABLE** AND **EFFICIENT** WAY TO MAKE CHANGES TO YOUR PLAN.

1 **Select the house plan that most closely meets your needs.** Purchase of a reproducible master is necessary in order to make changes to a plan.

2 **Call 1-877-671-6036 to place your order.** Tell the sales representative you're interested in customizing a plan. A $50 refundable consultation fee will be charged. You will then be instructed to complete a customization checklist indicating all the changes you wish to make to your plan. You may attach sketches if necessary. If you proceed with the custom changes the $50 will be credited to the total amount charged.

3 **FAX the completed customization checklist** to our design consultant at 1-866-477-5173 or e-mail **blarochelle@drummonddesigns.com.** Within *24-48 business hours you will be provided with a written cost estimate to modify your plan. Our design consultant will contact you by phone if you wish to discuss any of your changes in greater detail.

4 **Once you approve the estimate,** a 75% retainer fee is collected and customization work gets underway. Preliminary drawings can usually be completed within *5-10 business days. Following approval of the preliminary drawings your design changes are completed within *5-10 business days. Your remaining 25% balance due is collected prior to shipment of your completed drawings. You will be shipped five sets of revised blueprints or a reproductible master, plus a customized materials list if required.

*Terms are subject to change without notice.

BEFORE

Plan 2829

Customized Versi
of Plan 28

AFTER

MODIFICATION PRICING GUIDE

CATEGORIES	Average Cost from...	to
Adding or removing living space (square footage)	Quote required	
Adding or removing a garage	$400	$680
Garage: Front entry to side load or vice versa	Starting at $300	
Adding a screened porch	$280	$600
Adding a bonus room in the attic	$450	$780
Changing full basement to crawl space or vice versa	Starting at $220	
Changing full basement to slab or vice versa	Starting at $260	
Changing exterior building material	Starting at $200	
Changing roof lines	$360	$630
Adjusting ceiling height	$280	$500
Adding, moving or removing an exterior opening	$55 per opening	
Adding or removing a fireplace	$90	$200
Modifying a non-bearing wall or room	$55 per rooom	
Changing exterior walls from 2"x4" to 2"x6"	Starting at $200	
Redesigning a bathroom or a kitchen	$120	$280
Reverse plan right reading	Quote required	
Adapting plans for local building code requirements	Quote required	
Engineering stamping only	$450 / any state	
Any other engineering services	Quote required	
Adjust plan for handicapped accessibility	Quote required	
Interactive illustrations (choices of exterior materials)	Quote required	
Metric conversion of home plan	$400	

Note: Any home plan can be customized to accommodate your desired changes. The average prices specifed above are provided only as examples for the most commonly requested changes, and are subject to change without notice. Prices for changes will vary according to the number of modifications requested, plan size, style, and metod of design used by the original designer. To obtain a detailed cost estimate, please contact us.

The Family
Handyman

Plan #702-HP-C316

A Charming Home Loaded With Extras

1,997 total square feet of living area | **Price Code C**

32'8"
TERRACE
UP
BREAKFAST RM
16⁸ x 10⁶
SLOPED CEILING
SCREENED PORCH
11¹⁰ x 11²
SNACK BAR
PASS THRU
RANGE
DESK
BC
KITCHEN
16⁸ x 11²
FLOWER BOX
DW
REF'G
PANTRY
DINING RM
12⁰ x 12⁸
PDR RM
50'0"
DN
OPEN ABOVE
CL
CURIO
FOYER
LIVING RM
18⁴ x 14⁰
VERANDA
RAILING
ROOF
WALL BELOW
RECESSED ROOF
UPPER BREAKFAST RM
BEDROOM
11¹⁰ x 11⁴
BEDROOM
11⁴ x 11⁴
WALK-IN CLOSET
LINEN
BATH
WHIRLPOOL
RAILING
OPEN BELOW
UPPER FOYER
MASTER BEDROOM
12⁴ x 16⁰
DRESS. RM
WALK-IN CLOSET

First Floor
1,111 sq. ft.

Second Floor
886 sq. ft.

Special features

- Screened porch leads to a rear terrace with access to the breakfast room
- Living and dining rooms combine adding spaciousness to the floor plan
- Other welcome amenities include boxed windows in breakfast and dining rooms, a fireplace in living room and a pass-through snack bar in the kitchen
- 3 bedrooms, 2 1/2 baths
- Basement foundation

Plan #702-0201

Two-Story Foyer Adds Spacious Feeling

1,814 total square feet of living area

Price Code D

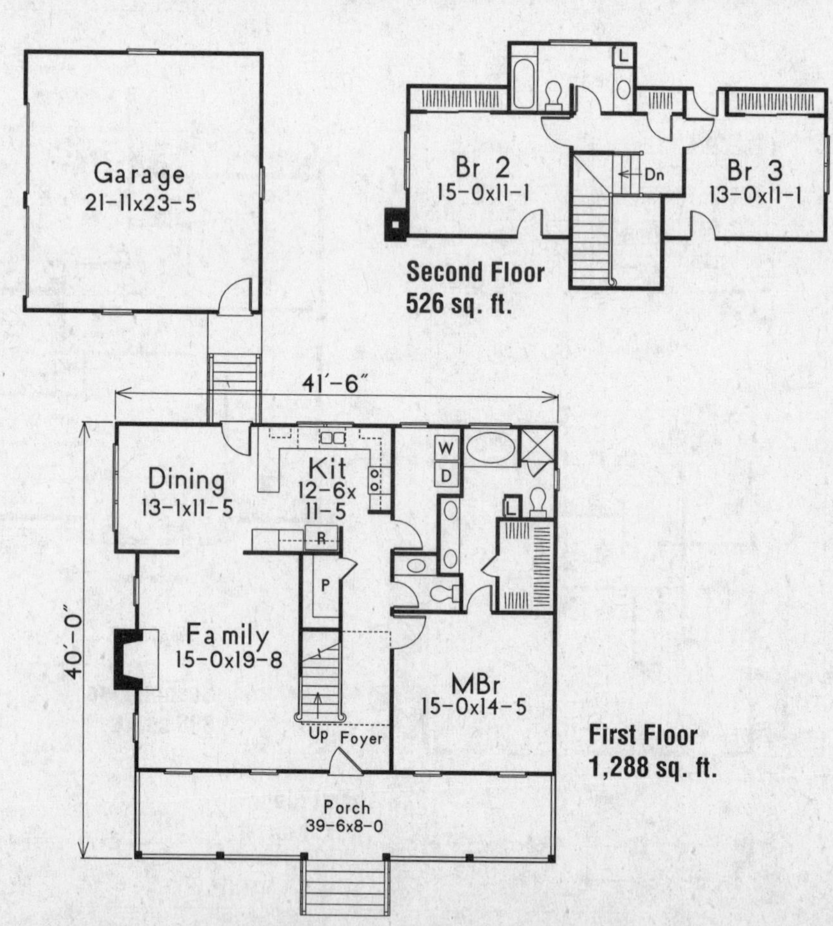
Garage
21-11x23-5
Br 2
15-0x11-1
Dn
Br 3
13-0x11-1
Second Floor
526 sq. ft.
41'-6"
40'-0"
Dining
13-1x11-5
Kit
12-6x
11-5
W
D
R
P
L
Family
15-0x19-8
MBr
15-0x14-5
Up
Foyer
Porch
39-6x8-0
First Floor
1,288 sq. ft.

Special features

- Large master suite includes a spacious bath with garden tub, separate shower and large walk-in closet
- Spacious kitchen and dining area brightened by large windows and patio access
- Detached two-car garage with walkway leading to house adds charm to this country home
- Large front porch
- 3 bedrooms, 2 1/2 baths, 2-car detached garage
- Crawl space foundation, drawings also include slab foundation

TO ORDER BLUEPRINTS USE THE FORM ON PAGE 19 OR CALL TOLL-FREE 1-877-671-6036

The Family
Handyman

Two-Story Foyer Adds To Country Charm

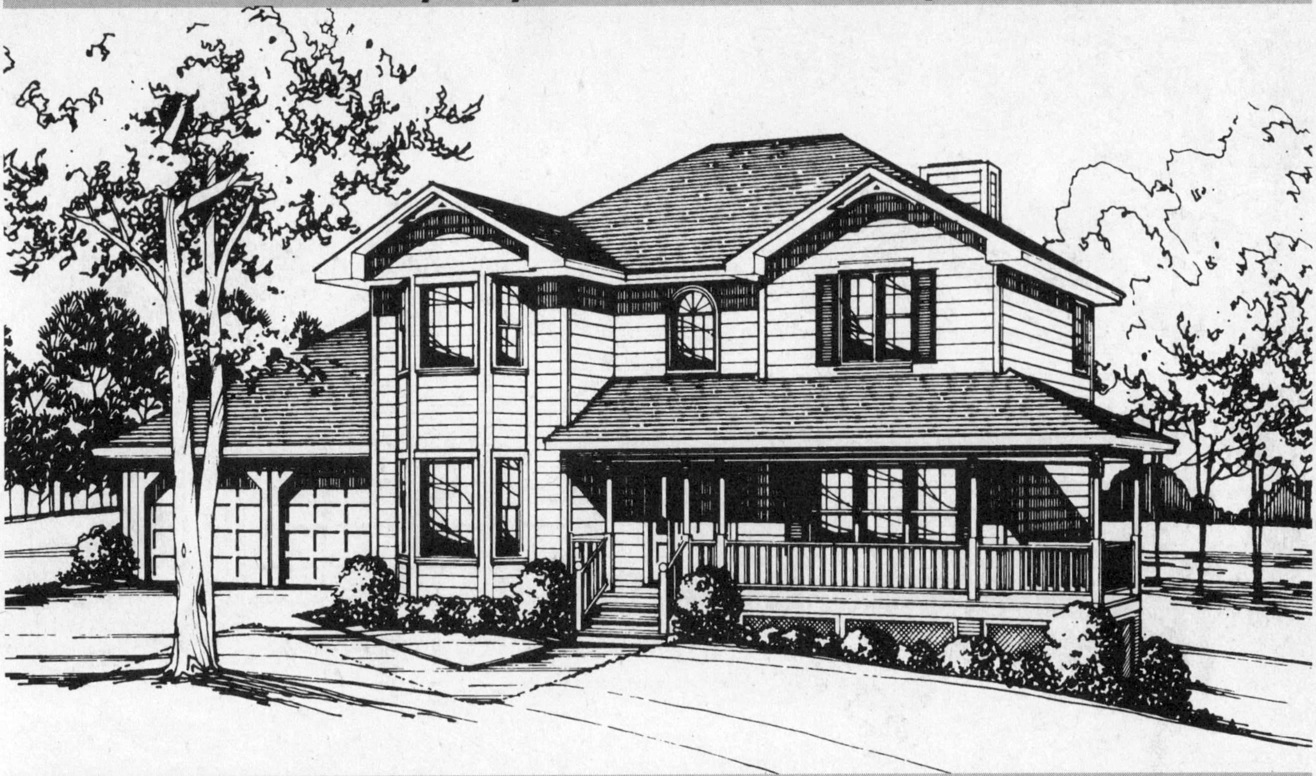

1,922 total square feet of living area | **Price Code C**

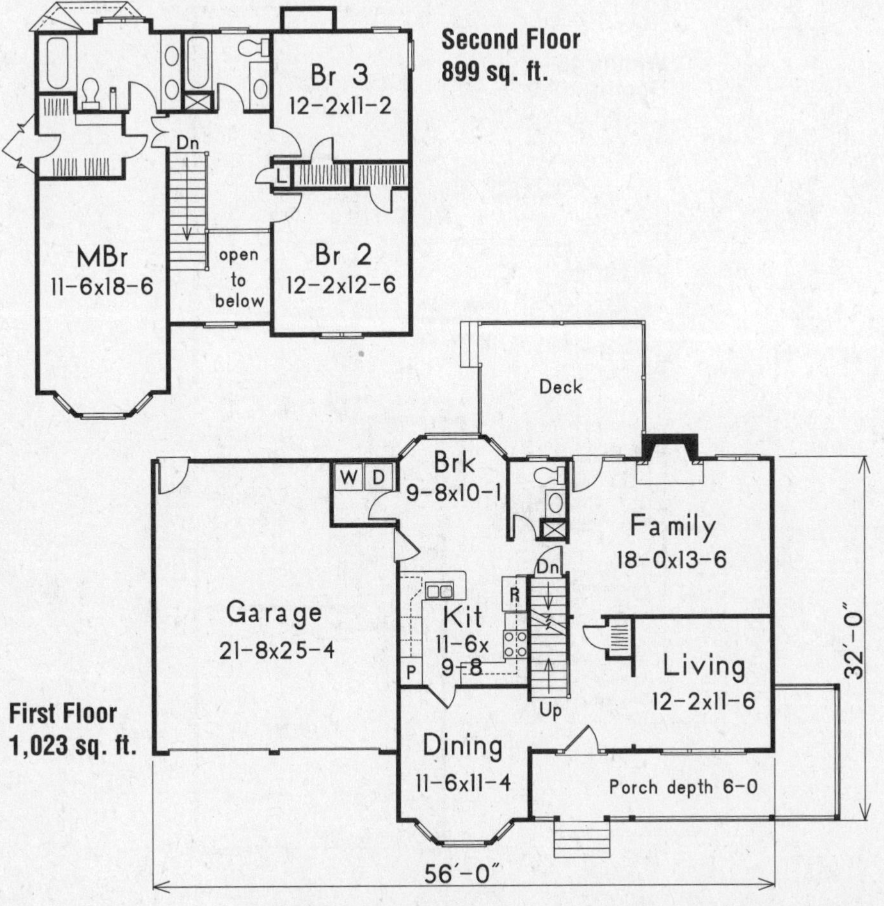
Second Floor
899 sq. ft.
Br 3
12-2x11-2
Dn
L
MBr
11-6x18-6
open
to
below
Br 2
12-2x12-6
Deck
Brk
9-8x10-1
W D
Family
18-0x13-6
Dn
R
Garage
21-8x25-4
Kit
11-6x
9-8
P
Up
Living
12-2x11-6
32'-0"
First Floor
1,023 sq. ft.
Dining
11-6x11-4
Porch depth 6-0
56'-0"

Special features

- Varied front elevation features numerous accents
- Master bedroom suite well secluded with double-door entry and private bath
- Formal living and dining rooms located off the entry
- 3 bedrooms, 2 1/2 baths, 2-car garage
- Basement foundation

The Family
Handyman

Plan #702-HDS-1627

Ranch Design With All The Luxuries

© HOME DESIGN SERVICES, INC.

1,627 total square feet of living area **Price Code B**

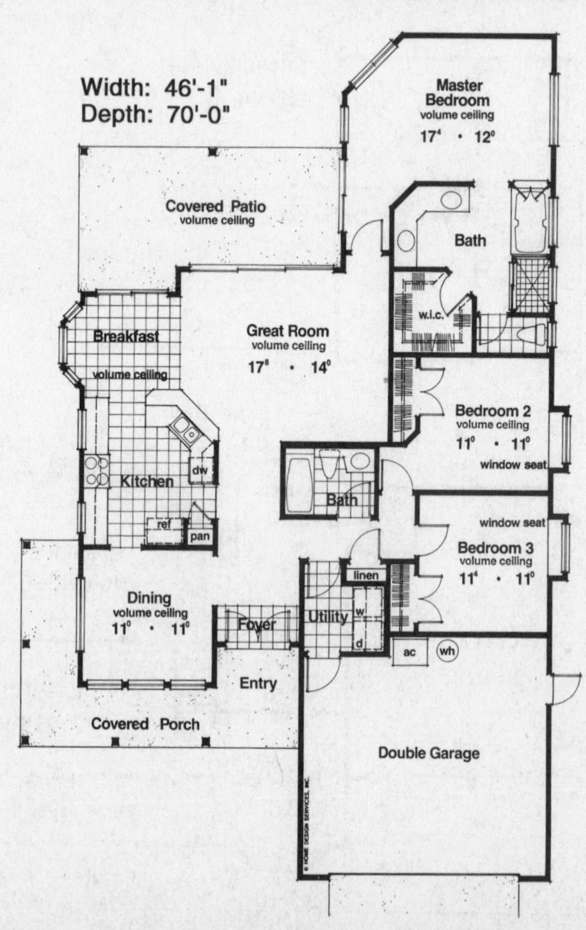
Width: 46'-1"
Depth: 70'-0"
Master Bedroom
volume ceiling
$17^{4} \cdot 12^{0}$
Covered Patio
volume ceiling
Bath
w.i.c.
Breakfast
volume ceiling
Great Room
volume ceiling
$17^{8} \cdot 14^{0}$
Bedroom 2
volume ceiling
$11^{0} \cdot 11^{0}$
window seat
Kitchen
dw
ref
pan
Bath
window seat
Bedroom 3
volume ceiling
$11^{4} \cdot 11^{0}$
linen
Dining
volume ceiling
$11^{0} \cdot 11^{0}$
Foyer
Utility
w
d
ac
wh
Entry
Covered Porch
Double Garage
© HOME DESIGN SERVICES, INC.

Special features

- Bay-shaped breakfast room is sunny and bright
- Angled window wall and volume ceiling in master bedroom adds interest
- Box bay windows are featured in secondary bedrooms
- 3 bedrooms, 2 baths, 2-car garage
- Slab foundation

TO ORDER BLUEPRINTS USE THE FORM ON PAGE 19 OR CALL TOLL-FREE 1-877-671-6036

View thousands more home plans online at www.familyhandyman.com/homeplans

The Family
Handyman

Plan #702-BF-2108

Two-Story Living Room

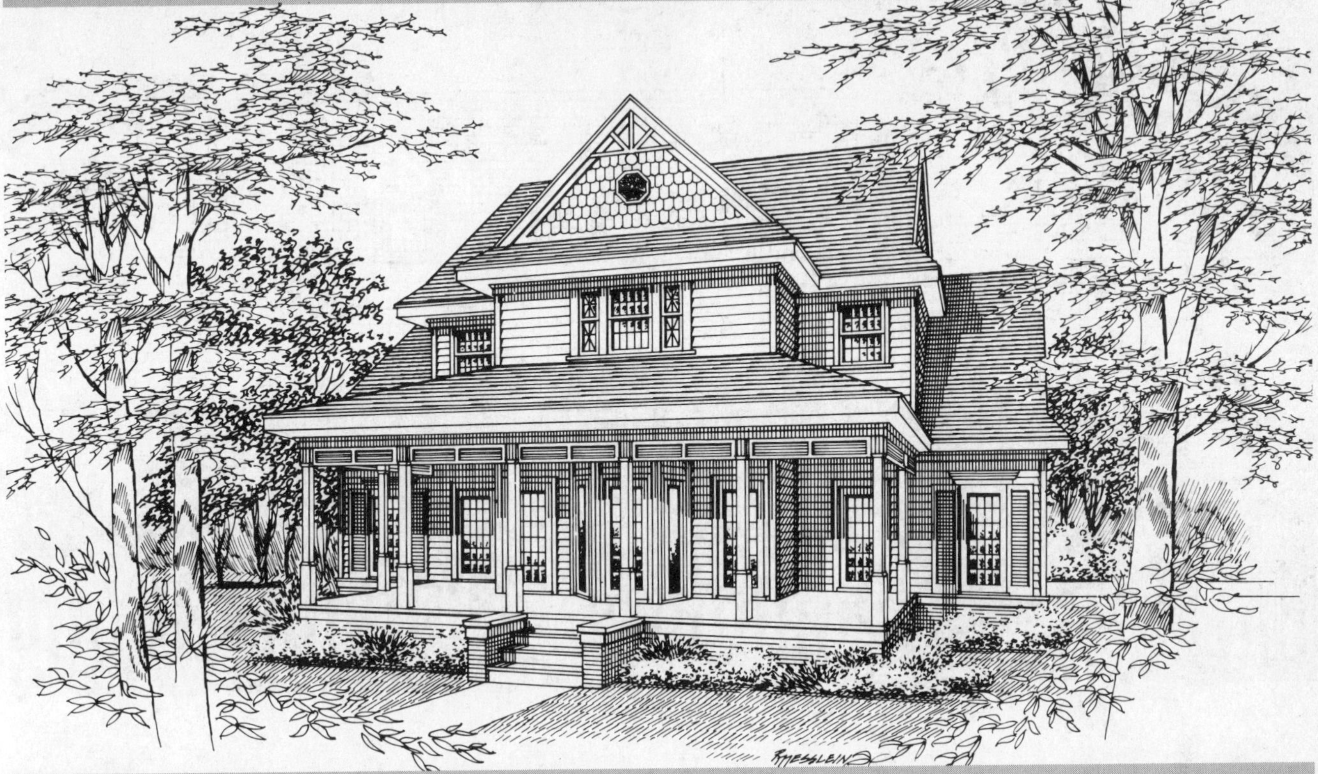

2,194 total square feet of living area

Price Code C

Second Floor
663 sq. ft.

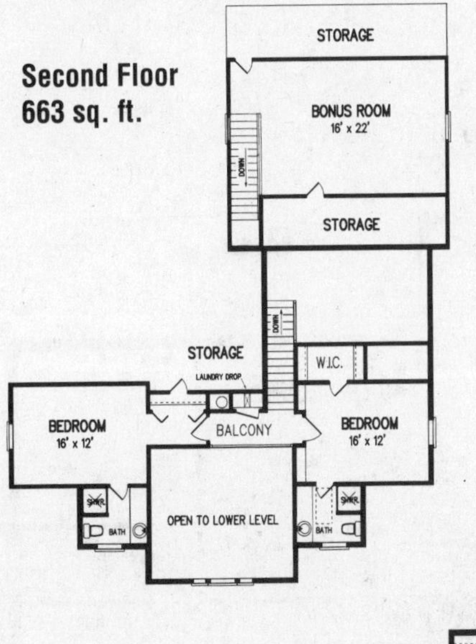
STORAGE
BONUS ROOM
16' x 22'
DOWN
STORAGE
DOWN
STORAGE
LAUNDRY DROP
W.I.C.
BEDROOM
16' x 12'
BALCONY
BEDROOM
16' x 12'
BATH
OPEN TO LOWER LEVEL
BATH

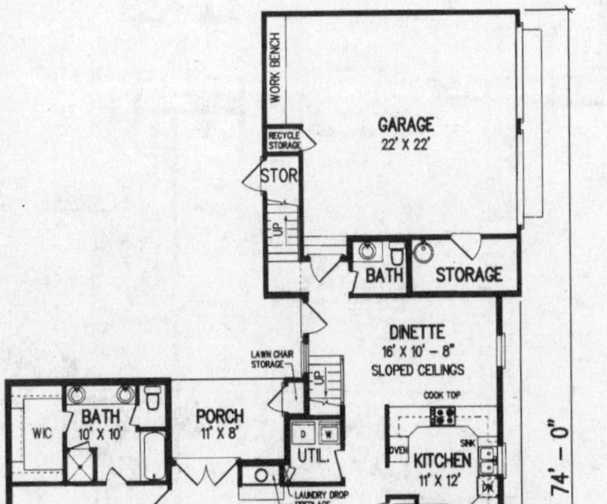

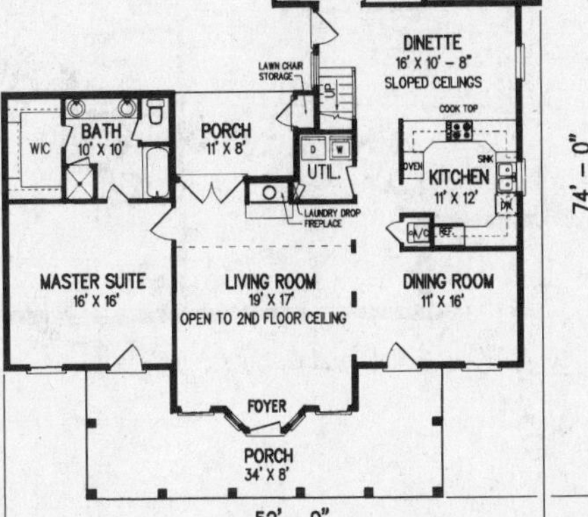
WORK BENCH
RECYCLE STORAGE
STOR
UP
GARAGE
22' X 22'
BATH
STORAGE
DINETTE
16' X 10' – 8"
SLOPED CEILINGS
LAWN CHAIR STORAGE
WIC
BATH
10' X 10'
PORCH
11' X 8'
UTIL.
LAUNDRY DROP
FIREPLACE
COOK TOP
OVEN
KITCHEN
11' X 12'
MASTER SUITE
16' X 16'
LIVING ROOM
19' X 17'
OPEN TO 2ND FLOOR CEILING
DINING ROOM
11' X 16'
FOYER
PORCH
34' X 8'
52' – 0"
74' – 0"

First Floor
1,531 sq. ft.

Special features

- Energy efficient home with 2" x 6" exterior walls
- Utility room has laundry drop conveniently located next to kitchen
- Both second floor bedrooms have large closets and their own bath
- 3 bedrooms, 3 1/2 baths, 2-car side entry garage
- Crawl space, slab or basement foundation, please specify when ordering

The Family
Handyman

Plan #702-DL-21644L1

Trio Of Dormers Add Appeal

2,164 total square feet of living area **Price Code C**

Special features

- Country-styled front porch adds charm
- Plenty of counterspace in kitchen
- Large utility area meets big families laundry needs
- Double-doors lead to covered rear porch
- 4 bedrooms, 2 1/2 baths, 2-car garage
- Slab foundation

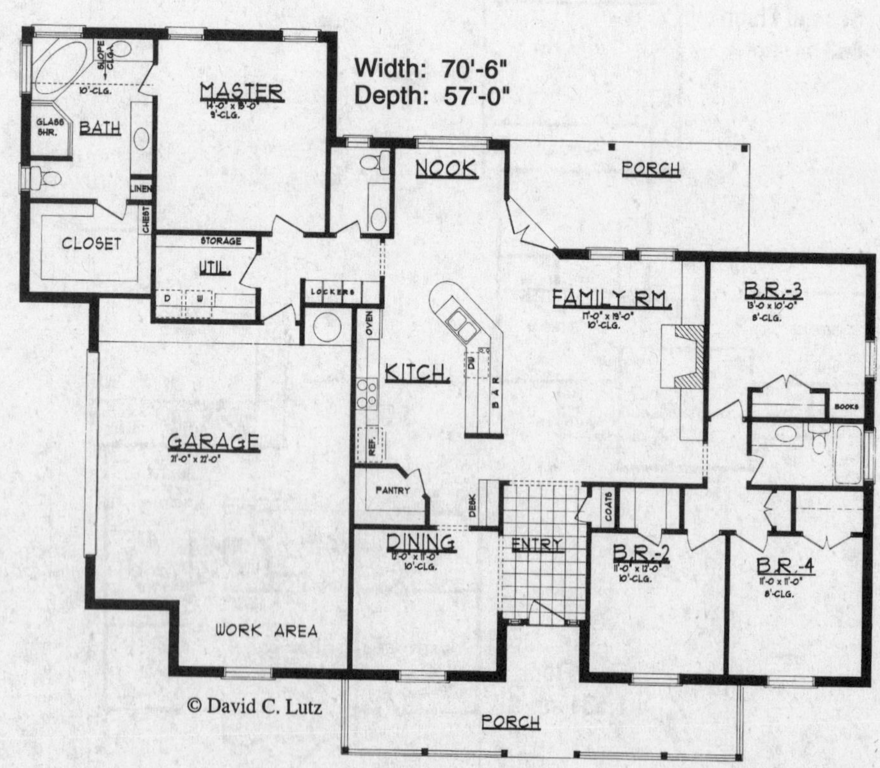
Width: 70'-6"
Depth: 57'-0"
MASTER
BATH
GLASS SHR.
LINEN
CLOSET
STORAGE
UTIL.
LOCKERS
NOOK
PORCH
FAMILY RM.
B.R.-3
BOOKS
KITCH.
OVEN
BAR
GARAGE
PANTRY
DESK
COATS
DINING
ENTRY
B.R.-2
B.R.-4
WORK AREA
PORCH
© David C. Lutz

TO ORDER BLUEPRINTS USE THE FORM ON PAGE 19 OR CALL TOLL-FREE 1-877-671-6036

The Family
Handyman

Wrap-Around Veranda Softens Country-Style Home

2,449 total square feet of living area | **Price Code E**

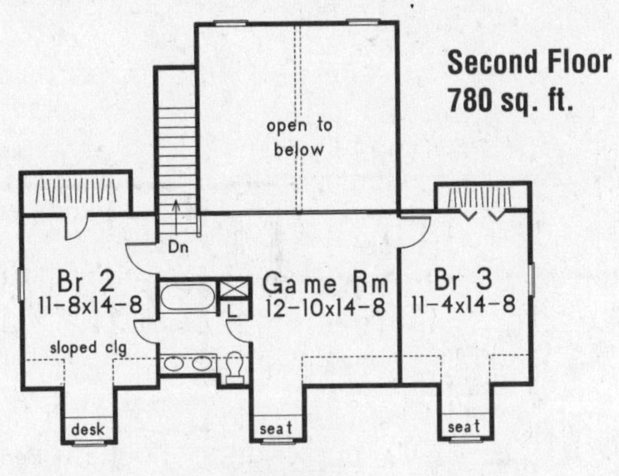
open to
below
Dn
Br 2
11-8x14-8
sloped clg
Game Rm
12-10x14-8
L
Br 3
11-4x14-8
desk
seat
seat

Second Floor
780 sq. ft.

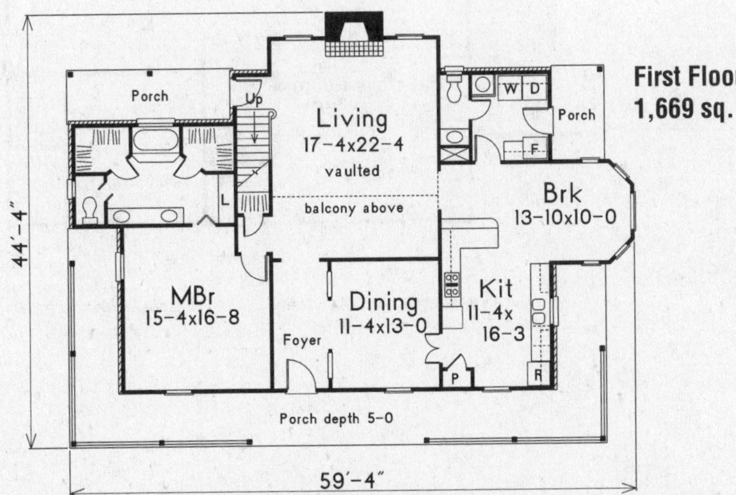
Porch
Up
Living
17-4x22-4
vaulted
balcony above
W
D
Porch
F
Brk
13-10x10-0
L
MBr
15-4x16-8
Dining
11-4x13-0
Foyer
Kit
11-4x
16-3
P
R
Porch depth 5-0
44'-4"
59'-4"

First Floor
1,669 sq. ft.

Special features

- Striking living area features fireplace flanked with windows, cathedral ceiling and balcony
- First floor master bedroom with twin walk-in closets and large linen storage
- Dormers add space for desks or seats
- 3 bedrooms, 2 1/2 baths, 2-car detached garage
- Slab foundation, drawings also include crawl space foundation

TO ORDER BLUEPRINTS USE THE FORM ON PAGE 19 OR CALL TOLL-FREE 1-877-671-6036

Covered Rear Porch

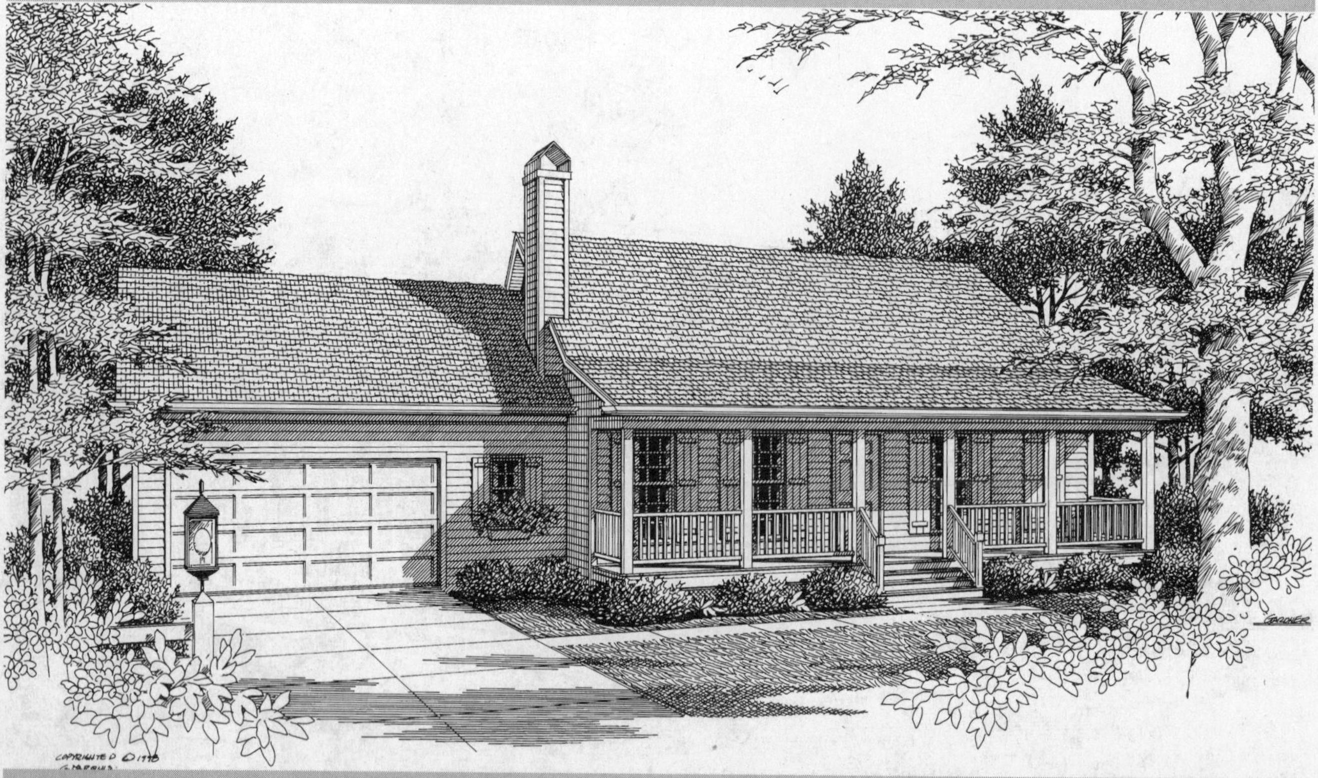

1,253 total square feet of living area **Price Code A**

Special features

- Sloped ceiling and fireplace in family room add drama
- U-shaped kitchen efficiently designed
- Large walk-in closets are found in all the bedrooms
- 3 bedrooms, 2 baths, 2-car garage
- Crawl space or slab foundation, please specify when ordering

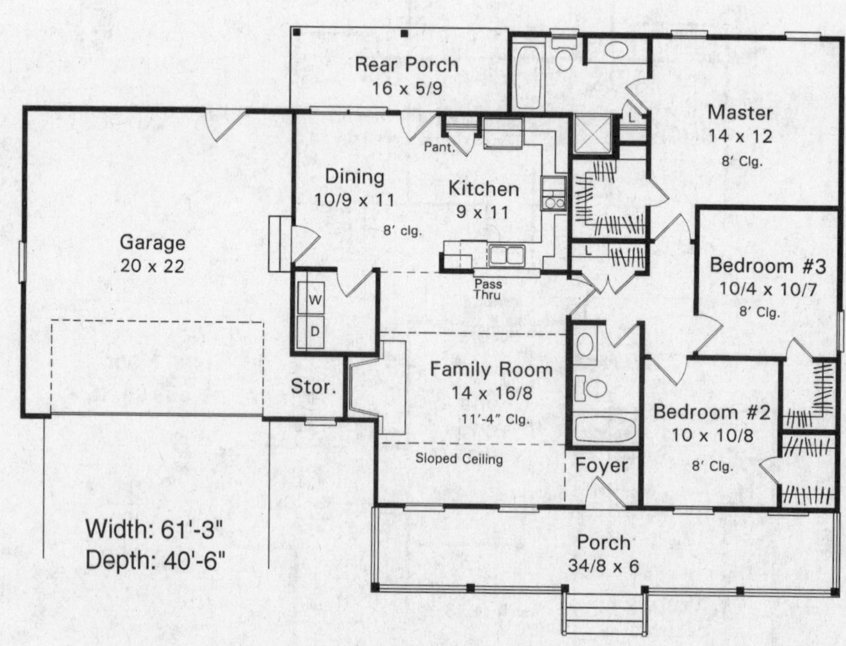
Rear Porch
16 x 5/9
Master
14 x 12
8' Clg.
Pant.
Dining
10/9 x 11
Kitchen
9 x 11
8' clg.
Garage
20 x 22
Bedroom #3
10/4 x 10/7
8' Clg.
Pass Thru
W
D
Family Room
14 x 16/8
11'-4" Clg.
Stor.
Bedroom #2
10 x 10/8
8' Clg.
Sloped Ceiling
Foyer
Width: 61'-3"
Depth: 40'-6"
Porch
34/8 x 6

The Family
Handyman

Plan #702-HDS-1668

Expansive Wrap-Around Porch

1,668 total square feet of living area **Price Code B**

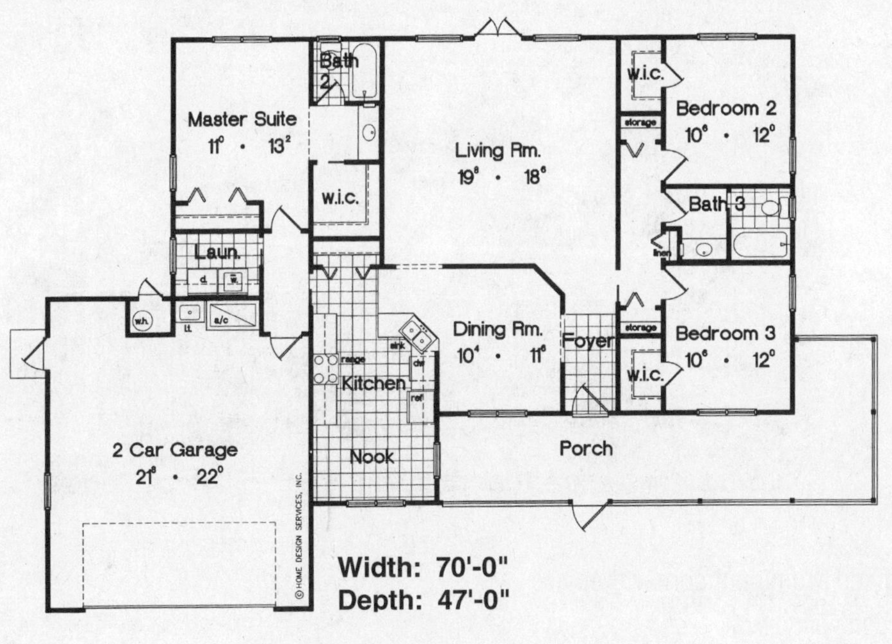
Bath 2
Master Suite
11^{0} · 13^{2}
w.i.c.
Laun.
w.h.
Living Rm.
19^{8} · 18^{6}
w.i.c.
storage
Bedroom 2
10^{6} · 12^{0}
Bath 3
linen
Dining Rm.
10^{4} · 11^{6}
Foyer
storage
Bedroom 3
10^{6} · 12^{0}
w.i.c.
range
sink
dw
Kitchen
ref
2 Car Garage
21^{8} · 22^{0}
Nook
Porch
© HOME DESIGN SERVICES, INC.

Width: 70'-0"
Depth: 47'-0"

Special features

- Master suite separated from other bedrooms for privacy
- Breakfast nook is an added bonus in kitchen
- All bedrooms include walk-in closets as well as additional storage space
- 3 bedrooms, 2 baths, 2-car garage
- Slab foundation

Charming Country Styling In This Ranch Plan #702-0190

1,600 total square feet of living area Price Code C

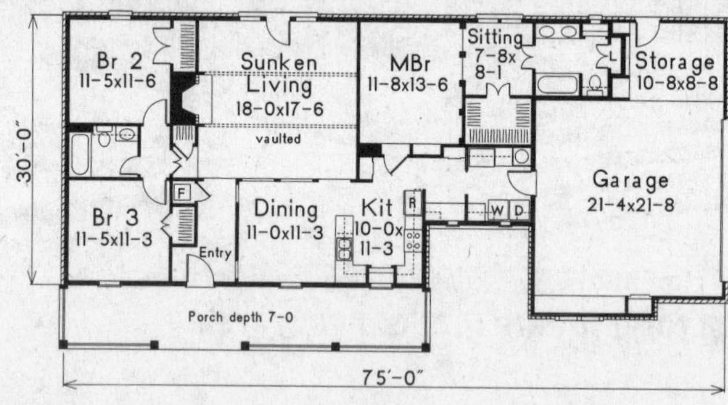
Br 2
11-5x11-6
Sunken
Living
18-0x17-6
vaulted
MBr
11-8x13-6
Sitting
7-8x
8-1
Storage
10-8x8-8
Garage
21-4x21-8
Br 3
11-5x11-3
F
Entry
Dining
11-0x11-3
Kit
10-0x
11-3
W D
Porch depth 7-0
30'-0"
75'-0"

Special features

- Energy efficient home with 2" x 6" exterior walls
- Impressive sunken living room has massive stone fireplace and 16' vaulted ceilings
- Dining room conveniently located next to kitchen and divided for privacy
- Special amenities include sewing room, glass shelves in kitchen and master bath and a large utility area
- Sunken master bedroom features a distinctive sitting room
- 3 bedrooms, 2 baths, 2-car side entry garage
- Slab foundation, drawings also include crawl space and basement foundations

Rambling Country Bungalow Plan #702-0203

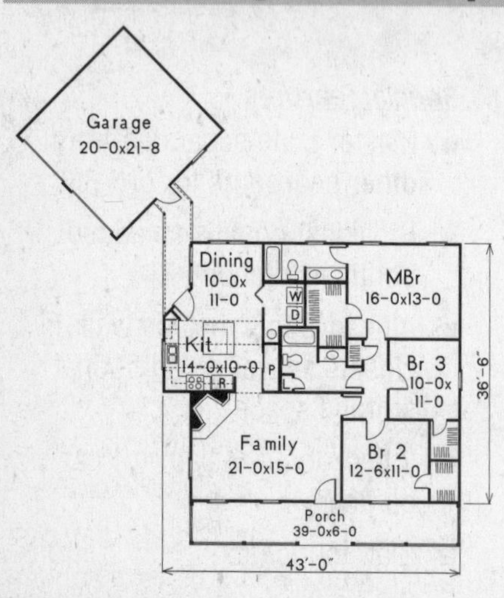
Garage
20-0x21-8
Dining
10-0x
11-0
MBr
16-0x13-0
W
D
Kit
14-0x10-0
P
Br 3
10-0x
11-0
Family
21-0x15-0
Br 2
12-6x11-0
Porch
39-0x6-0
36'-6"
43'-0"

1,475 total square feet of living area Price Code B

Special features

- Family room features a high ceiling and prominent corner fireplace
- Kitchen has island counter and garden window
- Hallway leads to three bedrooms all with large walk-in closets
- Covered breezeway joins main house and garage
- 3 bedrooms, 2 baths, 2-car side entry garage
- Slab foundation, drawings also include crawl space foundation

TO ORDER BLUEPRINTS USE THE FORM ON PAGE 19 OR CALL TOLL-FREE 1-877-671-6036

View thousands more home plans online at www.familyhandyman.com/homeplans

The Family
Handyman

Plan #702-0784

Wrap-Around Porch And Turret Accent Design

3,556 total square feet of living area | **Price Code F**

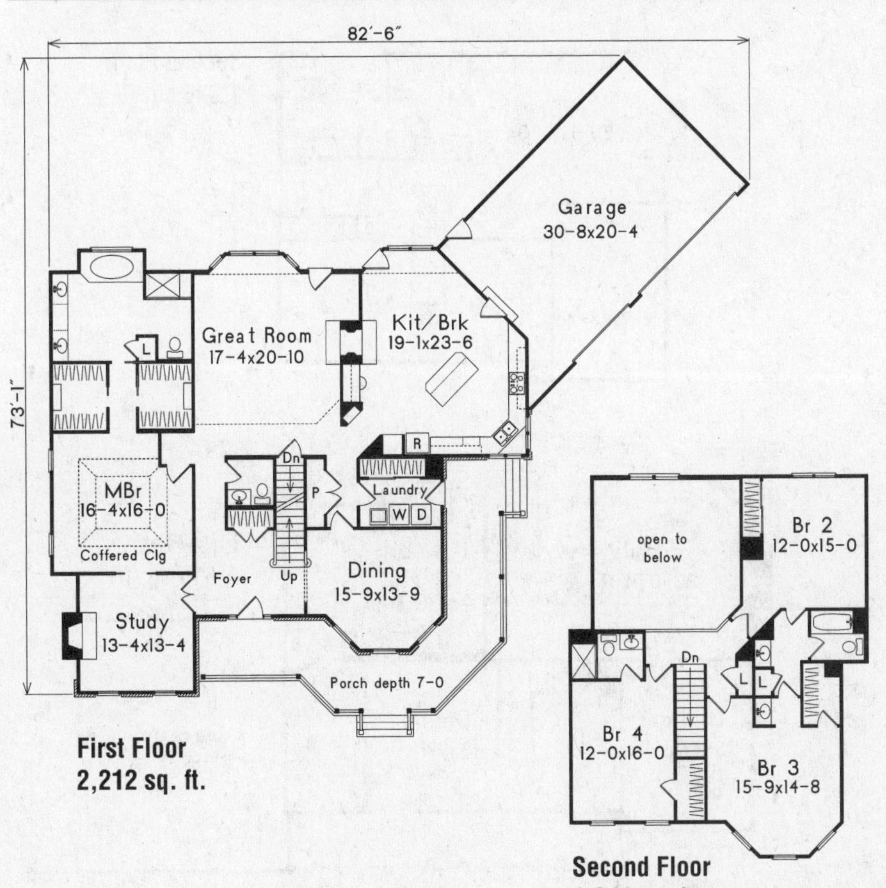
82'-6"
73'-1"
Garage
30-8x20-4
Great Room
17-4x20-10
Kit/Brk
19-1x23-6
R
Dn
P
Laundry
W D
MBr
16-4x16-0
Coffered Clg
Foyer
Up
Dining
15-9x13-9
Study
13-4x13-4
Porch depth 7-0
open to
below
Br 2
12-0x15-0
Dn
L L
Br 4
12-0x16-0
Br 3
15-9x14-8

First Floor
2,212 sq. ft.

Second Floor
1,344 sq. ft.

Special features

- Jack and jill bath located between two of the bedrooms on the second floor
- Second floor features three bedrooms overlooking the great room
- Formal entrance and additional family entrance from covered porch to laundry/mud room
- First floor master suite features coffered ceiling, his and hers walk-in closets, luxury bath and direct access to study
- 4 bedrooms, 3 1/2 baths, 3-car side entry garage
- Basement foundation

TO ORDER BLUEPRINTS USE THE FORM ON PAGE 19 OR CALL TOLL-FREE 1-877-671-6036

View thousands more home plans online at www.familyhandyman.com/homeplans

Charming Victorian Has Unexpected Pleasures

2,935 total square feet of living area **Price Code E**

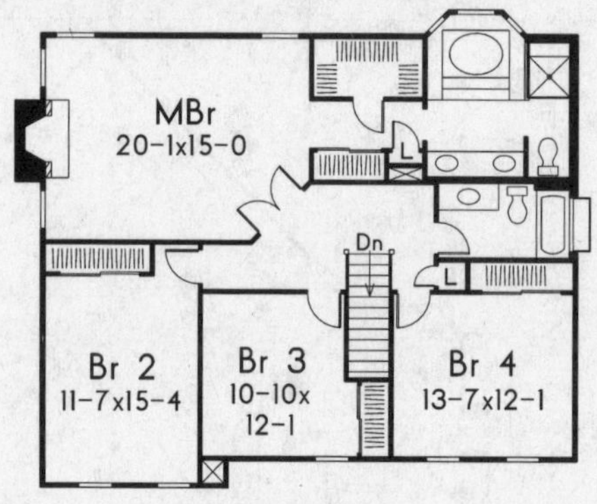
MBr
20-1x15-0
Dn
L
Br 2
11-7x15-4
Br 3
10-10x
12-1
Br 4
13-7x12-1

Second Floor
1,320 sq. ft.

Special features

- Gracious entry foyer with handsome stairway opens to separate living and dining rooms
- Kitchen has vaulted ceiling and skylight, island worktop, breakfast area with bay window and two separate pantries
- Large second floor master bedroom suite with fireplace, raised tub, dressing area with vaulted ceiling and skylight
- 4 bedrooms, 2 1/2 baths, 2-car side entry garage
- Basement foundation

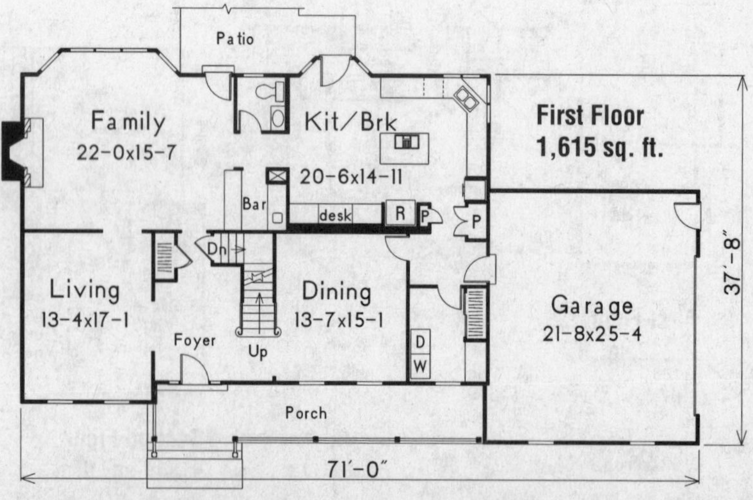
Patio
Family
22-0x15-7
Kit/Brk
20-6x14-11
Bar
desk
R
P
P
Dn
Living
13-4x17-1
Dining
13-7x15-1
Foyer
Up
D
W
Garage
21-8x25-4
Porch
71'-0"
37'-8"

First Floor
1,615 sq. ft.

The Family
Handyman

Plan #702-RJ-A1387

Great Family Plan

1,382 total square feet of living area **Price Code A**

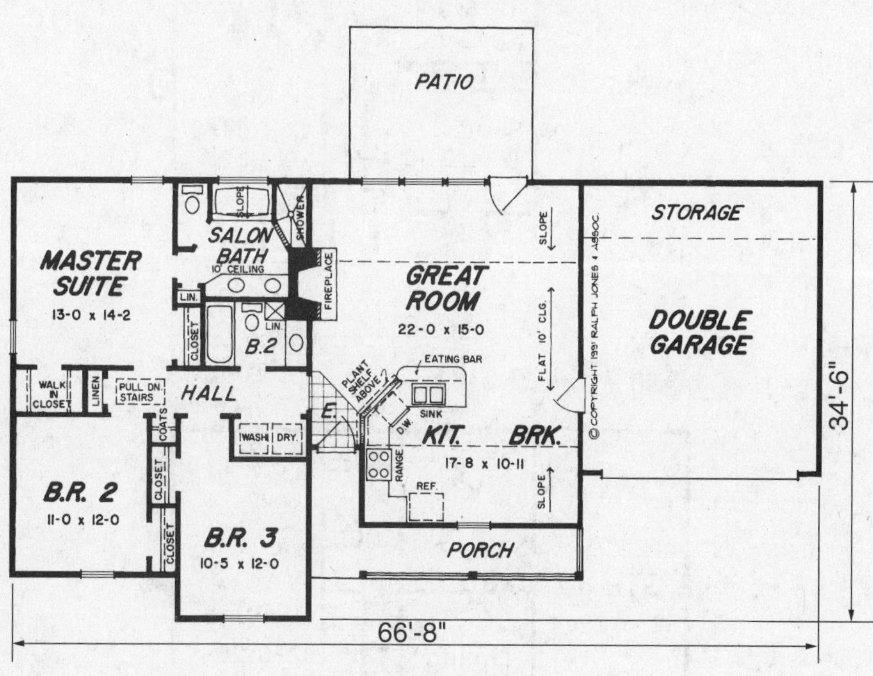

PATIO
STORAGE
SALON BATH
10' CEILING
SLOPE
SHOWER
MASTER SUITE
13-0 x 14-2
FIREPLACE
GREAT ROOM
22-0 x 15-0
SLOPE
FLAT 10' CLG.
© COPYRIGHT 1991 RALPH JONES & ASSOC.
DOUBLE GARAGE
LIN.
CLOSET
LIN.
B.2
PLANT SHELF ABOVE
EATING BAR
WALK IN CLOSET
LINEN
PULL DN. STAIRS
HALL
E.
SINK
D.W.
COATS
WASH
DRY.
KIT.
BRK.
17-8 x 10-11
RANGE
REF.
SLOPE
34'-6"
CLOSET
B.R. 2
11-0 x 12-0
CLOSET
B.R. 3
10-5 x 12-0
PORCH
66'-8"

__Special features__

- An appealing open feel with kitchen, breakfast room and great room combining for the ultimate use of space
- All bedrooms separate from living areas for privacy
- Extra storage in garage
- 3 bedrooms, 2 baths, 2-car garage
- Slab or crawl space foundation, please specify when ordering

TO ORDER BLUEPRINTS USE THE FORM ON PAGE 19 OR CALL TOLL-FREE 1-877-671-6036

Plan #702-0111

Trim Colonial For Practical Living

1,582 total square feet of living area **Price Code B**

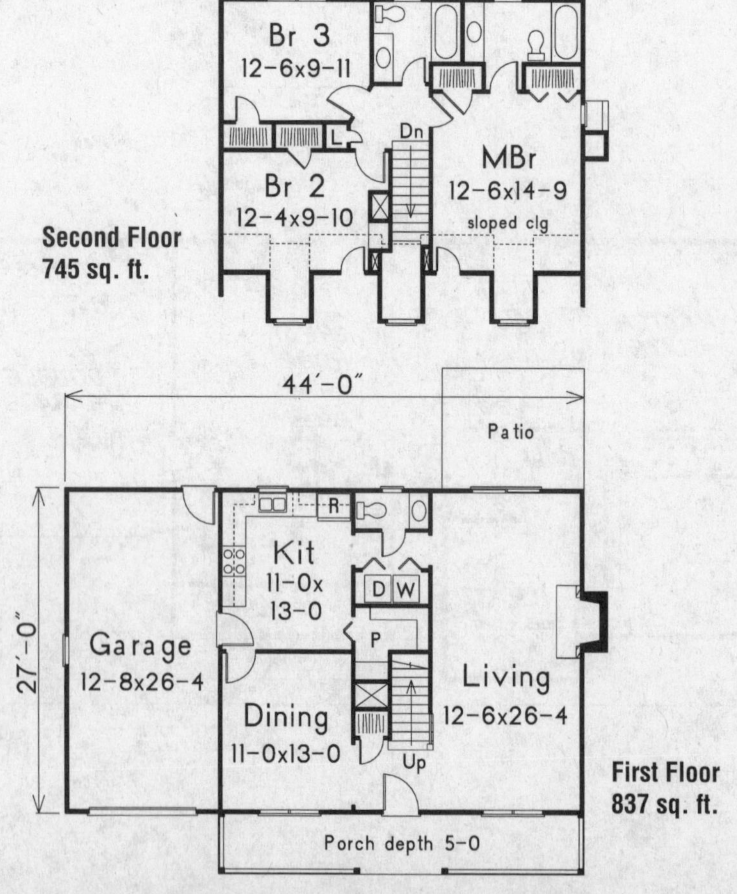
Br 3
12-6x9-11
L
Dn
MBr
12-6x14-9
sloped clg
Br 2
12-4x9-10
Second Floor
745 sq. ft.
44'-0"
Patio
R
Kit
11-0x
13-0
D W
P
27'-0"
Garage
12-8x26-4
Living
12-6x26-4
Dining
11-0x13-0
Up
First Floor
837 sq. ft.
Porch depth 5-0

Special features

- Conservative layout gives privacy to living and dining areas
- Large fireplace and windows enhance the living area
- Rear door in garage is convenient to the garden and kitchen
- Full front porch adds charm
- Dormers add light to the foyer and bedrooms
- 3 bedrooms, 2 1/2 baths, 1-car garage
- Slab foundation, drawings also include crawl space foundation

TO ORDER BLUEPRINTS USE THE FORM ON PAGE 19 OR CALL TOLL-FREE 1-877-671-6036

Massive Ranch With Classy Features

2,874 total square feet of living area **Price Code E**

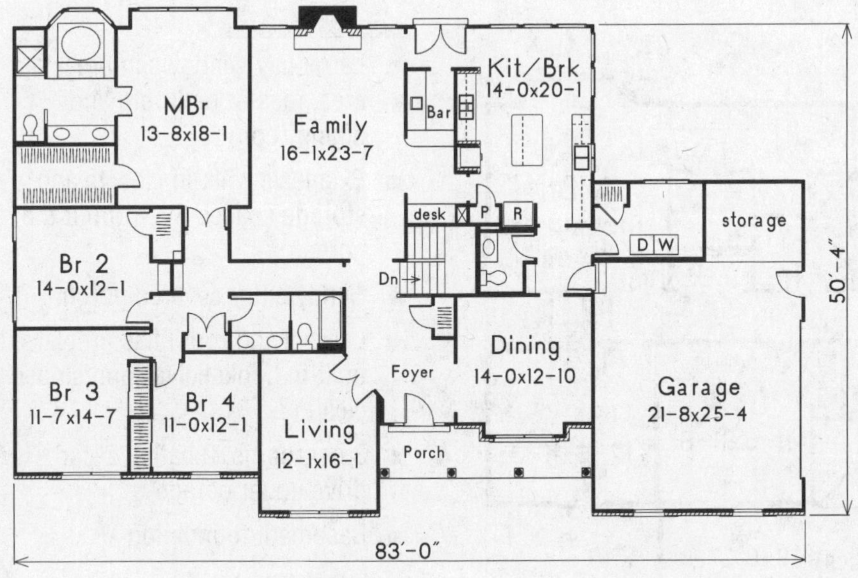
MBr
13-8x18-1
Family
16-1x23-7
Kit/Brk
14-0x20-1
Bar
desk
P
R
storage
D W
Br 2
14-0x12-1
Dn
50'-4"
Dining
14-0x12-10
Foyer
Br 3
11-7x14-7
Br 4
11-0x12-1
L
Garage
21-8x25-4
Living
12-1x16-1
Porch
83'-0"

Special features

- Large family room with sloped ceiling and wood beams adjoins the kitchen and breakfast area with windows on two walls
- Large foyer opens to family room with massive stone fireplace and open stairs to the basement
- Private master bedroom with raised tub under the bay window, dramatic dressing area and a huge walk-in closet
- 4 bedrooms, 2 1/2 baths, 2-car side entry garage
- Basement foundation

Plan #702-0112

Bay Window Graces Luxury Master Bedroom

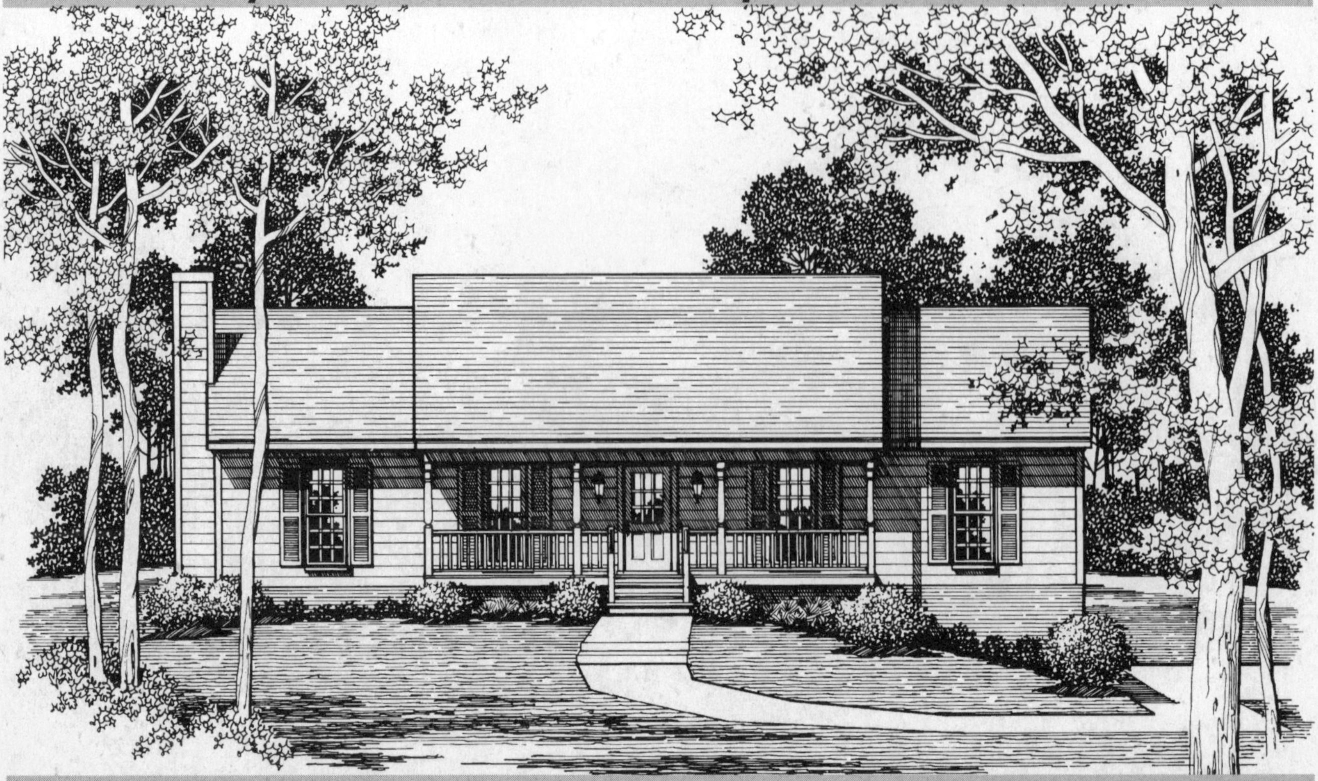

1,668 total square feet of living area | **Price Code C**

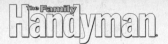

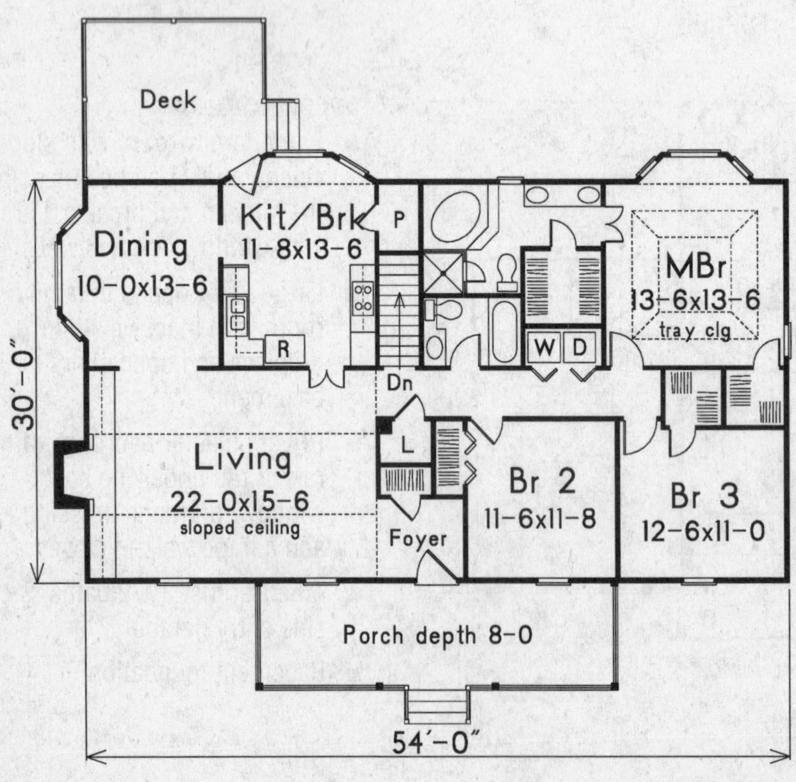
Deck
Kit/Brk
11-8x13-6
P
Dining
10-0x13-6
R
MBr
13-6x13-6
tray clg
W
D
Dn
30'-0"
L
Living
22-0x15-6
sloped ceiling
Br 2
11-6x11-8
Br 3
12-6x11-0
Foyer
Porch depth 8-0
54'-0"

Special features

- Large bay windows in breakfast area, master bedroom and dining room
- Extensive walk-in closets and storage spaces throughout the home
- Handy entry covered porch
- Large living room has fireplace, built-in bookshelves and sloped ceiling
- 3 bedrooms, 2 baths, 2-car drive under garage
- Basement foundation

The Family
Handyman

Plan #702-AX-7944

Rustic Feel With Stone Accent

1,648 total square feet of living area

Price Code B

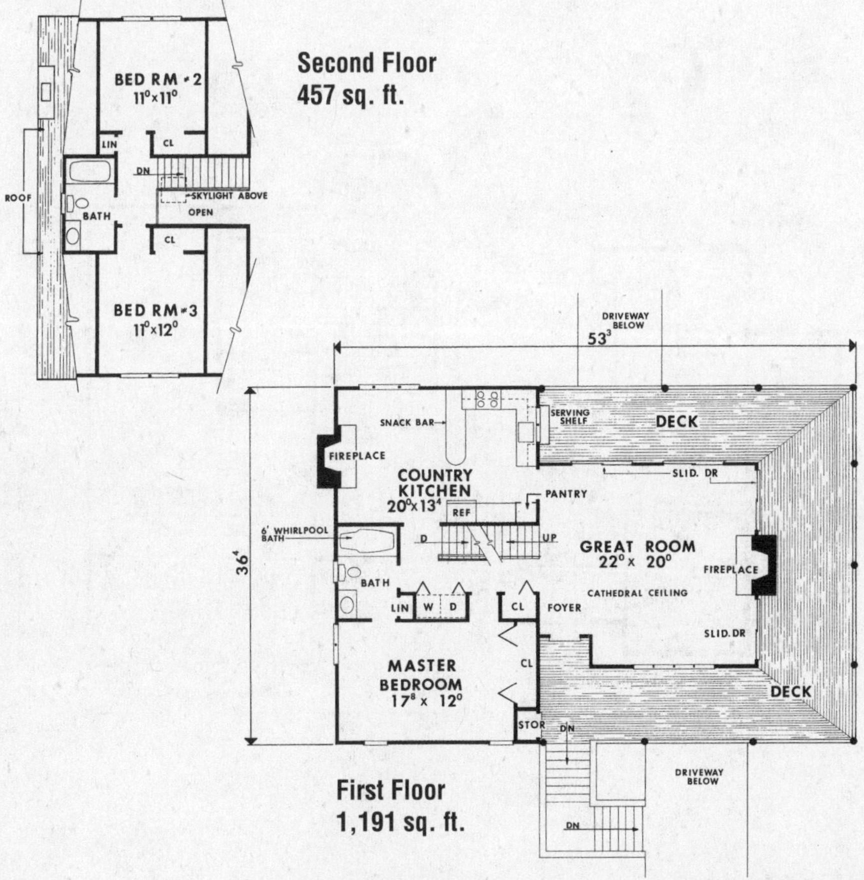
BED RM • 2
11⁰×11⁰
LIN
CL
DN
ROOF
BATH
SKYLIGHT ABOVE
OPEN
CL
BED RM • 3
11⁰×12⁰
DRIVEWAY BELOW
53³
36⁴
SNACK BAR
SERVING SHELF
DECK
FIREPLACE
COUNTRY KITCHEN
20⁰×13⁴
SLID. DR
PANTRY
REF
6' WHIRLPOOL BATH
D
UP
GREAT ROOM
22⁰ x 20⁰
FIREPLACE
BATH
CATHEDRAL CEILING
LIN
W
D
CL
FOYER
SLID. DR
CL
MASTER BEDROOM
17⁸ x 12⁰
DECK
STOR
DN
DRIVEWAY BELOW
DN

Second Floor
457 sq. ft.

First Floor
1,191 sq. ft.

Special features

- Enormous country kitchen has fireplace and a snack bar
- Four sets of sliding glass doors fill this home full of light and make the deck convenient from any room
- Secondary bedrooms both located on second floor along with a full bath
- 3 bedrooms, 2 baths, 2-car drive under garage
- Basement, crawl space or slab foundation, please specify when ordering

Distinctive Ranch

FREILING

1,962 total square feet of living area **Price Code C**

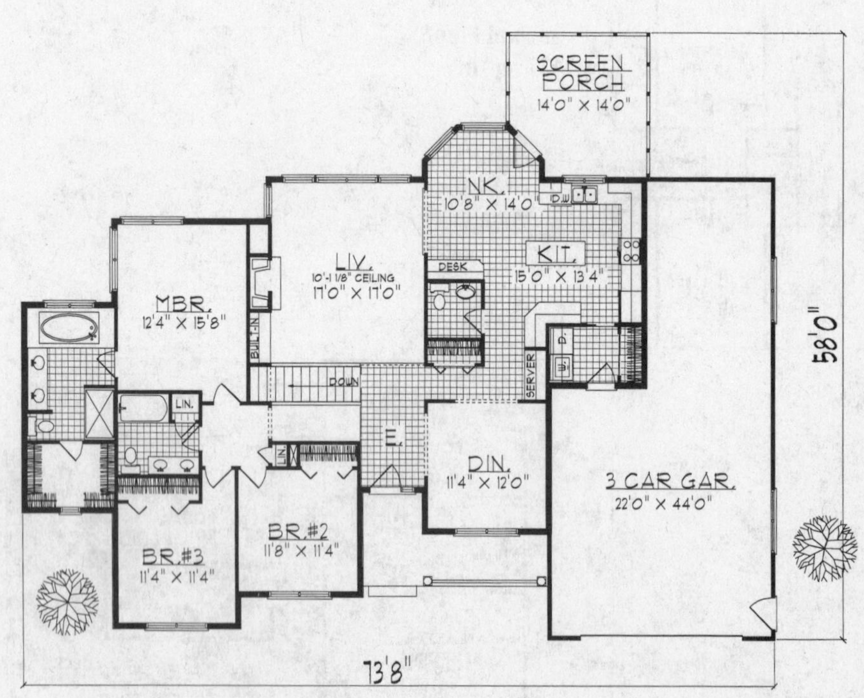
SCREEN PORCH
14'0" X 14'0"
NK.
10'8" X 14'0"
LIV.
10'-1 1/8" CEILING
17'0" X 17'0"
DESK
KIT.
15'0" X 13'4"
MBR.
12'4" X 15'8"
BUILT-IN
DOWN
SERVER
LIN.
E.
DIN.
11'4" X 12'0"
3 CAR GAR.
22'0" X 44'0"
BR.#2
11'8" X 11'4"
BR.#3
11'4" X 11'4"
58'0"
73'8"

Special features

- Formal dining room has a butler's pantry for entertaining
- Open living room offers a fireplace, built-in cabinetry and exceptional views to the outdoors
- Kitchen has work island and planning desk
- 3 bedrooms, 2 1/2 baths, 3-car garage
- Basement foundation

Plan #702-0221

Wrap-Around Porch Adds Country Charm

1,619 total square feet of living area — **Price Code B**

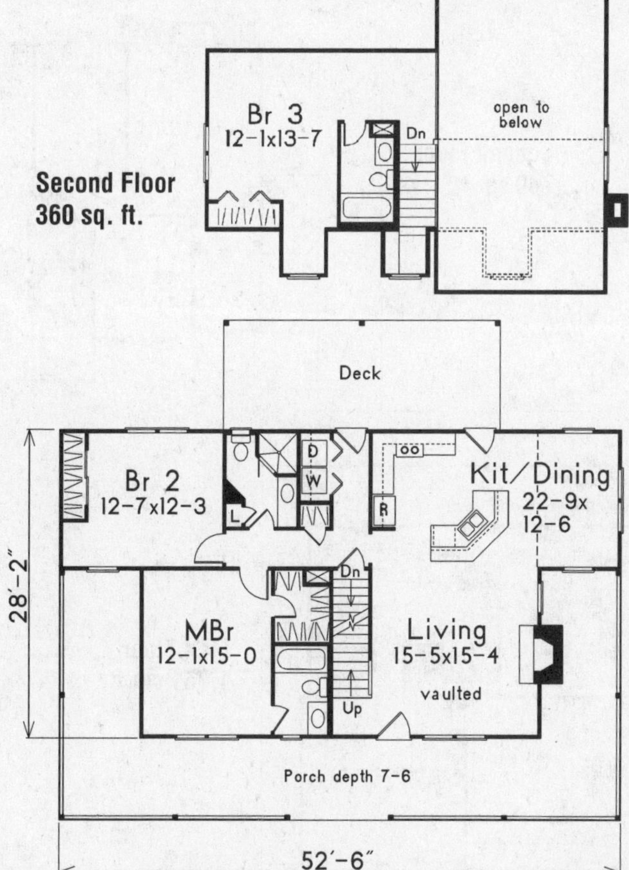
Br 3
12-1x13-7
Dn
open to
below
Deck
Br 2
12-7x12-3
D
W
L
R
Kit/Dining
22-9x
12-6
Dn
MBr
12-1x15-0
Living
15-5x15-4
vaulted
Up
Porch depth 7-6
28'-2"
52'-6"

Second Floor
360 sq. ft.

First Floor
1,259 sq. ft.

Special features

- Private second floor bedroom and bath
- Kitchen features a snack bar and adjacent dining area
- Master bedroom has a private bath
- Centrally located washer and dryer
- 3 bedrooms, 3 baths
- Basement foundation, drawings also include crawl space and slab foundations

TO ORDER BLUEPRINTS USE THE FORM ON PAGE 19 OR CALL TOLL-FREE 1-877-671-6036
View thousands more home plans online at www.familyhandyman.com/homeplans

Plan #702-MG-96132

Windows Add Plenty Of Light

2,450 total square feet of living area **Price Code D**

Special features

- Convenient first floor master bedroom has double walk-in closets and an optional sitting area/study
- Two-story breakfast and grand room are open and airy
- Laundry room has a sink and overhead cabinets for convenience
- 4 bedrooms, 2 1/2 baths, 2-car garage
- Basement or slab foundation, please specify when ordering

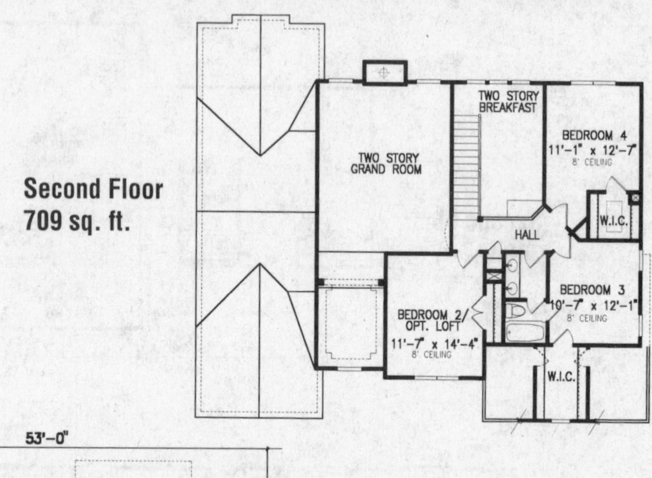
TWO STORY
BREAKFAST
BEDROOM 4
11'-1" x 12'-7"
8' CEILING
TWO STORY
GRAND ROOM
W.I.C.
HALL
BEDROOM 3
10'-7" x 12'-1"
8' CEILING
BEDROOM 2/
OPT. LOFT
11'-7" x 14'-4"
8' CEILING
W.I.C.

Second Floor
709 sq. ft.

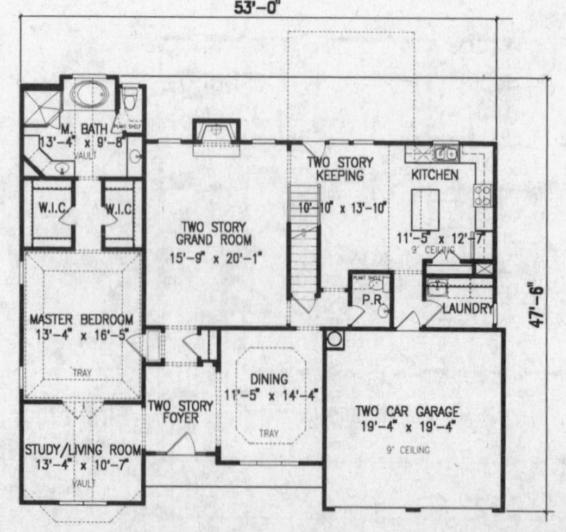
53'-0"
M. BATH
13'-4" x 9'-8"
VAULT
W.I.C.
W.I.C.
TWO STORY
GRAND ROOM
15'-9" x 20'-1"
TWO STORY
KEEPING
10'-10" x 13'-10"
KITCHEN
11'-5" x 12'-7"
9' CEILING
P.R.
LAUNDRY
47'-6"
MASTER BEDROOM
13'-4" x 16'-5"
TRAY
DINING
11'-5" x 14'-4"
TRAY
TWO STORY
FOYER
TWO CAR GARAGE
19'-4" x 19'-4"
9' CEILING
STUDY/LIVING ROOM
13'-4" x 10'-7"
VAULT

First Floor
1,751 sq. ft.

TO ORDER BLUEPRINTS USE THE FORM ON PAGE 19 OR CALL TOLL-FREE 1-877-671-6036

View thousands more home plans online at www.familyhandyman.com/homeplans

Plan #702-FB-676

Vaulted Rooms Throughout

1,373 total square feet of living area **Price Code A**

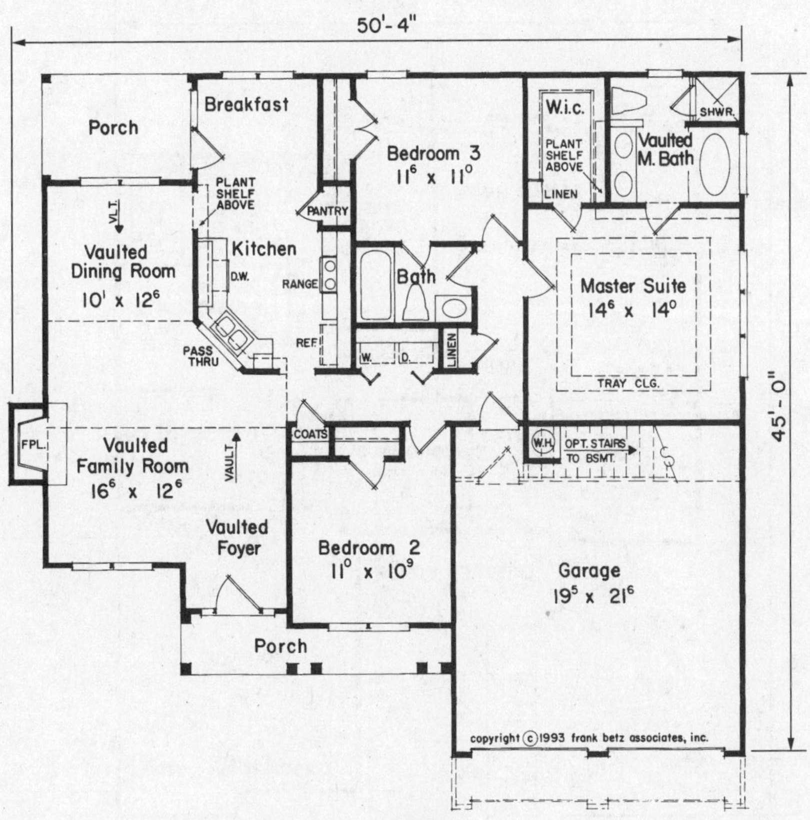
50'-4"
Porch
Breakfast
Bedroom 3
11⁶ x 11⁰
W.i.c.
PLANT SHELF ABOVE
LINEN
Vaulted M. Bath
SHWR.
PLANT SHELF ABOVE
PANTRY
VLT.
Vaulted Dining Room
10¹ x 12⁶
Kitchen
D.W.
RANGE
Bath
Master Suite
14⁶ x 14⁰
PASS THRU
REF.
W.
D.
LINEN
TRAY CLG.
45'-0"
FPL.
Vaulted Family Room
16⁶ x 12⁶
VAULT
COATS
W.H.
OPT. STAIRS TO BSMT.
Vaulted Foyer
Bedroom 2
11⁰ x 10⁹
Garage
19⁵ x 21⁶
Porch
copyright © 1993 frank betz associates, inc.

Special features

- 9' ceilings throughout this home
- Sunny breakfast room is very accessible to kitchen
- Kitchen has pass-through to vaulted family room
- 3 bedrooms, 2 baths, 2-car garage
- Crawl space or walk-out basement foundation, please specify when ordering

Plan #702-GSD-1748

Cottage-Style Adds Charm

1,496 total square feet of living area — **Price Code A**

<u>*Special features*</u>

- Large utility room with sink and extra counterspace
- Covered patio off breakfast nook extends dining to the outdoors
- Eating counter in kitchen overlooks vaulted family room
- 3 bedrooms, 2 baths, 2-car side entry garage
- Crawl space foundation

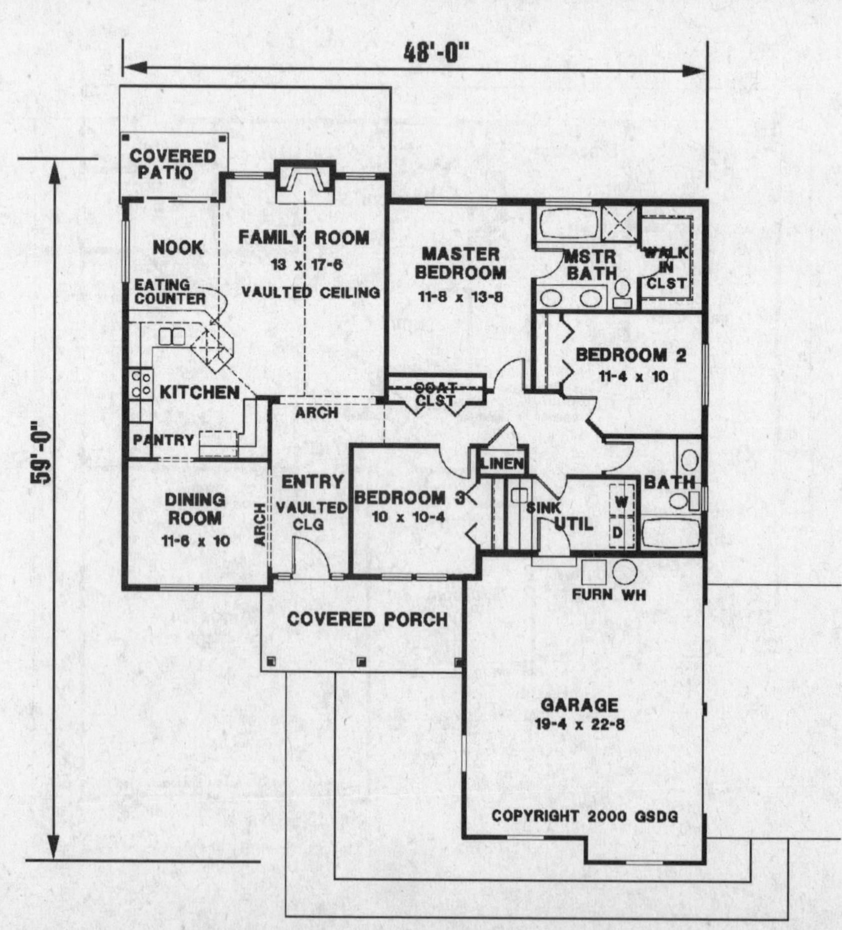
48'-0"
59'-0"
COVERED PATIO
NOOK
EATING COUNTER
FAMILY ROOM
13 x 17-6
VAULTED CEILING
MASTER BEDROOM
11-8 x 13-8
MSTR BATH
WALK IN CLST
BEDROOM 2
11-4 x 10
KITCHEN
PANTRY
ARCH
COAT CLST
LINEN
DINING ROOM
11-6 x 10
ARCH
ENTRY
VAULTED CLG
BEDROOM 3
10 x 10-4
SINK
UTIL
W
D
BATH
FURN
WH
COVERED PORCH
GARAGE
19-4 x 22-8
COPYRIGHT 2000 GSDG

TO ORDER BLUEPRINTS USE THE FORM ON PAGE 19 OR CALL TOLL-FREE 1-877-671-6036

Large Sundeck Creates Outdoor Living Area

1,732 total square feet of living area **Price Code B**

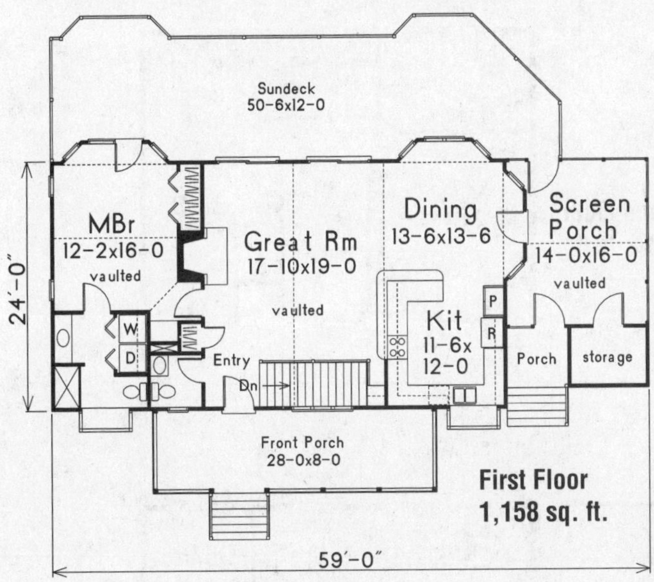

Sundeck
50-6x12-0
MBr
12-2x16-0
vaulted
Great Rm
17-10x19-0
vaulted
Dining
13-6x13-6
Screen
Porch
14-0x16-0
vaulted
Kit
11-6x
12-0
P
R
W
D
Entry
Dn
Porch
storage
Front Porch
28-0x8-0
24'-0"
59'-0"
First Floor
1,158 sq. ft.

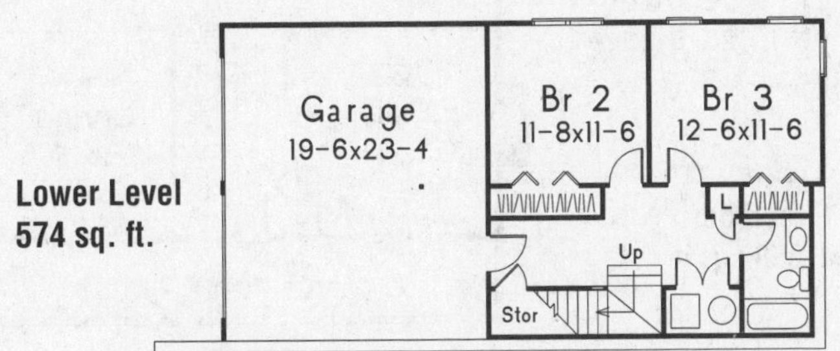

Lower Level
574 sq. ft.
Garage
19-6x23-4
Br 2
11-8x11-6
Br 3
12-6x11-6
L
Up
Stor

Special features

- Spacious great room with vaulted ceiling and fireplace overlooks large sundeck
- Dramatic dining room boasts extensive windows and angled walls
- Vaulted master bedroom includes private bath with laundry area and accesses sun deck
- Convenient second entrance
- 3 bedrooms, 2 1/2 baths, 2-car drive under garage
- Basement foundation

Country Classic With Modern Floor Plan

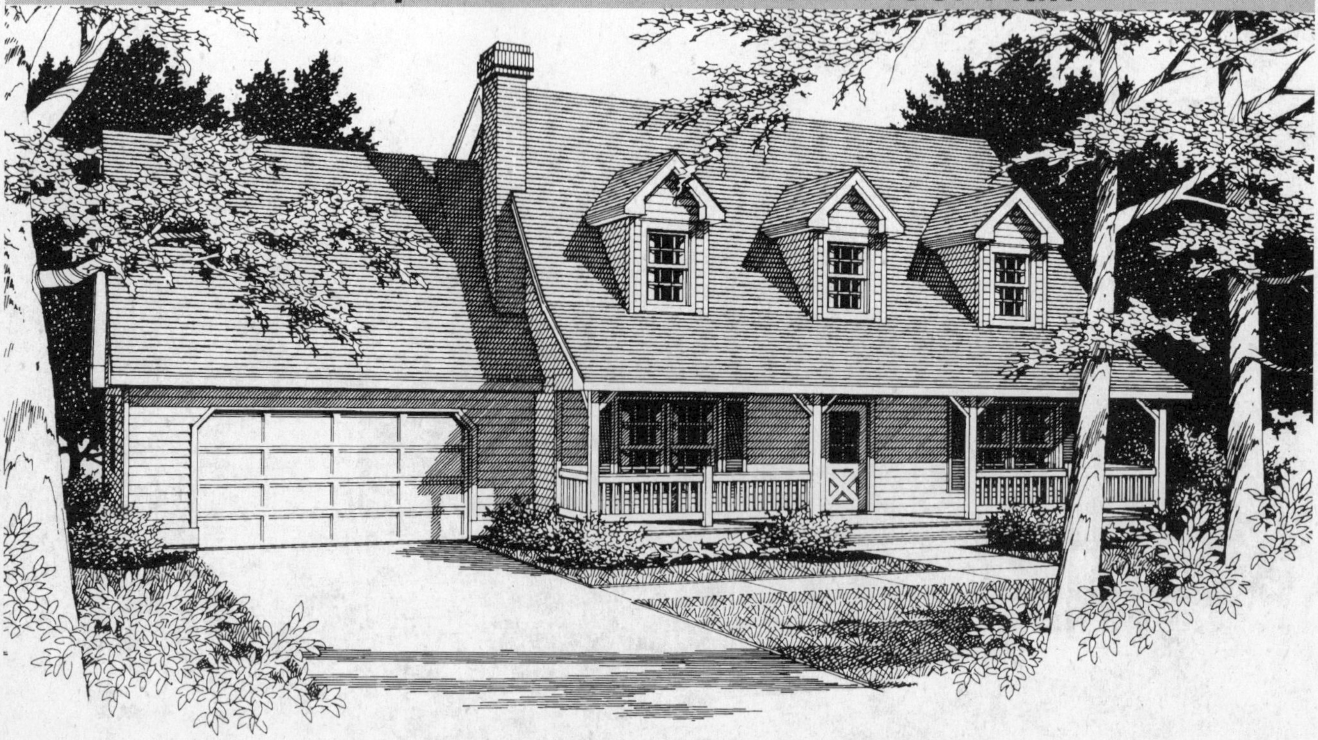

1,921 total square feet of living area **Price Code D**

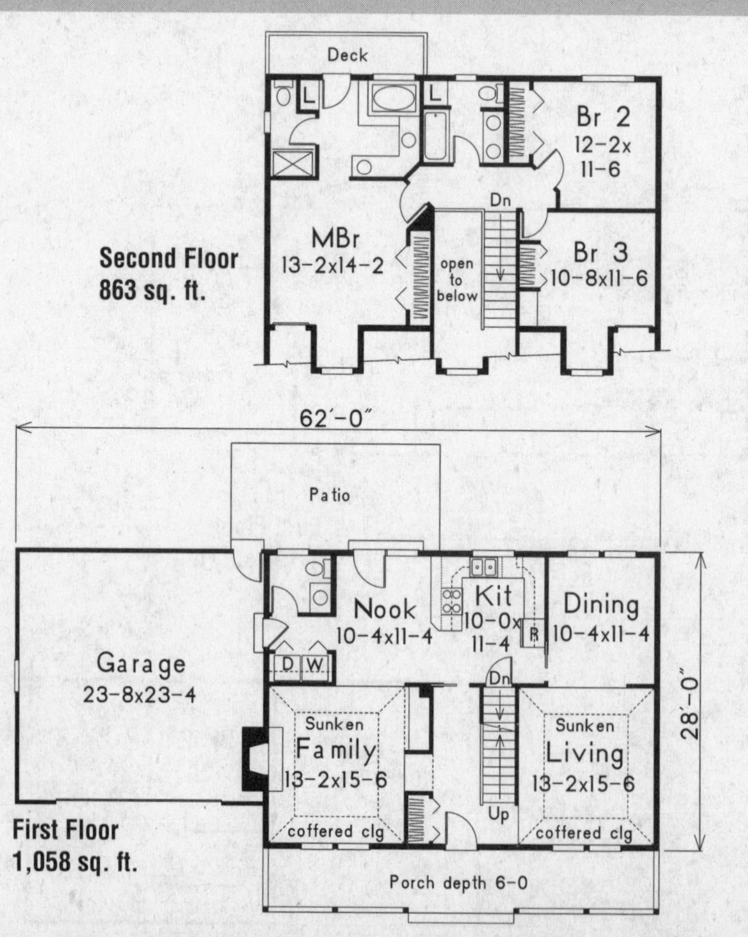
Deck
L
L
Br 2
12-2x
11-6
Dn
MBr
13-2x14-2
open
to
below
Br 3
10-8x11-6
Second Floor
863 sq. ft.
62'-0"
Patio
Nook
10-4x11-4
Kit
10-0x
11-4
R
Dining
10-4x11-4
Garage
23-8x23-4
D W
Dn
Sunken
Family
13-2x15-6
coffered clg
Up
Sunken
Living
13-2x15-6
coffered clg
28'-0"
Porch depth 6-0
First Floor
1,058 sq. ft.

Special features

- Energy efficient home with 2" x 6" exterior walls
- Sunken family room includes a built-in entertainment center and coffered ceiling
- Sunken formal living room features a coffered ceiling
- Dressing area has double sinks, spa tub, shower and French door to private deck
- Large front porch adds to home's appeal
- 3 bedrooms, 2 1/2 baths, 2-car garage
- Basement foundation

Plan #702-SH-SEA-405

Distinctive Country Victorian Design

2,693 total square feet of living area

Price Code E

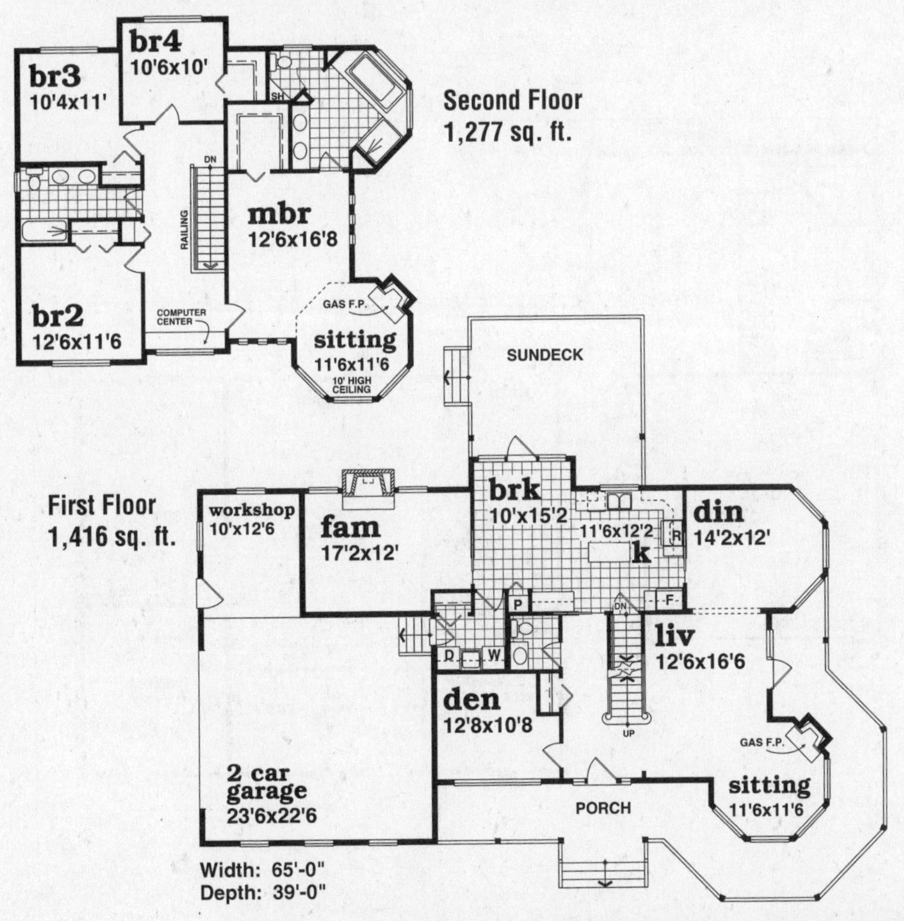

br3
10'4x11'
br4
10'6x10'
SH
DN
RAILING
mbr
12'6x16'8
br2
12'6x11'6
COMPUTER CENTER
GAS F.P.
sitting
11'6x11'6
10' HIGH CEILING
Second Floor
1,277 sq. ft.
SUNDECK
First Floor
1,416 sq. ft.
workshop
10'x12'6
fam
17'2x12'
brk
10'x15'2
11'6x12'2
k
R
din
14'2x12'
P
F
DN
D
W
liv
12'6x16'6
den
12'8x10'8
UP
GAS F.P.
2 car garage
23'6x22'6
PORCH
sitting
11'6x11'6
Width: 65'-0"
Depth: 39'-0"

Special features

- Energy efficient home with 2" x 6" exterior walls
- A private den is tucked into a corner off the entry
- Master suite has sitting area with fireplace and a lavish bath
- 4 bedrooms, 2 1/2 baths, 2-car side entry garage
- Basement or crawl space foundation, please specify when ordering

TO ORDER BLUEPRINTS USE THE FORM ON PAGE 19 OR CALL TOLL-FREE 1-877-671-6036

View thousands more home plans online at www.familyhandyman.com/homeplans

The Family
Handyman

Plan #702-VL2069

Covered Porch Adds Charm

2,069 total square feet of living area

Price Code C

Special features

- 9' ceilings throughout this home
- Kitchen has many amenities including a snack bar
- Large front and rear porches
- 3 bedrooms, 2 1/2 baths, 2-car garage
- Slab or crawl space foundation, please specify when ordering

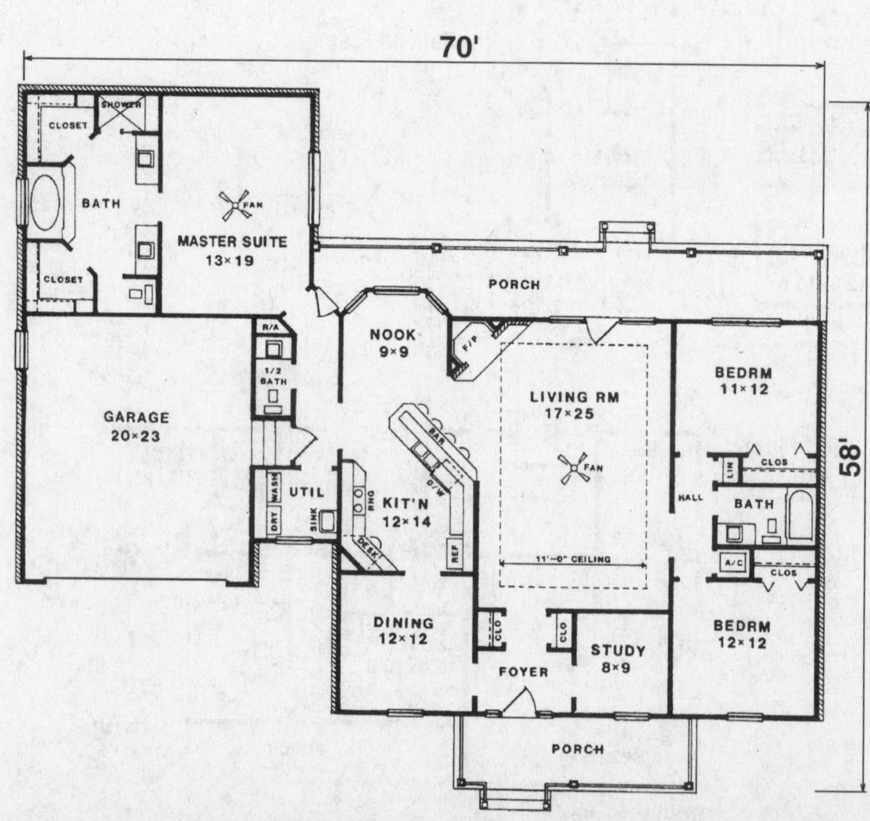

70'
58'
CLOSET
SHOWER
BATH
FAN
MASTER SUITE
13×19
CLOSET
PORCH
NOOK
9×9
F/P
R/A
1/2 BATH
GARAGE
20×23
LIVING RM
17×25
BEDRM
11×12
BAR
D/W
FAN
LIN
CLOS
UTIL
WASH
DRY
SINK
RNG
KIT'N
12×14
DESK
REF
HALL
BATH
A/C
CLOS
11'-0" CEILING
DINING
12×12
CLO
CLO
STUDY
8×9
FOYER
BEDRM
12×12
PORCH

TO ORDER BLUEPRINTS USE THE FORM ON PAGE 19 OR CALL TOLL-FREE 1-877-671-6036

View thousands more home plans online at www.familyhandyman.com/homeplans

Living Room Has Balcony Overlook

2,498 total square feet of living area

Price Code D

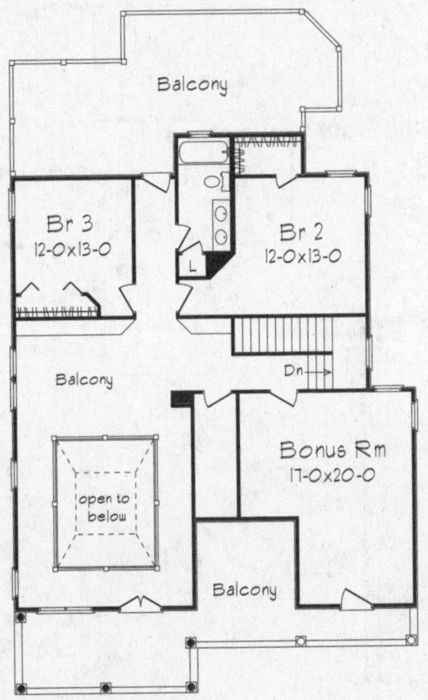
Balcony
Br 3
12-0x13-0
Br 2
12-0x13-0
L
Balcony
Dn
open to below
Bonus Rm
17-0x20-0
Balcony

Second Floor
968 sq. ft.

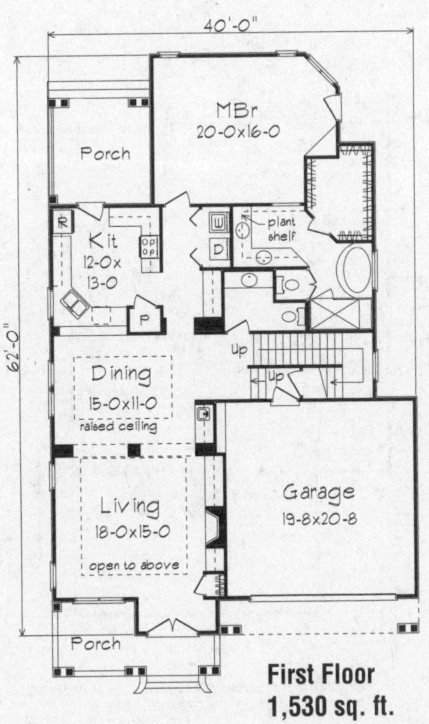
40'-0"
62'-0"
MBr
20-0x16-0
Porch
R
Kit
12-0x
13-0
W
D
plant shelf
P
Up
Dining
15-0x11-0
raised ceiling
Up
Living
18-0x15-0
open to above
Garage
19-8x20-8
Porch

First Floor
1,530 sq. ft.

Special features

- 10' ceilings on first floor and 9' ceilings on second floor
- Dining room has raised ceiling and convenient wet bar
- Master suite features oversized walk-in closet and bath with garden tub
- 3 bedrooms, 2 1/2 baths, 2-car garage
- Crawl space foundation, drawings also include slab and basement foundations

TO ORDER BLUEPRINTS USE THE FORM ON PAGE 19 OR CALL TOLL-FREE 1-877-671-6036

View thousands more home plans online at www.familyhandyman.com/homeplans

Plan #702-VL3011

Trio Of Dormers Add Appeal

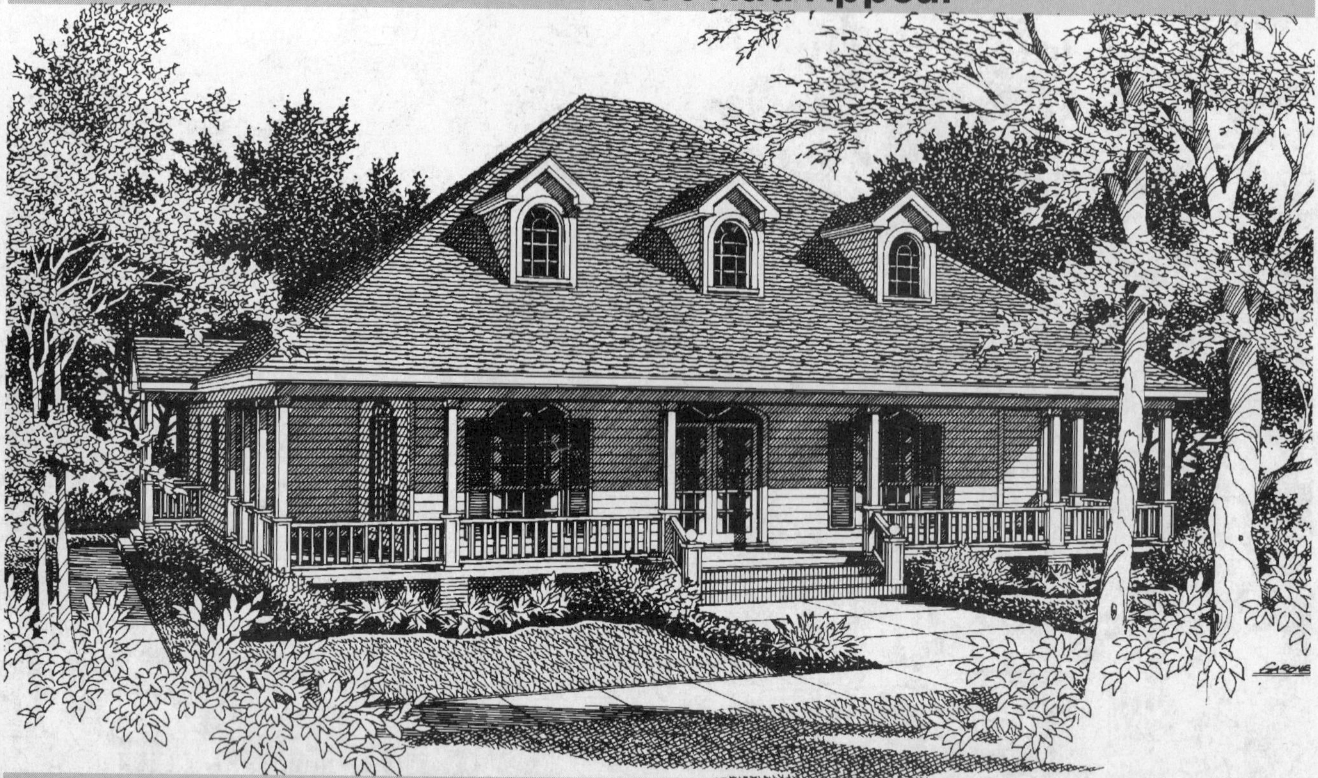

3,011 total square feet of living area **Price Code E**

Special features

- 9' ceilings on the first floor
- Formal dining room has decorative columns separating it from foyer and great room
- Two secondary bedrooms share a full bath on the second floor
- Spacious master suite accesses sun room through double-doors and has a spacious master bath
- 3 bedrooms, 2 1/2 baths
- Slab or crawl space foundation, please specify when ordering

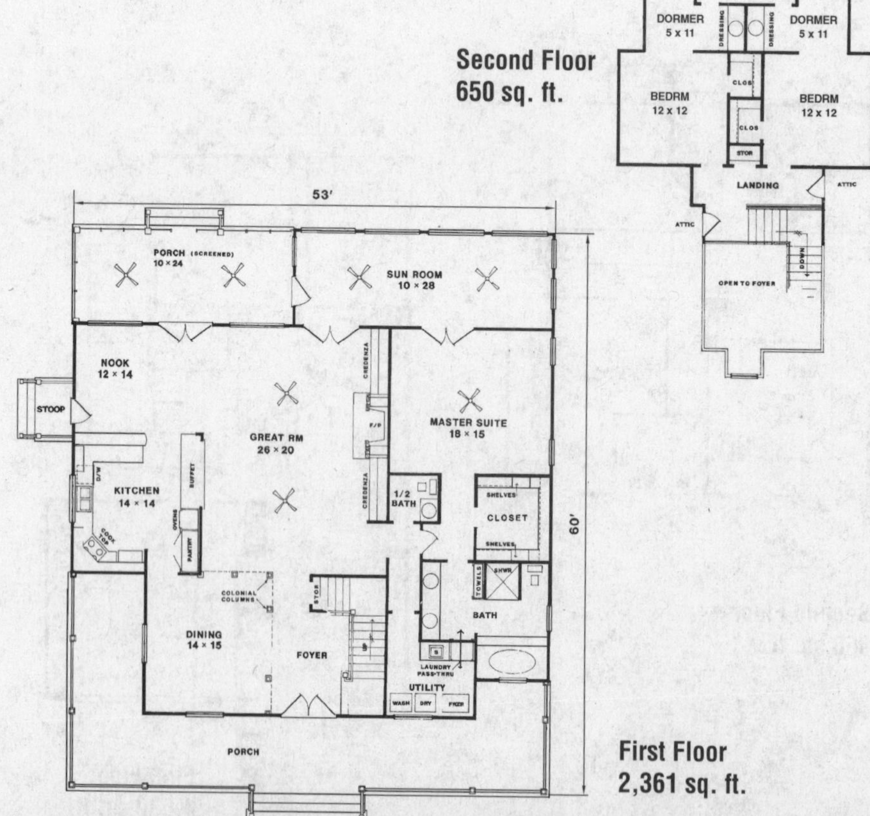
BATH
DORMER 5 x 11
DORMER 5 x 11
BEDRM 12 x 12
BEDRM 12 x 12
LANDING
ATTIC
ATTIC
OPEN TO FOYER
DOWN
53'
60'
PORCH (SCREENED) 10 x 24
SUN ROOM 10 x 28
NOOK 12 x 14
STOOP
GREAT RM 26 x 20
MASTER SUITE 18 x 15
KITCHEN 14 x 14
1/2 BATH
CLOSET
SHELVES
BATH
DINING 14 x 15
COLONIAL COLUMNS
FOYER
UTILITY
WASH
DRY
FREZR
PORCH

Second Floor
650 sq. ft.

First Floor
2,361 sq. ft.

TO ORDER BLUEPRINTS USE THE FORM ON PAGE 19 OR CALL TOLL-FREE 1-877-671-6036

View thousands more home plans online at www.familyhandyman.com/homeplans

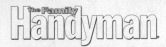

Windows Frame Fireplace

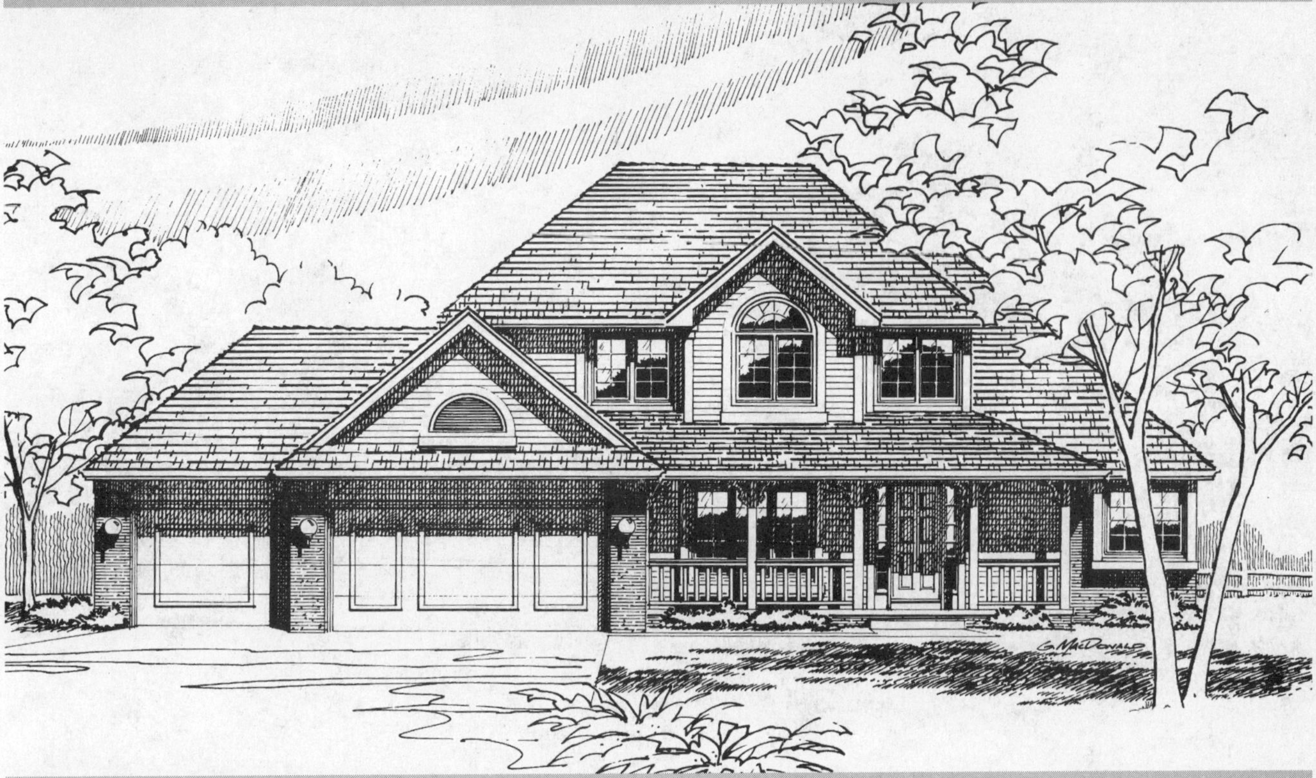

2,115 total square feet of living area **Price Code C**

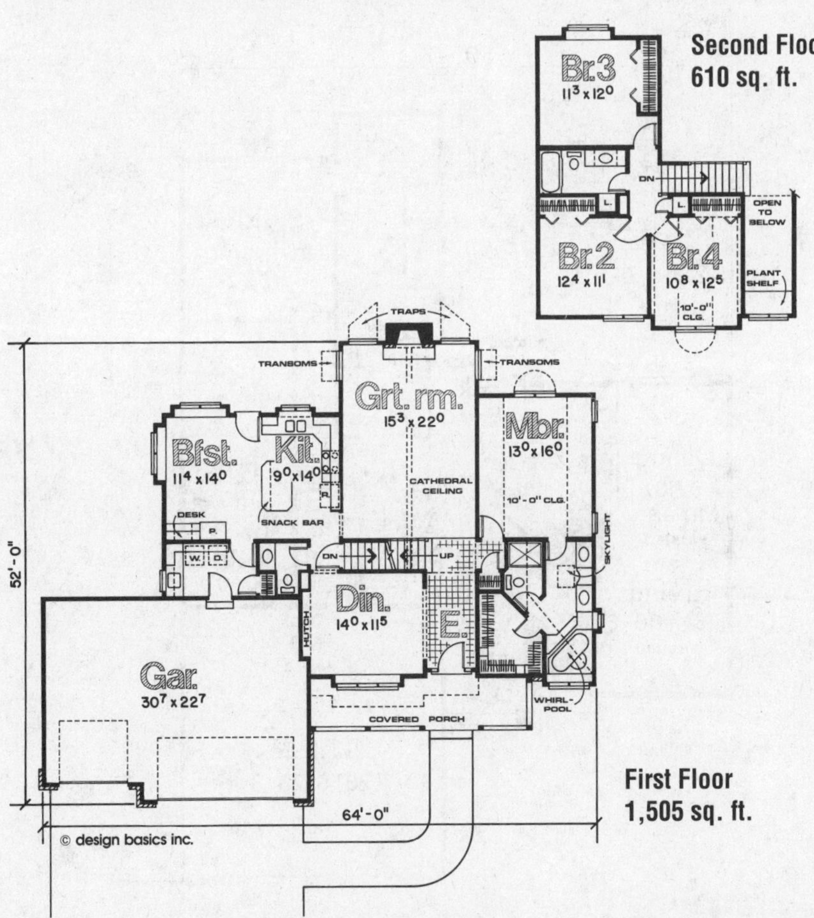
Second Floor
610 sq. ft.
Br.3
Br.2
Br.4
DN
OPEN TO BELOW
PLANT SHELF
Grt. rm.
CATHEDRAL CEILING
TRANSOMS
TRAPS
Mbr.
Bfst.
Kit.
DESK
SNACK BAR
Din.
HUTCH
Gar.
COVERED PORCH
WHIRL-POOL
SKYLIGHT
52'-0"
64'-0"
First Floor
1,505 sq. ft.
© design basics inc.

Special features

- Cathedral ceiling in great room adds spaciousness
- Two-story foyer is a grand entrance
- Efficiently designed kitchen with breakfast area, snack bar and built-in desk
- 4 bedrooms, 2 1/2 baths, 3-car garage
- Basement foundation

Plan #702-0264

Vaulted Living Area Adds Appeal

1,689 total square feet of living area **Price Code B**

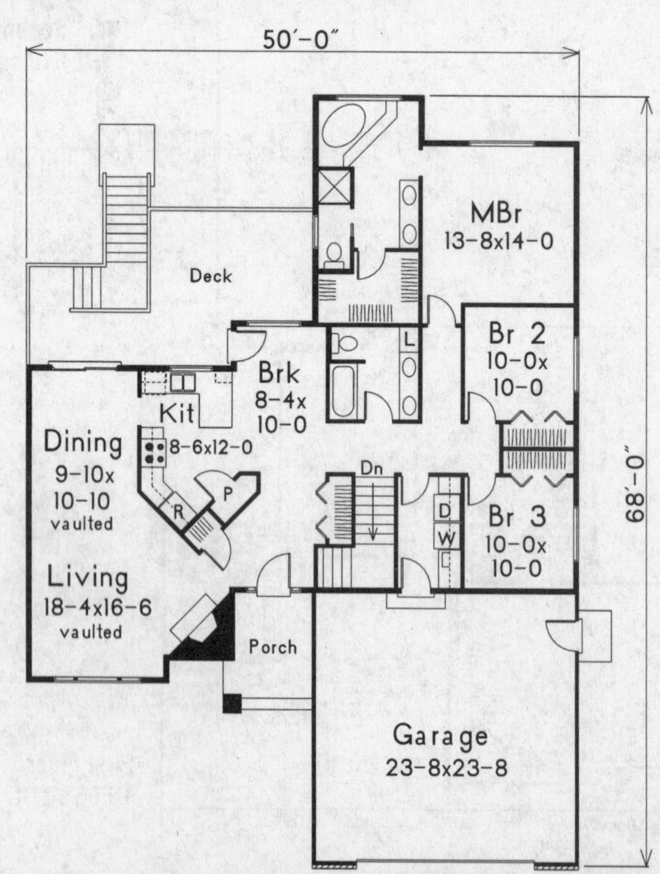
50'-0"
68'-0"
Deck
MBr
13-8x14-0
L
Br 2
10-0x
10-0
Brk
8-4x
10-0
Kit
8-6x12-0
Dining
9-10x
10-10
vaulted
P
R
Dn
D
W
Br 3
10-0x
10-0
Living
18-4x16-6
vaulted
Porch
Garage
23-8x23-8

Special features

- Distinct covered entrance
- Large, open living and dining area including vaulted ceiling, corner fireplace and access to the rear deck
- Stylish angled kitchen offers large counter work space and nook
- Master bedroom boasts spacious bath with step-up tub, separate shower and large walk-in closet
- 3 bedrooms, 2 baths, 2-car garage
- Basement foundation, drawings also include slab and crawl space foundations

Plan #702-GH-24724

Two-Story With Victorian Feel

1,982 total square feet of living area

Price Code C

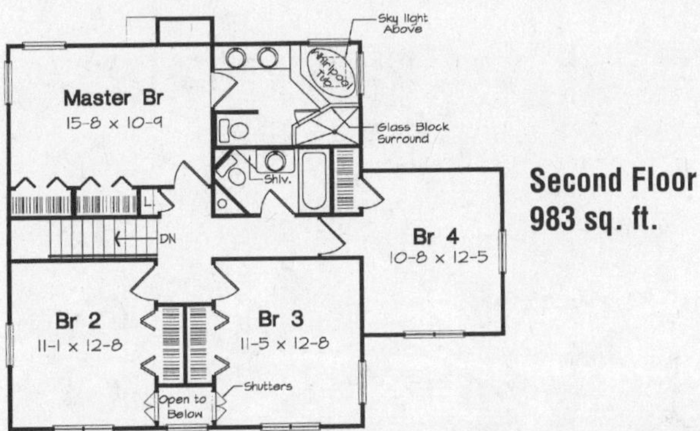
Sky light Above
Master Br
15-8 x 10-9
Whirlpool Tub
Glass Block Surround
Shlv.
DN
Br 4
10-8 x 12-5
Br 2
11-1 x 12-8
Br 3
11-5 x 12-8
Shutters
Open to Below

Second Floor
983 sq. ft.

51'-0"
36'-0"
Wood Box
Ent. Center
Great Rm
19-5 x 13-1
Brkfst
7-8 x 7-0
Screened Porch
10-8 x 9-8
Sky light Above
UP
DN
Kitchen
10-8 x 12-5
Ref
Decor Clg
Parlor
11-5 x 12-8
Dining
11-5 x 10-2

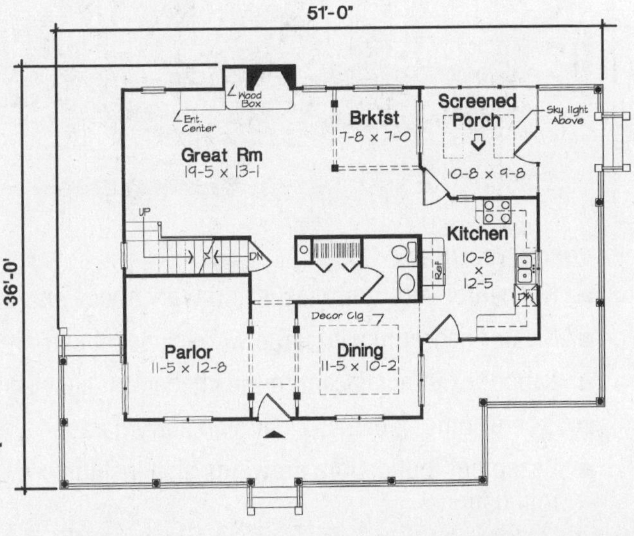

First Floor
999 sq. ft.

Special features

- Spacious master bedroom has bath with corner whirlpool tub and sunny skylight above
- Breakfast area overlooks into great room
- Screened porch with skylight above extends the home outdoors and allows for entertainment area
- 4 bedrooms, 2 1/2 baths
- Crawl space or slab foundation, please specify when ordering

Easy-To-Build Plan — Plan #702-SH-SEA-023

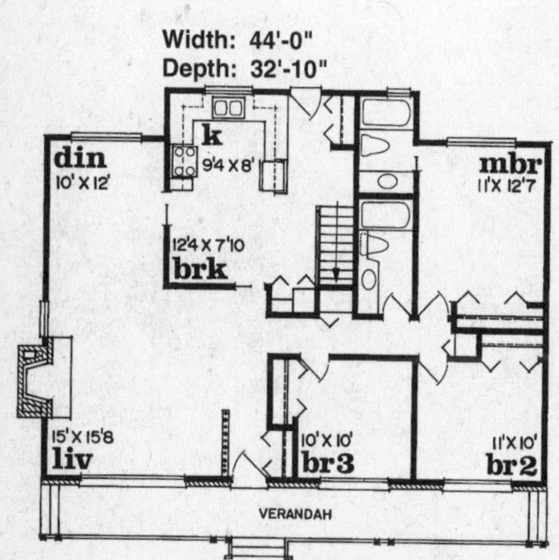
Width: 44'-0"
Depth: 32'-10"
k
9'4 X 8'
din
10' X 12'
mbr
11'X 12'7
12'4 X 7'10
brk
15' X 15'8
liv
10' X 10'
br3
11' X 10'
br2
VERANDAH

1,358 total square feet of living area **Price Code A**

Special features

- Energy efficient home with 2" x 6" exterior walls
- Covered verandah invites outdoor relaxation
- Living room is warmed by masonry fireplace
- 3 bedrooms, 2 baths
- Basement or crawl space foundation, please specify when ordering

Layout For Comfortable Living — Plan #702-0217

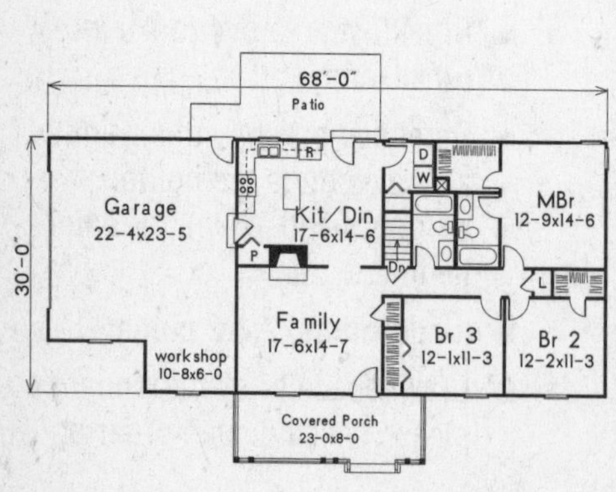
68'-0"
Patio
30'-0"
Garage
22-4x23-5
Kit/Din
17-6x14-6
MBr
12-9x14-6
Family
17-6x14-7
workshop
10-8x6-0
Br 3
12-1x11-3
Br 2
12-2x11-3
Covered Porch
23-0x8-0

1,360 total square feet of living area **Price Code A**

Special features

- Kitchen/dining room has island work space and plenty of dining area
- Master bedroom with large walk-in closet and private bath
- Laundry room adjacent to the kitchen for easy access
- 3 bedrooms, 2 baths, 2-car side entry garage
- Basement foundation, drawings also include crawl space and slab foundations

TO ORDER BLUEPRINTS USE THE FORM ON PAGE 19 OR CALL TOLL-FREE 1-877-671-6036

View thousands more home plans online at www.familyhandyman.com/homeplans

The Family
Handyman

Lovely Full-Width Column Porch

1,097 total square feet of living area **Price Code AA**

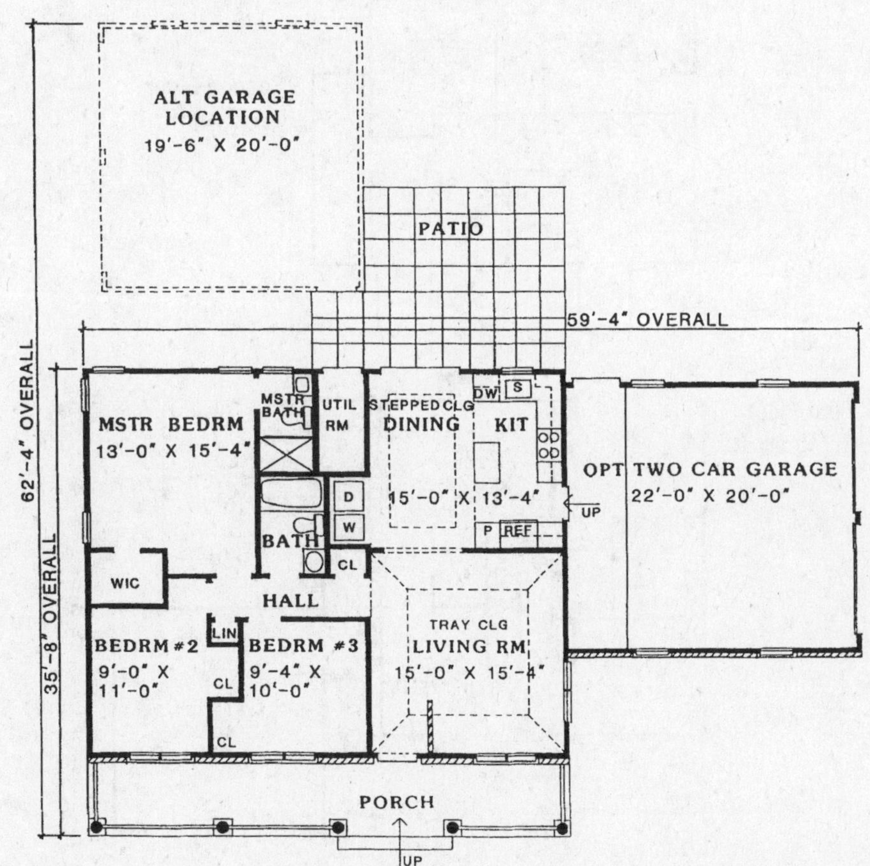
ALT GARAGE
LOCATION
19'-6" X 20'-0"
PATIO
59'-4" OVERALL
62'-4" OVERALL
35'-8" OVERALL
MSTR BEDRM
13'-0" X 15'-4"
MSTR BATH
UTIL RM
STEPPED CLG
DINING
KIT
DW
S
15'-0" X 13'-4"
D
W
P
REF
UP
OPT TWO CAR GARAGE
22'-0" X 20'-0"
BATH
CL
WIC
HALL
LIN
BEDRM #2
9'-0" X
11'-0"
CL
BEDRM #3
9'-4" X
10'-0"
TRAY CLG
LIVING RM
15'-0" X 15'-4"
CL
PORCH
UP

Special features

- U-shaped kitchen wraps around center island
- Master suite includes its own private bath and walk-in closet
- Living room provides expansive view to the rear
- 3 bedrooms, 2 baths, optional 2-car garage
- Basement, crawl space or slab foundation, please specify when ordering

Plan #702-0183

Compact Design Offers Privacy

2,847 total square feet of living area **Price Code E**

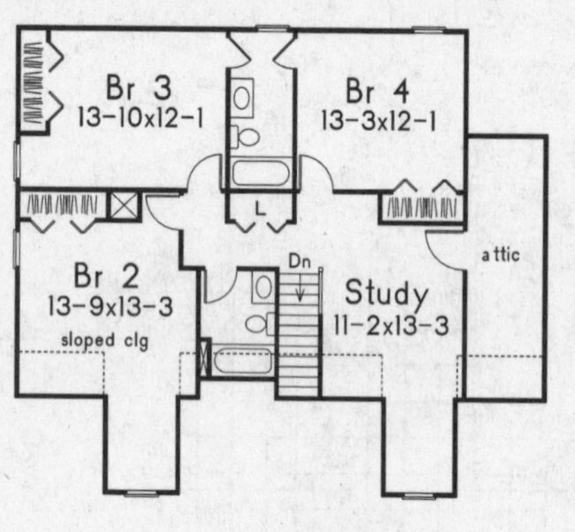
Br 3
13-10x12-1
Br 4
13-3x12-1
L
Br 2
13-9x13-3
sloped clg
Dn
Study
11-2x13-3
attic

Second Floor
1,102 sq. ft.

Special features

- Secluded first floor master bedroom includes an oversized window and a large walk-in closet
- Extensive attic storage and closet space
- Spacious second floor bedrooms, two of which share a private bath
- Great starter home with option to finish the second floor as needed
- 4 bedrooms, 3 1/2 baths, 2-car garage
- Basement foundation, drawings also include slab and crawl space foundations

First Floor
1,745 sq. ft.

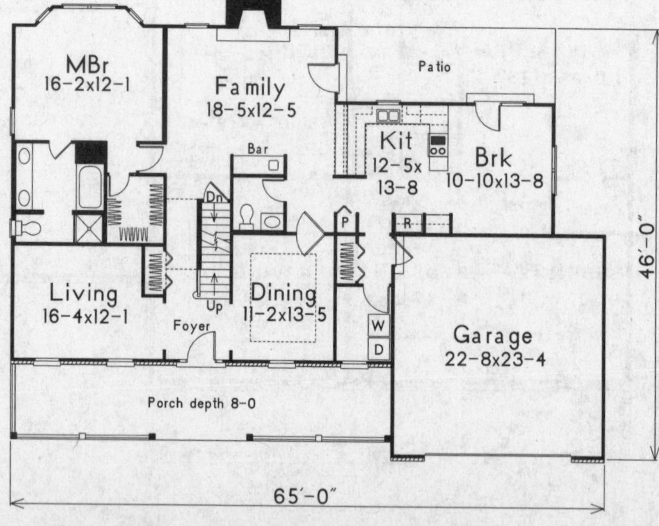
MBr
16-2x12-1
Family
18-5x12-5
Patio
Bar
Kit
12-5x
13-8
Brk
10-10x13-8
Dn
P
R
Living
16-4x12-1
Up
Foyer
Dining
11-2x13-5
W
D
Garage
22-8x23-4
Porch depth 8-0
46'-0"
65'-0"

TO ORDER BLUEPRINTS USE THE FORM ON PAGE 19 OR CALL TOLL-FREE 1-877-671-6036

The Family
Handyman

Plan #702-0134

Stately Colonial Features Porch With Overhead Balcony

2,216 total square feet of living area — **Price Code D**

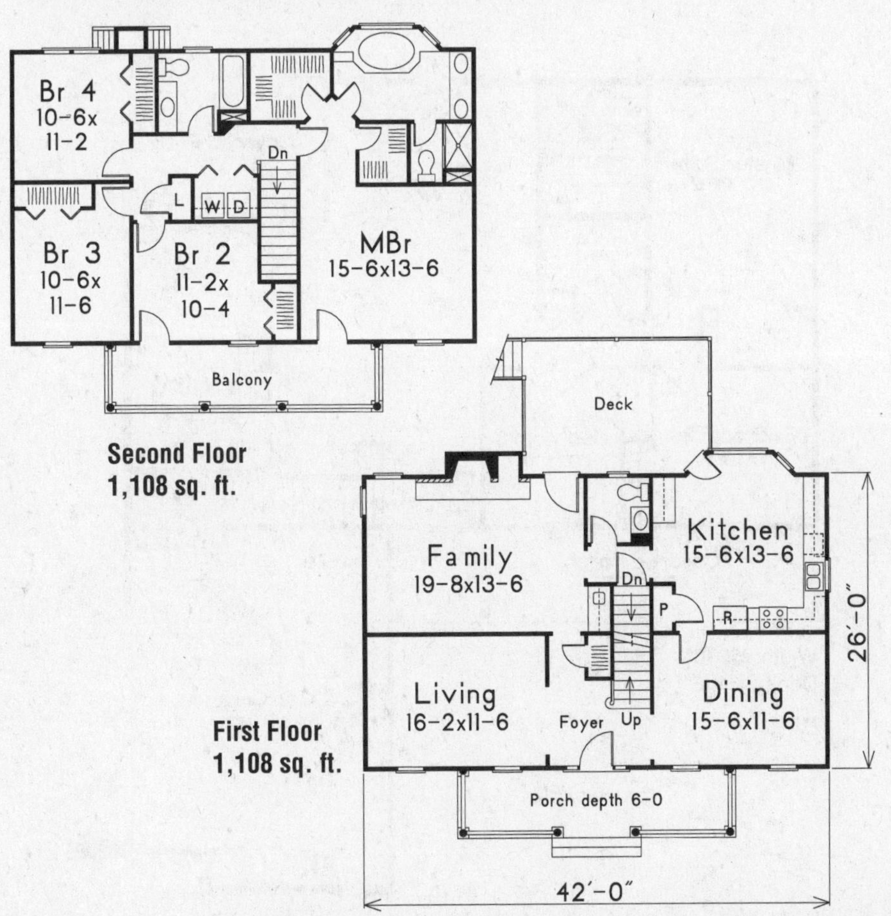
Br 4
10-6x
11-2
Dn
Br 3
10-6x
11-6
L
W D
Br 2
11-2x
10-4
MBr
15-6x13-6
Balcony
Deck
Family
19-8x13-6
Kitchen
15-6x13-6
Dn
P
R
26'-0"
Living
16-2x11-6
Foyer
Up
Dining
15-6x11-6
Porch depth 6-0
42'-0"

Second Floor
1,108 sq. ft.

First Floor
1,108 sq. ft.

Special features

- Luxury master bedroom suite features full-windowed bathtub bay, double walk-in closets and access to the front balcony
- Spacious kitchen/breakfast room combination
- Second floor laundry facility
- 4 bedrooms, 2 1/2 baths, 2-car drive under garage
- Basement foundation

Plan #702-HDS-1558-2

Rustic Styling With All The Comforts

J.N. HANSENS.D.G.

1,885 total square feet of living area **Price Code C**

Special features

- Enormous covered patio
- Dining and great rooms combine to create one large and versatile living area
- Utility room directly off kitchen for convenience
- 3 bedrooms, 2 baths, 2-car side entry garage
- Basement foundation

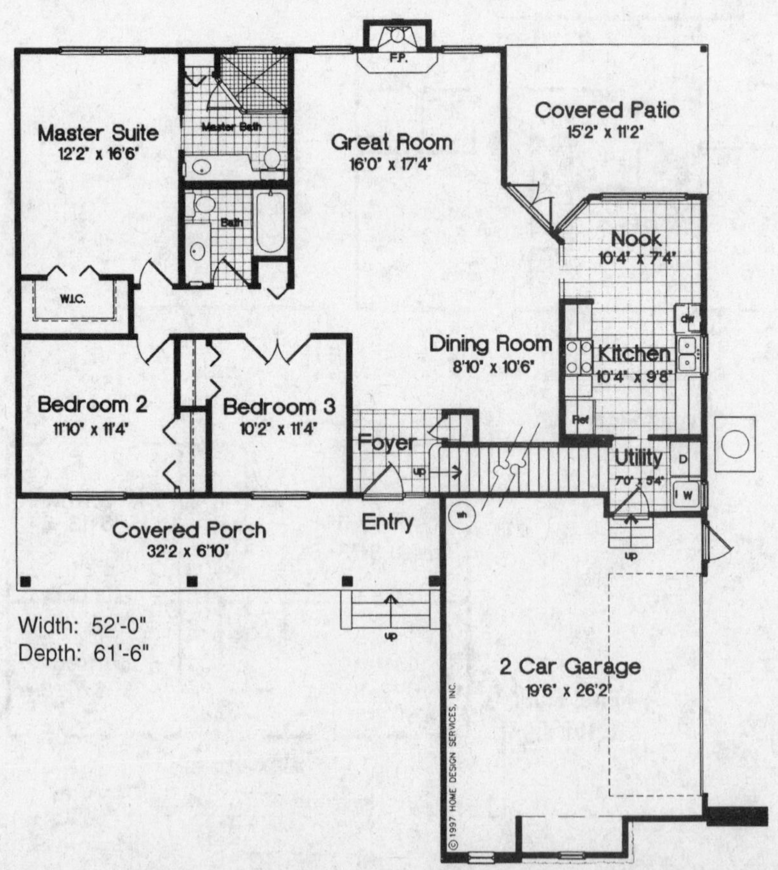

F.P.
Covered Patio
15'2" x 11'2"
Master Suite
12'2" x 16'6"
Master Bath
Great Room
16'0" x 17'4"
Bath
Nook
10'4" x 7'4"
W.I.C.
Dining Room
8'10" x 10'6"
Kitchen
10'4" x 9'8"
Bedroom 2
11'10" x 11'4"
Bedroom 3
10'2" x 11'4"
Foyer
Ref
Utility
7'0" x 5'4"
D
W
up
Entry
Covered Porch
32'2 x 6'10"
up
up
Width: 52'-0"
Depth: 61'-6"
2 Car Garage
19'6" x 26'2"
© 1997 HOME DESIGN SERVICES, INC.

TO ORDER BLUEPRINTS USE THE FORM ON PAGE 19 OR CALL TOLL-FREE 1-877-671-6036

View thousands more home plans online at www.familyhandyman.com/homeplans

The Family
Handyman

Plan #702-0804

Cozy Country-Style Home

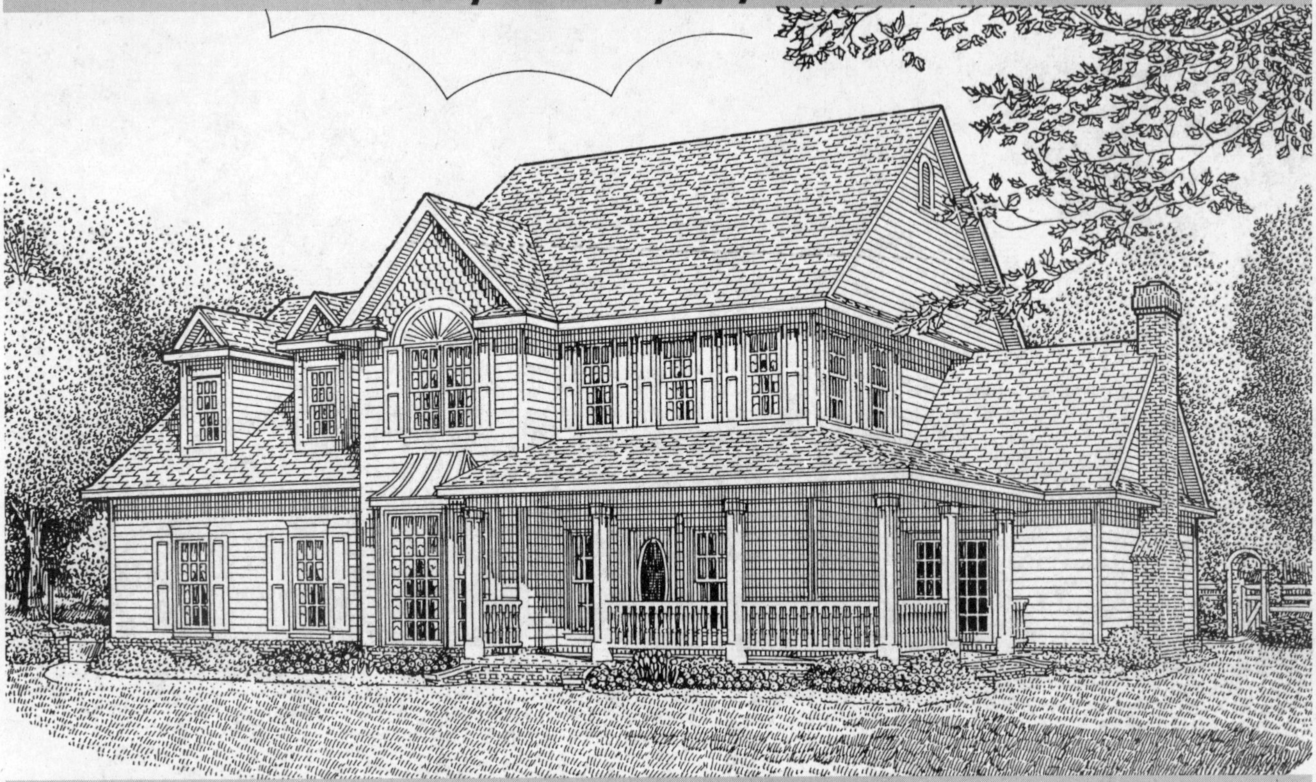

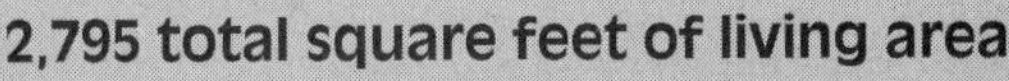

2,795 total square feet of living area

Price Code E

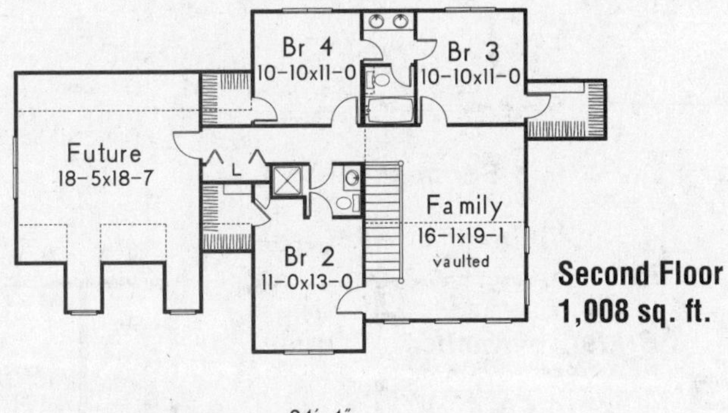
Br 4
10-10x11-0
Br 3
10-10x11-0
Future
18-5x18-7
L
Family
16-1x19-1
vaulted
Br 2
11-0x13-0

Second Floor
1,008 sq. ft.

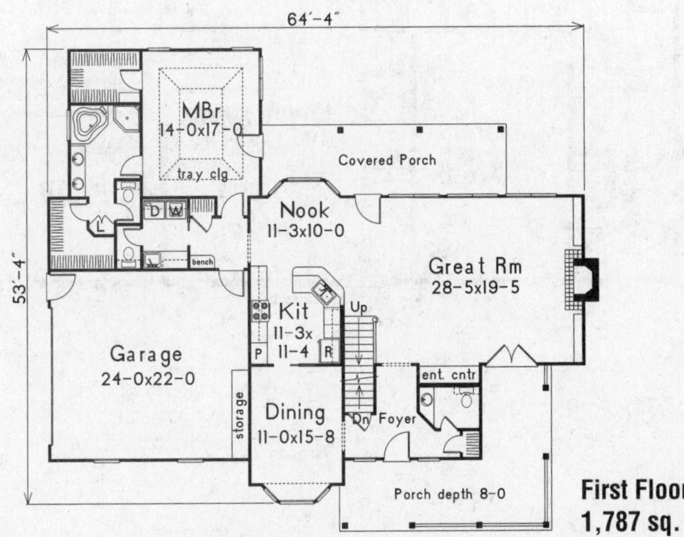
64'-4"
53'-4"
MBr
14-0x17-0
tray clg
Covered Porch
D W
L
bench
Nook
11-3x10-0
Great Rm
28-5x19-5
Kit
11-3x
11-4
Up
P
R
Garage
24-0x22-0
storage
Dining
11-0x15-8
Dn
Foyer
ent. cntr
Porch depth 8-0

First Floor
1,787 sq. ft.

Special features

- Second floor has cozy vaulted family room
- Formal dining room directly off kitchen
- Spacious great room with fireplace has built-in entertainment center
- Bonus room on the second floor has an additional 387 square feet of living area
- 4 bedrooms, 3 1/2 baths, 2-car side entry garage
- Basement foundation, drawings also include crawl space or slab foundation

Formal Country Charm

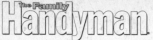

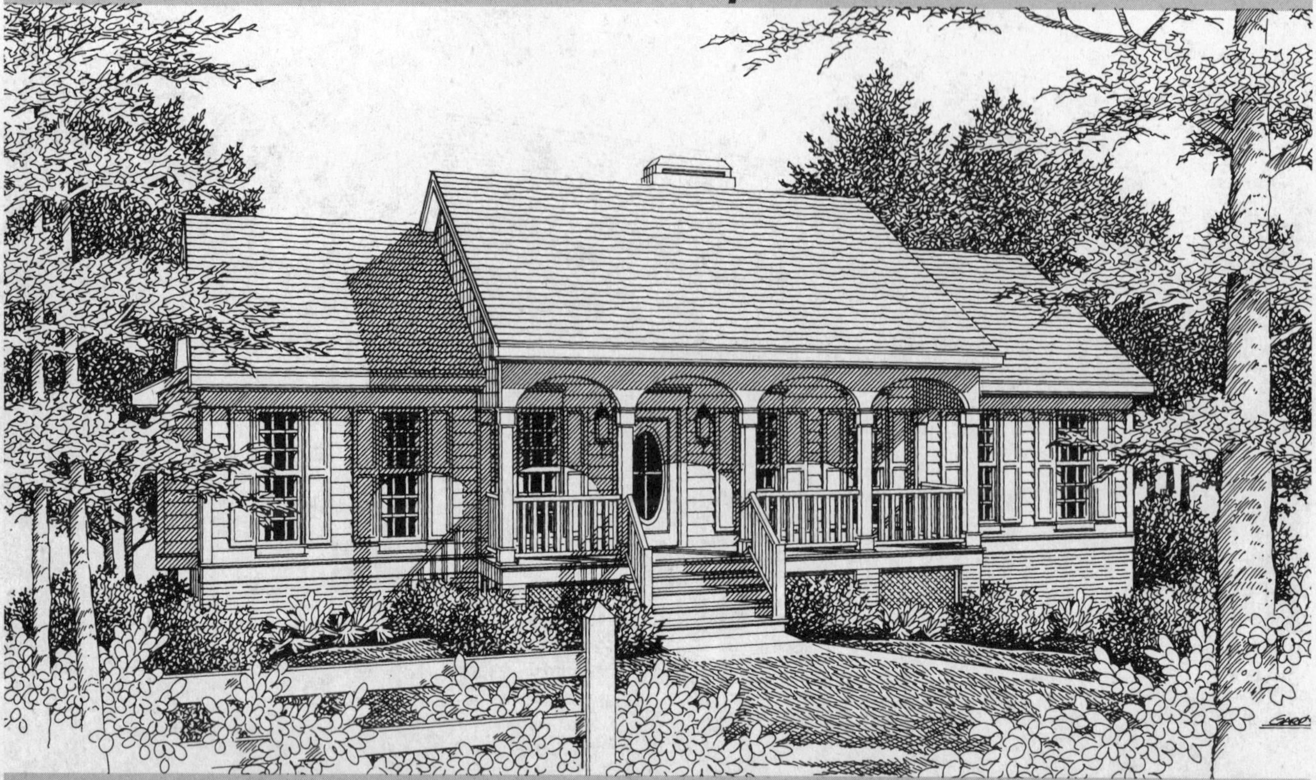

1,325 total square feet of living area **Price Code A**

Special features

- Sloped ceiling and a fireplace in living area creates a cozy feeling
- Formal dining and breakfast areas have an efficiently designed kitchen between them
- Master bedroom has walk-in closet with luxurious private bath
- 3 bedrooms, 2 baths, 2-car drive under garage
- Basement foundation

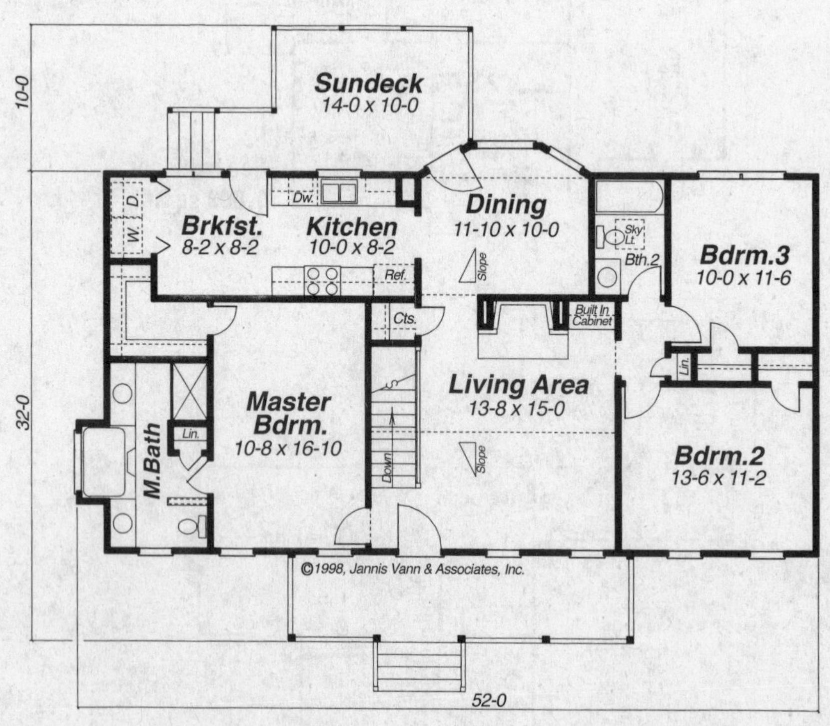
Sundeck
14-0 x 10-0
10-0
W. D.
Brkfst.
8-2 x 8-2
Dw.
Kitchen
10-0 x 8-2
Ref.
Dining
11-10 x 10-0
Slope
Sky Lt.
Bth.2
Bdrm.3
10-0 x 11-6
Cts.
Built In Cabinet
Lin.
Living Area
13-8 x 15-0
Slope
Down
32-0
Master Bdrm.
10-8 x 16-10
Lin.
M.Bath
Bdrm.2
13-6 x 11-2
©1998, Jannis Vann & Associates, Inc.
52-0

Plan #702-0528

Impressive Exterior, Spacious Interior

2,511 total square feet of living area

Price Code D

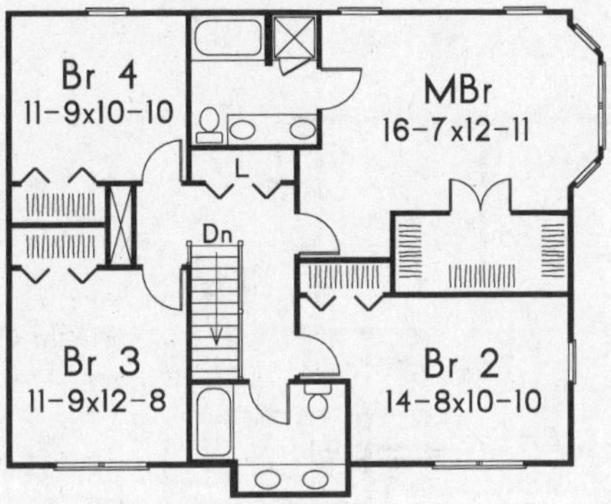

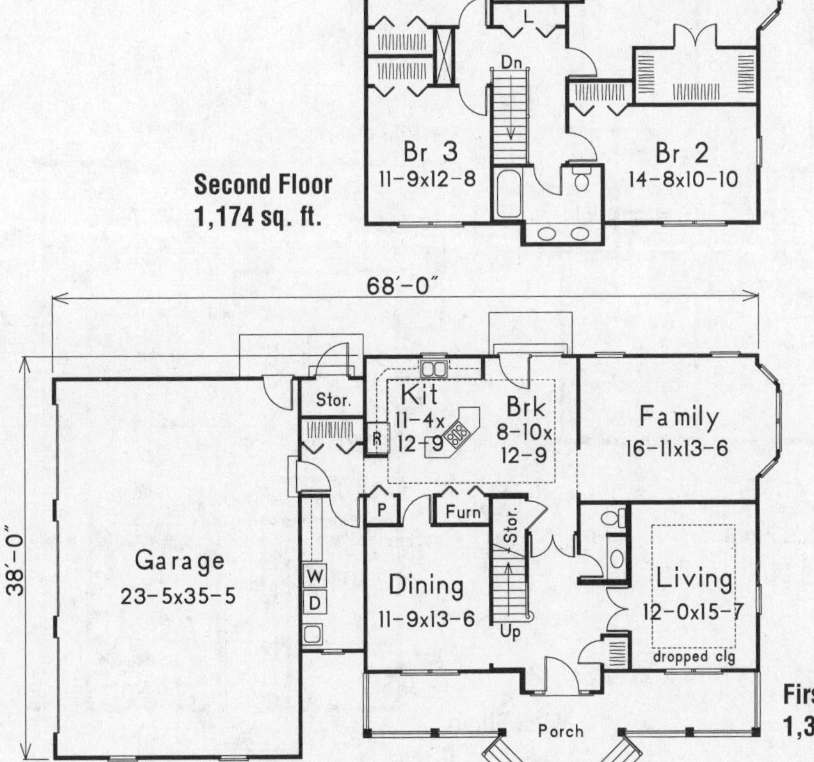
Br 4
11-9x10-10
MBr
16-7x12-11
L
Dn
Br 3
11-9x12-8
Br 2
14-8x10-10
68'-0"
38'-0"
Stor.
Kit
11-4x
12-9
Brk
8-10x
12-9
Family
16-11x13-6
R
P
Furn
Stor.
Garage
23-5x35-5
W
D
Dining
11-9x13-6
Up
Living
12-0x15-7
dropped clg
Porch

Second Floor
1,174 sq. ft.

First Floor
1,337 sq. ft.

Special features

- Both kitchen/breakfast area and living room feature tray ceilings
- Various architectural elements combine to create impressive exterior
- Master bedroom includes large walk-in closet, oversized bay window and private bath with shower and tub
- Large utility room with convenient workspace
- 4 bedrooms, 2 1/2 baths, 3-car side entry garage
- Basement foundation, drawings also include crawl space and slab foundations

TO ORDER BLUEPRINTS USE THE FORM ON PAGE 19 OR CALL TOLL-FREE 1-877-671-6036

Warm And Cozy Feeling

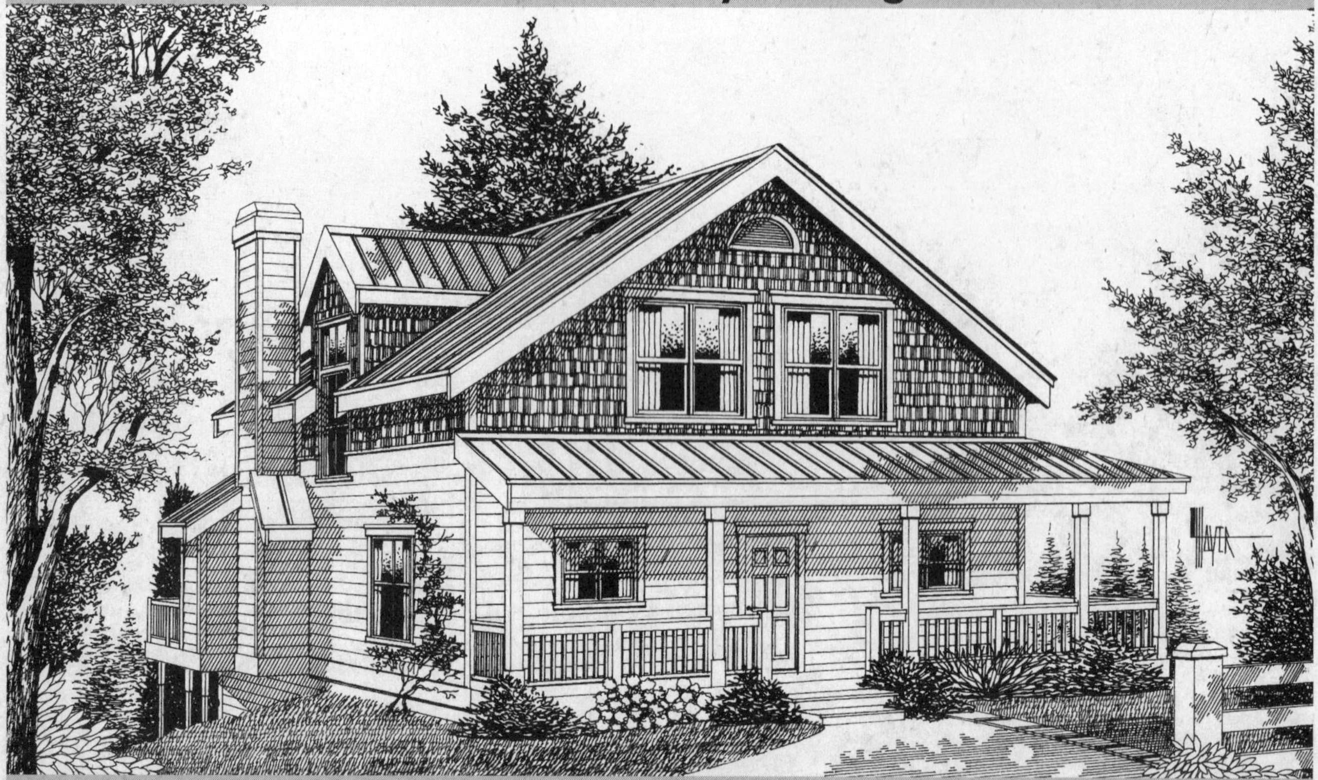

2,202 total square feet of living area

Price Code D

Special features

- 9' ceilings on first floor
- Guest bedroom located on the first floor for convenience could easily be converted to an office area
- Large kitchen with oversized island overlooks dining area
- 5 bedrooms, 4 full baths, 2 half baths, 2-car drive under garage
- Basement or walk-out basement foundation, please specify when ordering

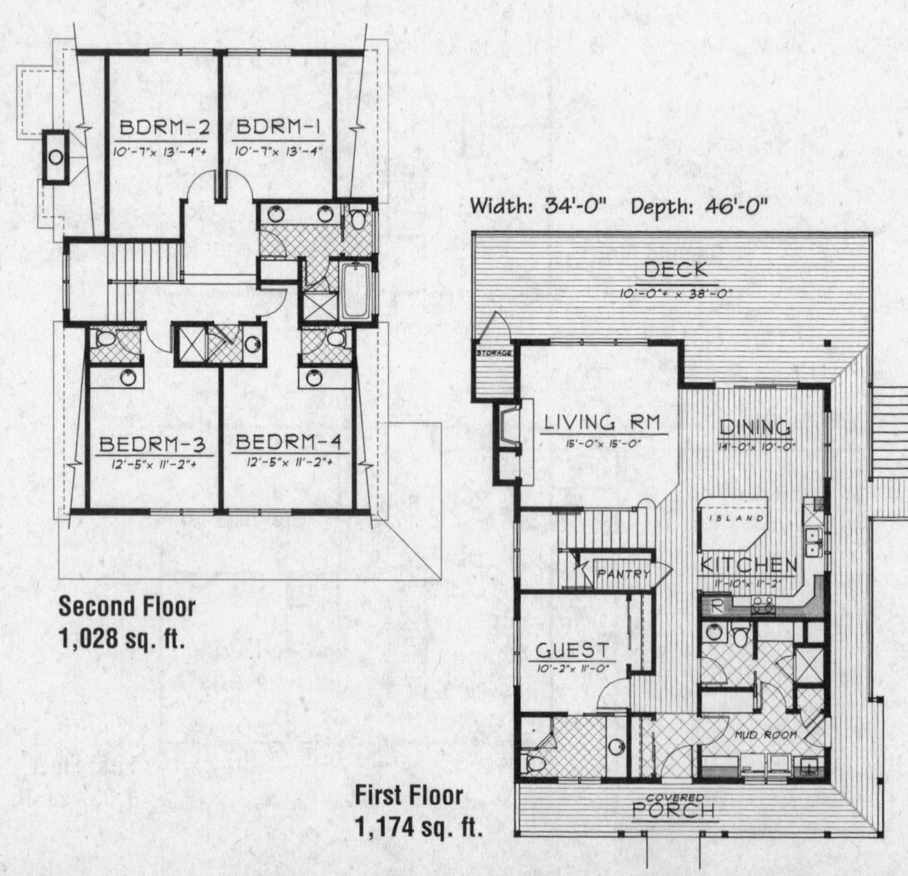

BDRM-2
10'-7"x 13'-4"+
BDRM-1
10'-7"x 13'-4"
BEDRM-3
12'-5"x 11'-2"+
BEDRM-4
12'-5"x 11'-2"+
Width: 34'-0" Depth: 46'-0"
DECK
10'-0"+ x 38'-0"
STORAGE
LIVING RM
15'-0"x 15'-0"
DINING
14'-0"x 10'-0"
ISLAND
PANTRY
KITCHEN
11'-10"x 11'-2"
GUEST
10'-2"x 11'-0"
MUD ROOM
COVERED
PORCH

Second Floor
1,028 sq. ft.

First Floor
1,174 sq. ft.

Modern Rustic Design — Plan #702-HP-C659

44'4"
47'4"
MASTER SUITE
15^{10}x 12^{8}
SLOPED CLG
COVERED PATIO
LIVING RM
15^{0}x 14^{0}
SLOPED CLG
MASTER BATH
BEDRM
9^{0}x 9^{8}
SLOPED CLG
BATH
KITCHEN
8^{0}x 14^{8}
FOYER
DINING RM
9^{10}x 9^{4}
COFFERED CLG
COVERED PORCH
GARAGE
19^{4}x 22^{10}

1,118 total square feet of living area **Price Code AA**

Special features

- Great room offers a sloped ceiling, fireplace with extended hearth and built-in shelves for an entertainment center
- Gourmet kitchen has a cooktop island counter and a morning room
- Master suite features a sloped ceiling, cozy sitting room, walk-in closet and a private bath with whirlpool tub
- 2 bedrooms, 2 baths, 2-car side entry garage
- Slab foundation

Inviting Victorian Details — Plan #702-VL947

947 total square feet of living area **Price Code AA**

Special features

- Efficiently designed kitchen/dining area accesses the outdoors onto a rear porch
- Future expansion plans included which allow the home to become 392 square feet larger with 3 bedrooms and 2 baths
- 2 bedrooms, 1 bath
- Crawl space or slab foundation, please specify when ordering

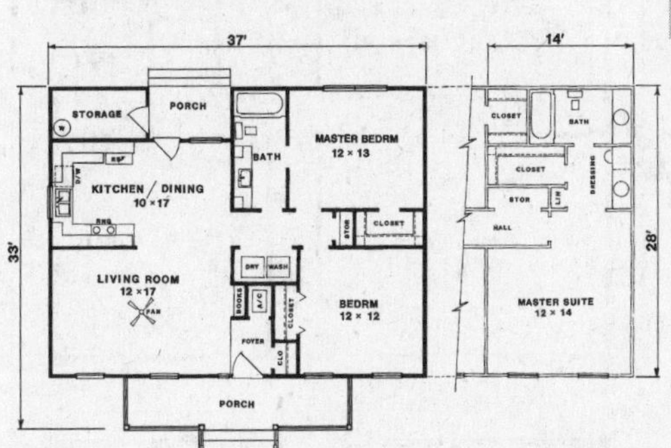
37'
14'
33'
28'
STORAGE
PORCH
MASTER BEDRM
12 × 13
BATH
KITCHEN / DINING
10 × 17
LIVING ROOM
12 × 17
BEDRM
12 × 12
FOYER
PORCH
MASTER SUITE
12 × 14

TO ORDER BLUEPRINTS USE THE FORM ON PAGE 19 OR CALL TOLL-FREE 1-877-671-6036

View thousands more home plans online at www.familyhandyman.com/homeplans

Plan #702-FB-1148

Southern Styling With Covered Porch

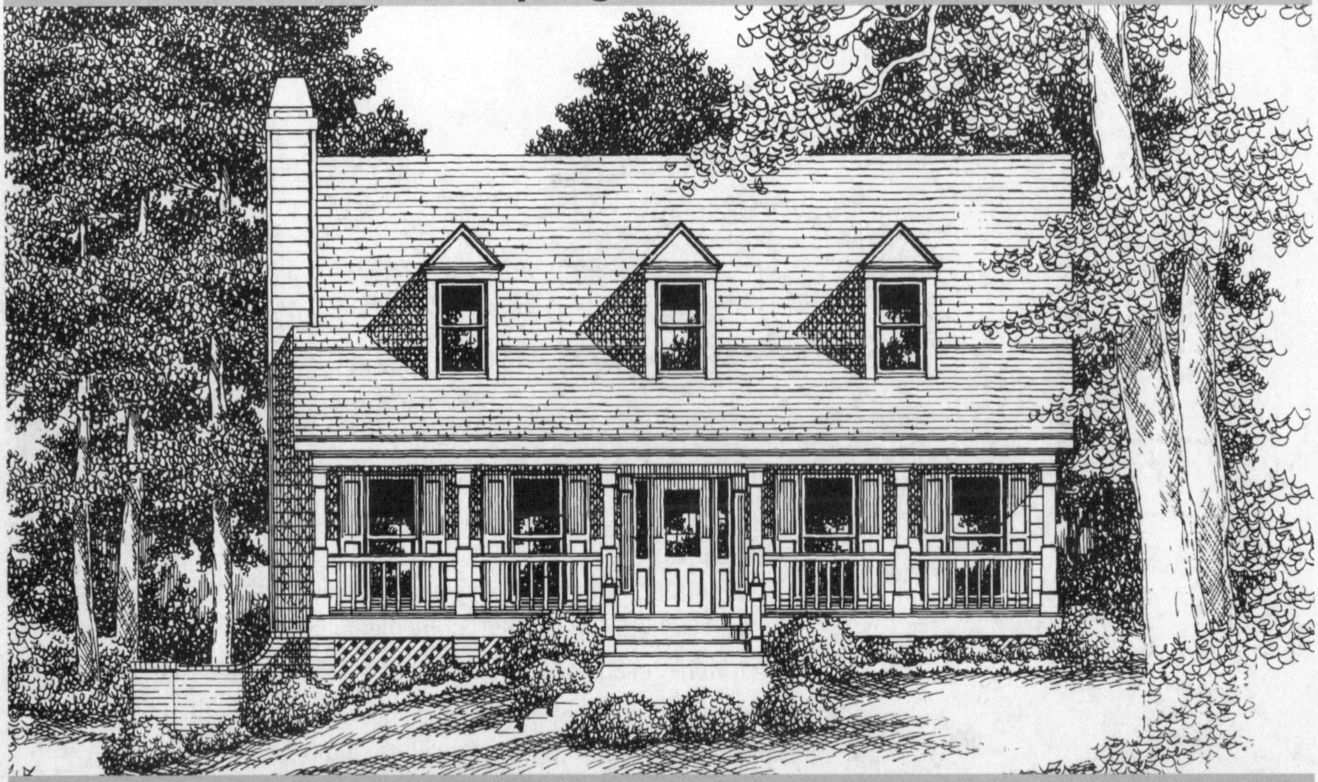

1,491 total square feet of living area

Price Code A

Special features

- Two-story family room has vaulted ceiling
- Well-organized kitchen has serving bar which overlooks family and dining rooms
- First floor master suite has tray ceiling, walk-in closet and master bath
- 3 bedrooms, 2 1/2 baths, 2-car drive under garage
- Walk-out basement foundation

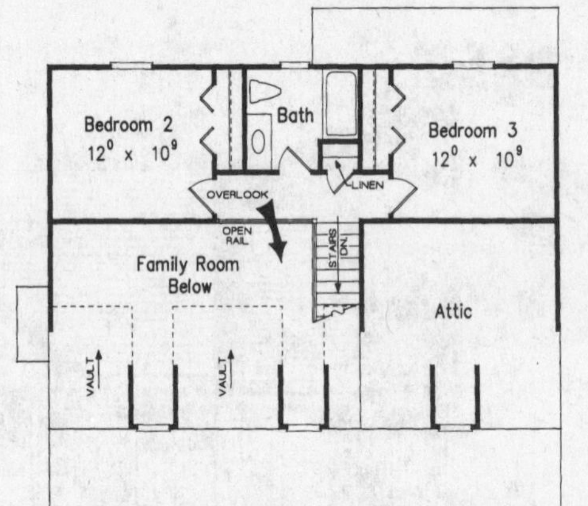
Bedroom 2
12⁰ x 10⁹
Bath
Bedroom 3
12⁰ x 10⁹
LINEN
OVERLOOK
OPEN RAIL
STAIRS DN
Family Room Below
Attic
VAULT
VAULT

Second Floor
430 sq. ft.

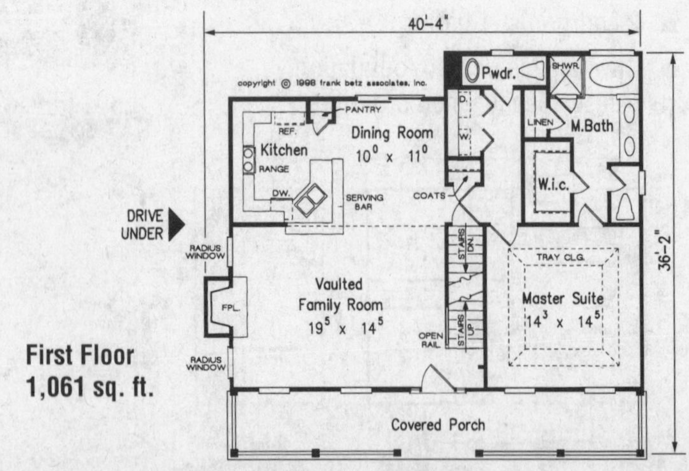
40'-4"
copyright © 1998 frank betz associates, inc.
PANTRY
REF.
Kitchen
RANGE
DW.
Dining Room
10⁰ x 11⁰
SERVING BAR
COATS
Pwdr.
SHWR
LINEN
M.Bath
W.i.c.
DRIVE UNDER
RADIUS WINDOW
FPL.
Vaulted Family Room
19⁵ x 14⁵
STAIRS DN
STAIRS UP
OPEN RAIL
TRAY CLG.
Master Suite
14³ x 14⁵
RADIUS WINDOW
Covered Porch
36'-2"

First Floor
1,061 sq. ft.

TO ORDER BLUEPRINTS USE THE FORM ON PAGE 19 OR CALL TOLL-FREE 1-877-671-6036

View thousands more home plans online at www.familyhandyman.com/homeplans

Plan #702-0106

Gabled Front Porch Adds Charm And Value

1,443 total square feet of living area **Price Code A**

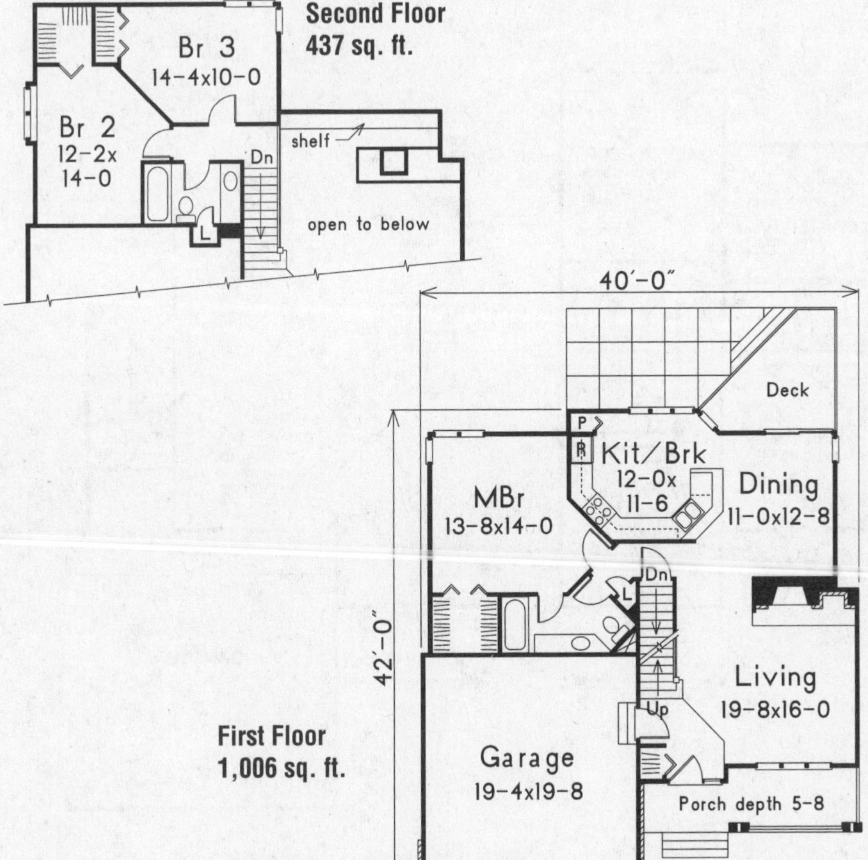
Second Floor
437 sq. ft.
Br 3
14-4x10-0
Br 2
12-2x
14-0
Dn
shelf
open to below
40'-0"
42'-0"
Deck
P
R
Kit/Brk
12-0x
11-6
Dining
11-0x12-8
MBr
13-8x14-0
Dn
L
Living
19-8x16-0
Up
Garage
19-4x19-8
Porch depth 5-8
First Floor
1,006 sq. ft.

Special features

- Raised foyer and cathedral ceiling in living room
- Impressive tall-wall fireplace between living and dining rooms
- Open U-shaped kitchen with breakfast bay
- Angular side deck accentuates patio and garden
- First floor master bedroom suite has a walk-in closet and a corner window
- 3 bedrooms, 2 baths, 2-car garage
- Basement foundation

TO ORDER BLUEPRINTS USE THE FORM ON PAGE 19 OR CALL TOLL-FREE 1-877-671-6036

The Family
Handyman

Plan #702-LBD-19-15A

Warm And Inviting

1,955 total square feet of living area **Price Code C**

Special features

- Porch adds outdoor area to this design
- Dining and great rooms visible from foyer through a series of elegant archways
- Kitchen overlooks great room and breakfast room
- 3 bedrooms, 2 baths, 2-car side entry garage
- Crawl space or slab foundation, please specify when ordering

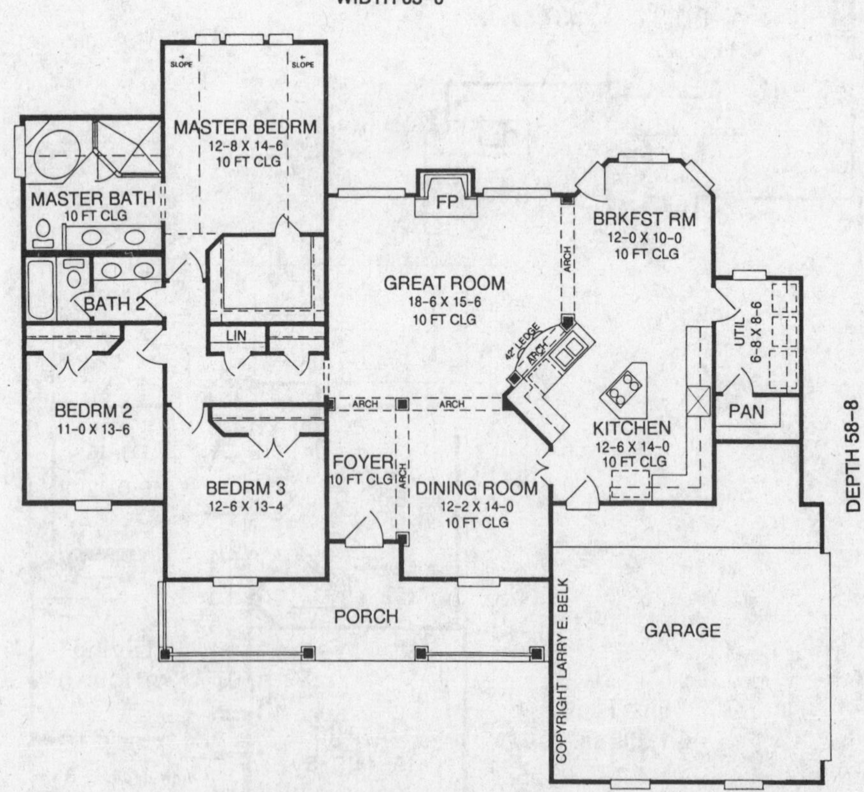
WIDTH 65-0
SLOPE
SLOPE
MASTER BEDRM
12-8 X 14-6
10 FT CLG
MASTER BATH
10 FT CLG
BATH 2
LIN
FP
GREAT ROOM
18-6 X 15-6
10 FT CLG
BRKFST RM
12-0 X 10-0
10 FT CLG
ARCH
42" LEDGE
UTIL
6-8 X 8-6
PAN
KITCHEN
12-6 X 14-0
10 FT CLG
ARCH
ARCH
BEDRM 2
11-0 X 13-6
BEDRM 3
12-6 X 13-4
FOYER
10 FT CLG
ARCH
DINING ROOM
12-2 X 14-0
10 FT CLG
PORCH
GARAGE
COPYRIGHT LARRY E. BELK
DEPTH 58-8

TO ORDER BLUEPRINTS USE THE FORM ON PAGE 19 OR CALL TOLL-FREE 1-877-671-6036

View thousands more home plans online at www.familyhandyman.com/homeplans

Plan #702-GH-34901

Unique, Traditional Style, Farmhouse Flavor

Rear View

1,763 total square feet of living area | **Price Code C**

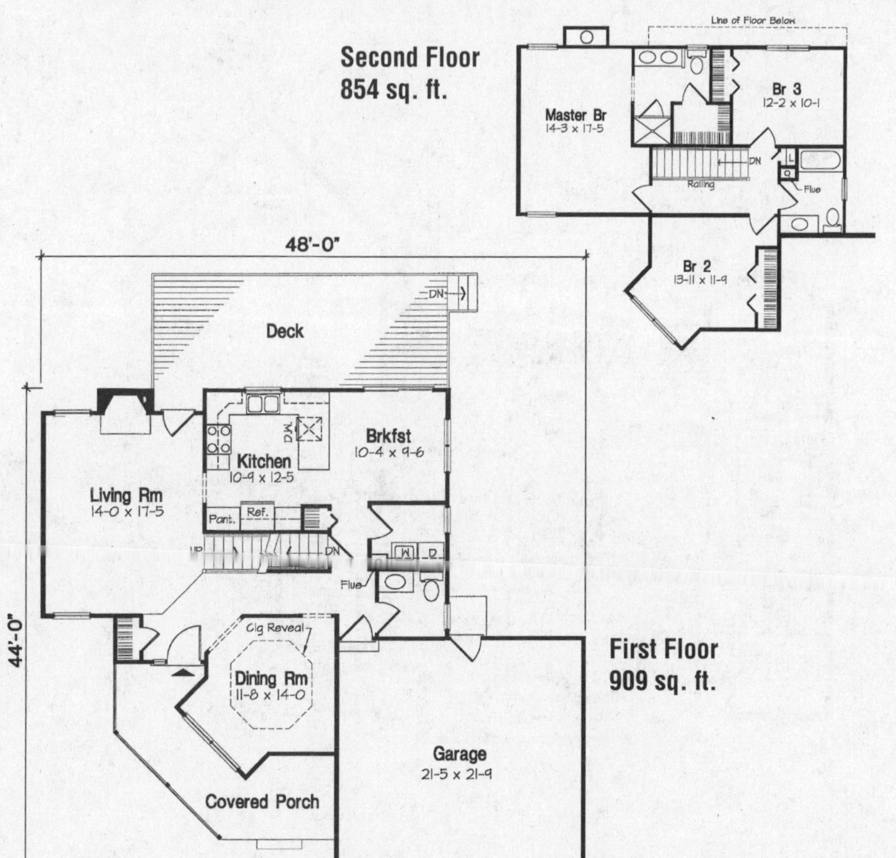

Second Floor
854 sq. ft.
Line of Floor Below
Master Br
14-3 x 17-5
Br 3
12-2 x 10-1
DN
Railing
Flue
Br 2
13-11 x 11-9
48'-0"
44'-0"
Deck
DN
Kitchen
10-9 x 12-5
Brkfst
10-4 x 9-6
Living Rm
14-0 x 17-5
Pant.
Ref.
UP
DN
Flue
Clg Reveal
Dining Rm
11-8 x 14-0
Garage
21-5 x 21-9
Covered Porch
First Floor
909 sq. ft.

Special features

- Dining room has a large box bay window and a recessed ceiling
- Living room includes a large fireplace
- Kitchen has plenty of workspace, a pantry and a double sink overlooking the deck
- Master suite features a large bath with walk-in closet
- 3 bedrooms, 2 1/2 baths, 2-car garage
- Basement foundation, drawings also include crawl space and slab foundations

TO ORDER BLUEPRINTS USE THE FORM ON PAGE 19 OR CALL TOLL-FREE 1-877-671-6036

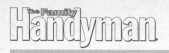

Plan #702-FDG-8729-L

Double Bays Accent Front

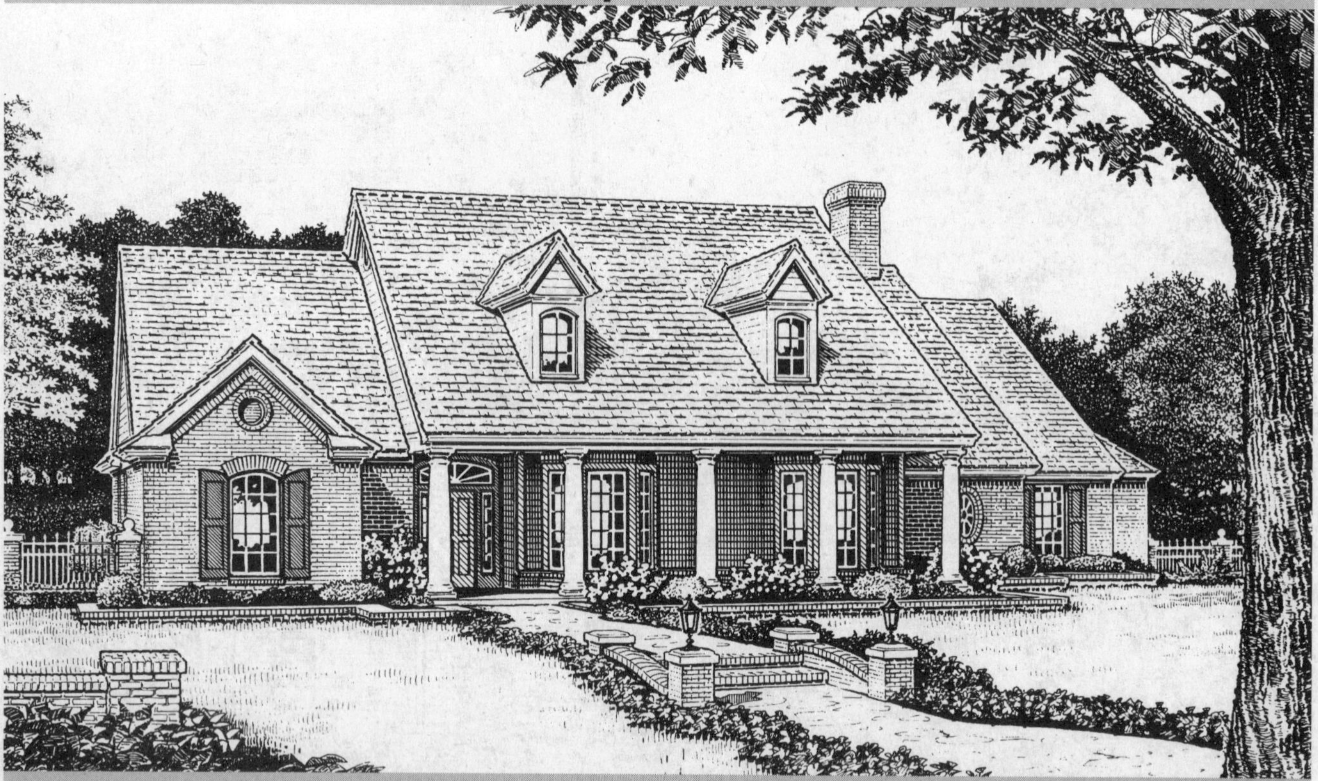

2,529 total square feet of living area

Price Code D

Special features

- Kitchen and breakfast area are located between the family and living rooms for easy access
- Master bedroom includes sitting area, private bath and access to covered patio
- 4 bedrooms, 3 baths, 3-car side entry garage
- Slab foundation

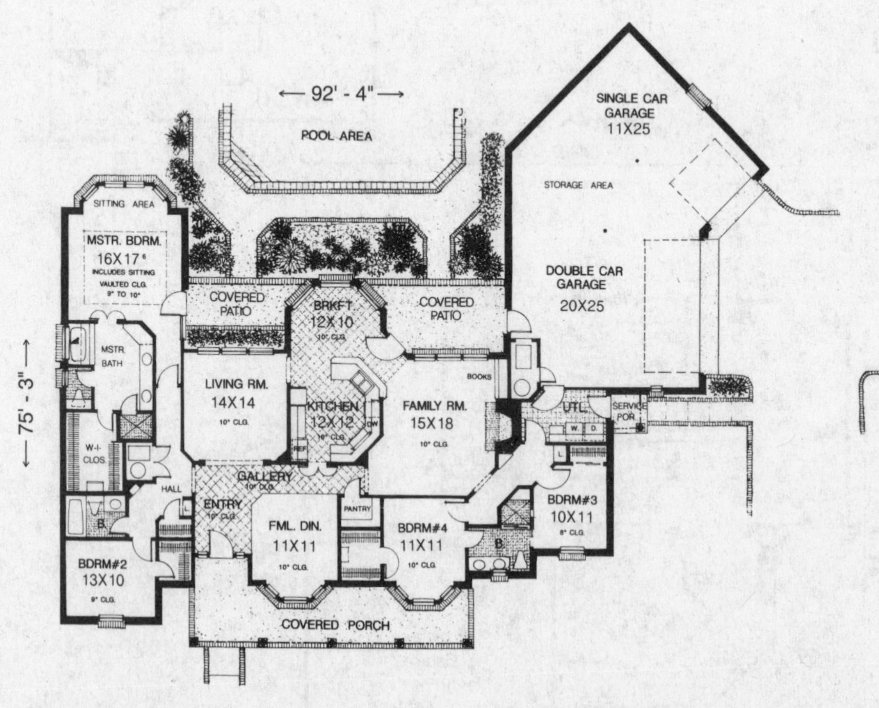
92' - 4"
75' - 3"
POOL AREA
SINGLE CAR GARAGE 11X25
STORAGE AREA
DOUBLE CAR GARAGE 20X25
SITTING AREA
MSTR. BDRM. 16X17
COVERED PATIO
BRKFT 12X10
COVERED PATIO
MSTR. BATH
LIVING RM. 14X14
KITCHEN 12X12
FAMILY RM. 15X18
BOOKS
UTL.
SERVICE POR.
W-I- CLOS.
GALLERY
HALL
ENTRY
FML. DIN. 11X11
PANTRY
BDRM#4 11X11
BDRM#3 10X11
BDRM#2 13X10
COVERED PORCH

The Family
Handyman

Plan #702-DDI-101-205

Ultimate Curb Appeal

2,487 total square feet of living area **Price Code D**

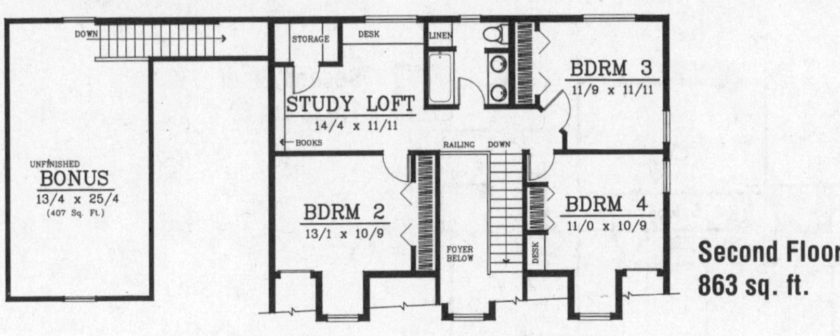
DOWN
UNFINISHED
BONUS
13/4 x 25/4
(407 Sq. Ft.)
STORAGE
DESK
LINEN
STUDY LOFT
14/4 x 11/11
BOOKS
BDRM 3
11/9 x 11/11
RAILING
DOWN
BDRM 2
13/1 x 10/9
FOYER BELOW
DESK
BDRM 4
11/0 x 10/9

Second Floor
863 sq. ft.

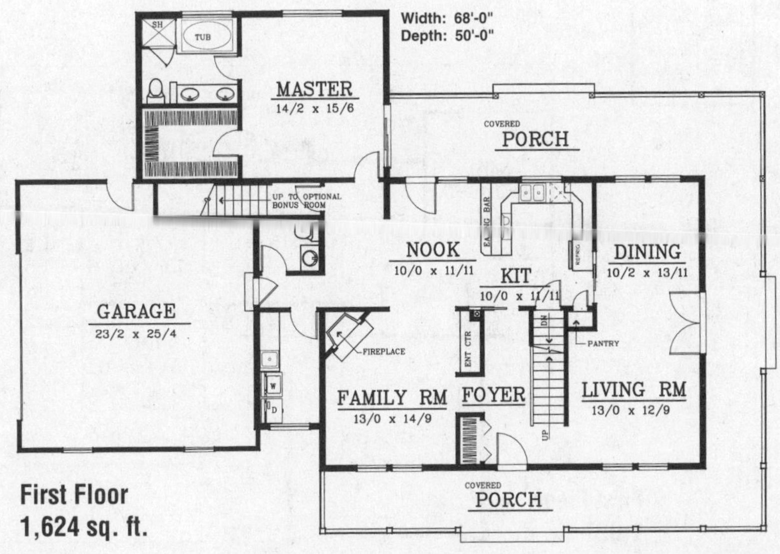
SH
TUB
MASTER
14/2 x 15/6
Width: 68'-0"
Depth: 50'-0"
COVERED
PORCH
UP TO OPTIONAL BONUS ROOM
EATING BAR
NOOK
10/0 x 11/11
KIT
10/0 x 11/11
DINING
10/2 x 13/11
GARAGE
23/2 x 25/4
FIREPLACE
ENT CTR
DN
PANTRY
W
D
FAMILY RM
13/0 x 14/9
FOYER
LIVING RM
13/0 x 12/9
UP
COVERED
PORCH

First Floor
1,624 sq. ft.

Special features

- Three second floor bedrooms and a convenient study/office share a hall bath
- Dining/living area features French doors leading to a covered porch and cozy family room with corner fireplace
- First floor living spaces offer formal dining as well as a casual nook and kitchen with eating bar and pantry
- 4 bedrooms, 2 1/2 baths, 2-car side entry garage
- Basement foundation

Plan #702-0359

Fireplaces Accent Gathering Rooms

2,659 total square feet of living area **Price Code E**

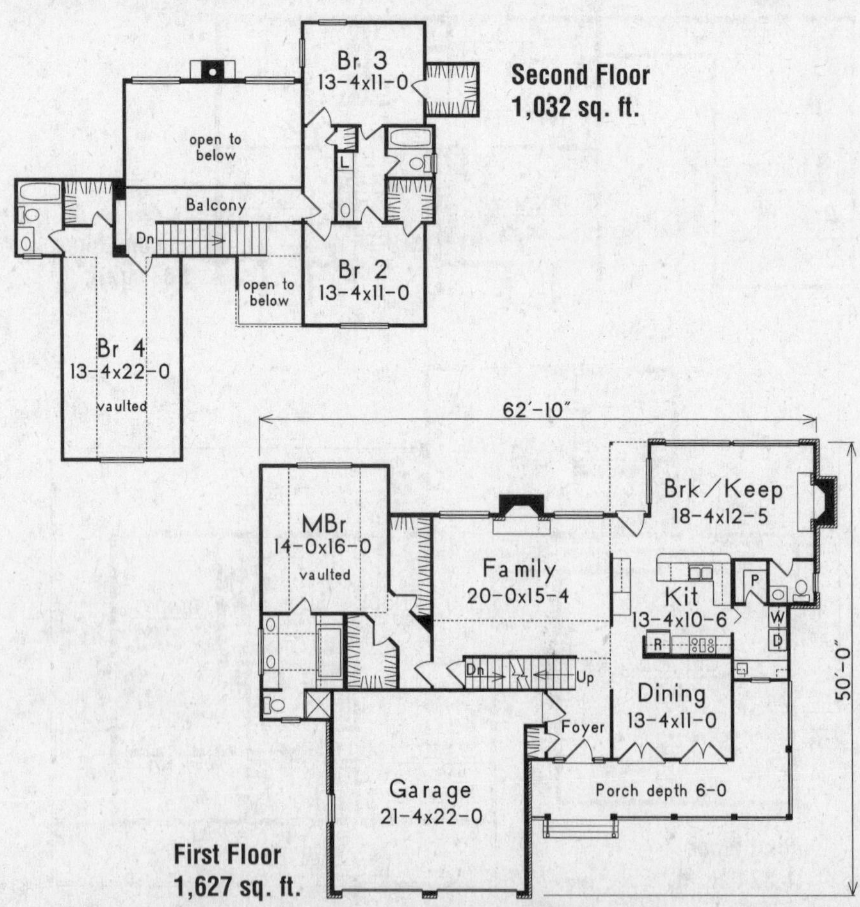
Second Floor
1,032 sq. ft.
Br 3
13-4x11-0
open to below
Balcony
Dn
L
Br 2
13-4x11-0
open to below
Br 4
13-4x22-0
vaulted
62'-10"
50'-0"
MBr
14-0x16-0
vaulted
Family
20-0x15-4
Brk/Keep
18-4x12-5
Kit
13-4x10-6
P
W
D
R
Dn
Up
Dining
13-4x11-0
Foyer
Porch depth 6-0
Garage
21-4x22-0
First Floor
1,627 sq. ft.

Special features

- 9' ceilings throughout first floor
- Balcony overlooks large family room
- Private first floor master suite features double walk-in closets, sloped ceilings and luxury bath
- Double French doors in dining room open onto porch
- 4 bedrooms, 3 1/2 baths, 2-car garage
- Basement foundation

TO ORDER BLUEPRINTS USE THE FORM ON PAGE 19 OR CALL TOLL-FREE 1-877-671-6036

The Family
Handyman

Plan #702-0739

A Special Home For Views

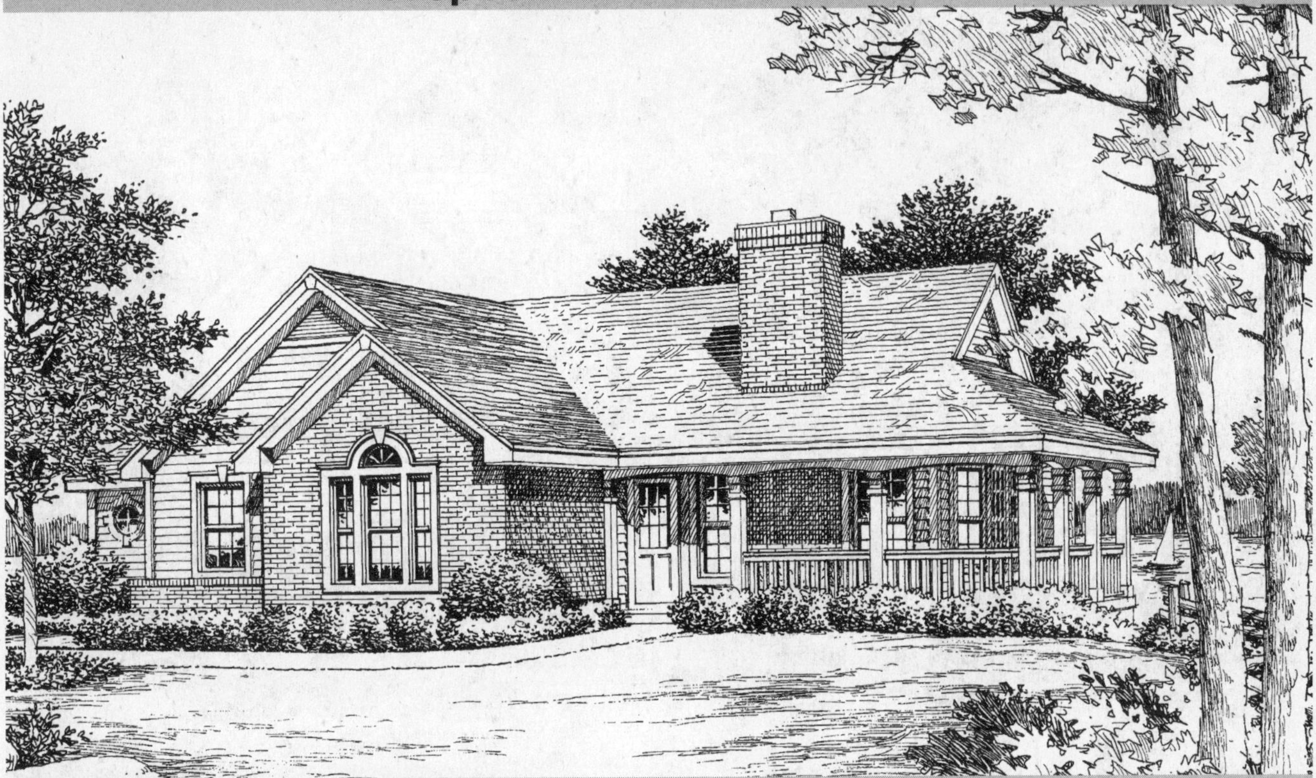

1,684 total square feet of living area

Price Code B

Rear View

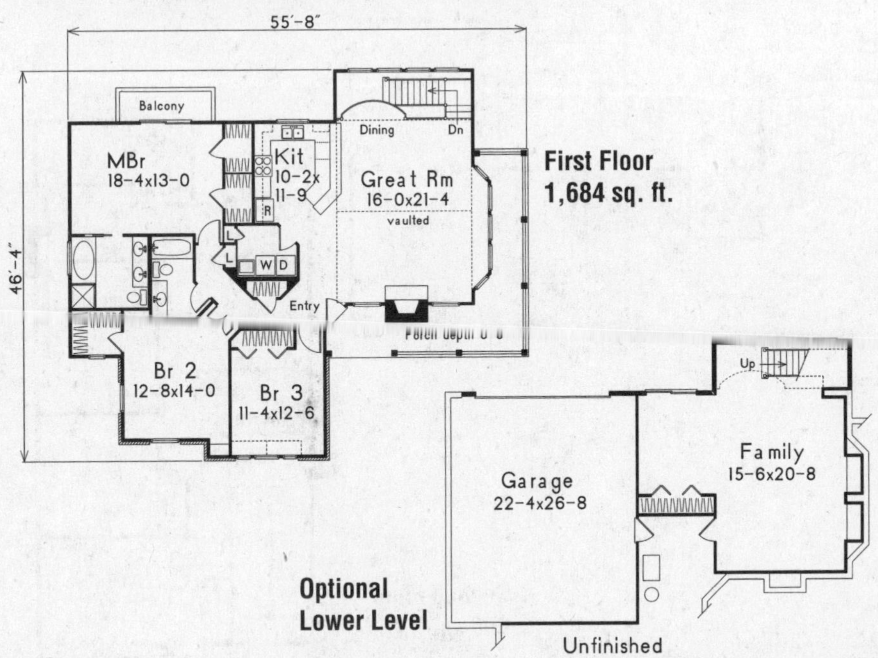
55'-8"
46'-4"
Balcony
MBr
18-4x13-0
Kit
10-2x
11-9
Dining
Dn
Great Rm
16-0x21-4
vaulted
W D
Entry
Br 2
12-8x14-0
Br 3
11-4x12-6
First Floor
1,684 sq. ft.
Up
Family
15-6x20-8
Garage
22-4x26-8
Optional
Lower Level
Unfinished

Special features

- Delightful wrap-around porch anchored by full masonry fireplace
- The vaulted great room includes a large bay window, fireplace, dining balcony and atrium window wall
- His and hers walk-in closets, large luxury bath and sliding doors to exterior balcony are a few fantastic features of the master bedroom
- Atrium open to 611 square feet of optional living area on the lower level
- 3 bedrooms, 2 baths, 2-car drive under garage
- Walk-out basement foundation

The Family
Handyman

Plan #702-JFD-20-2097-1

Comfortable Family Living

2,097 total square feet of living area

Price Code C

Special features

- Formal living room connects with dining room, perfect for entertaining
- Elegant two-story foyer
- Spacious entry off garage near bath and laundry area
- Family room has cozy fireplace
- 4 bedrooms, 2 1/2 baths, 2-car side entry garage
- Basement foundation

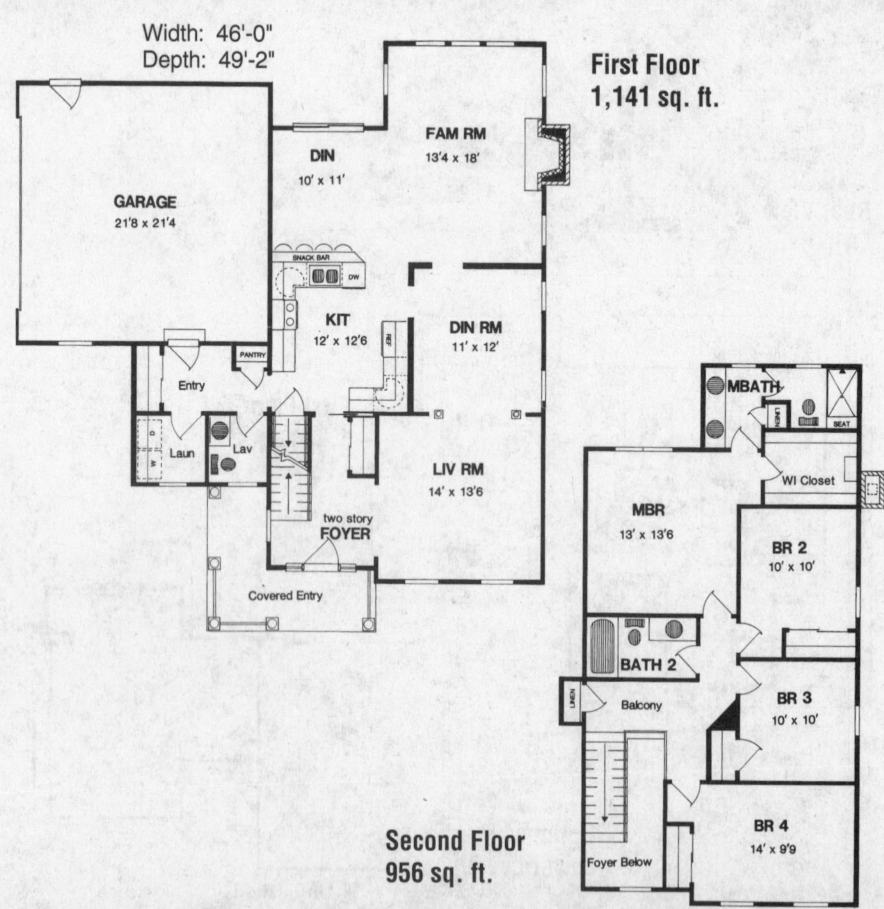

Width: 46'-0"
Depth: 49'-2"
First Floor
1,141 sq. ft.
GARAGE
21'8 x 21'4
DIN
10' x 11'
FAM RM
13'4 x 18'
SNACK BAR
DW
KIT
12' x 12'6
REF
DIN RM
11' x 12'
PANTRY
Entry
Laun
Lav
LIV RM
14' x 13'6
two story
FOYER
Covered Entry
MBATH
SEAT
WI Closet
MBR
13' x 13'6
BR 2
10' x 10'
BATH 2
Balcony
BR 3
10' x 10'
BR 4
14' x 9'9
Foyer Below
Second Floor
956 sq. ft.

TO ORDER BLUEPRINTS USE THE FORM ON PAGE 19 OR CALL TOLL-FREE 1-877-671-6036

View thousands more home plans online at www.familyhandyman.com/homeplans

The Family
Handyman

Plan #702-0712

Country Home With Front Orientation

2,029 total square feet of living area

Price Code C

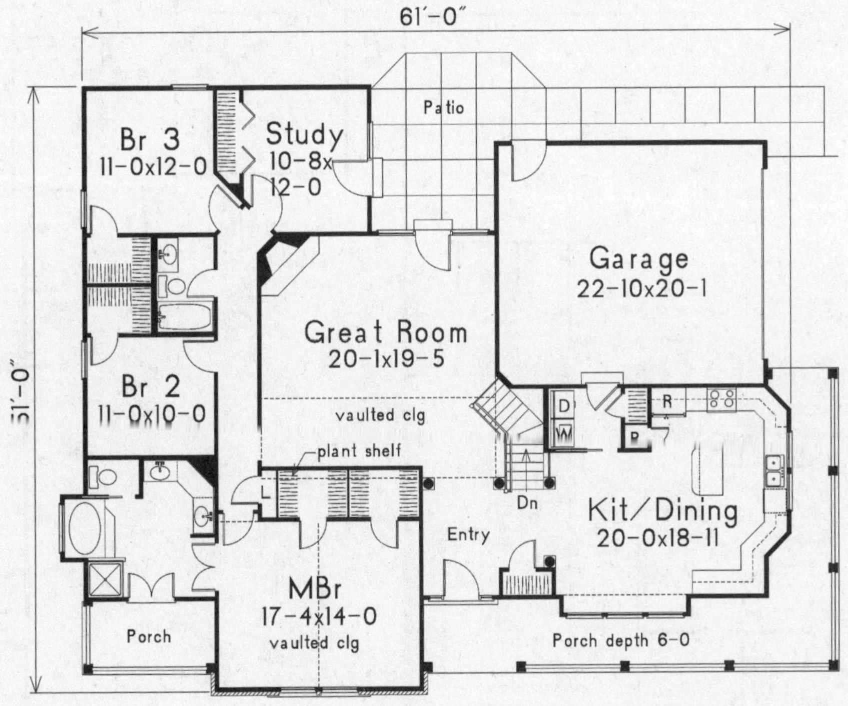
61'-0"
51'-0"
Patio
Br 3
11-0x12-0
Study
10-8x
12-0
Garage
22-10x20-1
Great Room
20-1x19-5
vaulted clg
plant shelf
Br 2
11-0x10-0
D
W
R
P
L
Dn
Kit/Dining
20-0x18-11
Entry
MBr
17-4x14-0
vaulted clg
Porch
Porch depth 6-0

Special features

- Stonework, gables, roof dormer and double porches create a country flavor
- Kitchen enjoys extravagant cabinetry and counterspace in a bay, island snack bar, built-in pantry and cheery dining area with multiple tall windows
- Angled stair descends from large entry with wood columns and is open to vaulted great room with corner fireplace
- Master bedroom boasts his and hers walk-in closets, double-doors leading to an opulent master bath and private porch
- 4 bedrooms, 2 baths, 2-car side entry garage
- Basement foundation

The Family
Handyman

Plan #702-0436

Spectacular Five Bedroom Home

2,801 total square feet of living area **Price Code E**

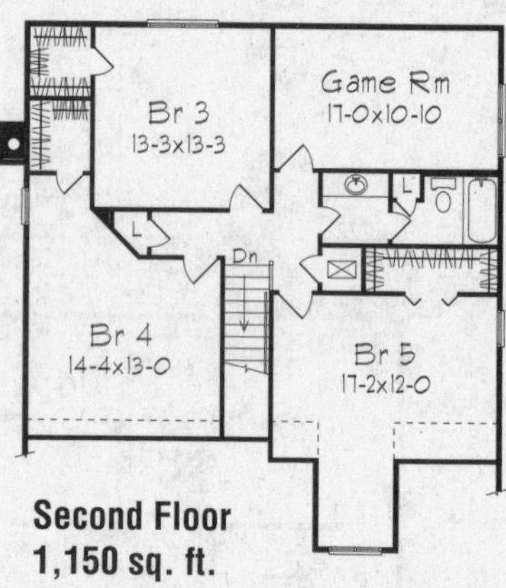
Br 3
13-3x13-3
Game Rm
17-0x10-10
L
Dn
Br 4
14-4x13-0
Br 5
17-2x12-0

Second Floor
1,150 sq. ft.

Special features

- 9' ceilings on first floor
- Full view dining bay with elegant circle-top windows
- Wrap-around porches provide outdoor exposure in all directions
- Secluded master bedroom with double vanities and walk-in closets
- Convenient game room
- 5 bedrooms, 3 baths, 2-car side entry garage
- Slab foundation

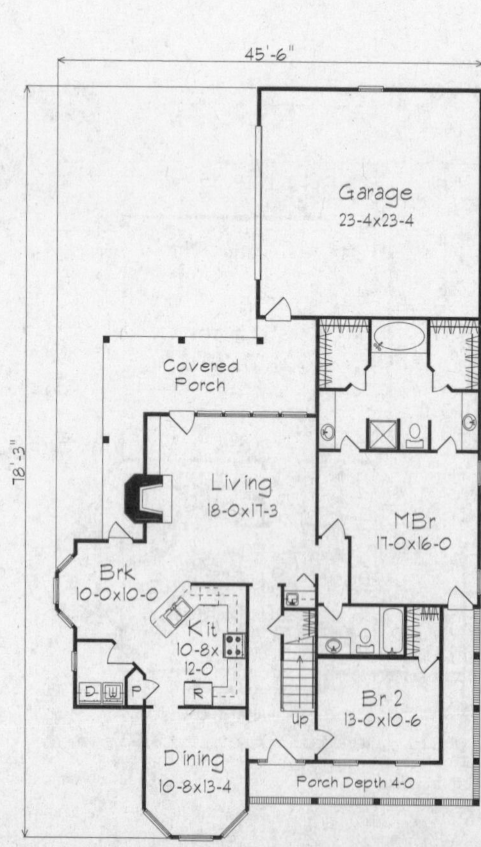
45'-6"
78'-3"
Garage
23-4x23-4
Covered
Porch
Living
18-0x17-3
MBr
17-0x16-0
Brk
10-0x10-0
Kit
10-8x
12-0
R
P
Up
Br 2
13-0x10-6
Dining
10-8x13-4
Porch Depth 4-0

First Floor
1,651 sq. ft.

TO ORDER BLUEPRINTS USE THE FORM ON PAGE 19 OR CALL TOLL-FREE 1-877-671-6036

View thousands more home plans online at www.familyhandyman.com/homeplans

The Family
Handyman

Plan #702-0449

Charming House, Spacious And Functional

2,505 total square feet of living area

Price Code D

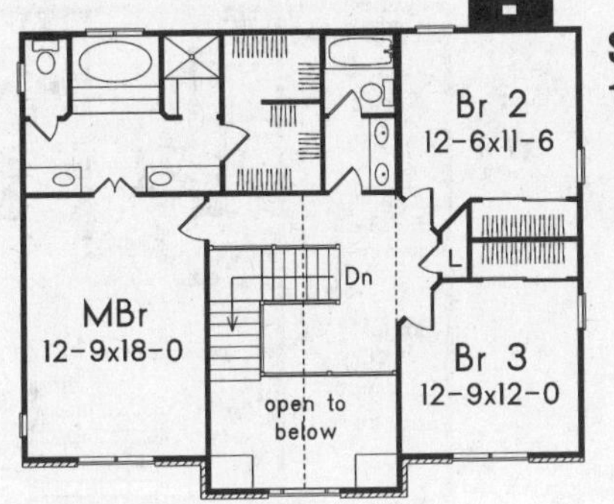

Br 2
12-6x11-6
L
Dn
MBr
12-9x18-0
Br 3
12-9x12-0
open to below

Second Floor
1,069 sq. ft.

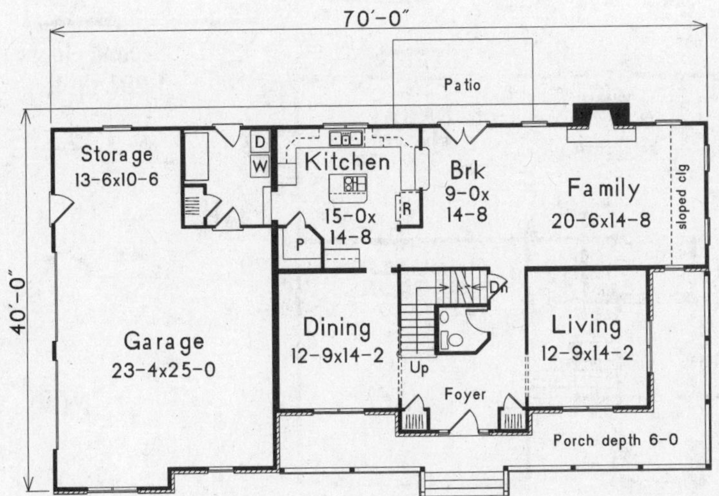

70'-0"
40'-0"
Patio
Storage
13-6x10-6
D
W
Kitchen
15-0x
14-8
P
Brk
9-0x
14-8
R
Family
20-6x14-8
sloped clg
Dn
Garage
23-4x25-0
Dining
12-9x14-2
Up
Living
12-9x14-2
Foyer
Porch depth 6-0

First Floor
1,436 sq. ft.

Special features

- The garage features extra storage area and ample work space
- Laundry room accessible from the garage and the outdoors
- Deluxe raised tub and immense walk-in closet grace master bath
- 3 bedrooms, 2 1/2 baths, 2-car side entry garage
- Basement foundation, drawings also include crawl space foundation

TO ORDER BLUEPRINTS USE THE FORM ON PAGE 19 OR CALL TOLL-FREE 1-877-671-6036

View thousands more home plans online at www.familyhandyman.com/homeplans

Plan #702-CHD-18-53

Lovely Entry Highlighted With Large Window

2,310 total square feet of living area

Price Code D

Special features

- 9' ceilings on first floor
- Fireplace in great room is flanked by windows creating a sunny atmosphere
- Large playroom on second floor is convenient to secondary bedrooms
- Second floor utility room provides convenience
- 3 bedrooms, 2 1/2 baths, 2-car garage
- Slab foundation

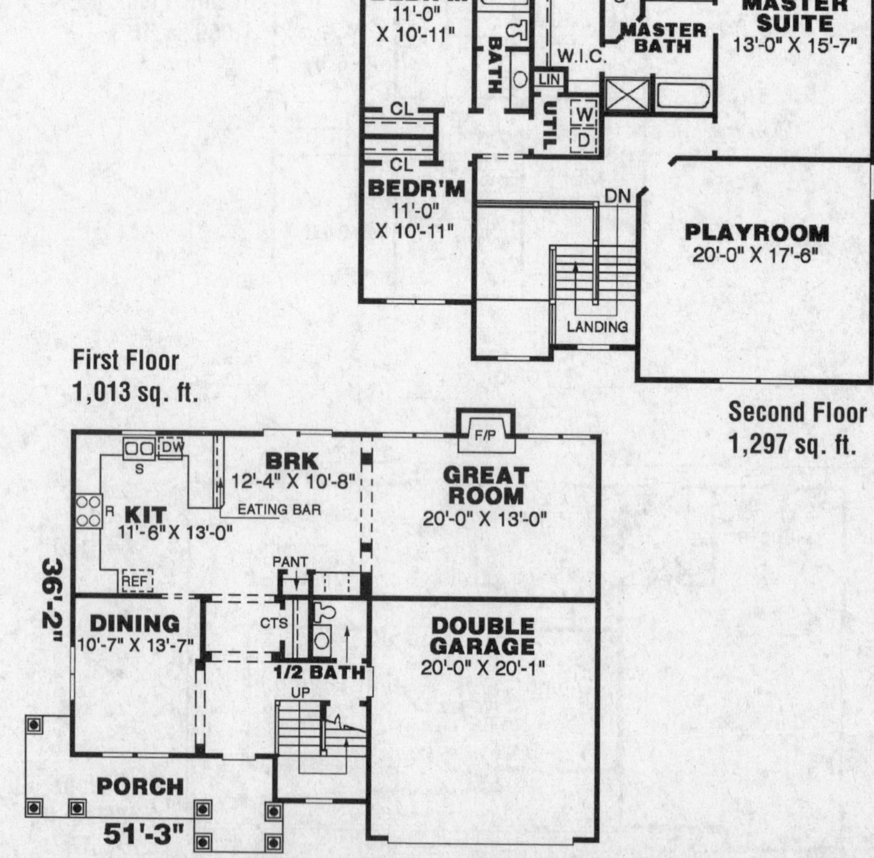

BEDR'M
11'-0" X 10'-11"
BATH
W.I.C.
LIN
MASTER BATH
MASTER SUITE
13'-0" X 15'-7"
CL
UTIL
W
D
CL
BEDR'M
11'-0" X 10'-11"
DN
PLAYROOM
20'-0" X 17'-6"
LANDING
Second Floor
1,297 sq. ft.
First Floor
1,013 sq. ft.
DW
S
BRK
12'-4" X 10'-8"
EATING BAR
F/P
GREAT ROOM
20'-0" X 13'-0"
R
KIT
11'-6" X 13'-0"
REF
PANT
36'-2"
DINING
10'-7" X 13'-7"
CTS
1/2 BATH
UP
DOUBLE GARAGE
20'-0" X 20'-1"
PORCH
51'-3"

TO ORDER BLUEPRINTS USE THE FORM ON PAGE 19 OR CALL TOLL-FREE 1-877-671-6036

View thousands more home plans online at www.familyhandyman.com/homeplans

The Family
Handyman

Plan #702-0434

Attractive Entry Created By Full-Length Porch

2,357 total square feet of living area **Price Code D**

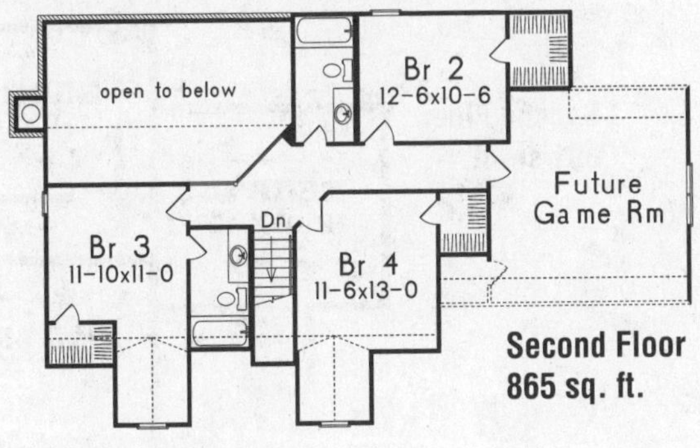
open to below
Br 2
12-6x10-6
Future
Game Rm
Br 3
11-10x11-0
Dn
Br 4
11-6x13-0

Second Floor
865 sq. ft.

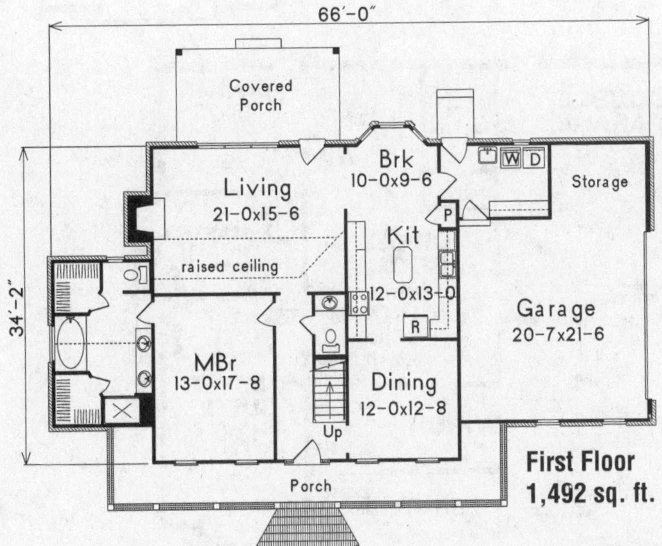
66'-0"
34'-2"
Covered
Porch
Living
21-0x15-6
Brk
10-0x9-6
W
D
Storage
P
Kit
12-0x13-0
raised ceiling
R
Garage
20-7x21-6
MBr
13-0x17-8
Dining
12-0x12-8
Up
Porch

First Floor
1,492 sq. ft.

Special features

- 9' ceilings on first floor
- Secluded master bedroom includes private bath with double walk-in closets and vanity
- Balcony overlooks living room with large fireplace
- Second floor has three bedrooms and an expansive game room
- 4 bedrooms, 3 1/2 baths, 2-car side entry garage
- Slab foundation, drawings also include crawl space foundation

TO ORDER BLUEPRINTS USE THE FORM ON PAGE 19 OR CALL TOLL-FREE 1-877-671-6036

The Family
Handyman

Plan #702-CHD-20-51

Victorian Styled Gazebo Enhances Front Porch

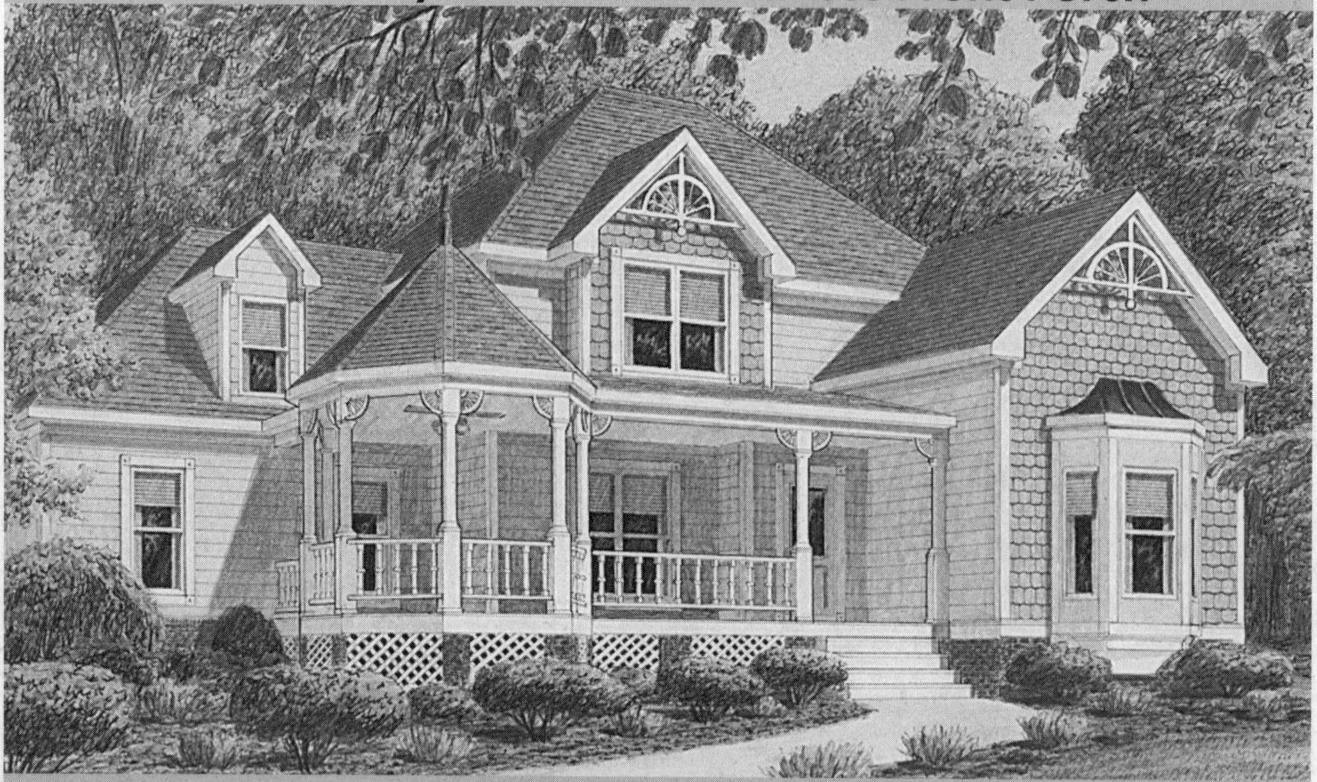

2,084 total square feet of living area

Price Code C

Special features

- Charming bay window in master suite allows sunlight in as well as style
- Great room accesses front cvered porch extending the living area to the outdoors
- Large playroom on second floor is ideal for family living
- 3 bedrooms, 2 1/2 baths, 2-car side entry garage
- Slab, crawl space or basement foundation, please specify when ordering

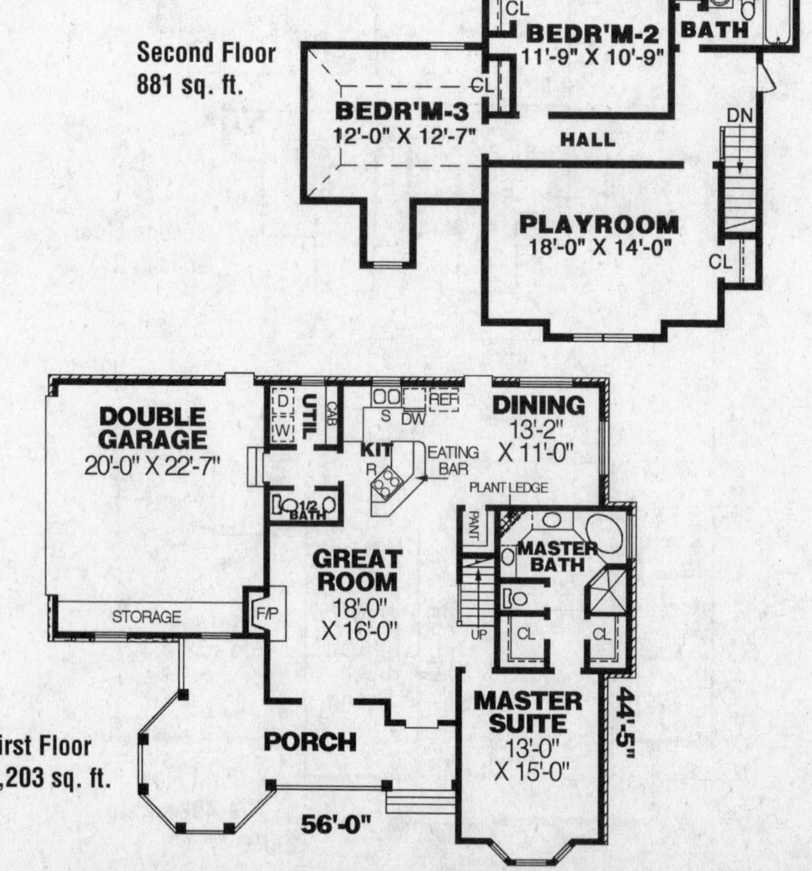
Second Floor
881 sq. ft.
CL
BEDR'M-2
11'-9" X 10'-9"
BATH
CL
BEDR'M-3
12'-0" X 12'-7"
HALL
DN
PLAYROOM
18'-0" X 14'-0"
CL
DOUBLE GARAGE
20'-0" X 22'-7"
D
W
UTIL
CAB
S
DW
REF
DINING
13'-2"
X 11'-0"
KIT
R
EATING BAR
PLANT LEDGE
1/2 BATH
PANT
MASTER BATH
GREAT ROOM
18'-0"
X 16'-0"
STORAGE
F/P
UP
CL
CL
MASTER SUITE
13'-0"
X 15'-0"
44'-5"
PORCH
First Floor
1,203 sq. ft.
56'-0"

Plan #702-0127

Garden Courtyard Lends Distinction, Privacy

1,996 total square feet of living area **Price Code D**

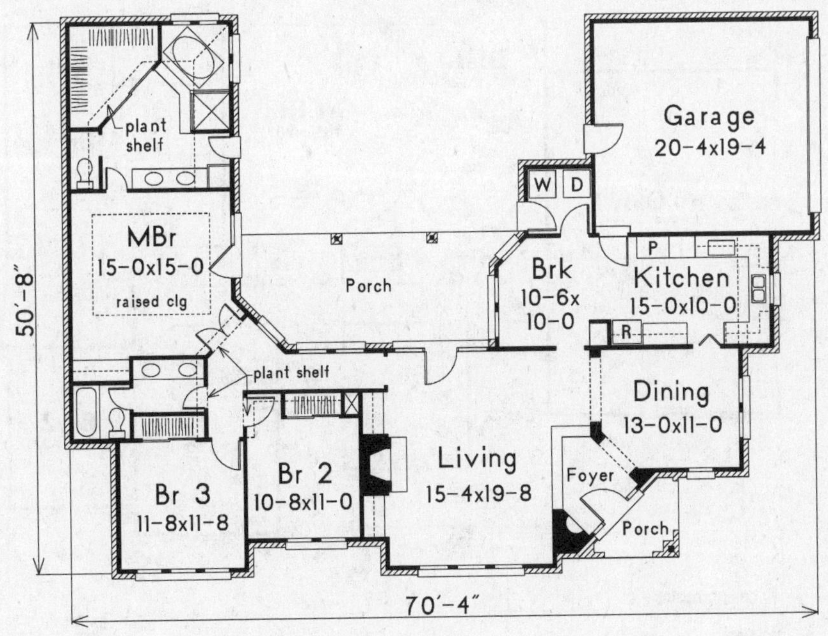

Garage
20-4x19-4
W D
P
Brk
10-6x
10-0
Kitchen
15-0x10-0
R
plant shelf
MBr
15-0x15-0
raised clg
Porch
plant shelf
Dining
13-0x11-0
Living
15-4x19-8
Foyer
Porch
Br 3
11-8x11-8
Br 2
10-8x11-0
50'-8"
70'-4"

Special features

- Garden courtyard comes with large porch and direct access to master bedroom suite, breakfast room and garage
- Sculptured entrance has artful plant shelves and special niche in foyer
- Master bedroom boasts French doors, garden tub, desk with bookshelves and generous storage
- Plant shelves and high ceilings grace hallway
- 3 bedrooms, 2 baths, 2-car side entry garage
- Slab foundation, drawings also include crawl space foundation

The Family
Handyman

Plan #702-DBI-5498

Master Suite With Sitting Area

2,188 total square feet of living area

Price Code C

Special features

- Master suite includes private covered porch, sitting area and two large walk-in closets
- Spacious kitchen has center island, snack bar and laundry access
- Kitchen has center island, snack bar and laundry access
- 3 bedrooms, 2 baths, 3-car side entry garage
- Basement foundation

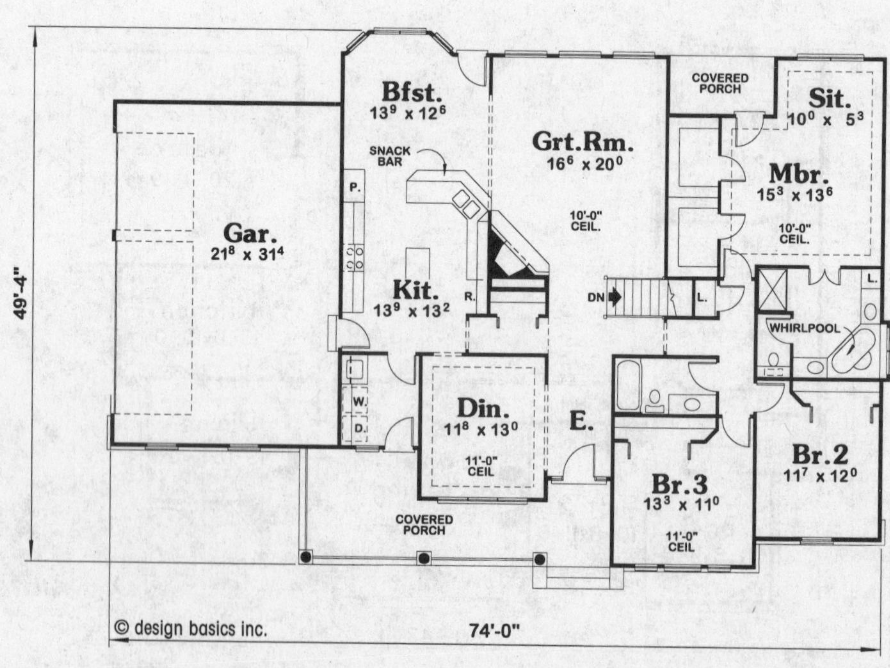
Bfst.
13⁹ x 12⁶
SNACK BAR
Grt.Rm.
16⁶ x 20⁰
10'-0" CEIL.
COVERED PORCH
Sit.
10⁰ x 5³
Mbr.
15³ x 13⁶
10'-0" CEIL.
Gar.
21⁸ x 31⁴
P.
Kit.
13⁹ x 13²
R.
DN
L.
WHIRLPOOL
W.
D.
Din.
11⁸ x 13⁰
11'-0" CEIL
E.
Br.3
13³ x 11⁰
11'-0" CEIL
Br.2
11⁷ x 12⁰
COVERED PORCH
49'-4"
© design basics inc.
74'-0"

The Family
Handyman

Plan #702-0676

Comfortable One-Story Country Home

1,367 total square feet of living area

Price Code A

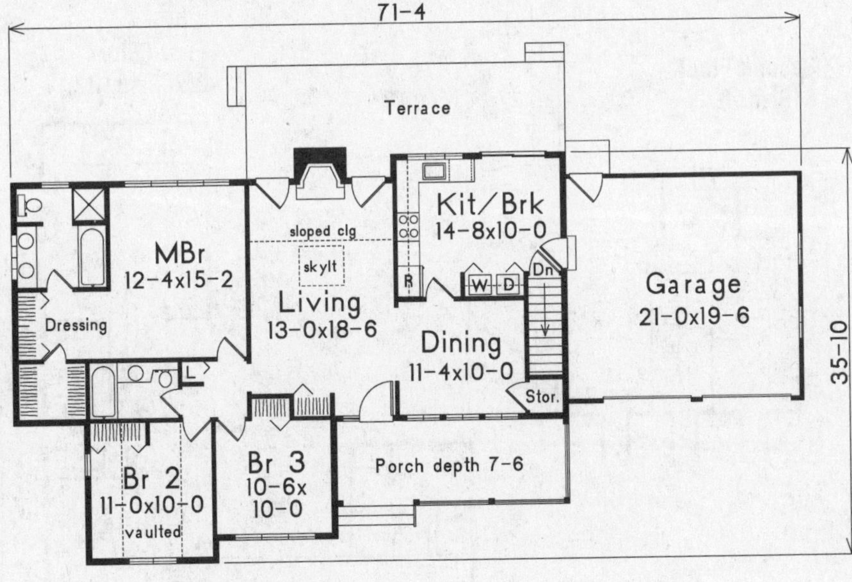
71-4
Terrace
MBr
12-4x15-2
Dressing
sloped clg
skylt
Living
13-0x18-6
Kit/Brk
14-8x10-0
R
W
D
Dn
Dining
11-4x10-0
Stor.
Garage
21-0x19-6
35-10
L
Br 2
11-0x10-0
vaulted
Br 3
10-6x
10-0
Porch depth 7-6

Special features

- Neat front porch shelters the entrance
- Dining room has full wall of windows and convenient storage area
- Breakfast area leads to the rear terrace through sliding doors
- Large living room with high ceiling, skylight and fireplace
- 3 bedrooms, 2 baths, 2-car garage
- Basement foundation, drawings also include slab foundation

Plan #702-BF-3007

Plenty Of Built-Ins

3,012 total square feet of living area

Price Code E

Special features

- Master suite has sitting area with entertainment center/ library
- Utility room has a sink and includes lots of storage and counterspace
- Future space above garage has its own stairway
- Bonus area has an additional 336 square feet of living area
- 4 bedrooms, 3 1/2 baths, 2-car side entry garage
- Crawl space, slab or basement foundation, please specify when ordering

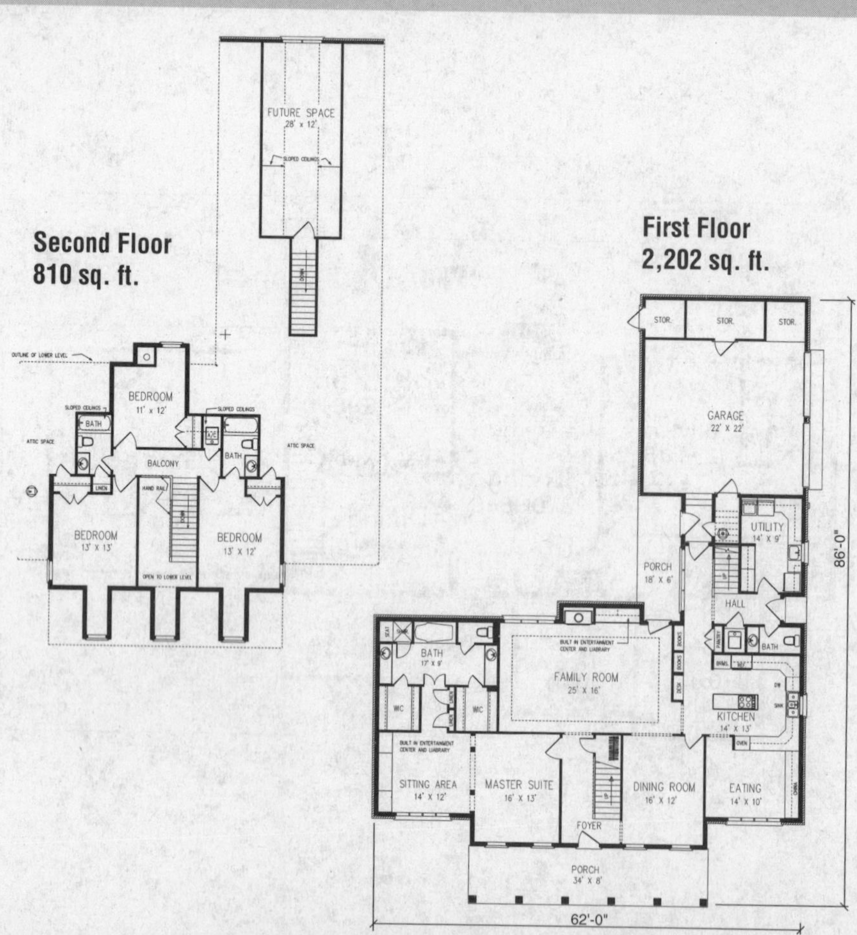
FUTURE SPACE
28' x 12'
BEDROOM
11' x 12'
BATH
BALCONY
BATH
BEDROOM
13' x 13'
BEDROOM
13' x 12'
STOR.
STOR.
STOR.
GARAGE
22' X 22'
UTILITY
14' X 9'
PORCH
18' X 6'
HALL
BATH
BATH
17' X 9'
FAMILY ROOM
25' X 16'
KITCHEN
14' X 13'
SITTING AREA
14' X 12'
MASTER SUITE
16' X 13'
DINING ROOM
16' X 12'
EATING
14' X 10'
FOYER
PORCH
34' X 8'
86'-0"
62'-0"

Second Floor
810 sq. ft.

First Floor
2,202 sq. ft.

Plan #702-SH-SEA-208

Appealing Victorian Accents

2,516 total square feet of living area **Price Code D**

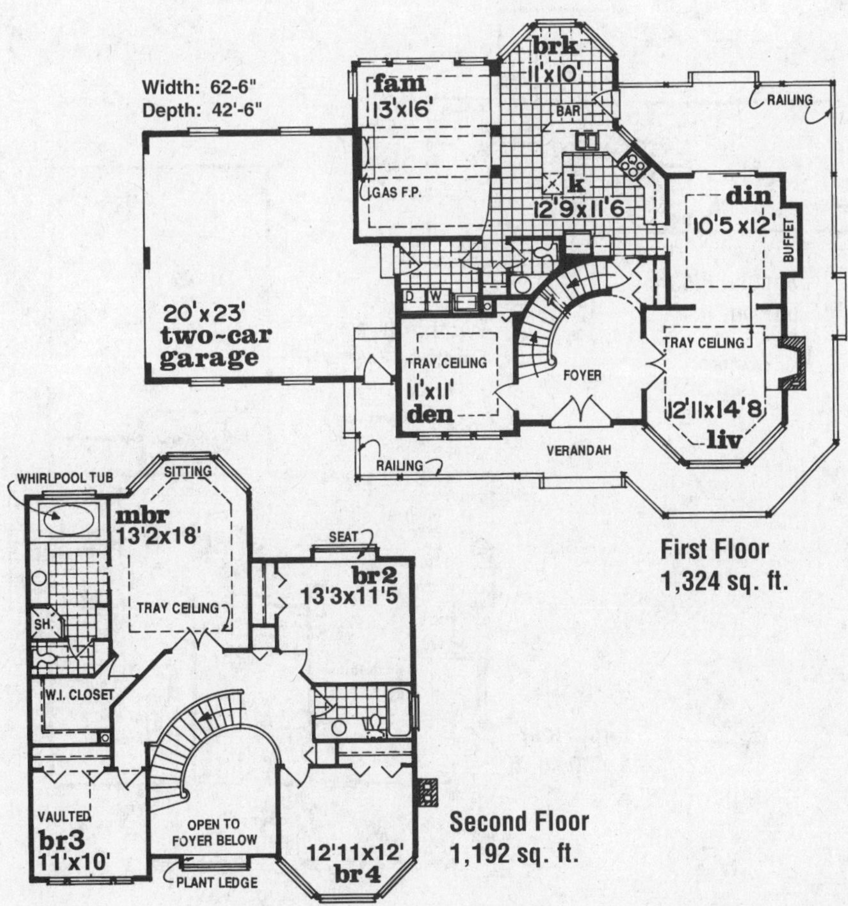
Width: 62-6"
Depth: 42'-6"
brk
11'x10'
fam
13'x16'
RAILING
BAR
GAS F.P.
k
12'9x11'6
din
10'5x12'
BUFFET
20'x23'
two-car
garage
TRAY CEILING
11'x11'
den
FOYER
TRAY CEILING
12'11x14'8
liv
VERANDAH
RAILING
WHIRLPOOL TUB
SITTING
mbr
13'2x18'
SEAT
br2
13'3x11'5
TRAY CEILING
SH.
W.I. CLOSET
VAULTED
br3
11'x10'
OPEN TO
FOYER BELOW
12'11x12'
br4
PLANT LEDGE

First Floor
1,324 sq. ft.

Second Floor
1,192 sq. ft.

Special features

- Living room has a fireplace, while the formal dining room has a buffet alcove and access to the verandah
- A cozy sitting area and tray ceiling accent the master bedroom
- Spacious bedrooms make this a wonderful family home
- 4 bedrooms, 2 1/2 baths, 2-car side entry garage
- Basement or crawl space foundation, please specify when ordering

TO ORDER BLUEPRINTS USE THE FORM ON PAGE 19 OR CALL TOLL-FREE 1-877-671-6036

The Family
Handyman

Plan #702-GM-1966

Covered Front Porch

1,966 total square feet of living area

Price Code C

Special features

- Private dining room remains focal point when entering the home
- Kitchen and breakfast room join to create a functional area
- Lots of closet space in second floor bedrooms
- 3 bedrooms, 2 1/2 baths, 2-car side entry garage
- Basement foundation

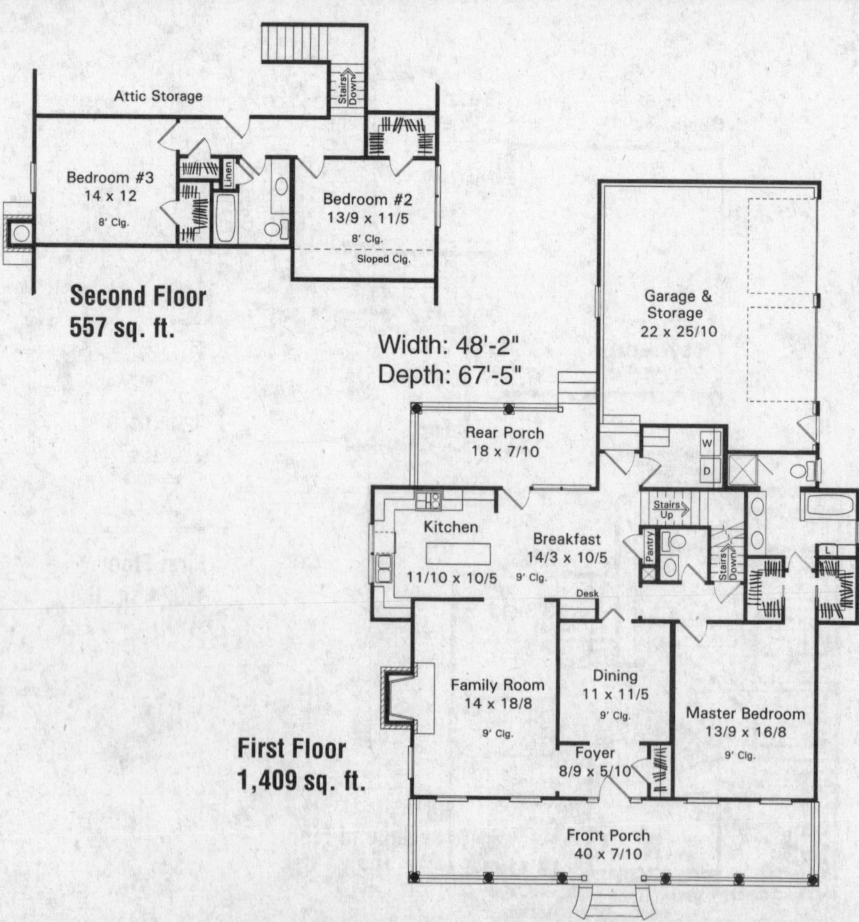
Attic Storage
Stairs Down
Bedroom #3
14 x 12
8' Clg.
Linen
Bedroom #2
13/9 x 11/5
8' Clg.
Sloped Clg.
Second Floor
557 sq. ft.
Width: 48'-2"
Depth: 67'-5"
Garage & Storage
22 x 25/10
Rear Porch
18 x 7/10
W
D
Kitchen
11/10 x 10/5
Breakfast
14/3 x 10/5
9' Clg.
Stairs Up
Pantry
Stairs Down
Desk
L
Family Room
14 x 18/8
9' Clg.
Dining
11 x 11/5
9' Clg.
Master Bedroom
13/9 x 16/8
9' Clg.
Foyer
8/9 x 5/10
First Floor
1,409 sq. ft.
Front Porch
40 x 7/10

TO ORDER BLUEPRINTS USE THE FORM ON PAGE 19 OR CALL TOLL-FREE 1-877-671-6036

View thousands more home plans online at www.familyhandyman.com/homeplans

Plan #702-0133

Victorian Turret Provides Dramatic Focus

e feet of living area

Price Code D

loor
ft.

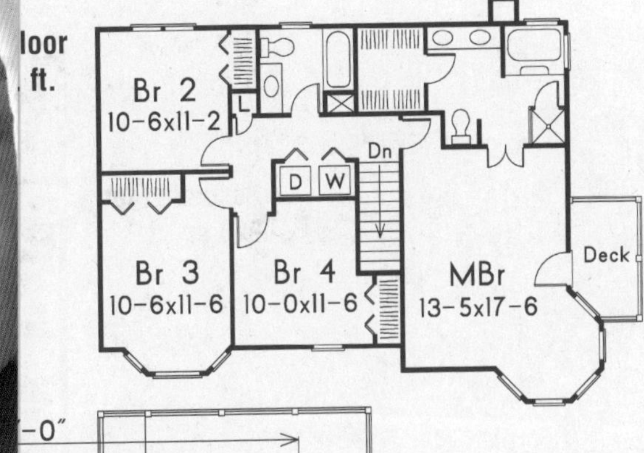

Br 2
10-6x11-2
Dn
D
W
Br 3
10-6x11-6
Br 4
10-0x11-6
MBr
13-5x17-6
Deck

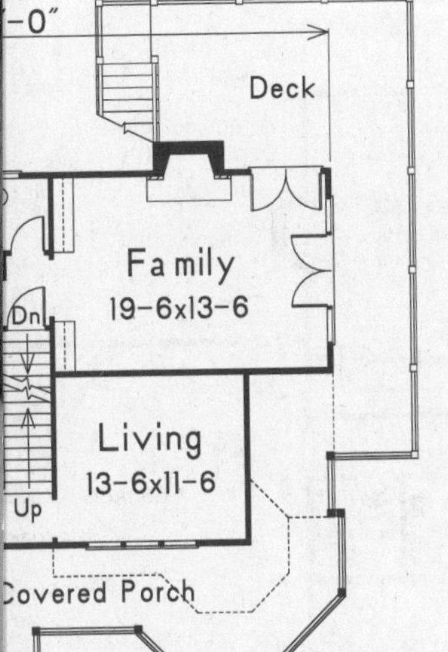

-0″
Deck
Family
19-6x13-6
Dn
Living
13-6x11-6
Up
Covered Porch

Special features

- Victorian accents dominate facade
- Covered porches and decks fan out to connect front and rear entries and add to outdoor living space
- Elegant master bedroom suite features a five-sided windowed alcove and private deck
- Corner kitchen with a sink-top peninsula
- 4 bedrooms, 2 1/2 baths, 2-car drive under garage
- Basement foundation

Plan #702-JFD-20-1887-1

Enhanced By Columned Porch

1,887 total square feet of living area

Price Code C

Special features

- Enormous great room is the heart of this home with an overlooking kitchen and dining room
- Formal dining room has lovely bay window
- Master bedroom has spacious bath with corner step-up tub, double vanity and walk-in closet
- 3 bedrooms, 2 1/2 baths, 2-car garage
- Basement foundation

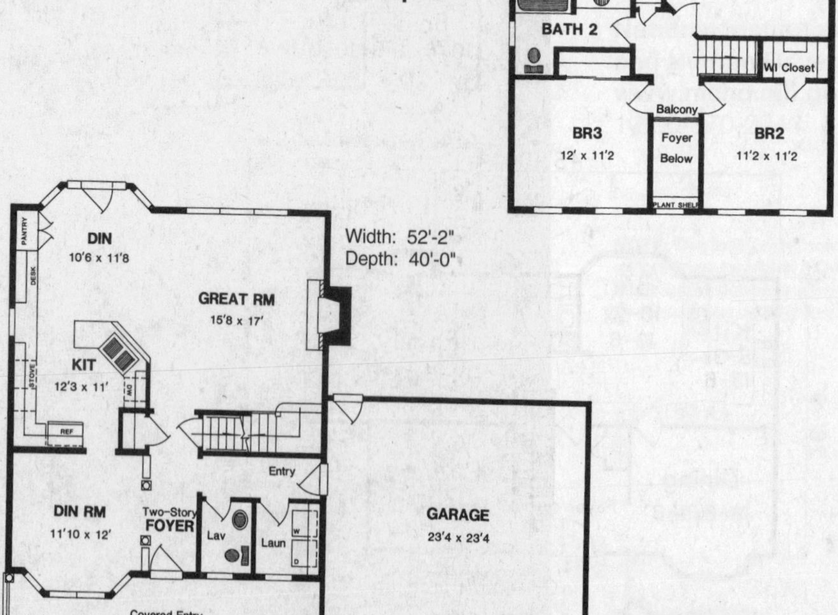

MBATH
MBR
14'8 x 17'
WI Closet
BATH 2
WI Closet
Balcony
BR3
12' x 11'2
Foyer
Below
BR2
11'2 x 11'2
PLANT SHELF
PANTRY
DESK
DIN
10'6 x 11'8
GREAT RM
15'8 x 17'
KIT
12'3 x 11'
STOVE
MO
REF
Entry
DIN RM
11'10 x 12'
Two-Story
FOYER
Lav
Laun
W
D
GARAGE
23'4 x 23'4
Covered Entry

Second Floor
926 sq. ft.

Width: 52'-2"
Depth: 40'-0"

First Floor
961 sq. ft.

The Family
Handyman

Plan #702-0348

Open Living Centers On Windowed Dining Room

2,003 total square feet of living area

Price Code D

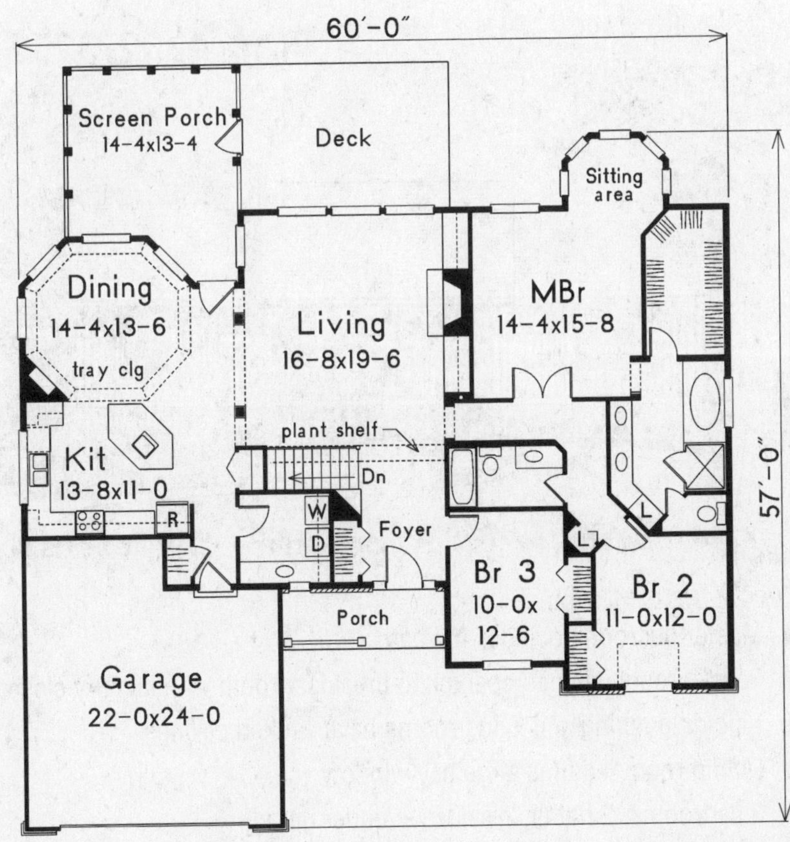

60′-0″
57′-0″
Screen Porch
14-4x13-4
Deck
Sitting area
Dining
14-4x13-6
tray clg
Living
16-8x19-6
MBr
14-4x15-8
plant shelf
Kit
13-8x11-0
R
Dn
W
D
Foyer
Br 3
10-0x
12-6
Br 2
11-0x12-0
L
L
Porch
Garage
22-0x24-0

Special features

- Octagon-shaped dining room with tray ceiling and deck overlook
- L-shaped island kitchen serves living and dining rooms
- Master bedroom boasts luxury bath and walk-in closet
- Living room features columns, elegant fireplace and 10' ceiling
- 3 bedrooms, 2 baths, 2-car garage
- Basement foundation

Covered Porch Adds Charm To Entrance   Plan #702-0294

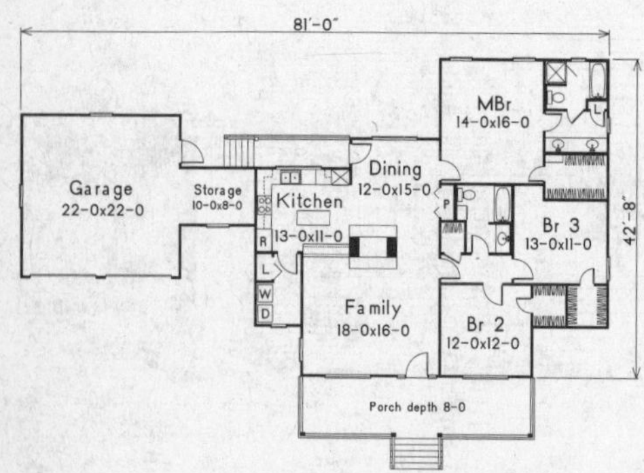
81'-0"
MBr
14-0x16-0
Dining
12-0x15-0
Garage
22-0x22-0
Storage
10-0x8-0
Kitchen
13-0x11-0
Br 3
13-0x11-0
42'-8"
Family
18-0x16-0
Br 2
12-0x12-0
Porch depth 8-0

1,655 total square feet of living area   Price Code B

Special features

- Master bedroom features 9' ceiling, walk-in closet and private bath
- Large family room has 10' ceiling and masonry see-through fireplace
- Island kitchen with convenient access to laundry room
- Handy covered walkway from garage to kitchen and dining area
- 3 bedrooms, 2 baths, 2-car garage
- Crawl space foundation

Central Living Space   Plan #702-0252

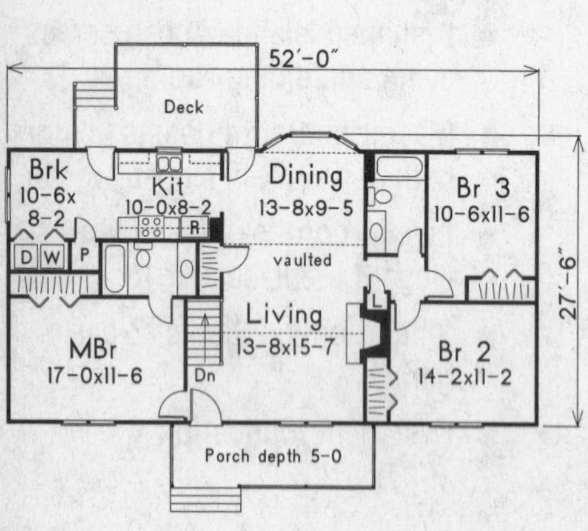
52'-0"
Deck
Brk
10-6x
8-2
Kit
10-0x8-2
Dining
13-8x9-5
Br 3
10-6x11-6
vaulted
27'-6"
Living
13-8x15-7
MBr
17-0x11-6
Br 2
14-2x11-2
Dn
Porch depth 5-0

1,364 total square feet of living area   Price Code A

Special features

- Master bedroom includes full bath
- Pass-through kitchen opens into breakfast room with laundry closet
- Adjoining dining and living rooms have vaulted ceilings
- Dining room features large bay window
- 3 bedrooms, 2 baths, 2-car drive under garage
- Basement foundation

TO ORDER BLUEPRINTS USE THE FORM ON PAGE 19 OR CALL TOLL-FREE 1-877-671-6036

View thousands more home plans online at www.familyhandyman.com/homeplans

The Family
Handyman

Plan #702-DR-2884

Inviting Oversized Porch

2,135 total square feet of living area

Price Code C

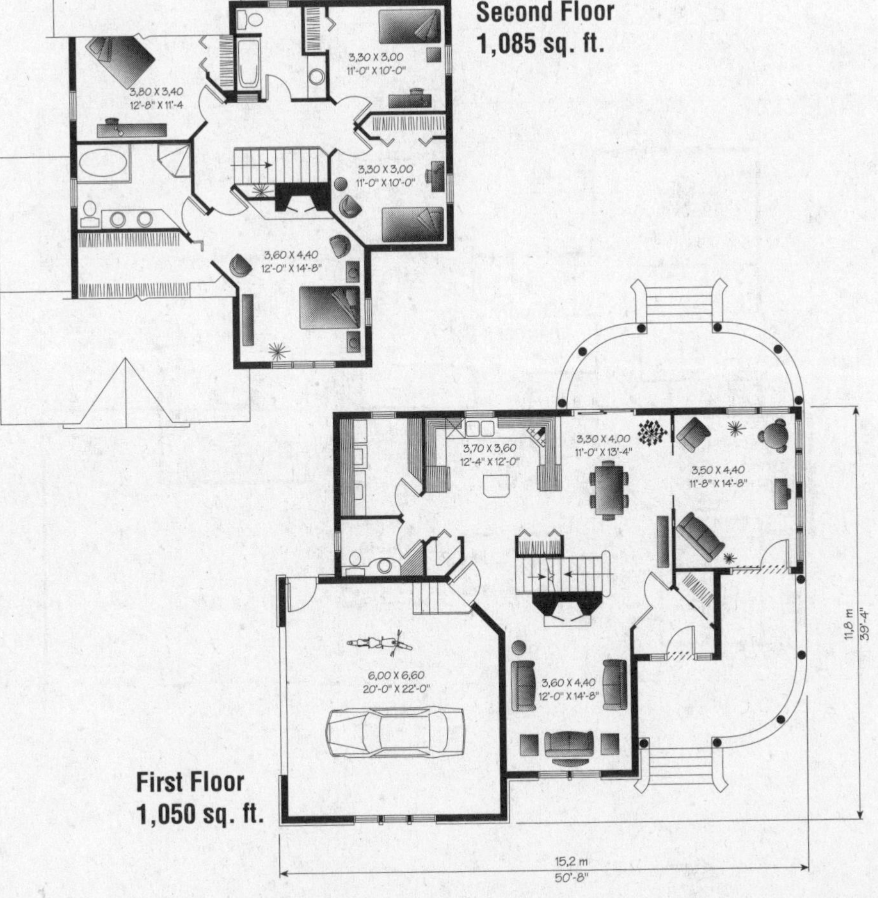
3,80 X 3,40
12'-8" X 11'-4
3,30 X 3,00
11'-0" X 10'-0"
3,30 X 3,00
11'-0" X 10'-0"
3,60 X 4,40
12'-0" X 14'-8"
3,70 X 3,60
12'-4" X 12'-0"
3,30 X 4,00
11'-0" X 13'-4"
3,50 X 4,40
11'-8" X 14'-8"
6,00 X 6,60
20'-0" X 22'-0"
3,60 X 4,40
12'-0" X 14'-8"
11,8 m
39'-4"
15,2 m
50'-8"

Second Floor
1,085 sq. ft.

First Floor
1,050 sq. ft.

Special features

- All bedrooms on second floor for privacy
- 9' ceilings on first floor
- Energy efficient home has 2" x 6" exterior walls
- 4 bedrooms, 2 1/2 baths, 2-car side entry garage
- Basement foundation

TO ORDER BLUEPRINTS USE THE FORM ON PAGE 19 OR CALL TOLL-FREE 1-877-671-6036

View thousands more home plans online at www.familyhandyman.com/homeplans

Plan #702-0263

High Styling Wraps Central Kitchen

3,003 total square feet of living area **Price Code E**

Special features

- Vaulted master bedroom features large walk-in closet, spa, separate shower room and access to rear patio
- Covered entrance opens into foyer with large greeting area
- Formal living room with 12' ceiling and 36" walls on two sides
- Island kitchen features large pantry and nook
- Cozy fireplace accents vaulted family room that opens onto a covered deck
- Utility room with generous space is adjacent to a half bath
- 3 bedrooms, 2 1/2 baths, 3-car garage
- Crawl space foundation

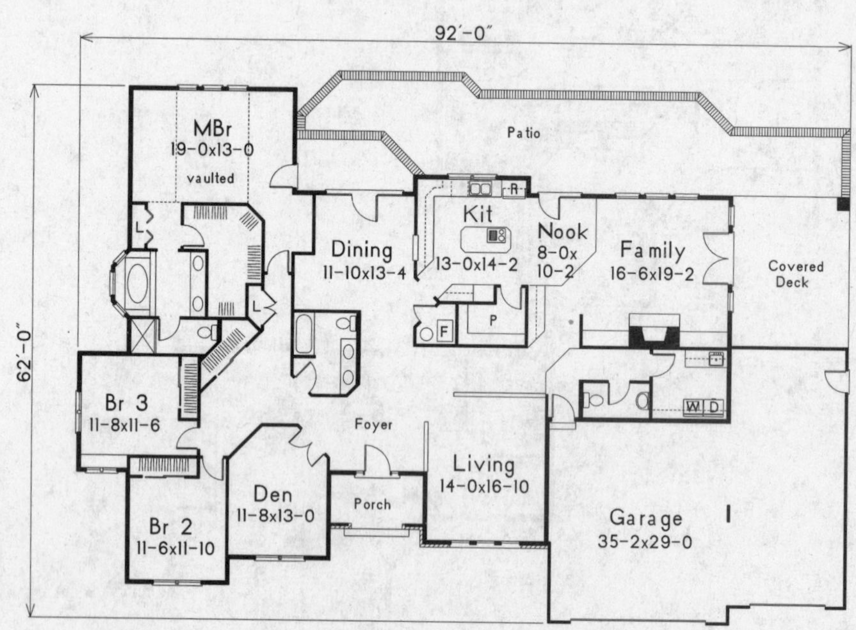
92'-0"
62'-0"
Patio
MBr
19-0x13-0
vaulted
Kit
13-0x14-2
Nook
8-0x
10-2
Family
16-6x19-2
Covered
Deck
Dining
11-10x13-4
Br 3
11-8x11-6
Foyer
Living
14-0x16-10
Den
11-8x13-0
Porch
Br 2
11-6x11-10
Garage
35-2x29-0

The Family
Handyman

Plan #702-AX-93308

Wrap-Around Porch Adds To Farmhouse Style

1,793 total square feet of living area **Price Code B**

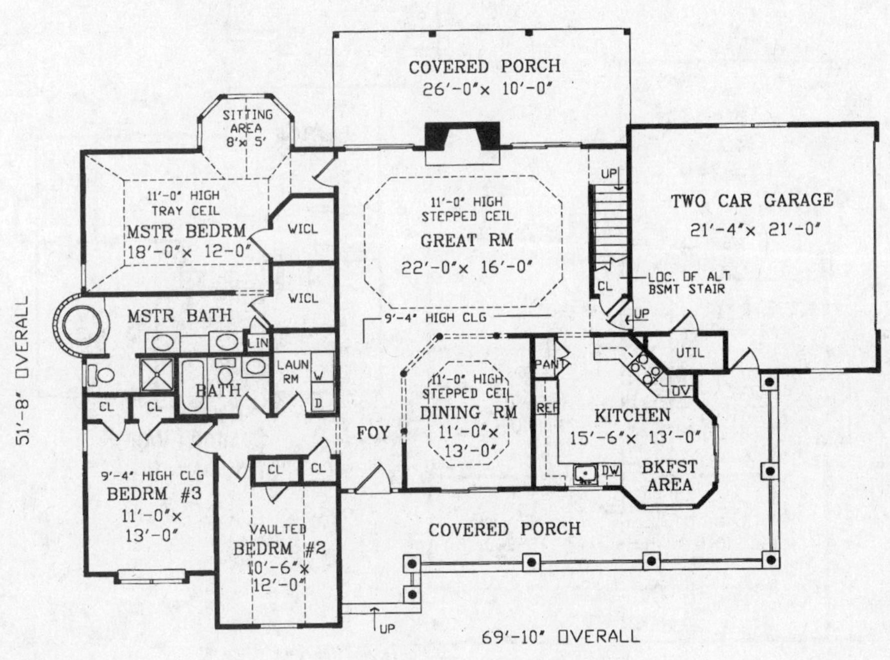
COVERED PORCH
26'-0"× 10'-0"
SITTING AREA
8'× 5'
11'-0" HIGH
TRAY CEIL
MSTR BEDRM
18'-0"× 12-0"
WICL
WICL
11'-0" HIGH
STEPPED CEIL
GREAT RM
22'-0"× 16'-0"
UP
TWO CAR GARAGE
21'-4"× 21'-0"
CL
LOC. OF ALT
BSMT STAIR
UP
9'-4" HIGH CLG
MSTR BATH
LIN
UTIL
LAUN
RM
W
D
BATH
PAN
DV
11'-0" HIGH
STEPPED CEIL
DINING RM
11'-0"×
13'-0"
REF
KITCHEN
15'-6"× 13'-0"
CL
CL
FOY
BKFST
AREA
DW
9'-4" HIGH CLG
BEDRM #3
11'-0"×
13'-0"
CL
CL
VAULTED
BEDRM #2
10'-6"×
12'-0"
COVERED PORCH
51'-8" OVERALL
UP
69'-10" OVERALL

Special features

- A beautiful foyer leads into the great room which has a fireplace flanked by two sets of beautifully transomed doors both leading to a large covered porch
- Dramatic eat-in kitchen includes an abundance of cabinets and workspace in an exciting angled shape
- Delightful master suite has many amenities
- Optional bonus room has an additional 779 square feet of living area
- 3 bedrooms, 2 baths, 2-car side entry garage
- Basement, crawl space or slab foundation, please specify when ordering

Plan #702-0141

Country-Style Comfort

2,826 total square feet of living area

Price Code E

Special features

- Wrap-around covered porch is accessible from family and breakfast rooms in addition to front entrance
- Bonus room with separate entrance suitable for an office or private accommodations
- Large, full-windowed breakfast room
- 4 bedrooms, 2 1/2 baths, 2-car side entry garage
- Basement foundation

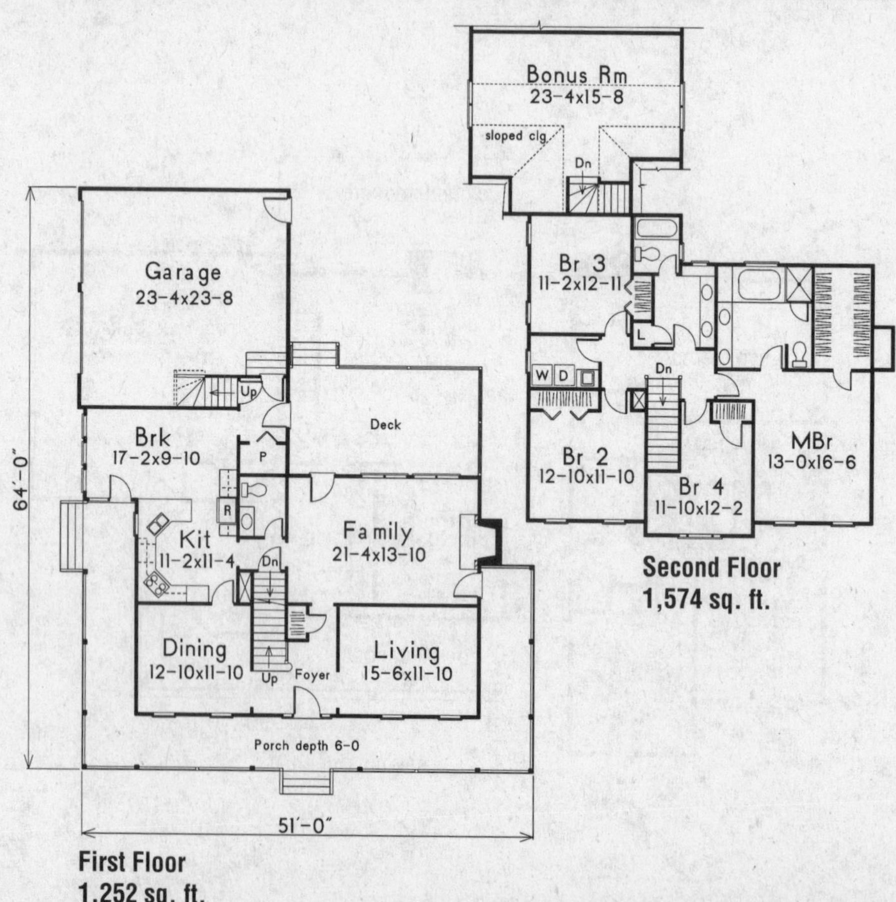
Bonus Rm
23-4x15-8
sloped clg.
Dn
Br 3
11-2x12-11
L
W D
Dn
Br 2
12-10x11-10
Br 4
11-10x12-2
MBr
13-0x16-6
Garage
23-4x23-8
Up
Deck
Brk
17-2x9-10
P
R
Kit
11-2x11-4
Dn
Family
21-4x13-10
Dining
12-10x11-10
Up
Foyer
Living
15-6x11-10
Porch depth 6-0
64'-0"
51'-0"

Second Floor
1,574 sq. ft.

First Floor
1,252 sq. ft.

Plan #702-JV-2008-B

Foyer Is Open To Loft Above

GARDNER

2,008 total square feet of living area **Price Code C**

Second Floor
876 sq. ft.

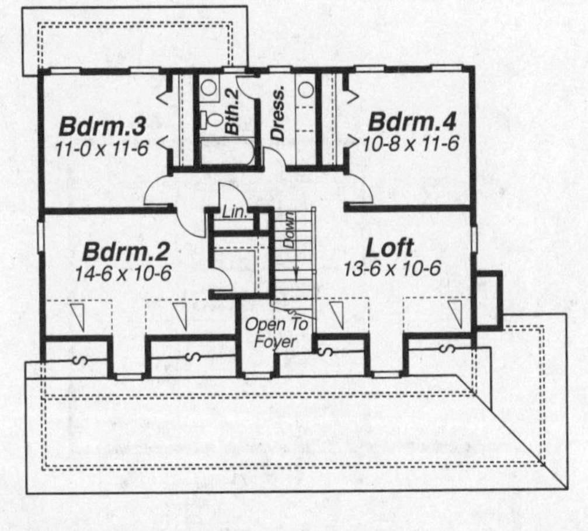
Bdrm.3
11-0 x 11-6
Bth.2
Dress.
Bdrm.4
10-8 x 11-6
Lin.
Down
Bdrm.2
14-6 x 10-6
Loft
13-6 x 10-6
Open To
Foyer

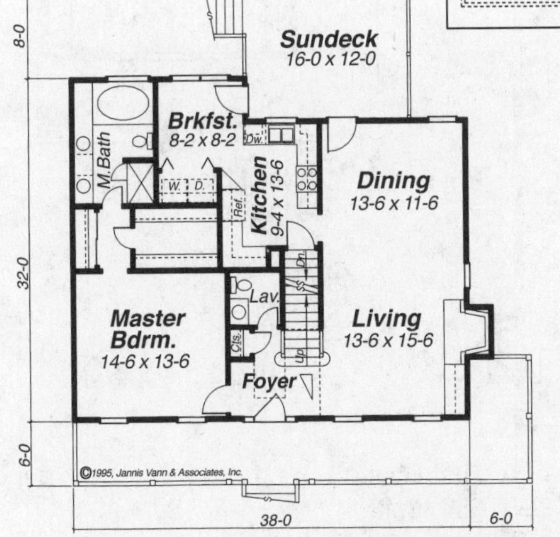
Sundeck
16-0 x 12-0
8-0
Brkfst.
8-2 x 8-2
DW.
M.Bath
W. D.
Kitchen
9-4 x 13-6
Ref.
Dining
13-6 x 11-6
32-0
Dn
Lav.
Master
Bdrm.
14-6 x 13-6
Cls.
Up
Living
13-6 x 15-6
Foyer
6-0
©1995, Jannis Vann & Associates, Inc.
38-0
6-0

First Floor
1,132 sq. ft.

Special features

- Living and dining areas join to create wonderful space for entertaining
- Master bedroom includes bath with large tub and separate shower
- Second floor includes loft space perfect for home office or playroom
- 4 bedrooms, 2 1/2 baths, 2-car drive under garage
- Basement foundation

Plan #702-DDI-95-234

Craftsman Cottage

1,649 total square feet of living area — **Price Code B**

Special features

- Energy efficient home with 2" x 6" exterior walls
- Ideal design for a narrow lot
- Country kitchen includes an island and eating bar
- Master bedroom has 12' vaulted ceiling and a charming arched window
- 4 bedrooms, 2 1/2 baths, 2-car side entry garage
- Basement or crawl space foundation, please specify when ordering

Width: 30'
Depth: 52'

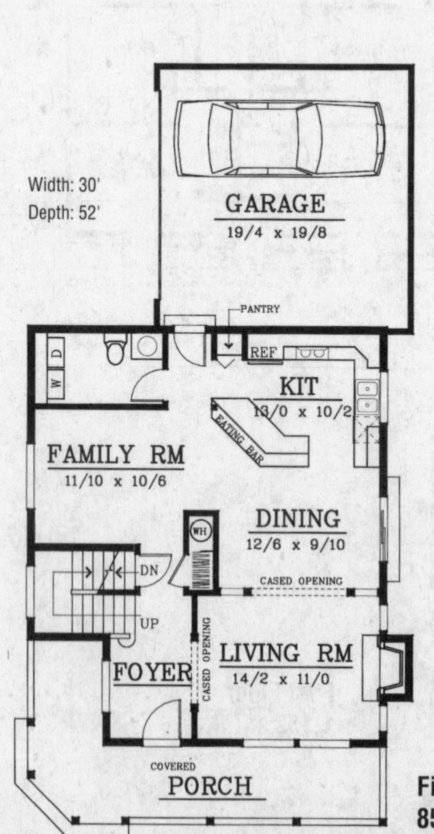
GARAGE
19/4 x 19/8
PANTRY
REF
W
D
KIT
13/0 x 10/2
EATING BAR
FAMILY RM
11/10 x 10/6
WH
DINING
12/6 x 9/10
CASED OPENING
DN
UP
FOYER
CASED OPENING
LIVING RM
14/2 x 11/0
COVERED
PORCH

First Floor
858 sq. ft.

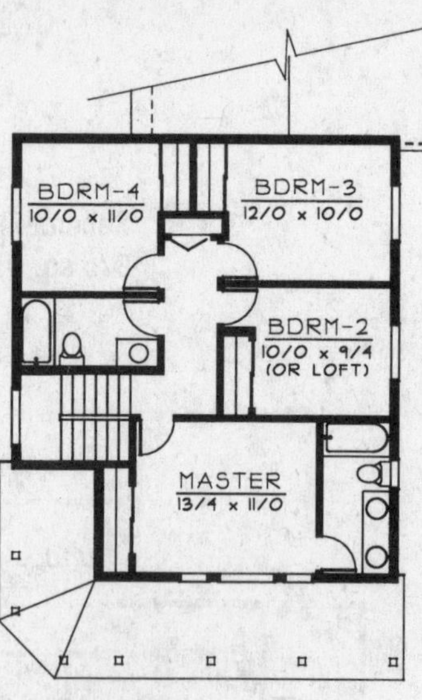
BDRM-4
10/0 x 11/0
BDRM-3
12/0 x 10/0
BDRM-2
10/0 x 9/4
(OR LOFT)
MASTER
13/4 x 11/0

Second Floor
791 sq. ft.

Plan #702-0672

Welcoming Front Porch, A Country Touch

2,043 total square feet of living area **Price Code C**

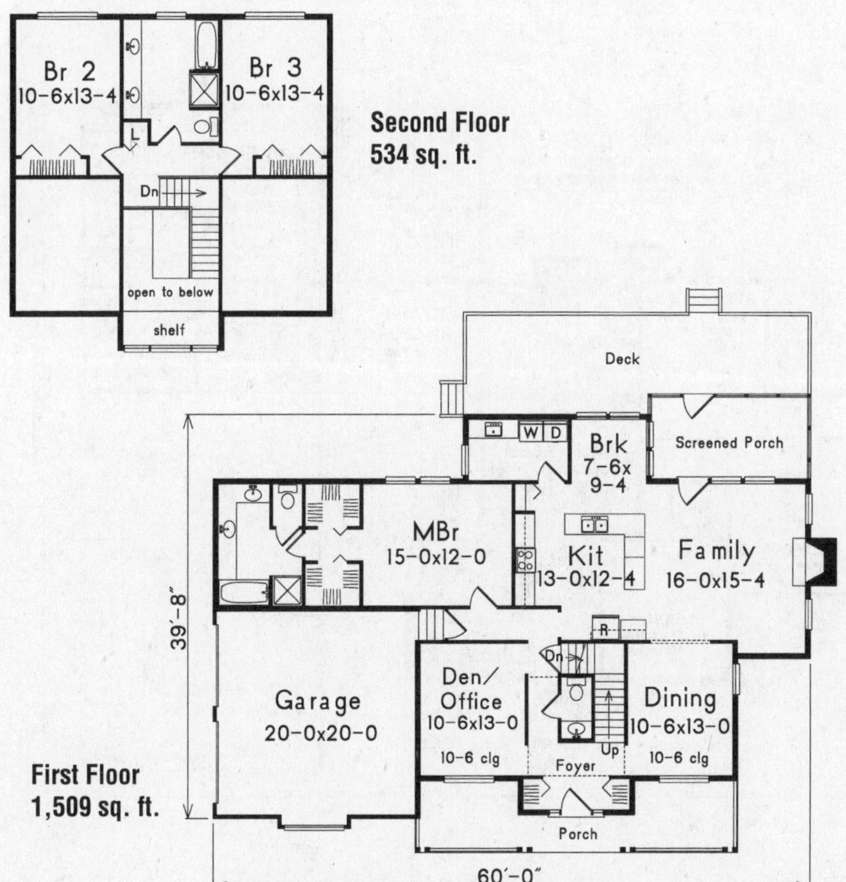
Br 2
10-6x13-4
Br 3
10-6x13-4
L
Dn
open to below
shelf
Deck
W D
Brk
7-6x
9-4
Screened Porch
MBr
15-0x12-0
Kit
13-0x12-4
Family
16-0x15-4
39'-8"
R
Dn
Garage
20-0x20-0
Den/
Office
10-6x13-0
10-6 clg
Dining
10-6x13-0
10-6 clg
Up
Foyer
Porch
60'-0"

Second Floor
534 sq. ft.

First Floor
1,509 sq. ft.

Special features

- Energy efficient home with 2" x 6" exterior walls
- Two-story central foyer includes two coat closets
- Large combined space provided by the kitchen, family and breakfast rooms
- Breakfast nook for informal dining looks out to the deck and screened porch
- 3 bedrooms, 2 1/2 baths, 2-car side entry garage
- Basement foundation, drawings also include slab foundation

Inviting Vaulted Entry

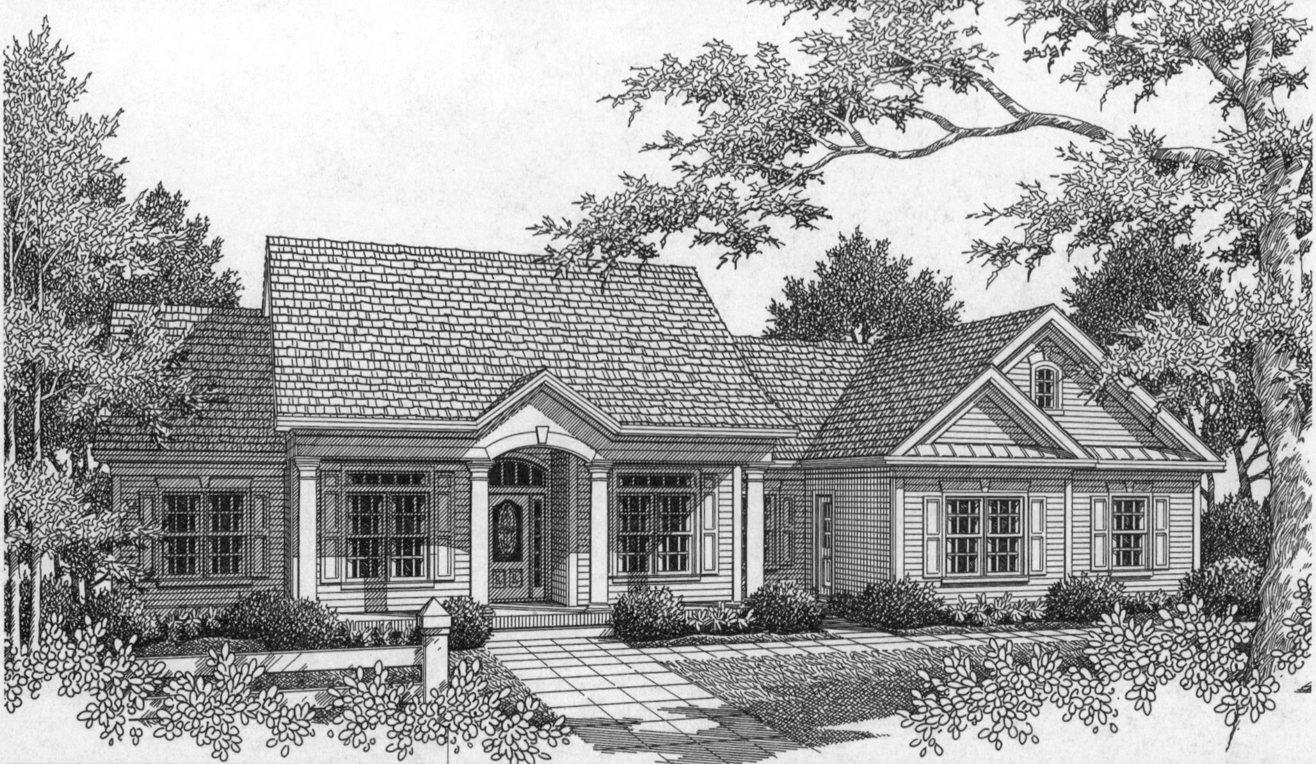

2,097 total square feet of living area **Price Code C**

Special features

- Angled kitchen, family room and eating areas add interest to this home
- Family room includes a TV niche making this a cozy place to relax
- Sumptuous master suite includes sitting area, walk-in closet, and a full bath with double vanities
- 3 bedrooms, 3 baths, 3-car side entry garage
- Crawl space or slab foundation, please specify when ordering

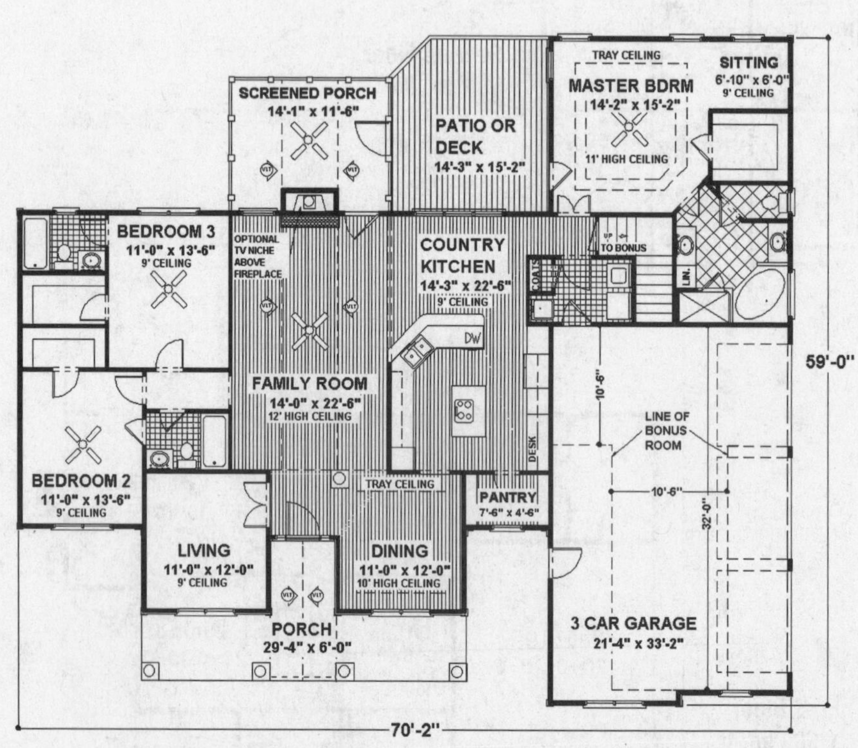
SCREENED PORCH
14'-1" x 11'-6"
PATIO OR DECK
14'-3" x 15'-2"
TRAY CEILING
MASTER BDRM
14'-2" x 15'-2"
11' HIGH CEILING
SITTING
6'-10" x 6'-0"
9' CEILING
BEDROOM 3
11'-0" x 13'-6"
9' CEILING
OPTIONAL TV NICHE ABOVE FIREPLACE
COUNTRY KITCHEN
14'-3" x 22'-6"
9' CEILING
UP TO BONUS
COATS
DW
LIN.
FAMILY ROOM
14'-0" x 22'-6"
12' HIGH CEILING
DESK
10'-6"
LINE OF BONUS ROOM
59'-0"
BEDROOM 2
11'-0" x 13'-6"
9' CEILING
TRAY CEILING
PANTRY
7'-6" x 4'-6"
10'-6"
32'-0"
LIVING
11'-0" x 12'-0"
9' CEILING
DINING
11'-0" x 12'-0"
10' HIGH CEILING
PORCH
29'-4" x 6'-0"
3 CAR GARAGE
21'-4" x 33'-2"
70'-2"

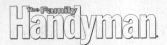

Plan #702-0598

Dormers Accent Country Home

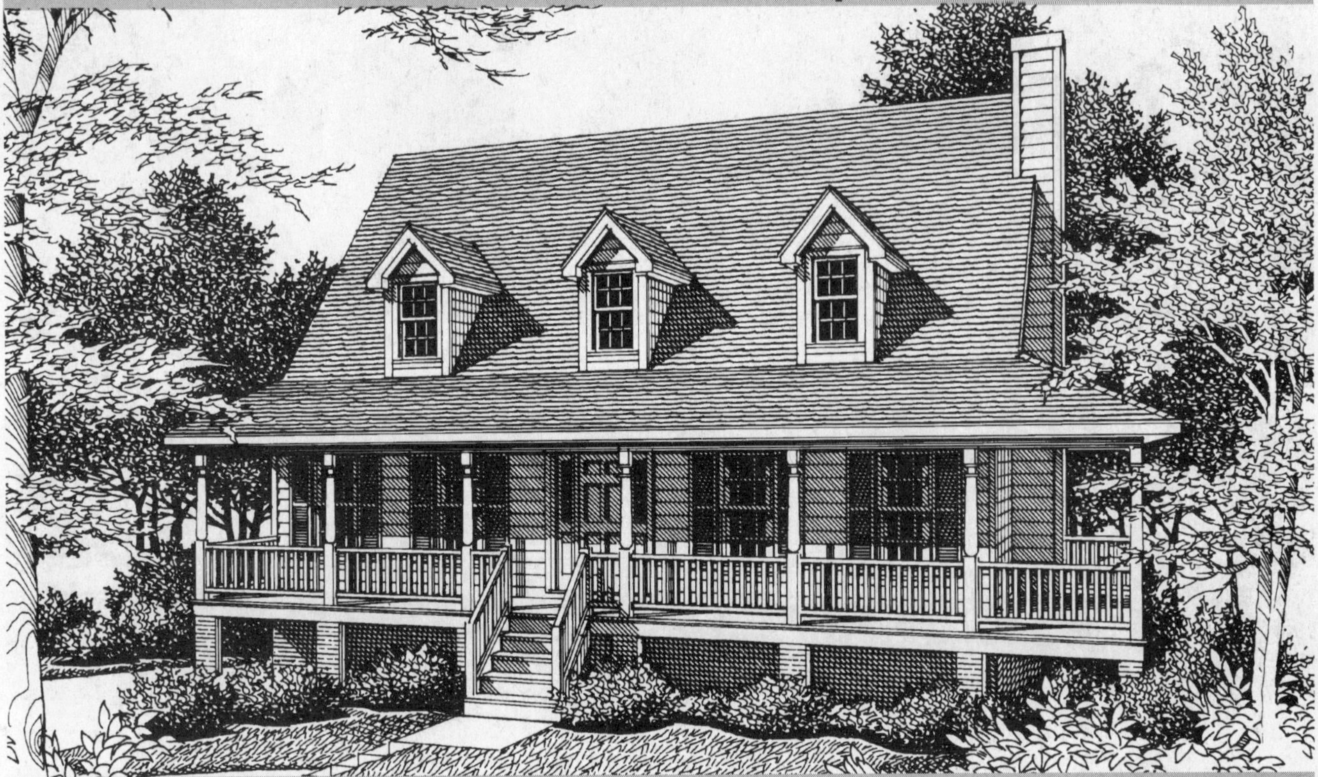

1,818 total square feet of living area

Price Code C

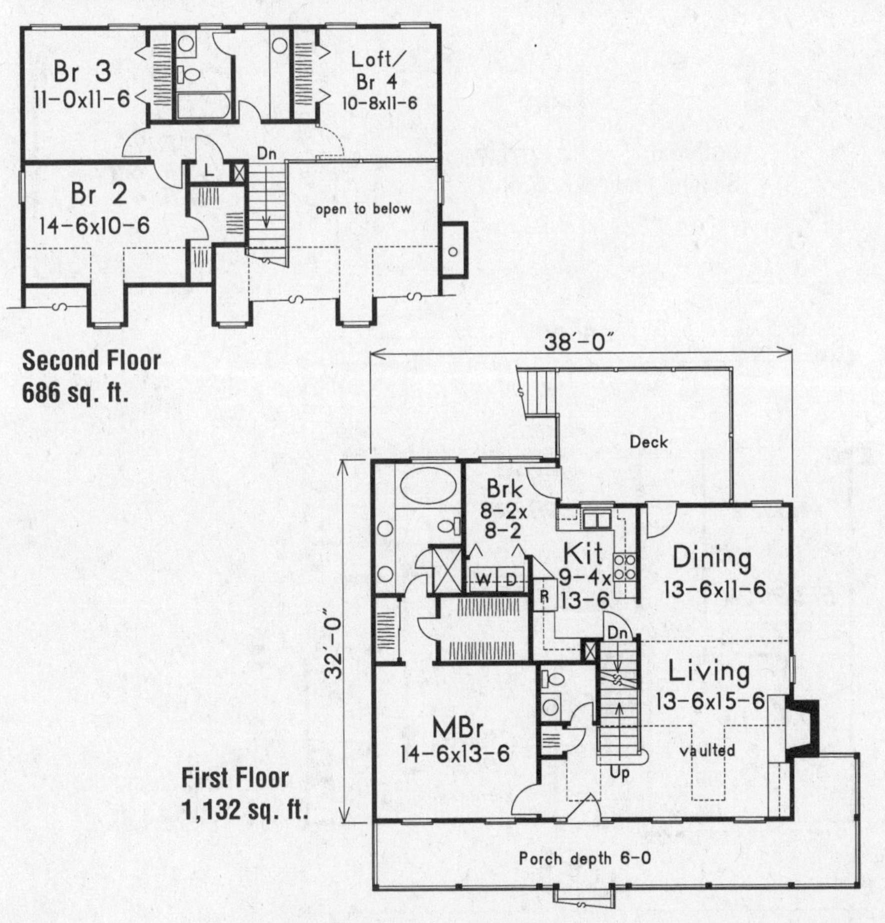
Br 3
11-0x11-6
Loft/
Br 4
10-8x11-6
Dn
L
Br 2
14-6x10-6
open to below
Second Floor
686 sq. ft.
38′-0″
Deck
Brk
8-2x
8-2
Kit
9-4x
13-6
Dining
13-6x11-6
W
D
R
Dn
32′-0″
Living
13-6x15-6
MBr
14-6x13-6
vaulted
Up
First Floor
1,132 sq. ft.
Porch depth 6-0

Special features

- Breakfast room is tucked behind the kitchen and has laundry closet and deck access
- Living and dining areas share vaulted ceiling and fireplace
- Master bedroom has two closets, large double-bowl vanity, separate tub and shower
- Large front porch wraps around home
- 4 bedrooms, 2 1/2 baths, 2-car drive under garage
- Basement foundation

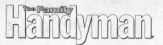

Plan #702-RJ-B1416

Decorative Accents Featured On Front Porch

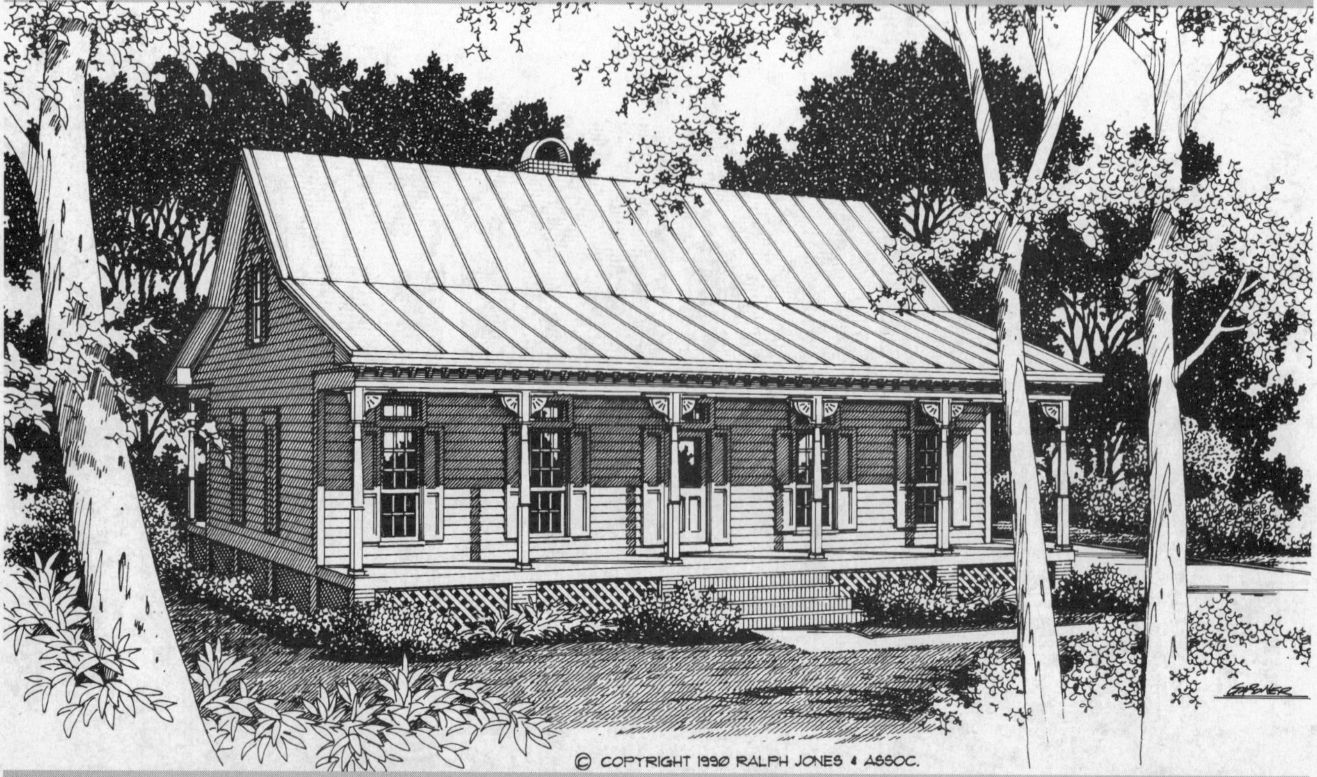

1,455 total square feet of living area

Price Code A

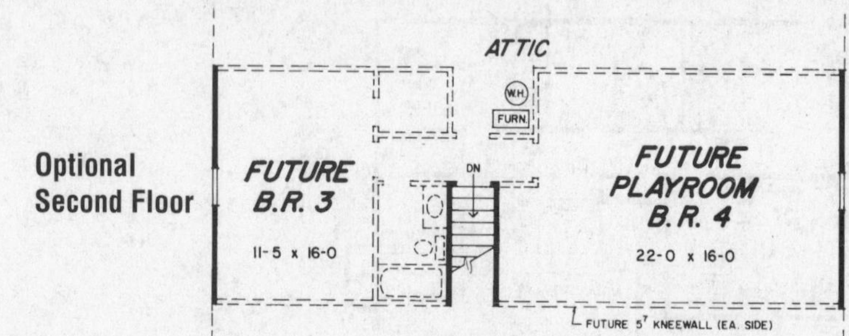

ATTIC
W.H.
FURN
DN
FUTURE B.R. 3
11-5 x 16-0
FUTURE PLAYROOM B.R. 4
22-0 x 16-0
FUTURE 5' KNEEWALL (EA. SIDE)

Optional Second Floor

Special features

- Spacious mud room has a large pantry, space for a freezer, sink/ counter area and bath with shower
- Bedroom #2 can easily be converted to a study or office area
- Optional second floor bedroom and playroom have an additional 744 square feet of living area
- 2 bedrooms, 2 baths
- Slab or crawl space foundation, please specify when ordering

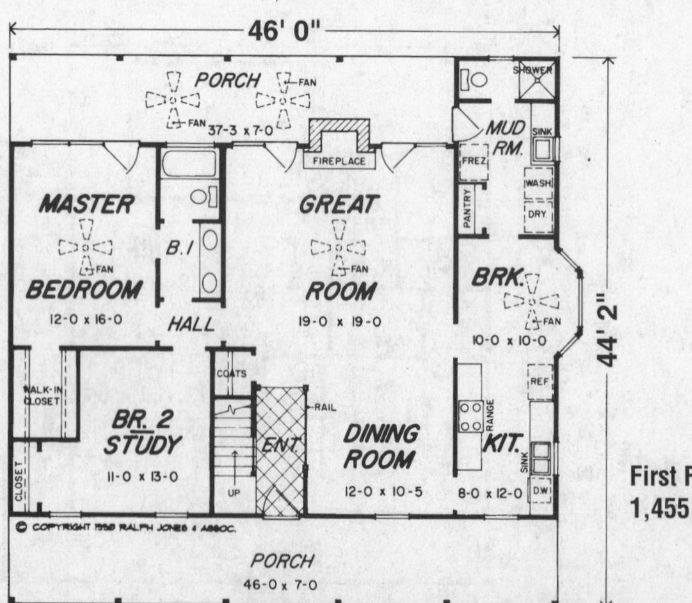

46' 0"
44' 2"
PORCH
37-3 x 7-0
FAN
FIREPLACE
SHOWER
MUD RM.
SINK
FREZ
WASH
DRY
PANTRY
MASTER BEDROOM
12-0 x 16-0
B.1
HALL
GREAT ROOM
19-0 x 19-0
BRK.
10-0 x 10-0
REF
WALK-IN CLOSET
COATS
RAIL
BR. 2 STUDY
11-0 x 13-0
ENT.
UP
DINING ROOM
12-0 x 10-5
RANGE
KIT.
8-0 x 12-0
SINK
DW
CLOSET
© COPYRIGHT 1990 RALPH JONES & ASSOC.
PORCH
46-0 x 7-0

First Floor
1,455 sq. ft.

Double Atrium Embraces The Sun

3,199 total square feet of living area

Price Code E

Rear View

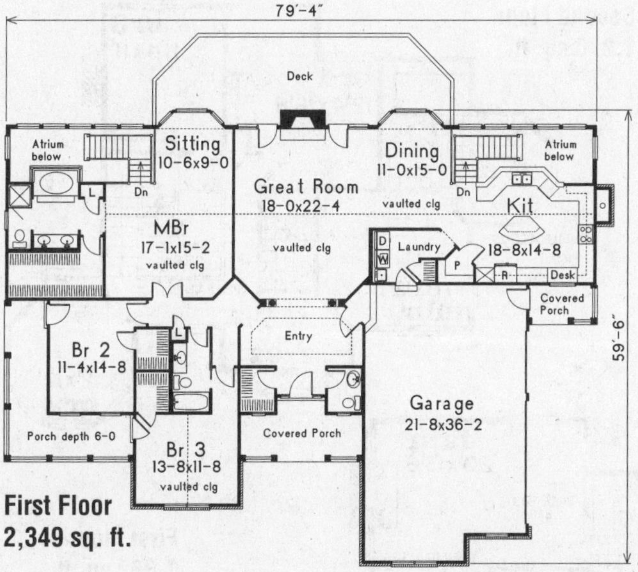

First Floor
2,349 sq. ft.

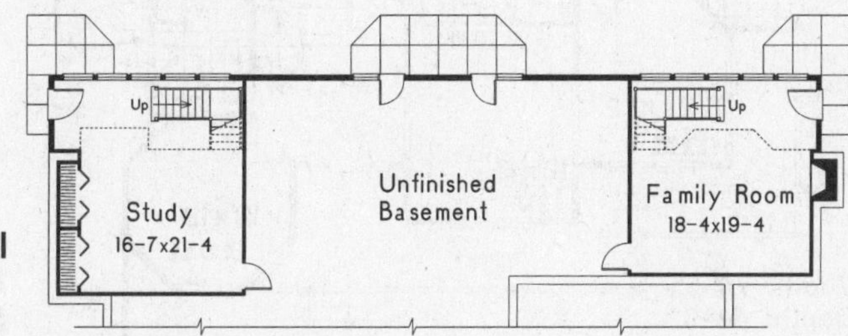
Up
Up
Study
16-7x21-4
Unfinished
Basement
Family Room
18-4x19-4

Lower Level
850 sq. ft.

Special features

- Grand scale kitchen features bay-shaped cabinetry built over atrium that overlooks two-story window wall
- A second atrium dominates the master suite which boasts a sitting area with bay window and luxurious bath, which has whirlpool tub open to the garden atrium and lower level study
- 3 bedrooms, 2 1/2 baths, 3-car side entry garage
- Walk-out basement foundation

TO ORDER BLUEPRINTS USE THE FORM ON PAGE 19 OR CALL TOLL-FREE 1-877-671-6036

Rich With Victorian Details

2,632 total square feet of living area

Price Code E

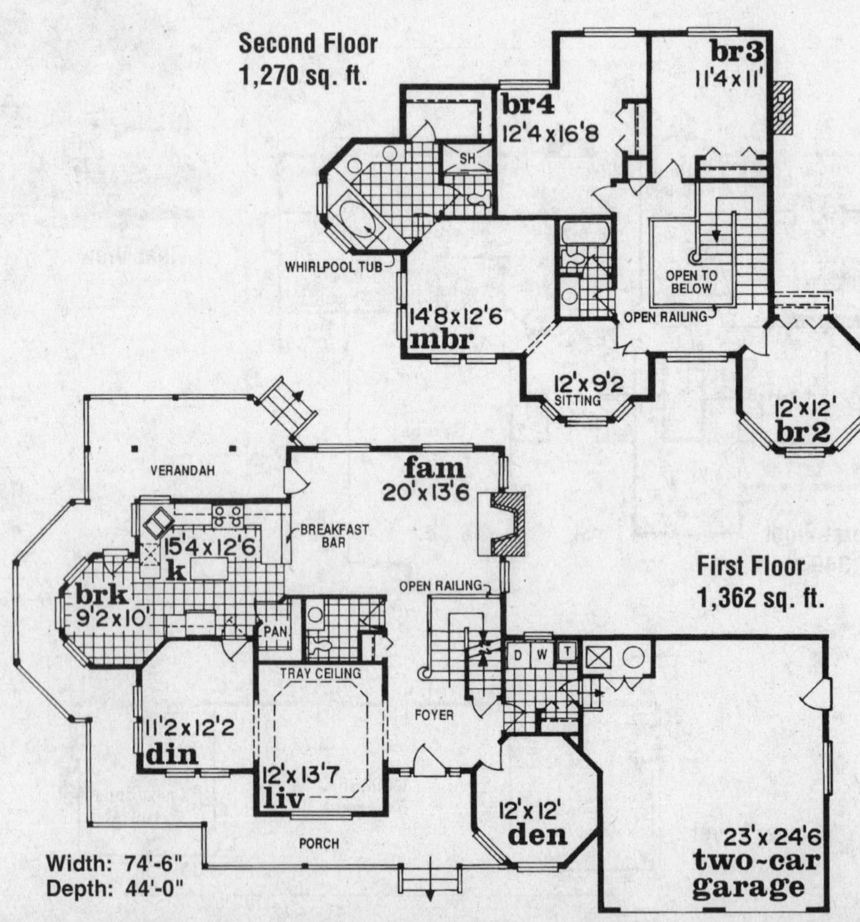
Second Floor
1,270 sq. ft.
br3
11'4 x 11'
br4
12'4 x 16'8
SH
WHIRLPOOL TUB
OPEN TO BELOW
OPEN RAILING
14'8 x 12'6
mbr
12'x 9'2
SITTING
12'x 12'
br2
VERANDAH
fam
20' x 13'6
BREAKFAST BAR
15'4 x 12'6
k
brk
9'2 x 10'
PAN.
OPEN RAILING
First Floor
1,362 sq. ft.
D
W
T
TRAY CEILING
FOYER
11'2 x 12'2
din
12' x 13'7
liv
12' x 12'
den
PORCH
23' x 24'6
two-car garage
Width: 74'-6"
Depth: 44'-0"

Special features

- Energy efficient home with 2" x 6" exterior walls
- Master bedroom has cheerful octagon-shaped sitting area
- Arched entrances create a distinctive living room with a lovely tray ceiling and help define the dining room
- 4 bedrooms, 2 1/2 baths, 2-car garage
- Basement or crawl space foundation, please specify when ordering

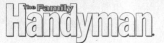

Plan #702-0249

Country-Style Home With Large Front Porch

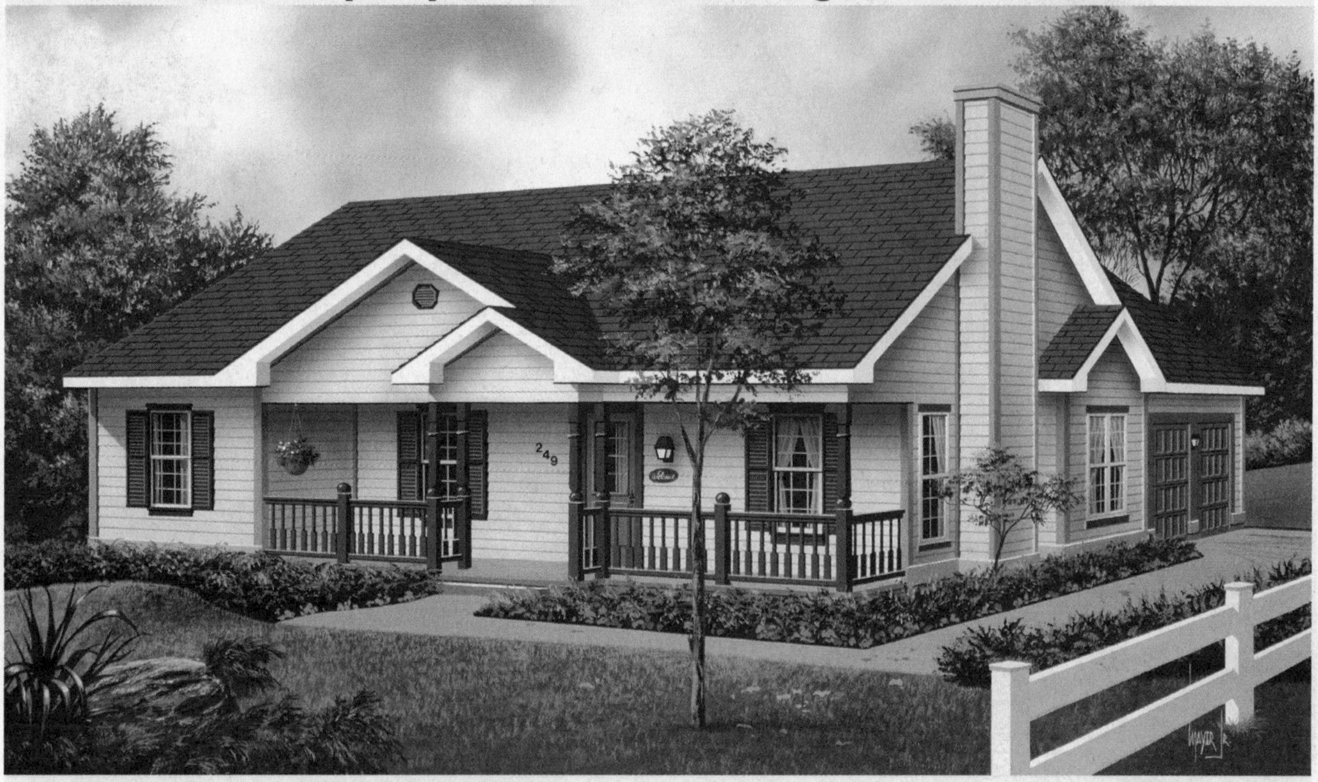

1,501 total square feet of living area **Price Code B**

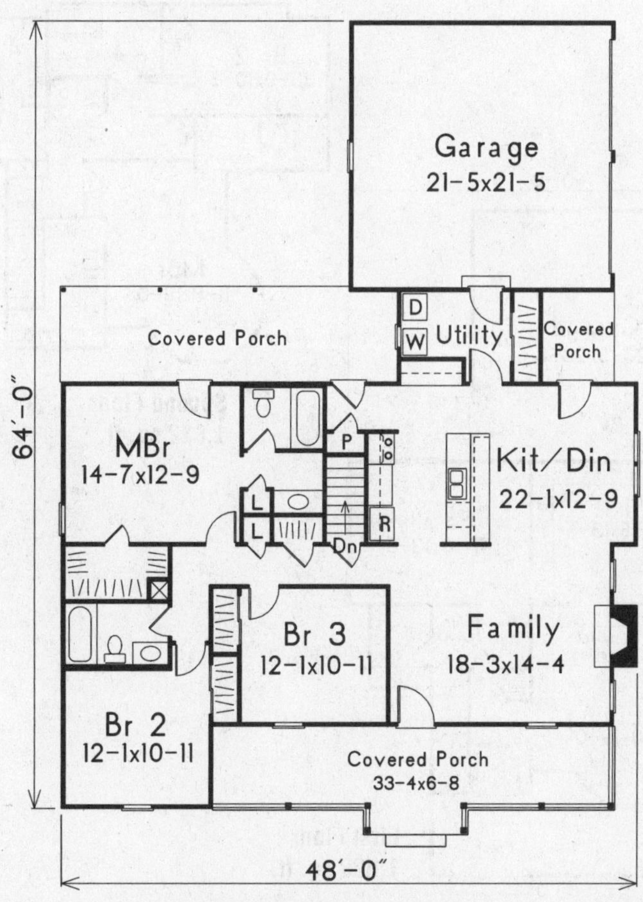

Garage
21-5x21-5
D
W
Utility
Covered Porch
Covered Porch
MBr
14-7x12-9
P
Kit/Din
22-1x12-9
L
L
R
Dn
Br 3
12-1x10-11
Family
18-3x14-4
Br 2
12-1x10-11
Covered Porch
33-4x6-8
64'-0"
48'-0"

Special features

- Spacious kitchen with dining area is open to the outdoors
- Convenient utility room is adjacent to garage
- Master suite with private bath, dressing area and access to large covered porch
- Large family room creates openness
- 3 bedrooms, 2 baths, 2-car side entry garage
- Basement foundation, drawings also include crawl space and slab foundations

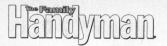

Dramatic Layout Created By Victorian Turret

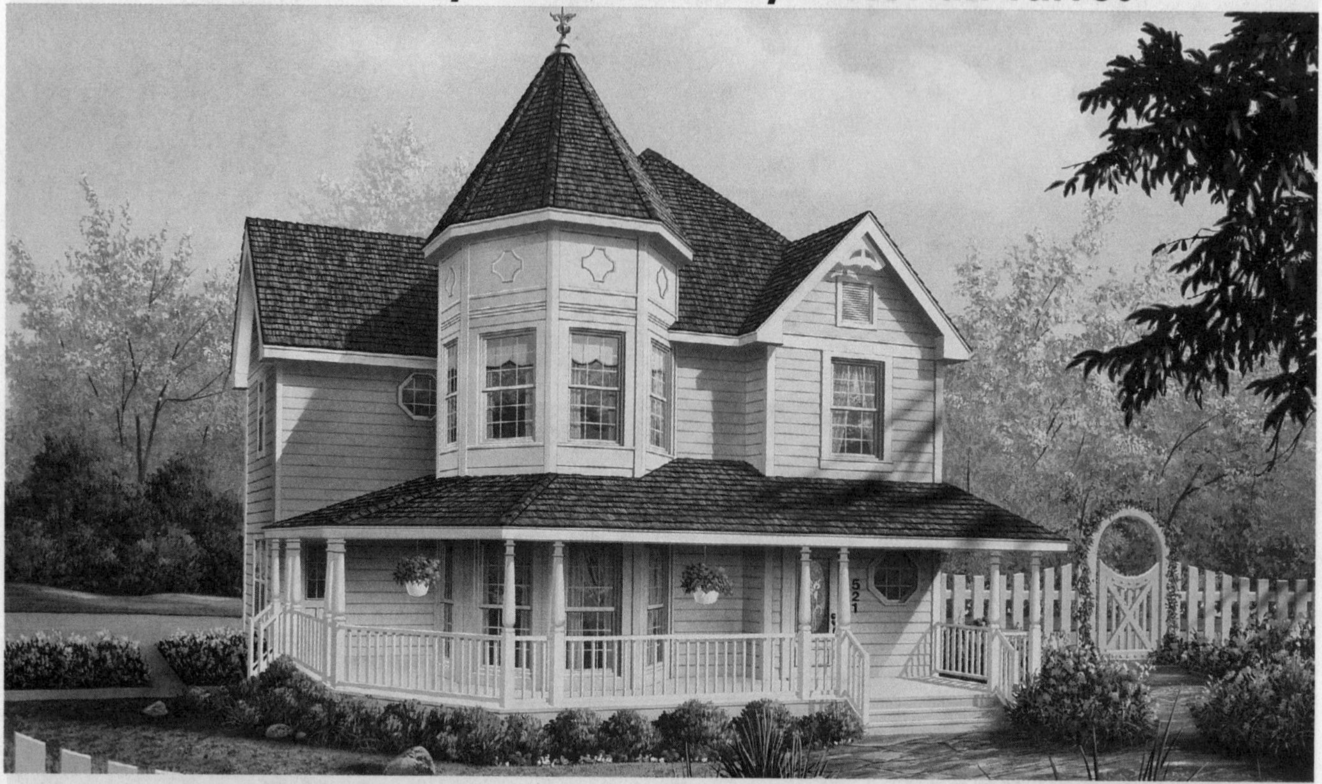

2,050 total square feet of living area

Price Code C

Special features

- Large kitchen/dining area with access to garage and porch
- Master bedroom suite features unique turret design, private bath and large walk-in closet
- Laundry facilities conveniently located near bedrooms
- 3 bedrooms, 2 1/2 baths, 2-car side entry garage
- Basement foundation, drawings also include crawl space and slab foundations

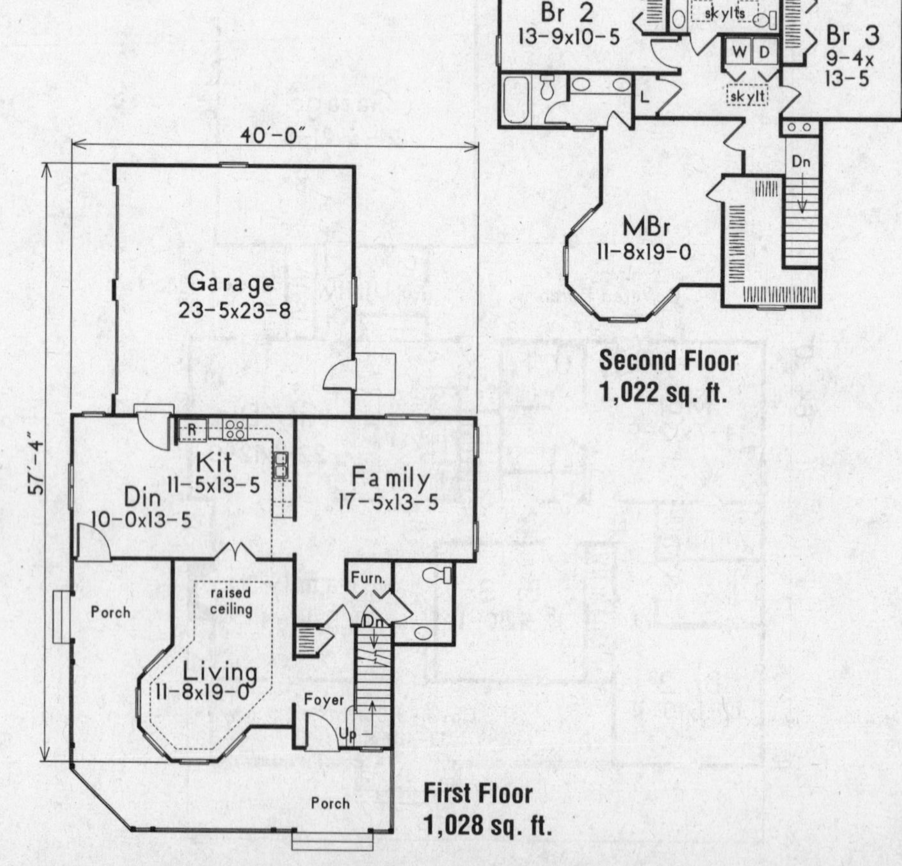
Br 2
13-9x10-5
skylts
W D
Br 3
9-4x
13-5
L
skylt
Dn
MBr
11-8x19-0
40'-0"
57'-4"
Garage
23-5x23-8
R
Kit
11-5x13-5
Din
10-0x13-5
Family
17-5x13-5
Furn.
raised
ceiling
Porch
Dn
Living
11-8x19-0
Foyer
Up
Porch

Second Floor
1,022 sq. ft.

First Floor
1,028 sq. ft.

Plan #702-DR-3814

Grand Victorian Home

2,590 total square feet of living area

Price Code D

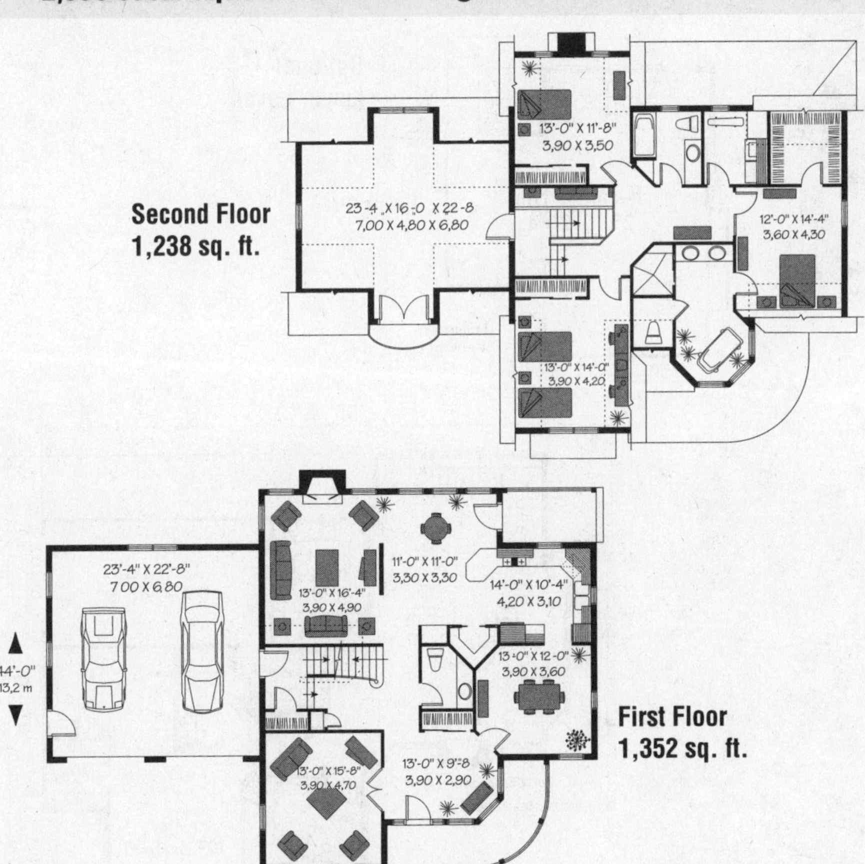
Second Floor
1,238 sq. ft.
23'-4" X 16'-0" X 22'-8"
7,00 X 4,80 X 6,80
13'-0" X 11'-8"
3,90 X 3,50
12'-0" X 14'-4"
3,60 X 4,30
13'-0" X 14'-0"
3,90 X 4,20
23'-4" X 22'-8"
7,00 X 6,80
13'-0" X 16'-4"
3,90 X 4,90
11'-0" X 11'-0"
3,30 X 3,30
14'-0" X 10'-4"
4,20 X 3,10
13'-0" X 12'-0"
3,90 X 3,60
13'-0" X 15'-8"
3,90 X 4,70
13'-0" X 9'-8"
3,90 X 2,90
44'-0"
13,2 m
62'-0"
18,6 m
First Floor
1,352 sq. ft.

Special features

- Energy efficient home with 2" x 6" exterior walls
- Utility room is located on the second floor for convenience
- Master bedroom has private bath with double vanity, oversized shower and freestanding tub in bay window
- Bonus room above the garage has an additional 459 square feet of living area
- 3 bedrooms, 2 1/2 baths, 2-car garage
- Basement foundation

TO ORDER BLUEPRINTS USE THE FORM ON PAGE 19 OR CALL TOLL-FREE 1-877-671-6036

View thousands more home plans online at www.familyhandyman.com/homeplans

The Family Handyman

Plan #702-0732

Tranquility Of An Atrium Cottage

1,384 total square feet of living area

Price Code A

Rear View

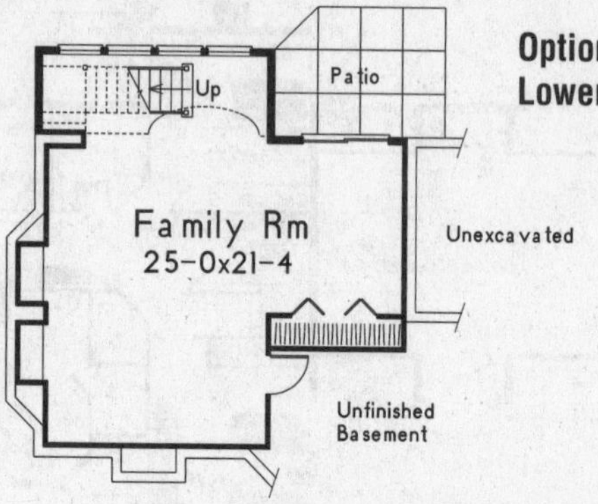

Optional Lower Level

Patio
Up
Family Rm
25-0x21-4
Unexcavated
Unfinished Basement

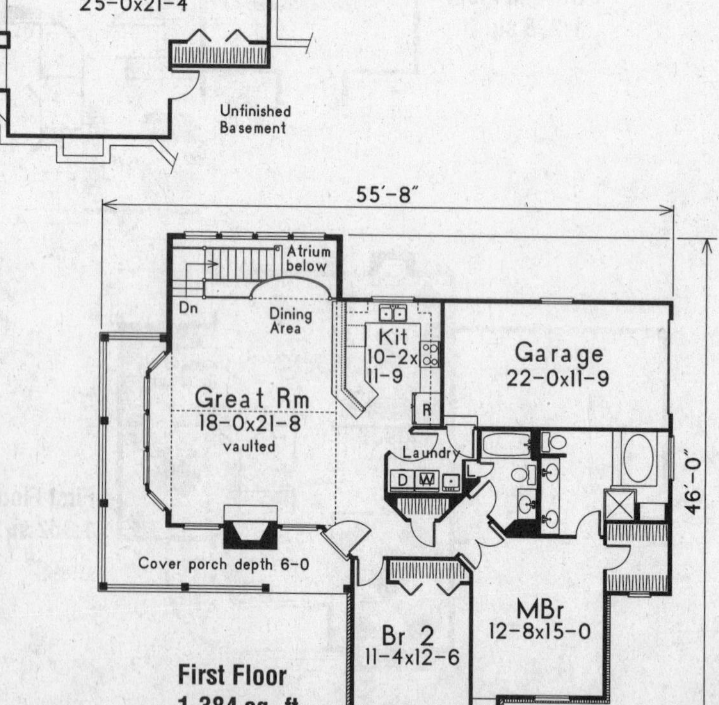

55'-8"
46'-0"
Atrium below
Dn
Dining Area
Kit
10-2x
11-9
Garage
22-0x11-9
Great Rm
18-0x21-8
vaulted
R
Laundry
D W
Cover porch depth 6-0
Br 2
11-4x12-6
MBr
12-8x15-0

First Floor
1,384 sq. ft.

Special features

- Wrap-around country porch for peaceful evenings
- Vaulted great room enjoys a large bay window, stone fireplace, pass-through kitchen and awesome rear views through atrium window wall
- Master suite features double entry doors, walk-in closet and a fabulous bath
- Atrium open to 611 square feet of optional living area below
- 2 bedrooms, 2 baths, 1-car side entry garage
- Walk-out basement foundation

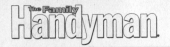

Marvelous Curb Appeal

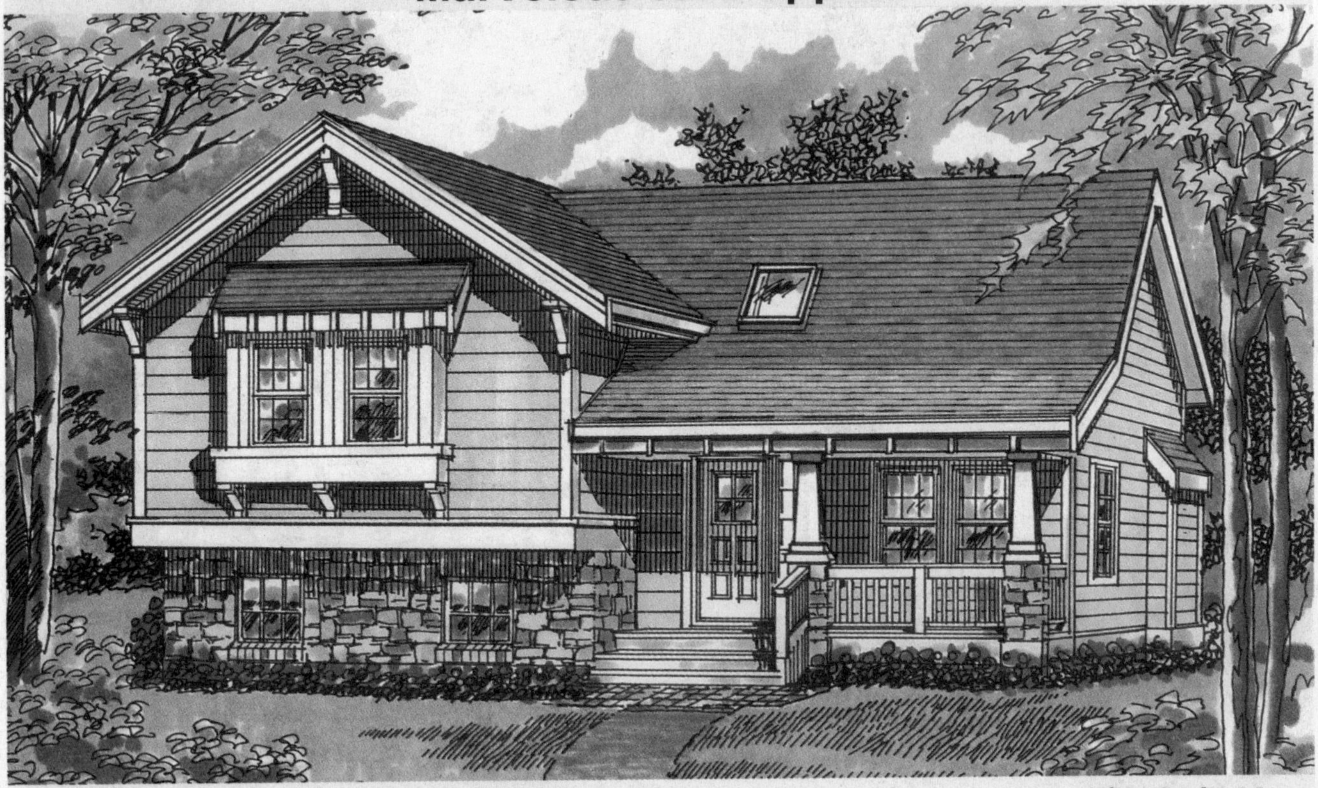

1,108 total square feet of living area

Price Code AA

Width: 38'-0"
Depth: 32'-0"

First Floor
1,108 sq. ft.

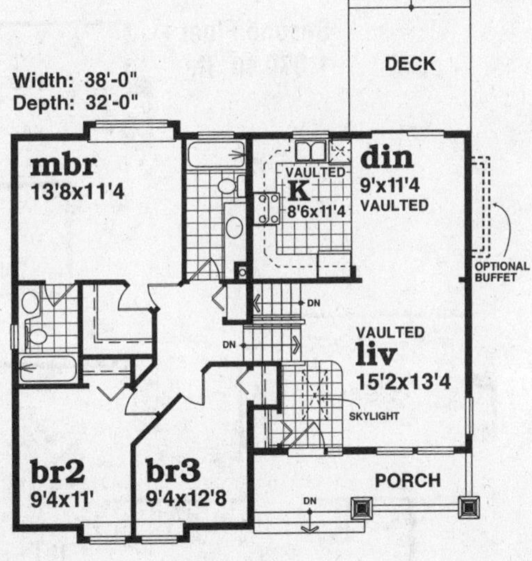
DECK
mbr
13'8x11'4
VAULTED
K
8'6x11'4
din
9'x11'4
VAULTED
OPTIONAL BUFFET
DN
DN
VAULTED
liv
15'2x13'4
SKYLIGHT
br2
9'4x11'
br3
9'4x12'8
PORCH
DN

Optional
Lower Level

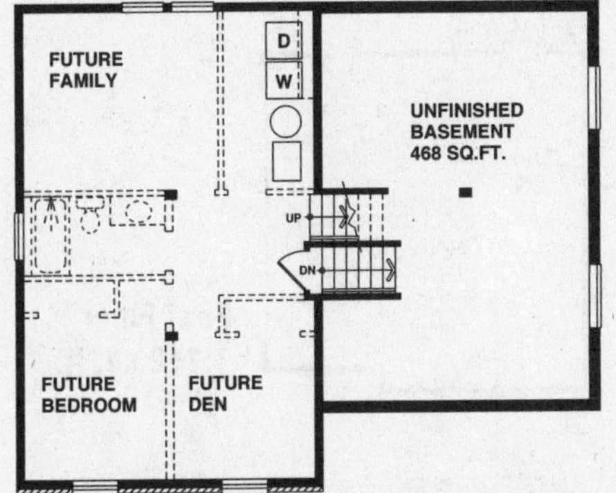
FUTURE FAMILY
D
W
UNFINISHED BASEMENT 468 SQ.FT.
UP
DN
FUTURE BEDROOM
FUTURE DEN

Special features

- Master bedroom offers a walk-in closet, a full bath and a box bay window
- Vaulted ceilings in kitchen, living and dining rooms make this home appear larger than its actual size
- Compact, but efficient kitchen is U-shaped so everything is within reach
- Optional lower level has an additional 1,108 square feet of living area
- 3 bedrooms, 2 baths
- Basement or crawl space foundation, please specify when ordering

The Family Handyman

Plan #702-0413

Distinctive Country Porch

2,182 total square feet of living area

Price Code C

Special features

- Meandering porch creates an inviting look
- Generous great room has four double-hung windows and gliding doors to exterior
- Highly functional kitchen features island/breakfast bar, menu desk and convenient pantry
- Each secondary bedroom includes generous closet and private bath
- 3 bedrooms, 3 1/2 baths, 2-car side entry garage
- Basement foundation

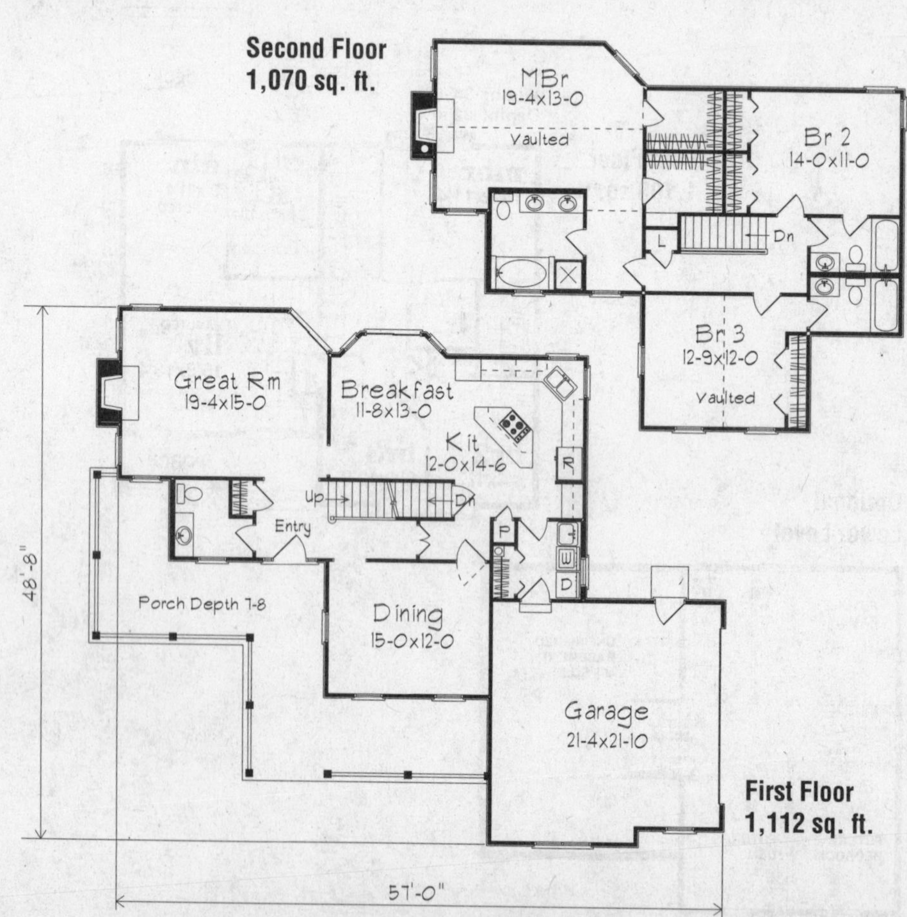
Second Floor
1,070 sq. ft.
MBr
19-4x13-0
Vaulted
Br 2
14-0x11-0
Dn
L
Br 3
12-9x12-0
Vaulted
Great Rm
19-4x15-0
Breakfast
11-8x13-0
Kit
12-0x14-6
R
Up
Dn
Entry
P
W
D
Porch Depth 7-8
Dining
15-0x12-0
Garage
21-4x21-10
48'-8"
57'-0"
First Floor
1,112 sq. ft.

The Family
Handyman

Plan #702-HDS-2802-2

Pillars And Dormers Create A Charming Feel

2,802 total square feet of living area

Price Code E

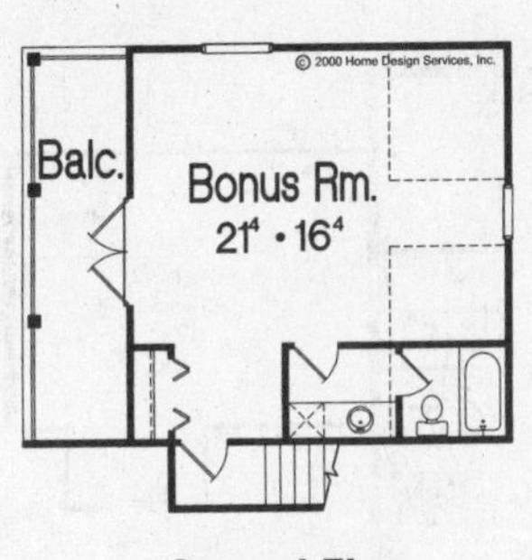

© 2000 Home Design Services, Inc.
Balc.
Bonus Rm.
$21^4 \cdot 16^4$

Second Floor
509 sq. ft.

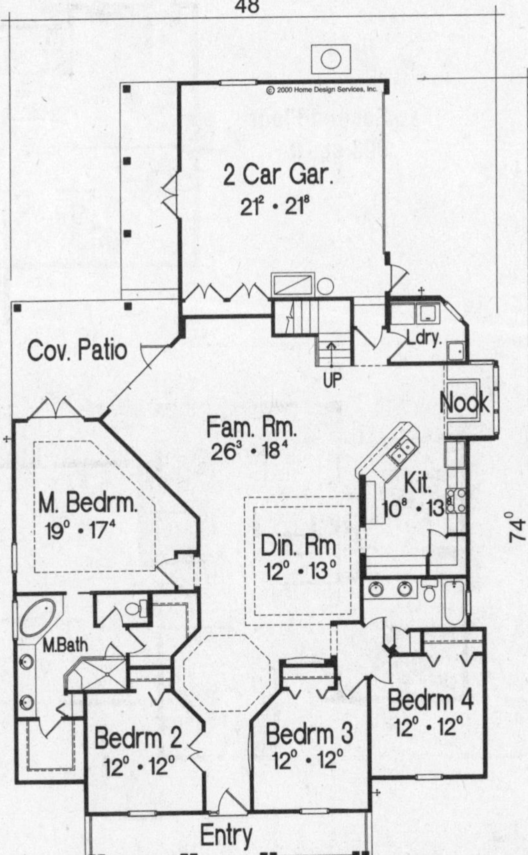

48^0
© 2000 Home Design Services, Inc.
2 Car Gar.
$21^2 \cdot 21^8$
Cov. Patio
Ldry.
UP
Nook
Fam. Rm.
$26^3 \cdot 18^4$
Kit.
$10^8 \cdot 13^8$
M. Bedrm.
$19^0 \cdot 17^4$
Din. Rm
$12^0 \cdot 13^0$
74^0
M.Bath
Bedrm 4
$12^0 \cdot 12^0$
Bedrm 2
$12^0 \cdot 12^0$
Bedrm 3
$12^0 \cdot 12^0$
Entry

First Floor
2,293 sq. ft.

Special features

- Formal dining area flows into large family room making great use of space
- Cozy nook off kitchen would make an ideal breakfast dining area
- Covered patio attaches to master bedroom and family room
- Framing - only concrete block available
- 4 bedrooms, 2 baths, 2-car side entry garage
- Slab foundation

TO ORDER BLUEPRINTS USE THE FORM ON PAGE 19 OR CALL TOLL-FREE 1-877-671-6036

View thousands more home plans online at www.familyhandyman.com/homeplans

The Family
Handyman

Plan #702-DR-3812

Perfect Farmhouse For Family Living

2,129 total square feet of living area

Price Code C

Special features

- Energy efficient home with 2" x 6" exterior walls
- Home office has a double-door entry and is secluded from other living areas
- Corner fireplace in living area is a nice focal point
- Bonus room above the garage has an additional 407 square feet of living area
- 3 bedrooms, 2 1/2 baths, 2-car side entry garage
- Basement foundation

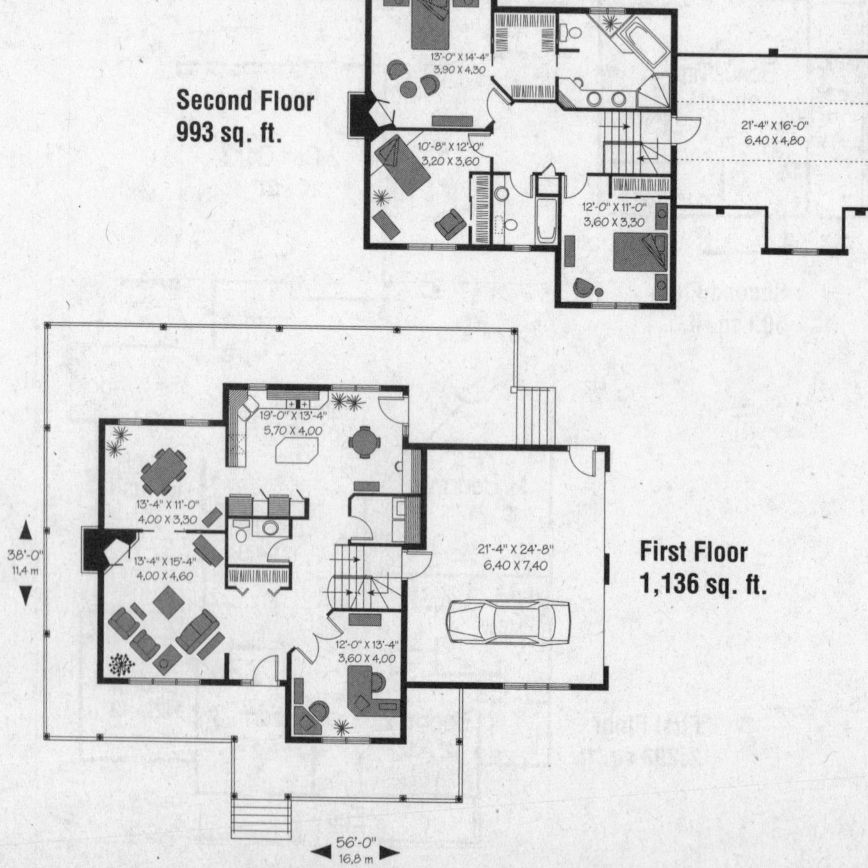

Second Floor
993 sq. ft.
13'-0" X 14'-4"
3,90 X 4,30
10'-8" X 12'-0"
3,20 X 3,60
12'-0" X 11'-0"
3,60 X 3,30
21'-4" X 16'-0"
6,40 X 4,80
19'-0" X 13'-4"
5,70 X 4,00
13'-4" X 11'-0"
4,00 X 3,30
13'-4" X 15'-4"
4,00 X 4,60
21'-4" X 24'-8"
6,40 X 7,40
12'-0" X 13'-4"
3,60 X 4,00
38'-0"
11,4 m
56'-0"
16,8 m
First Floor
1,136 sq. ft.

Plan #702-NDG-619

Triple Dormers Add Charm To This Country Home

3,060 total square feet of living area

Price Code E

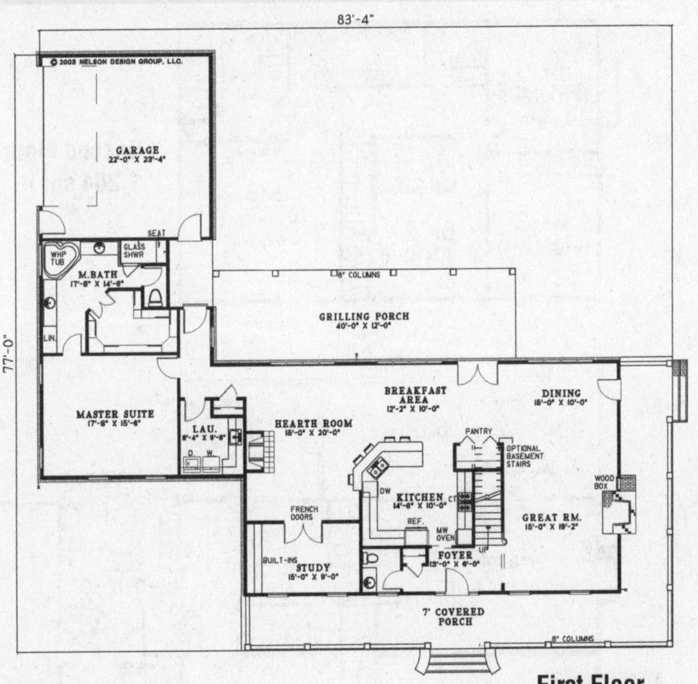
83'-4"
77'-0"
GARAGE
22'-0" X 23'-4"
M.BATH
17'-8" X 14'-6"
GRILLING PORCH
40'-0" X 12'-0"
BREAKFAST AREA
12'-2" X 10'-0"
DINING
18'-0" X 10'-0"
MASTER SUITE
17'-8" X 15'-6"
LAU.
HEARTH ROOM
18'-0" X 20'-0"
PANTRY
OPTIONAL BASEMENT STAIRS
KITCHEN
14'-8" X 10'-0"
WOOD BOX
GREAT RM.
18'-0" X 19'-2"
FRENCH DOORS
BUILT-INS
STUDY
15'-0" X 9'-0"
FOYER
7' COVERED PORCH

First Floor
2,204 sq. ft.

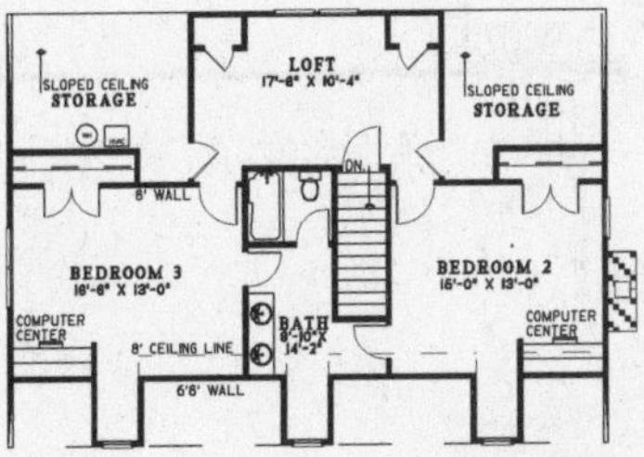

Second Floor
856 sq. ft.

Special features

- Double-doors in hearth room lead into a private study with built-in shelves
- Kitchen includes a large wrap-around style eating counter capable of serving five
- Breakfast area has access onto a large covered grilling porch
- 3 bedrooms, 2 1/2 baths, 2-car side entry garage
- Crawl space or slab foundation, please specify when ordering

TO ORDER BLUEPRINTS USE THE FORM ON PAGE 19 OR CALL TOLL-FREE 1-877-671-6036

View thousands more home plans online at www.familyhandyman.com/homeplans

Plan #702-0749

Stately Country Home For The "Spacious Age"

2,727 total square feet of living area **Price Code E**

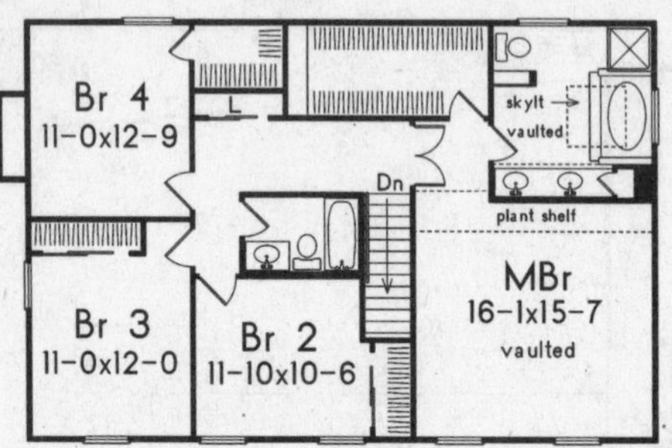
Br 4
11-0x12-9
L
skylt
vaulted
Dn
plant shelf
MBr
16-1x15-7
vaulted
Br 3
11-0x12-0
Br 2
11-10x10-6

Second Floor
1,204 sq. ft.

__Special features__

- Wrap-around porch and large foyer create impressive entrance
- A state-of-the-art vaulted kitchen has walk-in pantry and is open to the breakfast room and adjoining screened porch
- A walk-in wet bar, fireplace bay window and deck access are features of the family room
- Vaulted master bedroom suite enjoys a luxurious bath with skylight and an enormous 13' deep walk-in closet
- 4 bedrooms, 2 1/2 baths, 2-car side entry garage
- Walk-out basement foundation

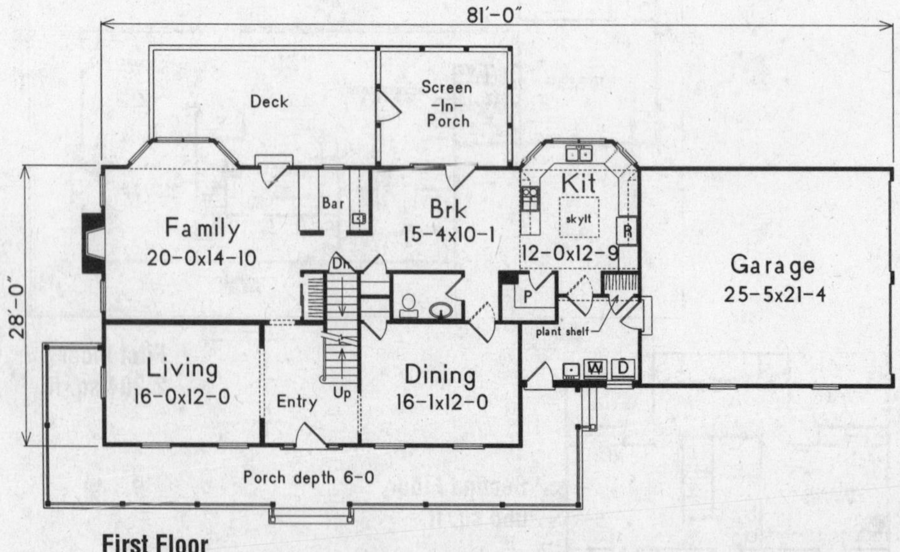
81'-0"
Deck
Screen
-In-
Porch
Kit
skylt
R
Bar
Brk
15-4x10-1
12-0x12-9
Family
20-0x14-10
Garage
25-5x21-4
28'-0"
Dn
P
plant shelf
W
D
Living
16-0x12-0
Entry
Up
Dining
16-1x12-0
Porch depth 6-0

First Floor
1,523 sq. ft.

The Family
Handyman

Plan #702-DH-2313J

Spacious Country Home Could Easily Fit On A Narrow Lot

2,123 total square feet of living area **Price Code C**

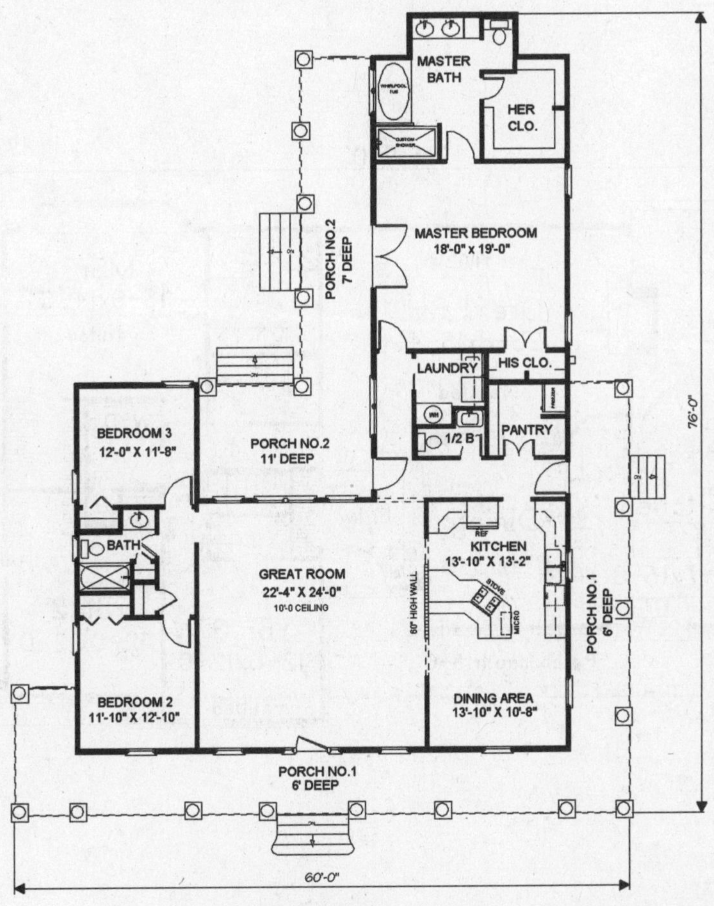
MASTER BATH
HER CLO.
MASTER BEDROOM
18'-0" x 19'-0"
PORCH NO.2
7' DEEP
LAUNDRY
HIS CLO.
1/2 B
PANTRY
BEDROOM 3
12'-0" X 11'-8"
PORCH NO.2
11' DEEP
76'-0"
KITCHEN
13'-10" X 13'-2"
BATH
GREAT ROOM
22'-4" X 24'-0"
10'-0 CEILING
PORCH NO.1
6' DEEP
BEDROOM 2
11'-10" X 12'-10"
DINING AREA
13'-10" X 10'-8"
PORCH NO.1
6' DEEP
60'-0"

<u>*Special features*</u>

- L-shaped porch extends the entire length of this home creating lots of extra space for outdoor living
- Master bedroom is secluded for privacy and has his and hers closets, double vanity in bath and a double-door entry onto covered porch
- Efficiently designed kitchen
- 3 bedrooms, 2 1/2 baths
- Crawl space foundation

Ranch Offers Country Elegance

1,787 total square feet of living area **Price Code B**

Special features

- Large great room with fireplace and vaulted ceiling features three large skylights and windows galore
- Cooking is sure to be a pleasure in this L-shaped well-appointed kitchen which includes bayed breakfast area with access to rear deck
- Every bedroom offers a spacious walk-in closet with a convenient laundry room just steps away
- 415 square feet of optional living area on the lower level
- 3 bedrooms, 2 baths, 2-car drive under rear entry garage
- Walk-out basement foundation

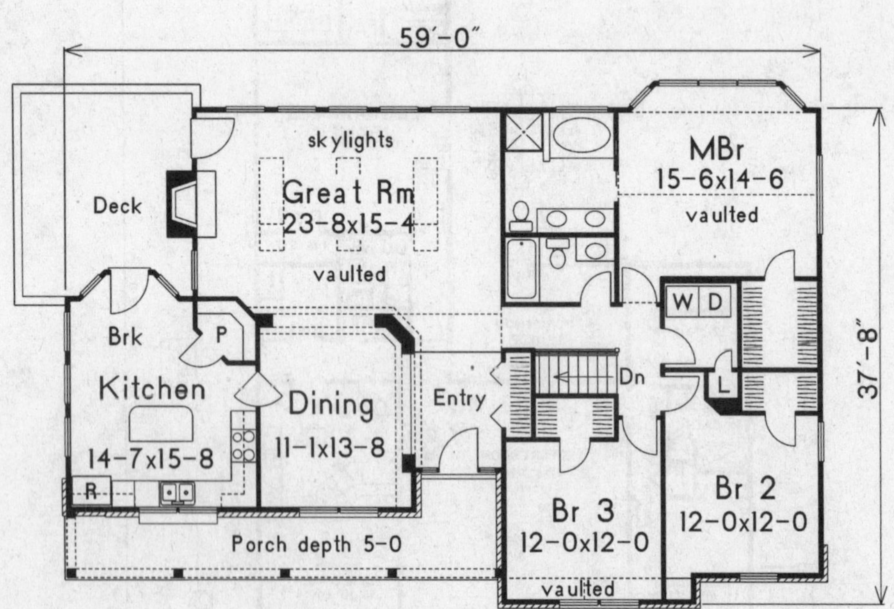
59′-0″
37′-8″
Deck
skylights
Great Rm
23-8x15-4
vaulted
MBr
15-6x14-6
vaulted
W D
Brk
P
Kitchen
14-7x15-8
R
Dining
11-1x13-8
Entry
Dn
L
Br 2
12-0x12-0
Br 3
12-0x12-0
vaulted
Porch depth 5-0

TO ORDER BLUEPRINTS USE THE FORM ON PAGE 19 OR CALL TOLL-FREE 1-877-671-6036

View thousands more home plans online at www.familyhandyman.com/homeplans

The Family Handyman

Plan #702-0706

Classic Exterior Employs Innovative Planning

1,791 total square feet of living area **Price Code B**

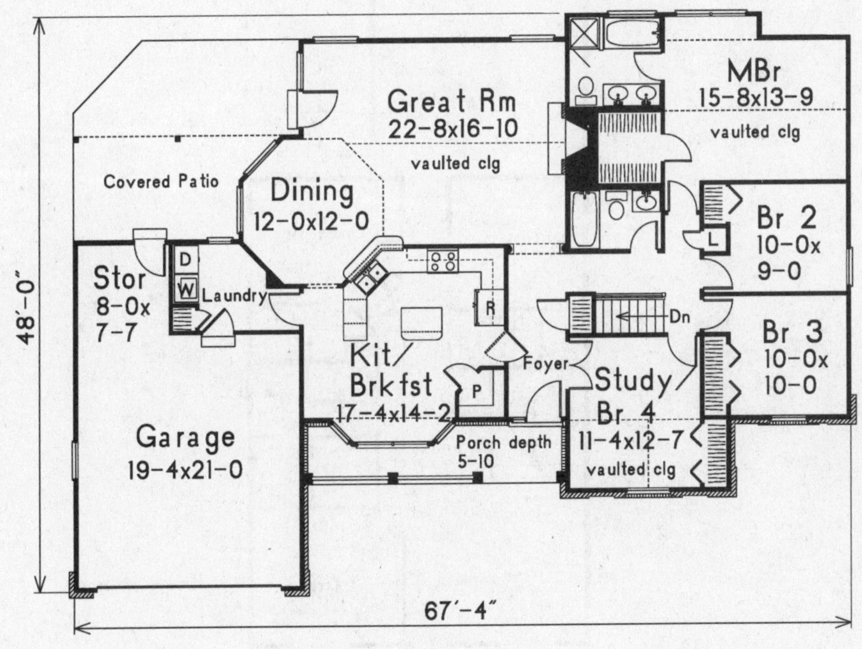
Great Rm
22-8x16-10
vaulted clg
MBr
15-8x13-9
vaulted clg
Covered Patio
Dining
12-0x12-0
Br 2
10-0x
9-0
Stor
8-0x
7-7
D
W
Laundry
R
Dn
Br 3
10-0x
10-0
Kit/
Brkfst
17-4x14-2
Foyer
P
Study/
Br 4
11-4x12-7
vaulted clg
Garage
19-4x21-0
Porch depth
5-10
L
48'-0"
67'-4"

Special features

- Vaulted great room and octagon-shaped dining area enjoy views of covered patio
- Kitchen features a pass-through to dining area, center island, large walk-in pantry and breakfast room with large bay window
- Master bedroom is vaulted with sitting area
- 4 bedrooms, 2 baths, 2-car garage with storage
- Basement foundation

Plan #702-NDG-795

Comfortable Living In This Narrow Lot Home

1,462 total square feet of living area

Price Code A

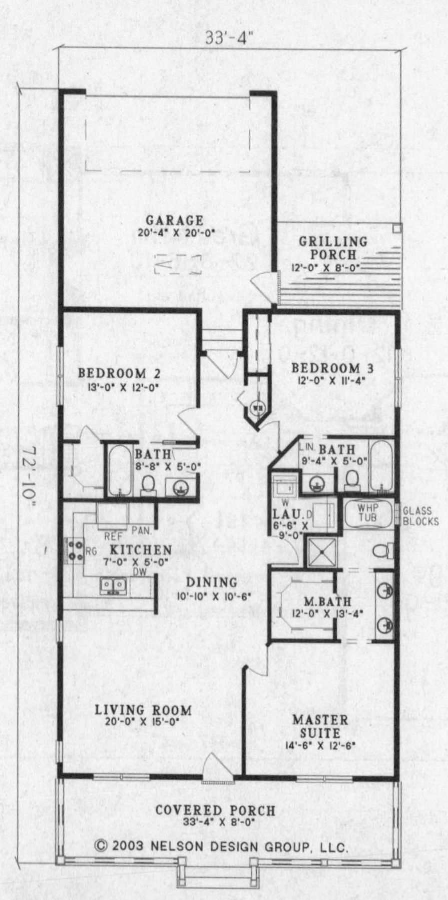
33'-4"
72'-10"
GARAGE
20'-4" X 20'-0"
GRILLING PORCH
12'-0" X 8'-0"
BEDROOM 2
13'-0" X 12'-0"
BEDROOM 3
12'-0" X 11'-4"
BATH
8'-8" X 5'-0"
LIN.
BATH
9'-4" X 5'-0"
LAU.
6'-6" X 9'-0"
WHP TUB
GLASS BLOCKS
REF
PAN.
RG
KITCHEN
7'-0" X 5'-0"
DW
DINING
10'-10" X 10'-6"
M.BATH
12'-0" X 13'-4"
LIVING ROOM
20'-0" X 15'-0"
MASTER SUITE
14'-6" X 12'-6"
COVERED PORCH
33'-4" X 8'-0"
© 2003 NELSON DESIGN GROUP, LLC.

Special features

- U-shaped kitchen has everything within reach
- All bedrooms have access to their own bath
- Master bath has double vanity, shower and a whirlpool tub with glass blaock window
- 3 bedrooms, 3 baths, 2-car rear entry garage
- Crawl space or slab foundation, please specify when ordering

Circular Stairway Adds To Front Entry

2,360 total square feet of living area **Price Code D**

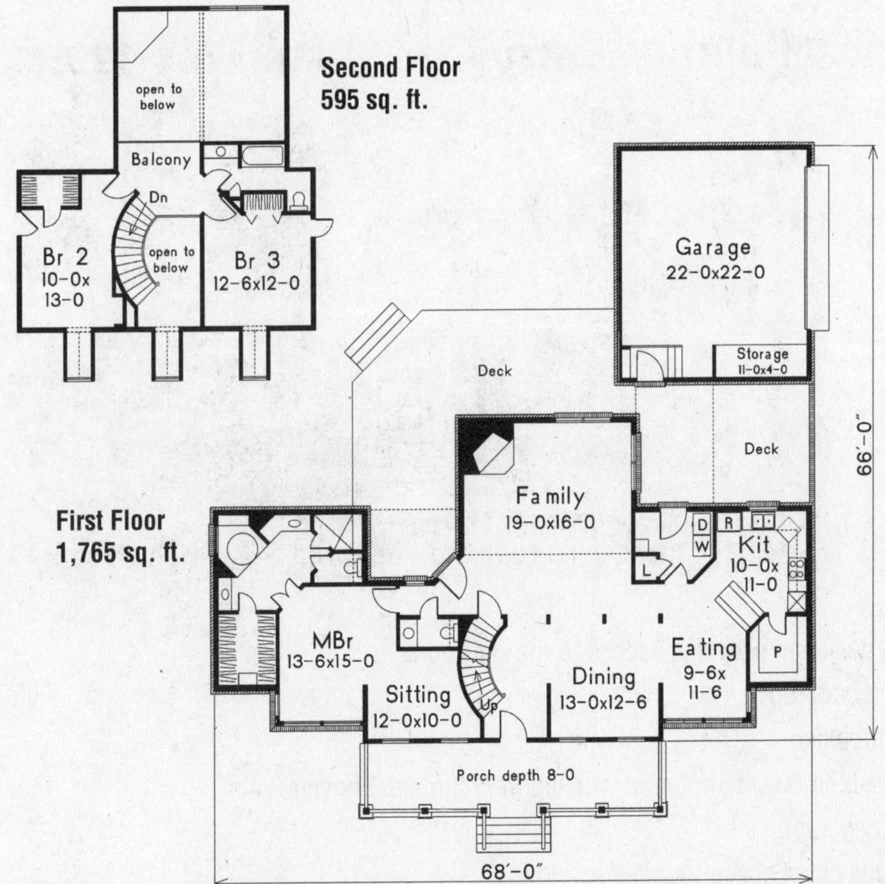

Second Floor
595 sq. ft.
open to below
Balcony
Dn
Br 2
10-0x
13-0
open to below
Br 3
12-6x12-0
Garage
22-0x22-0
Storage
11-0x4-0
Deck
Deck
Family
19-0x16-0
First Floor
1,765 sq. ft.
D
W
R
Kit
10-0x
11-0
L
MBr
13-6x15-0
Sitting
12-0x10-0
Up
Dining
13-0x12-6
Eating
9-6x
11-6
P
Porch depth 8-0
68'-0"
66'-0"

Special features

- Master suite includes sitting area and large bath
- Sloped family room ceiling provides view from second floor balcony
- Kitchen features island bar and walk-in butler's pantry
- 3 bedrooms, 2 1/2 baths, 2-car side entry garage
- Crawl space foundation, drawings also include slab and basement foundations

A Grand Full Pillared Porch — Plan #702-0188

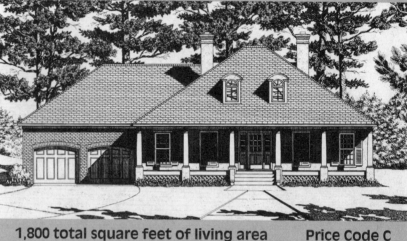

1,800 total square feet of living area — Price Code C

Special features

- Stylish kitchen and breakfast area feature large windows that allow great views outdoors
- Covered front and rear porches provide an added dimension to this home's living space
- Generous storage areas and large utility room
- Energy efficient home with 2" x 6" exterior walls
- Large separate master suite and adjoining bath with large tub and corner shower
- 3 bedrooms, 2 baths, 2-car garage
- Crawl space foundation, drawings also include slab foundation

Covered Porch Is Focal Point Of Entry — Plan #702-0293

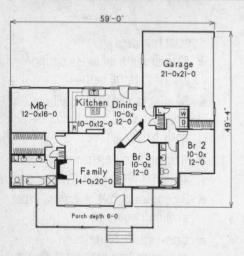

1,595 total square feet of living area — Price Code B

Special features

- Dining room has convenient built-in desk and provides access to the outdoors
- L-shaped kitchen area features island cooktop
- Family room has high ceiling and a fireplace
- Private master suite includes large walk-in closet and bath with separate tub and shower units
- 3 bedrooms, 2 baths, 2-car side entry garage
- Slab foundation, drawings also include crawl space foundation

The Family
Handyman

Plan #702-FDG-8701-L

Fireplace Warms Large Great Room

2,578 total square feet of living area

Price Code D

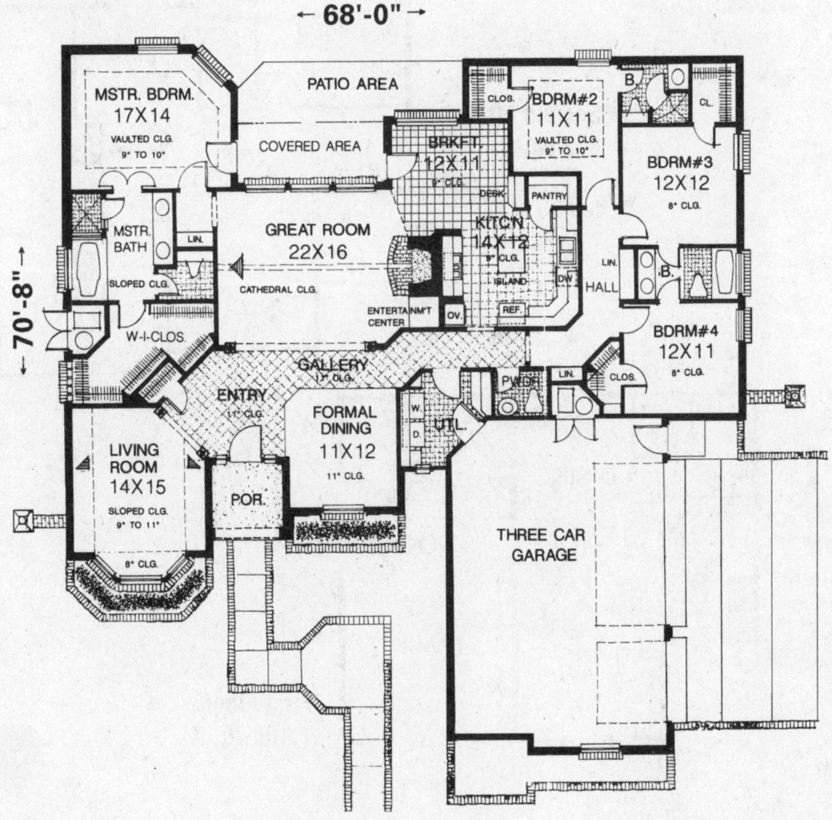
68'-0"
70'-8"
PATIO AREA
MSTR. BDRM.
17X14
VAULTED CLG.
9" TO 10"
COVERED AREA
BRKFT.
12X11
9" CLG.
CLOS.
BDRM#2
11X11
VAULTED CLG.
9" TO 10"
B.
CL.
BDRM#3
12X12
8" CLG.
DESK
PANTRY
KITC'N
14X12
9" CLG.
ISLAND
DW
REF.
OV.
MSTR.
BATH
LIN.
GREAT ROOM
22X16
CATHEDRAL CLG.
SLOPED CLG.
ENTERTAINMNT
CENTER
HALL
LIN.
B.
W-I-CLOS.
GALLERY
11" CLG.
BDRM#4
12X11
8" CLG.
CLOS.
LIN.
PWDR.
ENTRY
11" CLG.
FORMAL
DINING
11X12
11" CLG.
W.
D.
UTL.
LIVING
ROOM
14X15
SLOPED CLG.
9" TO 11"
8" CLG.
POR.
THREE CAR
GARAGE

Special features

- Enormous entry has an airy feel with gallery area nearby
- Living room with bay window is tucked away from traffic areas
- Large kitchen and breakfast area access covered patio
- Great room has entertainment center, fireplace and cathedral ceiling
- 4 bedrooms, 3 1/2 baths, 3-car side entry garage
- Slab foundation

Plan #702-AMD-2163

Three-Story Design

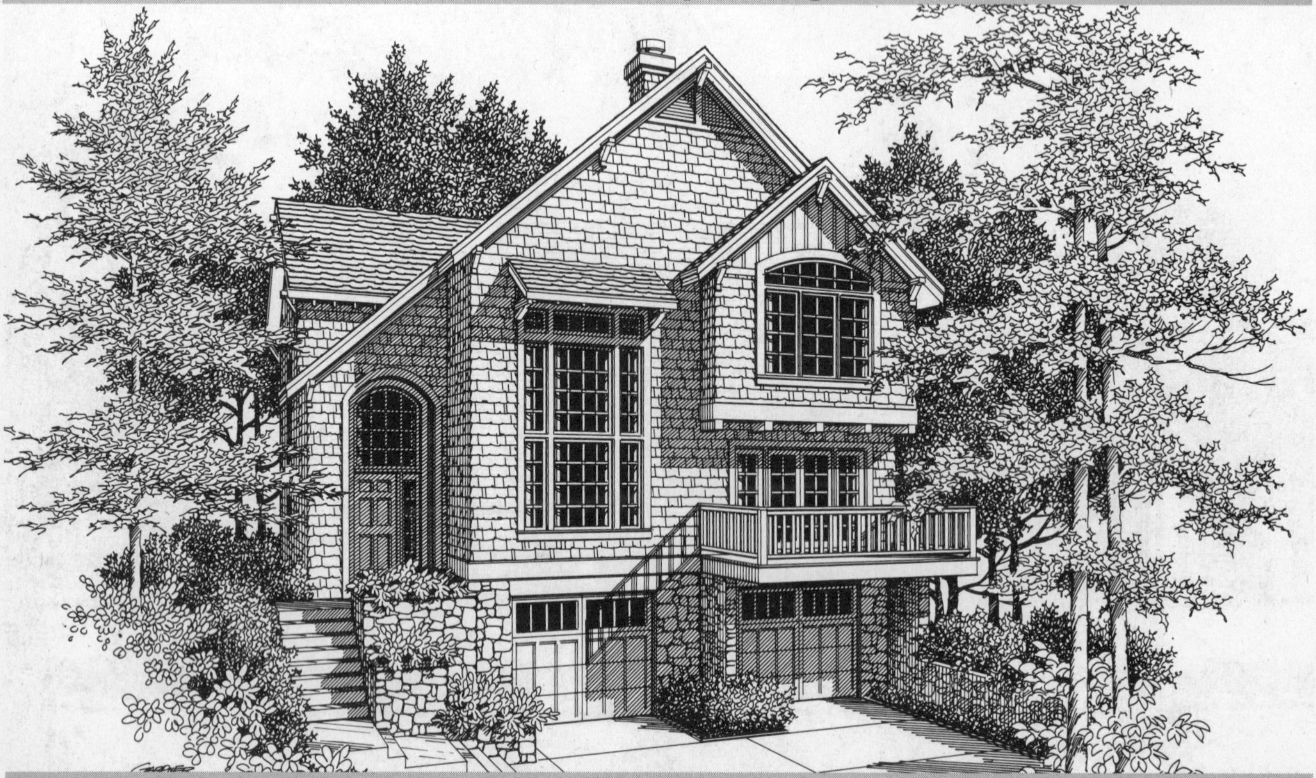

1,978 total square feet of living area **Price Code C**

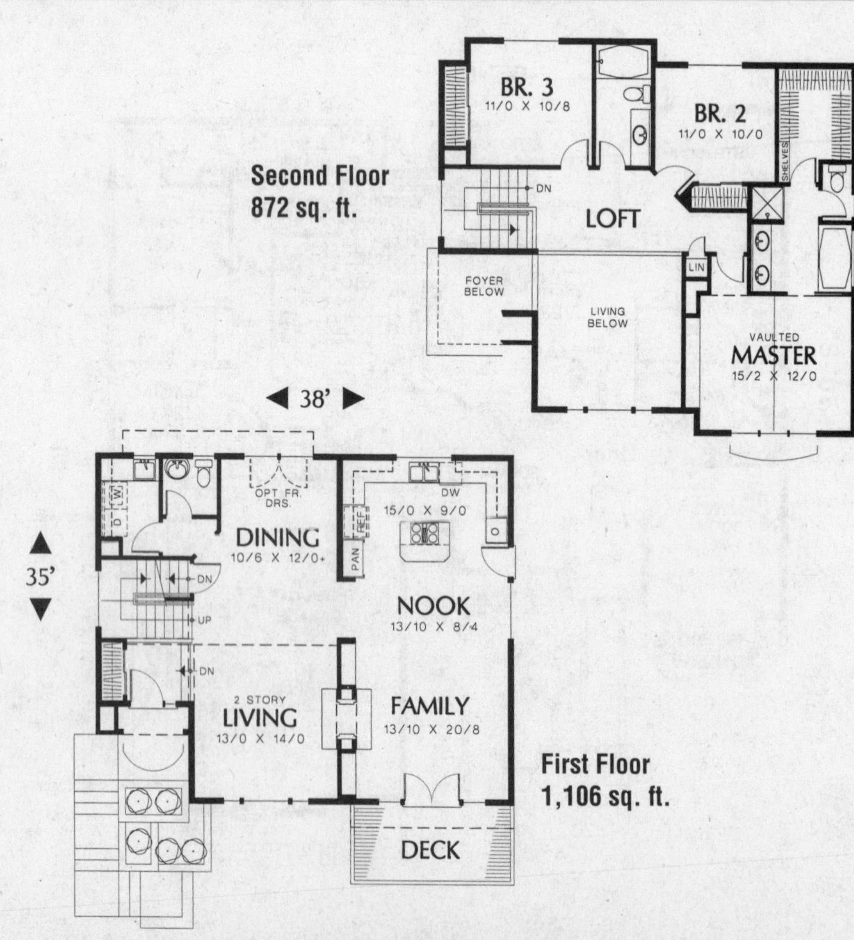
BR. 3
11/0 X 10/8
BR. 2
11/0 X 10/0
SHELVES
DN
LOFT
LIN
Second Floor
872 sq. ft.
FOYER
BELOW
LIVING
BELOW
VAULTED
MASTER
15/2 X 12/0
38'
35'
OPT FR.
DRS.
DW
15/0 X 9/0
DINING
10/6 X 12/0+
REF
PAN
NOOK
13/10 X 8/4
DN
UP
DN
2 STORY
LIVING
13/0 X 14/0
FAMILY
13/10 X 20/8
DECK
First Floor
1,106 sq. ft.

Special features

- Designed for a sloping lot, this multi-level home intrigues the eye
- Sunlight filters into the grand two-story foyer and living room from tall windows
- Master suite has elegant front facing windows and a private bath
- 3 bedrooms, 2 1/2 baths, 2-car drive under garage
- Walk-out basement foundation

Plan #702-FB-902

Impressive Foyer

1,856 total square feet of living area

Price Code C

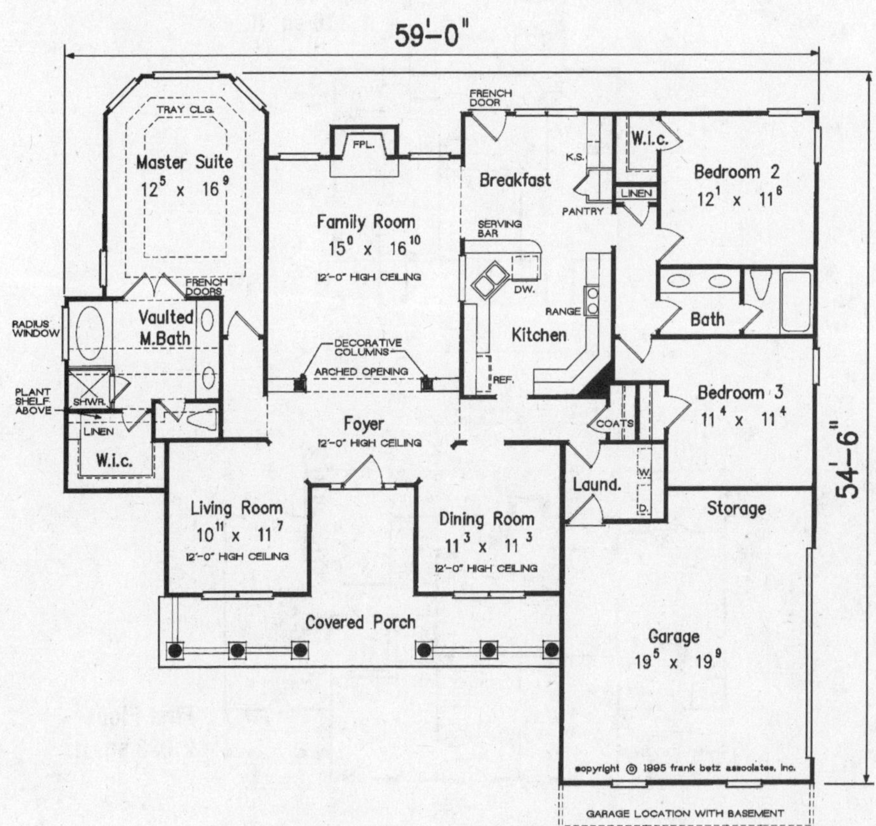
59'-0"
54'-6"
TRAY CLG.
Master Suite
12⁵ x 16⁹
FRENCH DOORS
RADIUS WINDOW
Vaulted M.Bath
PLANT SHELF ABOVE
SHWR.
LINEN
W.i.c.
FPL.
Family Room
15⁰ x 16¹⁰
12'-0" HIGH CEILING
DECORATIVE COLUMNS
ARCHED OPENING
Foyer
12'-0" HIGH CEILING
Living Room
10¹¹ x 11⁷
12'-0" HIGH CEILING
Dining Room
11³ x 11³
12'-0" HIGH CEILING
Covered Porch
FRENCH DOOR
Breakfast
K.S.
PANTRY
SERVING BAR
DW.
RANGE
Kitchen
REF.
COATS
Laund.
W.
D.
W.i.c.
LINEN
Bedroom 2
12¹ x 11⁶
Bath
Bedroom 3
11⁴ x 11⁴
Storage
Garage
19⁵ x 19⁹
copyright © 1995 frank betz associates, inc.
GARAGE LOCATION WITH BASEMENT

Special features

- Beautiful covered porch creates a Southern accent
- Kitchen has an organized feel with lots of cabinetry
- Large foyer has a grand entrance and leads into family room through columns and arched opening
- 3 bedrooms, 2 baths, 2-car side entry garage
- Walk-out basement, crawl space or slab foundation, please specify when ordering

TO ORDER BLUEPRINTS USE THE FORM ON PAGE 19 OR CALL TOLL-FREE 1-877-671-6036

View thousands more home plans online at www.familyhandyman.com/homeplans

Plan #702-0429

Outdoor Living Created By Decks And Porches

3,149 total square feet of living area

Price Code E

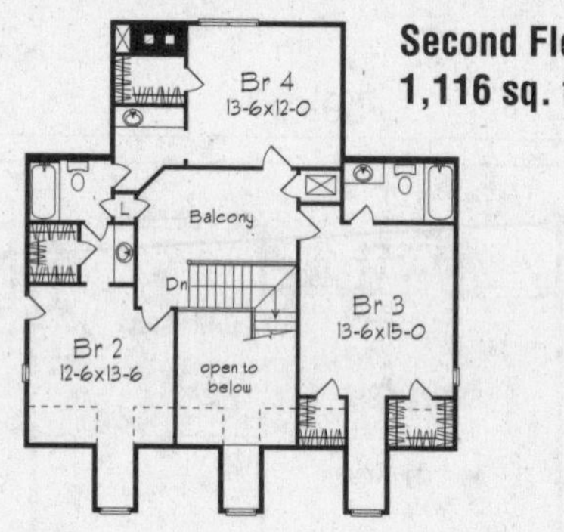
Br 4
13-6x12-0
Balcony
Dn
Br 2
12-6x13-6
open to below
Br 3
13-6x15-0

Second Floor
1,116 sq. ft.

Special features

- 10' ceilings on first floor and 9' ceilings on second floor
- All bedrooms include walk-in closets
- Formal living and dining rooms flank two-story foyer
- 4 bedrooms, 3 1/2 baths, 2-car detached garage
- Slab foundation, drawings also include crawl space foundation

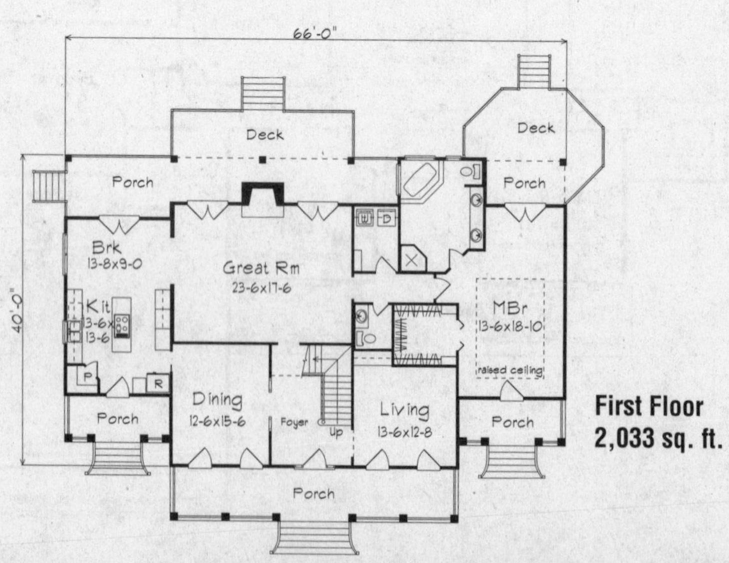
66'-0"
40'-0"
Deck
Deck
Porch
Porch
Brk
13-8x9-0
Great Rm
23-6x17-6
Kit
13-6x
13-6
MBr
13-6x18-10
raised ceiling
Dining
12-6x15-6
Foyer
Up
Living
13-6x12-8
Porch
Porch
Porch

First Floor
2,033 sq. ft.

The Family
Handyman

Plan #702-DL-25454L1

Sunny Sitting Area In Master Suite

2,545 total square feet of living area **Price Code D**

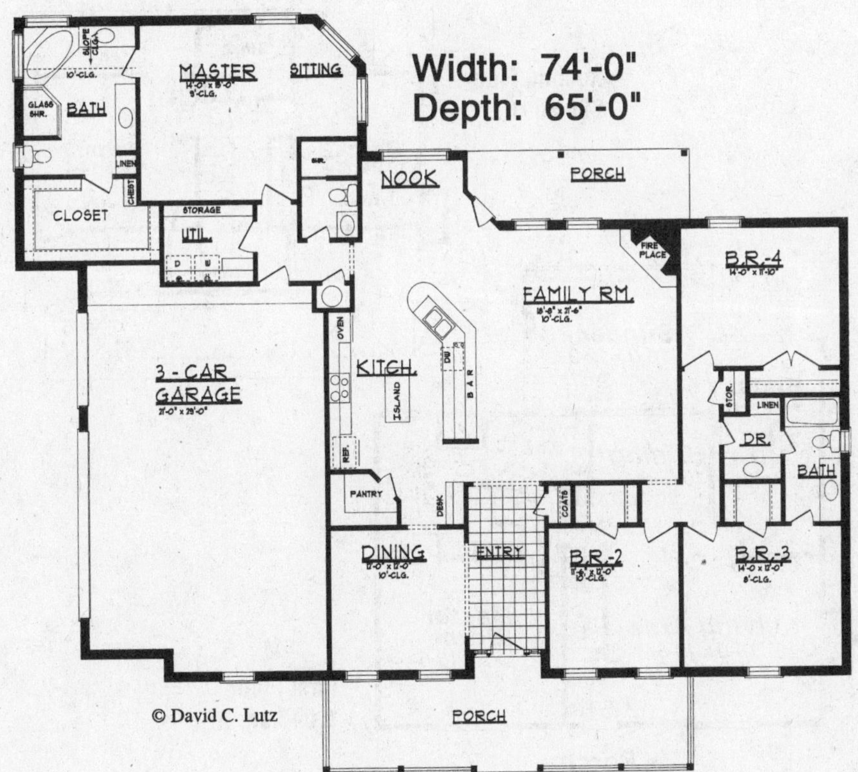
Width: 74'-0"
Depth: 65'-0"
MASTER
SITTING
BATH
GLASS SHR.
CLOSET
LINEN
CHEST
STORAGE
UTIL.
NOOK
PORCH
FIRE PLACE
FAMILY RM.
B.R.-4
KITCH.
ISLAND
BAR
OVEN
REF.
PANTRY
DESK
COATS
3 - CAR GARAGE
DINING
ENTRY
B.R.-2
B.R.-3
STOR.
LINEN
DR.
BATH
PORCH
© David C. Lutz

Special features

- Beautiful covered front porch gives country appeal
- Open family room has 10' ceiling
- Kitchen has abundant counterspace
- 4 bedrooms, 2 1/2 baths, 3-car side entry garage
- Slab foundation

TO ORDER BLUEPRINTS USE THE FORM ON PAGE 19 OR CALL TOLL-FREE 1-877-671-6036

Plan #702-JV-1735A

Quaint Porch Adds Charm

1,735 total square feet of living area

Price Code B

Special features

- Angled kitchen wall expands space into the dining room
- Second floor has cozy sitting area with cheerful window
- Two spacious bedrooms on second floor share a bath
- 3 bedrooms, 2 1/2 baths, 2-car drive under garage
- Basement foundation

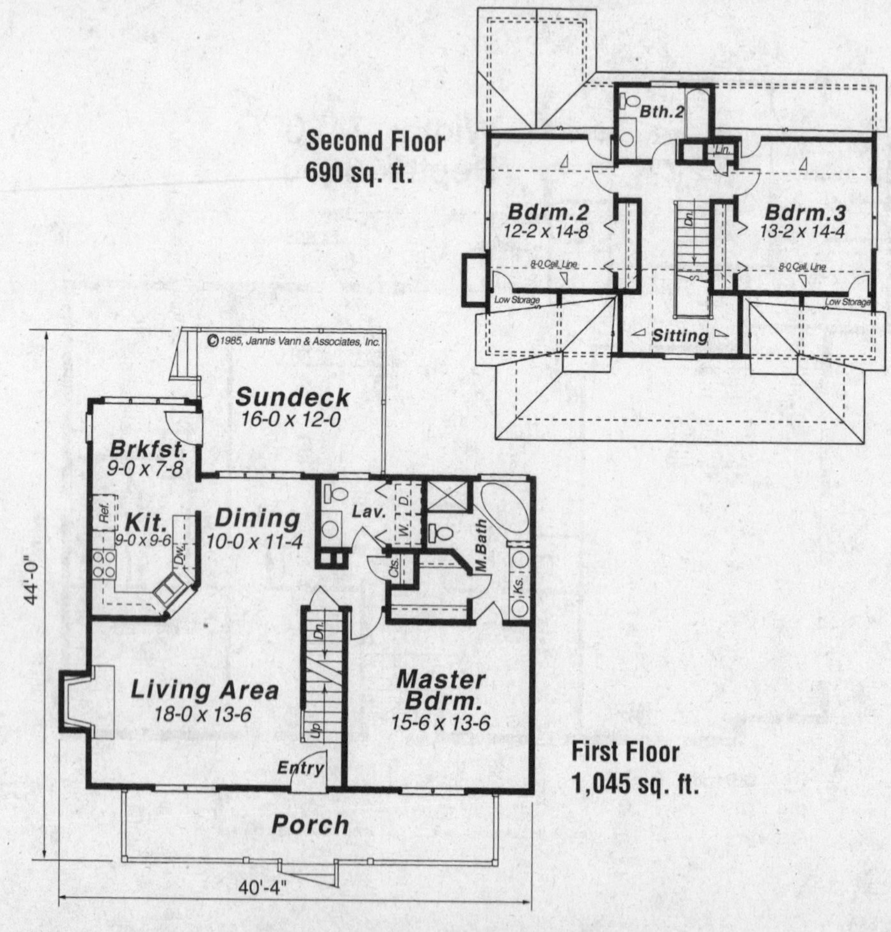
Bth.2
Bdrm.2
12-2 x 14-8
Bdrm.3
13-2 x 14-4
Low Storage
Low Storage
Sitting
©1985, Jannis Vann & Associates, Inc.
Sundeck
16-0 x 12-0
Brkfst.
9-0 x 7-8
Kit.
9-0 x 9-6
Dining
10-0 x 11-4
Lav.
M.Bath
Living Area
18-0 x 13-6
Master
Bdrm.
15-6 x 13-6
Entry
Porch
44'-0"
40'-4"

Second Floor
690 sq. ft.

First Floor
1,045 sq. ft.

TO ORDER BLUEPRINTS USE THE FORM ON PAGE 19 OR CALL TOLL-FREE 1-877-671-6036

View thousands more home plans online at www.familyhandyman.com/homeplans

Plan #702-0801

Plenty Of Seating At Breakfast Bar

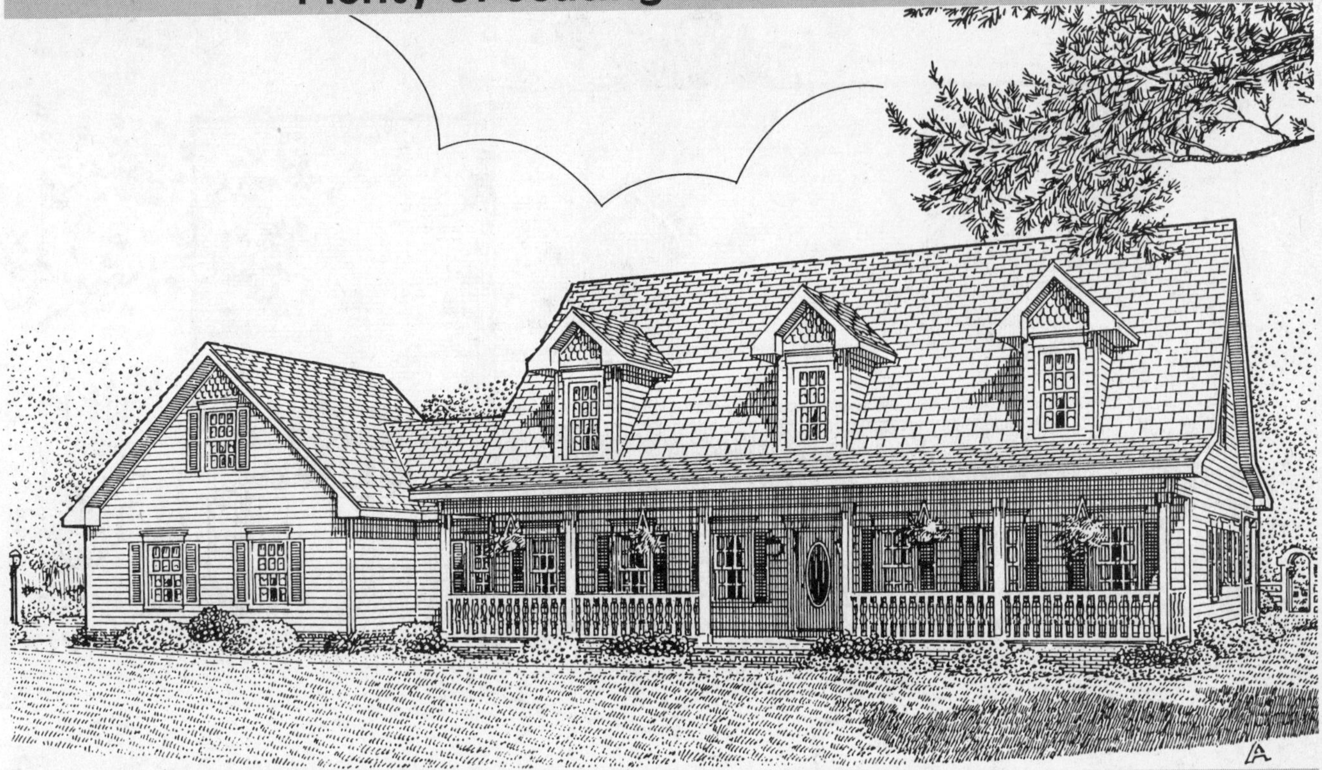

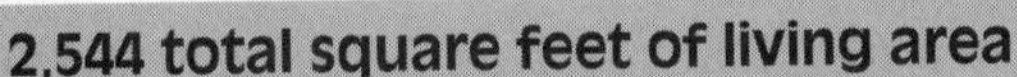

2,544 total square feet of living area

Price Code D

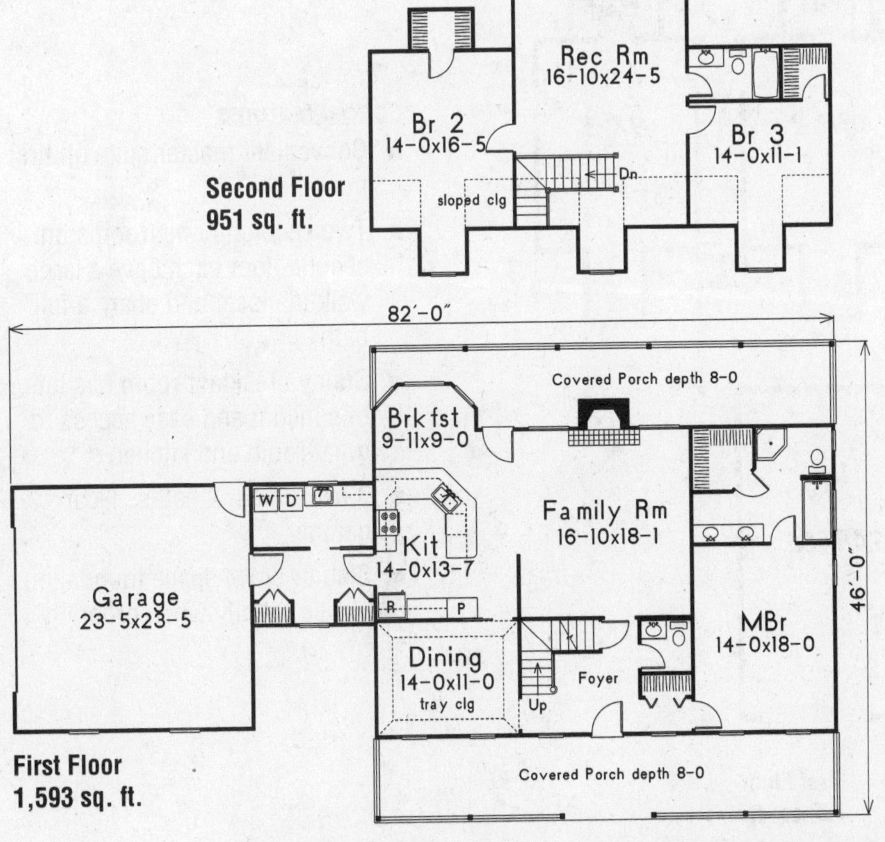

Rec Rm
16-10x24-5
Br 2
14-0x16-5
sloped clg
Dn
Br 3
14-0x11-1
Second Floor
951 sq. ft.
82'-0"
Covered Porch depth 8-0
Brkfst
9-11x9-0
W D
Family Rm
16-10x18-1
Kit
14-0x13-7
R P
Garage
23-5x23-5
MBr
14-0x18-0
46'-0"
Dining
14-0x11-0
tray clg
Up
Foyer
Covered Porch depth 8-0
First Floor
1,593 sq. ft.

Special features

- Central family room becomes gathering place
- Second floor recreation room is a great game room for children
- First floor master suite secluded from main living areas
- 3 bedrooms, 2 1/2 baths, 2-car side entry garage
- Basement foundation, drawings also include crawl space and slab foundations

Plan #702-RJ-B123

Lovely Front Dormers

1,270 total square feet of living area

Price Code A

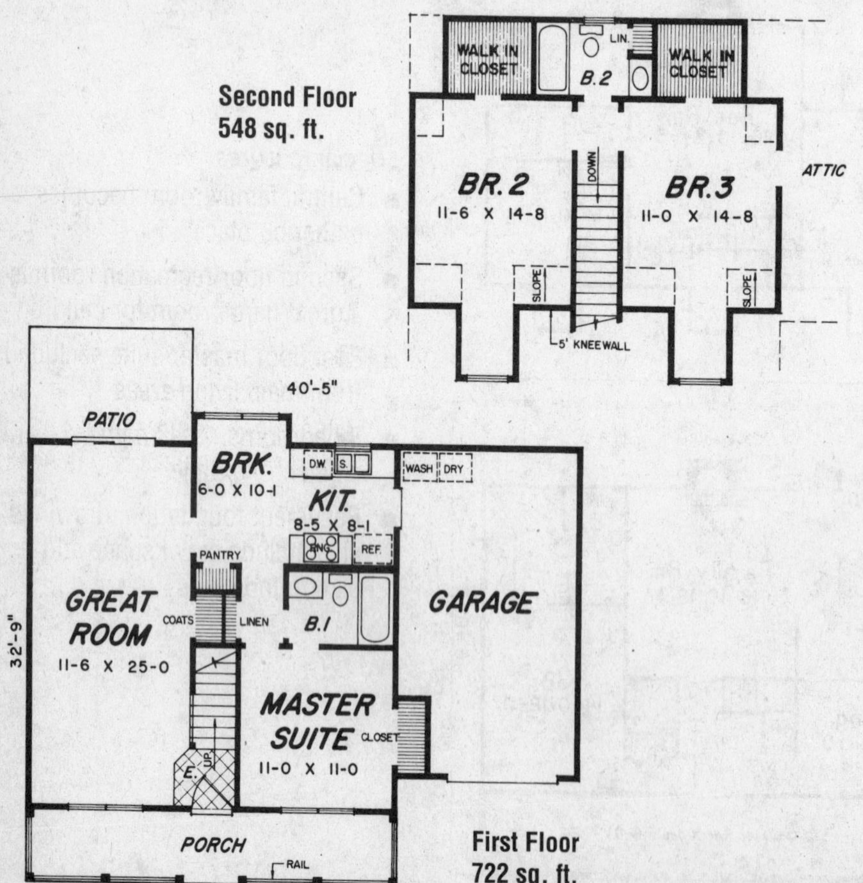

Second Floor
548 sq. ft.
WALK IN CLOSET
LIN.
B.2
WALK IN CLOSET
BR.2
11-6 X 14-8
DOWN
BR.3
11-0 X 14-8
ATTIC
SLOPE
SLOPE
5' KNEE WALL
40'-5"
PATIO
BRK.
6-0 X 10-1
DW
S.
WASH
DRY
KIT.
8-5 X 8-1
REF.
PANTRY
GREAT ROOM
11-6 X 25-0
COATS
LINEN
B.1
GARAGE
32'-9"
MASTER SUITE
11-0 X 11-0
CLOSET
UP
E.
PORCH
RAIL
First Floor
722 sq. ft.

Special features

- Convenient master suite on first floor
- Two secondary bedrooms on second floor each have a large walk-in closet and share a full bath
- Sunny breakfast room has lots of sunlight and easy access to great room and kitchen
- 3 bedrooms, 2 baths, 1-car garage
- Slab or crawl space foundation, please specify when ordering

Plan #702-0305

Distinctive Two-Level Porch

2,605 total square feet of living area **Price Code E**

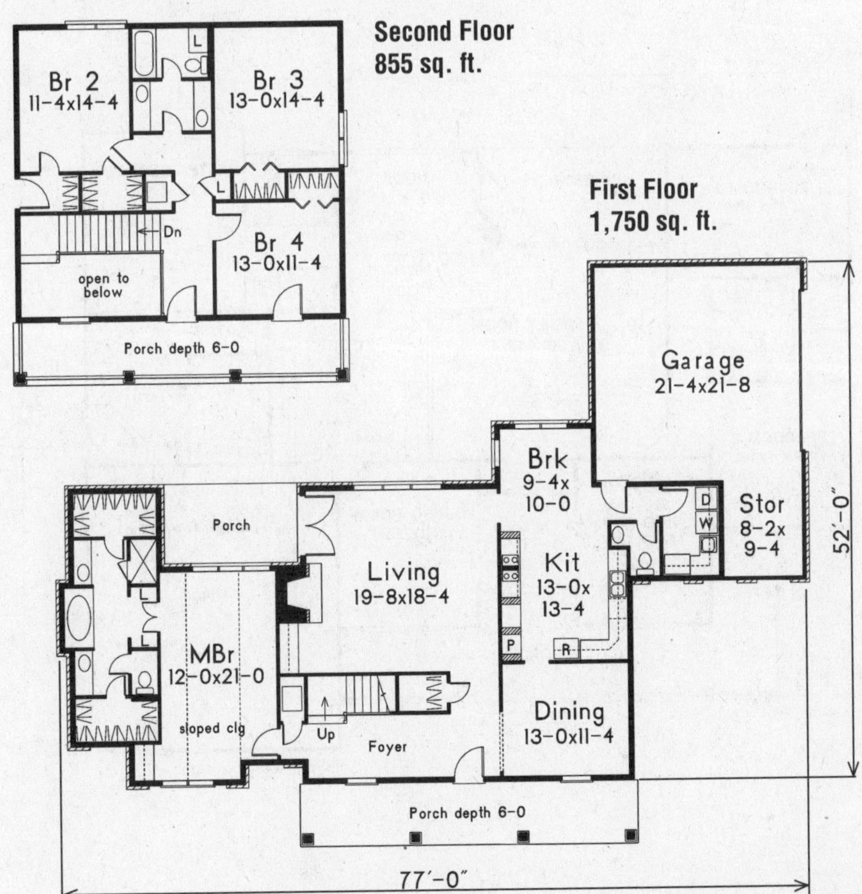
Second Floor
855 sq. ft.
Br 2
11-4x14-4
Br 3
13-0x14-4
Br 4
13-0x11-4
Dn
open to below
Porch depth 6-0
First Floor
1,750 sq. ft.
Garage
21-4x21-8
Brk
9-4x
10-0
Stor
8-2x
9-4
Porch
Living
19-8x18-4
Kit
13-0x
13-4
MBr
12-0x21-0
sloped clg
Up
Foyer
Dining
13-0x11-4
Porch depth 6-0
52'-0"
77'-0"

Special features

- Master bedroom boasts vaulted ceiling and transom picture window which lights sitting area
- Country kitchen features appliances set in between brick dividers and beamed ceiling
- Living room features built-in bookcases, fireplace and raised tray ceiling
- 4 bedrooms, 2 1/2 baths, 2-car side entry garage
- Slab foundation, drawings also include crawl space and basement foundations

The Family
Handyman

Plan #702-DBI-24038-9P

Unique Three-Way Fireplace

2,126 total square feet of living area **Price Code C**

Special features

- Elegant bay windows in master bedroom welcome the sun
- Double vanities in master bath separated by large whirlpool tub
- 3 bedrooms, 2 baths, 2-car side entry garage
- Basement foundation

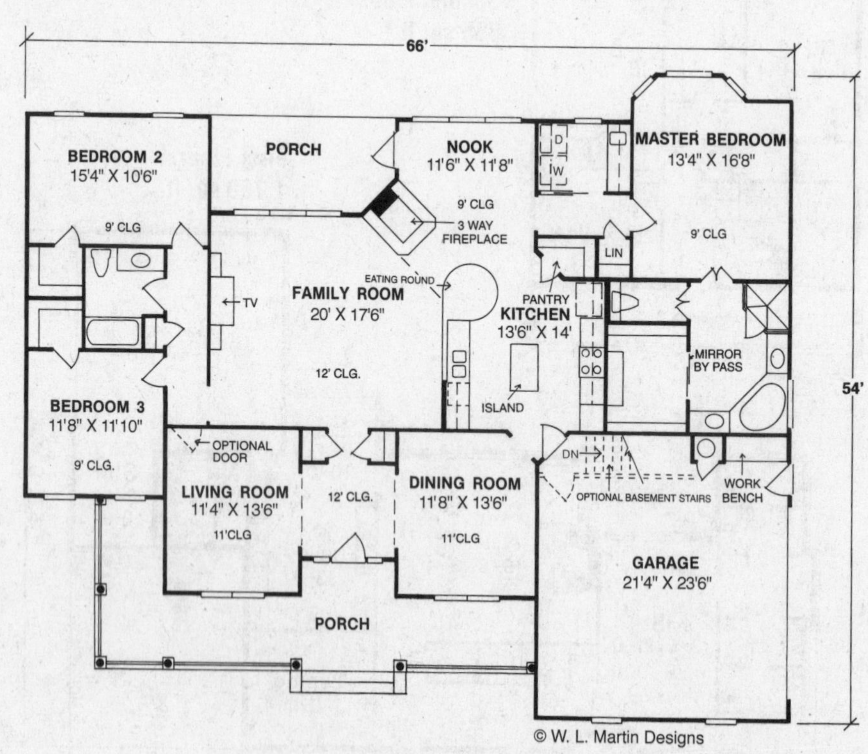
66'
54'
BEDROOM 2
15'4" X 10'6"
9' CLG
PORCH
NOOK
11'6" X 11'8"
9' CLG
3 WAY
FIREPLACE
MASTER BEDROOM
13'4" X 16'8"
9' CLG
LIN
EATING ROUND
FAMILY ROOM
20' X 17'6"
TV
12' CLG.
PANTRY
KITCHEN
13'6" X 14'
ISLAND
MIRROR
BY PASS
BEDROOM 3
11'8" X 11'10"
9' CLG.
OPTIONAL
DOOR
LIVING ROOM
11'4" X 13'6"
11'CLG
12' CLG.
DINING ROOM
11'8" X 13'6"
11'CLG
DN
OPTIONAL BASEMENT STAIRS
WORK
BENCH
GARAGE
21'4" X 23'6"
PORCH

The Family
Handyman

Plan #702-0736

Two-Story Atrium For Great Views

J.N. HANSEN S.D.G.

2,900 total square feet of living area — **Price Code E**

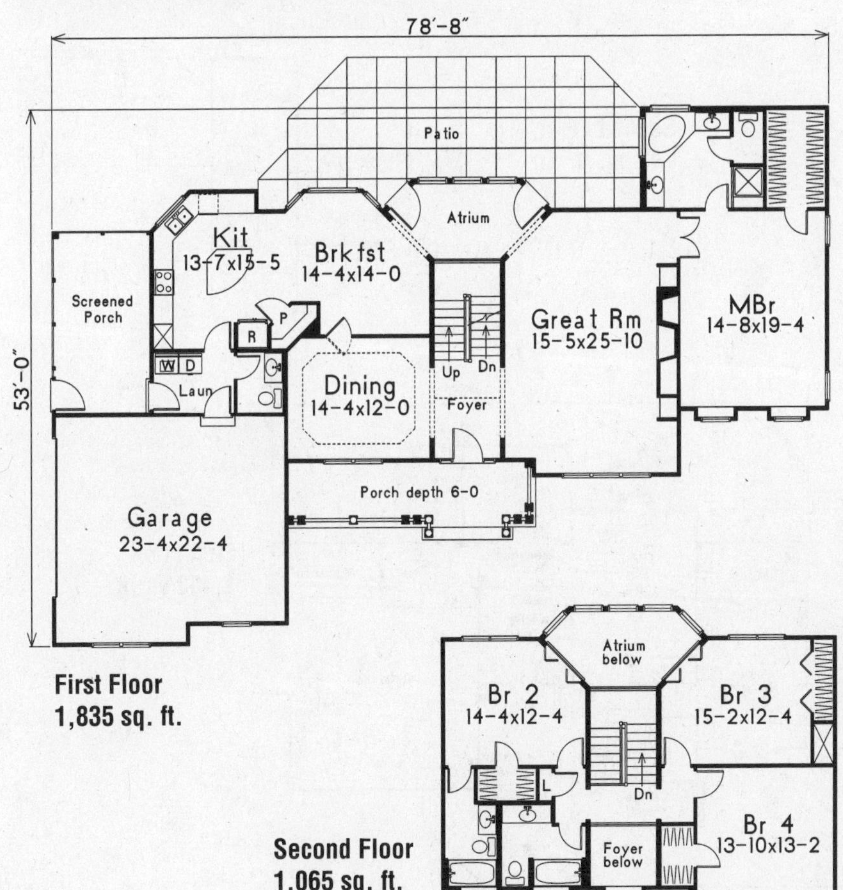
78'-8"
53'-0"
Patio
Atrium
Kit
13-7x15-5
Brkfst
14-4x14-0
Screened Porch
P
R
W D
Laun
Dining
14-4x12-0
Up
Dn
Foyer
Great Rm
15-5x25-10
MBr
14-8x19-4
Porch depth 6-0
Garage
23-4x22-4
Atrium below
Br 2
14-4x12-4
Br 3
15-2x12-4
L
Dn
Foyer below
Br 4
13-10x13-2

First Floor
1,835 sq. ft.

Second Floor
1,065 sq. ft.

Special features

- Elegant entry foyer leads to balcony overlook of vaulted two-story atrium
- Spacious kitchen features an island breakfast bar, walk-in pantry, bayed breakfast room and adjoining screened porch
- Two large second floor bedrooms and stair balconies overlook a sun drenched two-story vaulted atrium
- 4 bedrooms, 3 1/2 baths, 2-car side entry garage
- Basement foundation

The Family
Handyman

Plan #702-GH-24736

Unique Octagon-Shaped Porch

2,044 total square feet of living area

Price Code C

Special features

- Formal dining area easily accesses kitchen through double-doors
- Two-car garage features a workshop area for projects or extra storage
- Second floor includes loft space ideal for office area and a handy computer center
- Colossal master bedroom with double walk-in closets, private bath bay window seat
- 3 bedrooms, 2 1/2 baths, 2-car side entry garage
- Basement, crawl space or slab foundation, please specify when ordering

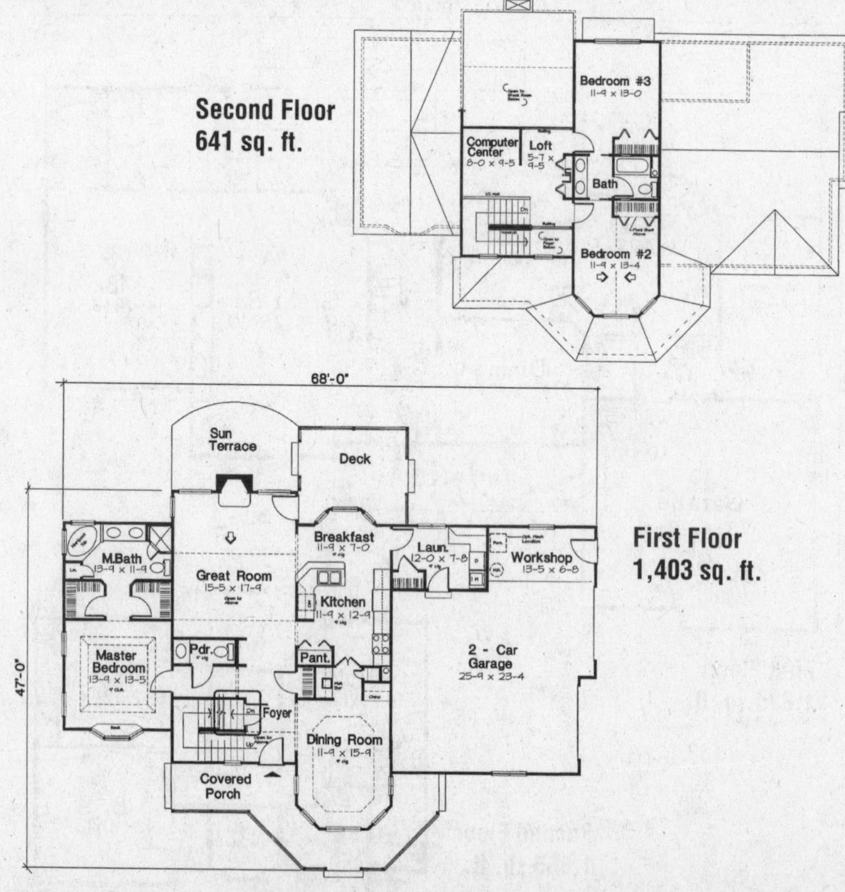
Second Floor
641 sq. ft.
Bedroom #3
11-9 x 13-0
Computer Center
8-0 x 9-5
Loft
5-7 x 9-5
Bath
Bedroom #2
11-9 x 13-4
68'-0"
47'-0"
Sun Terrace
Deck
Breakfast
11-9 x 7-0
Laun.
12-0 x 7-8
Workshop
13-5 x 6-8
M.Bath
13-9 x 11-9
Great Room
15-5 x 17-9
Kitchen
11-9 x 12-9
Master Bedroom
13-9 x 13-5
Pdr.
Pant.
2 - Car Garage
25-9 x 23-4
Foyer
Dining Room
11-9 x 15-9
Covered Porch
First Floor
1,403 sq. ft.

Plan #702-AMD-2229

Dramatic U-Shaped Stairs

2,287 total square feet of living area

Price Code D

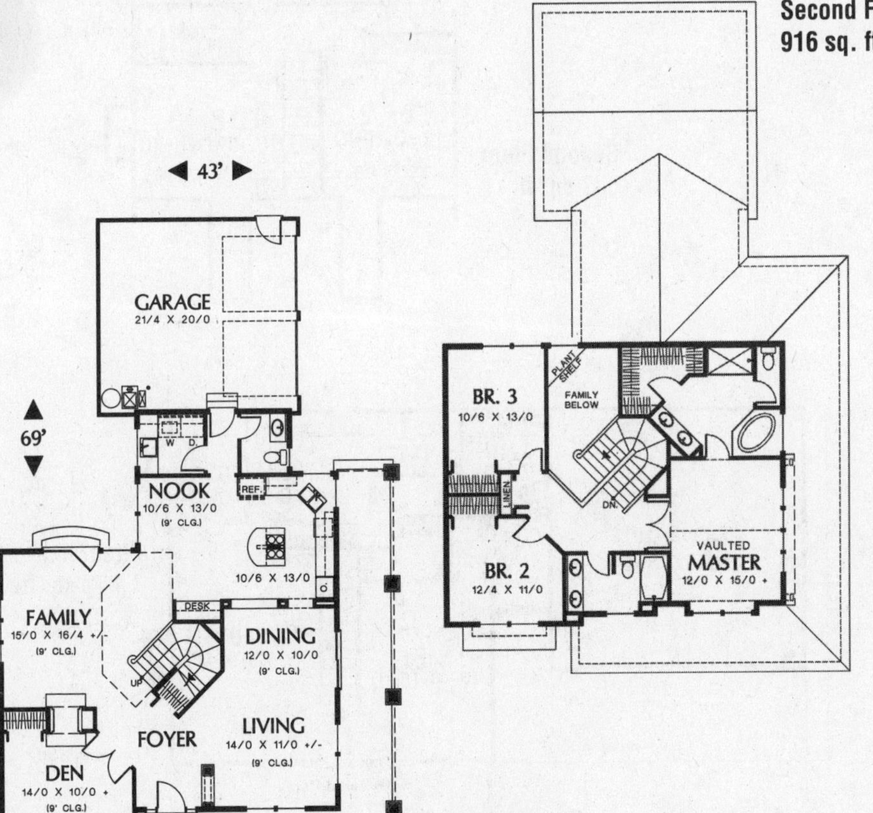
43'
69'
GARAGE
21/4 X 20/0
W D
NOOK
10/6 X 13/0
(9' CLG.)
REF.
10/6 X 13/0
FAMILY
15/0 X 16/4 +/-
(9' CLG.)
DESK
DINING
12/0 X 10/0
(9' CLG.)
UP
FOYER
LIVING
14/0 X 11/0 +/-
(9' CLG.)
DEN
14/0 X 10/0 +
(9' CLG.)
BR. 3
10/6 X 13/0
PLANT SHELF
FAMILY BELOW
LINEN
DN.
BR. 2
12/4 X 11/0
VAULTED
MASTER
12/0 X 15/0 +

Second Floor
916 sq. ft.

First Floor
1,371 sq. ft.

Special features

- Wrap-around porch creates inviting feeling
- First floor windows have transom windows above
- Den has see-through fireplace into the family area
- 4 bedrooms, 2 1/2 baths, 2-car side entry garage
- Crawl space foundation

The Family
Handyman

Plan #702-0686

Charming Home Arranged For Open Living

1,609 total square feet of living area | **Price Code B**

Special features

- Kitchen captures full use of space with pantry, ample cabinets and workspace
- Master bedroom is well-secluded with walk-in closet and private bath
- Large utility room includes sink and extra storage
- Attractive bay window in dining area provides light
- 3 bedrooms, 2 1/2 baths, 2-car garage
- Slab foundation

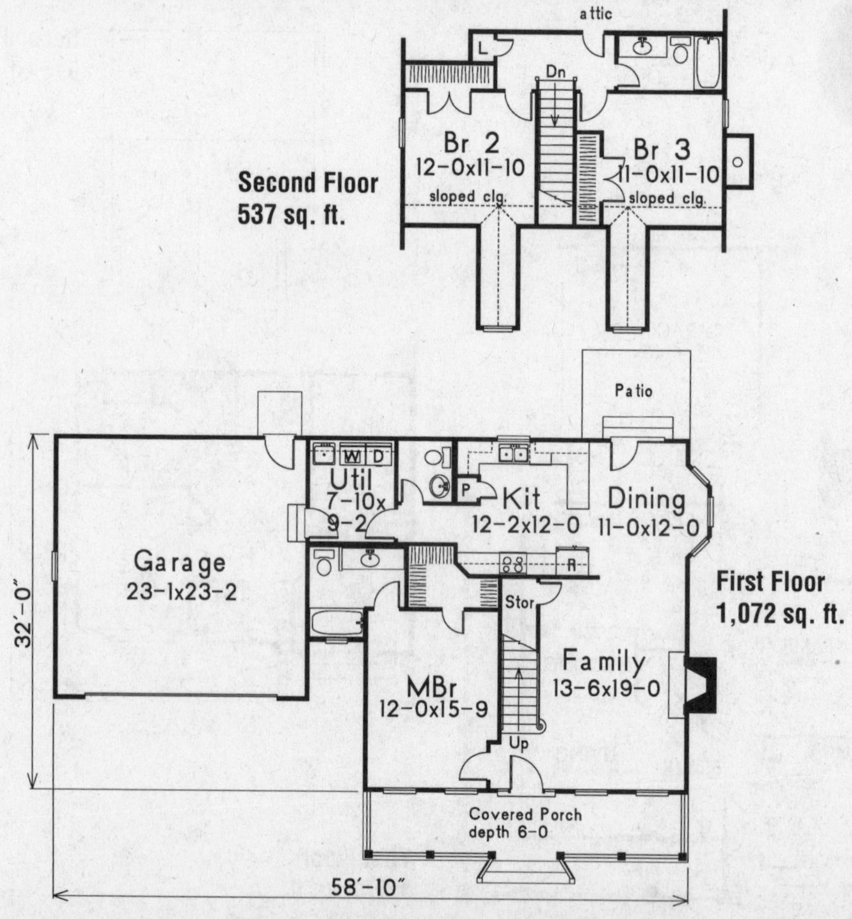

attic
L
Dn
Br 2
12-0x11-10
sloped clg.
Br 3
11-0x11-10
sloped clg.
Second Floor
537 sq. ft.
Patio
W D
Util
7-10x
9-2
P
Kit
12-2x12-0
Dining
11-0x12-0
Garage
23-1x23-2
Stor
32'-0"
First Floor
1,072 sq. ft.
Family
13-6x19-0
MBr
12-0x15-9
Up
Covered Porch
depth 6-0
58'-10"

TO ORDER BLUEPRINTS USE THE FORM ON PAGE 19 OR CALL TOLL-FREE 1-877-671-6036

The Family
Handyman

Plan #702-RDD-1753-9

Easy Living

1,753 total square feet of living area

Price Code B

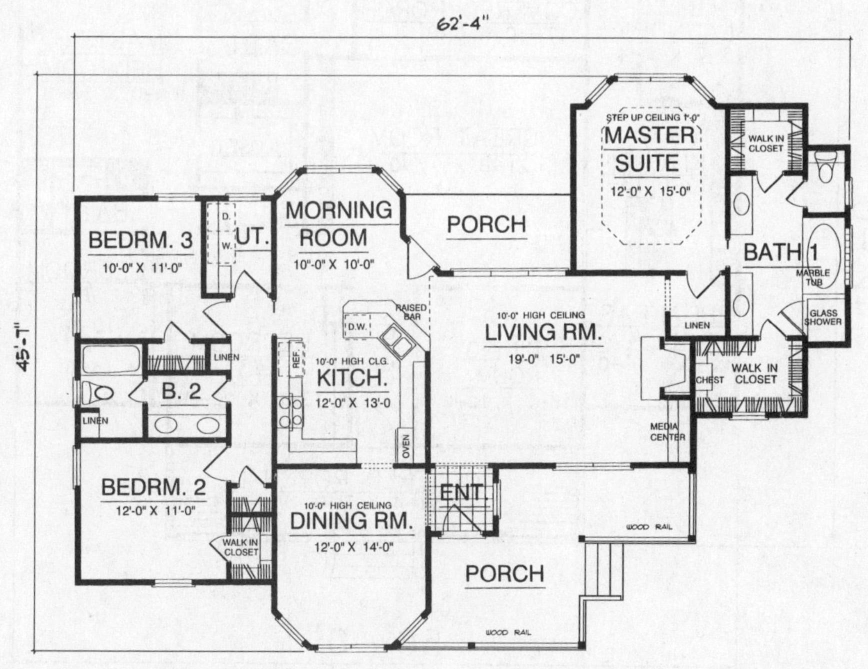
62'-4"
45'-1"
STEP UP CEILING 1'-0"
MASTER
SUITE
12'-0" X 15'-0"
WALK IN CLOSET
BATH 1
MARBLE TUB
GLASS SHOWER
LINEN
WALK IN CLOSET
CHEST
MEDIA CENTER
PORCH
MORNING ROOM
10'-0" X 10'-0"
BEDRM. 3
10'-0" X 11'-0"
UT.
D.
W.
RAISED BAR
D.W.
10'-0" HIGH CEILING
LIVING RM.
19'-0" 15'-0"
10'-0" HIGH CLG.
KITCH.
12'-0" X 13'-0
REF.
OVEN
LINEN
B. 2
LINEN
BEDRM. 2
12'-0" X 11'-0"
WALK IN CLOSET
10'-0" HIGH CEILING
DINING RM.
12'-0" X 14'-0"
ENT.
WOOD RAIL
PORCH
WOOD RAIL

Special features

- Large front porch has charming appeal
- Kitchen with breakfast bar overlooks morning room and accesses covered porch
- Master suite with amenities like private bath, spacious closets and sunny bay window
- 3 bedrooms, 2 baths
- Slab or crawl space foundation, please specify when ordering

The Family
Handyman

Plan #702-DH-1786

Traditional Southern Style Home

1,785 total square feet of living area

Price Code B

Special features

- 9' ceilings throughout home
- Luxurious master bath includes whirlpool tub and separate shower
- Cozy breakfast area is convenient to kitchen
- 3 bedrooms, 3 baths, 2-car detached garage
- Basement, crawl space or slab foundation, please specify when ordering

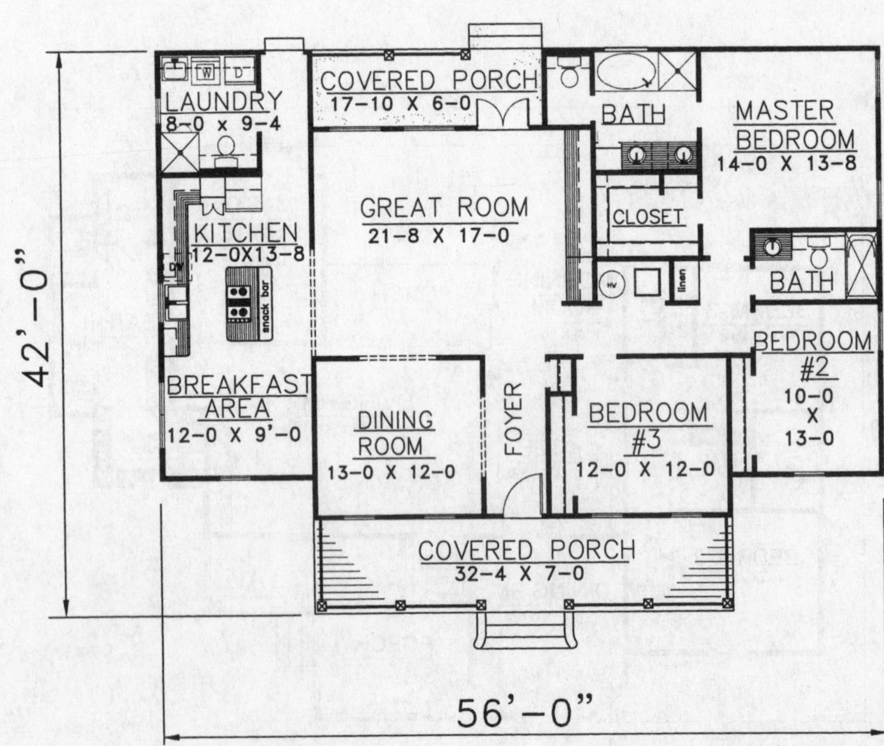
LAUNDRY
8-0 x 9-4
COVERED PORCH
17-10 X 6-0
BATH
MASTER
BEDROOM
14-0 X 13-8
KITCHEN
12-0X13-8
snack bar
GREAT ROOM
21-8 X 17-0
CLOSET
BATH
BEDROOM
#2
10-0
X
13-0
BREAKFAST
AREA
12-0 X 9'-0
DINING
ROOM
13-0 X 12-0
FOYER
BEDROOM
#3
12-0 X 12-0
COVERED PORCH
32-4 X 7-0
42'-0"
56'-0"

The Family
Handyman

Plan #702-0537

Old-Fashioned Porches Gives Welcoming Appeal

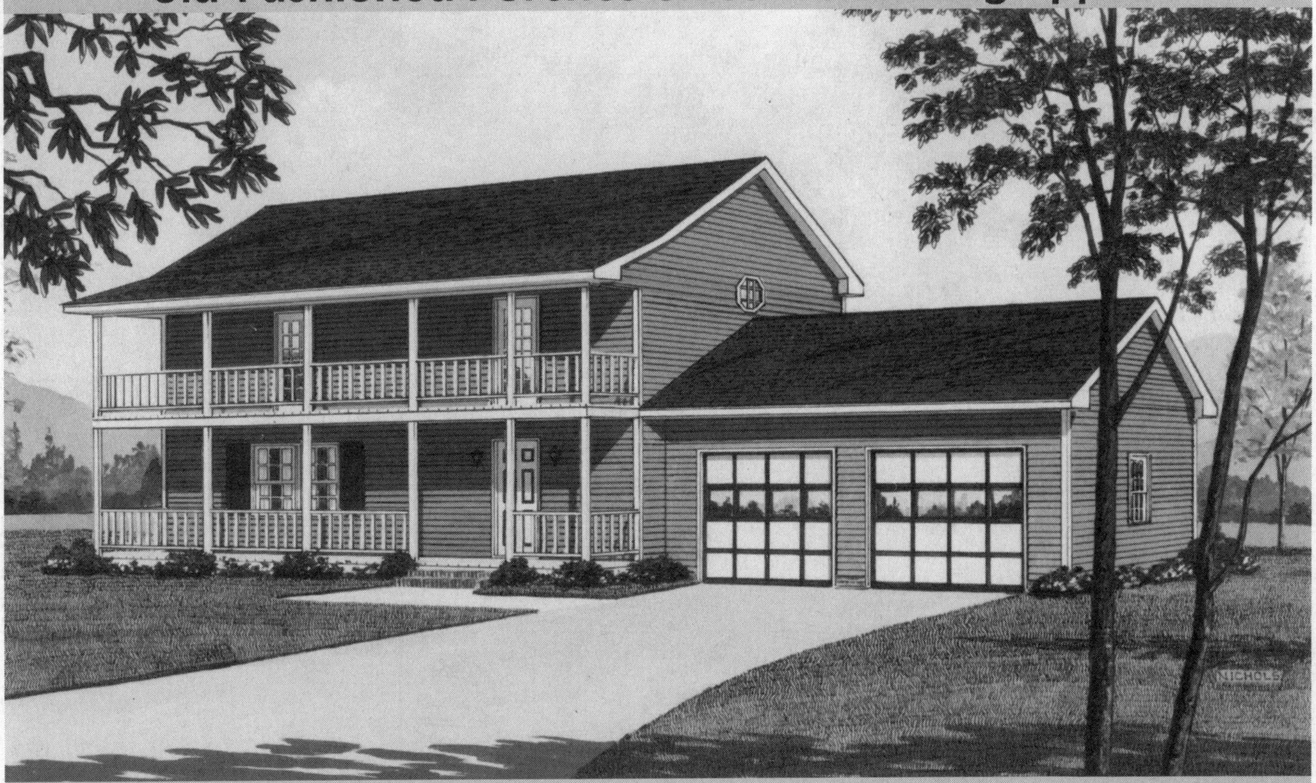

1,664 total square feet of living area **Price Code B**

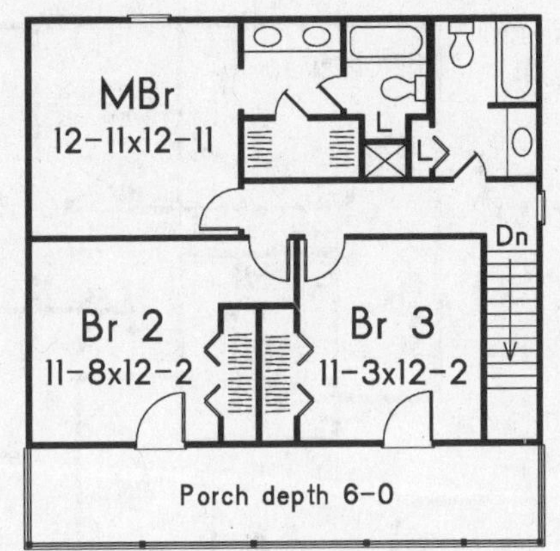
MBr
12-11x12-11
L
L
Dn
Br 2
11-8x12-2
Br 3
11-3x12-2
Porch depth 6-0

Second Floor
832 sq. ft.

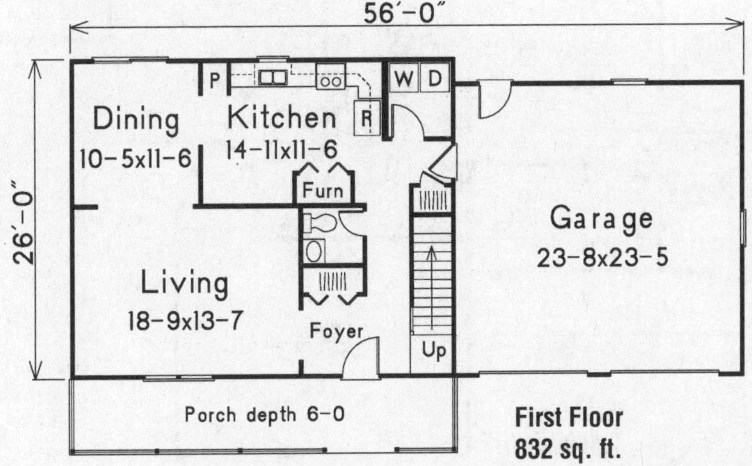
56′-0″
26′-0″
P
W
D
Dining
10-5x11-6
Kitchen
14-11x11-6
R
Furn
Garage
23-8x23-5
Living
18-9x13-7
Foyer
Up
Porch depth 6-0

First Floor
832 sq. ft.

Special features

- L-shaped country kitchen includes pantry and cozy breakfast area
- Bedrooms located on second floor for privacy
- Master bedroom includes walk-in closet, dressing area and bath
- 3 bedrooms, 2 1/2 baths, 2-car garage
- Crawl space foundation, drawings also include basement and slab foundations

The Family
Handyman

Plan #702-DDI-98-203

Convenient First Floor Master Suite

2,504 total square feet of living area

Price Code D

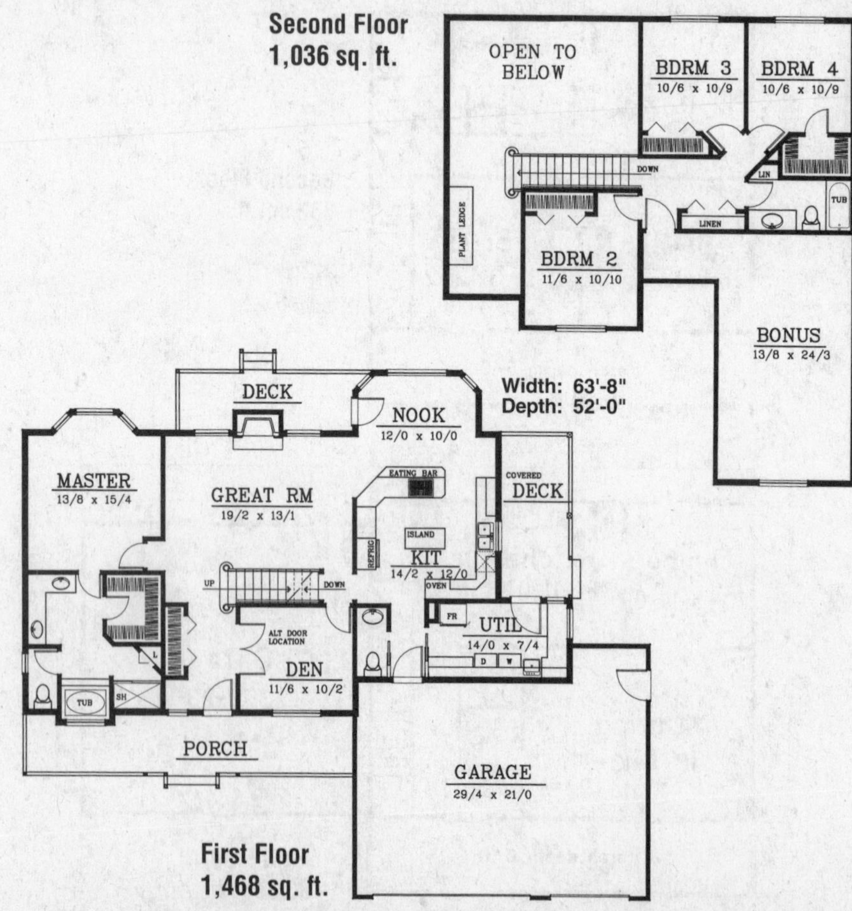
Second Floor
1,036 sq. ft.
OPEN TO BELOW
BDRM 3
10/6 x 10/9
BDRM 4
10/6 x 10/9
DOWN
LIN
TUB
PLANT LEDGE
LINEN
BDRM 2
11/6 x 10/10
BONUS
13/8 x 24/3
Width: 63'-8"
Depth: 52'-0"
DECK
NOOK
12/0 x 10/0
MASTER
13/8 x 15/4
GREAT RM
19/2 x 13/1
EATING BAR
COVERED DECK
ISLAND
REFRIG
KIT
14/2 x 12/0
OVEN
UP
DOWN
FR
UTIL
14/0 x 7/4
D
W
ALT DOOR LOCATION
DEN
11/6 x 10/2
TUB
SH
PORCH
GARAGE
29/4 x 21/0
First Floor
1,468 sq. ft.

Special features

- Efficient kitchen boasts a peninsula counter adding workspace as well as an eating bar
- The nook and kitchen blend nicely into the great room for family gathering
- The utility room has a soaking sink, extra counterspace and plenty of room for an additional refrigerator
- 4 bedrooms, 2 1/2 baths, 3-car garage
- Basement foundation

The Family
Handyman

Plan #702-0677

Spacious Room Around A Central Foyer

3,006 total square feet of living area

Price Code E

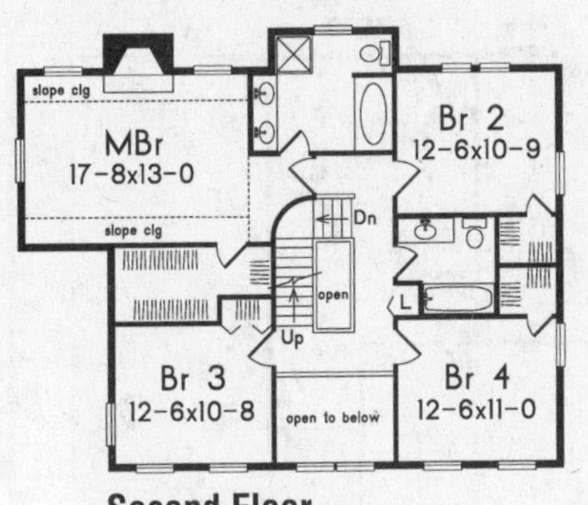
slope clg
MBr
17-8x13-0
Br 2
12-6x10-9
slope clg
Dn
open
Up
L
Br 3
12-6x10-8
open to below
Br 4
12-6x11-0

Second Floor
1,138 sq. ft.

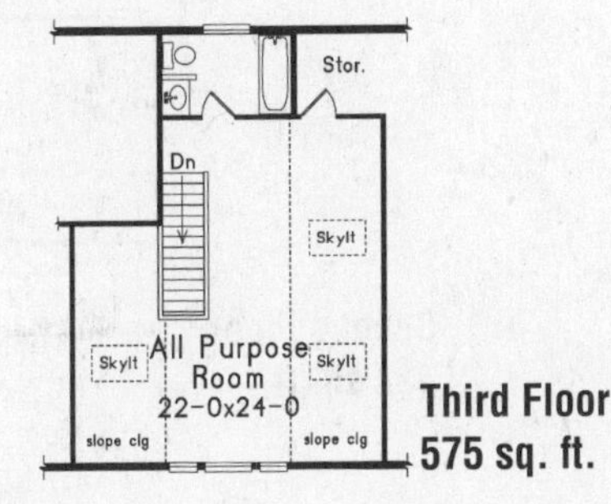
Stor.
Dn
Skylt
Skylt
All Purpose
Room
22-0x24-0
Skylt
slope clg
slope clg

Third Floor
575 sq. ft.

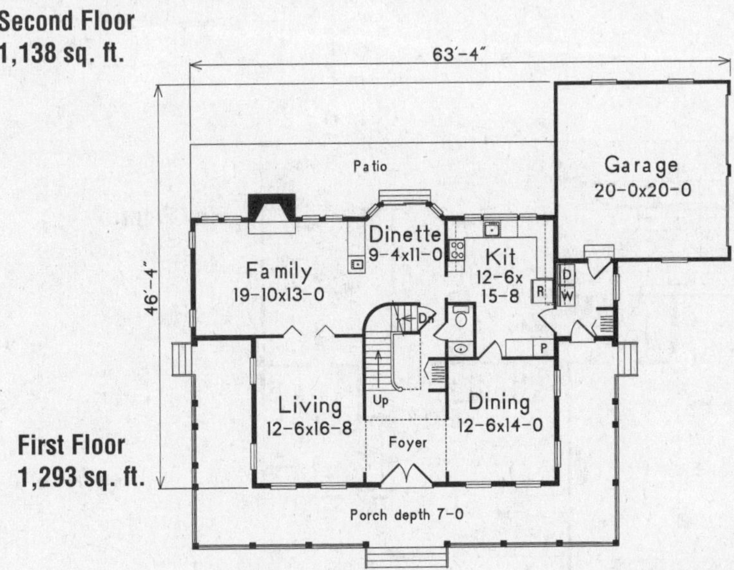
63'-4"
46'-4"
Patio
Garage
20-0x20-0
Dinette
9-4x11-0
Kit
12-6x
15-8
Family
19-10x13-0
R
D
W
Dn
P
Up
Living
12-6x16-8
Dining
12-6x14-0
Foyer
Porch depth 7-0

First Floor
1,293 sq. ft.

Special features

- Energy efficient home with 2" x 6" exterior walls
- Large all purpose room and bath on third floor
- Efficient U-shaped kitchen includes a pantry and adjacent planning desk
- 4 bedrooms, 3 1/2 baths, 2-car side entry garage
- Basement foundation, drawings also include slab foundation

TO ORDER BLUEPRINTS USE THE FORM ON PAGE 19 OR CALL TOLL-FREE 1-877-671-6036

The Family
Handyman

Plan #702-FB-582

Country Charm With Dormers And Covered Porch

1,497 total square feet of living area **Price Code A**

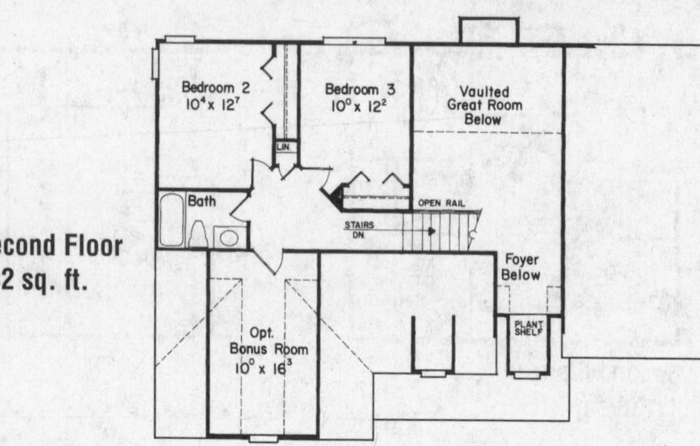
Bedroom 2
$10^{4} \times 12^{7}$
Bedroom 3
$10^{0} \times 12^{2}$
Vaulted
Great Room
Below
LIN
Bath
OPEN RAIL
STAIRS
DN.
Foyer
Below
PLANT
SHELF
Opt.
Bonus Room
$10^{0} \times 16^{3}$

Second Floor
432 sq. ft.

Special features

- Master suite has private luxurious bath with spacious walk-in closet
- Formal dining room has tray ceiling and views onto front covered porch
- Bonus room on second floor has an additional 175 square feet of living area
- 3 bedrooms, 2 1/2 baths, 2-car garage
- Crawl space or walk-out basement foundation, please specify when ordering

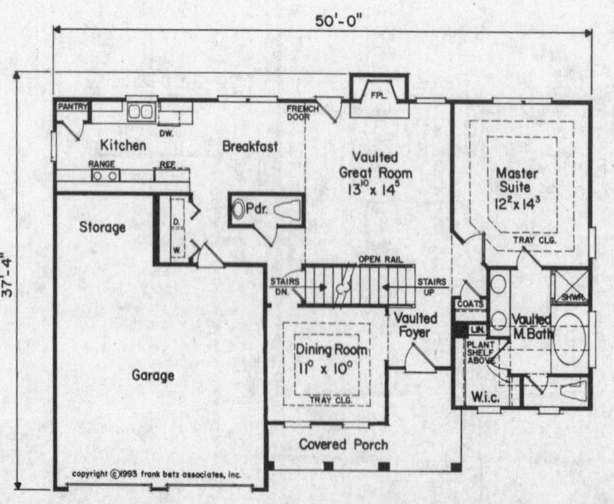
50'-0"
37'-4"
PANTRY
Kitchen
DW.
RANGE
REF.
FRENCH
DOOR
Breakfast
FPL.
Vaulted
Great Room
$13^{10} \times 14^{5}$
Master
Suite
$12^{2} \times 14^{3}$
TRAY CLG.
Storage
Pdr.
OPEN RAIL
STAIRS
DN.
STAIRS
UP
COATS
LIN.
SHWR.
Vaulted
M.Bath
Vaulted
Foyer
PLANT
SHELF
ABOVE
Dining Room
$11^{0} \times 10^{0}$
TRAY CLG.
Garage
W.i.c.
Covered Porch
copyright © 1993 frank betz associates, inc.

First Floor
1,065 sq. ft.

TO ORDER BLUEPRINTS USE THE FORM ON PAGE 19 OR CALL TOLL-FREE 1-877-671-6036

View thousands more home plans online at www.familyhandyman.com/homeplans

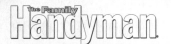

Plan #702-0167

Open Format For Easy Living

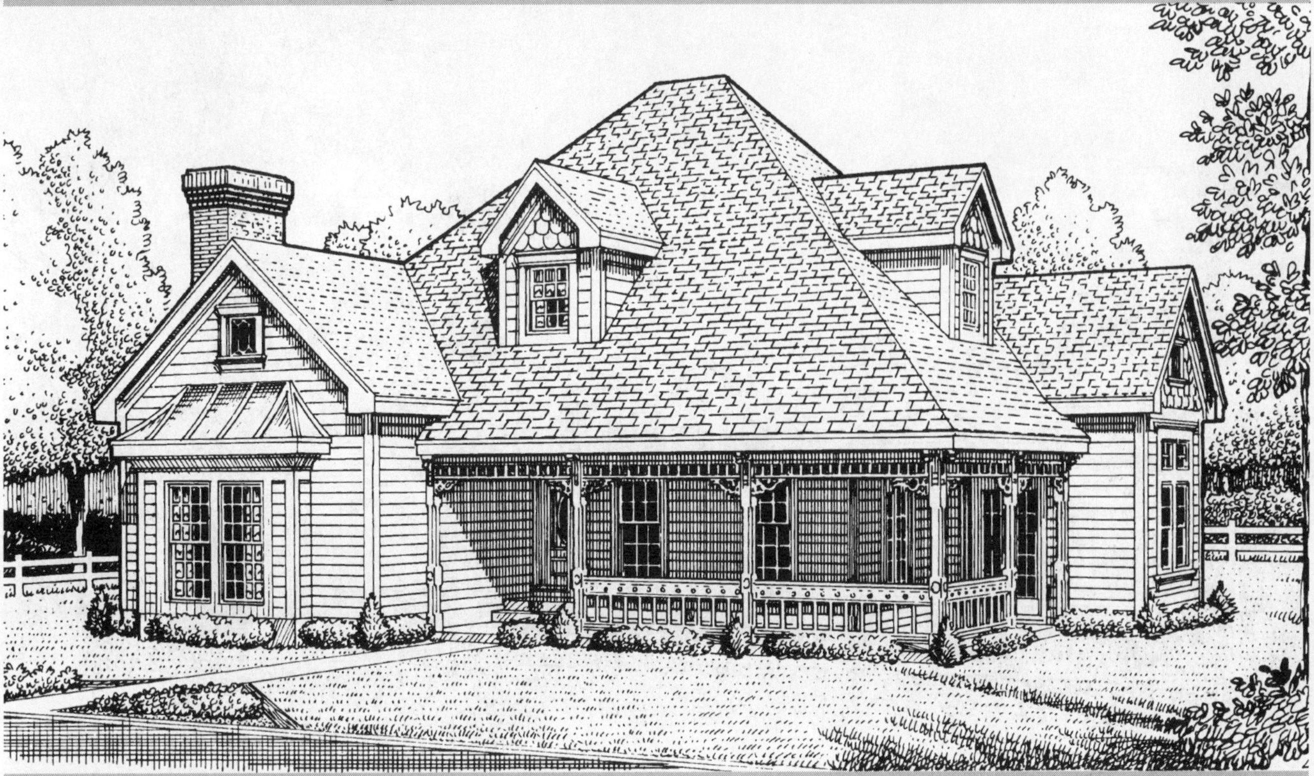

2,282 total square feet of living area **Price Code D**

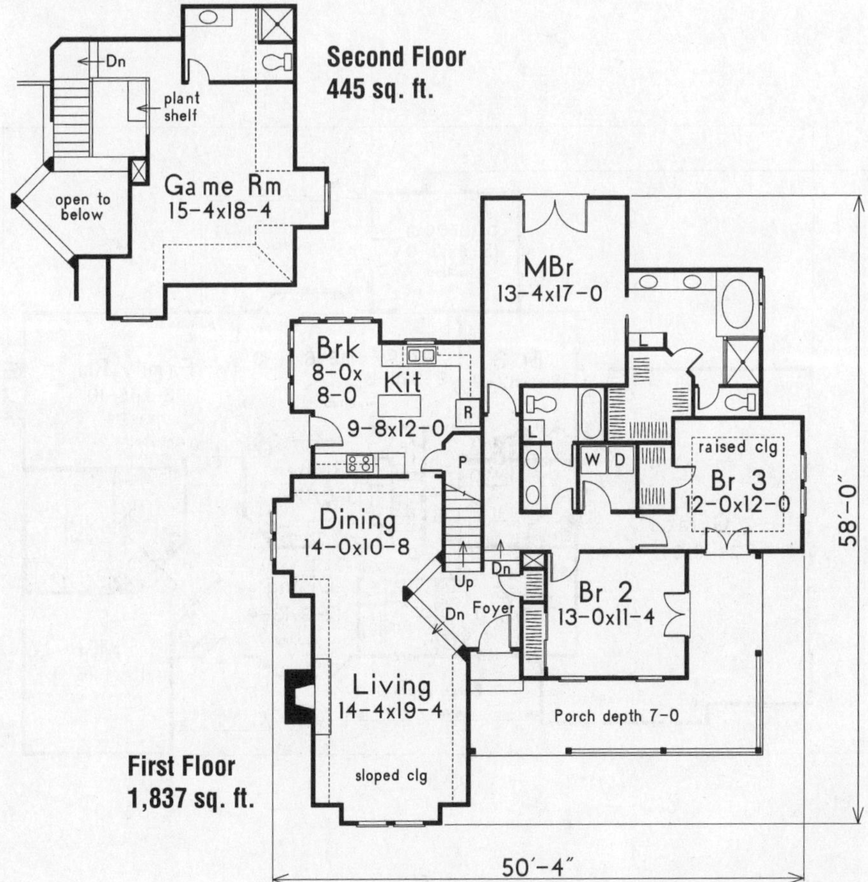
Second Floor
445 sq. ft.
Dn
plant shelf
open to below
Game Rm
15-4x18-4
MBr
13-4x17-0
Brk
8-0x
8-0
Kit
9-8x12-0
R
P
L
W
D
raised clg
Br 3
12-0x12-0
Dining
14-0x10-8
Up
Dn
Foyer
Br 2
13-0x11-4
Living
14-4x19-4
Porch depth 7-0
sloped clg
58'-0"
50'-4"
First Floor
1,837 sq. ft.

Special features

- Living and dining rooms combine to create a large, convenient entertaining area that includes a fireplace
- Comfortable veranda allows access from secondary bedrooms
- Second floor game room overlooks foyer and includes a full bath
- Kitchen and breakfast areas are surrounded by mullioned windows
- 3 bedrooms, 3 baths, 2-car detached garage
- Slab foundation, drawings also include crawl space foundation

The Family
Handyman

Plan #702-0748

Rambling Ranch With Country Charm

2,514 total square feet of living area **Price Code D**

Special features

- Expansive porch welcomes you to the foyer, spacious dining area with bay and a gallery-sized hall with plant shelf above
- A highly functional U-shaped kitchen is open to a bayed breakfast room, study and family room with a 46' vista
- Vaulted rear sunroom has fireplace
- 1,509 square feet of optional living area on the lower level with recreation room, bedroom #4 with bath and an office with storage closet
- 3 bedrooms, 2 baths, 3-car oversized side entry garage with workshop/storage area
- Walk-out basement foundation

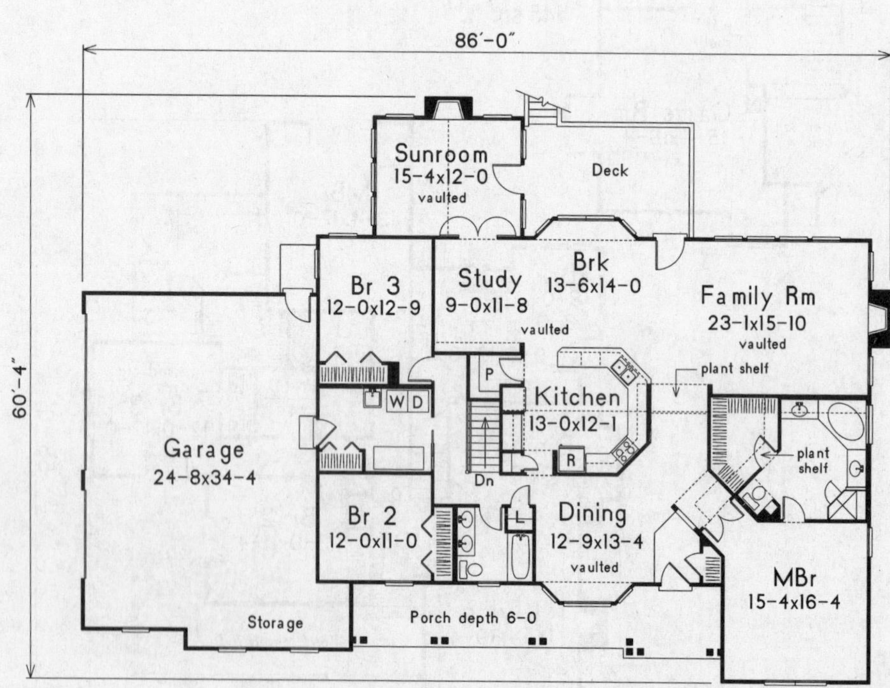
86'-0"
60'-4"
Sunroom
15-4x12-0
vaulted
Deck
Br 3
12-0x12-9
Study
9-0x11-8
Brk
13-6x14-0
vaulted
Family Rm
23-1x15-10
vaulted
plant shelf
Kitchen
13-0x12-1
P
W D
R
Dn
plant shelf
Garage
24-8x34-4
Br 2
12-0x11-0
Dining
12-9x13-4
vaulted
MBr
15-4x16-4
Storage
Porch depth 6-0

Kitchen Overlooks Living Area

1,815 total square feet of living area — **Price Code C**

Second Floor
570 sq. ft.

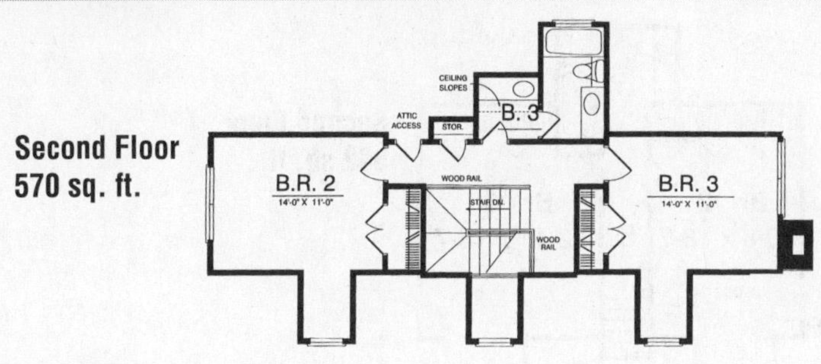
CEILING SLOPES
ATTIC ACCESS
STOR.
B. 3
B.R. 2
14'-0" X 11'-0"
WOOD RAIL
STAIR DN.
WOOD RAIL
B.R. 3
14'-0" X 11'-0"

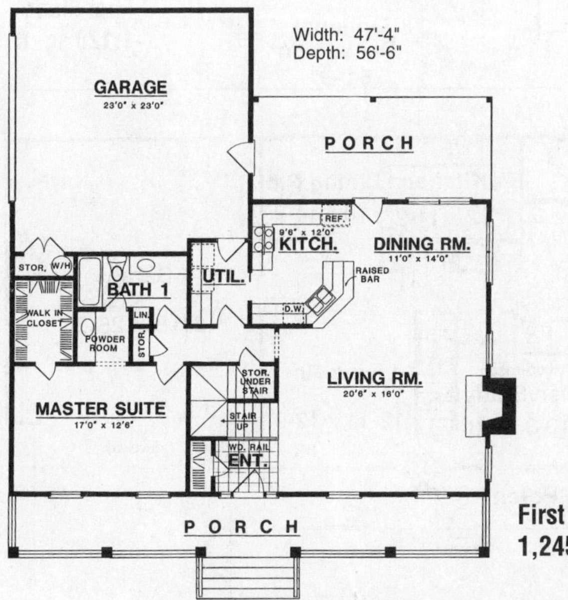
Width: 47'-4"
Depth: 56'-6"
GARAGE
23'0" x 23'0"
PORCH
REF.
9'6" x 12'0"
KITCH.
DINING RM.
11'0" x 14'0"
RAISED BAR
D.W.
STOR.
W/H
BATH 1
UTIL.
LIN.
WALK IN CLOSET
POWDER ROOM
STOR.
STOR. UNDER STAIR
LIVING RM.
20'6" x 16'0"
MASTER SUITE
17'0" x 12'6"
STAIR UP
WD. RAIL
ENT.
PORCH

First Floor
1,245 sq. ft.

Special features

- Well-designed kitchen opens to dining room and features raised breakfast bar
- First floor master suite has walk-in closet
- Front and back porches unite this home with the outdoors
- 3 bedrooms, 2 baths, 2-car side entry garage
- Basement, crawl space or slab foundation, please specify when ordering

Plan #702-GH-35002

Double Dormers Add Country Charm

1,712 total square feet of living area **Price Code B**

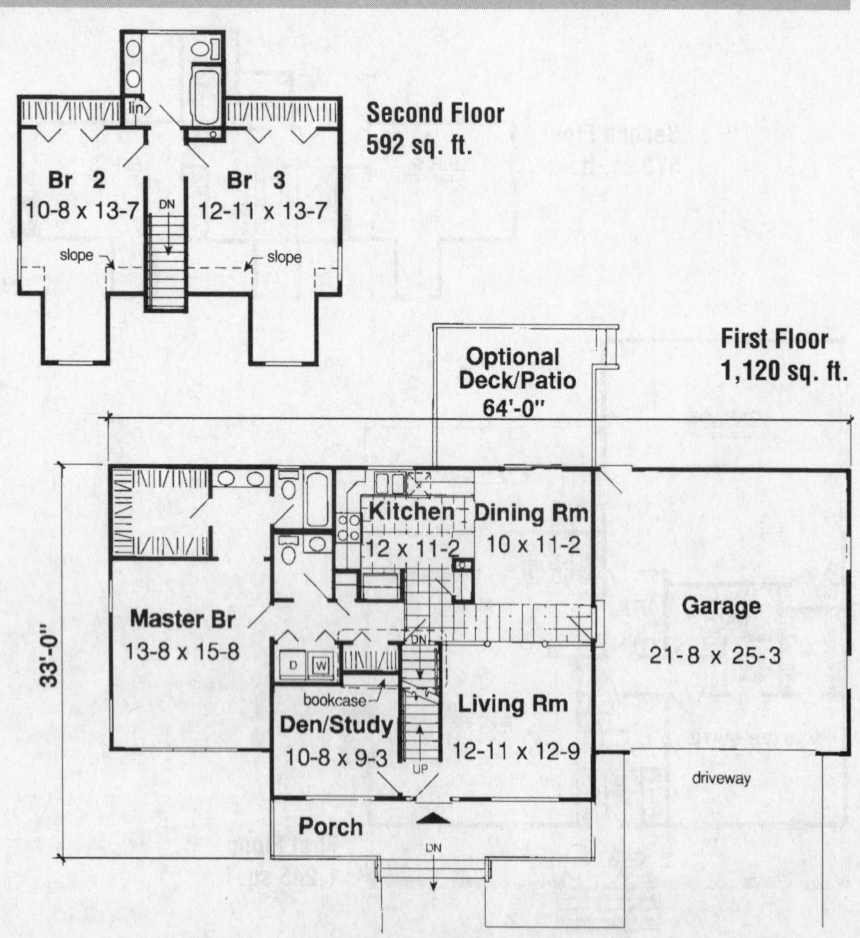
Second Floor
592 sq. ft.
lin
Br 2
10-8 x 13-7
DN
Br 3
12-11 x 13-7
slope
slope
Optional
Deck/Patio
64'-0"
First Floor
1,120 sq. ft.
Kitchen
12 x 11-2
Dining Rm
10 x 11-2
Garage
21-8 x 25-3
Master Br
13-8 x 15-8
33'-0"
D W
DN
bookcase
Den/Study
10-8 x 9-3
UP
Living Rm
12-11 x 12-9
driveway
Porch
DN

Special features

- Laundry closet conveniently located near bedrooms
- Formal living room connects to the dining room and kitchen area
- Den/study makes a cozy retreat with built-in bookcases
- 3 bedrooms, 2 1/2 baths, 2-car garage
- Basement, crawl space or slab foundation, please specify when ordering

TO ORDER BLUEPRINTS USE THE FORM ON PAGE 19 OR CALL TOLL-FREE 1-877-671-6036

View thousands more home plans online at www.familyhandyman.com/homeplans

Plan #702-AP-1914

Triple Dormers Create Terrific Curb Appeal

1,992 total square feet of living area **Price Code C**

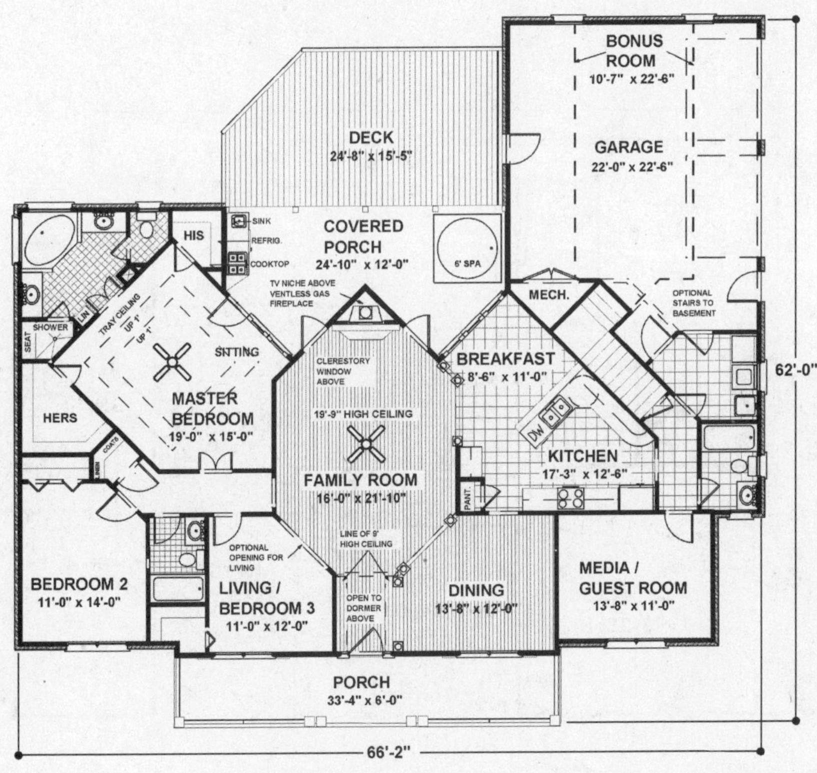
BONUS ROOM
10'-7" x 22'-6"
GARAGE
22'-0" x 22'-6"
DECK
24'-8" x 15'-5"
COVERED PORCH
24'-10" x 12'-0"
SINK
REFRIG.
COOKTOP
6' SPA
HIS
HERS
SHOWER
SEAT
TRAY CEILING
MASTER BEDROOM
19'-0" x 15'-0"
SITTING
TV NICHE ABOVE VENTLESS GAS FIREPLACE
CLERESTORY WINDOW ABOVE
19'-9" HIGH CEILING
FAMILY ROOM
16'-0" x 21'-10"
MECH.
OPTIONAL STAIRS TO BASEMENT
BREAKFAST
8'-6" x 11'-0"
KITCHEN
17'-3" x 12'-6"
DW
PANT.
62'-0"
OPTIONAL OPENING FOR LIVING
LINE OF 9' HIGH CEILING
BEDROOM 2
11'-0" x 14'-0"
LIVING / BEDROOM 3
11'-0" x 12'-0"
OPEN TO DORMER ABOVE
DINING
13'-8" x 12'-0"
MEDIA / GUEST ROOM
13'-8" x 11'-0"
PORCH
33'-4" x 6'-0"
66'-2"

Special features

- Interesting angled walls add drama to many of the living areas including family room, master bedroom and breakfast area
- Covered porch includes spa and an outdoor kitchen with sink, refridgerator and cooktop
- Enter majestic master bath to find a dramatic corner oversized tub
- 4 bedrooms, 3 baths, 2-car side entry garage
- Basement, crawl space or slab foundation, please specify when ordering

The Family
Handyman

Plan #702-0287

Striking Front Facade With Arched Entry

2,718 total square feet of living area **Price Code E**

Special features

- Master suite has tray ceiling, access to the rear deck, walk-in closet and impressive private bath
- Dining and living rooms flank the foyer and both feature tray ceilings
- Spacious family room features 12' ceiling, fireplace and access to the rear deck
- Kitchen has a 9' ceiling, large pantry and bar overlooking the breakfast room
- 4 bedrooms, 2 1/2 baths, 2-car side entry garage
- Basement foundation

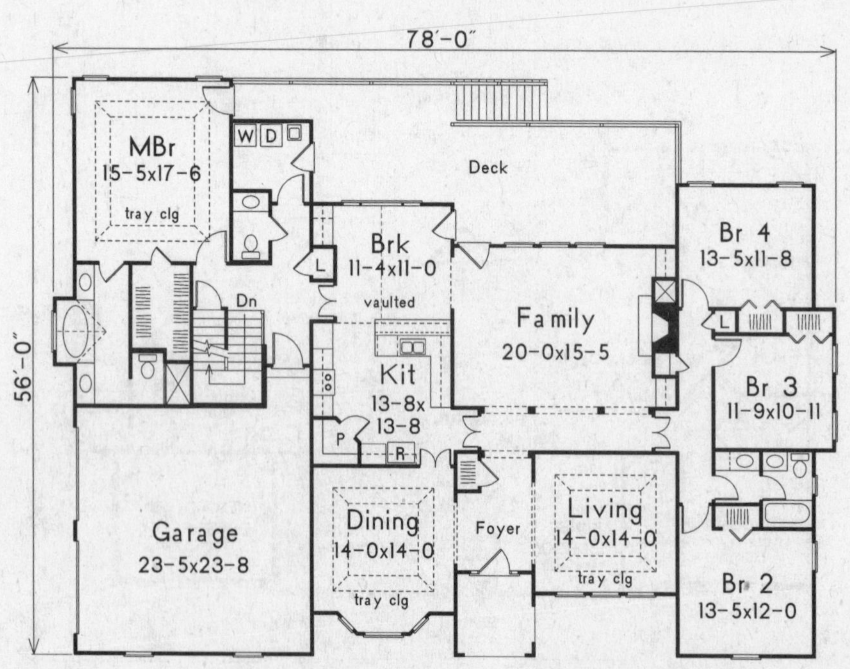
78'-0"
56'-0"
MBr
15-5x17-6
tray clg
W D
Deck
Brk
11-4x11-0
L
Dn
vaulted
Family
20-0x15-5
Br 4
13-5x11-8
L
Br 3
11-9x10-11
Kit
13-8x
13-8
P
R
Garage
23-5x23-8
Dining
14-0x14-0
tray clg
Foyer
Living
14-0x14-0
tray clg
Br 2
13-5x12-0

TO ORDER BLUEPRINTS USE THE FORM ON PAGE 19 OR CALL TOLL-FREE 1-877-671-6036

Plan #702-GM-1815

Large Built-In Desk

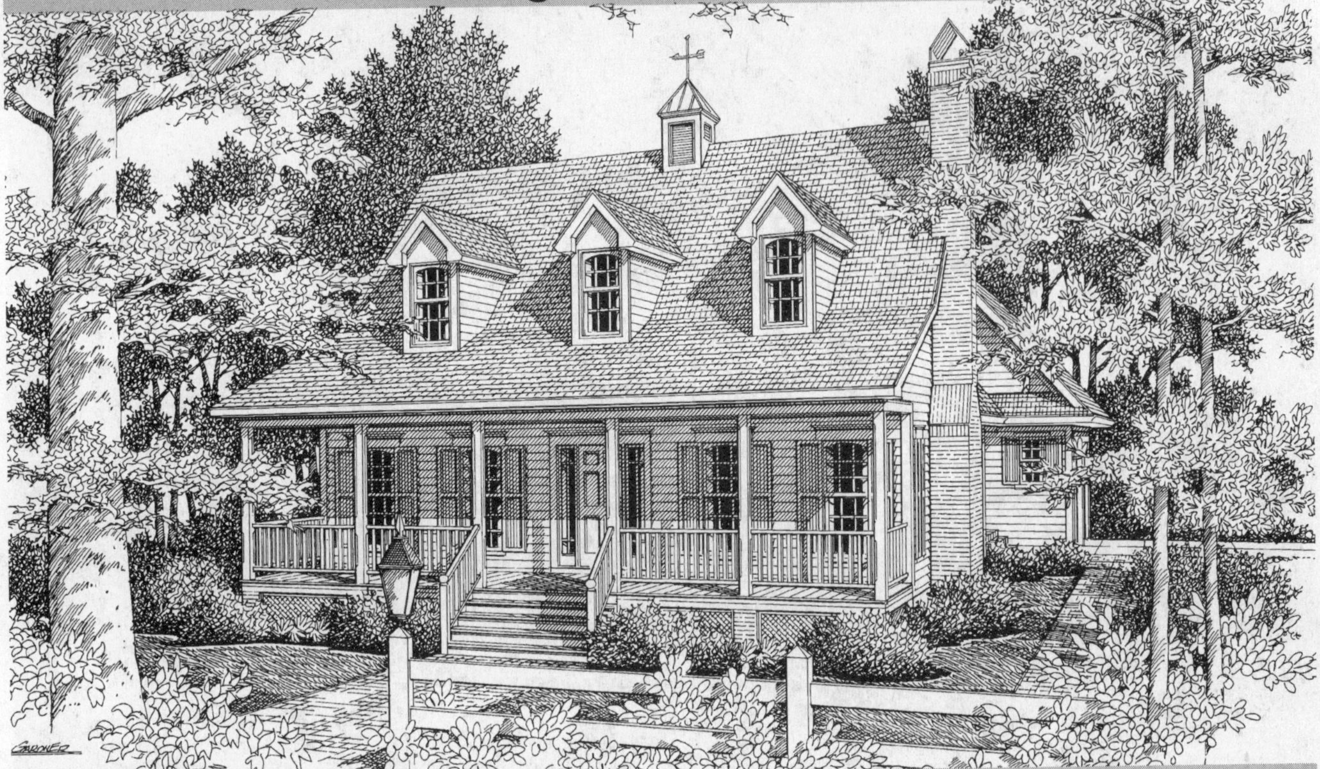

1,815 total square feet of living area

Price Code C

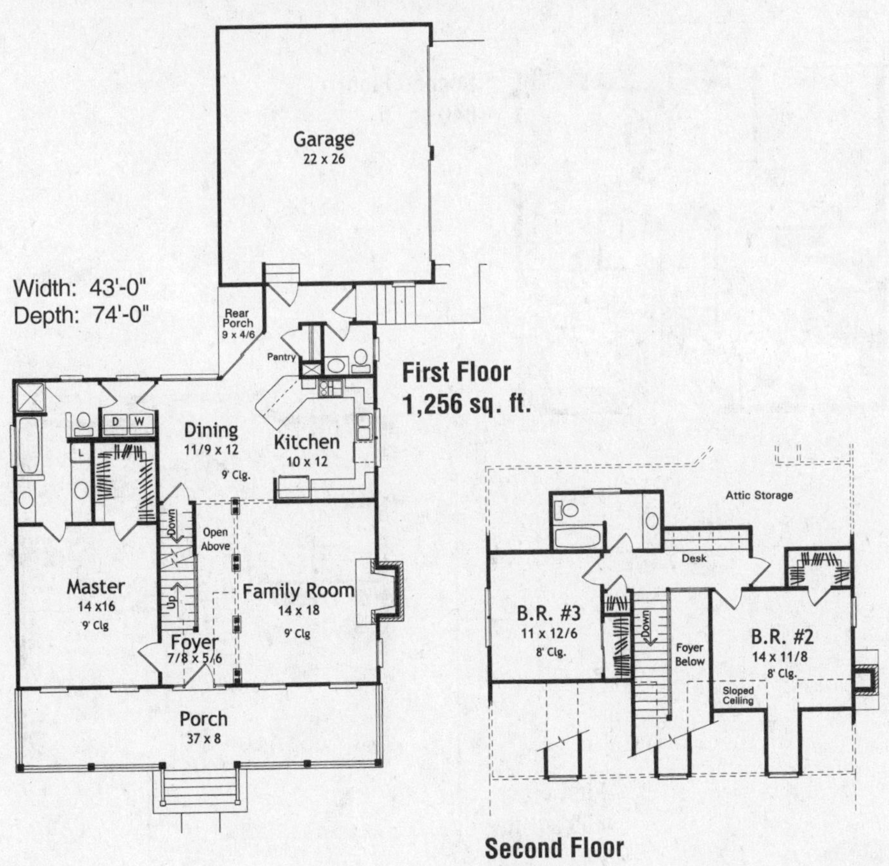

Garage
22 x 26
Width: 43'-0"
Depth: 74'-0"
Rear Porch
9 x 4/6
Pantry
Dining
11/9 x 12
9' Clg.
Kitchen
10 x 12
Master
14 x16
9' Clg
Open Above
Family Room
14 x 18
9' Clg
Foyer
7/8 x 5/6
Porch
37 x 8
First Floor
1,256 sq. ft.
Attic Storage
Desk
B.R. #3
11 x 12/6
8' Clg.
Foyer Below
B.R. #2
14 x 11/8
8' Clg.
Sloped Ceiling
Second Floor
559 sq. ft.

Special features

- Second floor has built-in desk in hall; ideal as a computer work station or mini office area
- Two doors into laundry area make it handy from master bedroom and the rest of the home
- Inviting covered porch
- Lots of counterspace and cabinetry in kitchen
- 3 bedrooms, 2 1/2 baths, 2-car side entry garage
- Basement foundation

Plan #702-DR-2590

Charming Wrap-Around Porch

1,700 total square feet of living area

Price Code B

Special features

- Energy efficient home with 2" x 6" exterior walls
- Cozy living area has plenty of space for entertaining
- Snack bar in kitchen provides extra dining area
- 3 bedrooms, 1 1/2 baths
- Basement foundation

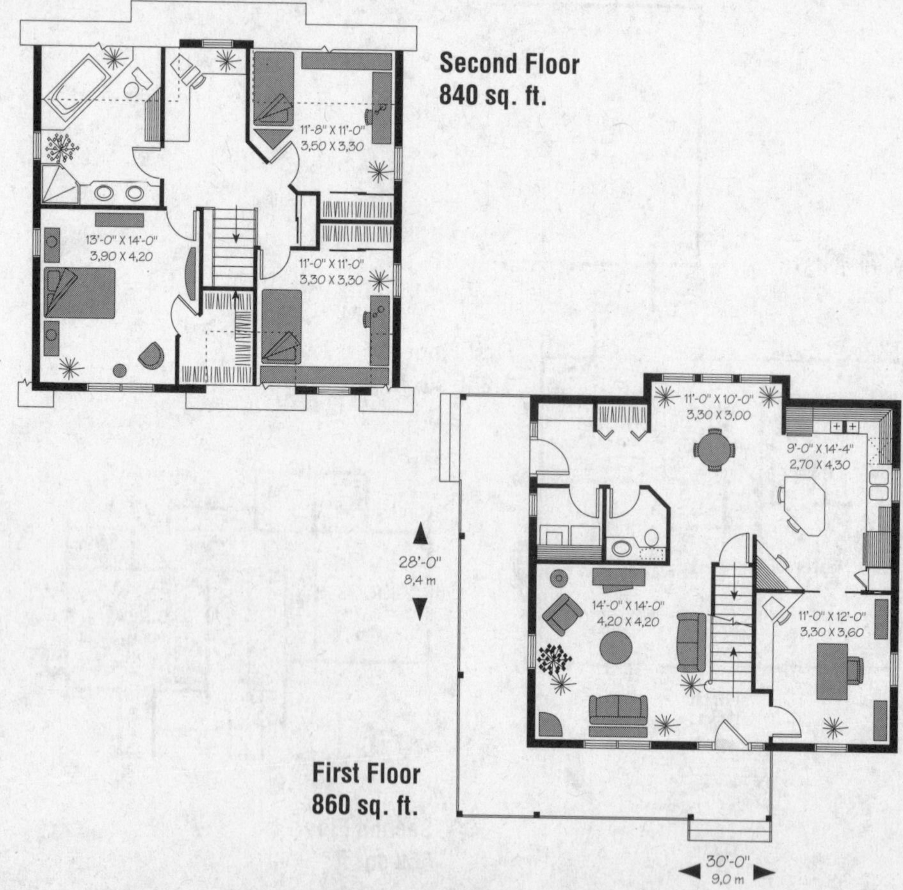
Second Floor
840 sq. ft.
11'-8" X 11'-0"
3,50 X 3,30
13'-0" X 14'-0"
3,90 X 4,20
11'-0" X 11'-0"
3,30 X 3,30
11'-0" X 10'-0"
3,30 X 3,00
9'-0" X 14'-4"
2,70 X 4,30
28'-0"
8,4 m
14'-0" X 14'-0"
4,20 X 4,20
11'-0" X 12'-0"
3,30 X 3,60
First Floor
860 sq. ft.
30'-0"
9,0 m

The Family
Handyman

Plan #702-0674

Columns Grace The Interior And Exterior

1,476 total square feet of living area

Price Code A

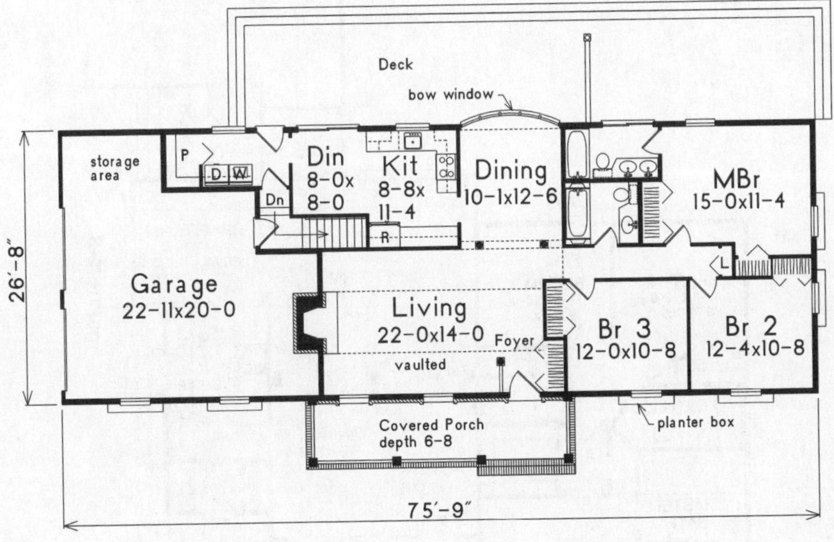

Deck
bow window
storage area
P
D W
Dn
Din 8-0x 8-0
Kit 8-8x 11-4
R
Dining 10-1x12-6
MBr 15-0x11-4
L
Garage 22-11x20-0
Living 22-0x14-0
vaulted
Foyer
Br 3 12-0x10-8
Br 2 12-4x10-8
26'-8"
Covered Porch depth 6-8
planter box
75'-9"

Special features

- Energy efficient home with 2" x 6" exterior walls
- Living room made more spacious by vaulted ceiling
- Laundry/mud room has a large pantry and accesses dining area, garage, stairs and the outdoors
- Master bedroom features bath and private deck
- Dining room is defined by columns and a large bow window
- 3 bedrooms, 2 baths, 2-car side entry garage
- Basement foundation, drawings also include slab foundation

Plan #702-LBD-17-14A

Covered Porches All Around

1,725 total square feet of living area

Price Code B

Special features

- Spectacular arches when entering foyer
- Dining room has double-doors leading to kitchen
- Unique desk area off kitchen ideal for computer work station
- 3 bedrooms, 2 baths, 2-car side entry garage
- Slab or crawl space foundation, please specify when ordering

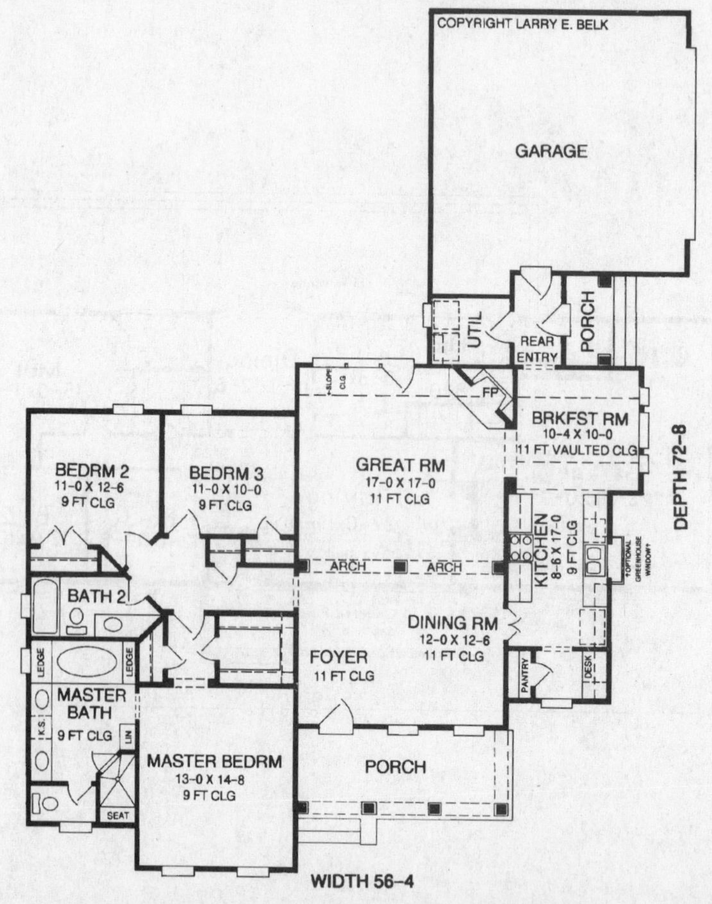

COPYRIGHT LARRY E. BELK
GARAGE
UTIL
REAR ENTRY
PORCH
FP
BRKFST RM
10-4 X 10-0
11 FT VAULTED CLG
GREAT RM
17-0 X 17-0
11 FT CLG
BEDRM 2
11-0 X 12-6
9 FT CLG
BEDRM 3
11-0 X 10-0
9 FT CLG
KITCHEN
8-6 X 17-0
9 FT CLG
DEPTH 72-8
ARCH
ARCH
BATH 2
DINING RM
12-0 X 12-6
11 FT CLG
LEDGE
LEDGE
FOYER
11 FT CLG
PANTRY
DESK
MASTER BATH
9 FT CLG
LIN
MASTER BEDRM
13-0 X 14-8
9 FT CLG
PORCH
SEAT
WIDTH 56-4

TO ORDER BLUEPRINTS USE THE FORM ON PAGE 19 OR CALL TOLL-FREE 1-877-671-6036

View thousands more home plans online at www.familyhandyman.com/homeplans

Plan #702-0210

Trim Layout Separates Living Area

2,361 total square feet of living area

Price Code D

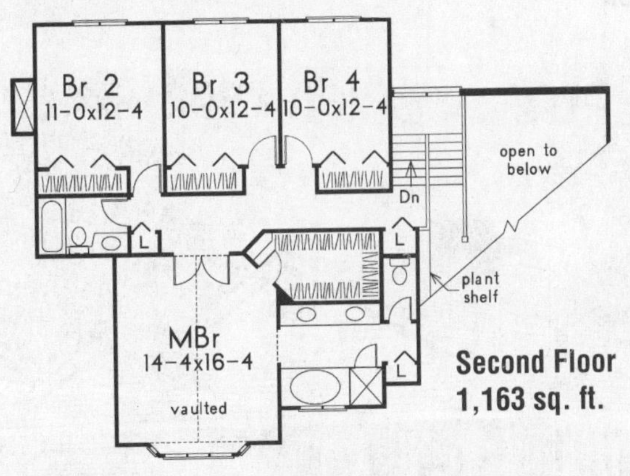
Br 2
11-0x12-4
Br 3
10-0x12-4
Br 4
10-0x12-4
open to below
Dn
plant shelf
MBr
14-4x16-4
vaulted

Second Floor
1,163 sq. ft.

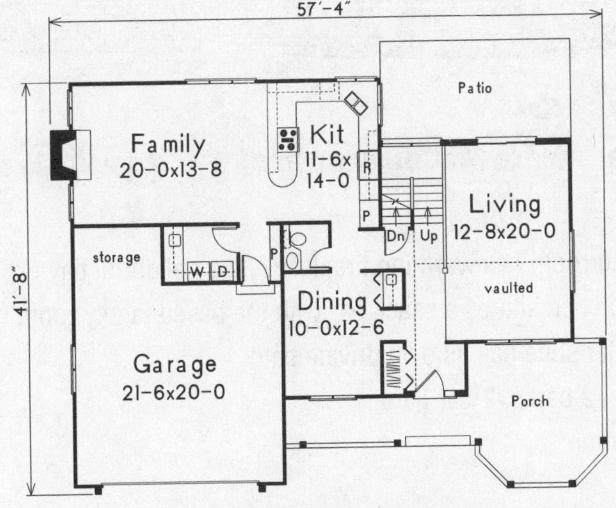
57'-4"
41'-8"
Patio
Family
20-0x13-8
Kit
11-6x
14-0
R
P
Dn
Up
Living
12-8x20-0
vaulted
storage
W D
P
Dining
10-0x12-6
Garage
21-6x20-0
Porch

First Floor
1,198 sq. ft.

Special features

- Octagon-shaped front porch is the focal point of this facade
- Large living room with a vaulted ceiling couples the front porch with the rear patio for open entertaining
- Family room with fireplace and kitchen with ample breakfast bar are situated in a secluded corner
- Master suite boasts a vaulted ceiling and oversized bay window
- 4 bedrooms, 2 1/2 baths, 2-car garage
- Basement foundation

Narrow Lot Design — Plan #702-MG-97099

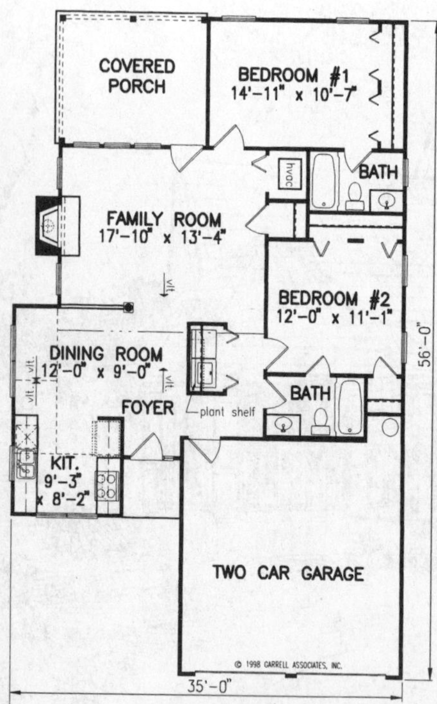
COVERED PORCH
BEDROOM #1
14'-11" x 10'-7"
BATH
hvac
FAMILY ROOM
17'-10" x 13'-4"
BEDROOM #2
12'-0" x 11'-1"
DINING ROOM
12'-0" x 9'-0"
FOYER
plant shelf
BATH
KIT.
9'-3" x 8'-2"
TWO CAR GARAGE
© 1998 GARRELL ASSOCIATES, INC.
35'-0"
56'-0"

1,093 total square feet of living area **Price Code AA**

Special features

- Family room with fireplace overlooks large covered porch
- Vaulted family and dining rooms are adjacent to kitchen
- Bedroom #2 has its own entrance into bath
- Plant shelf accents vaulted foyer
- Centrally located laundry area
- 2 bedrooms, 2 baths, 2-car garage
- Slab foundation

Simple Rooflines And Inviting Porch — Plan #702-HP-C460

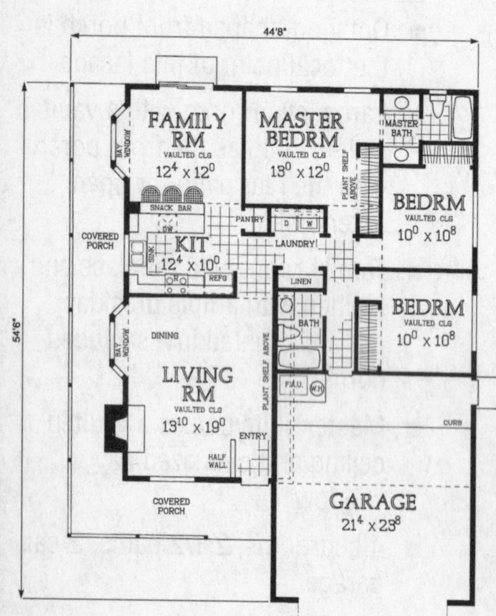
44'8"
54'6"
FAMILY RM
VAULTED CLG
12⁴ x 12⁰
MASTER BEDRM
VAULTED CLG
13⁰ x 12⁰
MASTER BATH
BEDRM
VAULTED CLG
10⁰ x 10⁸
SNACK BAR
PANTRY
KIT
12⁴ x 10⁰
LAUNDRY
REFG
COVERED PORCH
LINEN
BEDRM
VAULTED CLG
10⁰ x 10⁸
DINING
BATH
LIVING RM
VAULTED CLG
13¹⁰ x 19⁰
PLANT SHELF ABOVE
ENTRY
HALF WALL
CURB
COVERED PORCH
GARAGE
21⁴ x 23⁸

1,389 total square feet of living area **Price Code A**

Special features

- Formal living room has warming fireplace and a delightful bay window
- U-shaped kitchen shares a snack bar with the bayed family room
- Lovely master suite has its own private bath
- 3 bedrooms, 2 baths, 2-car garage
- Slab foundation

The Family
Handyman

Plan #702-HP-C619

Graceful Southern Hospitality

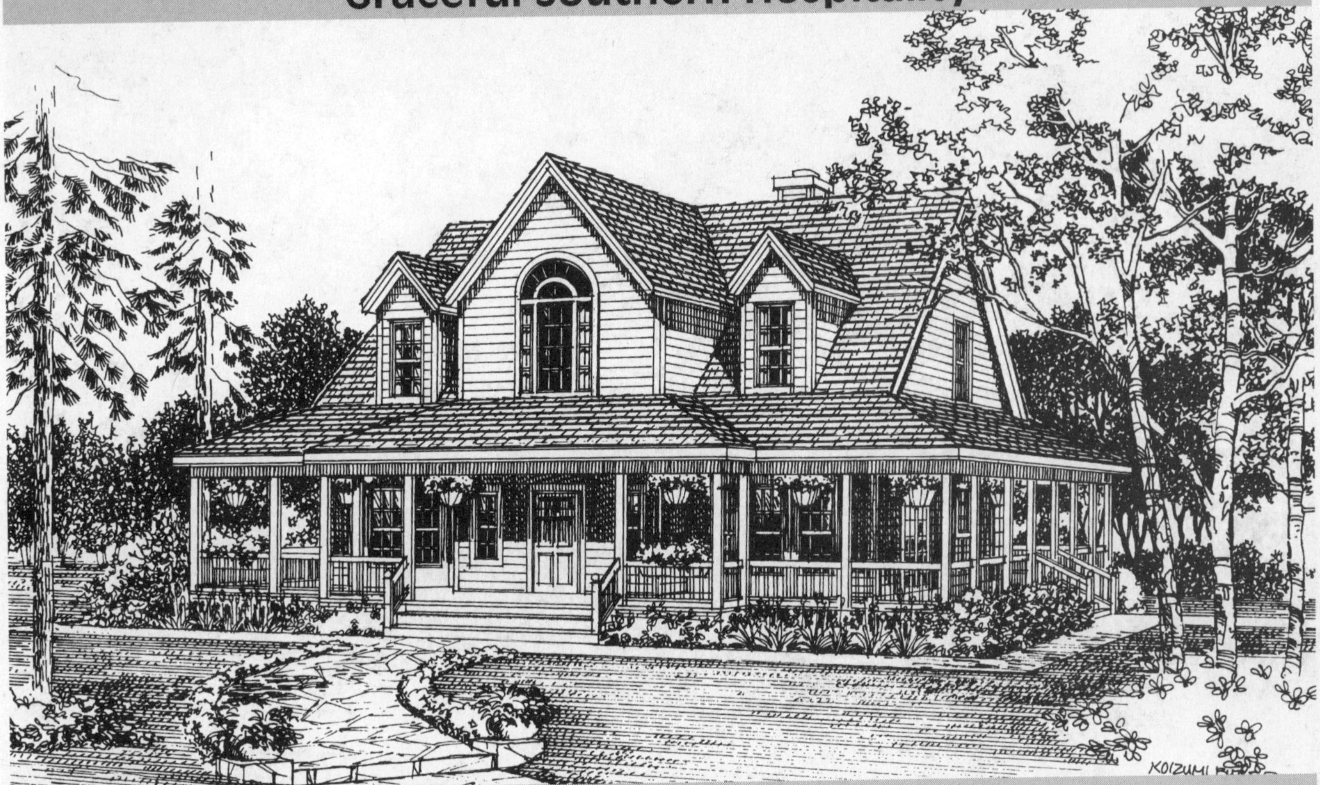

1,771 total square feet of living area

Price Code B

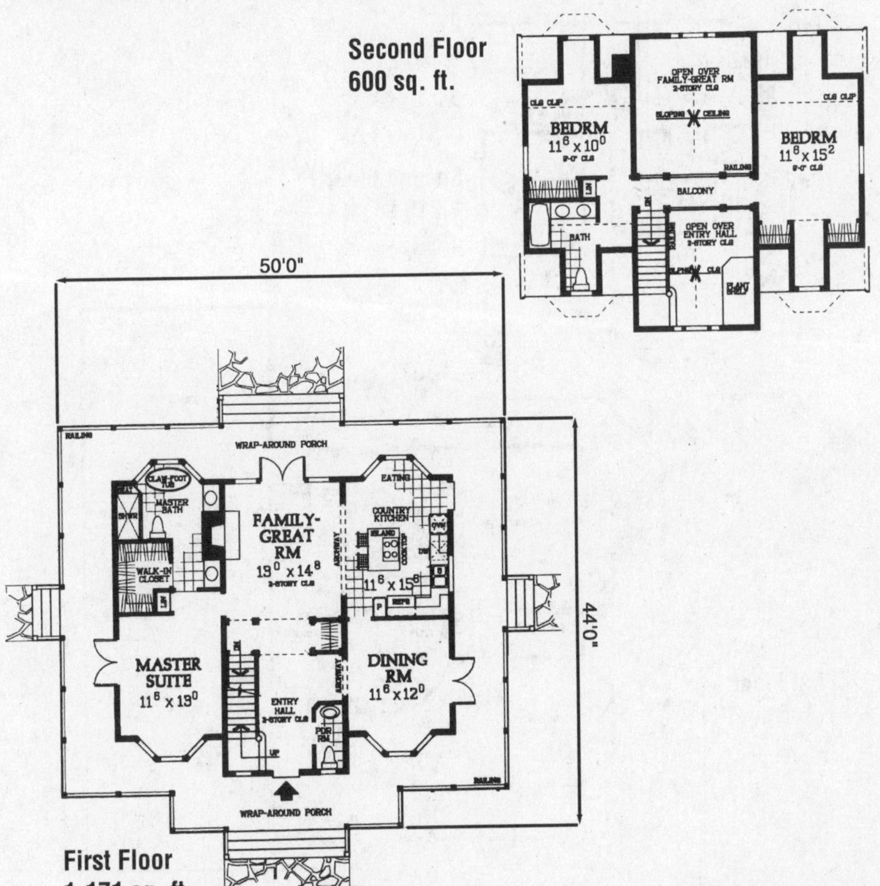
BEDRM
11⁶ x 10⁰
OPEN OVER
FAMILY-GREAT RM
2-STORY CLG
BEDRM
11⁸ x 15²
BALCONY
BATH
OPEN OVER
ENTRY HALL
2-STORY CLG
50'0"
44'0"
WRAP-AROUND PORCH
MASTER BATH
WALK-IN CLOSET
FAMILY-GREAT RM
13⁰ x 14⁸
2-STORY CLG
EATING
COUNTRY KITCHEN
11⁶ x 15⁸
MASTER SUITE
11⁸ x 13⁰
ENTRY HALL
2-STORY CLG
DINING RM
11⁶ x 12⁰
PDR RM
WRAP-AROUND PORCH

Second Floor
600 sq. ft.

First Floor
1,171 sq. ft.

Special features

- Efficient country kitchen shares space with a bayed eating area
- Two-story family/great room is warmed by a fireplace in winter and open to outdoor country comfort in the summer with double French doors
- First floor master suite offers a bay window and access to the porch through French doors
- 3 bedrooms, 2 1/2 baths, optional detached 2-car garage
- Basement foundation

Plan #702-1309

Terrific Custom-Style Victorian Makes Impression

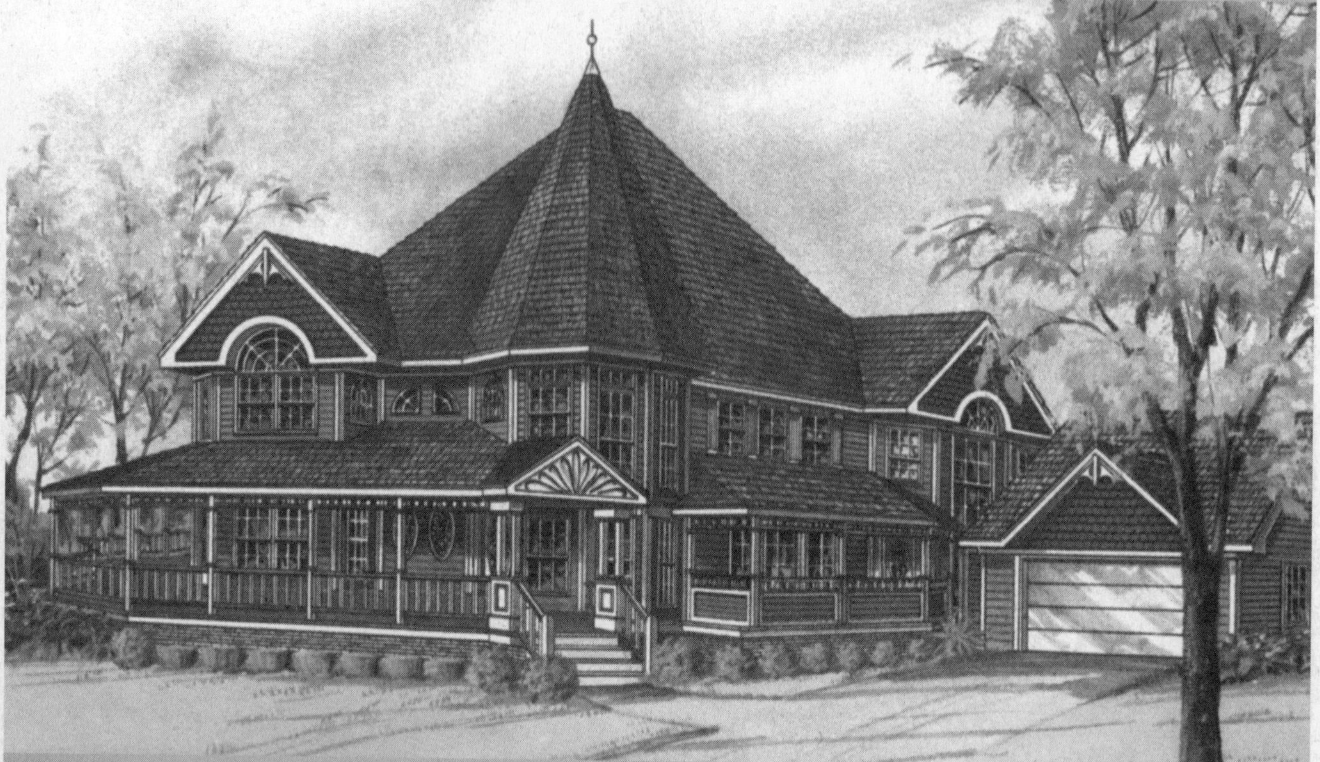

2,562 total square feet of living area

Price Code D

Special features

- Numerous bay windows create a design unlike any other
- Enormous master suite has private bath with step-up tub-in-a-bay
- Double stairways make any room easily accessible
- Cheerful breakfast room extends onto covered private porch
- 3 bedrooms, 2 1/2 baths, 2-car garage
- Basement foundation

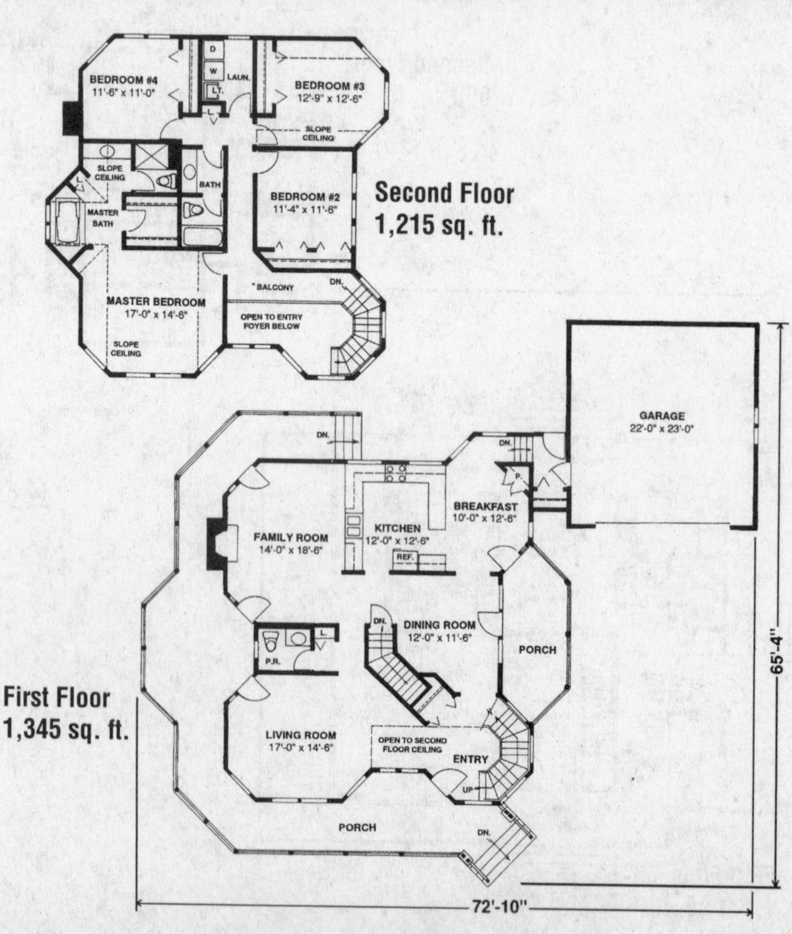
BEDROOM #4
11'-6" x 11'-0"
LAUN.
BEDROOM #3
12'-9" x 12'-6"
SLOPE CEILING
BATH
MASTER BATH
BEDROOM #2
11'-4" x 11'-6"
BALCONY
MASTER BEDROOM
17'-0" x 14'-6"
OPEN TO ENTRY FOYER BELOW
SLOPE CEILING
GARAGE
22'-0" x 23'-0"
BREAKFAST
10'-0" x 12'-6"
KITCHEN
12'-0" x 12'-6"
FAMILY ROOM
14'-0" x 18'-6"
REF.
DINING ROOM
12'-0" x 11'-6"
P.R.
PORCH
LIVING ROOM
17'-0" x 14'-6"
OPEN TO SECOND FLOOR CEILING
ENTRY
PORCH
65'-4"
72'-10"

Second Floor
1,215 sq. ft.

First Floor
1,345 sq. ft.

Plan #702-0491

Covered Porch Highlights This Home

1,808 total square feet of living area

Price Code C

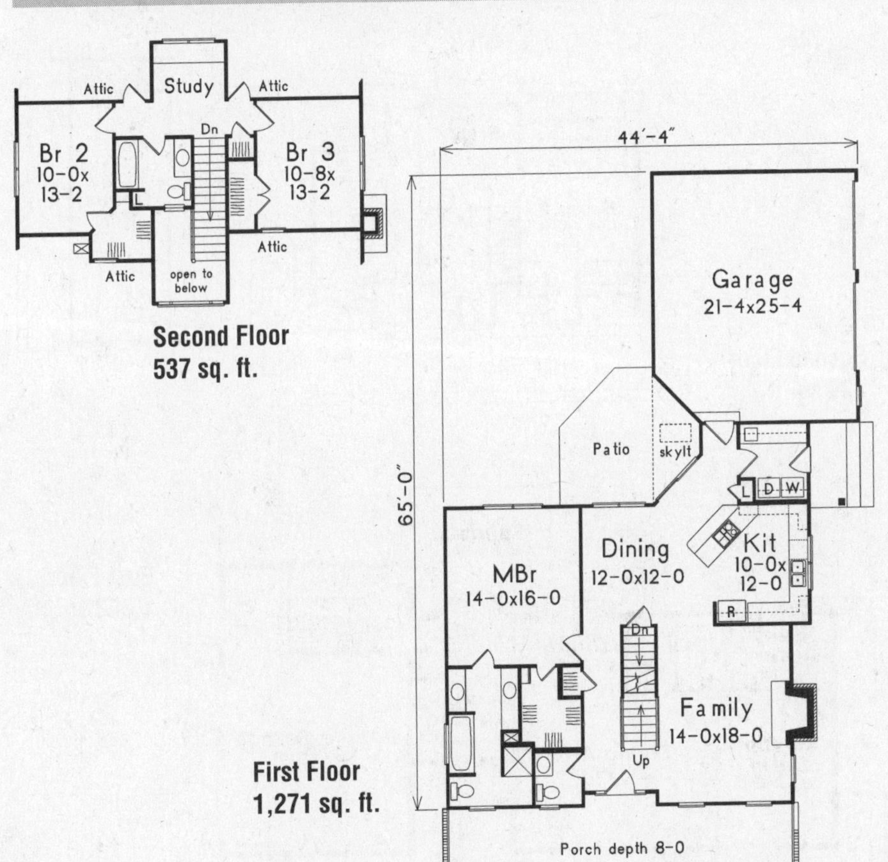
Study
Attic
Attic
Br 2
10-0x
13-2
Dn
Br 3
10-8x
13-2
Attic
Attic
open to below
44'-4"
65'-0"
Garage
21-4x25-4
Patio
skylt
L
D
W
Kit
10-0x
12-0
Dining
12-0x12-0
MBr
14-0x16-0
R
Dn
Family
14-0x18-0
Up
Porch depth 8-0

Second Floor
537 sq. ft.

First Floor
1,271 sq. ft.

Special features

- Master bedroom has a walk-in closet, double vanities and separate tub and shower
- Two second floor bedrooms share a study area and full bath
- Partially covered patio is complete with a skylight
- Side entrance opens to utility room with convenient counterspace and laundry sink
- 3 bedrooms, 2 1/2 baths, 2-car side entry garage
- Basement foundation

Plan #702-JV-2091-A

Open Floor Plan With Plenty Of Light

2,475 total square feet of living area

Price Code D

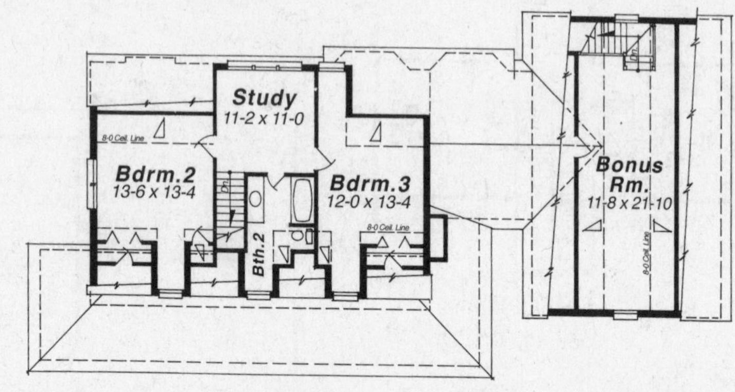
Study
11-2 x 11-0
Bdrm.2
13-6 x 13-4
Bdrm.3
12-0 x 13-4
Bth.2
Bonus Rm.
11-8 x 21-10

Second Floor
729 sq. ft.

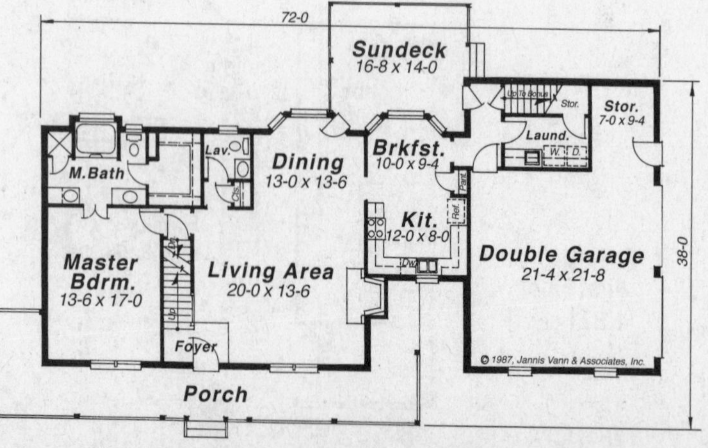
72-0
Sundeck
16-8 x 14-0
M.Bath
Lav.
Dining
13-0 x 13-6
Brkfst.
10-0 x 9-4
Laund.
Stor.
7-0 x 9-4
Kit.
12-0 x 8-0
Master Bdrm.
13-6 x 17-0
Living Area
20-0 x 13-6
Double Garage
21-4 x 21-8
38-0
Foyer
Porch
© 1987, Jannis Vann & Associates, Inc.

First Floor
1,362 sq. ft.

Special features

- Country feeling with wrap-around porch and dormered front
- Open floor plan with living and dining areas combined has access to a sun deck
- First floor master bedroom with many luxuries
- Bonus room on the second floor has an additional 384 square feet of living area
- 3 bedrooms, 2 1/2 baths, 2-car side entry garage
- Walk-out basement foundation

Plan #702-0285

Gallery Opens Into Grand Living Room

2,648 total square feet of living area **Price Code E**

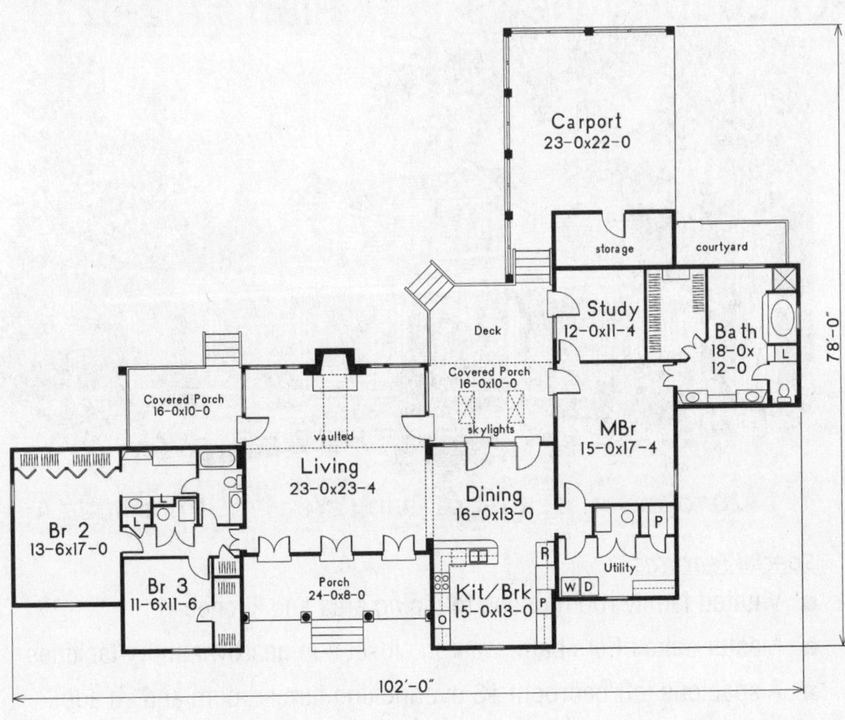

Carport
23-0x22-0
storage
courtyard
Study
12-0x11-4
Bath
18-0x
12-0
Deck
Covered Porch
16-0x10-0
skylights
Covered Porch
16-0x10-0
vaulted
Living
23-0x23-4
MBr
15-0x17-4
Dining
16-0x13-0
Br 2
13-6x17-0
Br 3
11-6x11-6
Porch
24-0x8-0
Kit/Brk
15-0x13-0
Utility
78'-0"
102'-0"

Special features

- Private study with access to master bedroom and porch
- Grand-sized living room with sloped ceiling, fireplace and entry to porches
- Energy efficient home with 2" x 6" exterior walls
- Master suite boasts expansive bath with separate vanities, large walk-in closet and separate tub and shower units
- Large kitchen with eating area and breakfast bar
- 3 bedrooms, 2 baths, 2-car carport
- Crawl space foundation, drawings also include slab foundation

Classic Ranch With Expansive Porch Plan #702-0690

1,400 total square feet of living area Price Code A

Special features

- Master bedroom is secluded for privacy
- Large utility room with additional cabinet space
- Covered porch provides an outdoor seating area
- Roof dormers add great curb appeal
- Vaulted ceilings in living room and master bedroom
- Oversized two-car garage with storage
- 3 bedrooms, 2 baths, 2-car garage
- Basement foundation, drawings also include crawl space foundation

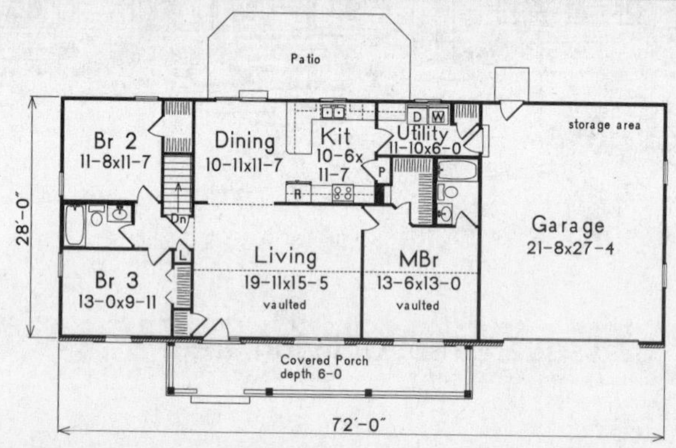
Patio
Br 2
11-8x11-7
Dining
10-11x11-7
Kit
10-6x
11-7
D W
Utility
11-10x6-0
storage area
Dn
P
R
28'-0"
Garage
21-8x27-4
Br 3
13-0x9-11
Living
19-11x15-5
vaulted
MBr
13-6x13-0
vaulted
Covered Porch
depth 6-0
72'-0"

Surrounding Porch For Country Views Plan #702-0726

1,428 total square feet of living area Price Code A

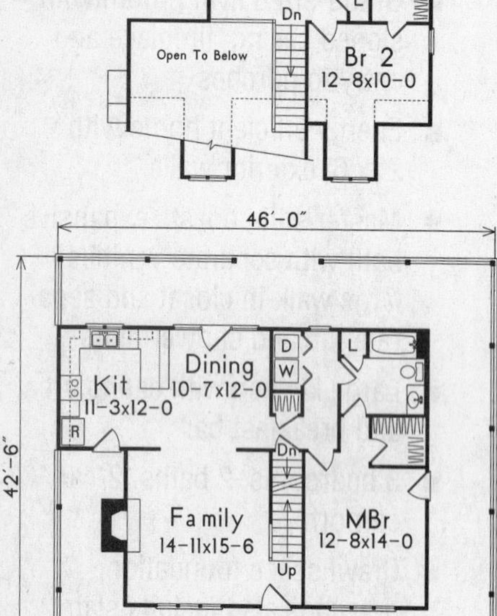
Second Floor
415 sq. ft.
Loft/
Br 3
10-7x11-11
Dn
L
Open To Below
Br 2
12-8x10-0
46'-0"
42'-6"
Kit
11-3x12-0
R
Dining
10-7x12-0
D
W
L
Dn
Family
14-11x15-6
MBr
12-8x14-0
Up
Covered Porch
depth 7-0

First Floor
1,013 sq. ft.

Special features

- Vaulted family room opens to dining area and kitchen
- Master suite offers bath, walk-in closet and nearby laundry facilities
- A spacious loft/bedroom #3 overlooking family room and an additional bedroom and bath conclude the second floor
- 3 bedrooms, 2 baths
- Basement foundation

Plan #702-0723

1,784 total square feet of living area

Price Code B

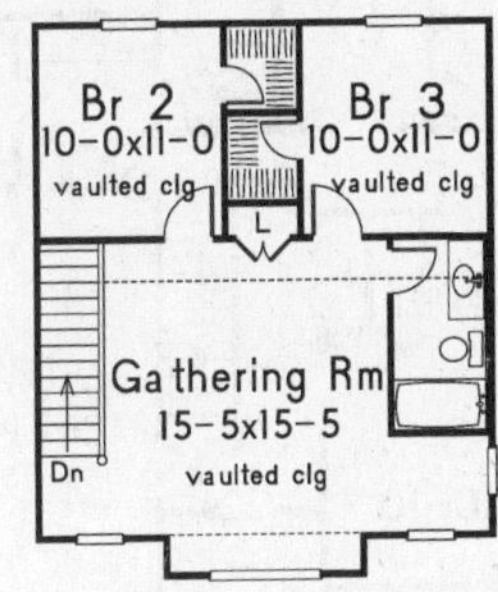
Br 2
10-0x11-0
vaulted clg
Br 3
10-0x11-0
vaulted clg
L
Gathering Rm
15-5x15-5
vaulted clg
Dn

Second Floor
672 sq. ft.

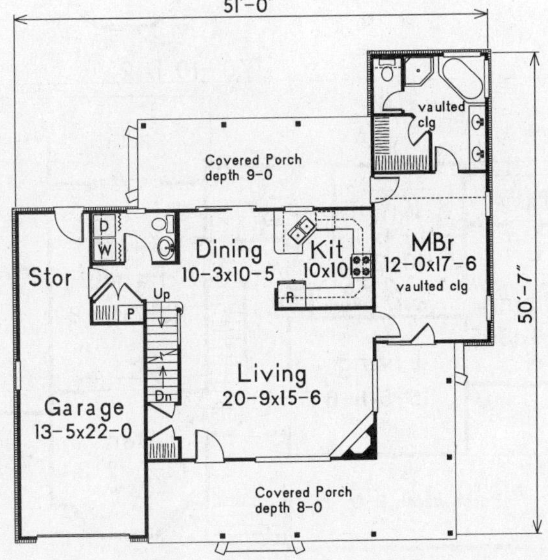
51'-0"
50'-7"
vaulted clg
Covered Porch
depth 9-0
D
W
Dining
10-3x10-5
Kit
10x10
R
MBr
12-0x17-6
vaulted clg
Stor
Up
P
Living
20-9x15-6
Dn
Garage
13-5x22-0
Covered Porch
depth 8-0

First Floor
1,112 sq. ft.

Special features

- Spacious living area with corner fireplace offers a cheerful atmosphere with large windows
- Large second floor gathering room is great for kid's play area
- Secluded master suite has separate porch entrances and large master bath with walk-in closet
- 3 bedrooms, 2 1/2 baths, 1-car garage
- Basement foundation, drawings also include crawl space foundation

Plan #702-0526

Two-Story Offers Attractive Exterior

2,262 total square feet of living area

Price Code D

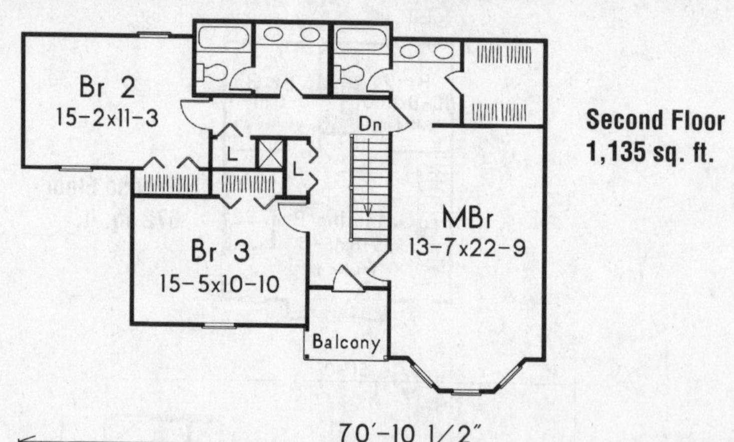
Br 2
15-2x11-3
Dn
L
L
MBr
13-7x22-9
Br 3
15-5x10-10
Balcony

Second Floor
1,135 sq. ft.

Special features

- Charming exterior features include large front porch, two patios, front balcony and double bay windows
- Den provides impressive entry to sunken family room
- Conveniently located first floor laundry
- Large master bedroom with walk-in closet, dressing area and bath
- 3 bedrooms, 2 1/2 baths, 2-car rear entry garage
- Crawl space foundation, drawings also include basement and slab foundations

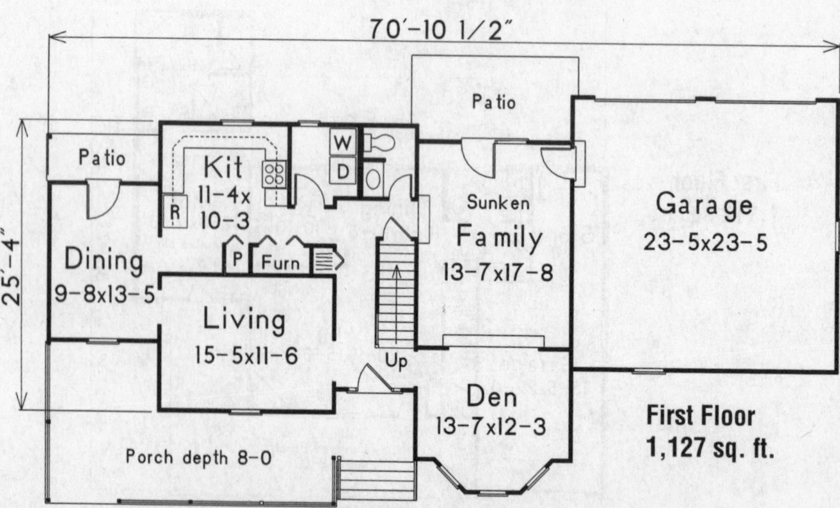
70'-10 1/2"
25'-4"
Patio
Patio
Kit
11-4x
10-3
W
D
R
Sunken
Family
13-7x17-8
Garage
23-5x23-5
Dining
9-8x13-5
P
Furn
Living
15-5x11-6
Up
Den
13-7x12-3
Porch depth 8-0

First Floor
1,127 sq. ft.

The Family
Handyman

Plan #702-AP-1612

Appealing Charming Porch

1,643 total square feet of living area

Price Code B

STORAGE
Second Floor
579 sq. ft.
BEDROOM 3
15X12
DN
OPEN TO BELOW
BEDROOM 2
15X12
DECK
SKYLIGHT
DINING
12x12
KITCHEN
10x12
VAULT
COATS
D
W
34
DN
VAULT
UP
MASTER BEDRM
15x13
FAMILY ROOM
18x15
First Floor
1,064 sq. ft.
38

Special features

- First floor master bedroom has private bath, walk-in closet and easy access to laundry closet
- Comfortable family room features a vaulted ceiling and a cozy fireplace
- Two bedrooms on the second floor share a bath
- 3 bedrooms, 2 1/2 baths, 2-car drive under garage
- Basement or crawl space foundation, please specify when ordering

Plan #702-SH-SEA-242

Vaulted Ceilings Add A Sense Of Spaciousness

1,408 total square feet of living area **Price Code A**

<u>*Special features*</u>

- A bright country kitchen boasts an abundance of counterspace and cupboards
- The front entry is sheltered by a broad verandah
- A spa tub is brightened by a box bay window in the master bath
- 3 bedrooms, 2 baths, 2-car side entry garage
- Basement or crawl space foundation, please specify when ordering

Width: 70'-0"
Depth: 28'-0"

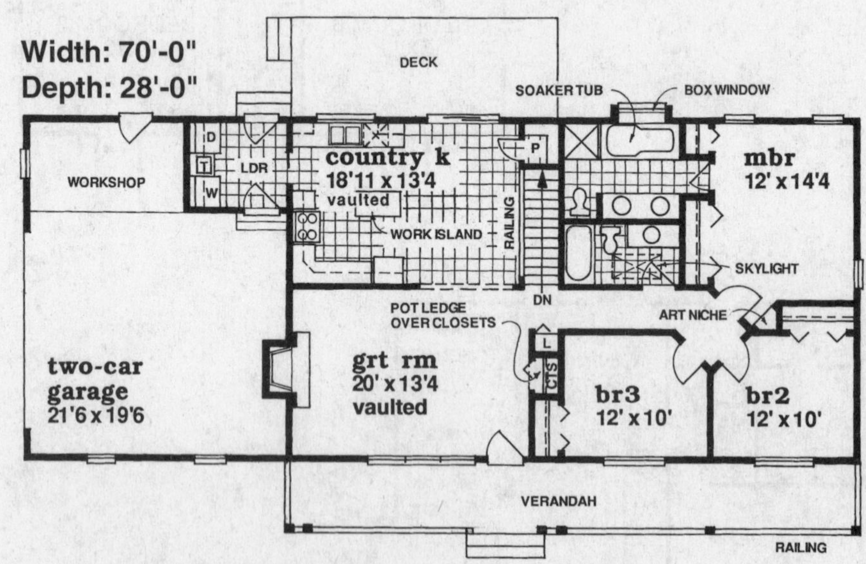
DECK
SOAKER TUB
BOX WINDOW
D
T
W
LDR
WORKSHOP
country k
18'11 x 13'4
vaulted
P
WORK ISLAND
RAILING
mbr
12' x 14'4
SKYLIGHT
DN
POT LEDGE OVER CLOSETS
ART NICHE
L
CTS
two-car garage
21'6 x 19'6
grt rm
20' x 13'4
vaulted
br3
12' x 10'
br2
12' x 10'
VERANDAH
RAILING

The Family
Handyman

Plan #702-0722

Wrap-Around Porch Creates A Comfortable Feel

2,266 total square feet of living area **Price Code D**

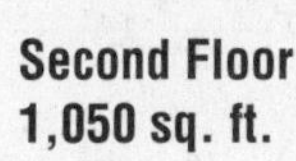
Second Floor
1,050 sq. ft.

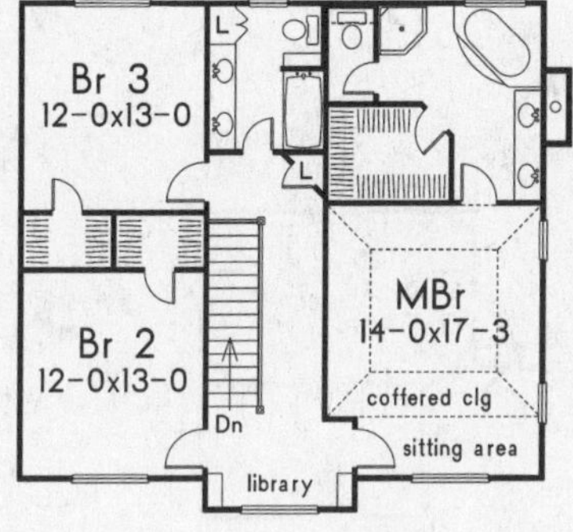
Br 3
12-0x13-0
Br 2
12-0x13-0
MBr
14-0x17-3
coffered clg
sitting area
library
Dn

First Floor
1,216 sq. ft.

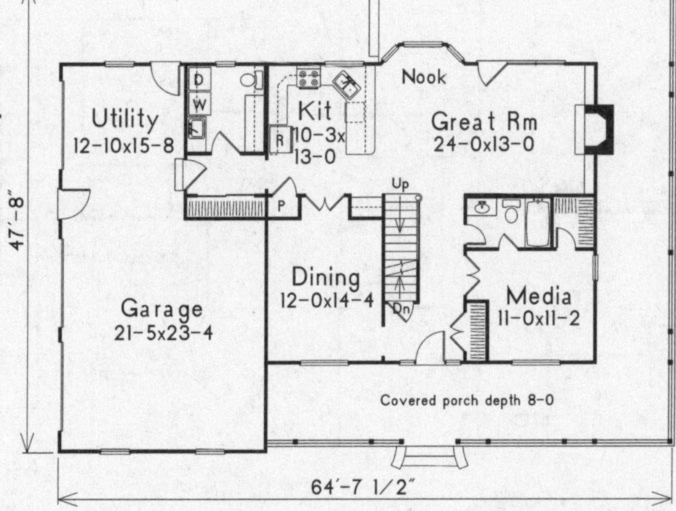
Utility
12-10x15-8
D
W
Kit
10-3x
13-0
R
Nook
Great Rm
24-0x13-0
P
Up
Dining
12-0x14-4
Dn
Media
11-0x11-2
Garage
21-5x23-4
Covered porch depth 8-0
47'-8"
64'-7 1/2"

Special features

- Great room includes fireplace flanked by built-in bookshelves and dining nook with bay window
- Unique media room includes double-door entrance, walk-in closet and access to full bath
- Master suite has lovely sitting area, walk-in closets and a private bath with step-up tub and double vanity
- 3 bedrooms, 3 baths, 2-car side entry garage
- Basement foundation, drawings also include crawl space foundation

TO ORDER BLUEPRINTS USE THE FORM ON PAGE 19 OR CALL TOLL-FREE 1-877-671-6036

Plan #702-CHP-3244-B-18

Two-Story Has A Farmhouse Feel

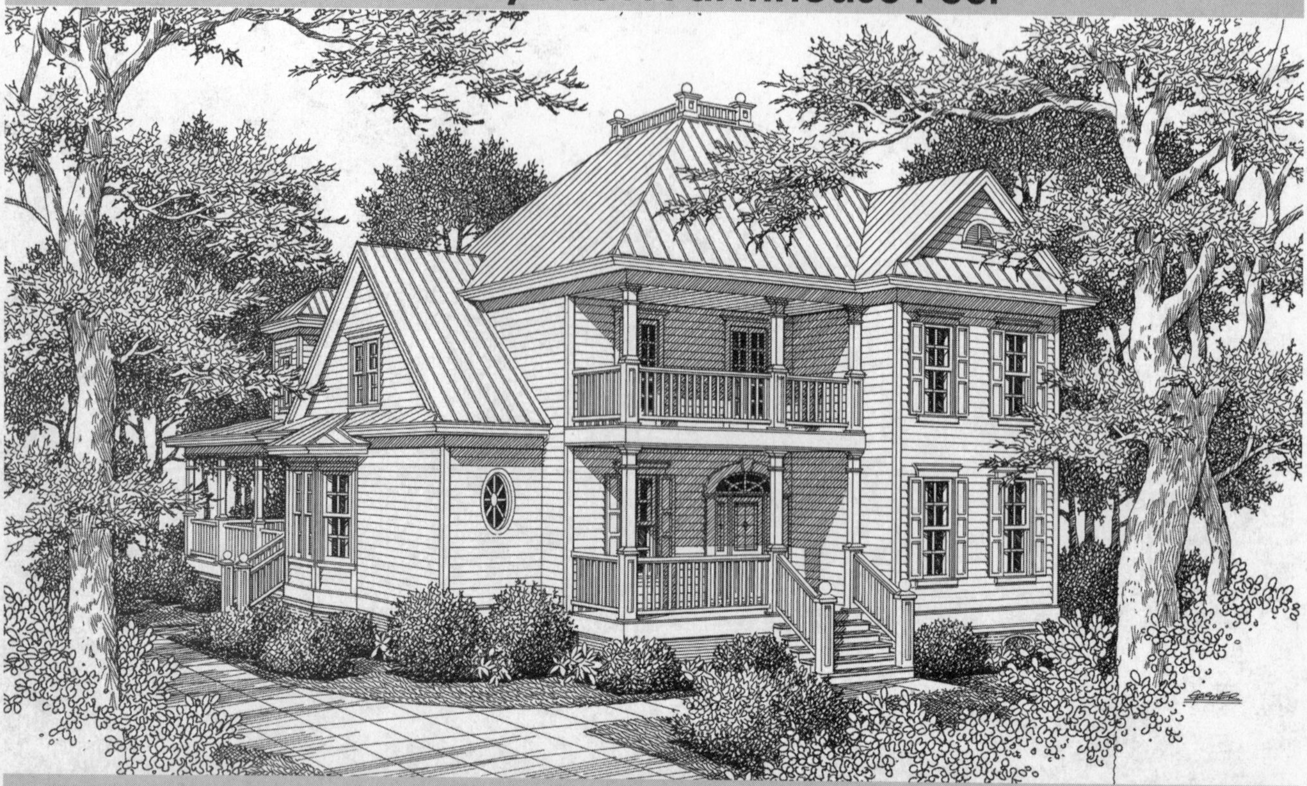

3,444 total square feet of living area

Price Code G

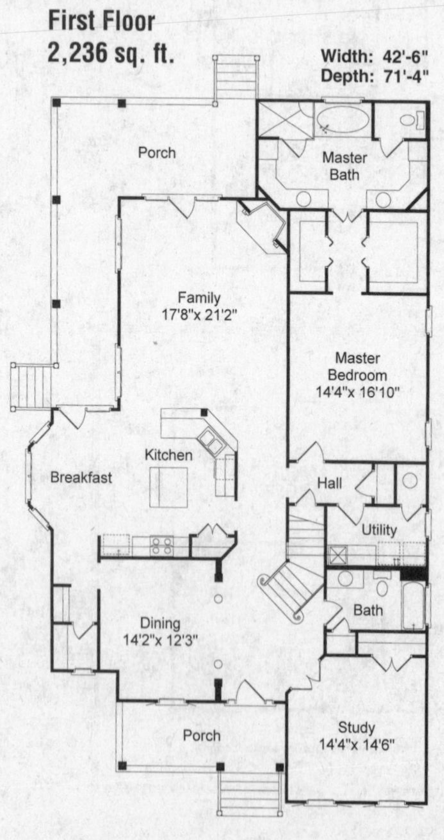
First Floor
2,236 sq. ft.
Width: 42'-6"
Depth: 71'-4"
Porch
Master Bath
Family
17'8"x 21'2"
Master Bedroom
14'4"x 16'10"
Kitchen
Breakfast
Hall
Utility
Bath
Dining
14'2"x 12'3"
Porch
Study
14'4"x 14'6"

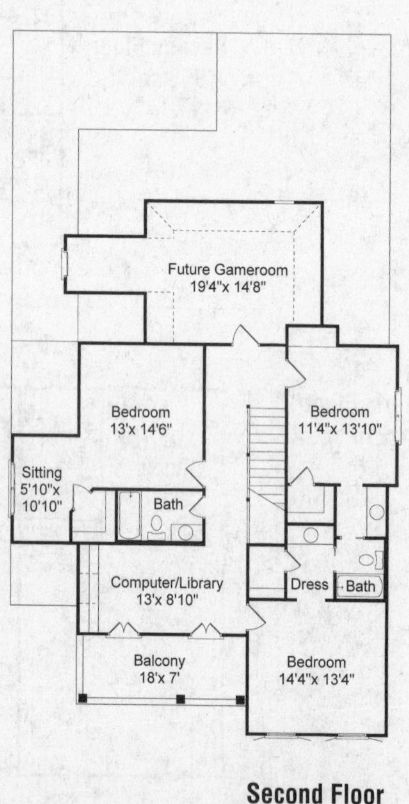
Future Gameroom
19'4"x 14'8"
Bedroom
13'x 14'6"
Bedroom
11'4"x 13'10"
Sitting
5'10"x 10'10"
Bath
Computer/Library
13'x 8'10"
Dress
Bath
Balcony
18'x 7'
Bedroom
14'4"x 13'4"
Second Floor
1,208 sq. ft.

Special features

- Lavish master bath has double vanities and walk-in closets
- Kitchen has a wonderful food preparation island that doubles as extra dining space
- Computer/library area on second floor has two sets of double-doors leading onto a second floor balcony
- Future gameroom on second floor has an additional 318 square feet of living area
- 5 bedrooms, 4 baths, 2-car detached garage
- Crawl space foundation

Plan #702-0156

Spacious Styling For Gracious Living

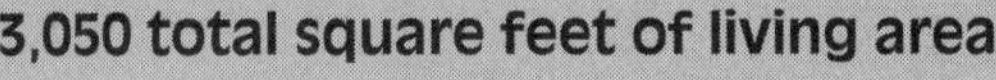

3,050 total square feet of living area **Price Code E**

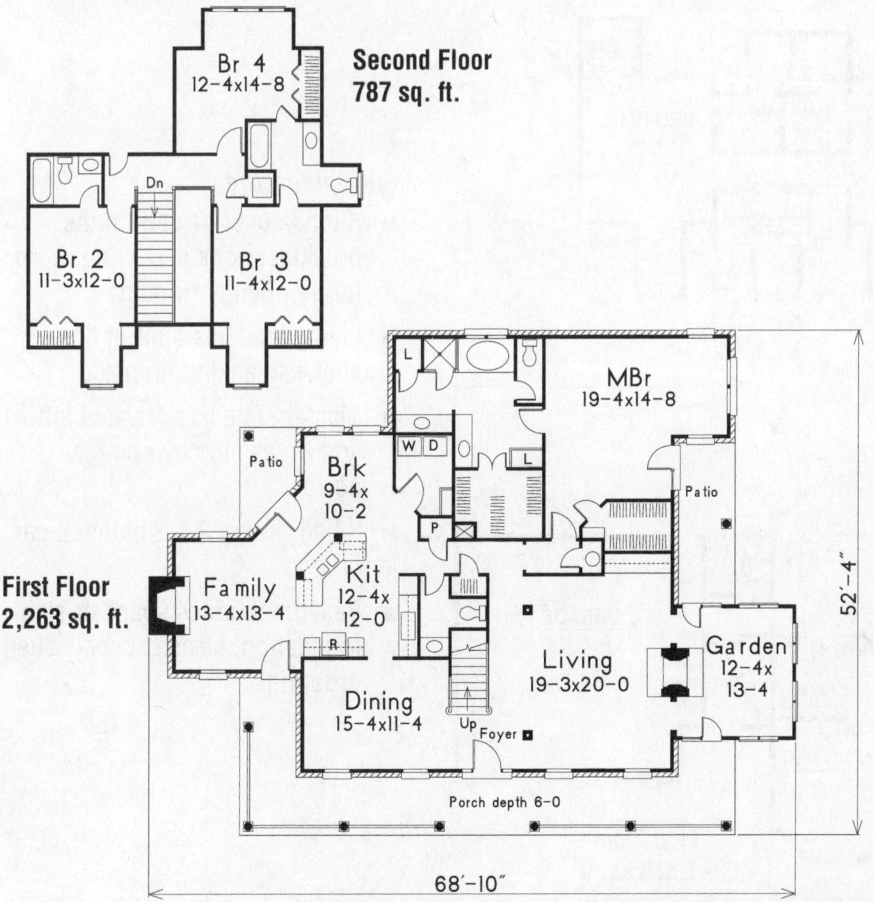
Br 4
12-4x14-8
Second Floor
787 sq. ft.
Dn
Br 2
11-3x12-0
Br 3
11-4x12-0
L
MBr
19-4x14-8
W D
L
P
Patio
Brk
9-4x
10-2
Patio
Kit
12-4x
12-0
First Floor
2,263 sq. ft.
Family
13-4x13-4
R
Living
19-3x20-0
Garden
12-4x
13-4
52'-4"
Dining
15-4x11-4
Up
Foyer
Porch depth 6-0
68'-10"

Special features

- Sunny garden room and two-way fireplace create a bright, airy living room
- Front porch enhanced by arched transom windows and bold columns
- Sitting alcove, French door access to side patio, walk-in closets and abundant storage in master bedroom
- 4 bedrooms, 3 1/2 baths, 2-car detached garage
- Slab foundation, drawings also include crawl space foundation

Plan #702-RDD-1895-9

Bath With Double Dressing Areas

1,895 total square feet of living area **Price Code C**

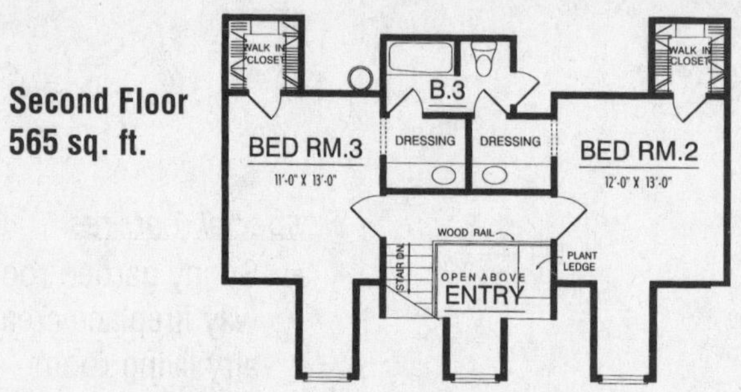
WALK IN CLOSET
B.3
WALK IN CLOSET
BED RM.3
11'-0" X 13'-0"
DRESSING
DRESSING
BED RM.2
12'-0" X 13'-0"
WOOD RAIL
STAIR DN
OPEN ABOVE
ENTRY
PLANT LEDGE

Second Floor
565 sq. ft.

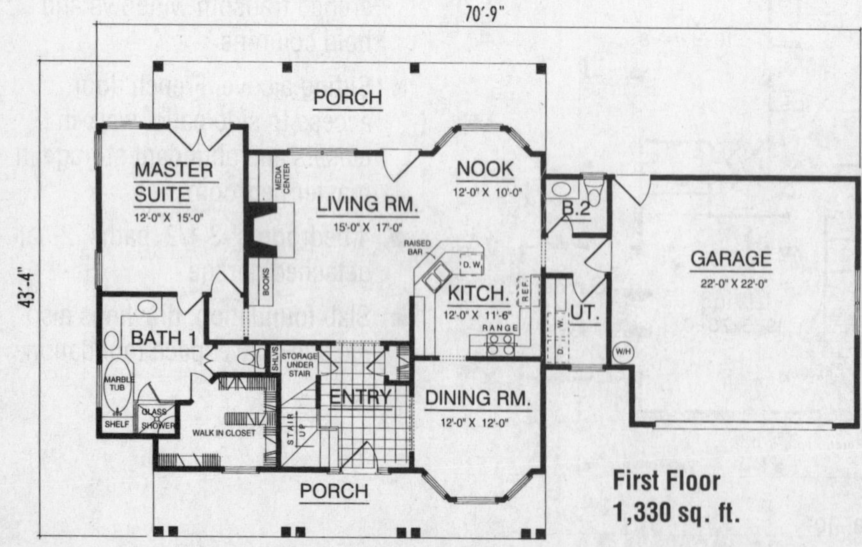
70'-9"
43'-4"
PORCH
MASTER SUITE
12'-0" X 15'-0"
MEDIA CENTER
LIVING RM.
15'-0" X 17'-0"
NOOK
12'-0" X 10'-0"
B.2
RAISED BAR
D.W.
KITCH.
12'-0" X 11'-6"
REF.
RANGE
UT.
W/H
GARAGE
22'-0" X 22'-0"
BOOKS
BATH 1
MARBLE TUB
GLASS SHOWER
SHELF
WALK IN CLOSET
SHLVS
STORAGE UNDER STAIR
ENTRY
DINING RM.
12'-0" X 12'-0"
STAIR UP
PORCH

First Floor
1,330 sq. ft.

Special features

- Kitchen overlooks both the breakfast nook and living room for an open floor plan
- Living area has built-in bookshelves flanking fireplace
- Master suite has private bath and access to covered rear porch
- 3 bedrooms, 2 1/2 baths, 2-car garage
- Basement, crawl space or slab foundation, please specify when ordering

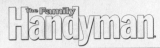

Cozy Columned Archway Defines Foyer

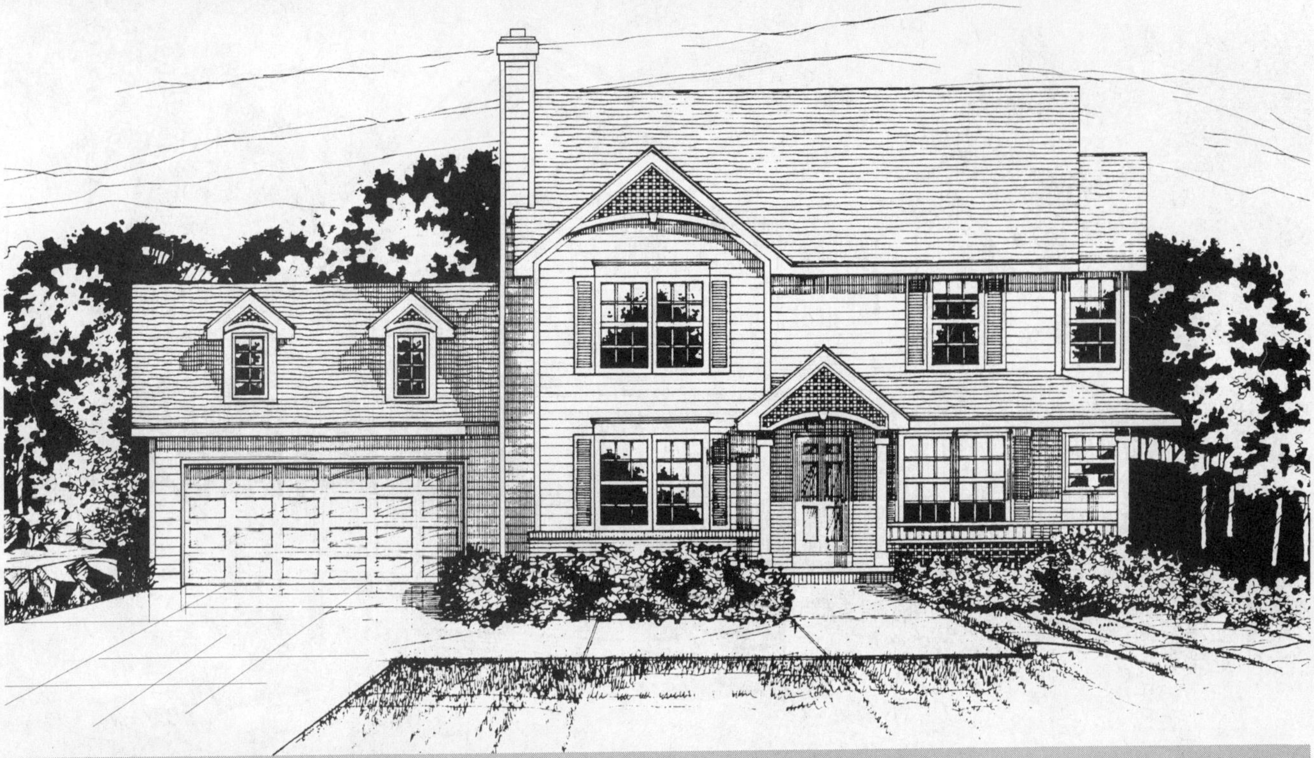

1,777 total square feet of living area **Price Code B**

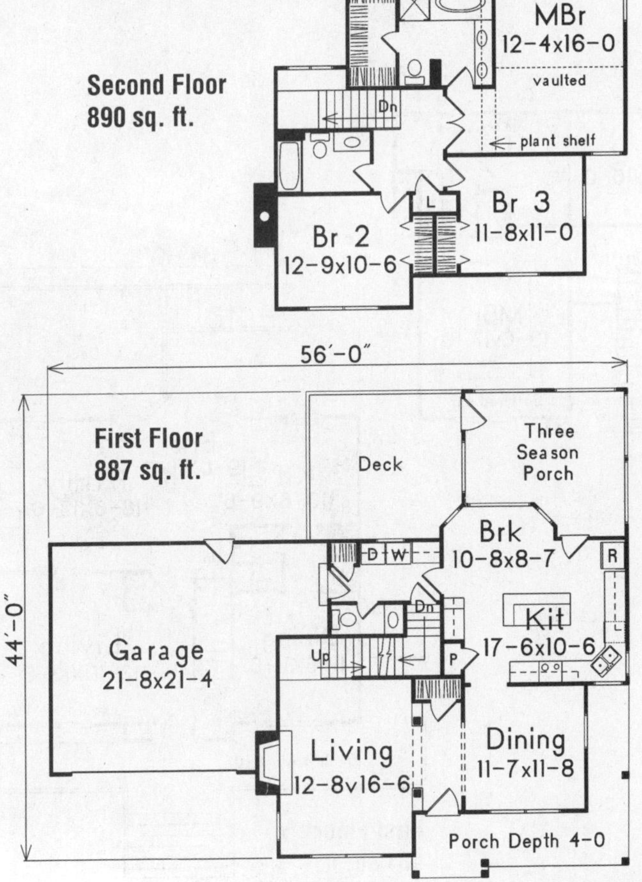
Second Floor
890 sq. ft.
MBr
12-4x16-0
vaulted
plant shelf
Dn
Br 3
11-8x11-0
L
Br 2
12-9x10-6
56'-0"
44'-0"
First Floor
887 sq. ft.
Deck
Three
Season
Porch
Brk
10-8x8-7
R
DW
Dn
Kit
17-6x10-6
Up
P
Garage
21-8x21-4
Living
12-8v16-6
Dining
11-7x11-8
Porch Depth 4-0

Special features

- Large master bedroom and bath with whirlpool tub, separate shower and spacious walk-in closet
- Large island kitchen with breakfast bay and access to the three-season porch
- Convenient laundry room with half bath
- 3 bedrooms, 2 1/2 baths, 2-car garage
- Basement foundation

Plan #702-0396

Charming Extras Add Character To This Home

1,880 total square feet of living area **Price Code C**

Special features

- Master suite enhanced with coffered ceiling
- Generous family and breakfast areas are modern and functional
- Front porch complements front facade
- 3 bedrooms, 2 1/2 baths, 2-car drive under garage
- Basement foundation

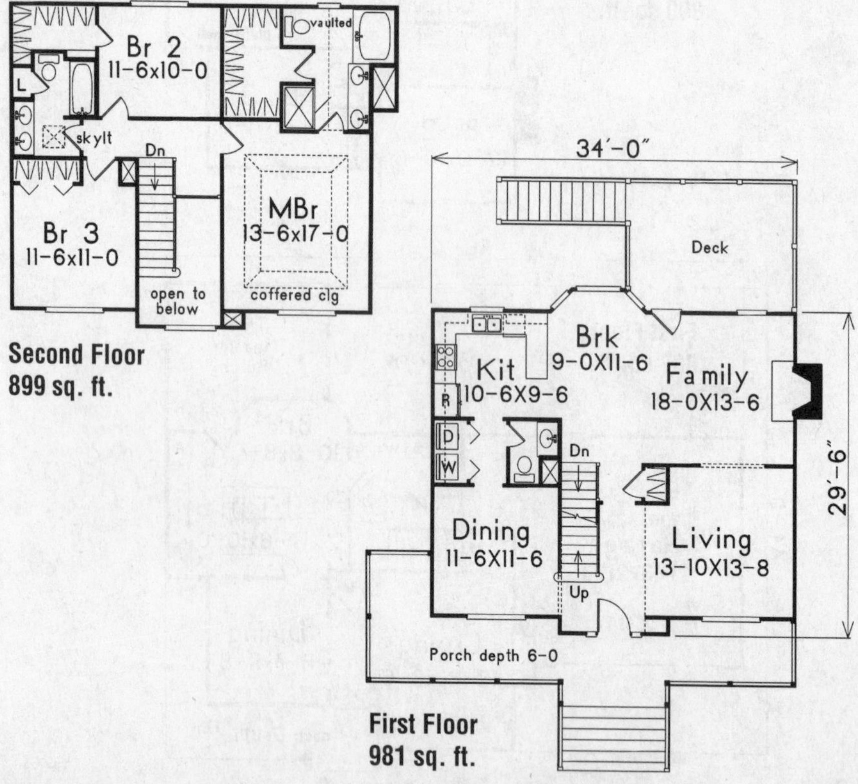
Br 2
11-6x10-0
vaulted
L
skylt
Dn
Br 3
11-6x11-0
MBr
13-6x17-0
open to below
coffered clg
34'-0"
Deck
Brk
9-0X11-6
Kit
10-6X9-6
Family
18-0X13-6
R
D
W
Dn
29'-6"
Dining
11-6X11-6
Living
13-10X13-8
Up
Porch depth 6-0

Second Floor
899 sq. ft.

First Floor
981 sq. ft.

The Family
Handyman

Plan #702-HP-C662

Wonderful, Compact Home

1,937 total square feet of living area **Price Code C**

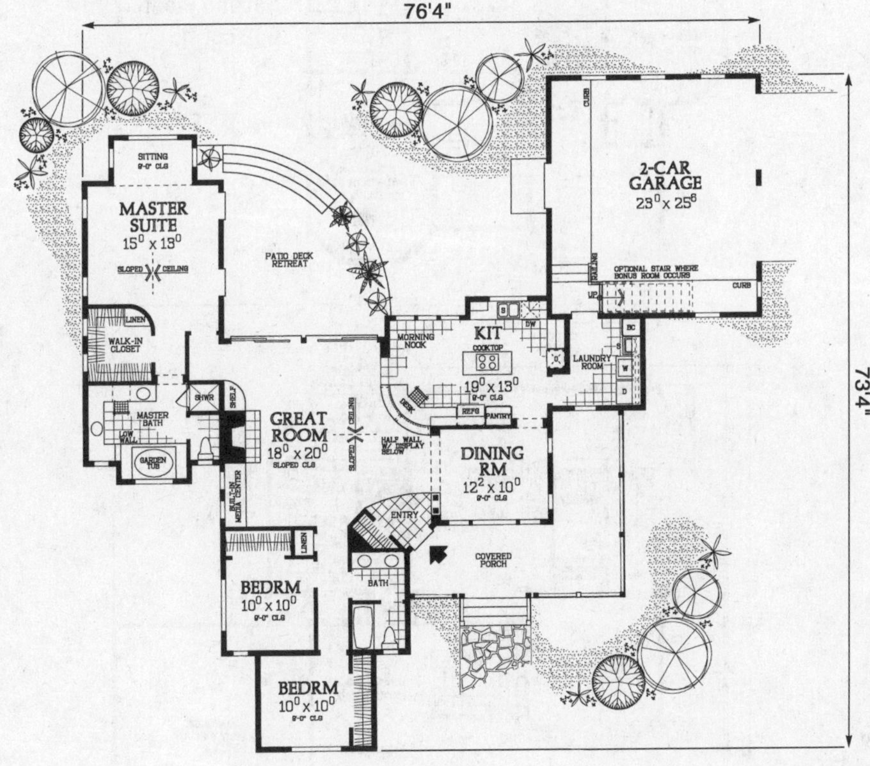

76'4"
73'4"
SITTING
MASTER SUITE
$15^{0} \times 13^{0}$
SLOPED CEILING
PATIO DECK RETREAT
2-CAR GARAGE
$23^{0} \times 25^{6}$
OPTIONAL STAIR WHERE BONUS ROOM OCCURS
CURB
MORNING NOOK
KIT
COOKTOP
$19^{0} \times 13^{0}$
LAUNDRY ROOM
WALK-IN CLOSET
LINEN
MASTER BATH
GARDEN TUB
GREAT ROOM
$18^{0} \times 20^{0}$
SLOPED CLG
DINING RM
$12^{2} \times 10^{0}$
PANTRY
ENTRY
COVERED PORCH
BEDRM
$10^{0} \times 10^{0}$
BATH
BEDRM
$10^{0} \times 10^{0}$

Special features

- Upscale great room offers a sloped ceiling, fireplace with extended hearth and built-in shelves for an entertainment center
- Gourmet kitchen includes a cooktop island counter and a quaint morning room
- Master suite features a sloped ceiling, cozy sitting room, walk-in closet and a private bath with whirlpool tub
- 3 bedrooms, 2 baths, 2-car side entry garage
- Crawl space foundation

TO ORDER BLUEPRINTS USE THE FORM ON PAGE 19 OR CALL TOLL-FREE 1-877-671-6036

View thousands more home plans online at www.familyhandyman.com/homeplans

The Family
Handyman

Plan #702-1307

Superb Home Accented With Victorian Details

2,420 total square feet of living area **Price Code D**

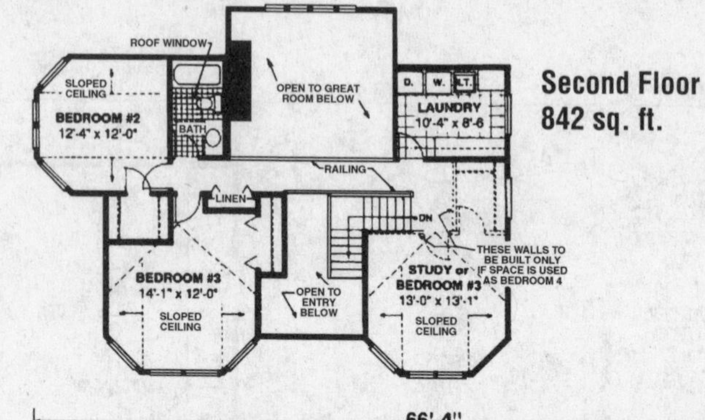
ROOF WINDOW
SLOPED CEILING
BEDROOM #2
12'-4" x 12'-0"
BATH
OPEN TO GREAT ROOM BELOW
D. W. L.T.
LAUNDRY
10'-4" x 8'-6"
RAILING
LINEN
DN
BEDROOM #3
14'-1" x 12'-0"
SLOPED CEILING
OPEN TO ENTRY BELOW
STUDY or BEDROOM #3
13'-0" x 13'-1"
SLOPED CEILING
THESE WALLS TO BE BUILT ONLY IF SPACE IS USED AS BEDROOM 4

Second Floor
842 sq. ft.

Special features

- Master suite filled with extras like unique master bath and lots of storage
- Extending off great room is a bright sunroom with access to a deck
- Compact kitchen with nook creates useful breakfast area
- 4 bedrooms, 2 1/2 baths, 2-car garage
- Basement foundation

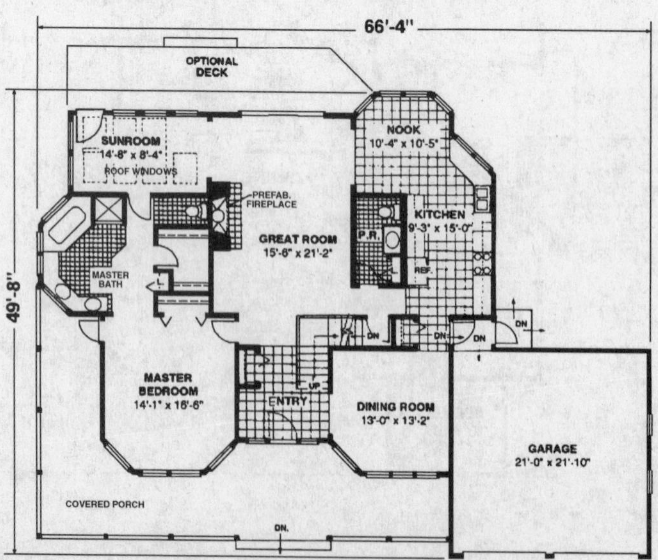
66'-4"
OPTIONAL DECK
NOOK
10'-4" x 10'-5"
SUNROOM
14'-8" x 8'-4"
ROOF WINDOWS
PREFAB. FIREPLACE
GREAT ROOM
15'-6" x 21'-2"
P.R.
KITCHEN
9'-3" x 15'-0"
REF.
MASTER BATH
49'-8"
DN
MASTER BEDROOM
14'-1" x 18'-6"
UP
ENTRY
DINING ROOM
13'-0" x 13'-2"
GARAGE
21'-0" x 21'-10"
COVERED PORCH
DN.

First Floor
1,578 sq. ft.

TO ORDER BLUEPRINTS USE THE FORM ON PAGE 19 OR CALL TOLL-FREE 1-877-671-6036
View thousands more home plans online at www.familyhandyman.com/homeplans

Fireplaces In Two Living Areas — Plan #702-SH-SEA-058

Special features

- Energy efficient home with 2" x 6" exterior walls
- Barrel vaulted two-story entrance foyer leads to an agled gallery
- Kitchen features a sunny bay window
- Bonus room with private staircase has an additional 390 square feet of living area
- 3 bedrooms, 2 1/2 baths, 2-car garage
- Basement foundation

2,170 total square feet of living area — **Price Code C**

First Floor
1,155 sq. ft.

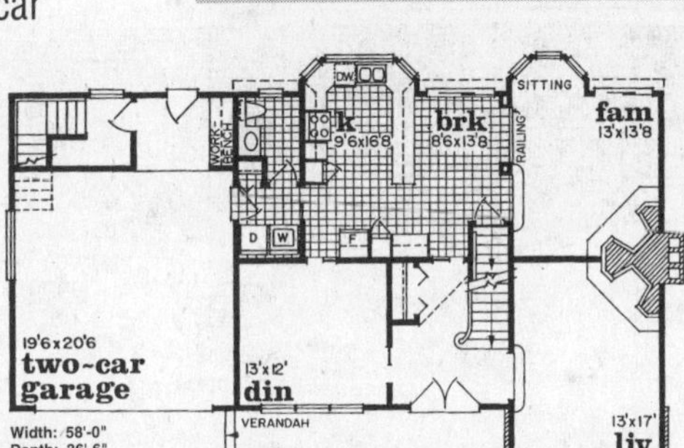

k 9'6x16'8
brk 8'6x13'8
SITTING
fam 13'x13'8
RAILING
19'6x20'6 two-car garage
13'x12' din
VERANDAH
13'x17' liv
Width: 58'-0"
Depth: 36'-6"

Second Floor
1,015 sq. ft.

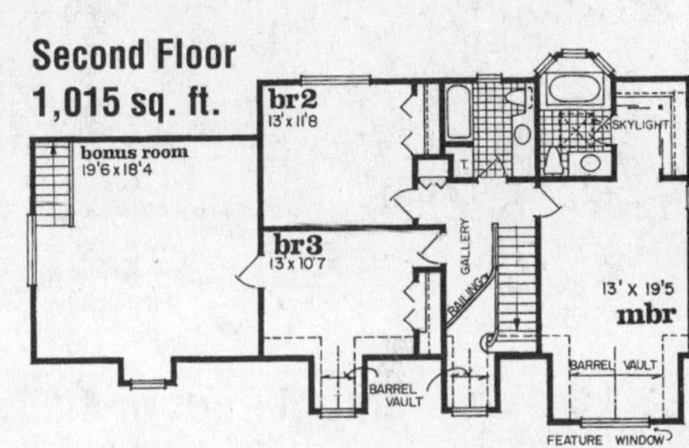

bonus room 19'6x18'4
br2 13'x11'8
SKYLIGHT
br3 13'x10'7
GALLERY
RAILING
13' x 19'5 mbr
BARREL VAULT
BARREL VAULT
FEATURE WINDOW

Double Bay Enhances Front Entry — Plan #702-0113

Special features

- Distinct living, dining and breakfast areas
- Master bedroom boasts full end bay window and a cathedral ceiling
- Storage and laundry area located adjacent to the garage
- Bonus room over the garage for future office or playroom
- 3 bedrooms, 2 1/2 baths, 2-car garage
- Crawl space foundation, drawings also include basement foundation

1,992 total square feet of living area — **Price Code C**

First Floor
868 sq. ft.

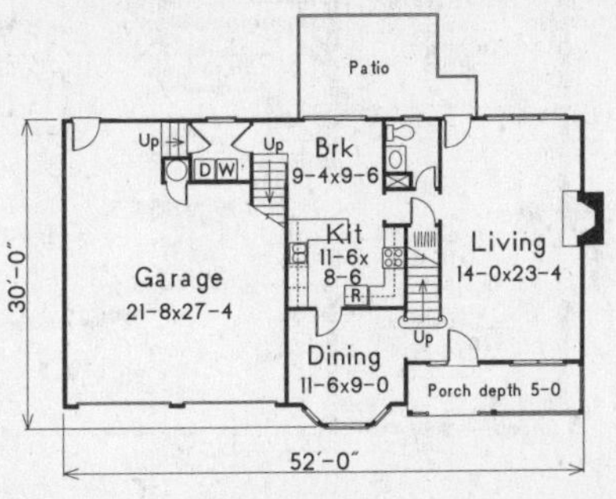

Patio
Up
DW
Up
Brk 9-4x9-6
Kit 11-6x 8-6
R
Living 14-0x23-4
Garage 21-8x27-4
30'-0"
Up
Dining 11-6x9-0
Porch depth 5-0
52'-0"

Second Floor
1,124 sq. ft.

Bonus 21-8x15-4 sloped clg
Dn
MBr 11-6x14-6
sloped clg
Dn
Br 3 10-6x10-8
Br 2 14-0x10-0

Plan #702-DDI-100-219

Charming Country Farmhouse

2,646 total square feet of living area **Price Code E**

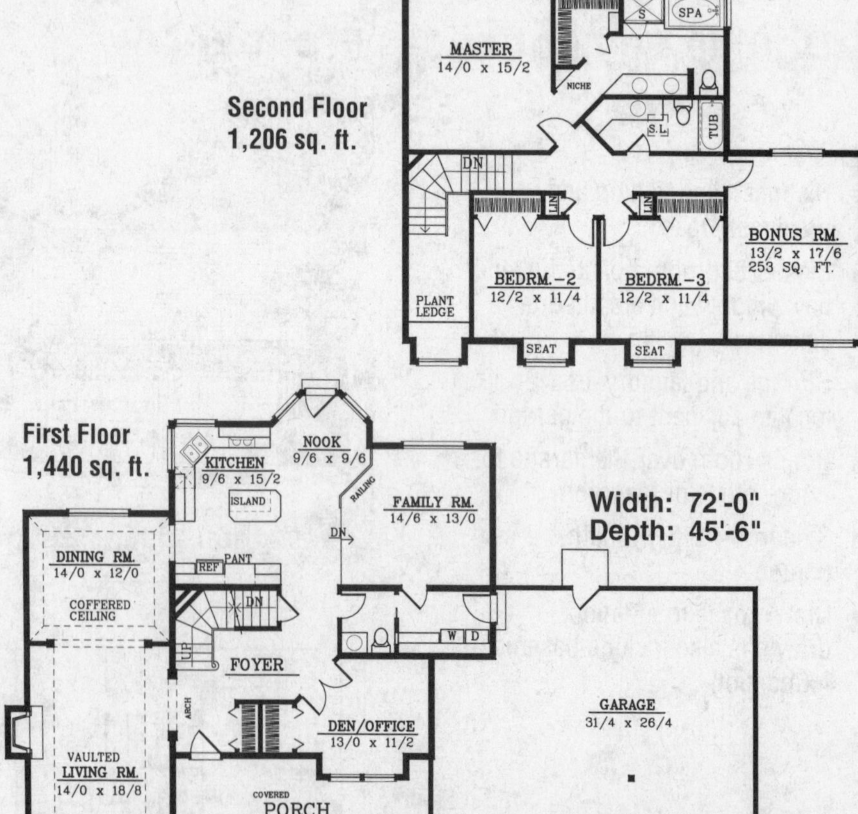
Second Floor
1,206 sq. ft.
MASTER
14/0 x 15/2
NICHE
SPA
S
S.L.
TUB
DN
BEDRM.-2
12/2 x 11/4
BEDRM.-3
12/2 x 11/4
BONUS RM.
13/2 x 17/6
253 SQ. FT.
PLANT LEDGE
SEAT
SEAT
First Floor
1,440 sq. ft.
NOOK
9/6 x 9/6
KITCHEN
9/6 x 15/2
ISLAND
RAILING
FAMILY RM.
14/6 x 13/0
DN
DINING RM.
14/0 x 12/0
COFFERED CEILING
REF
PANT
DN
UP
FOYER
W
D
ARCH
DEN/OFFICE
13/0 x 11/2
VAULTED LIVING RM.
14/0 x 18/8
COVERED PORCH
GARAGE
31/4 x 26/4
Width: 72'-0"
Depth: 45'-6"

Special features

- Casual living areas of home located in the rear including a kitchen with eating bar over-looking an angled nook
- Private second floor master suite has a large walk-in closet, double sinks, spa tub and separate shower
- Two additional generous-sized bedrooms with dormered window seats and a large bonus room share a hall bath
- 3 bedrooms, 2 1/2 baths, 3-car garage
- Basement foundation

Centralized Living Area Is Functional And Appealing

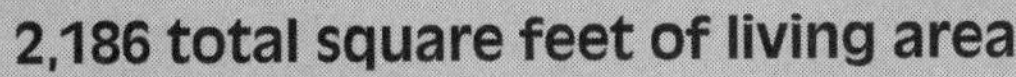

2,186 total square feet of living area

Price Code C

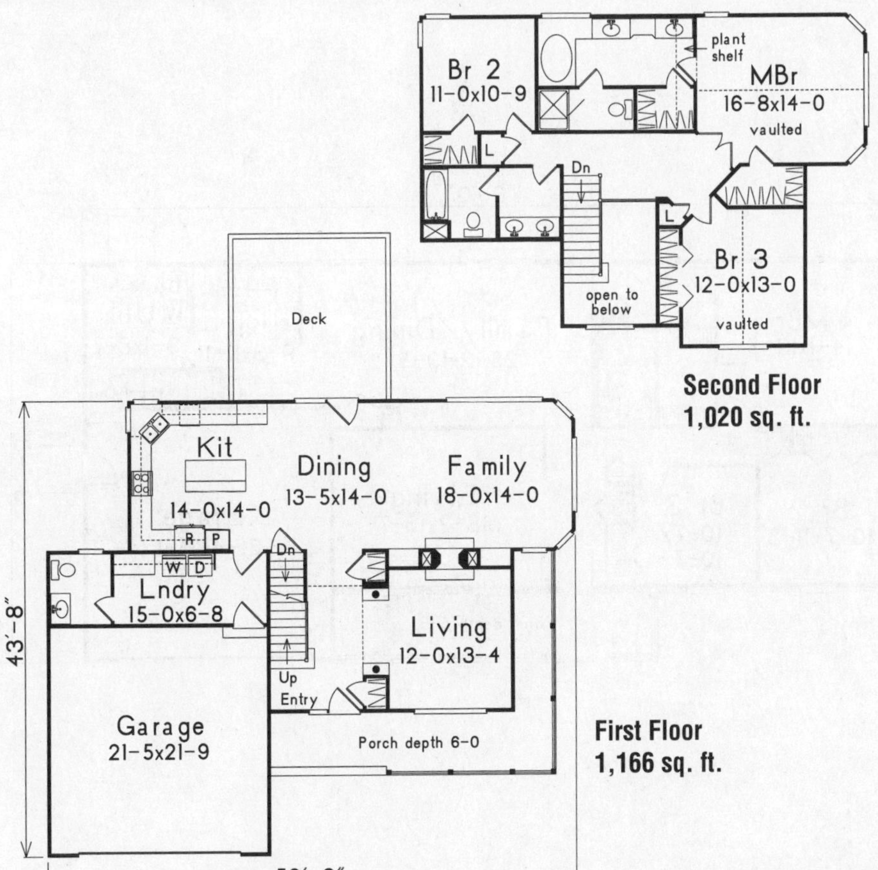

Br 2
11-0x10-9
plant shelf
MBr
16-8x14-0
vaulted
L
Dn
Br 3
12-0x13-0
vaulted
open to below
Deck
Kit
14-0x14-0
Dining
13-5x14-0
Family
18-0x14-0
R P
W D
Lndry
15-0x6-8
Dn
Living
12-0x13-4
Up
Entry
Garage
21-5x21-9
Porch depth 6-0
43'-8"
52'-0"

Second Floor
1,020 sq. ft.

First Floor
1,166 sq. ft.

Special features

- See-through fireplace is a focal point in family and living areas
- Colums grace the entrance into the living room
- Large laundry room with adjoining half bath
- Ideal second floor bath includes separate vanity with double sinks
- 3 bedrooms, 2 1/2 baths, 2-car garage
- Basement foundation

Plan #702-1101

Charming Country Facade

1,643 total square feet of living area **Price Code B**

Special features

- Attractive front entry porch gives this ranch a country accent
- Spacious family room is the focal point of this design
- Kitchen and utility room are conveniently located near gathering areas
- Formal living room in the front of the home provides area for quiet and privacy
- Master suite has view to the rear of the home and a generous walk-in closet
- 3 bedrooms, 2 baths, 2-car garage
- Basement foundation, drawings also include crawl space and slab foundations

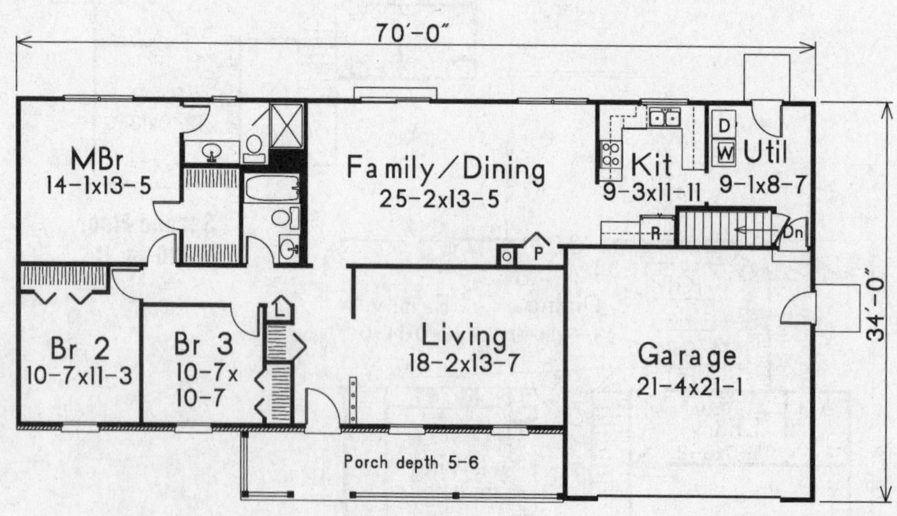
70'-0"
34'-0"
MBr
14-1x13-5
Family/Dining
25-2x13-5
Kit
9-3x11-11
Util
9-1x8-7
D
W
R
Dn
P
Br 2
10-7x11-3
Br 3
10-7x
10-7
Living
18-2x13-7
Garage
21-4x21-1
Porch depth 5-6

Plan #702-0207

Ornate Corner Porch Catches The Eye

1,550 total square feet of living area — **Price Code B**

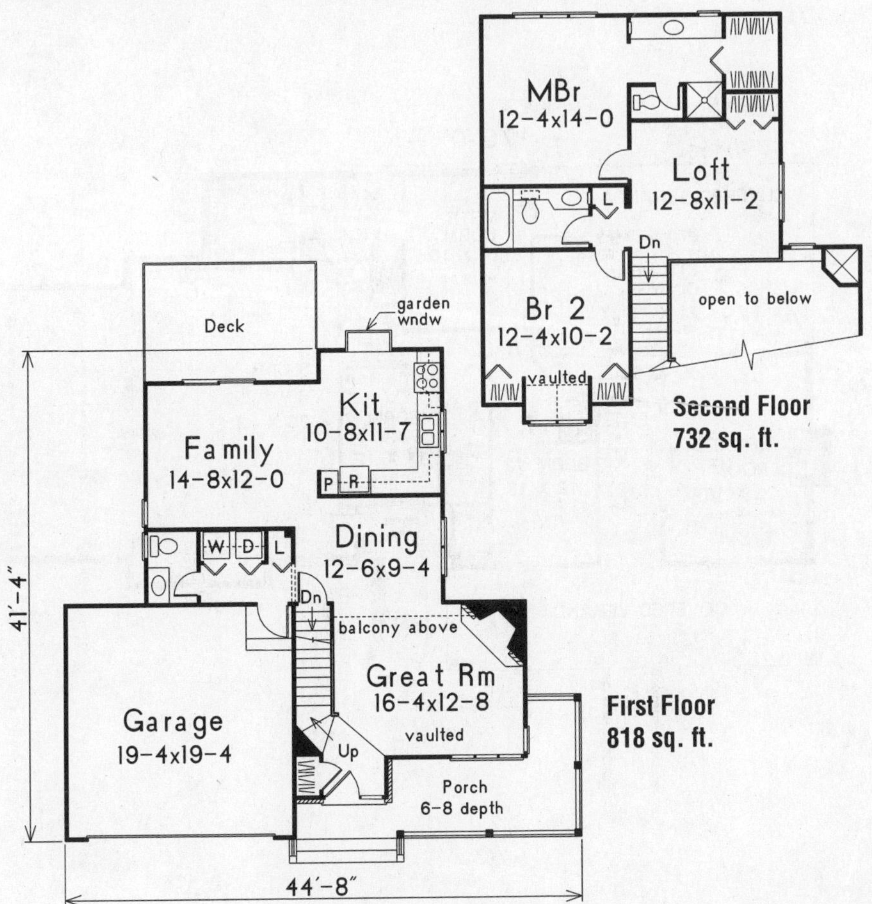
MBr
12-4x14-0
Loft
12-8x11-2
L
Dn
Br 2
12-4x10-2
open to below
vaulted
Second Floor
732 sq. ft.
Deck
garden
wndw
Kit
10-8x11-7
Family
14-8x12-0
P
R
W
D
L
Dining
12-6x9-4
Dn
balcony above
Great Rm
16-4x12-8
vaulted
Up
Garage
19-4x19-4
Porch
6-8 depth
41'-4"
44'-8"
First Floor
818 sq. ft.

Special features

- Impressive front entrance with a wrap-around covered porch and raised foyer
- Corner fireplace provides a focal point in the vaulted great room
- Loft is easily converted to a third bedroom or activity center
- Large family/kitchen area includes greenhouse windows and access to the deck and utility area
- Secondary bedroom has a large dormer and window seat
- 2 bedrooms, 2 1/2 baths, 2-car garage
- Basement foundation

Plan #702-FDG-7963-L

Inviting Covered Verandas

1,830 total square feet of living area **Price Code C**

Special features

- Inviting covered verandas in the front and rear of the home
- Great room has fireplace and cathedral ceiling
- Handy service porch allows easy access
- Master suite has vaulted ceiling and private bath
- 3 bedrooms, 2 baths, 3-car side entry garage
- Basement, crawl space or slab foundation, please specify when ordering

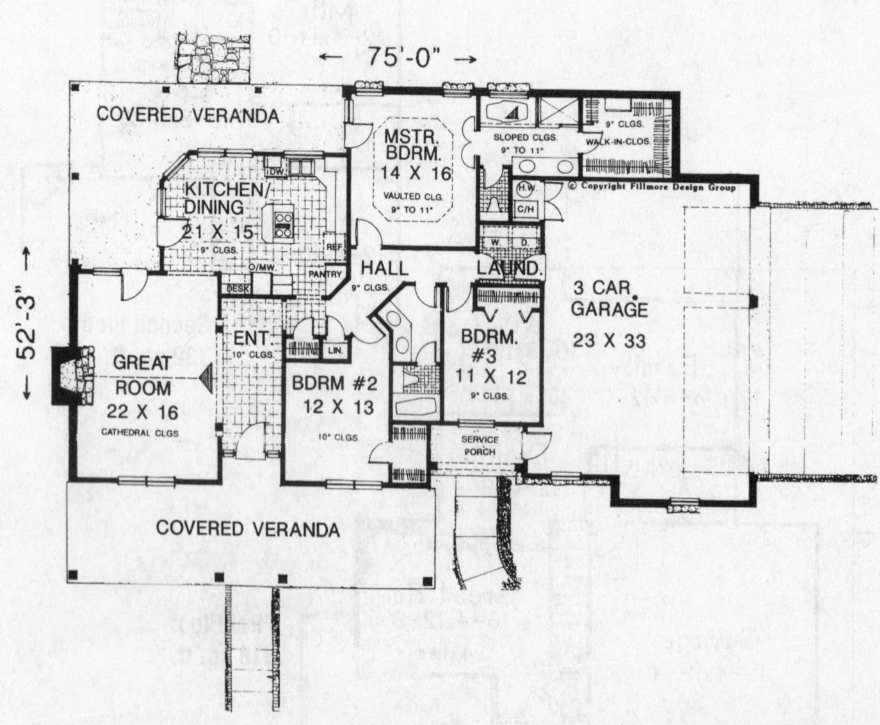

75'-0"
52'-3"
COVERED VERANDA
MSTR. BDRM. 14 X 16
VAULTED CLG. 9" TO 11"
SLOPED CLGS. 9" TO 11"
9" CLGS.
WALK-IN-CLOS.
© Copyright Fillmore Design Group
KITCHEN/ DINING 21 X 15
9" CLGS.
DW
REF.
PANTRY
O/MW
DESK
HALL
9" CLGS.
H.W.
C/H
W. D.
LAUND.
3 CAR GARAGE 23 X 33
ENT.
10" CLGS.
LIN.
GREAT ROOM 22 X 16
CATHEDRAL CLGS
BDRM #2 12 X 13
10" CLGS
BDRM. #3 11 X 12
9" CLGS.
SERVICE PORCH
COVERED VERANDA

Charming Wrap-Around Porch

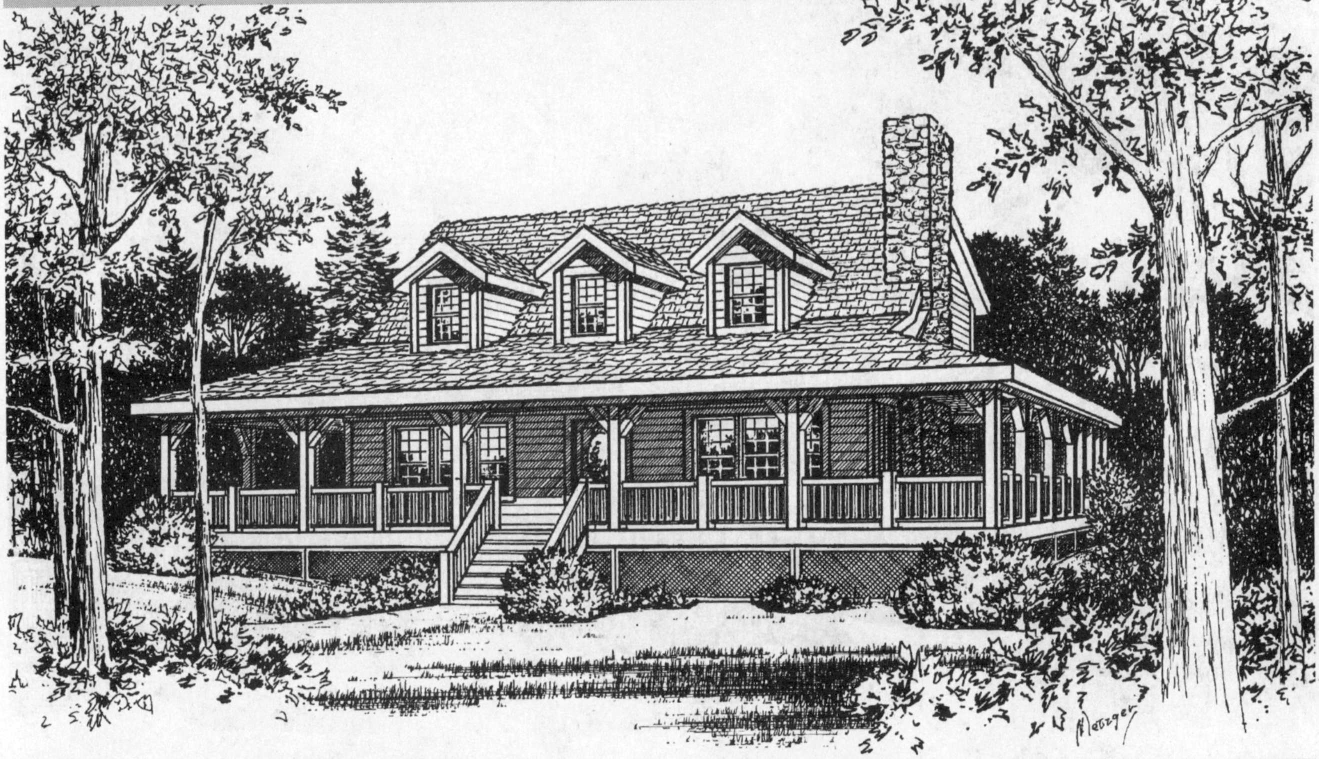

1,879 total square feet of living area

Price Code C

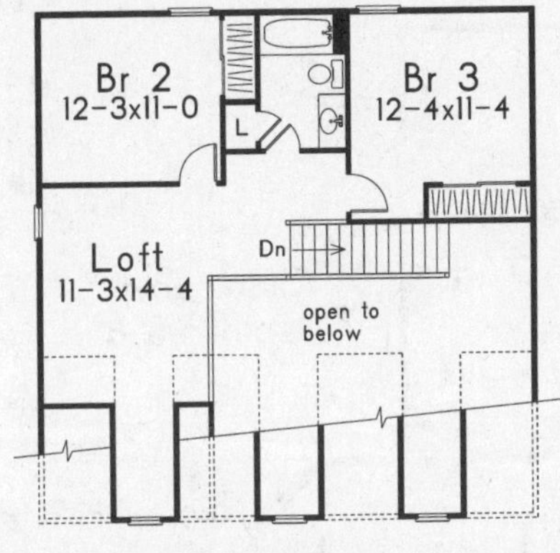
Br 2
12-3x11-0
Br 3
12-4x11-4
L
Dn
Loft
11-3x14-4
open to below

Second Floor
565 sq. ft.

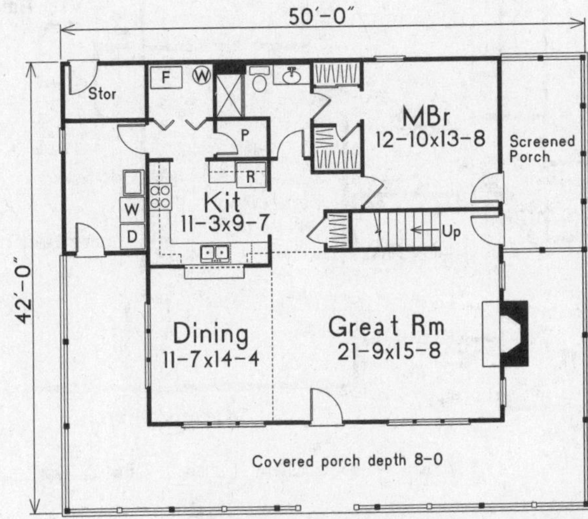
50'-0"
42'-0"
Stor
F
W
P
R
MBr
12-10x13-8
Screened Porch
Kit
11-3x9-7
W
D
Up
Dining
11-7x14-4
Great Rm
21-9x15-8
Covered porch depth 8-0

First Floor
1,314 sq. ft.

Special features

- Open floor plan on both floors makes home appear larger
- Loft area overlooks great room or can become an optional fourth bedroom
- Large walk-in pantry in kitchen and large storage in rear of home with access from exterior
- 3 bedrooms, 2 baths
- Crawl space foundation

Plan #702-HDS-1963

Charming Covered Porch

1,963 total square feet of living area **Price Code C**

Special features

- Spacious breakfast nook is a great gathering place
- Master bedroom has its own wing with private bath and lots of closet space
- Large laundry room with closet and sink
- 3 bedrooms, 2 baths, 2-car side entry garage
- Slab or crawl space foundation, please specify when ordering

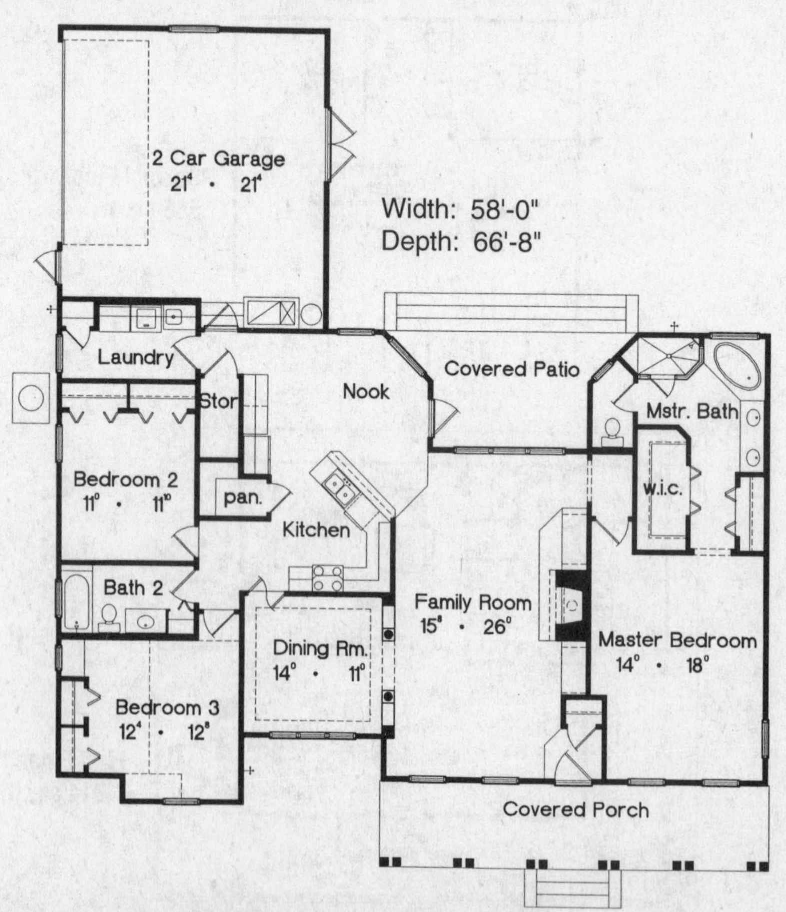
2 Car Garage
$21^{4} \cdot 21^{4}$
Width: 58'-0"
Depth: 66'-8"
Laundry
Stor
Nook
Covered Patio
Mstr. Bath
Bedroom 2
$11^{0} \cdot 11^{10}$
pan.
w.i.c.
Kitchen
Bath 2
Family Room
$15^{8} \cdot 26^{0}$
Master Bedroom
$14^{0} \cdot 18^{0}$
Dining Rm.
$14^{0} \cdot 11^{0}$
Bedroom 3
$12^{4} \cdot 12^{8}$
Covered Porch

TO ORDER BLUEPRINTS USE THE FORM ON PAGE 19 OR CALL TOLL-FREE 1-877-671-6036

View thousands more home plans online at www.familyhandyman.com/homeplans

Covered Deck Off Breakfast Room Plan #702-HDG-99004

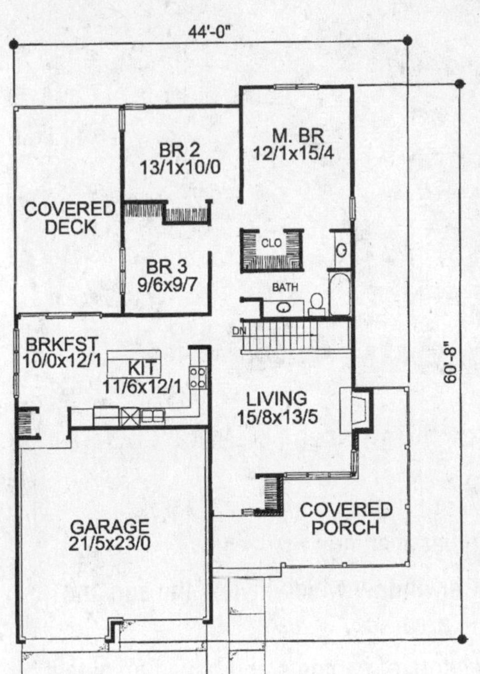
44'-0"
60'-8"
BR 2
13/1x10/0
M. BR
12/1x15/4
COVERED
DECK
BR 3
9/6x9/7
CLO
BATH
DN
BRKFST
10/0x12/1
KIT
11/6x12/1
LIVING
15/8x13/5
GARAGE
21/5x23/0
COVERED
PORCH

1,231 total square feet of living area **Price Code A**

Special features

- Covered front porch
- Master bedroom has separate sink area
- Large island in kitchen for eat-in dining or preparation area
- 3 bedrooms, 1 bath, 2-car garage
- Basement foundation

Perfect For A Narrow Lot Plan #702-HDG-97006

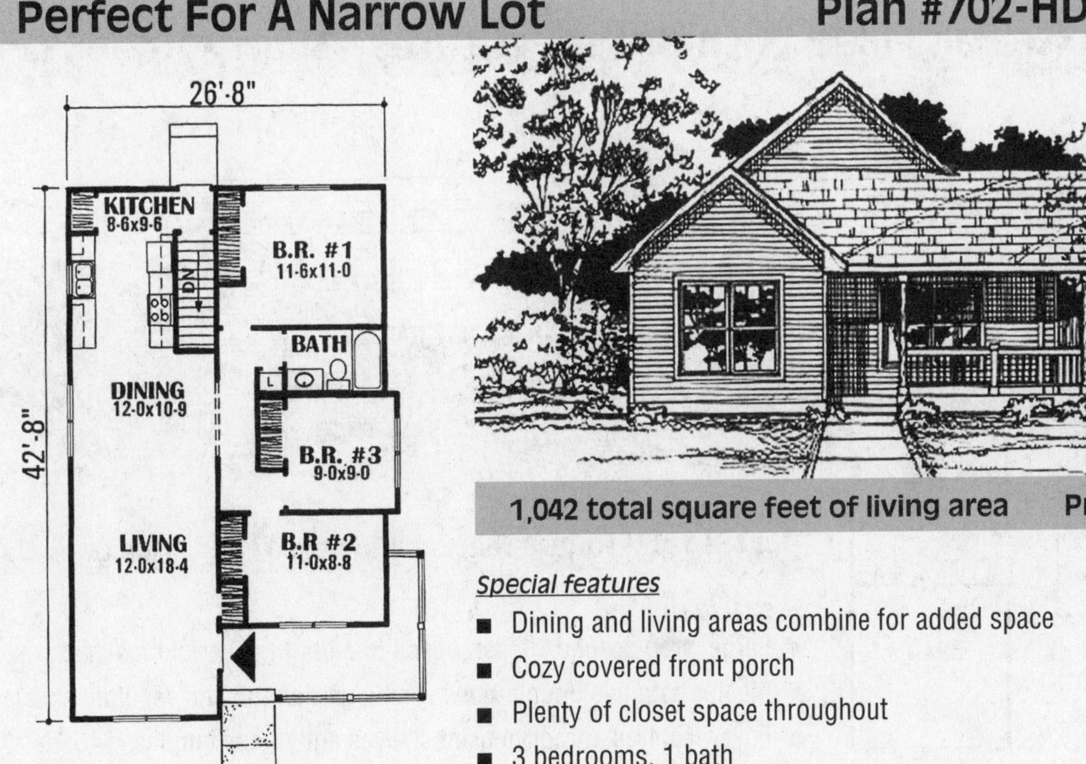
26'-8"
42'-8"
KITCHEN
8-6x9-6
DN
B.R. #1
11-6x11-0
BATH
L
DINING
12-0x10-9
B.R. #3
9-0x9-0
LIVING
12-0x18-4
B.R #2
11-0x8-8

1,042 total square feet of living area **Price Code AA**

Special features

- Dining and living areas combine for added space
- Cozy covered front porch
- Plenty of closet space throughout
- 3 bedrooms, 1 bath
- Basement foundation

Stylish Retreat For A Narrow Lot — Plan #702-0809

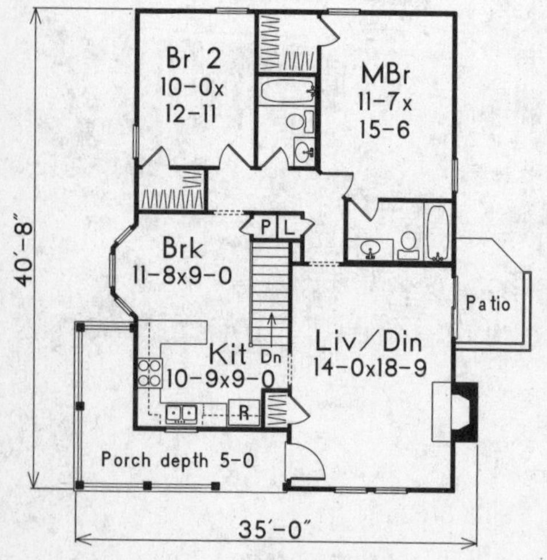
Br 2
10-0x
12-11
MBr
11-7x
15-6
P L
Brk
11-8x9-0
Patio
Kit Dn
10-9x9-0
Liv/Din
14-0x18-9
R
Porch depth 5-0
40'-8"
35'-0"

1,084 total square feet of living area — Price Code AA

Special features

- Delightful country porch for quiet evenings
- Living room has a front feature window which invites the sun and includes a fireplace and dining area
- The U-shaped kitchen features lots of cabinets and bayed breakfast room with built-in pantry
- Both bedrooms have walk-in closets and access to their own bath
- 2 bedrooms, 2 baths
- Basement foundation

Casual Exterior, Filled With Great Features — Plan #702-0387

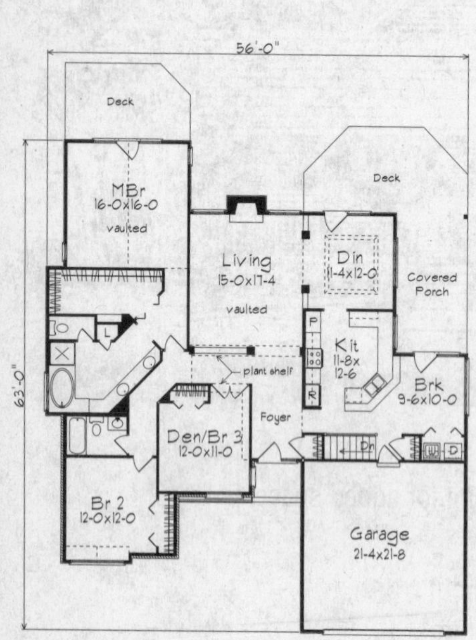
56'-0"
Deck
MBr
16-0x16-0
vaulted
Deck
Living
15-0x17-4
vaulted
Din
11-4x12-0
Covered
Porch
Kit
11-8x
12-6
plant shelf
Brk
9-6x10-0
Foyer
Den/Br 3
12-0x11-0
Br 2
12-0x12-0
Garage
21-4x21-8
63'-0"

1,958 total square feet of living area — Price Code C

Special features

- Large wrap-around kitchen opens to a bright cheerful breakfast area
- Master bath has double-bowl vanity, garden tub and separate shower
- Foyer features attractive plant shelves and opens into living room
- 3 bedrooms, 2 baths, 2-car garage
- Basement foundation

TO ORDER BLUEPRINTS USE THE FORM ON PAGE 19 OR CALL TOLL-FREE 1-877-671-6036

The Family
Handyman

Plan #702-0437

Double French Doors Grace Living Room

2,333 total square feet of living area

Price Code D

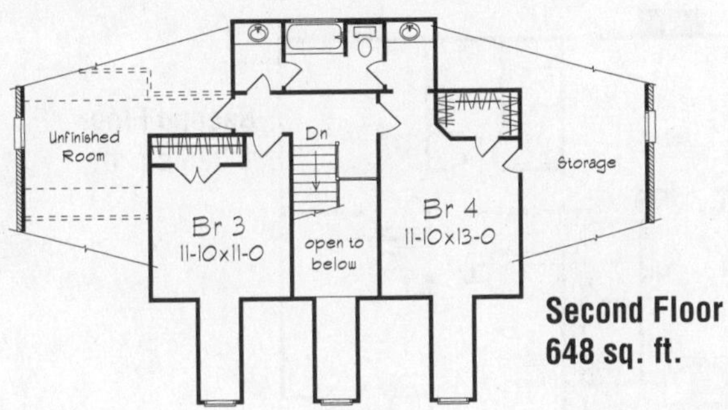
Unfinished Room
Dn
Storage
Br 3
11-10x11-0
open to below
Br 4
11-10x13-0

Second Floor
648 sq. ft.

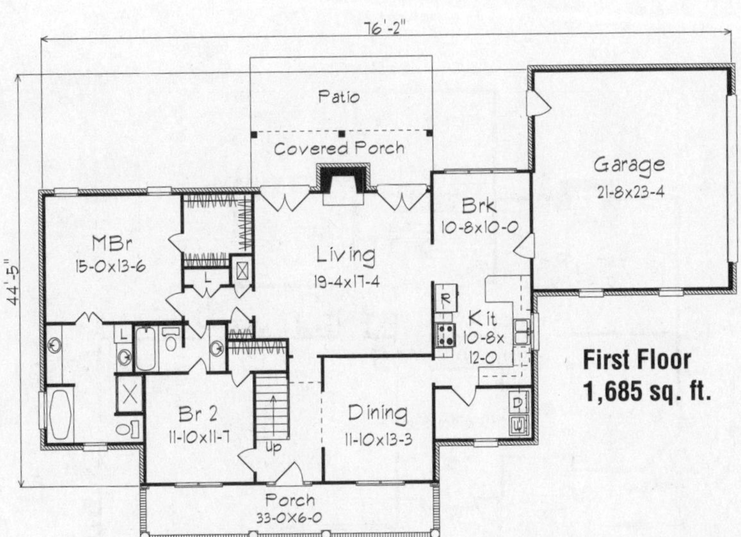
76'-2"
44'-5"
Patio
Covered Porch
Garage
21-8x23-4
Brk
10-8x10-0
MBr
15-0x13-6
Living
19-4x17-4
Kit
10-8x
12-0
Br 2
11-10x11-7
Dining
11-10x13-3
Up
Porch
33-0X6-0

First Floor
1,685 sq. ft.

Special features

- 9' ceilings on first floor
- Master bedroom features a large walk-in closet and an inviting double-door entry into a spacious bath
- Convenient laundry room located near kitchen
- 4 bedrooms, 3 baths, 2-car side entry garage
- Slab foundation, drawings also include crawl space and partial crawl space/basement foundations

The Family
Handyman

Plan #702-0391

Outdoor Exposure Front And Back

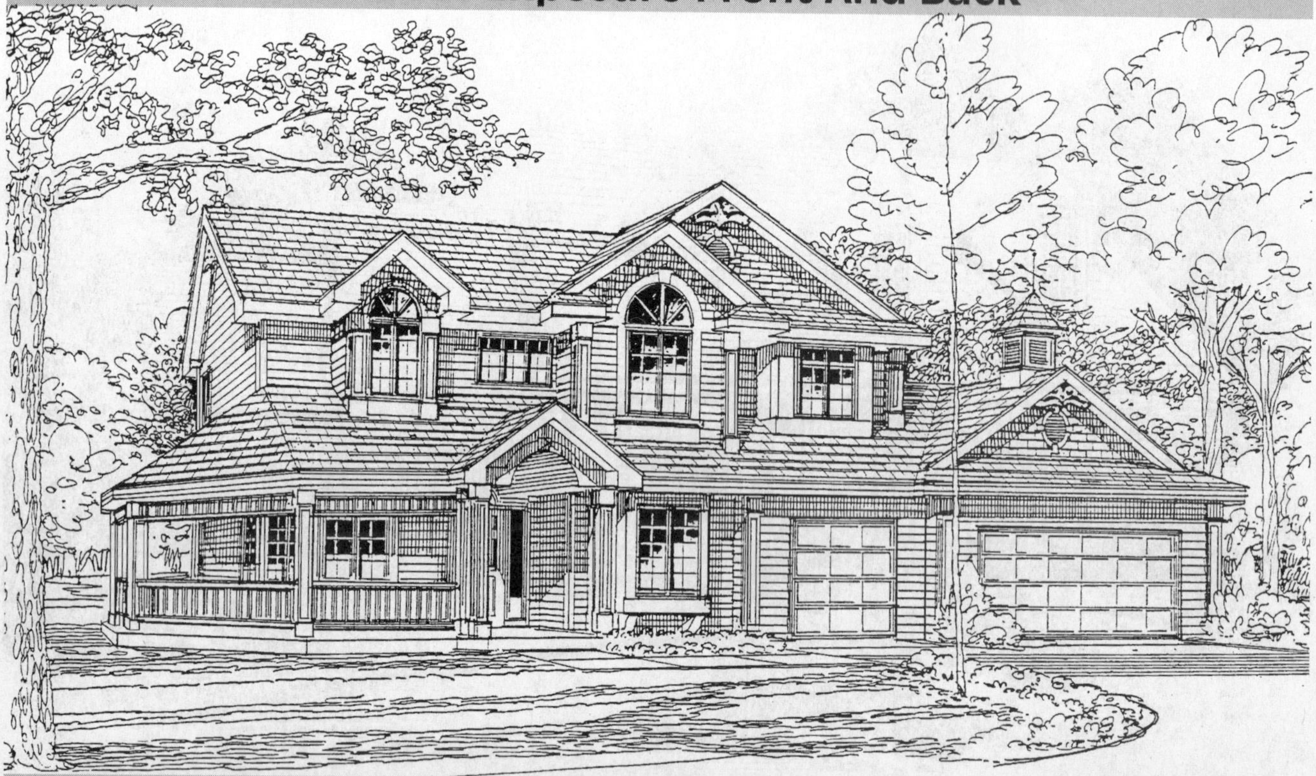

2,685 total square feet of living area **Price Code E**

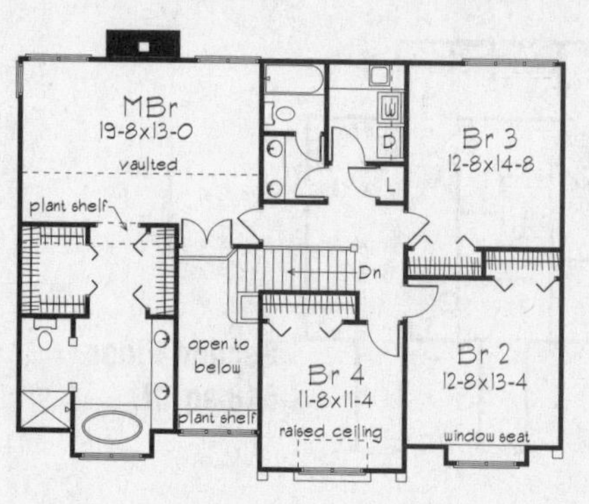
MBr
19-8x13-0
vaulted
plant shelf
open to below
plant shelf
Br 4
11-8x11-4
raised ceiling
Dn
Br 3
12-8x14-8
D
L
Br 2
12-8x13-4
window seat

Second Floor
1,325 sq. ft.

Special features

- 9' ceilings throughout first floor
- Vaulted master suite, isolated for privacy, boasts magnificent bath with garden tub, separate shower and two closets
- Laundry area near bedrooms
- Screened porch and morning room both located off well-planned kitchen
- 4 bedrooms, 2 1/2 baths, 3-car garage
- Basement foundation

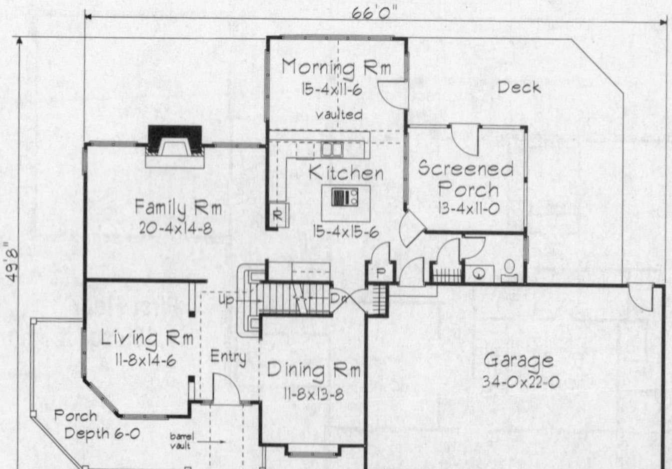

66'0"
Morning Rm
15-4x11-6
vaulted
Deck
Kitchen
15-4x15-6
Screened Porch
13-4x11-0
Family Rm
20-4x14-8
49'8"
Up
Dn
P
Living Rm
11-8x14-6
Entry
Dining Rm
11-8x13-8
Garage
34-0x22-0
Porch
Depth 6-0
barrel vault

First Floor
1,360 sq. ft.

Plan #702-HP-C681

A Great Country Farmhouse

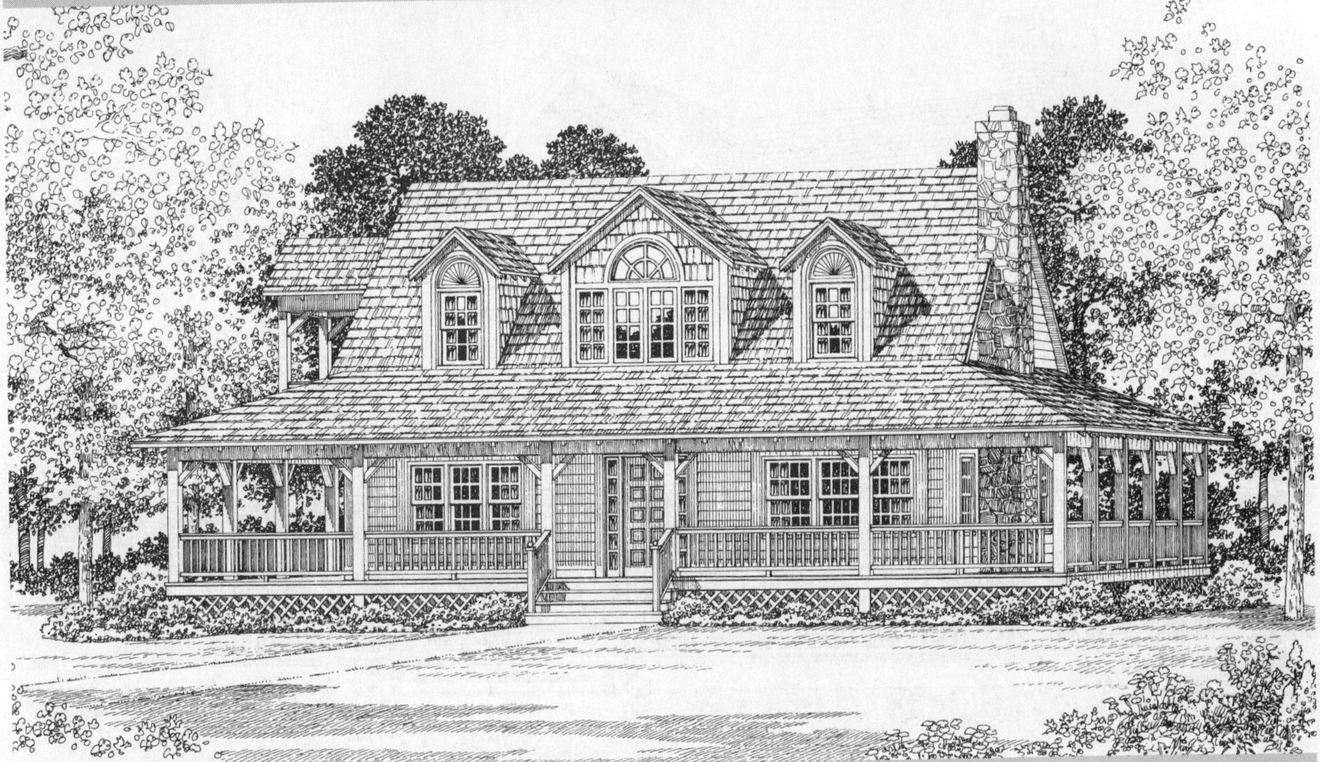

1,669 total square feet of living area | **Price Code B**

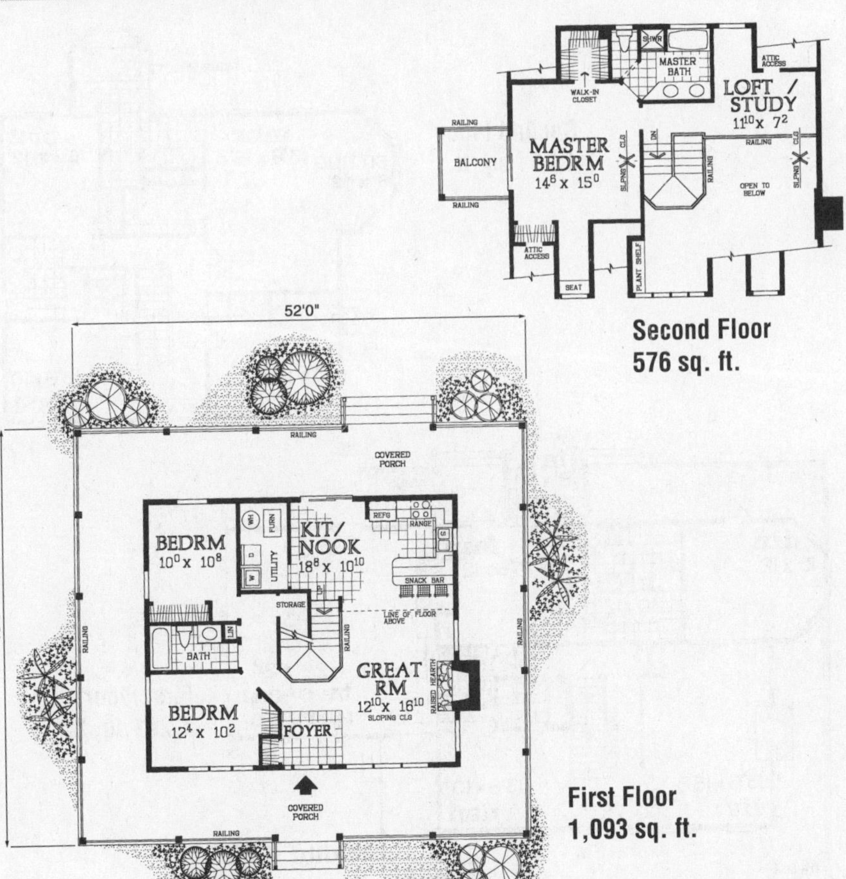
WALK-IN CLOSET
MASTER BATH
LOFT / STUDY
11¹⁰ x 7²
ATTIC ACCESS
RAILING
BALCONY
MASTER BEDRM
14⁶ x 15⁰
OPEN TO BELOW
ATTIC ACCESS
SEAT
PLANT SHELF
52'0"
46'0"
COVERED PORCH
BEDRM
10⁰ x 10⁸
UTILITY
KIT/ NOOK
18⁸ x 10¹⁰
SNACK BAR
STORAGE
LINE OF FLOOR ABOVE
BATH
GREAT RM
12¹⁰ x 16¹⁰
SLOPING CLG
RAISED HEARTH
BEDRM
12⁴ x 10²
FOYER
COVERED PORCH
RAILING

Second Floor
576 sq. ft.

First Floor
1,093 sq. ft.

Special features

- Generous use of windows adds exciting visual elements to the exterior as well as plenty of natural light to the interior
- Two-story great room has a raised hearth
- Second floor loft/study would easily make a terrific home office
- 3 bedrooms, 2 baths
- Crawl space foundation

The Family
Handyman

Plan #702-SH-SEA-100

Traditional Farmhouse Feeling With This Home

2,582 total square feet of living area

Price Code D

Special features

- Both the family and living rooms are warmed by hearths
- The master suite on the second floor has a bayed sitting room and a private bath with whirlpool tub
- Old-fashioned window seat in second floor landing is a charming touch
- 4 bedrooms, 3 baths, 2-car side entry garage
- Basement or crawl space foundation, please specify when ordering

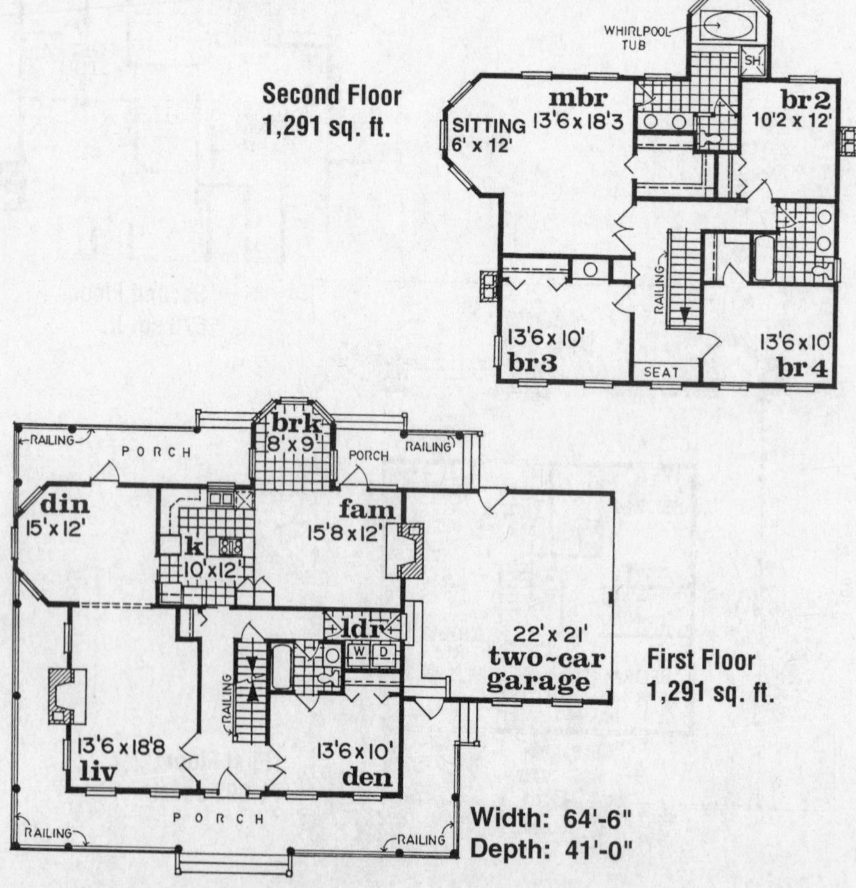
Second Floor
1,291 sq. ft.
WHIRLPOOL TUB
SH
mbr
13'6 x 18'3
SITTING
6' x 12'
br2
10'2 x 12'
RAILING
13'6 x 10'
br3
SEAT
13'6 x 10'
br4
brk
8' x 9'
RAILING
PORCH
PORCH
RAILING
din
15' x 12'
fam
15'8 x 12'
k
10' x 12'
ldr
W D
22' x 21'
two~car
garage
RAILING
13'6 x 18'8
liv
13'6 x 10'
den
PORCH
RAILING
RAILING
First Floor
1,291 sq. ft.
Width: 64'-6"
Depth: 41'-0"

The Family
Handyman

Plan #702-SH-SEA-303

1,583 total square feet of living area

Price Code B

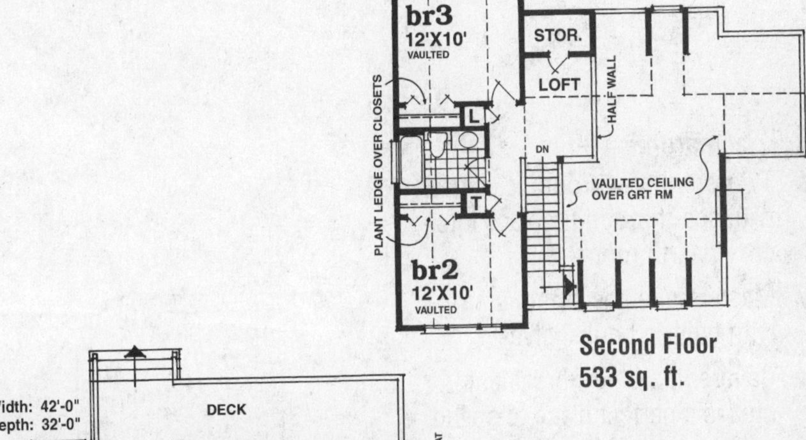
br3
12'X10'
VAULTED
STOR.
LOFT
HALF WALL
PLANT LEDGE OVER CLOSETS
L
T
DN
VAULTED CEILING OVER GRT RM
br2
12'X10'
VAULTED

Second Floor
533 sq. ft.

Special features

- Energy efficient home with 2" x 6" exterior walls
- Open kitchen includes preparation island
- Wrap-around railed porch and rear deck expand the living space for outdoor entertaining
- 3 bedrooms, 2 baths
- Basement or crawl space foundation, please specify when ordering

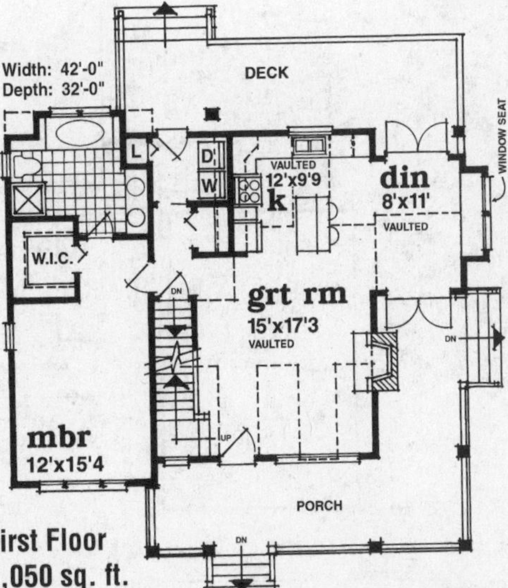
Width: 42'-0"
Depth: 32'-0"
DECK
WINDOW SEAT
L
D
W
VAULTED
12'x9'9
k
din
8'x11'
VAULTED
W.I.C.
DN
grt rm
15'x17'3
VAULTED
DN
UP
mbr
12'x15'4
PORCH
DN

First Floor
1,050 sq. ft.

The Family
Handyman

Plan #702-DBI-5520

Central Great Room

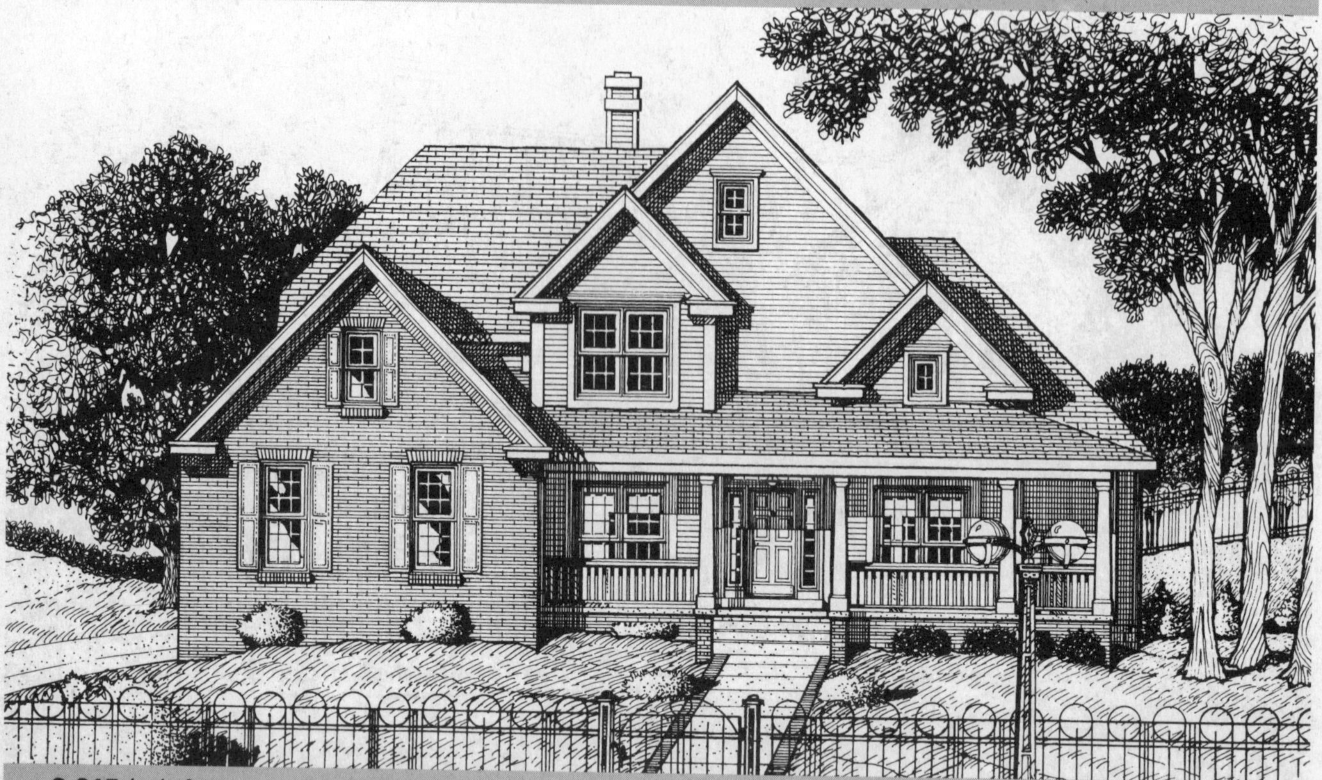

2,615 total square feet of living area

Price Code E

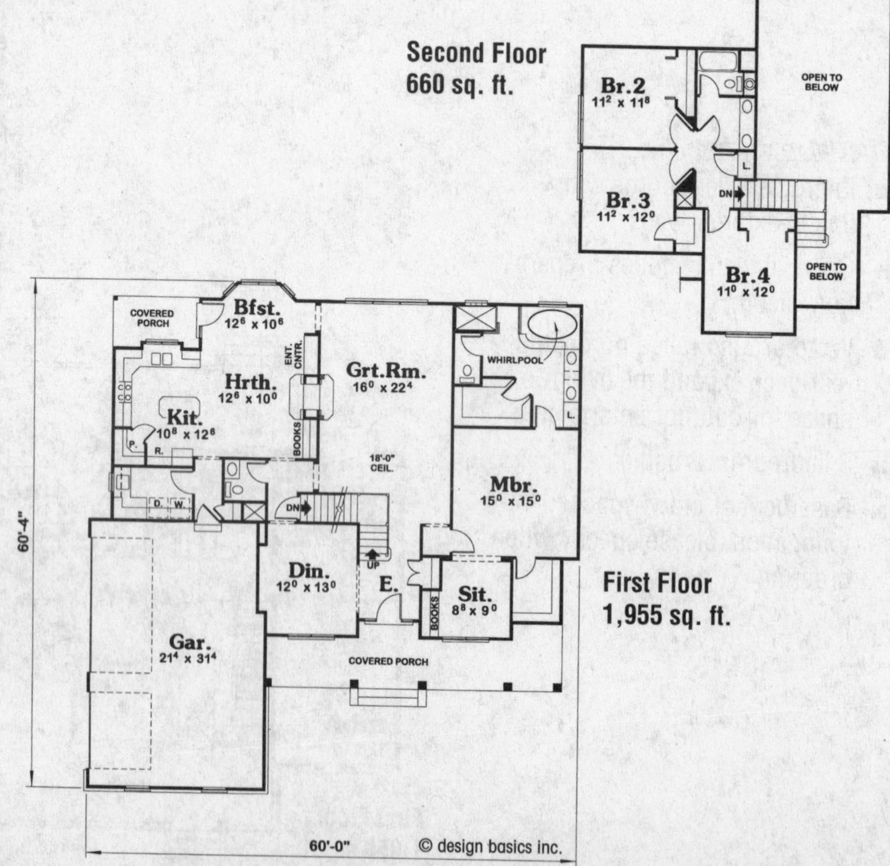
Second Floor
660 sq. ft.
Br.2
11^{2} x 11^{8}
OPEN TO BELOW
Br.3
11^{2} x 12^{0}
DN
Br.4
11^{0} x 12^{0}
OPEN TO BELOW
COVERED PORCH
Bfst.
12^{6} x 10^{6}
ENT. CNTR.
Grt.Rm.
16^{0} x 22^{4}
Hrth.
12^{6} x 10^{0}
Kit.
10^{8} x 12^{6}
P.
R.
BOOKS
18'-0" CEIL.
WHIRLPOOL
Mbr.
15^{0} x 15^{0}
D. W.
DN
UP
Din.
12^{0} x 13^{0}
E.
Sit.
8^{8} x 9^{0}
BOOKS
Gar.
21^{4} x 31^{4}
COVERED PORCH
60'-4"
60'-0"
© design basics inc.
First Floor
1,955 sq. ft.

Special features

- Two-story great room is elegant with see-through fireplace into cozy hearth room
- Master suite has sitting area with built-in bookshelves
- Covered porch off breakfast area is a perfect place to spend quiet mornings
- 4 bedrooms, 2 1/2 baths, 3-car side entry garage
- Basement foundation

The Family
Handyman

Plan #702-HDS-1571

Whirlpool Tub In Master Bath

1,571 total square feet of living area — **Price Code B**

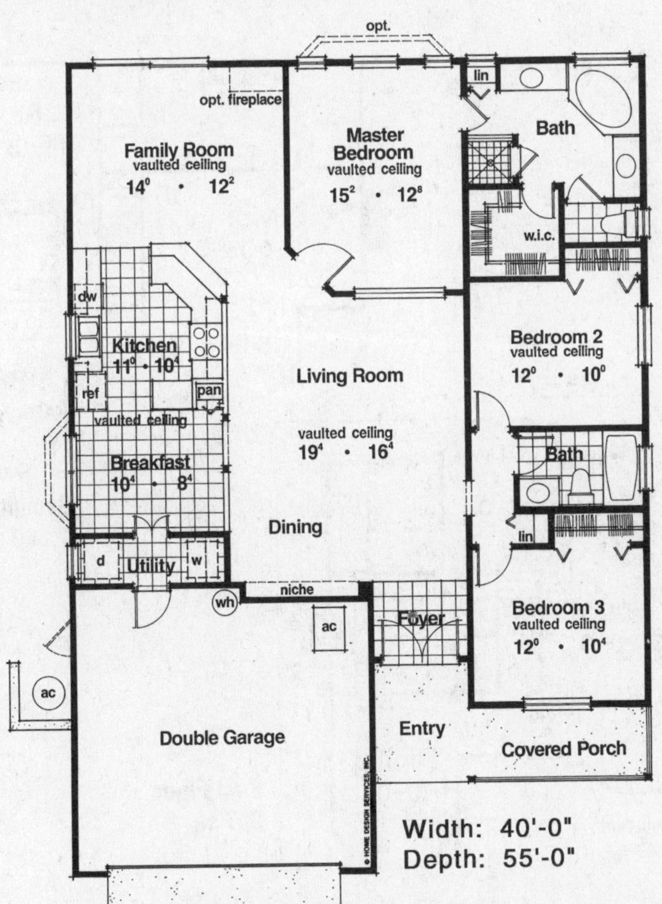

opt.
lin
opt. fireplace
Bath
Family Room
vaulted ceiling
14^0 · 12^2
Master
Bedroom
vaulted ceiling
15^2 · 12^8
w.i.c.
dw
Kitchen
11^0 · 10^4
ref
pan
vaulted ceiling
Breakfast
10^4 · 8^4
Living Room
vaulted ceiling
19^4 · 16^4
Dining
Bedroom 2
vaulted ceiling
12^0 · 10^0
Bath
lin
d
Utility
w
wh
niche
ac
Foyer
Bedroom 3
vaulted ceiling
12^0 · 10^4
ac
Double Garage
Entry
Covered Porch
© HOME DESIGN SERVICES, INC.

Width: 40'-0"
Depth: 55'-0"

Special features

- Bedrooms #2 and #3 share a bath in their own private hall
- Kitchen counter overlooks family room
- Open living area adds appeal with vaulted ceiling and display niche
- 3 bedrooms, 2 baths, 2-car garage
- Slab foundation

TO ORDER BLUEPRINTS USE THE FORM ON PAGE 19 OR CALL TOLL-FREE 1-877-671-6036

View thousands more home plans online at www.familyhandyman.com/homeplans

The Family
Handyman

Plan #702-0234

Victorian-Style Home Features Double Bays

2,066 total square feet of living area

Price Code C

Special features

- Large master bedroom includes sitting area and private bath
- Open living room features a fireplace with built-in bookshelves
- Spacious kitchen accesses formal dining area and breakfast room
- 3 bedrooms, 2 1/2 baths
- Slab foundation

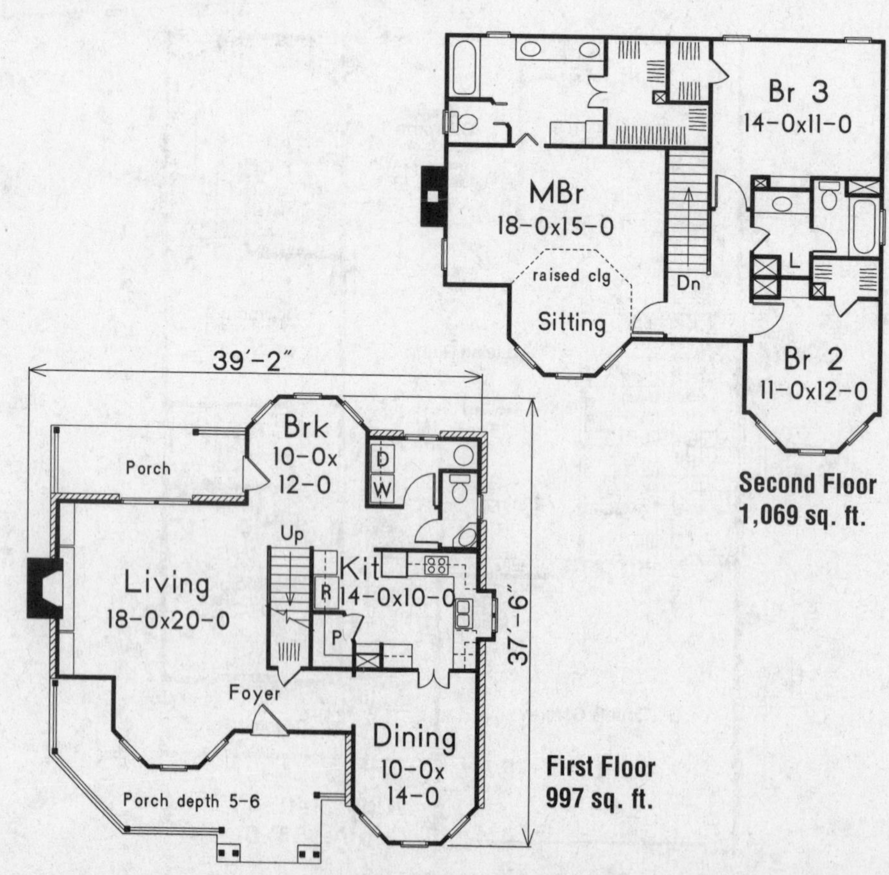

Br 3
14-0x11-0
MBr
18-0x15-0
raised clg
Sitting
Dn
L
Br 2
11-0x12-0
39'-2"
Brk
10-0x
12-0
Porch
D
W
Up
Kit
14-0x10-0
R
P
Living
18-0x20-0
37'-6"
Foyer
Dining
10-0x
14-0
Porch depth 5-6

Second Floor
1,069 sq. ft.

First Floor
997 sq. ft.

The Family
Handyman

Plan #702-0394

Innovative Design For That Narrow Lot

1,558 total square feet of living area

Price Code B

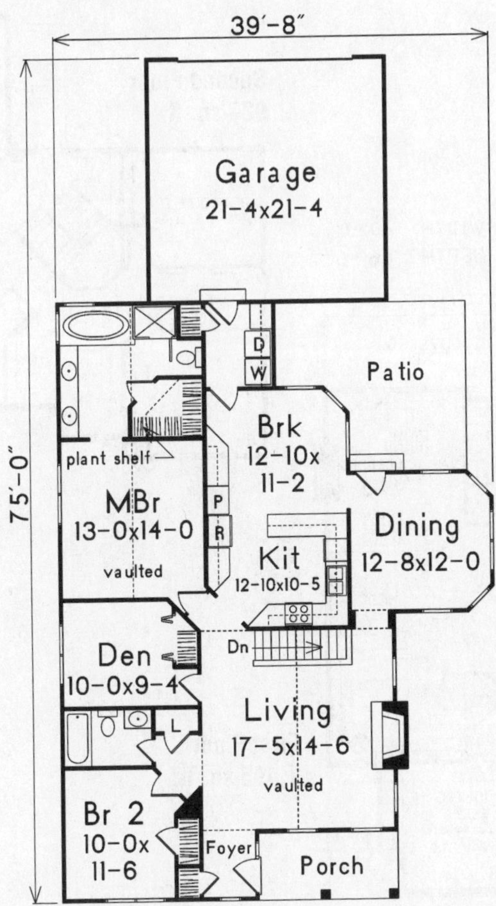
39'-8"
75'-0"
Garage
21-4x21-4
Patio
D
W
Brk
12-10x
11-2
plant shelf
MBr
13-0x14-0
vaulted
P
R
Kit
12-10x10-5
Dining
12-8x12-0
Den
10-0x9-4
Dn
Living
17-5x14-6
vaulted
L
Br 2
10-0x
11-6
Foyer
Porch

Special features

- Illuminated spaces created by visual access to outdoor living areas
- Vaulted master bedroom features private bath with whirlpool tub, separate shower and large walk-in closet
- Convenient first floor laundry has garage access
- Practical den or third bedroom
- U-shaped kitchen adjacent to sunny breakfast area
- 2 bedrooms, 2 baths, 2-car rear entry garage
- Basement foundation

TO ORDER BLUEPRINTS USE THE FORM ON PAGE 19 OR CALL TOLL-FREE 1-877-671-6036

Plan #702-GSD-2107

Vaulted Dining Room With Butler's Pantry

2,422 total square feet of living area **Price Code D**

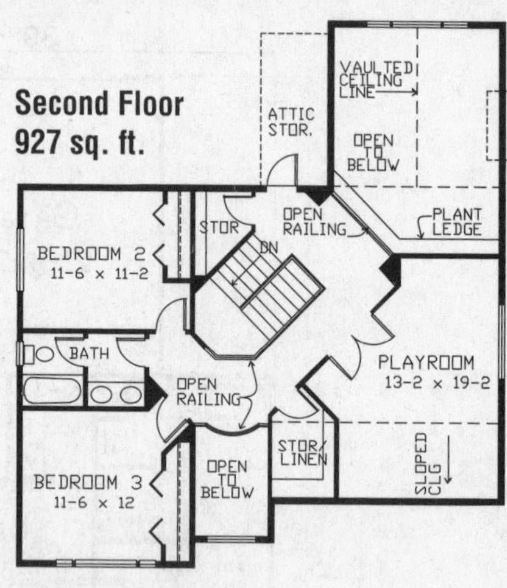
VAULTED CEILING LINE
ATTIC STOR.
OPEN TO BELOW
OPEN RAILING
PLANT LEDGE
STOR
DN
BEDROOM 2
11-6 x 11-2
BATH
OPEN RAILING
PLAYROOM
13-2 x 19-2
OPEN TO BELOW
STOR/LINEN
SLOPED CLG
BEDROOM 3
11-6 x 12

Second Floor
927 sq. ft.

Special features

- Covered porches invite guests into home
- Convenient and private first floor master suite
- Family room has vaulted ceiling
- 10' ceiling in dining room has formal feel
- Kitchen has walk-in pantry and eating bar
- 3 bedrooms, 2 1/2 baths, 3-car side entry garage
- Crawl space foundation

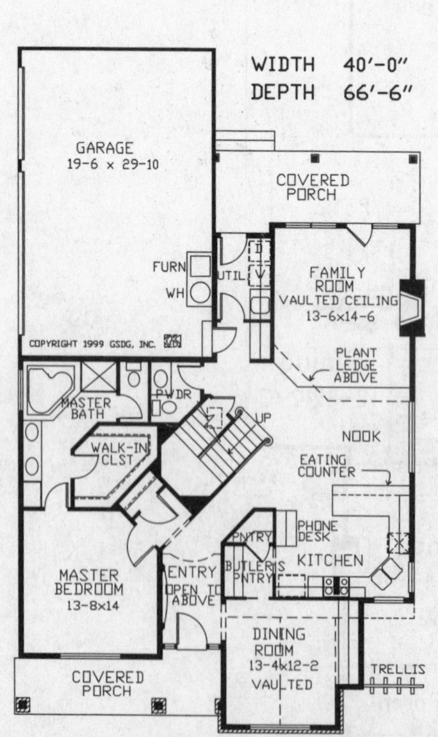
WIDTH 40'-0"
DEPTH 66'-6"
GARAGE
19-6 x 29-10
COVERED PORCH
FAMILY ROOM
VAULTED CEILING
13-6x14-6
FURN
WH
UTIL
COPYRIGHT 1999 GSDG, INC.
PLANT LEDGE ABOVE
MASTER BATH
PWDR
UP
NOOK
WALK-IN CLST
EATING COUNTER
PHONE DESK
PNTRY
KITCHEN
BUTLER'S PNTRY
MASTER BEDROOM
13-8x14
ENTRY
OPEN TO ABOVE
DINING ROOM
13-4x12-2
VAULTED
TRELLIS
COVERED PORCH

First Floor
1,495 sq. ft.

TO ORDER BLUEPRINTS USE THE FORM ON PAGE 19 OR CALL TOLL-FREE 1-877-671-6036

View thousands more home plans online at www.familyhandyman.com/homeplans

Plan #702-SH-SEA-245

Quaint Home Made For Country Living

1,578 total square feet of living area **Price Code B**

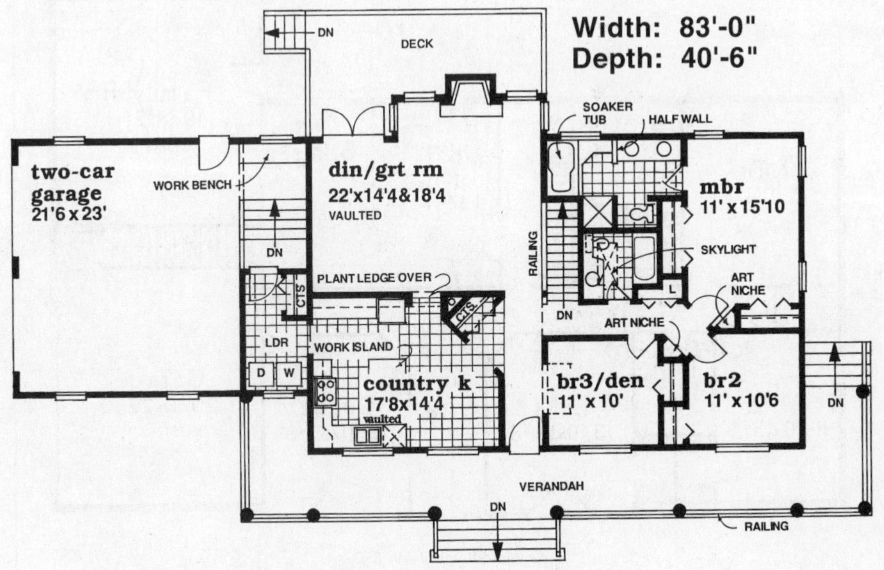
DN
DECK
SOAKER TUB
HALF WALL
two-car garage
21'6 x 23'
WORK BENCH
din/grt rm
22'x14'4&18'4
VAULTED
mbr
11' x 15'10
SKYLIGHT
RAILING
DN
PLANT LEDGE OVER
CTS
ART NICHE
LDR
WORK ISLAND
D W
country k
17'8x14'4
vaulted
br3/den
11' x 10'
br2
11' x 10'6
VERANDAH
RAILING

Width: 83'-0"
Depth: 40'-6"

Special features

- A fireplace warms the great room and is flanked by windows overlooking the rear deck
- Bedrooms are clustered on one side of the home for privacy from living areas
- Master bedroom has unique art niche at its entry and a private bath with separate tub and shower
- 3 bedrooms, 2 baths, 2-car side entry garage
- Basement or crawl space foundation, please specify when ordering

Plan #702-0797

Dormers Add Southern Accents

2,651 total square feet of living area

Price Code E

Special features

- Vaulted family room has corner fireplace and access to breakfast room and outdoor patio
- Dining room has double-door entry from covered front porch and a beautiful built-in corner display area
- Master bedroom has 10' tray ceiling, private bath and two walk-in closets
- Kitchen has enormous counterspace with plenty of eating area and overlooks a cheerful breakfast room
- 3 bedrooms, 2 baths, 2-car side entry garage
- Basement foundation, drawings also include crawl space and slab foundations

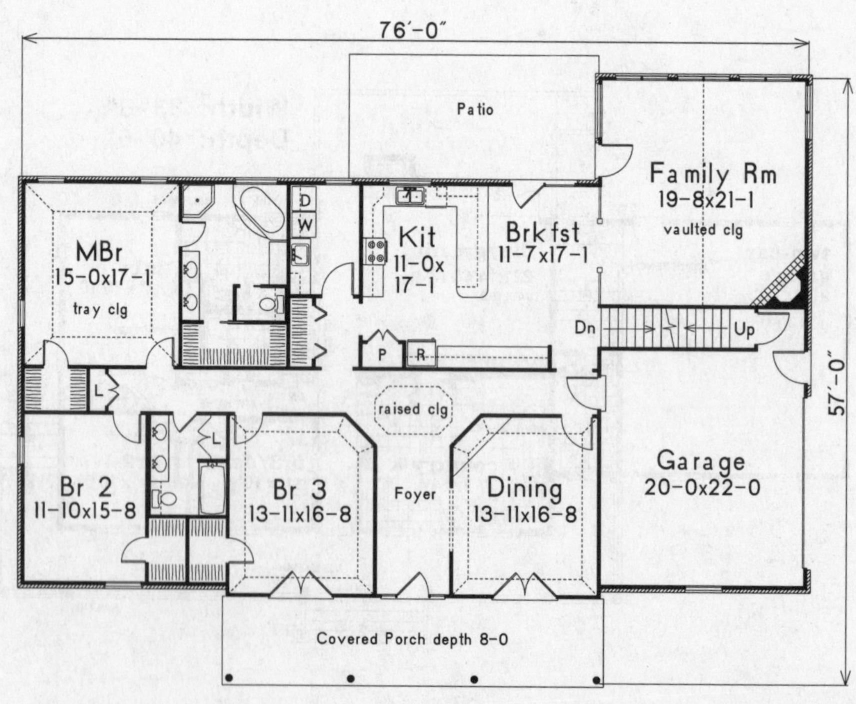
76'-0"
57'-0"
Patio
Family Rm
19-8x21-1
vaulted clg
MBr
15-0x17-1
tray clg
D
W
Kit
11-0x
17-1
Brkfst
11-7x17-1
Dn
Up
P
R
L
raised clg
Br 2
11-10x15-8
Br 3
13-11x16-8
Foyer
Dining
13-11x16-8
Garage
20-0x22-0
Covered Porch depth 8-0

Plan #702-1311

Attractive Dormers Enhance Facade

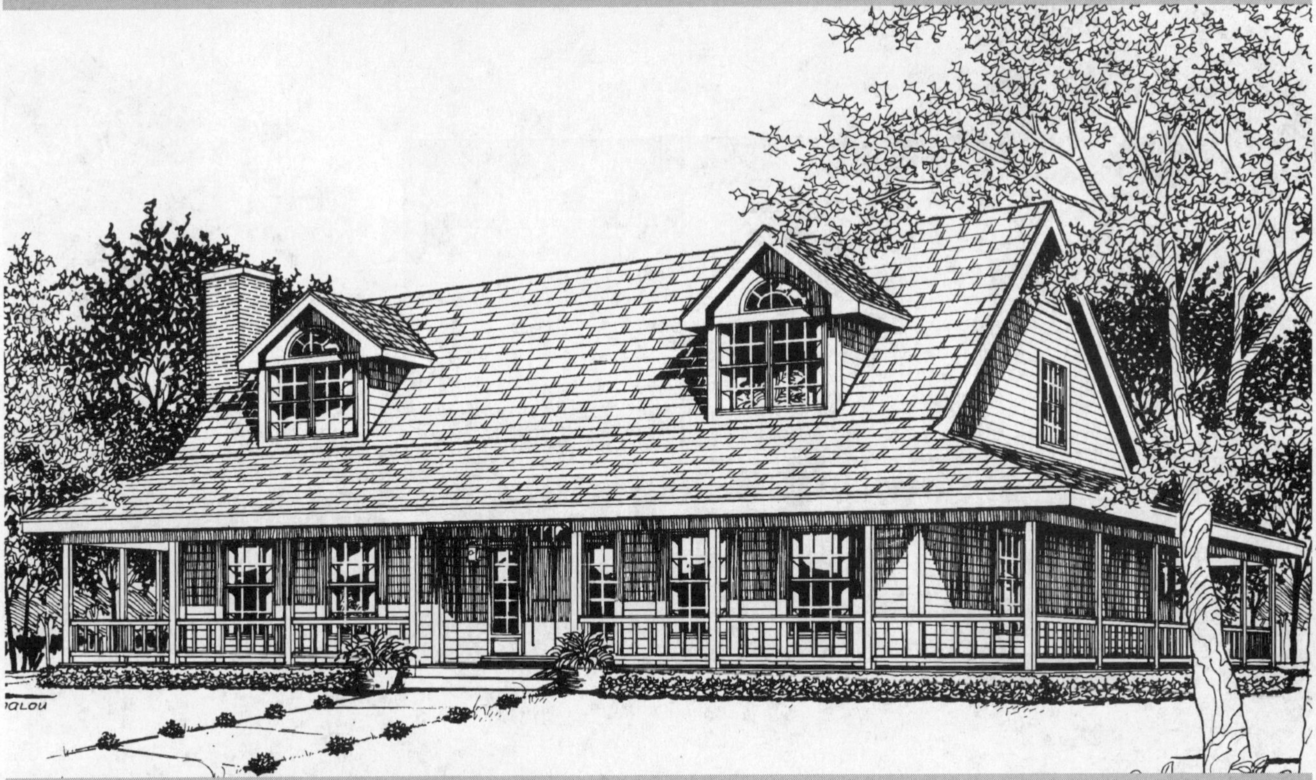

2,112 total square feet of living area **Price Code C**

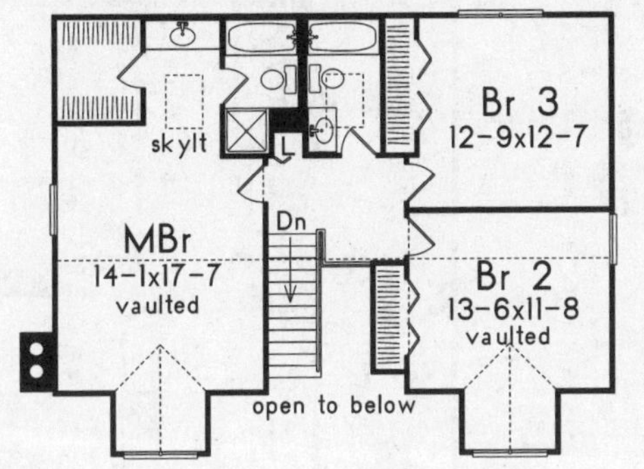
skylt
MBr
14-1x17-7
vaulted
Dn
L
Br 3
12-9x12-7
Br 2
13-6x11-8
vaulted
open to below

Second Floor
896 sq. ft.

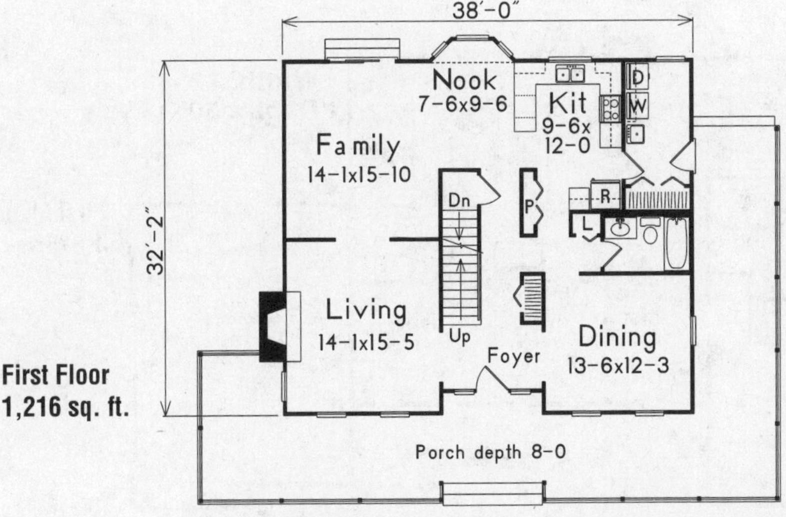
38'-0"
32'-2"
Nook
7-6x9-6
Kit
9-6x
12-0
D
W
Family
14-1x15-10
Dn
P
R
L
Living
14-1x15-5
Up
Foyer
Dining
13-6x12-3
Porch depth 8-0

First Floor
1,216 sq. ft.

Special features

- Double-door entrance from kitchen to dining area
- Nook located between family room and kitchen makes an ideal breakfast area
- Both baths on second floor feature skylights
- 3 bedrooms, 2 1/2 baths
- Basement foundation, drawings also include crawl space foundation

The Family
Handyman

Plan #702-JFD-20-2643-2

All The Features

2,643 total square feet of living area

Price Code E

Second Floor
768 sq. ft.

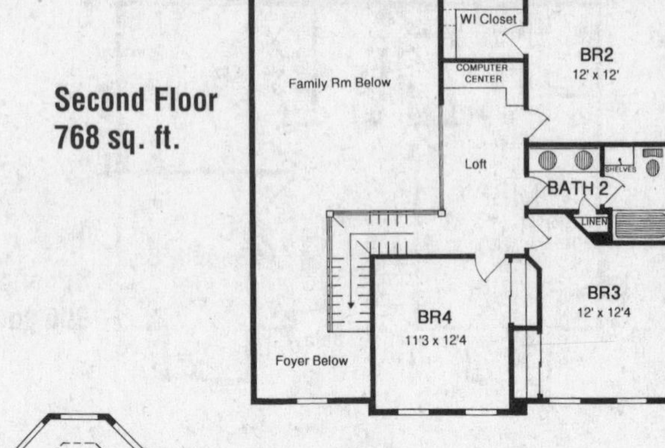
WI Closet
BR2
12' x 12'
COMPUTER CENTER
Family Rm Below
Loft
SHELVES
BATH 2
LINEN
BR4
11'3 x 12'4
BR3
12' x 12'4
Foyer Below

Special features

- Living and dining rooms combine to create a lovely area for entertaining
- Kitchen has snack bar which overlooks octagon shaped dining area
- Family room is centrally located with entertainment center
- Private study at rear of home
- 4 bedrooms, 2 1/2 baths, 2-car side entry garage
- Basement foundation

Width: 72'-8"
Depth: 50'-10"

First Floor
1,875 sq. ft.

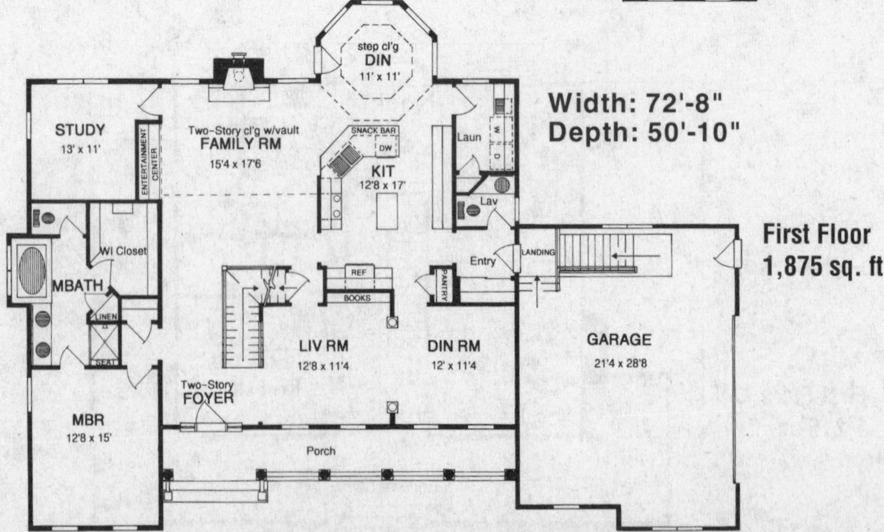
step cl'g
DIN
11' x 11'
STUDY
13' x 11'
ENTERTAINMENT CENTER
Two-Story cl'g w/vault
FAMILY RM
15'4 x 17'6
SNACK BAR
DW
KIT
12'8 x 17'
Laun
W
D
Lav
WI Closet
MBATH
LINEN
SEAT
Entry
LANDING
REF
BOOKS
PANTRY
LIV RM
12'8 x 11'4
DIN RM
12' x 11'4
GARAGE
21'4 x 28'8
Two-Story
FOYER
MBR
12'8 x 15'
Porch

TO ORDER BLUEPRINTS USE THE FORM ON PAGE 19 OR CALL TOLL-FREE 1-877-671-6036

View thousands more home plans online at www.familyhandyman.com/homeplans

Plan #702-0799

Bedrooms Separate From Rest Of Home

1,849 total square feet of living area **Price Code C**

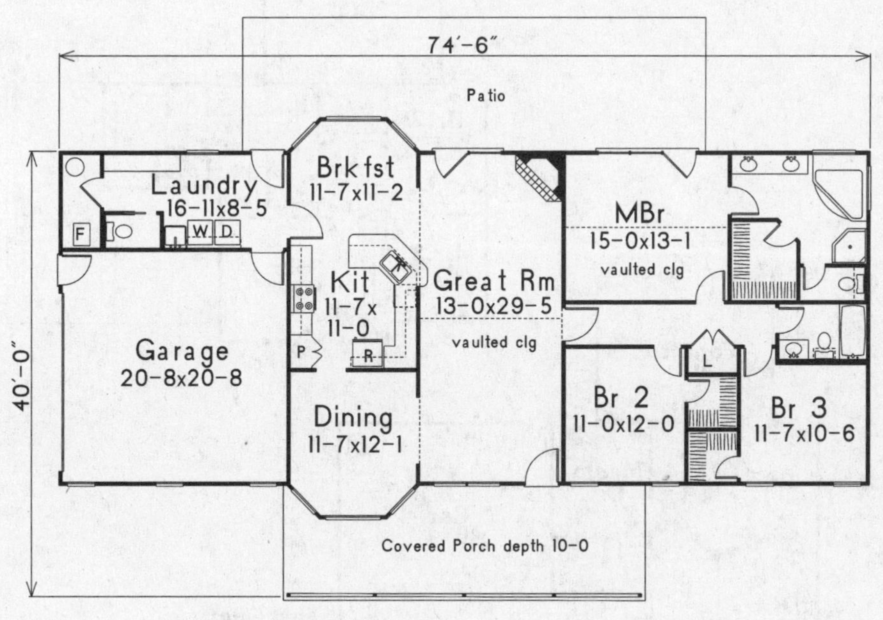

74'-6"
Patio
Brkfst
11-7x11-2
Laundry
16-11x8-5
F
W D
MBr
15-0x13-1
vaulted clg
Kit
11-7x
11-0
Great Rm
13-0x29-5
vaulted clg
P
R
Garage
20-8x20-8
40'-0"
L
Br 2
11-0x12-0
Br 3
11-7x10-6
Dining
11-7x12-1
Covered Porch depth 10-0

Special features

- Enormous laundry/mud room has many extras including storage area and half bath
- Lavish master bath has corner jacuzzi tub, double sinks, separate shower and walk-in closet
- Secondary bedrooms include walk-in closets
- Kitchen has wrap-around eating counter and is positioned between formal dining area and breakfast room for convenience
- 3 bedrooms, 2 1/2 baths, 2-car side entry garage
- Slab foundation, drawings also include crawl space foundation

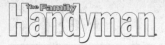

Plan #702-DBI-4642

Appealing Touches Abound

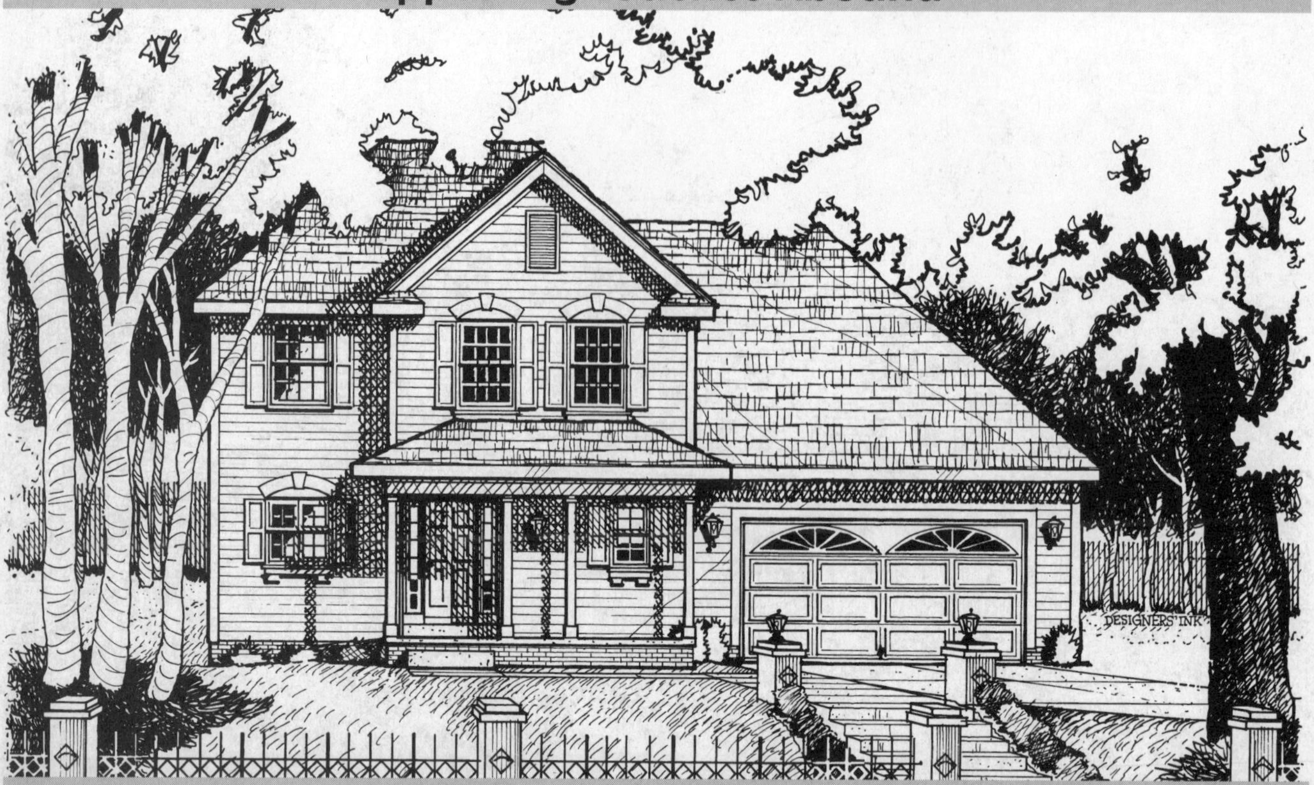

1,712 total square feet of living area

Price Code B

Special features

- Cathedral ceiling in family room adds drama and spaciousness
- Roomy utility area
- Master bedroom has a private bath, walk-in closet and whirlpool tub
- Efficient kitchen with snack bar
- 3 bedrooms, 2 1/2 baths, 2-car garage
- Basement foundation

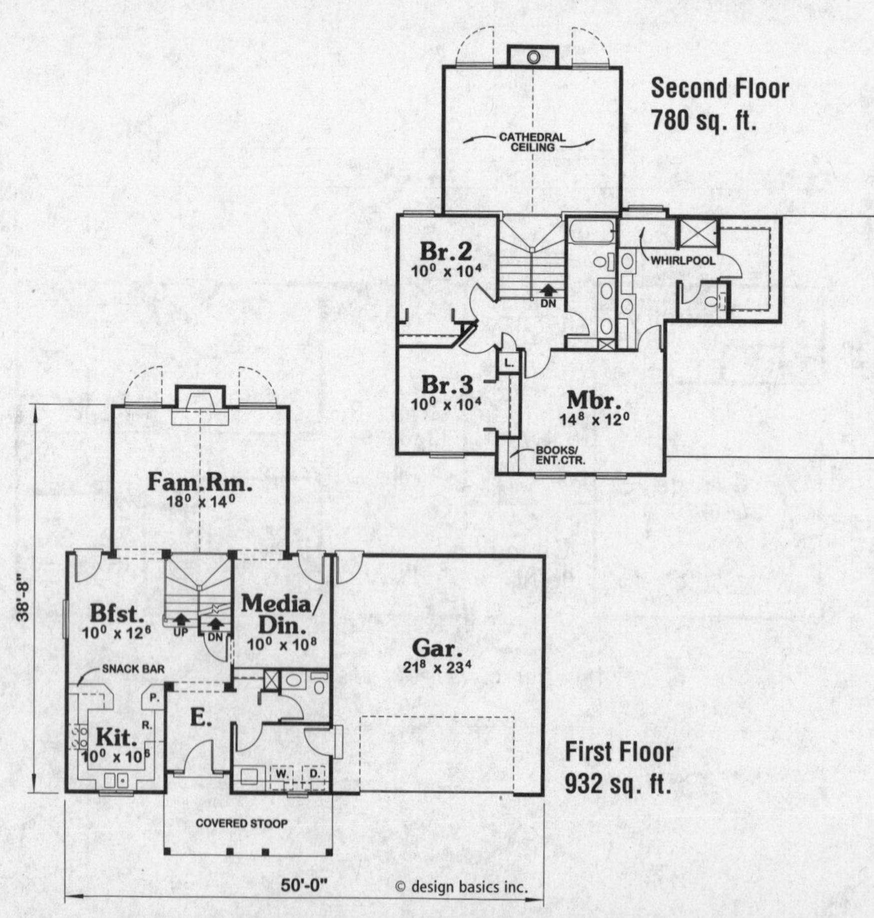

CATHEDRAL CEILING
Br.2 10⁰ x 10⁴
DN
WHIRLPOOL
L.
Br.3 10⁰ x 10⁴
Mbr. 14⁸ x 12⁰
BOOKS/ ENT.CTR.
Fam.Rm. 18⁰ x 14⁰
Bfst. 10⁰ x 12⁶
UP
DN
Media/ Din. 10⁰ x 10⁸
Gar. 21⁸ x 23⁴
SNACK BAR
P.
R.
Kit. 10⁰ x 10⁸
E.
W.
D.
COVERED STOOP
38'-8"
50'-0"
© design basics inc.

Second Floor
780 sq. ft.

First Floor
932 sq. ft.

Plan #702-0600

Country Comfort

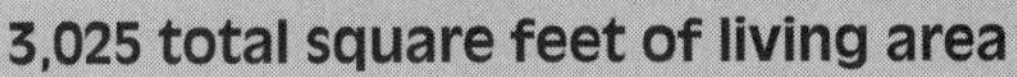

3,025 total square feet of living area **Price Code E**

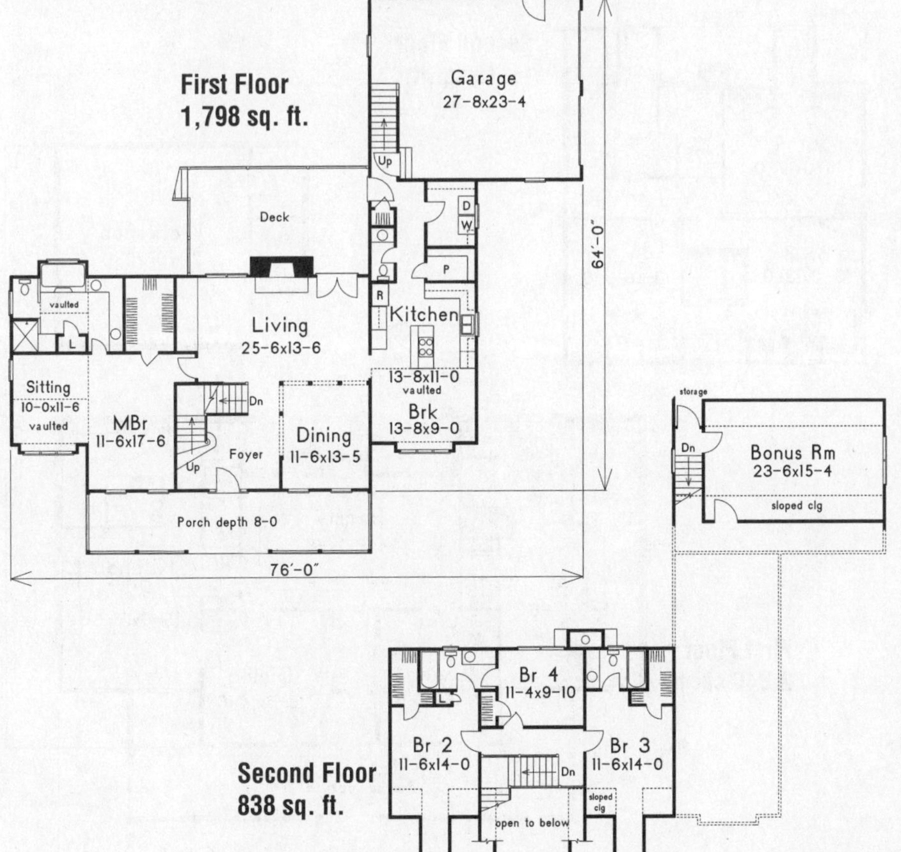

First Floor
1,798 sq. ft.
Garage
27-8x23-4
Up
D
W
P
R
Deck
Kitchen
Living
25-6x13-6
vaulted
L
13-8x11-0
vaulted
Sitting
10-0x11-6
vaulted
Dn
Brk
13-8x9-0
MBr
11-6x17-6
Dining
11-6x13-5
Up
Foyer
Porch depth 8-0
76'-0"
64'-0"
storage
Dn
Bonus Rm
23-6x15-4
sloped clg
Br 4
11-4x9-10
L
Br 2
11-6x14-0
Br 3
11-6x14-0
Dn
Second Floor
838 sq. ft.
sloped clg
open to below

Special features

- Bonus room above garage has its own private entrance - great for home office, hobby or exercise room
- Master suite has generous walk-in closet, luxurious bath and a vaulted sitting area
- Spacious kitchen has an island cooktop and vaulted breakfast nook
- Bonus room above garage has an additional 389 square feet of living area
- 4 bedrooms, 3 1/2 baths, 2-car side entry garage, 1-car drive under garage
- Basement foundation

Plan #702-0307

Large Porches Bring In The Outdoors

3,153 total square feet of living area **Price Code E**

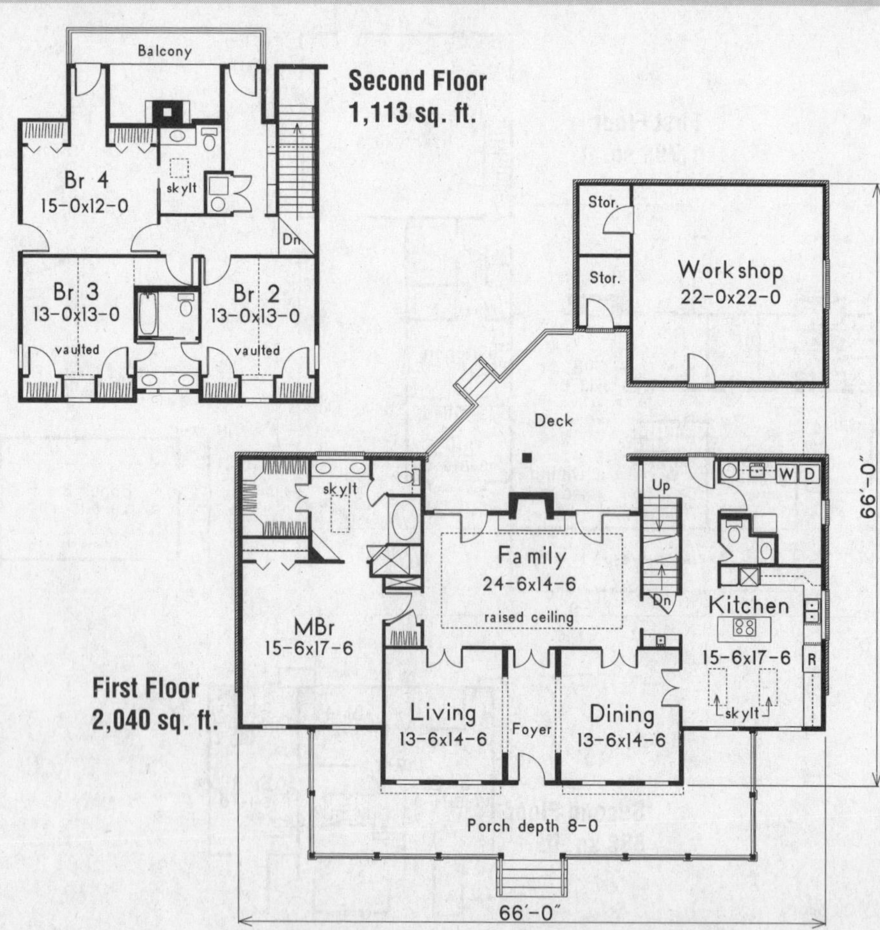

Balcony
Second Floor
1,113 sq. ft.
Br 4
15-0x12-0
skylt
Dn
Br 3
13-0x13-0
vaulted
Br 2
13-0x13-0
vaulted
Stor.
Stor.
Workshop
22-0x22-0
Deck
skylt
Up
W D
Family
24-6x14-6
raised ceiling
Dn
MBr
15-6x17-6
Kitchen
15-6x17-6
R
skylt
First Floor
2,040 sq. ft.
Living
13-6x14-6
Foyer
Dining
13-6x14-6
Porch depth 8-0
66'-0"
66'-0"

Special features

- Energy efficient home with 2" x 6" exterior walls
- Master suite with full amenities
- Covered breezeway and front and rear porches
- Full-sized workshop and storage with garage below, a unique combination
- 4 bedrooms, 3 1/2 baths, 2-car drive under garage
- Basement foundation, drawings also include crawl space and slab foundations

Plan #702-0705

Excellent Ranch For Country Setting

2,758 total square feet of living area

Price Code E

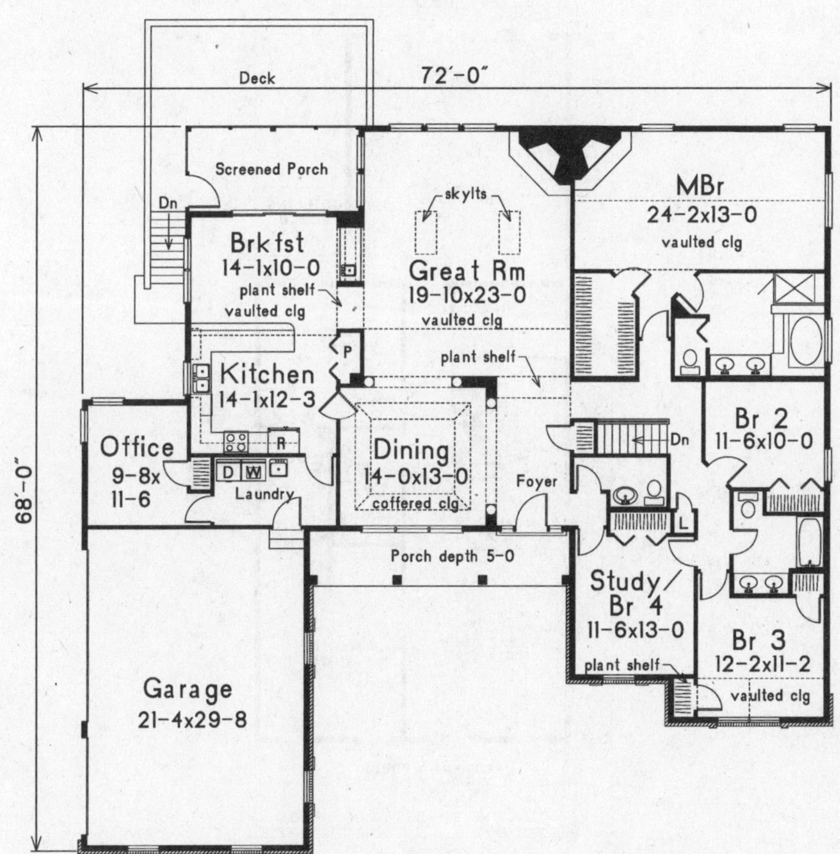
Deck
72'-0"
68'-0"
Screened Porch
Dn
Brkfst
14-1x10-0
plant shelf
vaulted clg
skylts
Great Rm
19-10x23-0
vaulted clg
plant shelf
MBr
24-2x13-0
vaulted clg
P
Kitchen
14-1x12-3
R
Office
9-8x
11-6
D W
Laundry
Dining
14-0x13-0
coffered clg
Foyer
Dn
Br 2
11-6x10-0
L
Porch depth 5-0
Study/
Br 4
11-6x13-0
plant shelf
Br 3
12-2x11-2
vaulted clg
Garage
21-4x29-8

Special features

- Vaulted great room excels with fireplace, wet bar, plant shelves and skylights
- Fabulous master suite enjoys a fireplace, large bath, walk-in closet and vaulted ceiling
- Trendsetting kitchen/breakfast room adjoins spacious screened porch
- Convenient office near kitchen is perfect for computer room, hobby enthusiast or fifth bedroom
- 4 bedrooms, 2 1/2 baths, 3-car side entry garage
- Basement foundation

TO ORDER BLUEPRINTS USE THE FORM ON PAGE 19 OR CALL TOLL-FREE 1-877-671-6036

View thousands more home plans online at www.familyhandyman.com/homeplans

The Family
Handyman

Plan #702-NDG-794

Country Charm Ideal For A Narrow Lot

1,120 total square feet of living area **Price Code AA**

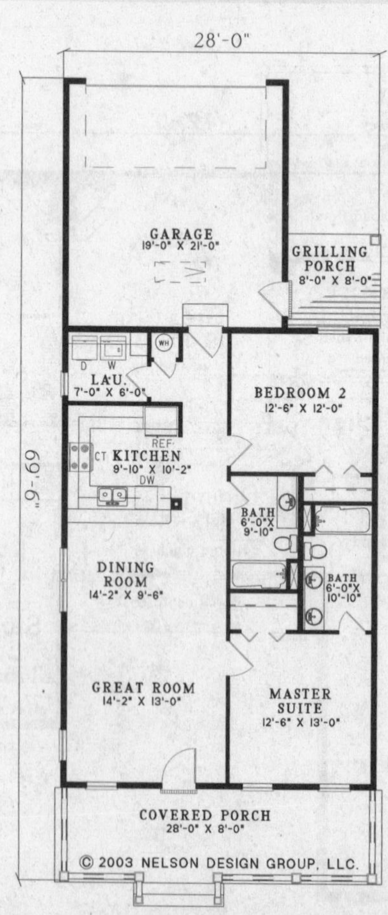
28'-0"
69'-6"
GARAGE
19'-0" X 21'-0"
GRILLING PORCH
8'-0" X 8'-0"
WH
D W
LAU.
7'-0" X 6'-0"
BEDROOM 2
12'-6" X 12'-0"
REF
CT KITCHEN
9'-10" X 10'-2"
DW
BATH
6'-0"X
9'-10"
BATH
6'-0"X
10'-10"
DINING ROOM
14'-2" X 9'-6"
GREAT ROOM
14'-2" X 13'-0"
MASTER SUITE
12'-6" X 13'-0"
COVERED PORCH
28'-0" X 8'-0"
© 2003 NELSON DESIGN GROUP, LLC.

Special features

- Open living has great room and dining room combining
- Private bath in the master suite
- Grilling porch in the rear of the home
- 2 bedrooms, 2 baths, 2-car rear entry garage
- Crawl space or slab foundation, please specify when ordering

TO ORDER BLUEPRINTS USE THE FORM ON PAGE 19 OR CALL TOLL-FREE 1-877-671-6036

View thousands more home plans online at www.familyhandyman.com/homeplans

Plan #702-SH-SEA-400

Country Accents Make This Home

1,568 total square feet of living area **Price Code B**

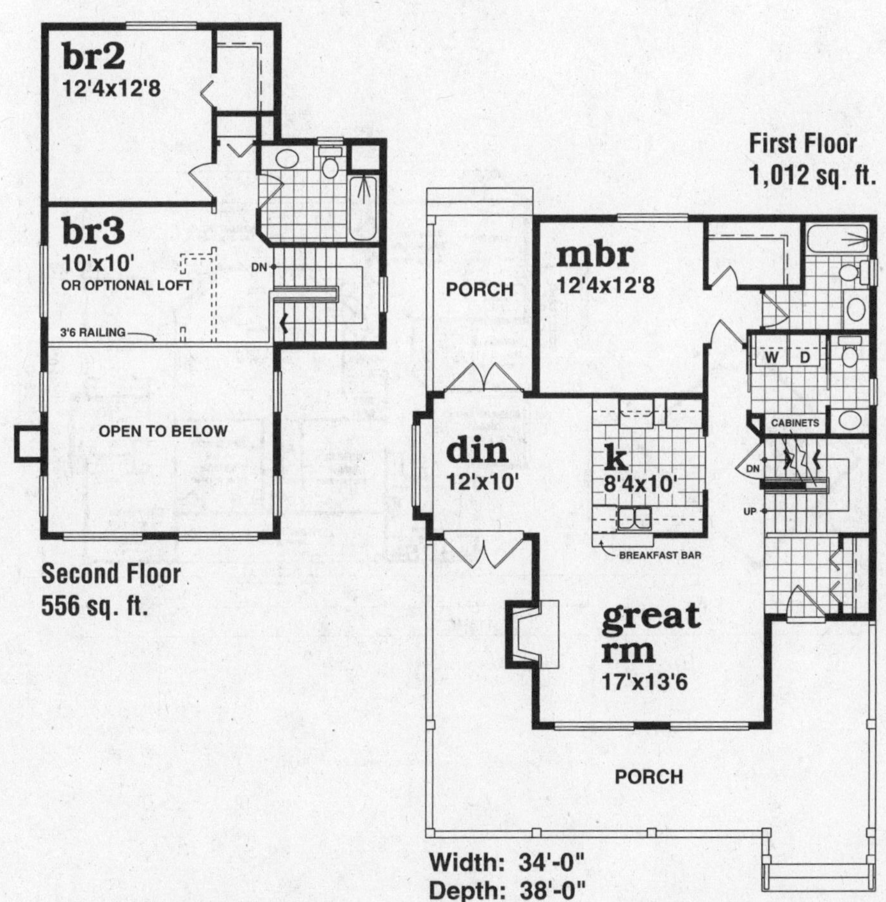
br2
12'4x12'8
br3
10'x10'
OR OPTIONAL LOFT
DN
3'6 RAILING
OPEN TO BELOW
Second Floor
556 sq. ft.
First Floor
1,012 sq. ft.
PORCH
mbr
12'4x12'8
W
D
CABINETS
din
12'x10'
k
8'4x10'
DN
UP
BREAKFAST BAR
great rm
17'x13'6
PORCH
Width: 34'-0"
Depth: 38'-0"

Special features

- Master bedroom is located on first floor for convenience
- Cozy great room has fireplace
- Dining room has access to both the front and rear porches
- Two secondary bedrooms and a bath complete the second floor
- 3 bedrooms, 2 1/2 baths
- Basement or crawl space foundation, please specify when ordering

TO ORDER BLUEPRINTS USE THE FORM ON PAGE 19 OR CALL TOLL-FREE 1-877-671-6036

The Family
Handyman

Plan #702-DH-2352

Sprawling Ranch Design

2,352 total square feet of living area **Price Code D**

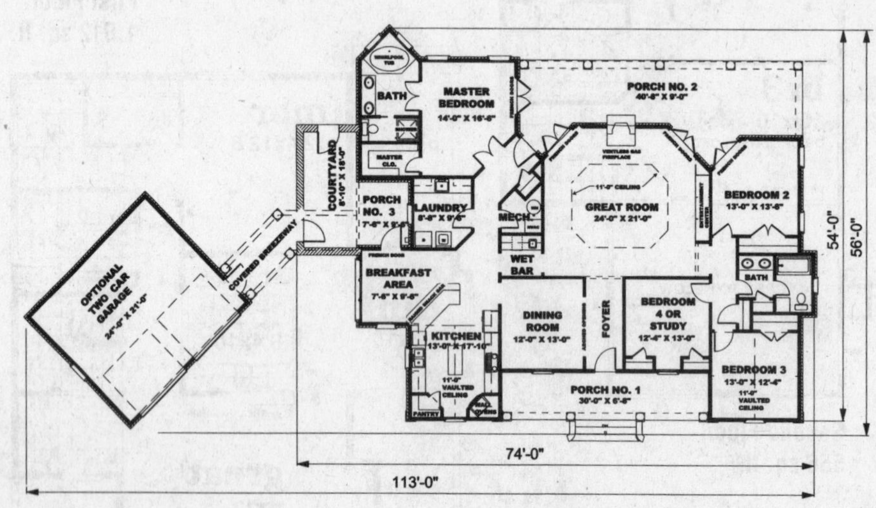
MASTER BEDROOM
14'-0" X 16'-5"
BATH
PORCH NO. 2
40'-0" X 9'-0"
GREAT ROOM
24'-0" X 21'-0"
BEDROOM 2
13'-0" X 13'-6"
COURTYARD
PORCH NO. 3
LAUNDRY
MECH.
WET BAR
BREAKFAST AREA
KITCHEN
13'-0" X 17'-10"
DINING ROOM
12'-0" X 13'-0"
FOYER
BEDROOM 4 OR STUDY
12'-4" X 13'-0"
BATH
BEDROOM 3
13'-0" X 12'-4"
PORCH NO. 1
30'-0" X 6'-8"
OPTIONAL TWO CAR GARAGE
24'-0" X 21'-0"
COVERED BREEZEWAY
74'-0"
113'-0"
54'-0"
56'-0"

Special features

- Charming courtyard on the side of the home easily accesses the porch leading into the breakfast area
- French doors throughout home create a sunny atmosphere
- Master bedroom accesses covered porch
- 4 bedrooms, 2 baths, optional 2-car garage
- Crawl space or slab foundation, please specify when ordering

The Family
Handyman

Plan #702-0322

Open Breakfast/Family Room Combination

2,135 total square feet of living area

Price Code D

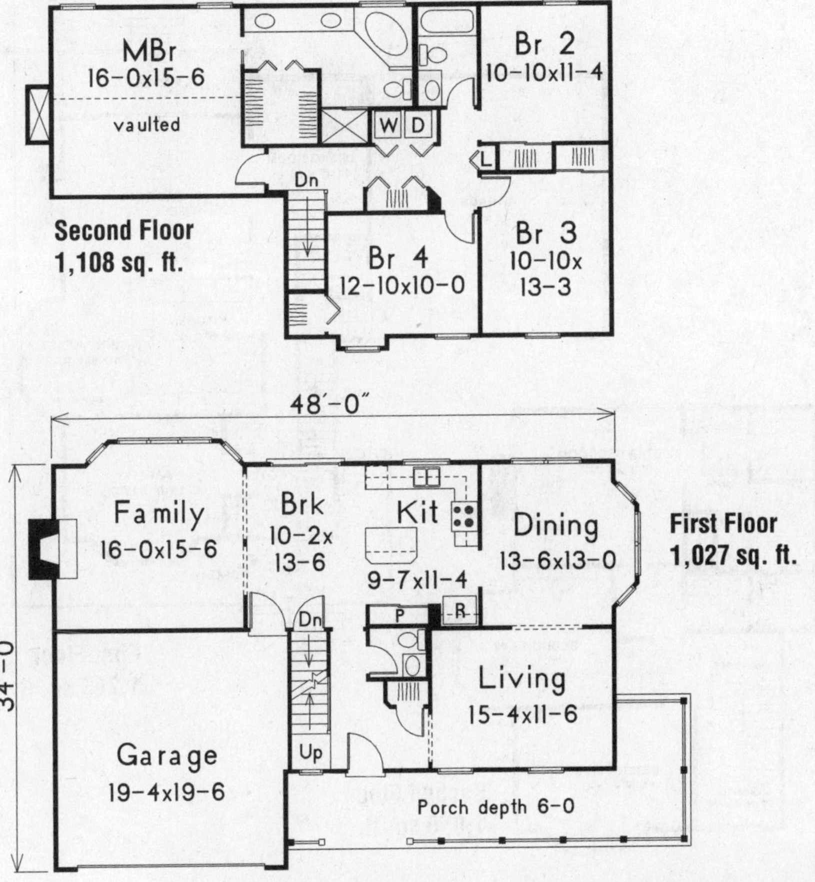
MBr
16-0x15-6
vaulted
W
D
Br 2
10-10x11-4
L
Dn
Br 4
12-10x10-0
Br 3
10-10x
13-3
Second Floor
1,108 sq. ft.
48′-0″
34′-0″
Family
16-0x15-6
Brk
10-2x
13-6
Kit
9-7x11-4
Dining
13-6x13-0
P
R
Dn
Up
Living
15-4x11-6
Garage
19-4x19-6
Porch depth 6-0

First Floor
1,027 sq. ft.

Special features

- Family room features extra space, impressive fireplace and full wall of windows that joins breakfast room creating a spacious entertainment area
- Washer and dryer conveniently located on the second floor
- Kitchen features island counter and pantry
- 4 bedrooms, 2 1/2 baths, 2-car garage
- Basement foundation

Plan #702-1300

Distinct Country Look And Feel

2,253 total square feet of living area

Price Code D

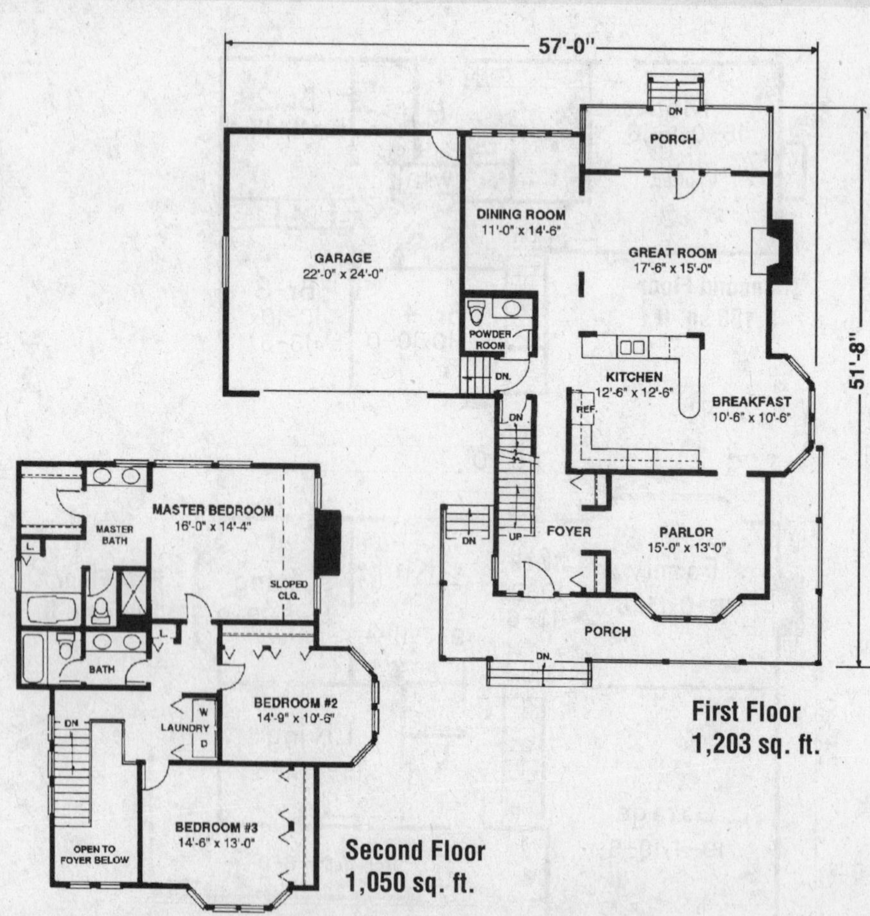
57'-0"
51'-8"
PORCH
DN
DINING ROOM
11'-0" x 14'-6"
GARAGE
22'-0" x 24'-0"
GREAT ROOM
17'-6" x 15'-0"
POWDER ROOM
KITCHEN
12'-6" x 12'-6"
REF.
BREAKFAST
10'-6" x 10'-6"
FOYER
UP
PARLOR
15'-0" x 13'-0"
PORCH
MASTER BEDROOM
16'-0" x 14'-4"
MASTER BATH
SLOPED CLG.
BATH
LAUNDRY
W
D
BEDROOM #2
14'-9" x 10'-6"
BEDROOM #3
14'-6" x 13'-0"
OPEN TO FOYER BELOW

First Floor
1,203 sq. ft.

Second Floor
1,050 sq. ft.

Special features

- Great room joined by covered porch
- Secluded parlor provides area for peace and quiet or private office
- Sloped ceiling adds drama to master suite
- Great room and kitchen/ breakfast area combine for large open living
- 3 bedrooms, 2 1/2 baths, 2-car garage
- Basement foundation

TO ORDER BLUEPRINTS USE THE FORM ON PAGE 19 OR CALL TOLL-FREE 1-877-671-6036
View thousands more home plans online at www.familyhandyman.com/homeplans

The Family
Handyman

Plan #702-NDG-111

Cozy Covered Porches

2,698 total square feet of living area

Price Code E

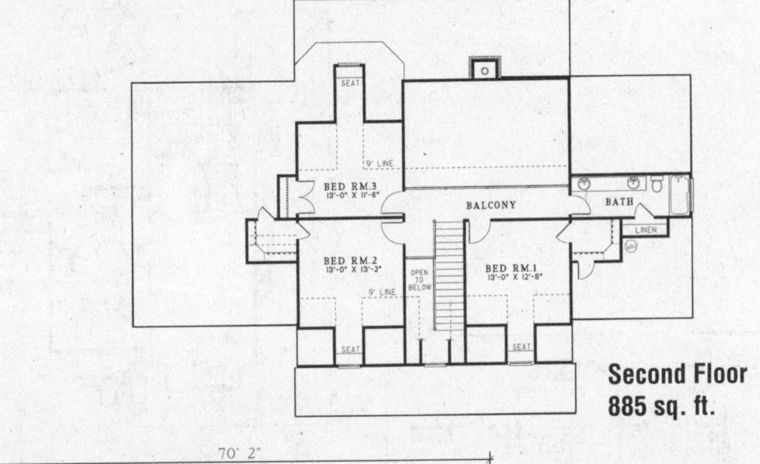
SEAT
9' LINE
BED RM.3
13'-0" X 11'-6"
BALCONY
BATH
LINEN
BED RM.2
13'-0" X 13'-2"
OPEN TO BELOW
9' LINE
BED RM.1
13'-0" X 12'-8"
SEAT
SEAT

Second Floor
885 sq. ft.

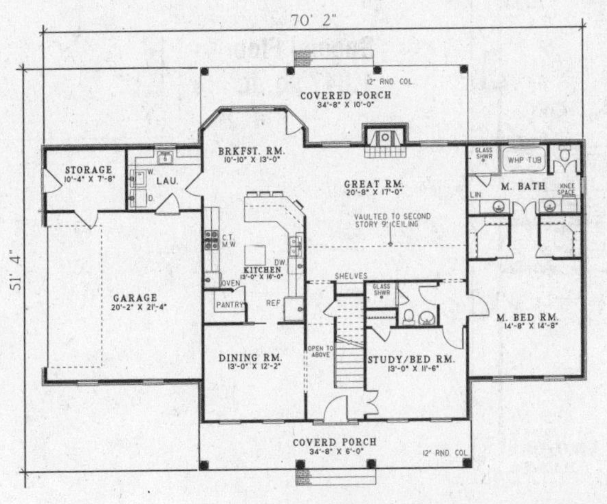
70' 2"
12" RND COL.
COVERED PORCH
34'-8" X 10'-0"
BRKFST. RM.
10'-10" X 13'-0"
GREAT RM.
20'-8" X 17'-0"
VAULTED TO SECOND STORY 9' CEILING
STORAGE
10'-4" X 7'-8"
LAU.
GLASS SHWR
WHP TUB
M. BATH
KNEE SPACE
LIN
KITCHEN
OVEN
PANTRY
REF
DW
SHELVES
GLASS SHWR
51' 4"
GARAGE
20'-2" X 21'-4"
M. BED RM.
14'-8" X 14'-8"
DINING RM.
13'-0" X 12'-2"
OPEN TO ABOVE
STUDY/BED RM.
13'-0" X 11'-6"
COVERD PORCH
34'-8" X 6'-0"
12" RND COL

First Floor
1,813 sq. ft.

Special features

- Great room feels spacious with vaulted ceiling and windows overlooking covered porch
- Master suite bath has a glass shower and whirlpool tub
- Laundry area includes counterspace and sink
- 4 bedrooms, 3 baths, 2-car side entry garage
- Basement, walk-out basement, crawl space or slab foundation, please specify when ordering

Plan #702-SH-SEA-061

Covered Verandah Wraps Three Sides Of Home

2,493 total square feet of living area

Price Code D

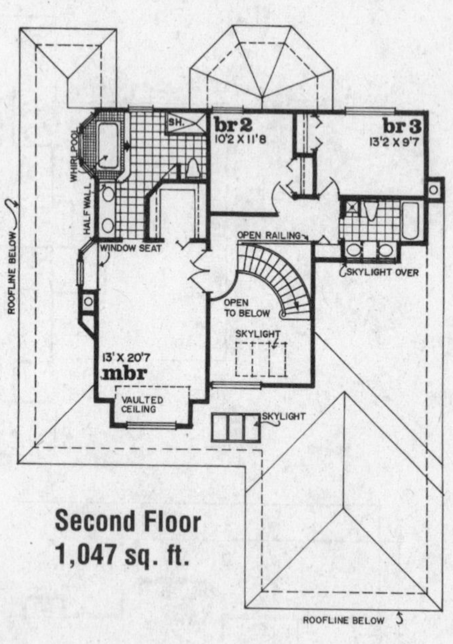
br 2
10'2 X 11'8
br 3
13'2 X 9'7
SH.
WHIRLPOOL
HALFWALL
WINDOW SEAT
OPEN RAILING
SKYLIGHT OVER
ROOFLINE BELOW
OPEN TO BELOW
SKYLIGHT
13' X 20'7
mbr
VAULTED CEILING
SKYLIGHT
ROOFLINE BELOW

Second Floor
1,047 sq. ft.

Special features

- Energy efficient home with 2" x 6" exterior walls
- Breakfast room is nestled in a bay window
- Master bedroom boasts a vaulted ceiling alcove, window seat and walk-in closet
- Sunken family room features a start-of-the-art built-in media center
- 3 bedrooms, 2 1/2 baths
- Basement foundation

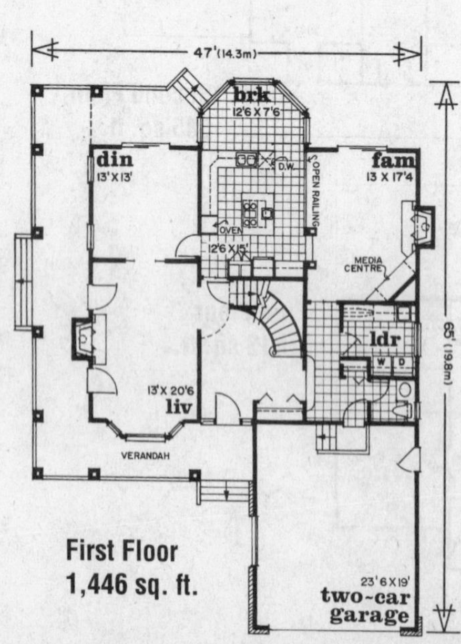
47' (14.3m)
brk
12'6 X 7'6
din
13' X 13'
fam
13 X 17'4
D.W.
OPEN RAILING
OVEN
12'6 X 15'
MEDIA CENTRE
ldr
W D
13' X 20'6
liv
VERANDAH
65' (19.8m)
23'6 X 19'
two-car garage

First Floor
1,446 sq. ft.

Plan #702-CHP-3054-B-3

Beautiful Entrance Is Graced With Southern Charm

3,266 total square feet of living area

Price Code H

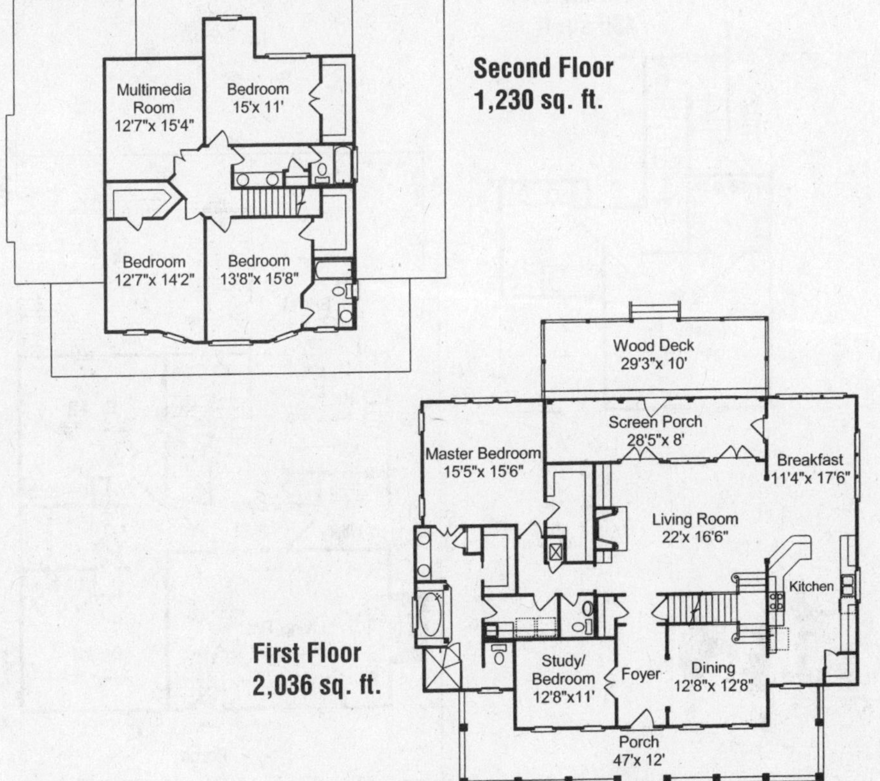

Multimedia Room 12'7"x 15'4"
Bedroom 15'x 11'
Bedroom 12'7"x 14'2"
Bedroom 13'8"x 15'8"
Second Floor
1,230 sq. ft.
Wood Deck 29'3"x 10'
Screen Porch 28'5"x 8'
Master Bedroom 15'5"x 15'6"
Breakfast 11'4"x 17'6"
Living Room 22'x 16'6"
Kitchen
Study/ Bedroom 12'8"x11'
Foyer
Dining 12'8"x 12'8"
Porch 47'x 12'
First Floor
2,036 sq. ft.
Width: 57'-4"
Depth: 41'-7"

Special features

- Screened porch has double-door entrances from living room
- Sunny breakfast room has lots of windows for a cheerful atmosphere
- All bedrooms on second floor have spacious walk-in closets
- Multimedia room makes a great casual family room
- 5 bedrooms, 3 1/2 baths, 2-car drive under garage
- Two-story pier foundation

TO ORDER BLUEPRINTS USE THE FORM ON PAGE 19 OR CALL TOLL-FREE 1-877-671-6036

View thousands more home plans online at www.familyhandyman.com/homeplans

Plan #702-GH-24706

An Open Feel With Vaulted Ceilings

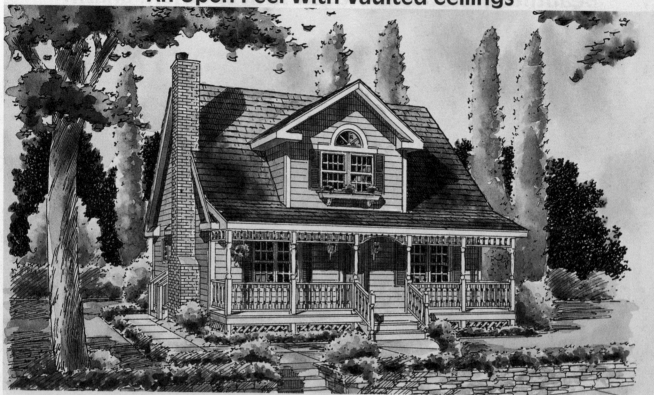

1,470 total square feet of living area

Price Code A

Special features

- Vaulted breakfast room is cheerful and sunny
- Private second floor master bedroom with bath and walk-in closet
- Large utility room has access to the outdoors
- 3 bedrooms, 2 baths
- Basement, crawl space or slab foundation, please specify when ordering

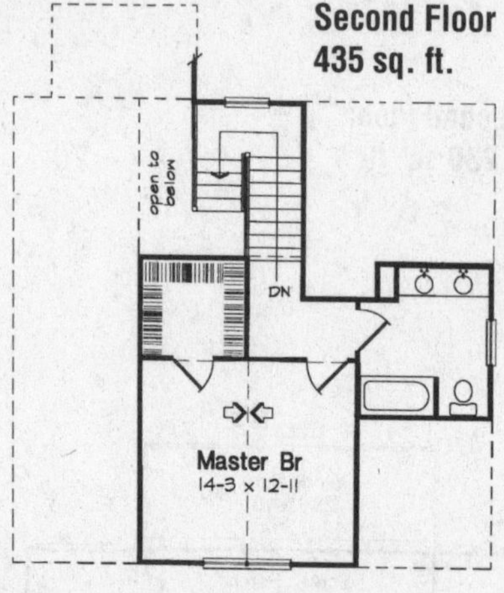
open to below
DN
Master Br
14-3 x 12-11

Second Floor
435 sq. ft.

Rear View

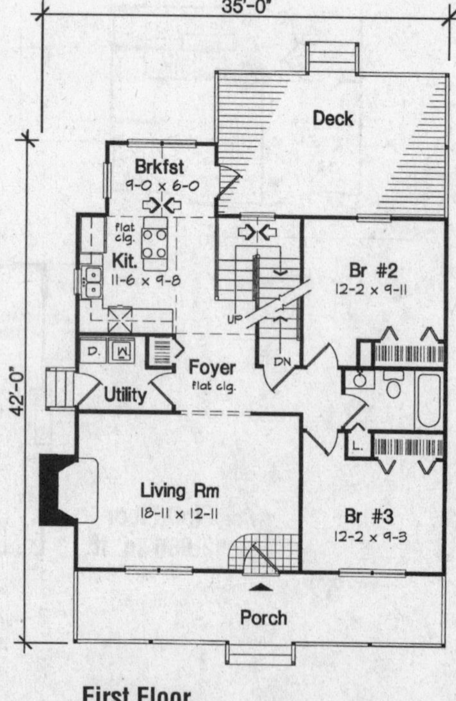
35'-0"
Deck
Brkfst
9-0 x 6-0
flat clg.
Kit.
11-6 x 9-8
UP
DN
Br #2
12-2 x 9-11
D.
W
Foyer
flat clg.
Utility
42'-0"
L.
Living Rm
18-11 x 12-11
Br #3
12-2 x 9-3
Porch

First Floor
1,035 sq. ft.

TO ORDER BLUEPRINTS USE THE FORM ON PAGE 19 OR CALL TOLL-FREE 1-877-671-6036

View thousands more home plans online at www.familyhandyman.com/homeplans

The Family
Handyman

Plan #702-0747

Classic Atrium Ranch With Rooms To Spare

1,977 total square feet of living area

Price Code C

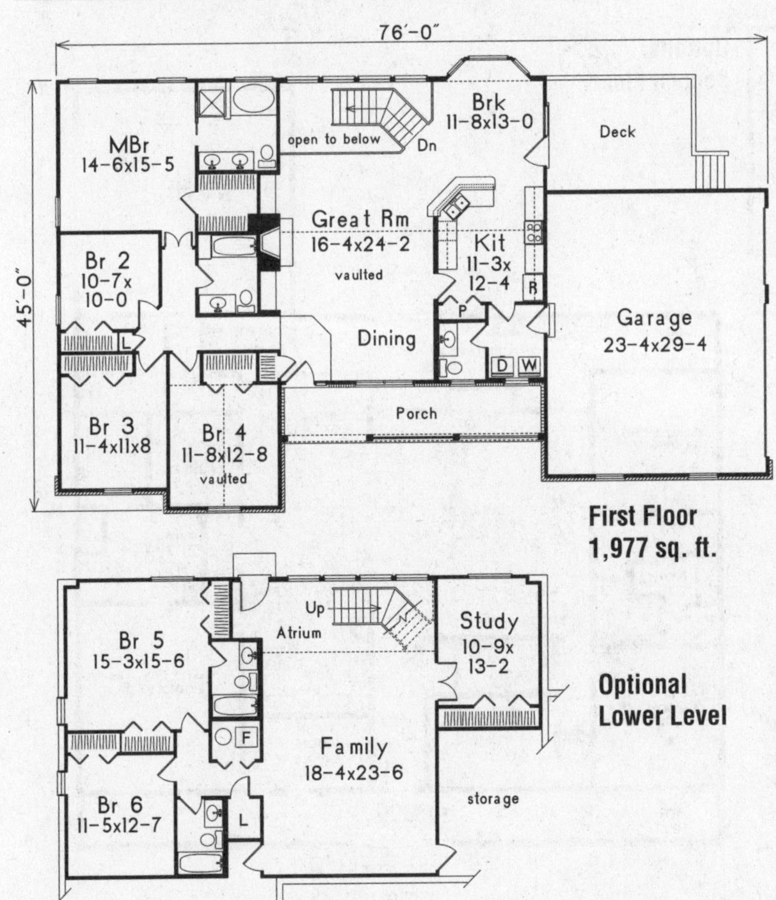
76'-0"
45'-0"
MBr
14-6x15-5
open to below
Dn
Brk
11-8x13-0
Deck
Great Rm
16-4x24-2
vaulted
Kit
11-3x
12-4
Br 2
10-7x
10-0
Dining
P
R
D
W
Garage
23-4x29-4
Porch
Br 3
11-4x11x8
Br 4
11-8x12-8
vaulted
First Floor
1,977 sq. ft.
Up
Atrium
Study
10-9x
13-2
Br 5
15-3x15-6
F
Family
18-4x23-6
Br 6
11-5x12-7
L
storage
storage
Optional
Lower Level

Special features

- Classic traditional exterior always in style
- Spacious great room boasts a vaulted ceiling, dining area, atrium with elegant staircase and feature windows
- Atrium open to 1,416 square feet of optional living area below which consists of an optional family room, two bedrooms, two baths and a study
- 4 bedrooms, 2 1/2 baths, 3-car side entry garage
- Walk-out basement foundation

Plan #702-DH-3329

Shaded Porches Perfect For Country Living

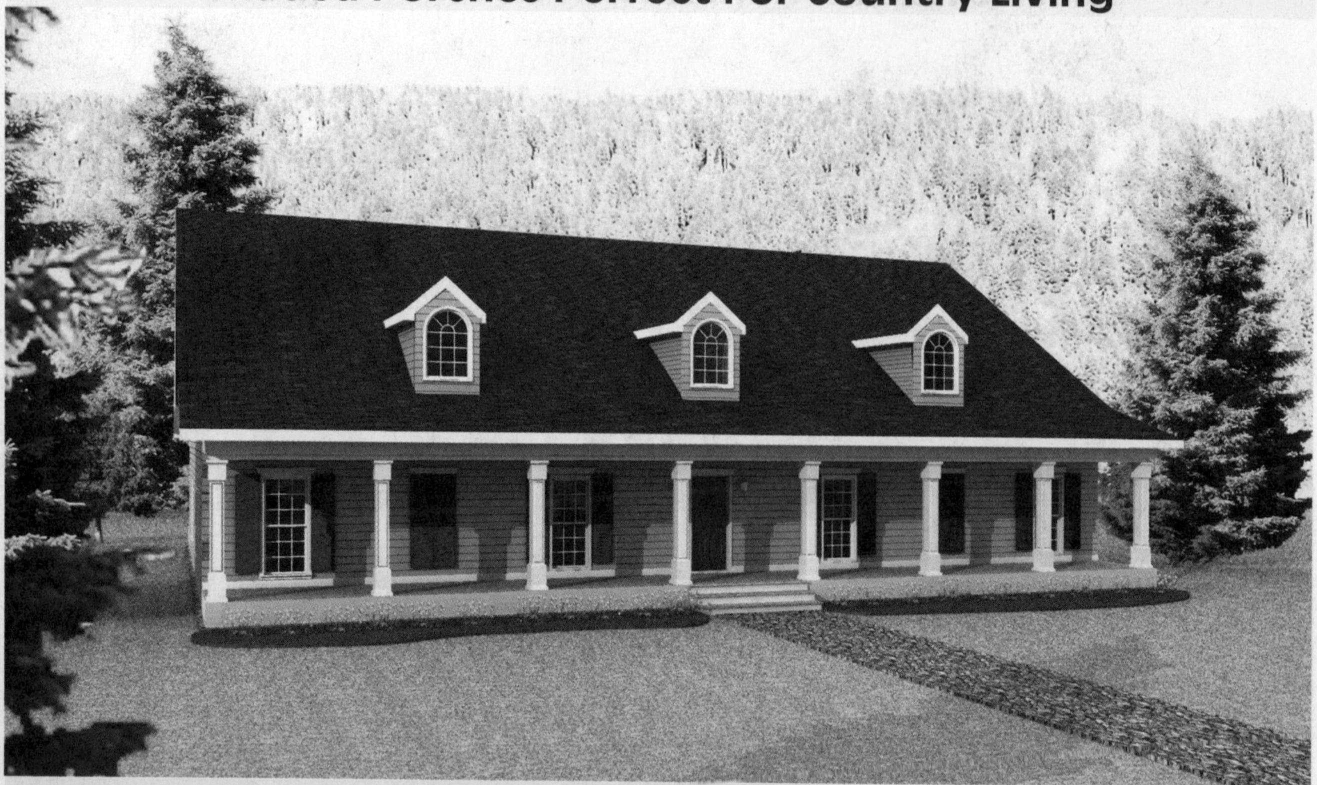

3,029 total square feet of living area

Price Code E

Special features

- Master bedroom is isolated from other bedrooms for privacy
- Bedroom #4 would make an ideal home office with plenty of storage
- Bonus room above garage has an additional 288 square feet of living area
- 4 bedrooms, 3 baths, 2-car garage
- Slab foundation

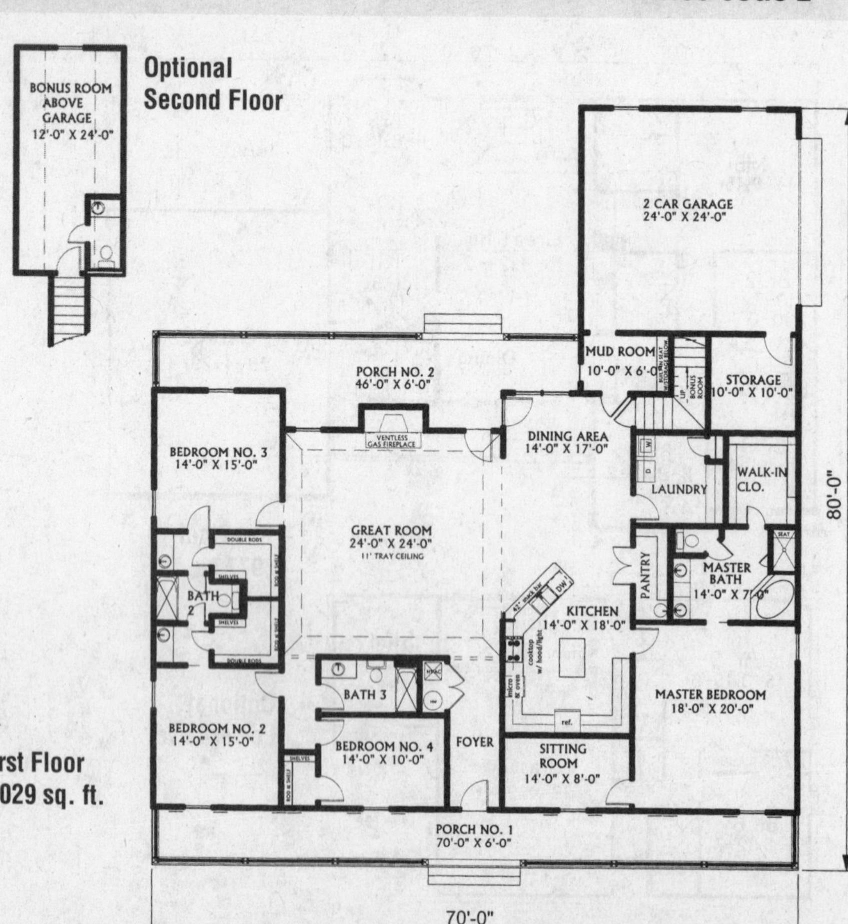
BONUS ROOM ABOVE GARAGE 12'-0" X 24'-0"
Optional Second Floor
2 CAR GARAGE 24'-0" X 24'-0"
MUD ROOM 10'-0" X 6'-0"
STORAGE 10'-0" X 10'-0"
PORCH NO. 2 46'-0" X 6'-0"
VENTLESS GAS FIREPLACE
DINING AREA 14'-0" X 17'-0"
BEDROOM NO. 3 14'-0" X 15'-0"
LAUNDRY
WALK-IN CLO.
GREAT ROOM 24'-0" X 24'-0" 11' TRAY CEILING
PANTRY
MASTER BATH 14'-0" X 7'-0"
BATH 2
KITCHEN 14'-0" X 18'-0"
BATH 3
MASTER BEDROOM 18'-0" X 20'-0"
BEDROOM NO. 2 14'-0" X 15'-0"
BEDROOM NO. 4 14'-0" X 10'-0"
FOYER
SITTING ROOM 14'-0" X 8'-0"
PORCH NO. 1 70'-0" X 6'-0"
80'-0"
70'-0"
First Floor 3,029 sq. ft.

Plan #702-CHP-1633-A-18

Nice-Sized Home Loaded With Charm

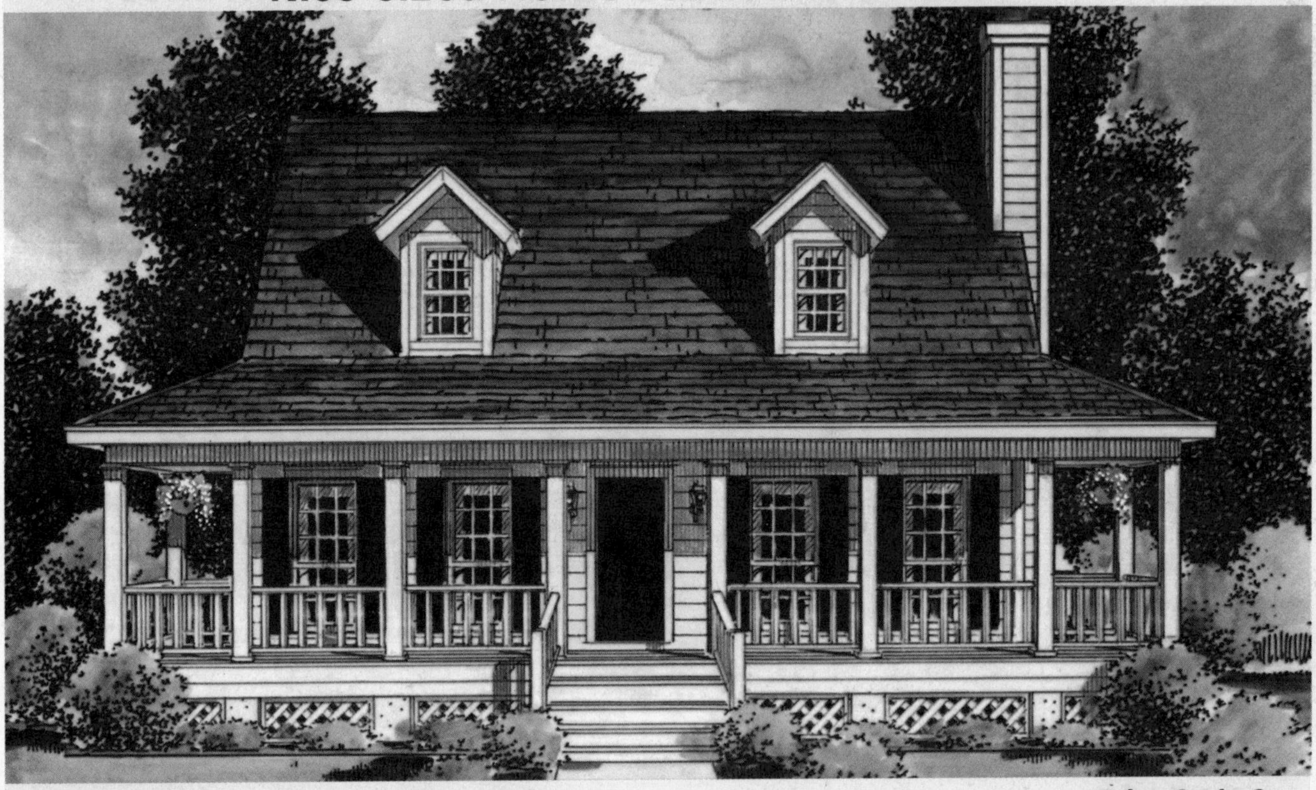

1,618 total square feet of living area

Price Code C

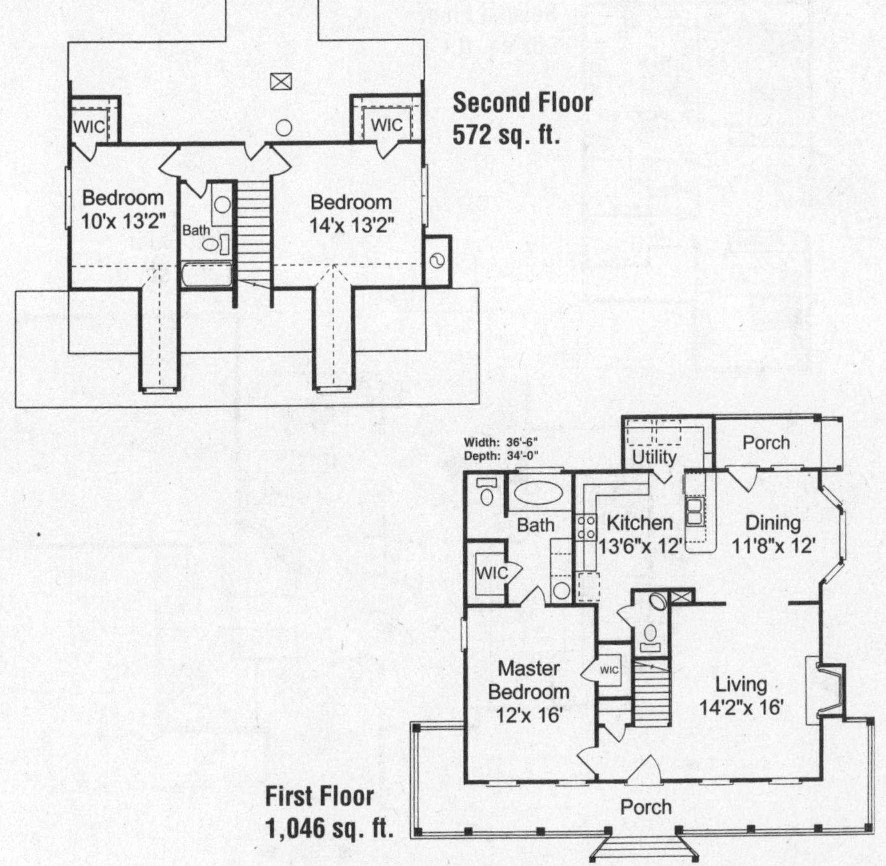

WIC
WIC
Bedroom
10'x 13'2"
Bath
Bedroom
14'x 13'2"
Width: 36'-6"
Depth: 34'-0"
Utility
Porch
Bath
Kitchen
13'6"x 12'
Dining
11'8"x 12'
WIC
WIC
Master
Bedroom
12'x 16'
Living
14'2"x 16'
Porch

Second Floor
572 sq. ft.

First Floor
1,046 sq. ft.

Special features

- Secondary bedrooms with walk-in closets are located on the second floor and share a bath
- Utility room is tucked away in kitchen for convenience but out-of-sight
- Dining area is brightened by large bay window
- 3 bedrooms, 2 1/2 baths
- Slab or crawl space foundation, please specify when ordering

The Family Handyman

Plan #702-DR-2615

Grand Curved Staircase Makes A Beautiful Entrance

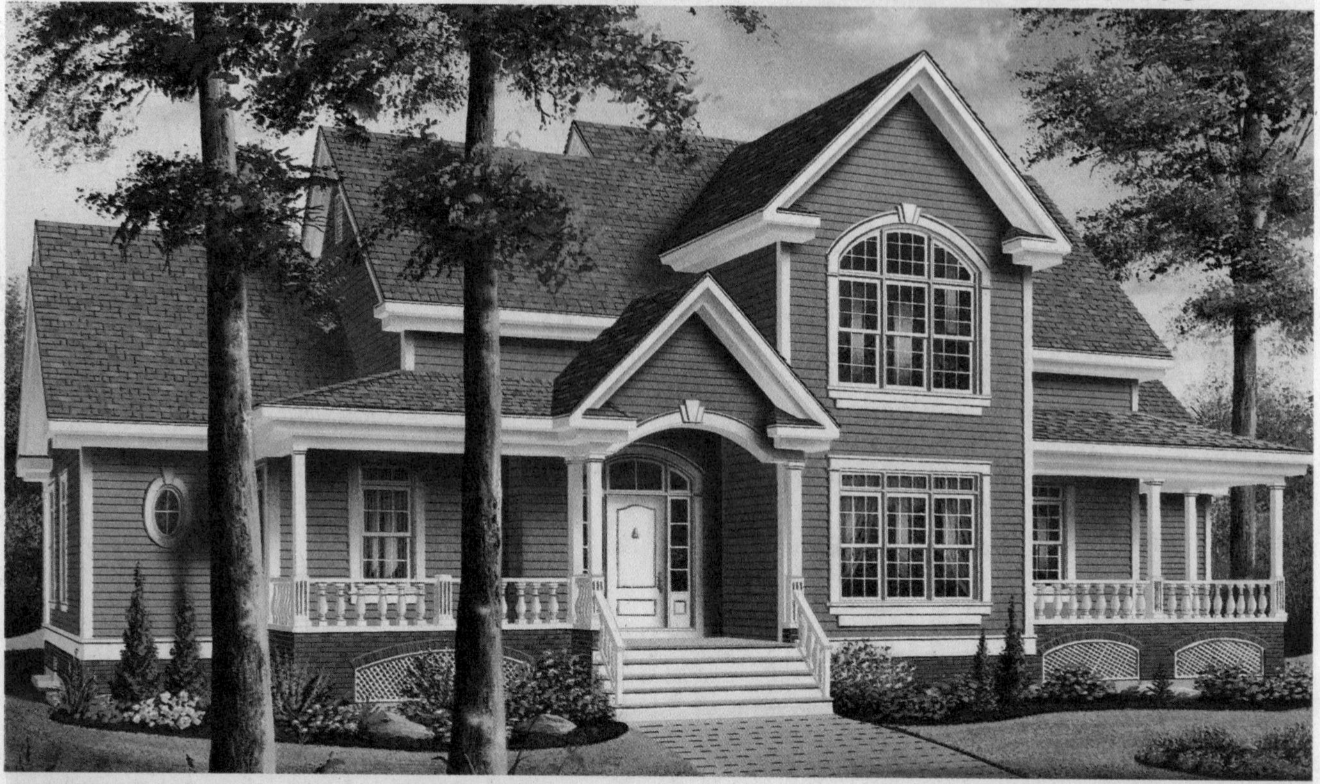

2,889 total square feet of living area **Price Code E**

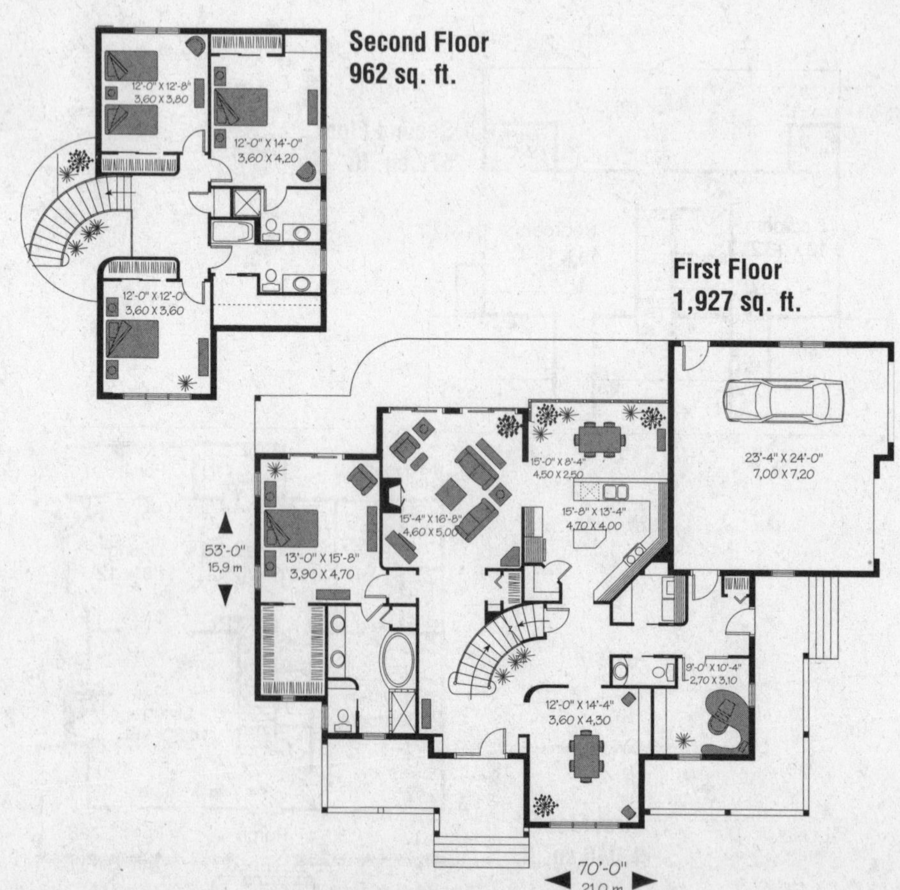

Second Floor
962 sq. ft.
12'-0" X 12'-8"
3,60 X 3,80
12'-0" X 14'-0"
3,60 X 4,20
12'-0" X 12'-0
3,60 X 3,60
First Floor
1,927 sq. ft.
23'-4" X 24'-0"
7,00 X 7,20
15'-0" X 8'-4"
4,50 X 2,50
15'-8" X 13'-4"
4,70 X 4,00
15'-4" X 16'-8"
4,60 X 5,00
13'-0" X 15'-8"
3,90 X 4,70
53'-0"
15,9 m
9'-0" X 10'-4"
2,70 X 3,10
12'-0" X 14'-4"
3,60 X 4,30
70'-0"
21,0 m

Special features

- Energy efficient home with 2" x 6" exterior walls
- Cathedral ceiling in family room is impressive
- 9' ceilings throughout first floor
- Private home office located away from traffic flow
- 4 bedrooms, 3 1/2 baths, 2-car side entry garage
- Basement foundation

Plan #702-1308

Wonderful Two-Story, Charming Yet Practical

2,280 total square feet of living area **Price Code D**

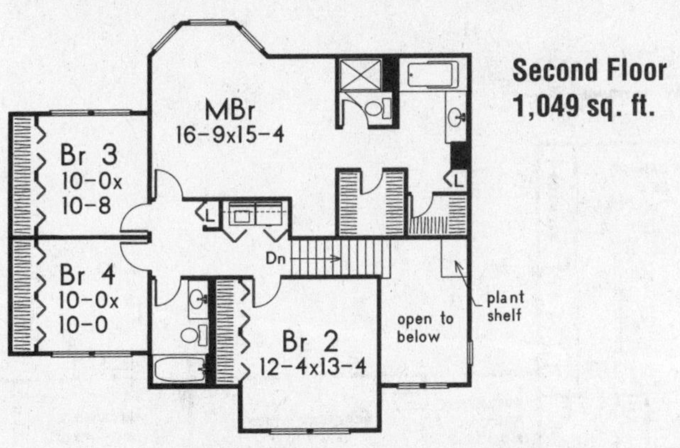
MBr
16-9x15-4
Br 3
10-0x
10-8
Br 4
10-0x
10-0
L
L
Dn
Br 2
12-4x13-4
open to
below
plant
shelf

Second Floor
1,049 sq. ft.

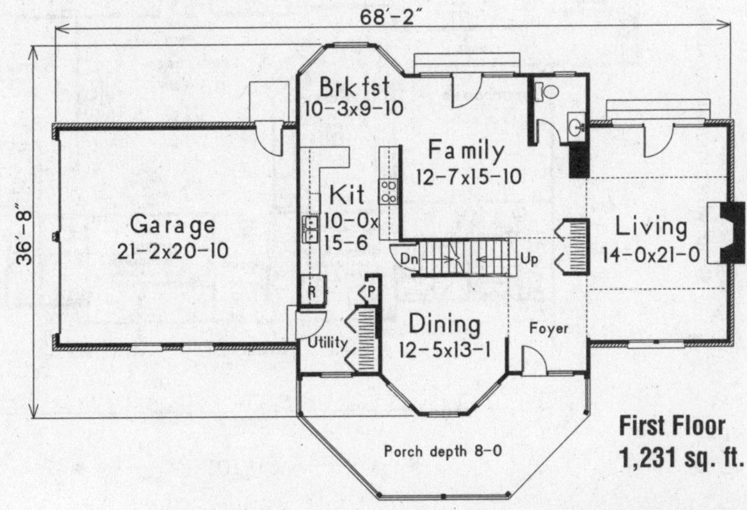
68'-2"
36'-8"
Brk fst
10-3x9-10
Family
12-7x15-10
Kit
10-0x
15-6
Garage
21-2x20-10
Living
14-0x21-0
Dn
Up
R
P
Utility
Dining
12-5x13-1
Foyer
Porch depth 8-0

First Floor
1,231 sq. ft.

Special features

- Laundry area conveniently located on second floor
- Compact yet efficient kitchen
- Unique shaped dining room overlooks front porch
- Cozy living room enhanced with sloped ceiling and fireplace
- 4 bedrooms, 2 1/2 baths, 2-car side entry garage
- Basement foundation

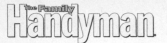

Plan #702-DH-2775A

Lots Of Outdoor Living Area On Porches

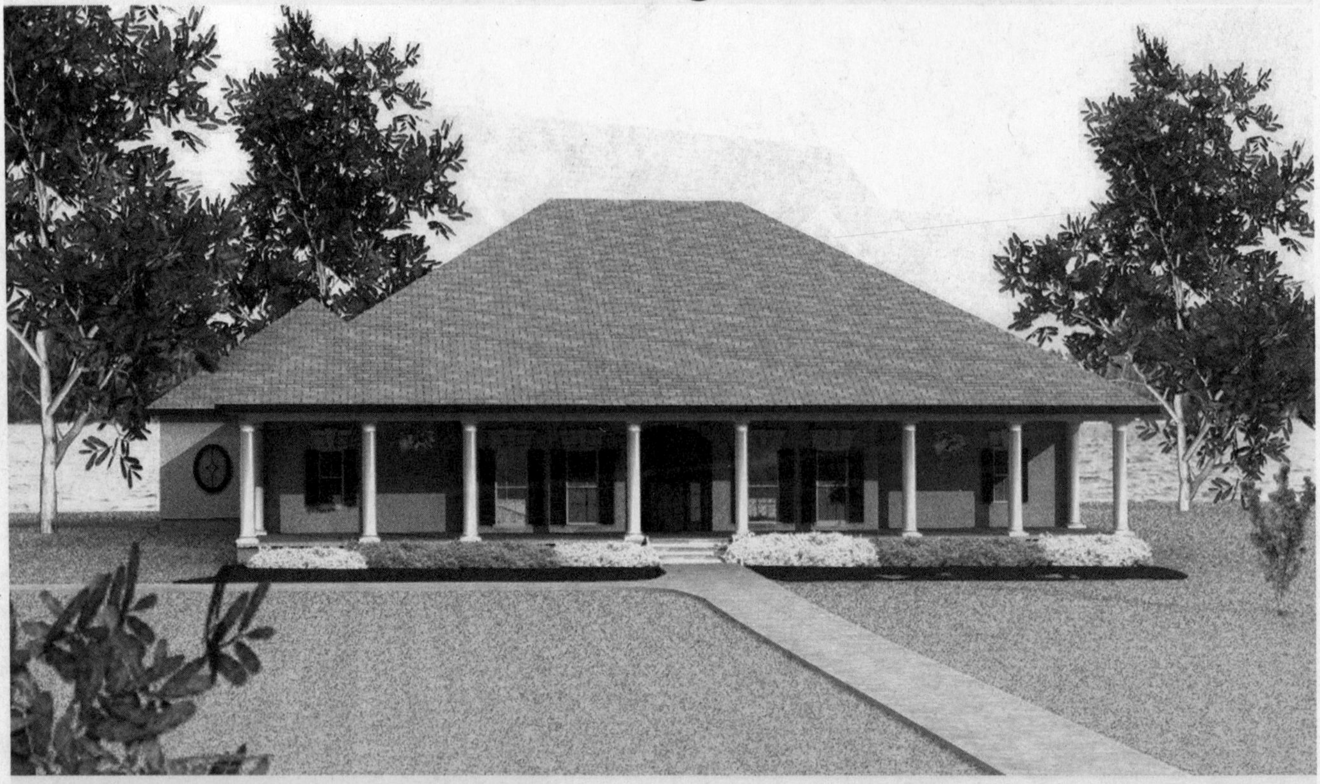

2,775 total square feet of living area

Price Code E

Special features

- Oversized laundry room is ideal for family living and includes plenty of extra closetspace
- Kitchen and great room combine creating plenty of space for entertaining
- Cozy breakfast room is sunny and bright with lots of windows and double-doors to a screened porch
- 3 bedrooms, 3 baths, 2-car garage
- Slab foundation

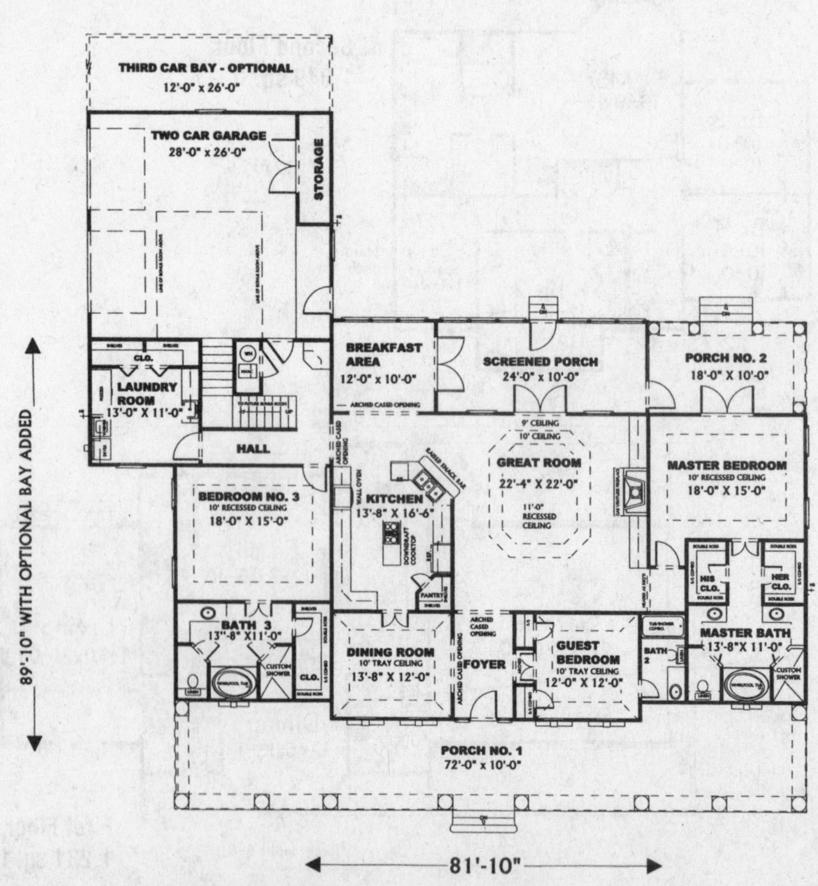
THIRD CAR BAY - OPTIONAL
12'-0" x 26'-0"
TWO CAR GARAGE
28'-0" x 26'-0"
STORAGE
CLO.
LAUNDRY ROOM
13'-0" X 11'-0"
HALL
BREAKFAST AREA
12'-0" x 10'-0"
SCREENED PORCH
24'-0" x 10'-0"
PORCH NO. 2
18'-0" X 10'-0"
9' CEILING
10' CEILING
GREAT ROOM
22'-4" X 22'-0"
11'-0" RECESSED CEILING
MASTER BEDROOM
10' RECESSED CEILING
18'-0" X 15'-0"
BEDROOM NO. 3
10' RECESSED CEILING
18'-0" X 15'-0"
KITCHEN
13'-8" X 16'-6"
PANTRY
HIS CLO.
HER CLO.
BATH 3
13'-8" X 11'-0"
CLO.
DINING ROOM
10' TRAY CEILING
13'-8" X 12'-0"
FOYER
GUEST BEDROOM
10' TRAY CEILING
12'-0" X 12'-0"
BATH 2
MASTER BATH
13'-8" X 11'-0"
PORCH NO. 1
72'-0" x 10'-0"
89'-10" WITH OPTIONAL BAY ADDED
81'-10"

The Family
Handyman

Charming Two-Story With Dormers And Porch

1,711 total square feet of living area

Price Code B

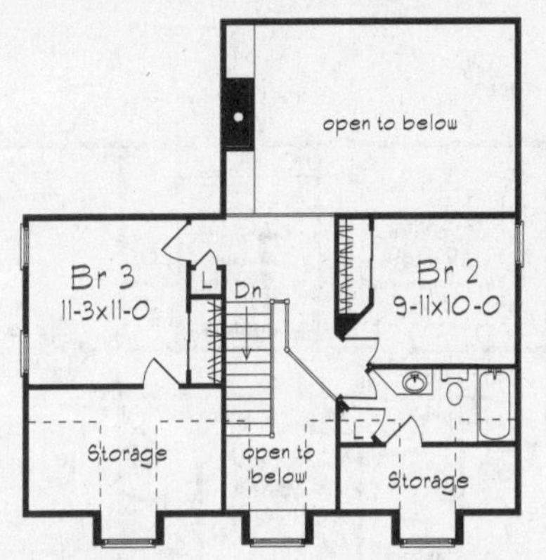
open to below
Br 3
11-3x11-0
Dn
Br 2
9-11x10-0
L
L
Storage
open to below
Storage

Second Floor
483 sq. ft.

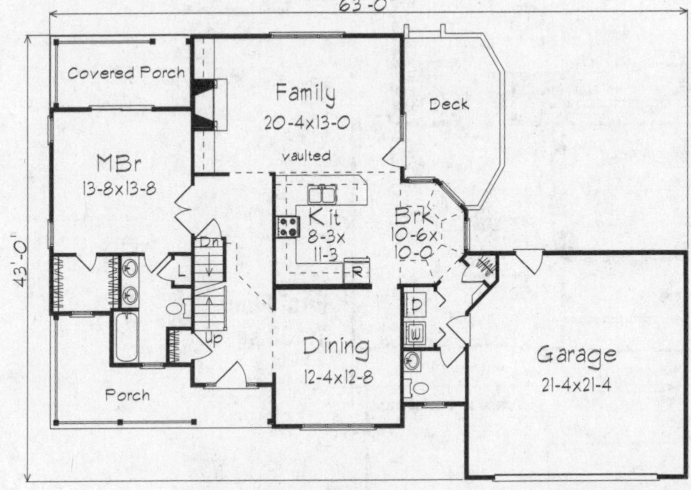
63'-0"
43'-0"
Covered Porch
Family
20-4x13-0
vaulted
Deck
MBr
13-8x13-8
Kit
8-3x
11-3
R
Brk
10-6x
10-0
Dn
L
Up
D
W
Dining
12-4x12-8
Garage
21-4x21-4
Porch

First Floor
1,228 sq. ft.

Special features

- U-shaped kitchen joins breakfast and family rooms for open living atmosphere
- Master bedroom has secluded covered porch and private bath
- Balcony overlooks family room that features a fireplace and accesses deck
- 3 bedrooms, 2 1/2 baths, 2-car garage
- Basement foundation

The Family
Handyman

Plan #702-DBI-2408

Cozy Family Home

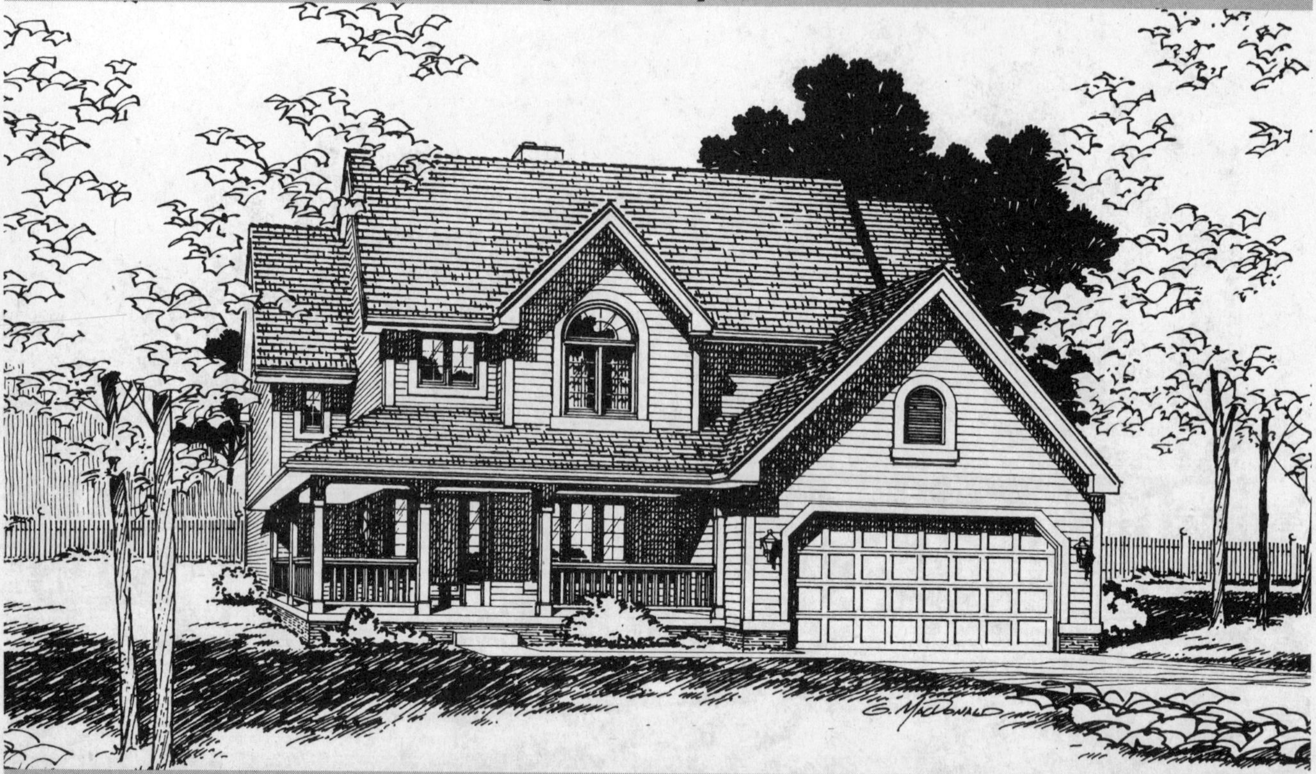

2,270 total square feet of living area | **Price Code D**

Special features

- Great room and hearth room share see-through fireplace
- Oversized rooms throughout
- First floor has terrific floor plan for entertaining with large kitchen/breakfast area and adjacent great room
- 4 bedrooms, 2 1/2 baths, 2-car garage
- Basement foundation

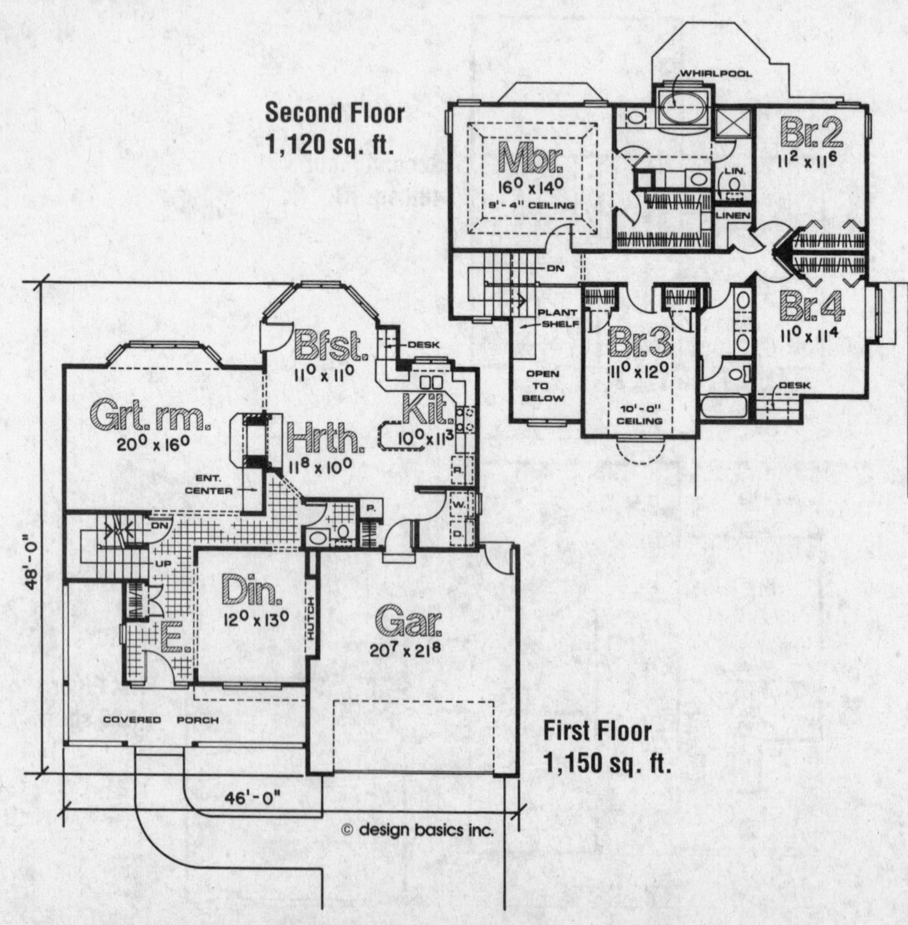
WHIRLPOOL
Mbr.
$16^{0} \times 14^{0}$
9'-4" CEILING
Br.2
$11^{2} \times 11^{6}$
LIN.
LINEN
DN
Br.4
$11^{0} \times 11^{4}$
PLANT SHELF
OPEN TO BELOW
Br.3
$11^{0} \times 12^{0}$
10'-0" CEILING
DESK
Bfst.
$11^{0} \times 11^{0}$
DESK
Grt. rm.
$20^{0} \times 16^{0}$
Kit.
$10^{0} \times 11^{3}$
Hrth.
$11^{8} \times 10^{0}$
ENT. CENTER
R.
P.
W.
D.
DN
UP
Din.
$12^{0} \times 13^{0}$
HUTCH
Gar.
$20^{7} \times 21^{8}$
E.
COVERED PORCH
48'-0"
46'-0"
© design basics inc.

Second Floor
1,120 sq. ft.

First Floor
1,150 sq. ft.

Plan #702-SH-SEA-078

Dormers Demand Attention

2,389 total square feet of living area **Price Code D**

Special features

- Energy efficient home with 2" x 6" exterior walls
- Full-width covered verandah invites outdoor relaxation
- Den can easily double as a guest room
- 3 bedrooms, 2 1/2 baths, 2-car garage
- Basement or crawl space foundation, please specify when ordering

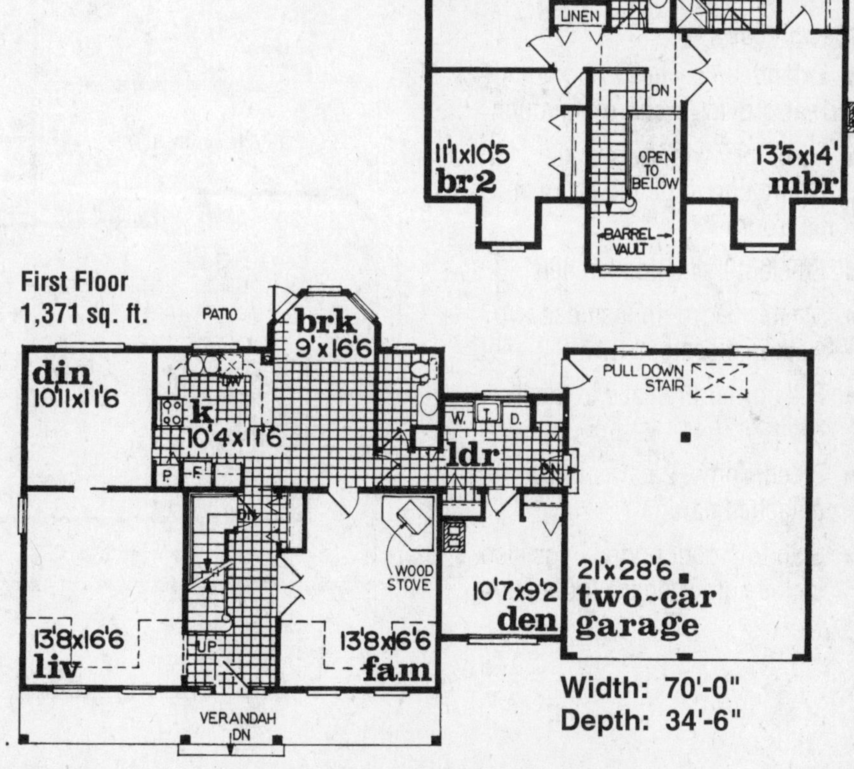
Second Floor
1,018 sq. ft.
br3
10'6x11'7
LINEN
SPA
TUB
STEP
WALK-IN CLOSET
DN
11'1x10'5
br2
OPEN TO BELOW
13'5x14'
mbr
BARREL VAULT
First Floor
1,371 sq. ft.
PATIO
brk
9'x16'6
din
10'11x11'6
k
10'4x11'6
DW
P
R
W.
D.
ldr
PULL DOWN STAIR
DN
WOOD STOVE
10'7x9'2
den
21'x28'6
two-car garage
13'8x16'6
liv
UP
13'8x16'6
fam
VERANDAH
DN

Width: 70'-0"
Depth: 34'-6"

TO ORDER BLUEPRINTS USE THE FORM ON PAGE 19 OR CALL TOLL-FREE 1-877-671-6036

View thousands more home plans online at www.familyhandyman.com/homeplans

The Family
Handyman

Plan #702-0163

Old-Fashioned Comfort And Privacy

1,772 total square feet of living area **Price Code C**

Special features

- Extended porches in front and rear provide a charming touch
- Large bay windows lend distinction to dining room and bedroom #3
- Efficient U-shaped kitchen
- Master bedroom includes two walk-in closets
- Full corner fireplace in family room
- 3 bedrooms, 2 baths, 2-car detached garage
- Slab foundation, drawings also include crawl space foundation

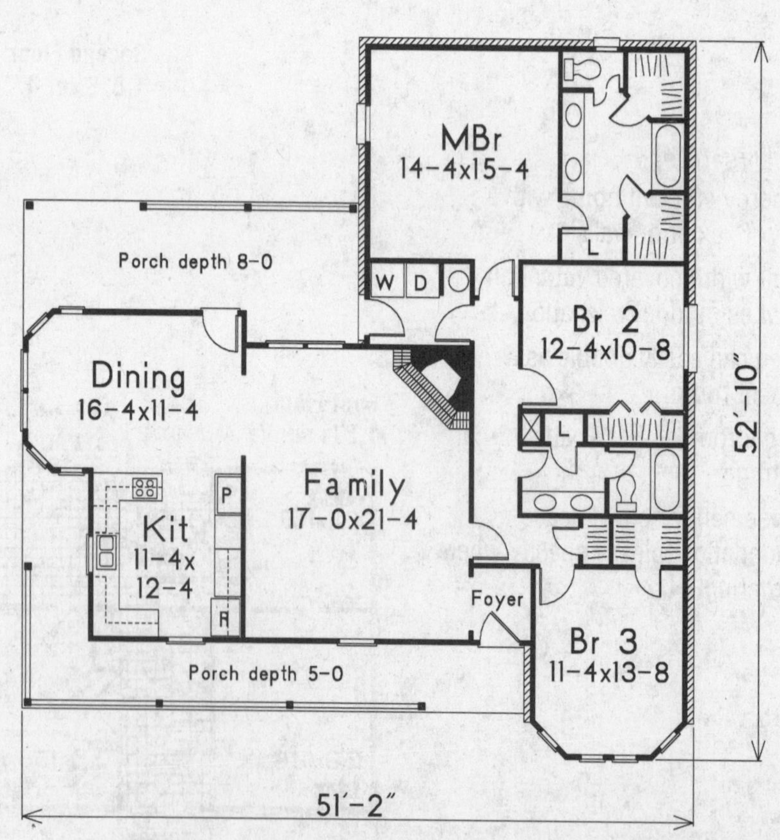
MBr
14-4x15-4
Porch depth 8-0
W
D
L
Br 2
12-4x10-8
52'-10"
Dining
16-4x11-4
L
P
Family
17-0x21-4
Kit
11-4x
12-4
R
Foyer
Br 3
11-4x13-8
Porch depth 5-0
51'-2"

Plan #702-CHD-29-58

Grand Covered Entry

3,369 total square feet of living area **Price Code F**

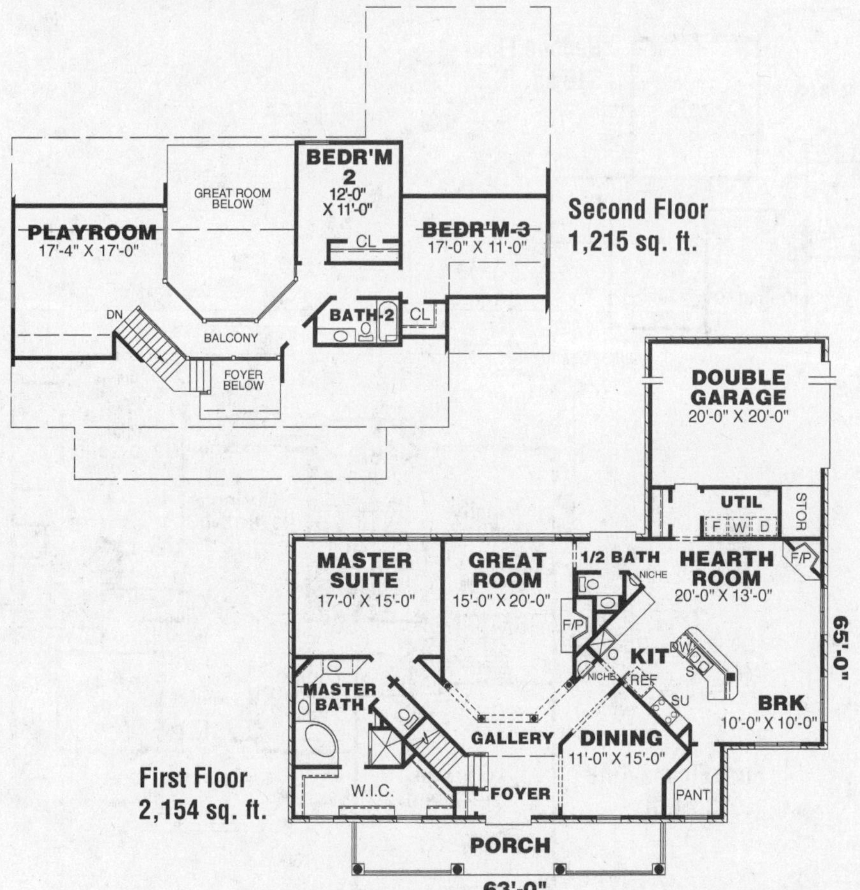
BEDR'M 2
12'-0" X 11'-0"
GREAT ROOM BELOW
PLAYROOM
17'-4" X 17'-0"
CL
BEDR'M-3
17'-0" X 11'-0"
Second Floor
1,215 sq. ft.
DN
BATH-2
CL
BALCONY
FOYER BELOW
DOUBLE GARAGE
20'-0" X 20'-0"
UTIL
F W D
STOR
MASTER SUITE
17'-0' X 15'-0"
GREAT ROOM
15'-0" X 20'-0"
1/2 BATH
NICHE
HEARTH ROOM
20'-0" X 13'-0"
F/P
F/P
KIT
DW
S
NICHE
REF
SU
BRK
10'-0" X 10'-0"
65'-0"
MASTER BATH
GALLERY
DINING
11'-0" X 15'-0"
W.I.C.
FOYER
PANT
PORCH
63'-0"
First Floor
2,154 sq. ft.

Special features

- Large playroom overlooks to great room below and makes a great casual family area
- Extra storage is located in garage
- Well-planned hearth room and kitchen are open and airy
- Foyer flows into unique diagonal gallery area creating a dramatic entrance into the great room
- 3 bedrooms, 2 1/2 baths, 2-car side entry garage
- Walk-out basement foundation

The Family Handyman

Plan #702-0350

Massive Double Columned Front Porch

2,452 total square feet of living area **Price Code D**

Special features

- Stairs balcony overlooks vaulted entry and two-story living room
- Living room features two-story glass rear wall
- Kitchen breakfast area open to family room with built-ins and fireplace
- Master bedroom and breakfast room provide access to rear deck
- 3 bedrooms, 2 1/2 baths, 2-car garage
- Basement foundation

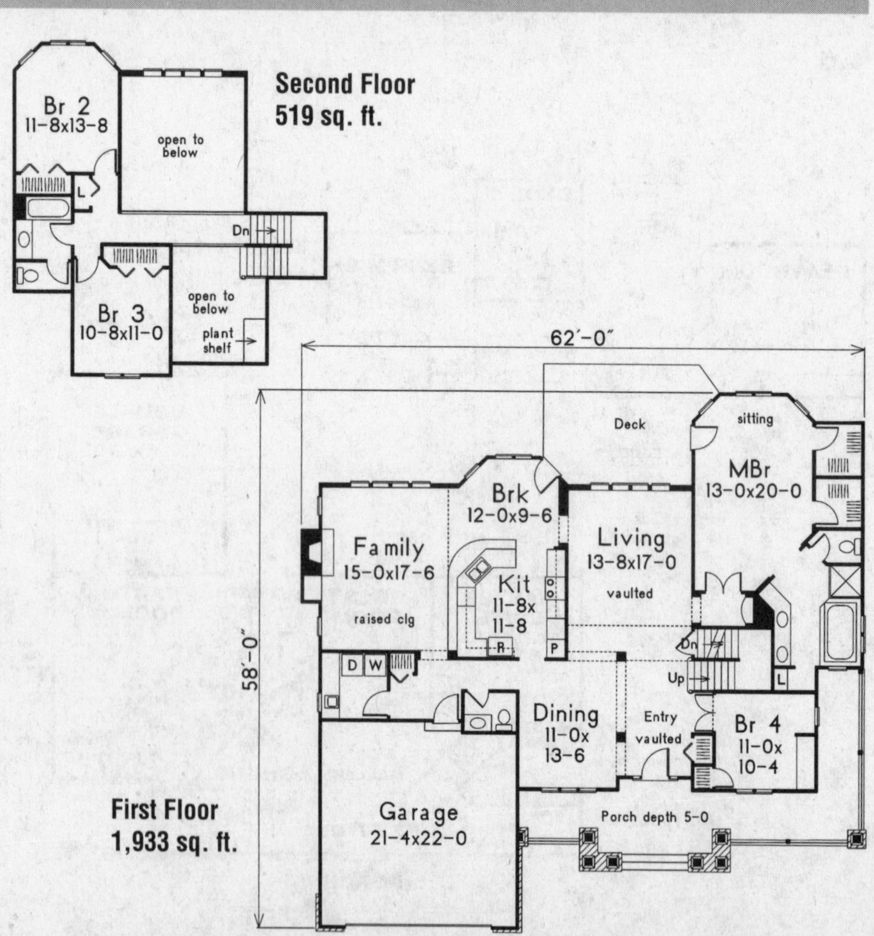
Second Floor
519 sq. ft.
Br 2
11-8x13-8
open to below
L
Dn
Br 3
10-8x11-0
open to below
plant shelf
62'-0"
58'-0"
Deck
sitting
MBr
13-0x20-0
Brk
12-0x9-6
Family
15-0x17-6
raised clg
Living
13-8x17-0
vaulted
Kit
11-8x
11-8
R
P
D
W
Dn
Up
L
Dining
11-0x
13-6
Entry
vaulted
Br 4
11-0x
10-4
Porch depth 5-0
Garage
21-4x22-0
First Floor
1,933 sq. ft.

TO ORDER BLUEPRINTS USE THE FORM ON PAGE 19 OR CALL TOLL-FREE 1-877-671-6036

View thousands more home plans online at www.familyhandyman.com/homeplans

Plan #702-0795

Covered Porch Surrounds Home

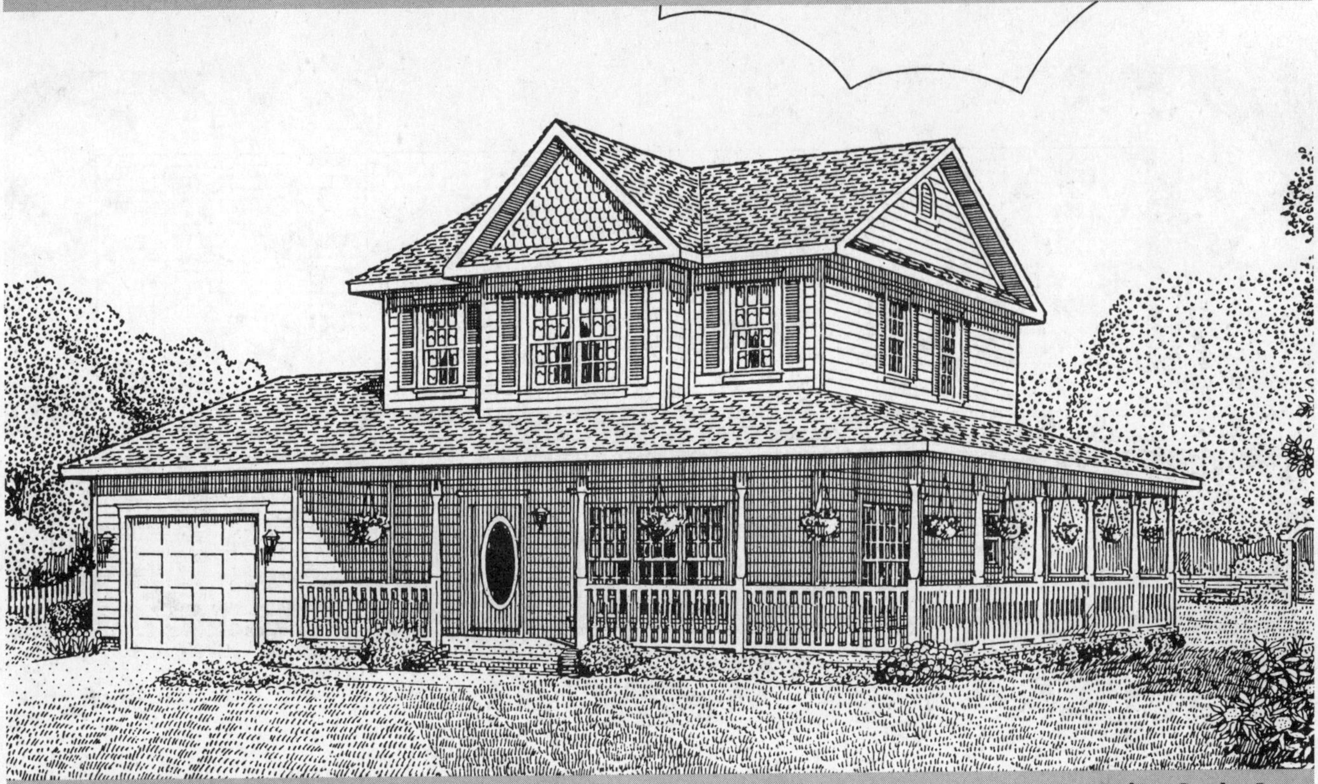

1,399 total square feet of living area

Price Code A

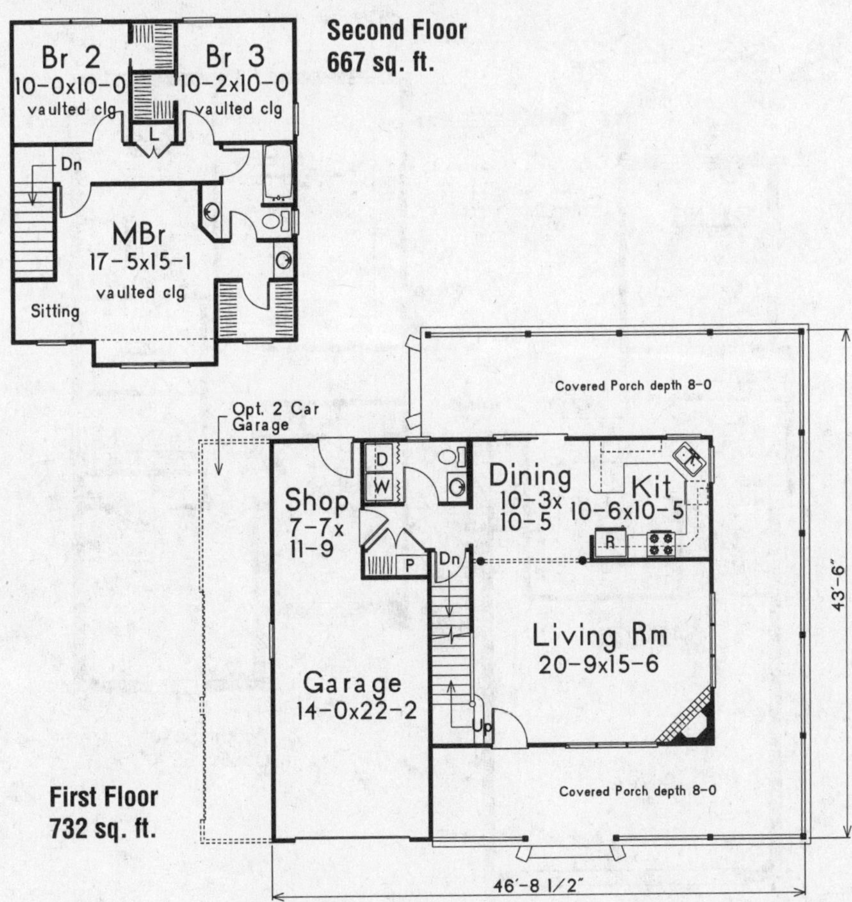

Br 2
10-0x10-0
vaulted clg
Br 3
10-2x10-0
vaulted clg
L
Dn
MBr
17-5x15-1
vaulted clg
Sitting
Second Floor
667 sq. ft.
Covered Porch depth 8-0
Opt. 2 Car Garage
D
W
Shop
7-7x
11-9
P
Dn
Dining
10-3x
10-5
Kit
10-6x10-5
R
Living Rm
20-9x15-6
Garage
14-0x22-2
Up
Covered Porch depth 8-0
43'-6"
46'-8 1/2"
First Floor
732 sq. ft.

Special features

- Living room overlooks dining area through arched columns
- Laundry room contains handy half bath
- Spacious master bedroom includes sitting area, walk-in closet and plenty of sunlight
- 3 bedrooms, 1 1/2 baths, 1-car garage
- Basement foundation, drawings also include crawl space and slab foundations

Sunny Dining Room

1,735 total square feet of living area **Price Code B**

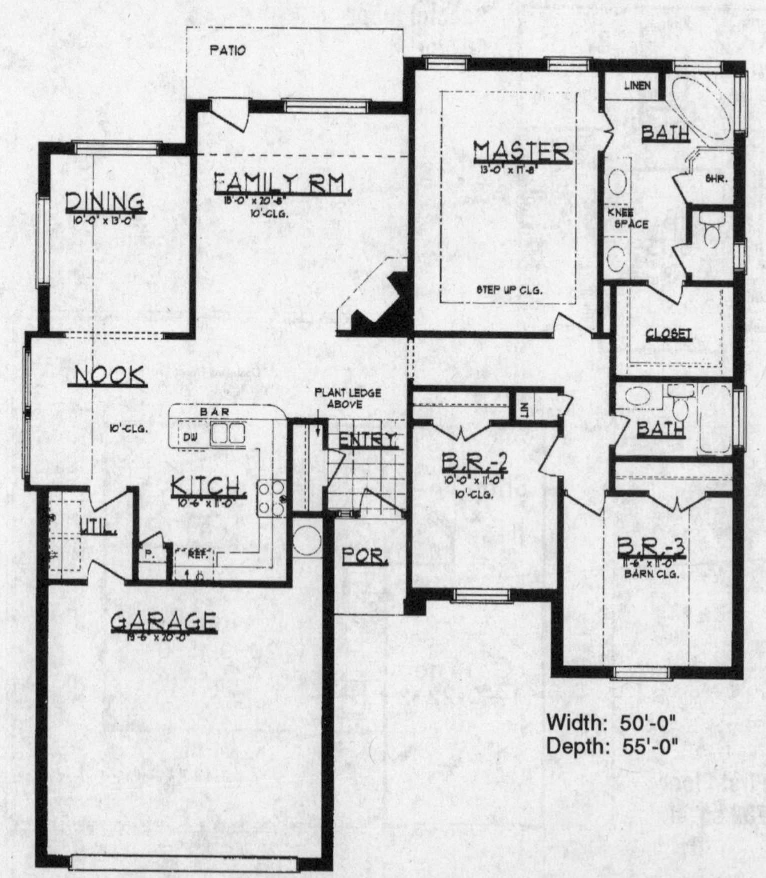
PATIO
MASTER
13'-0" x 17'-8"
STEP UP CLG.
LINEN
BATH
SHR.
KNEE SPACE
CLOSET
DINING
10'-0" x 13'-0"
FAMILY RM.
15'-0" x 20'-8"
10'-CLG.
NOOK
10'-CLG.
BAR
DW
PLANT LEDGE ABOVE
ENTRY
LIN
B.R.-2
10'-0" x 11'-0"
10'-CLG.
BATH
KITCH.
10'-6" x 11'-0"
UTIL.
REF.
POR.
B.R.-3
11'-6" x 11'-0"
BARN CLG.
GARAGE
19'-6" x 20'-0"

Width: 50'-0"
Depth: 55'-0"

Special features

- Luxurious master bath has spa tub, shower, double vanity and large walk-in closet
- Peninsula in kitchen has sink and dishwasher
- Massive master bedroom has step up ceiling and private location
- 3 bedrooms, 2 baths, 2-car garage
- Slab foundation

Plan #702-0177

Separate Living Areas Lend Privacy

2,562 total square feet of living area

Price Code D

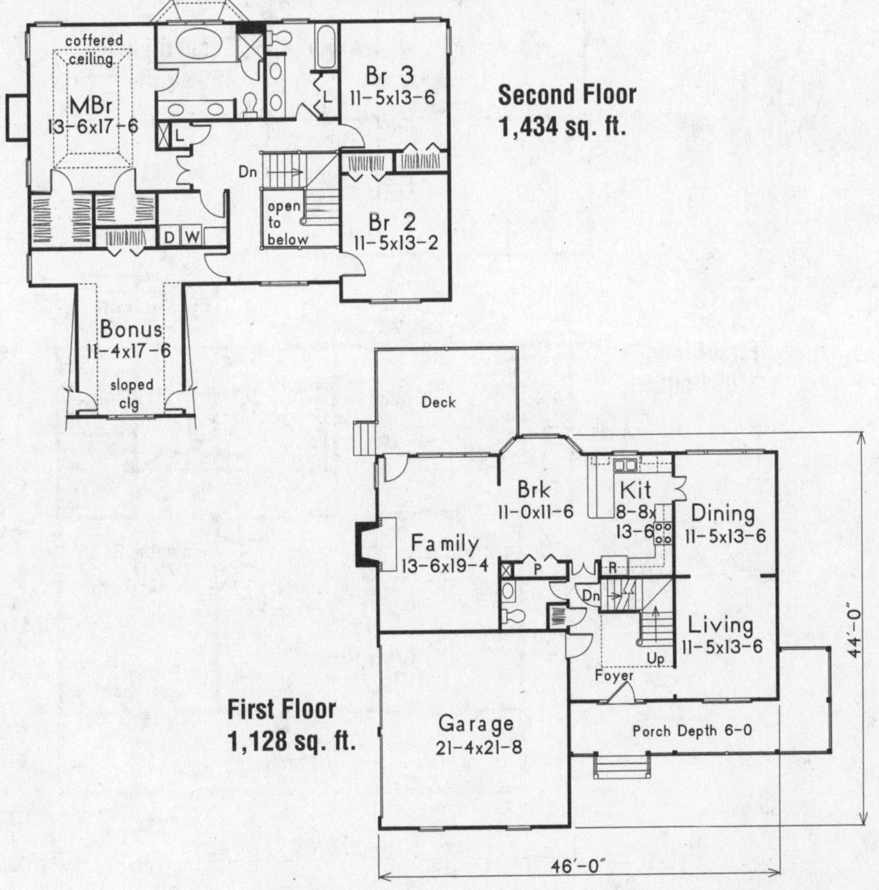

coffered ceiling
MBr 13-6x17-6
L
Dn
open to below
D W
Br 3 11-5x13-6
L
Br 2 11-5x13-2
Bonus 11-4x17-6
sloped clg
Second Floor
1,434 sq. ft.
Deck
Brk 11-0x11-6
Kit 8-8x 13-6
Dining 11-5x13-6
Family 13-6x19-4
P
R
Dn
Living 11-5x13-6
Up
Foyer
Porch Depth 6-0
Garage 21-4x21-8
44'-0"
46'-0"
First Floor
1,128 sq. ft.

Special features

- Large, open foyer creates a grand entrance
- Convenient open breakfast area includes peninsula counter, bay window and easy access to the sundeck
- Dining and living rooms flow together for expanded entertaining space
- 3 bedrooms, 2 1/2 baths, 2-car side entry garage
- Basement foundation, drawings also include slab and crawl space foundations

The Family
Handyman

Plan #702-GH-34603

1,560 total square feet of living area

Price Code B

Rear View

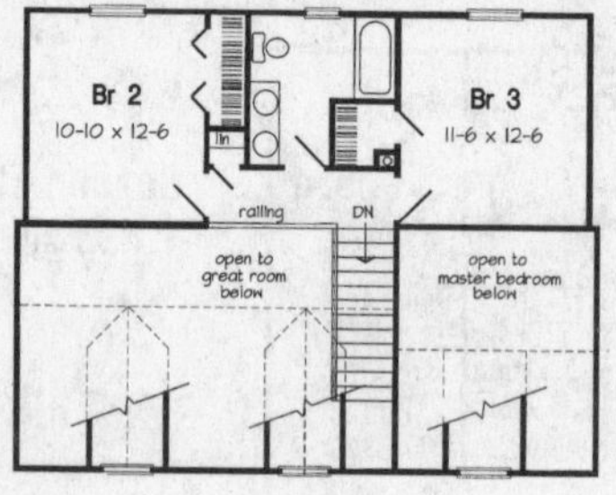
Br 2
10-10 x 12-6
Br 3
11-6 x 12-6
railing
DN
open to
great room
below
open to
master bedroom
below

Second Floor
499 sq. ft.

First Floor
1,061 sq. ft.

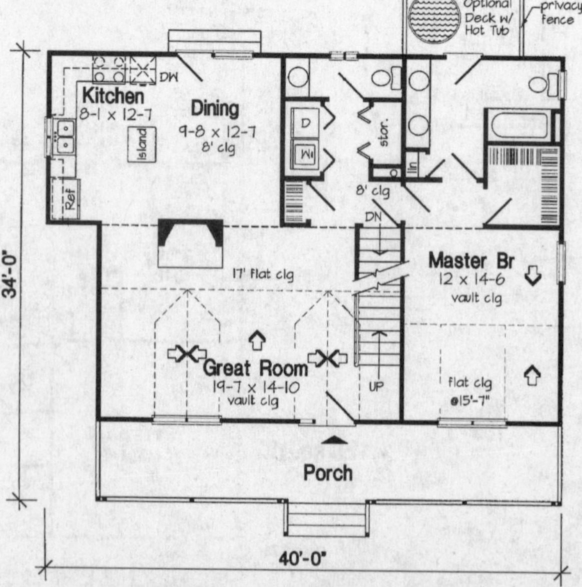
Optional
Deck w/
Hot Tub
privacy
fence
DW
Kitchen
8-1 x 12-7
Island
Ref
Dining
9-8 x 12-7
8' clg
D
W
stor.
8' clg
DN
17' Flat clg
Master Br
12 x 14-6
vault clg
Great Room
19-7 x 14-10
vault clg
UP
Flat clg
@15'-7"
Porch
34'-0"
40'-0"

Special features

- Two-story master bedroom has sunny dormer above, large walk-in closet and private bath
- Great room has unique two-story ceiling with dormers
- Spacious kitchen has large center island creating a ideal work space
- 3 bedrooms, 2 1/2 baths
- Basement, crawl space or slab foundation, please specify when ordering

Well-Designed Plan For Entertaining Plan #702-0688

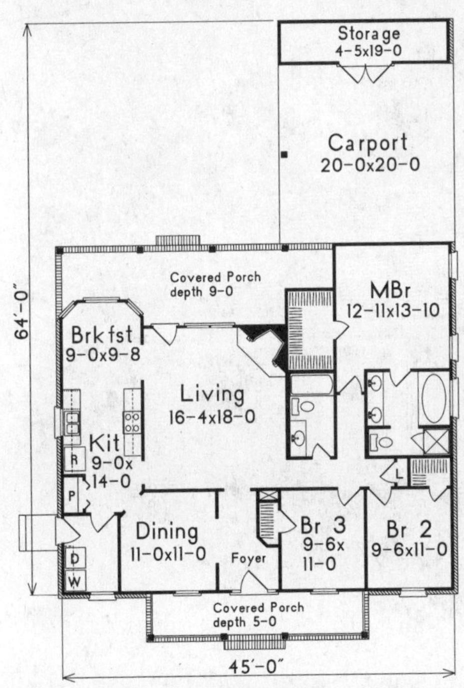
Storage
4-5x19-0
Carport
20-0x20-0
Covered Porch
depth 9-0
MBr
12-11x13-10
Brk fst
9-0x9-8
Living
16-4x18-0
Kit
9-0x
14-0
Dining
11-0x11-0
Foyer
Br 3
9-6x
11-0
Br 2
9-6x11-0
Covered Porch
depth 5-0
64'-0"
45'-0"

1,556 total square feet of living area **Price Code B**

Special features

- Corner fireplace in living area warms surroundings
- Spacious master suite has walk-in closet and private bath
- Compact kitchen designed for efficiency
- Covered porches in both front and back of home add coziness
- 3 bedrooms, 2 baths, 2-car attached carport
- Slab foundation

Circle-Top Windows Grace Facade Plan #702-0284

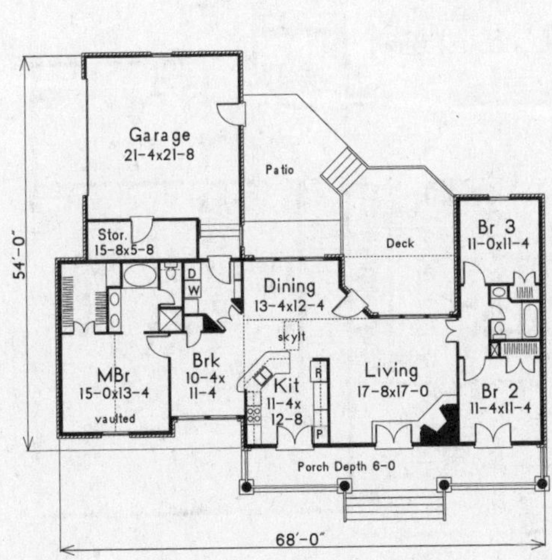
Garage
21-4x21-8
Patio
Stor.
15-8x5-8
Deck
Br 3
11-0x11-4
Dining
13-4x12-4
MBr
15-0x13-4
vaulted
Brk
10-4x
11-4
Kit
11-4x
12-8
Living
17-8x17-0
Br 2
11-4x11-4
Porch Depth 6-0
54'-0"
68'-0"

1,672 total square feet of living area **Price Code C**

Special features

- Master bath has a double-vanity and a separate tub and shower
- Energy efficient home with 2" x 6" exterior walls
- 12' ceilings in living room, kitchen and front secondary bedroom
- 3 bedrooms, 2 baths, 2-car side entry garage
- Crawl space foundation, drawings also include basement and slab foundations

The Family
Handyman

Plan #702-DH-2600

Southern Elegance

2,669 total square feet of living area | **Price Code E**

Special features

- Nice-sized corner pantry in kitchen
- Guest bedroom located off the great room with a full bath would make an excellent office
- Master bath has double walk-in closets, whirlpool bath and a large shower
- 3 bedrooms, 3 1/2 baths, 2-car side entry garage
- Basement or slab foundation, please specify when ordering

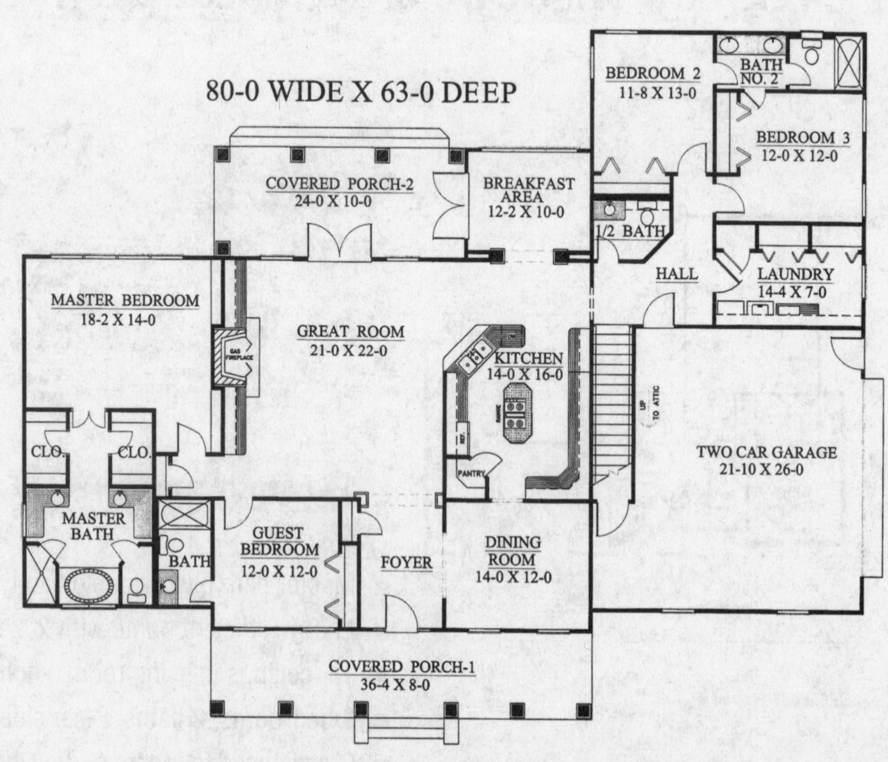
80-0 WIDE X 63-0 DEEP
BEDROOM 2
11-8 X 13-0
BATH NO. 2
BEDROOM 3
12-0 X 12-0
COVERED PORCH-2
24-0 X 10-0
BREAKFAST AREA
12-2 X 10-0
1/2 BATH
HALL
LAUNDRY
14-4 X 7-0
MASTER BEDROOM
18-2 X 14-0
GREAT ROOM
21-0 X 22-0
KITCHEN
14-0 X 16-0
TWO CAR GARAGE
21-10 X 26-0
CLO.
CLO.
PANTRY
MASTER BATH
BATH
GUEST BEDROOM
12-0 X 12-0
FOYER
DINING ROOM
14-0 X 12-0
COVERED PORCH-1
36-4 X 8-0

Plan #702-0805

Great Media Room

2,750 total square feet of living area — **Price Code E**

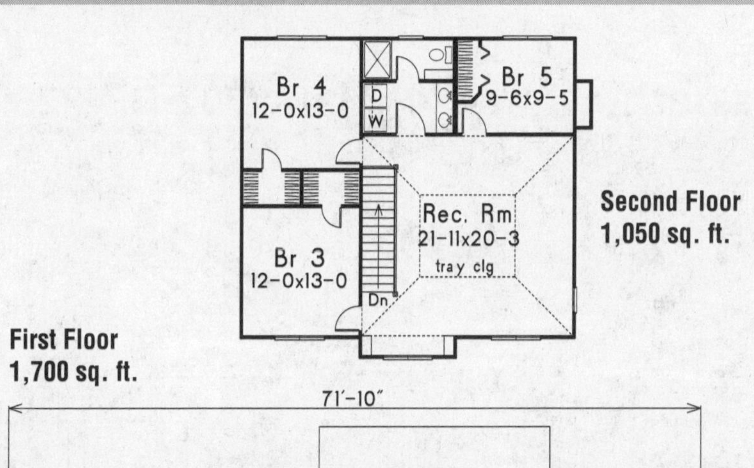

Br 4
12-0x13-0
D
W
Br 5
9-6x9-5
Rec. Rm
21-11x20-3
tray clg
Br 3
12-0x13-0
Dn

Second Floor
1,050 sq. ft.

First Floor
1,700 sq. ft.

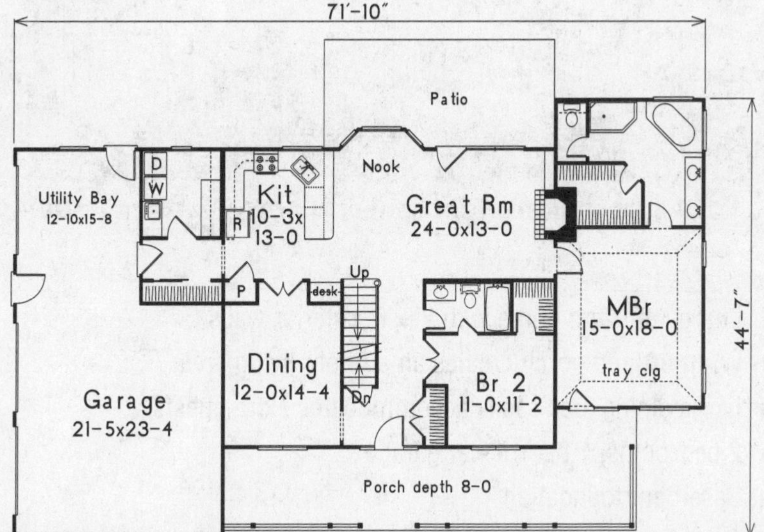

71'-10"
Patio
Nook
D
W
Utility Bay
12-10x15-8
Kit
10-3x
13-0
R
Great Rm
24-0x13-0
Up
P
desk
MBr
15-0x18-0
tray clg
44'-7"
Dining
12-0x14-4
Dn
Br 2
11-0x11-2
Garage
21-5x23-4
Porch depth 8-0

Special features

- Oversized rooms throughout
- 9' ceilings on first floor
- Unique utility bay workshop off garage
- Spacious master suite with luxurious bath
- Optional sixth bedroom plan also included
- 5 bedrooms, 3 1/2 baths, 2-car side entry garage
- Basement foundation, drawings also include crawl space and slab foundations

Vacation Home Or Year-Round Living — Plan #702-0767

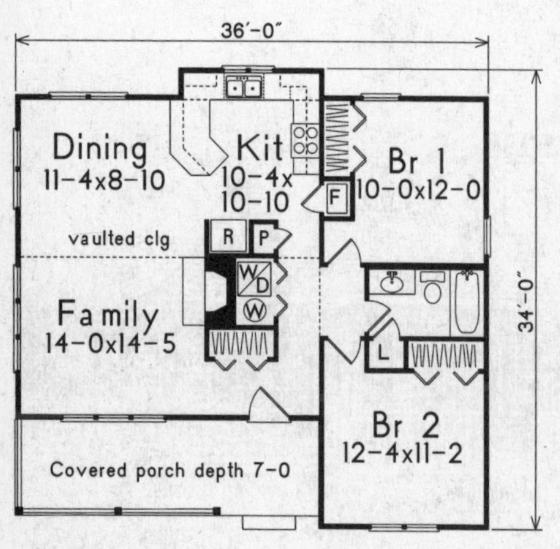
36'-0"
34'-0"
Dining
11-4x8-10
Kit
10-4x
10-10
Br 1
10-0x12-0
vaulted clg
R
P
F
W
D
Family
14-0x14-5
L
Br 2
12-4x11-2
Covered porch depth 7-0

990 total square feet of living area — **Price Code AA**

Special features

- Covered front porch adds charming feel
- Vaulted ceilings in kitchen, family and dining rooms creates a spacious feel
- Large linen, pantry and storage closets throughout
- 2 bedrooms, 1 bath
- Crawl space foundation

Eye-Catching Luxurious Bath

Plan #702-DR-2290

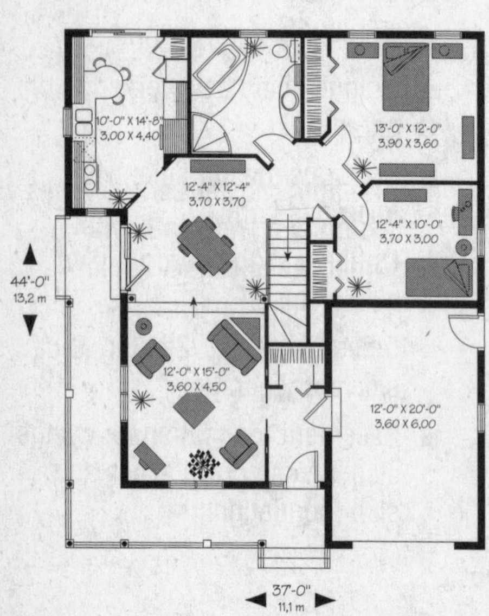
10'-0" X 14'-8"
3,00 X 4,40
13'-0" X 12'-0"
3,90 X 3,60
12'-4" X 12'-4"
3,70 X 3,70
12'-4" X 10'-0"
3,70 X 3,00
44'-0"
13,2 m
12'-0" X 15'-0"
3,60 X 4,50
12'-0" X 20'-0"
3,60 X 6,00
37'-0"
11,1 m

1,124 total square feet of living area — **Price Code AA**

Special features

- Energy efficient home with 2" x 6" exterior walls
- Wrap-around porch creates an outdoor living area
- Large dining area easily accommodates extra guests
- 2 bedrooms, 1 bath, 1-car garage
- Basement foundation

The Family
Handyman

Plan #702-0802

A Perfect Family Home

2,645 total square feet of living area

Price Code E

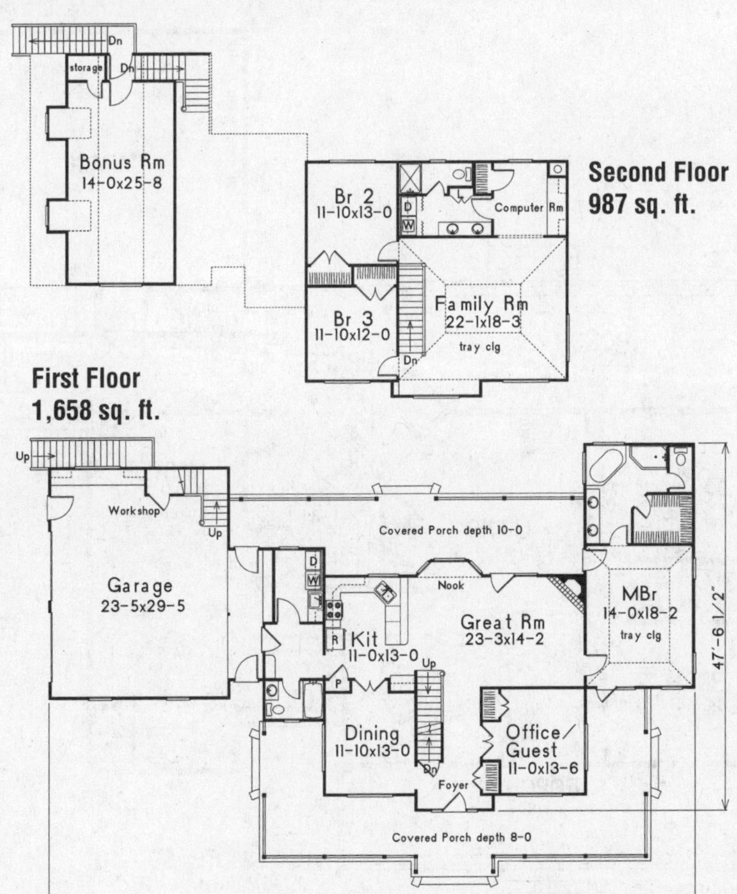

Dn
storage
Dn
Bonus Rm
14-0x25-8
Br 2
11-10x13-0
D
W
Computer Rm
Br 3
11-10x12-0
Family Rm
22-1x18-3
tray clg
Dn
Second Floor
987 sq. ft.
First Floor
1,658 sq. ft.
Up
Workshop
Up
Covered Porch depth 10-0
Garage
23-5x29-5
D
W
Nook
Great Rm
23-3x14-2
MBr
14-0x18-2
tray clg
R
Kit
11-0x13-0
Up
P
Dining
11-10x13-0
Dn
Office/
Guest
11-0x13-6
Foyer
Covered Porch depth 8-0
47'-6 1/2"
85'-6"

Special features

- Second floor has a second washer and dryer area ideal for convenience
- Second floor casual family room is ideal for children's play area with adjacent computer room
- First floor master bedroom has luxurious private bath with corner tub and walk-in closet
- Bonus room on second floor has an additional 438 square feet of living area
- 3 bedrooms, 2 1/2 baths, 2-car side entry garage
- Basement foundation, drawings also include crawl space and slab foundation

The Family
Handyman

Plan #702-LBD-19-16A

Country Farmhouse Appeal

1,993 total square feet of living area — **Price Code C**

Special features

- Charming front and rear porches
- 12' ceiling in living room
- Exquisite master bath with large walk-in closet
- 3 bedrooms, 2 baths, 2-car side entry garage
- Crawl space or slab foundation, please specify when ordering

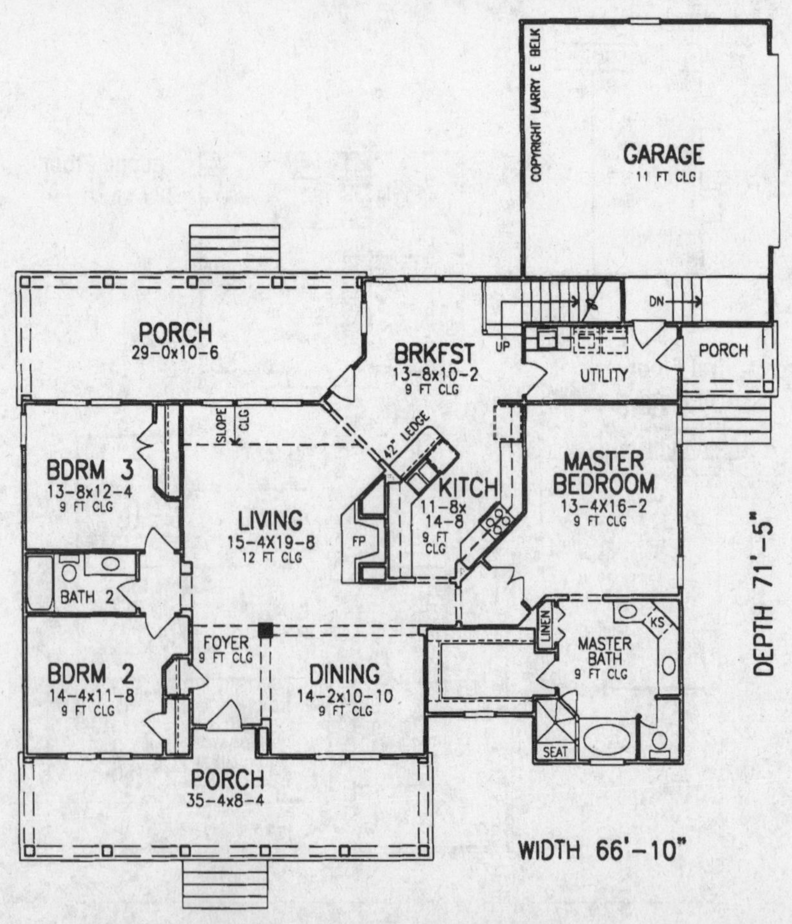
COPYRIGHT LARRY E BELK
GARAGE
11 FT CLG
PORCH
29-0x10-6
BRKFST
13-8x10-2
9 FT CLG
UP
DN
UTILITY
PORCH
SLOPE CLG
42" LEDGE
BDRM 3
13-8x12-4
9 FT CLG
LIVING
15-4X19-8
12 FT CLG
FP
KITCH
11-8x
14-8
9 FT
CLG
MASTER
BEDROOM
13-4X16-2
9 FT CLG
BATH 2
LINEN
KS
MASTER
BATH
9 FT CLG
FOYER
9 FT CLG
BDRM 2
14-4x11-8
9 FT CLG
DINING
14-2x10-10
9 FT CLG
SEAT
PORCH
35-4x8-4
DEPTH 71'-5"
WIDTH 66'-10"

TO ORDER BLUEPRINTS USE THE FORM ON PAGE 19 OR CALL TOLL-FREE 1-877-671-6036

View thousands more home plans online at www.familyhandyman.com/homeplans

The Family
Handyman

Plan #702-DR-2939

Covered Porch Adds Appeal

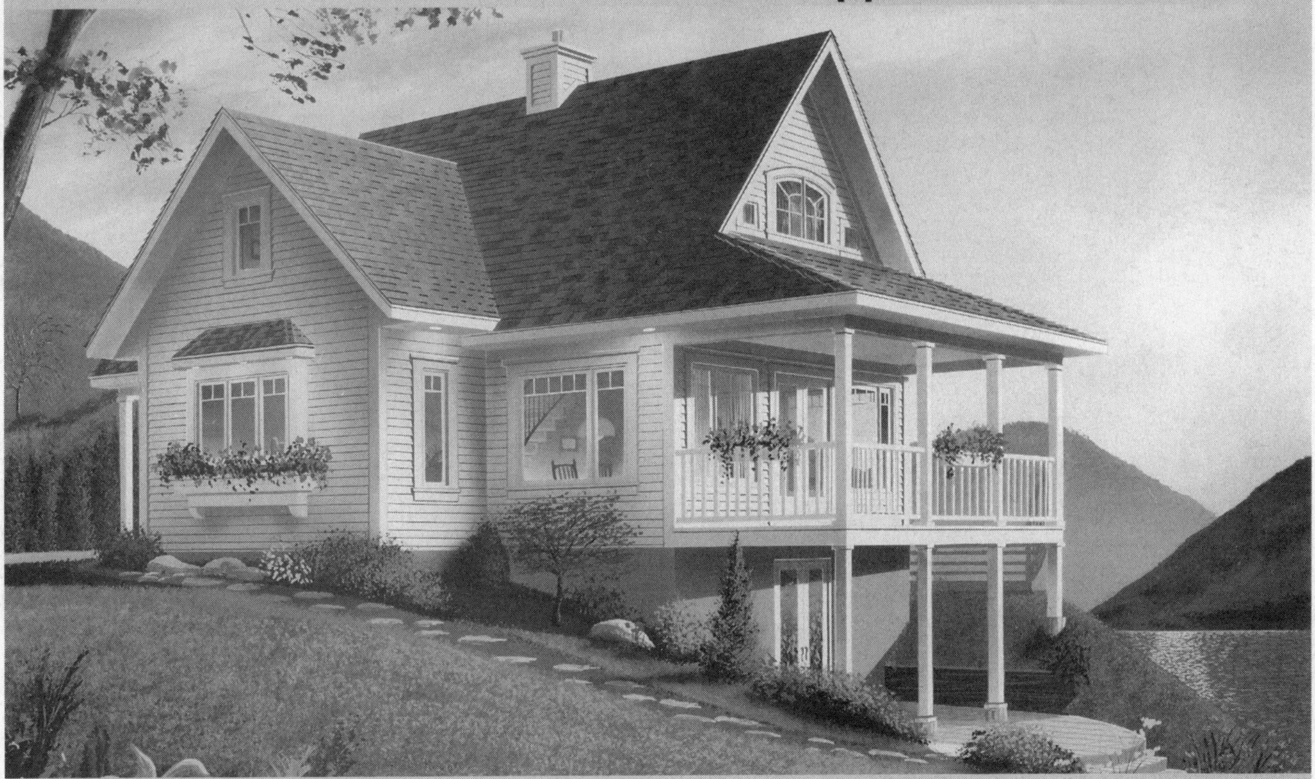

1,480 total square feet of living area

Price Code A

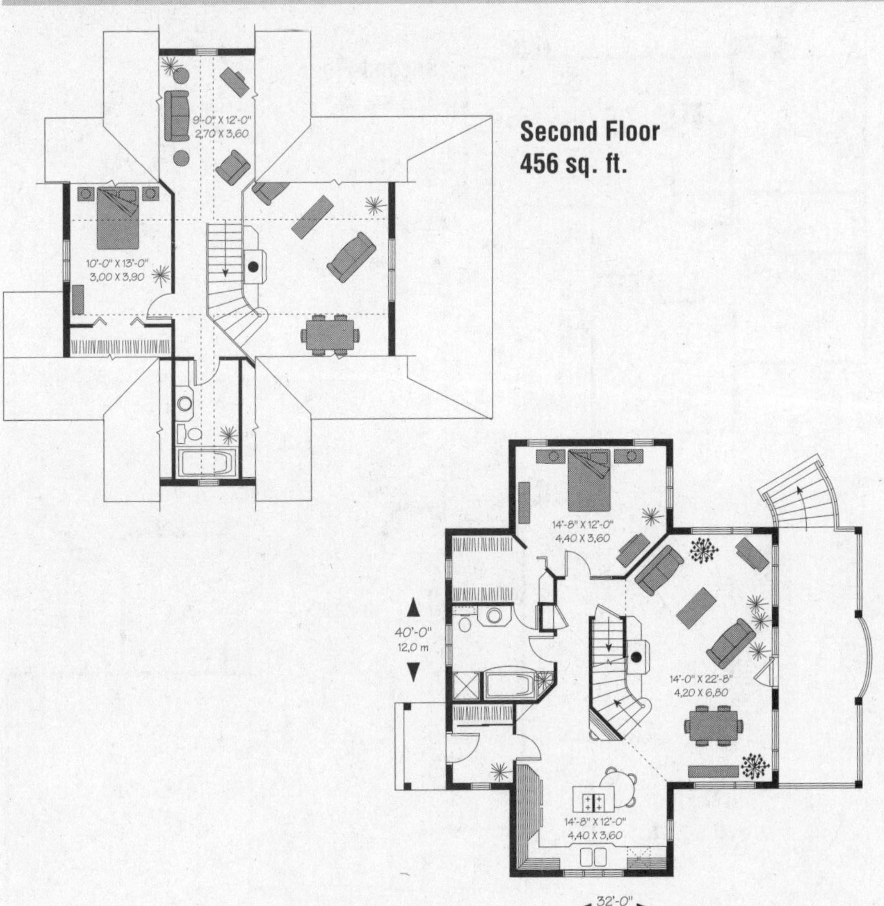
9'-0" X 12'-0"
2,70 X 3,60
10'-0" X 13'-0"
3,00 X 3,90
14'-8" X 12'-0"
4,40 X 3,60
40'-0"
12,0 m
14'-0" X 22'-8"
4,20 X 6,80
14'-8" X 12'-0"
4,40 X 3,60
32'-0"
9,6 m

Second Floor
456 sq. ft.

First Floor
1,024 sq. ft.

Special features

- Energy efficient home with 2" x 6" exterior walls
- Cathedral ceiling in family and dining rooms
- Master bedroom has walk-in closet and access to bath
- 2 bedrooms, 2 baths
- Basement foundation

Plan #702-0388

Two-Story Home With Uncommon Charm

1,695 total square feet of living area

Price Code B

Special features

- Facade features cozy wrap-around porch, projected living room window and repeating front gables
- Balcony overlooks to entry below
- Kitchen has full view corner window with adjacent eating space that opens to screened porch
- Vaulted master bedroom with his and her closets and private bath
- 3 bedrooms, 2 1/2 baths, 2-car garage
- Basement foundation

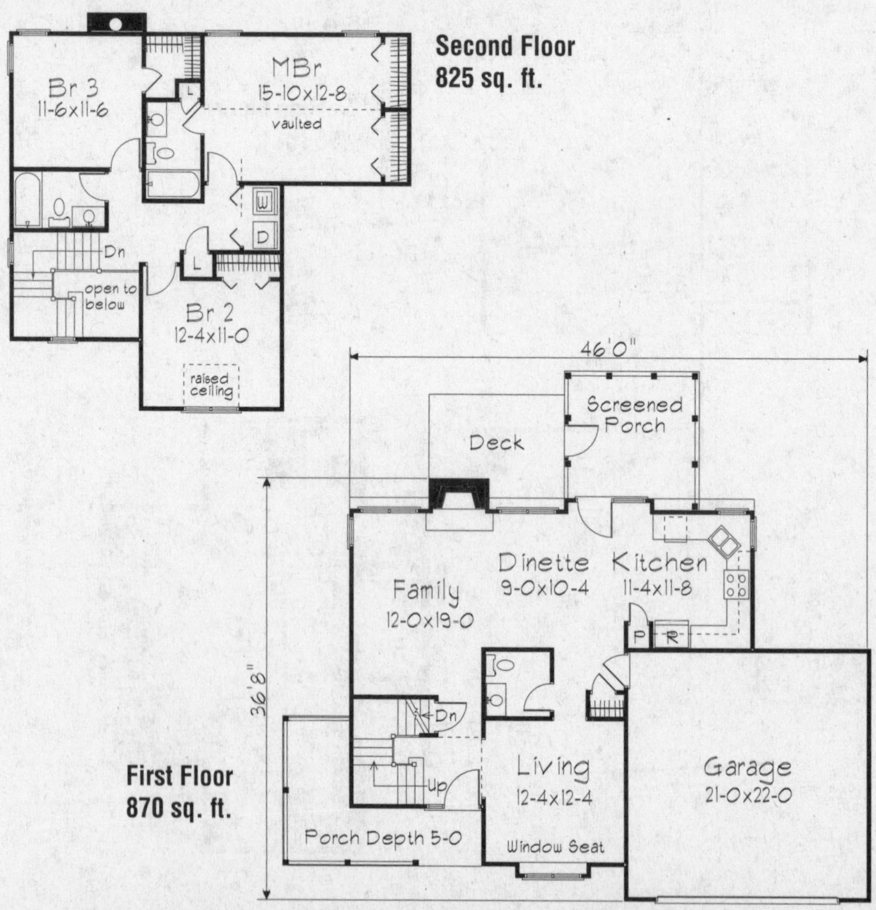
Br 3
11-6x11-6
MBr
15-10x12-8
vaulted
Dn
open to below
Br 2
12-4x11-0
raised ceiling
46'0"
Screened Porch
Deck
Dinette
9-0x10-4
Kitchen
11-4x11-8
Family
12-0x19-0
36'8"
Dn
Up
Living
12-4x12-4
Garage
21-0x22-0
Porch Depth 5-0
Window Seat

Second Floor
825 sq. ft.

First Floor
870 sq. ft.

The Family
Handyman

Plan #702-DDI-100-215

Inviting Country Home

1,757 total square feet of living area **Price Code B**

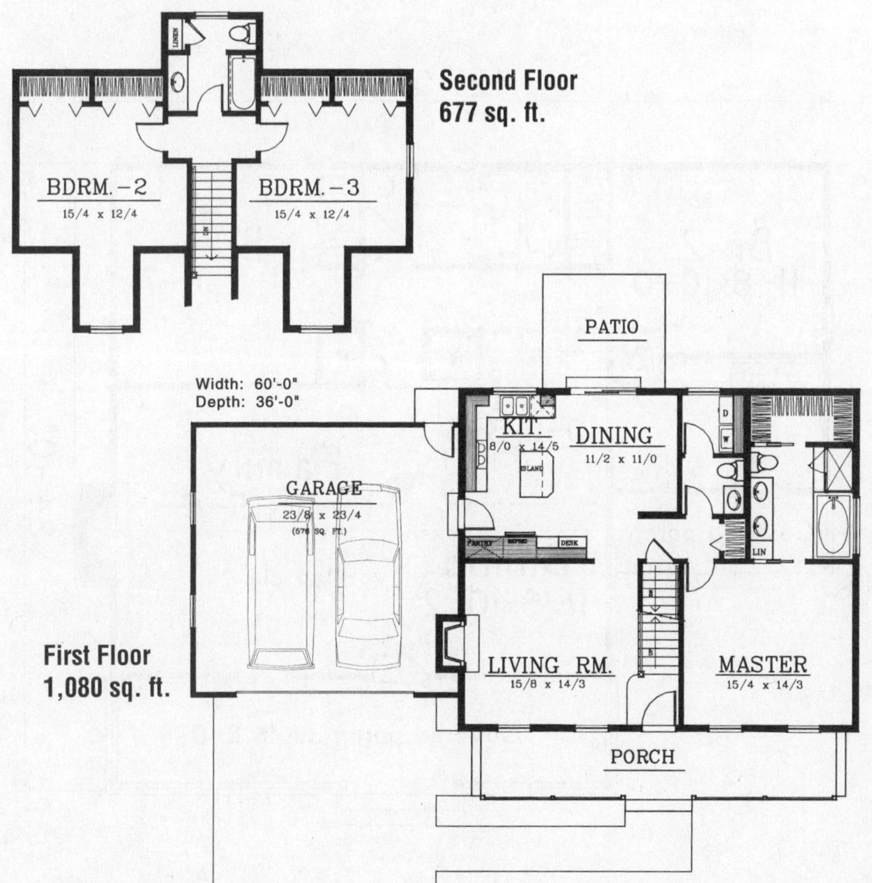
Second Floor
677 sq. ft.
LINEN
BDRM. – 2
15/4 x 12/4
BDRM. – 3
15/4 x 12/4
PATIO
Width: 60'-0"
Depth: 36'-0"
KIT.
8/0 x 14/5
ISLAND
DINING
11/2 x 11/0
GARAGE
23/8 x 23/4
(576 SQ. FT.)
PANTRY
DESK
D
W
LIN
LIVING RM.
15/8 x 14/3
MASTER
15/4 x 14/3
PORCH
First Floor
1,080 sq. ft.

Special features

- Energy efficient home with 2" x 6" exterior walls
- First floor master bedroom has privacy as well as its own bath and walk-in closet
- Cozy living room includes fireplace for warmth
- 3 bedrooms, 2 1/2 baths, 2-car garage
- Crawl space or slab foundation, please specify when ordering

Plan #702-0765

Rustic Design With Modern Features

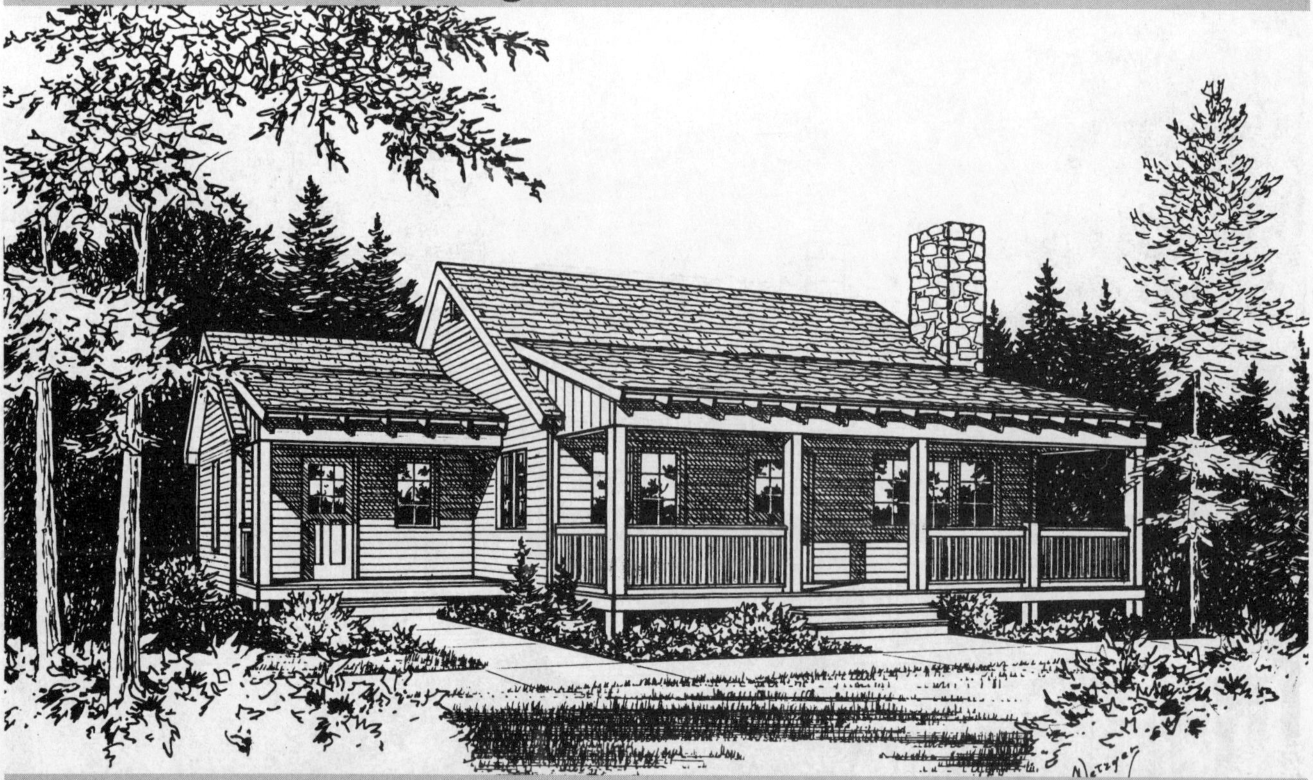

1,000 total square feet of living area

Price Code AA

Special features

- Large mud room with separate covered porch entrance
- Full-length covered front porch
- Bedrooms on opposite sides of the home for privacy
- Vaulted ceiling creates an open and spacious feeling
- 2 bedrooms, 1 bath
- Crawl space foundation

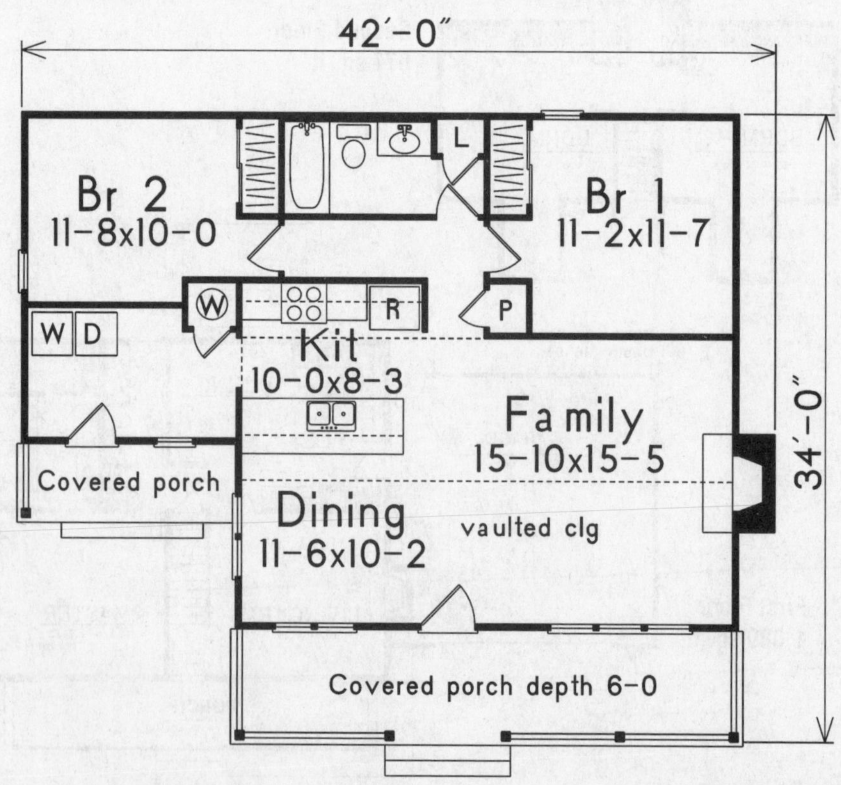
42′-0″
34′-0″
Br 2
11-8x10-0
L
Br 1
11-2x11-7
W
R
P
W D
Kit
10-0x8-3
Family
15-10x15-5
Covered porch
Dining
11-6x10-2
vaulted clg
Covered porch depth 6-0

The Family
Handyman

Plan #702-0220

Dramatic Entry With Soaring Staircase

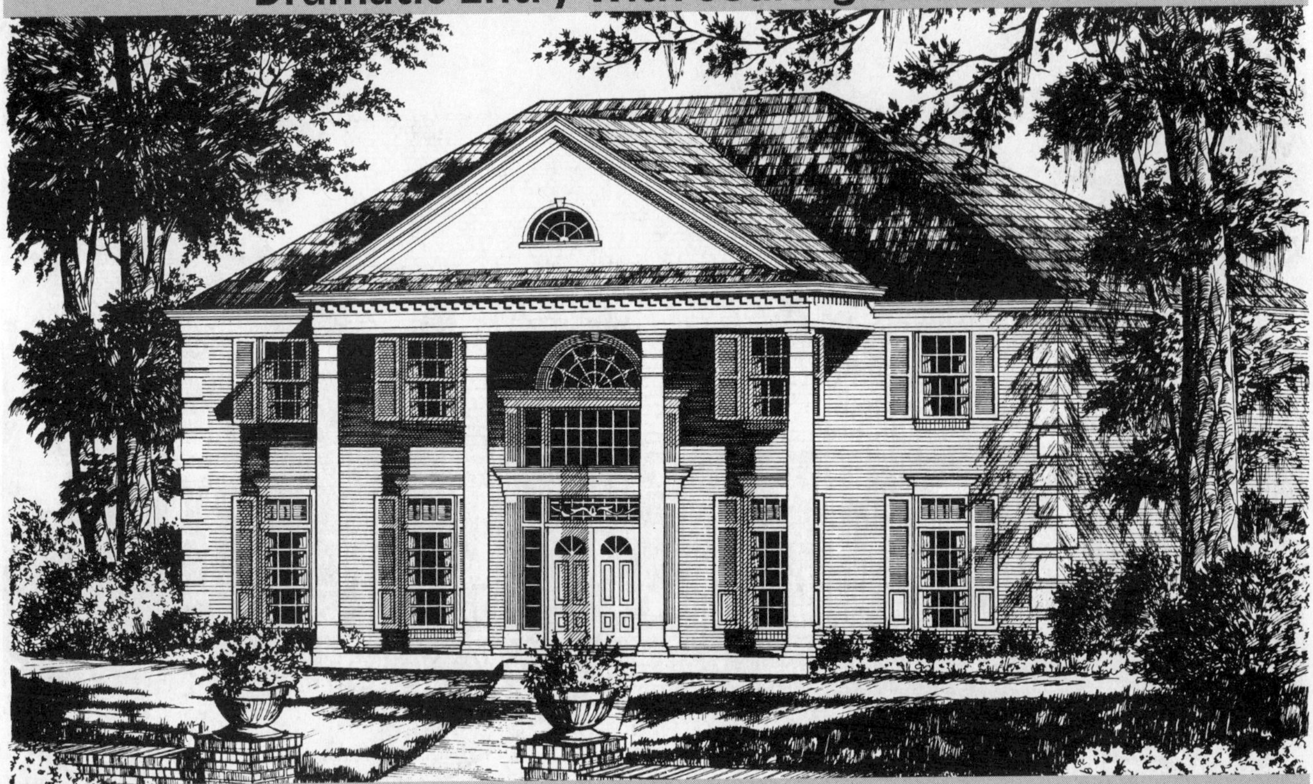

3,391 total square feet of living area

Price Code F

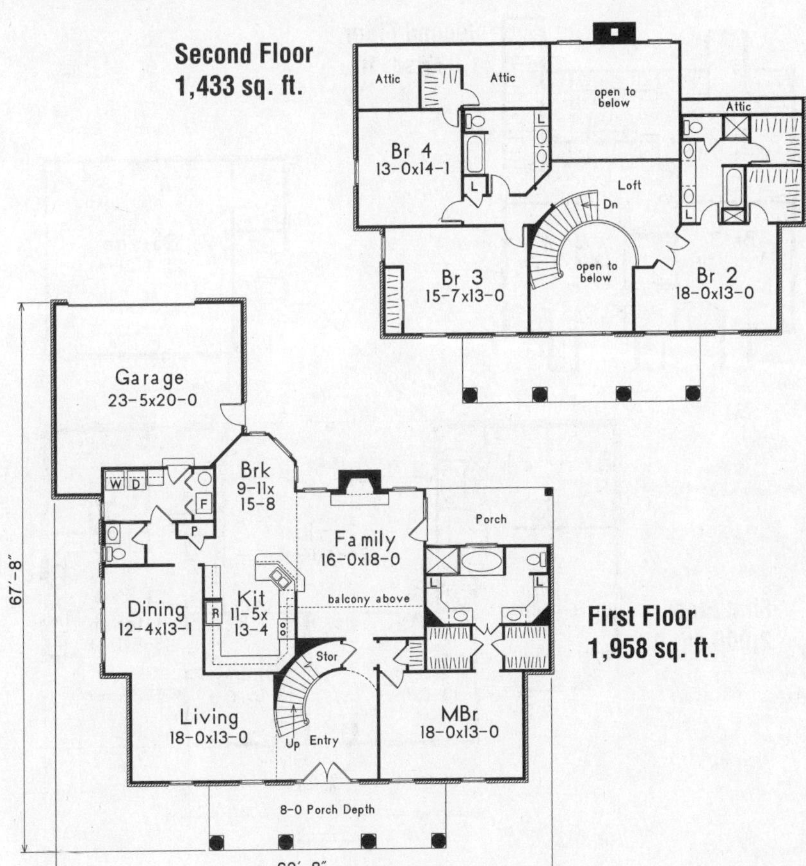
Attic
Attic
open to below
Attic
Br 4
13-0x14-1
Loft
Dn
Br 3
15-7x13-0
open to below
Br 2
18-0x13-0
Garage
23-5x20-0
Brk
9-11x
15-8
W D
F
P
Porch
Family
16-0x18-0
balcony above
Dining
12-4x13-1
R
Kit
11-5x
13-4
Stor
Living
18-0x13-0
Up
Entry
MBr
18-0x13-0
8-0 Porch Depth
67'-8"
62'-8"

Second Floor
1,433 sq. ft.

First Floor
1,958 sq. ft.

Special features

- Magnificent first floor master suite has two walk-in closets and double vanities
- Generous secondary bedrooms
- Bedroom #2 has private bath and plenty of closet space
- Two-story family room with fireplace and balcony above
- 4 bedrooms, 3 1/2 baths, 2-car rear entry garage
- Crawl space foundation, drawings also include slab foundation

Traditional Classic, Modern Features Abound

3,035 total square feet of living area

Price Code E

Special features

- Front facade includes large porch
- Private master bedroom with windowed sitting area, walk-in closet, sloped ceiling and skylight
- Formal living and dining rooms adjoin the family room through attractive French doors
- Energy efficient home with 2" x 6" exterior walls
- 4 bedrooms, 3 1/2 baths, 2-car side entry garage
- Crawl space foundation, drawings also include slab and basement foundations

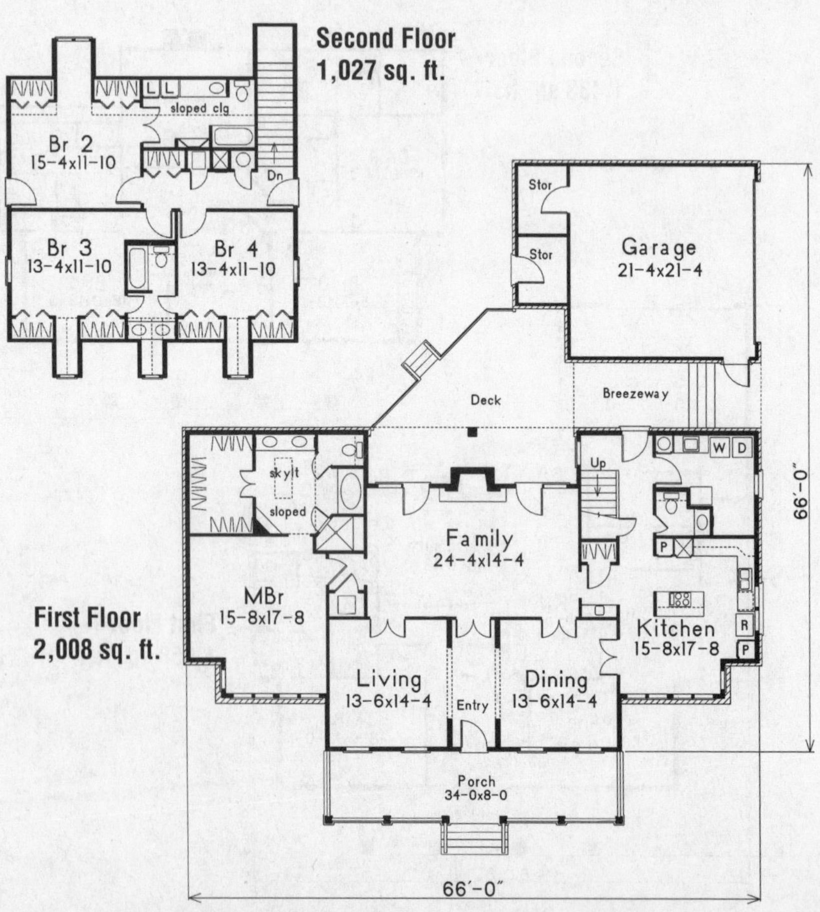
Second Floor
1,027 sq. ft.
sloped clg
Br 2
15-4x11-10
Dn
Br 3
13-4x11-10
Br 4
13-4x11-10
Stor
Stor
Garage
21-4x21-4
Deck
Breezeway
Up
W D
skylt
sloped
Family
24-4x14-4
MBr
15-8x17-8
Kitchen
15-8x17-8
First Floor
2,008 sq. ft.
Living
13-6x14-4
Entry
Dining
13-6x14-4
Porch
34-0x8-0
66'-0"
66'-0"

Plan #702-SH-SEA-307

Large Work Shop In Garage Is Ideal For Hobbies

2,462 total square feet of living area **Price Code D**

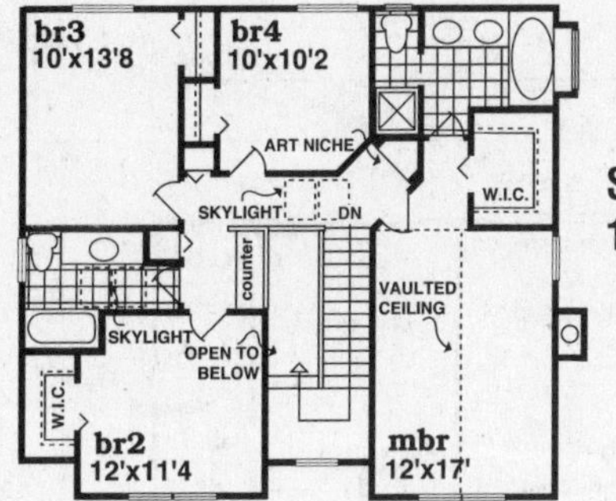
br3
10'x13'8
br4
10'x10'2
ART NICHE
SKYLIGHT
DN
W.I.C.
counter
VAULTED CEILING
SKYLIGHT
OPEN TO BELOW
W.I.C.
br2
12'x11'4
mbr
12'x17'

Second Floor
1,129 sq. ft.

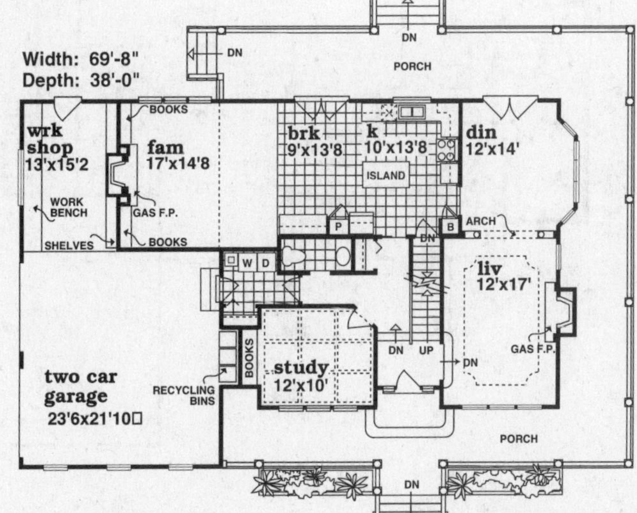
Width: 69'-8"
Depth: 38'-0"
DN
DN
PORCH
BOOKS
wrk shop
13'x15'2
fam
17'x14'8
brk
9'x13'8
k
10'x13'8
din
12'x14'
ISLAND
WORK BENCH
GAS F.P.
SHELVES
BOOKS
P
DN
B
ARCH
W
D
liv
12'x17'
DN
UP
DN
GAS F.P.
BOOKS
study
12'x10'
two car garage
23'6x21'10
RECYCLING BINS
PORCH
DN

First Floor
1,333 sq. ft.

Special features

- Energy efficient home with 2" x 6" exterior walls
- The front study has beamed ceilings and also has built-ins
- French doors open from the breakfast and dining rooms to the spacious porch
- 4 bedrooms, 2 1/2 baths, 2-car side entry garage
- Basement or crawl space foundation, please specify when ordering

TO ORDER BLUEPRINTS USE THE FORM ON PAGE 19 OR CALL TOLL-FREE 1-877-671-6036

View thousands more home plans online at www.familyhandyman.com/homeplans

The Family
Handyman

Plan #702-FB-1158

Serving Bar In Kitchen

2,072 total square feet of living area **Price Code C**

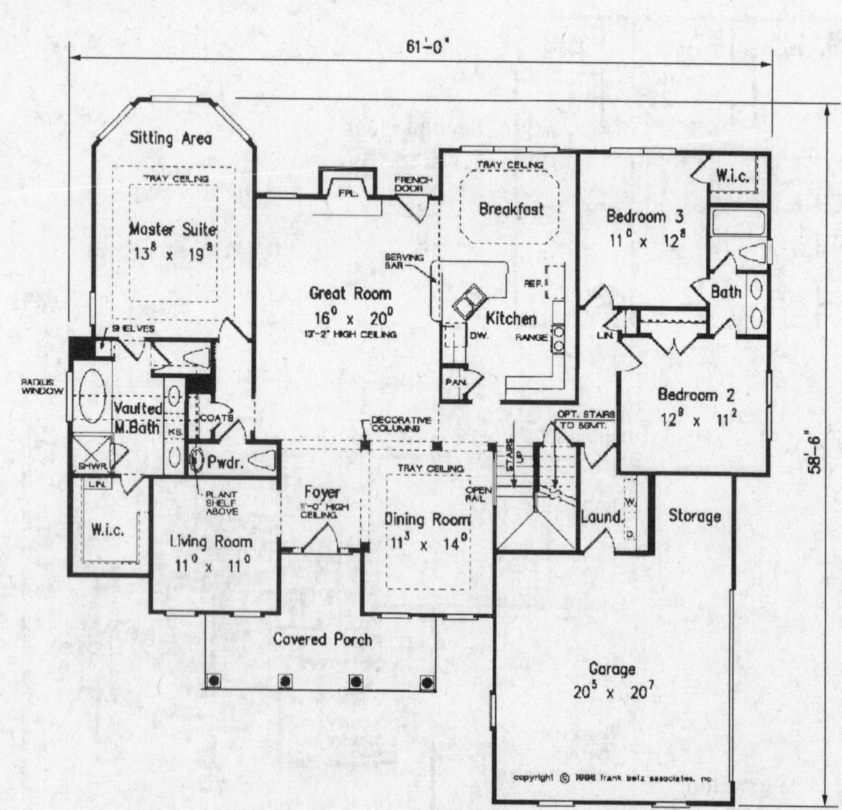
61'-0"
58'-6"
Sitting Area
TRAY CEILING
Master Suite
13^8 x 19^8
FPL.
FRENCH DOOR
TRAY CEILING
Breakfast
Bedroom 3
11^0 x 12^8
W.i.c.
SERVING BAR
Great Room
16^0 x 20^0
13'-2" HIGH CEILING
REF.
Kitchen
DW.
RANGE
Bath
LIN.
SHELVES
RADIUS WINDOW
Vaulted M.Bath
KS.
COATS
PAN.
DECORATIVE COLUMNS
OPT. STAIRS TO BSMT.
Bedroom 2
12^9 x 11^2
SHWR.
Pwdr.
STAIRS
LIN.
PLANT SHELF ABOVE
Foyer
11'-0" HIGH CEILING
TRAY CEILING
OPEN RAIL
W.i.c.
Living Room
11^0 x 11^0
Dining Room
11^3 x 14^0
Laund.
W.
D.
Storage
Covered Porch
Garage
20^5 x 20^7

Special features

- Master suite has large bay sitting area, private vaulted bath and enormous walk-in closet
- Tray ceiling in breakfast room and dining room is a charming touch
- Great room has a centered fireplace and a French door leading outdoors
- 3 bedrooms, 2 1/2 baths, 2-car side entry garage
- Walk-out basement or crawl space foundation, please specify when ordering

Plan #702-0774

Open Floor Plan With Extra Amenities

1,680 total square feet of living area

Price Code B

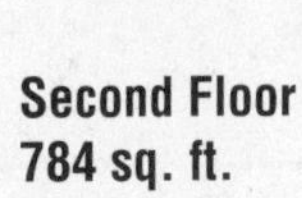

Second Floor
784 sq. ft.

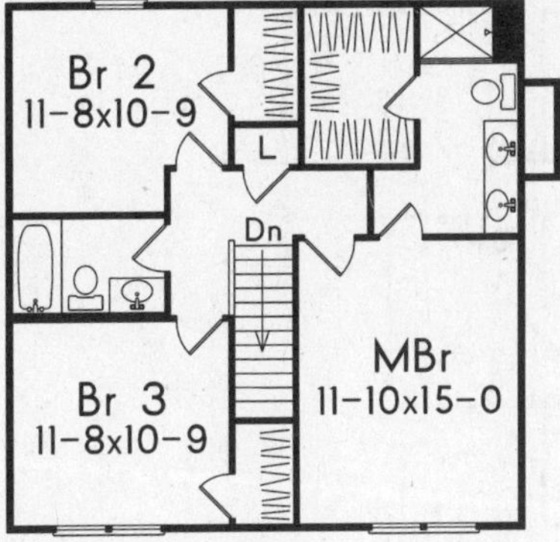

Br 2
11-8x10-9
L
Dn
Br 3
11-8x10-9
MBr
11-10x15-0

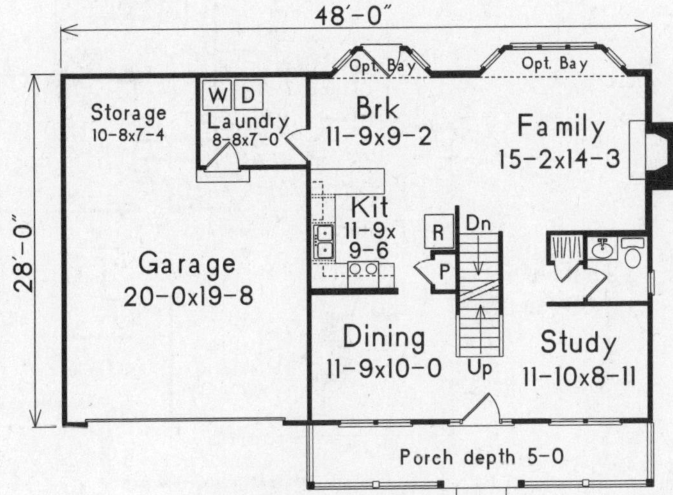

48'-0"
28'-0"
Opt. Bay
Opt. Bay
W D
Storage
10-8x7-4
Laundry
8-8x7-0
Brk
11-9x9-2
Family
15-2x14-3
Kit
11-9x
9-6
R
P
Dn
Garage
20-0x19-8
Dining
11-9x10-0
Up
Study
11-10x8-11
Porch depth 5-0

First Floor
896 sq. ft.

Special features

- Compact and efficient layout in an affordable package
- Second floor has three bedrooms all with oversized closets
- All bedrooms on second floor for privacy
- 3 bedrooms, 2 1/2 baths, 2-car garage
- Basement foundation

Plan #702-0231

Outdoor Living Area Created By Veranda

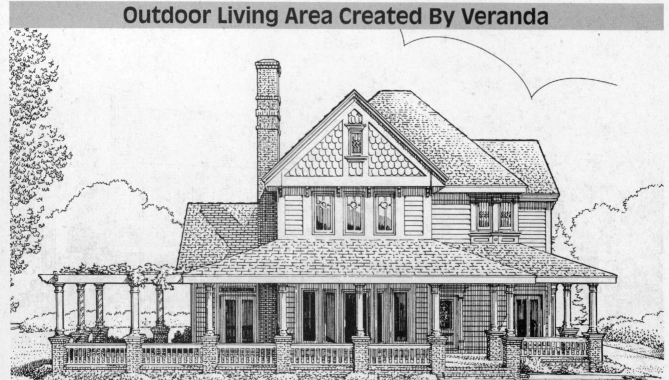

2,213 total square feet of living area **Price Code E**

Special features

- Master bedroom features full bath with separate vanities, large walk-in closet and access to veranda
- Living room enhanced by a fireplace, bay window and columns framing the gallery
- 9' ceilings throughout home add to open feeling
- 4 bedrooms, 2 1/2 baths, 2-car side entry garage
- Slab foundation

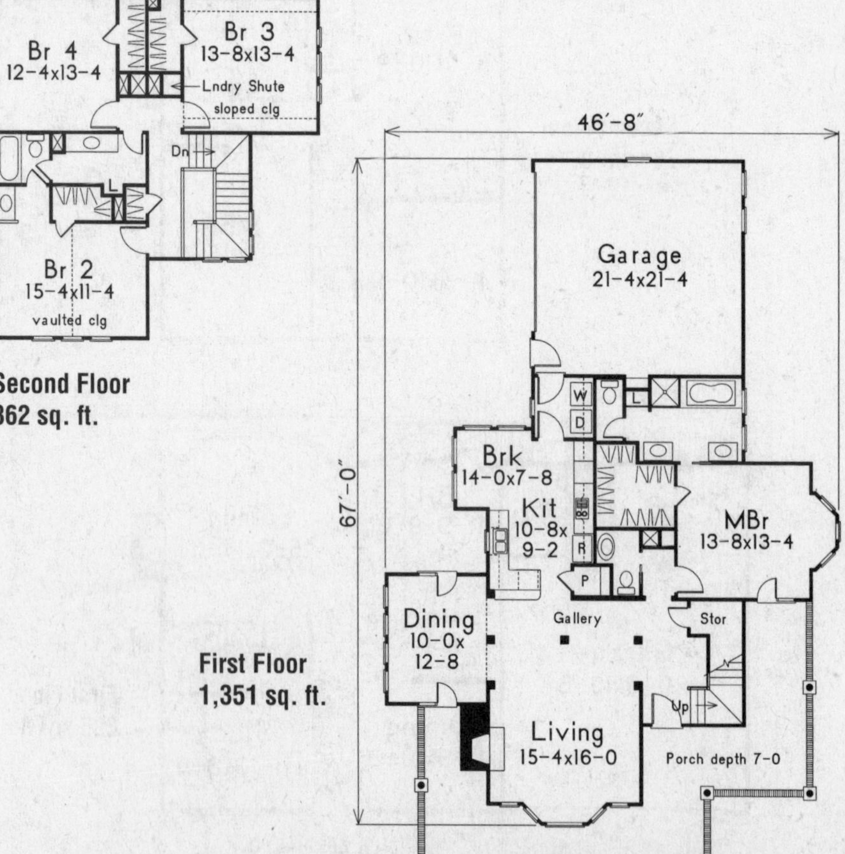
Br 4
12-4x13-4
Br 3
13-8x13-4
Lndry Shute
sloped clg
Dn
L
Br 2
15-4x11-4
vaulted clg
46'-8"
67'-0"
Garage
21-4x21-4
W
D
L
Brk
14-0x7-8
Kit
10-8x
9-2
R
P
MBr
13-8x13-4
Dining
10-0x
12-8
Gallery
Stor
Up
Living
15-4x16-0
Porch depth 7-0

Second Floor
862 sq. ft.

First Floor
1,351 sq. ft.

TO ORDER BLUEPRINTS USE THE FORM ON PAGE 19 OR CALL TOLL-FREE 1-877-671-6036

View thousands more home plans online at www.familyhandyman.com/homeplans

The Family
Handyman

Plan #702-1336

Efficient Ranch With Country Charm

1,364 total square feet of living area

Price Code A

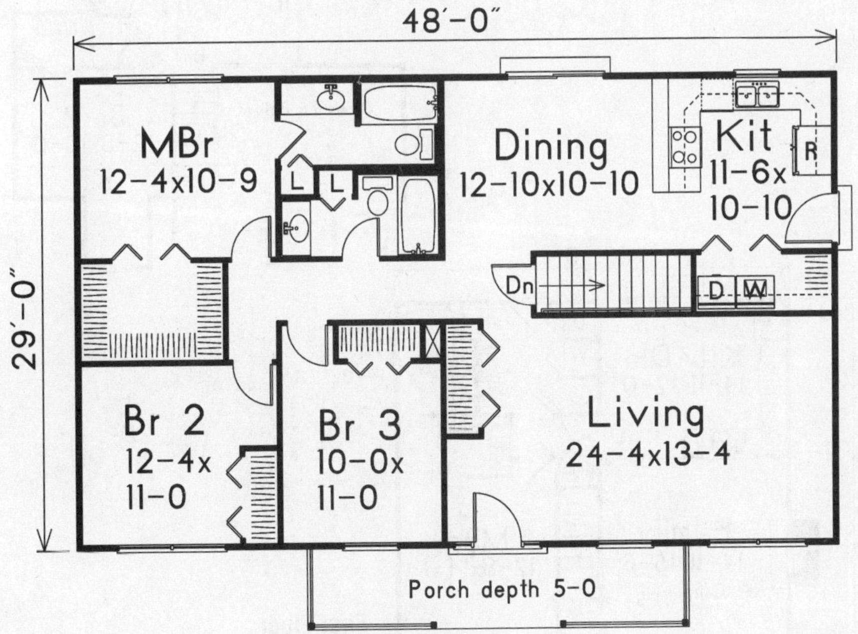
48'-0"
29'-0"
MBr
12-4x10-9
L
L
Dining
12-10x10-10
Kit
11-6x
10-10
R
Dn
D
W
Br 2
12-4x
11-0
Br 3
10-0x
11-0
Living
24-4x13-4
Porch depth 5-0

Special features

- Master suite features spacious walk-in closet and private bath
- Great room highlighted with several windows
- Kitchen with snack bar adjacent to dining area
- Plenty of storage space throughout
- 3 bedrooms, 2 baths, optional 2-car garage
- Basement foundation, drawings also include crawl space foundation

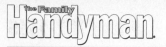

Plan #702-0692

Year-Round Or Weekend Getaway Home

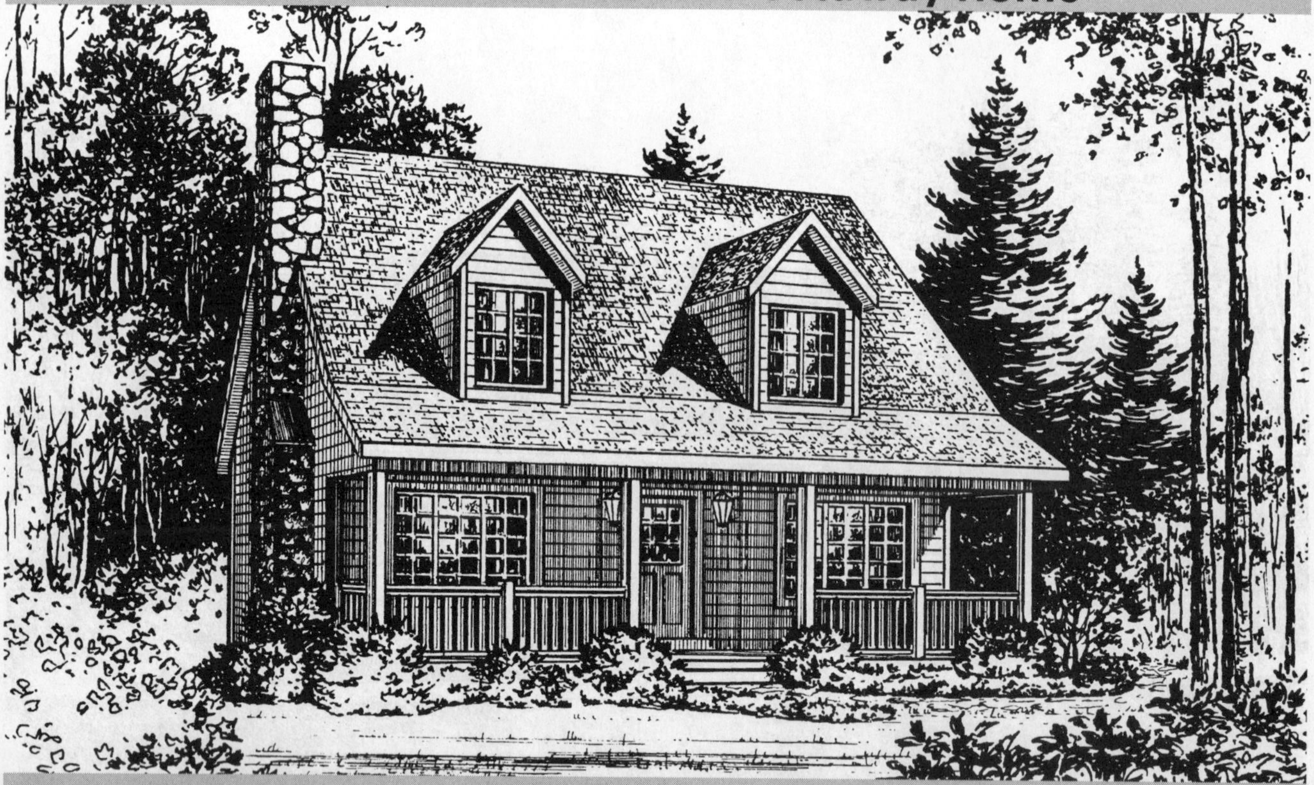

1,339 total square feet of living area

Price Code A

Special features

- Full-length covered porch enhances front facade
- Vaulted ceiling and stone fireplace add drama to family room
- Walk-in closets in bedrooms provide ample storage space
- Combined kitchen/dining area adjoins family room for perfect entertaining space
- 3 bedrooms, 2 1/2 baths
- Crawl space foundation

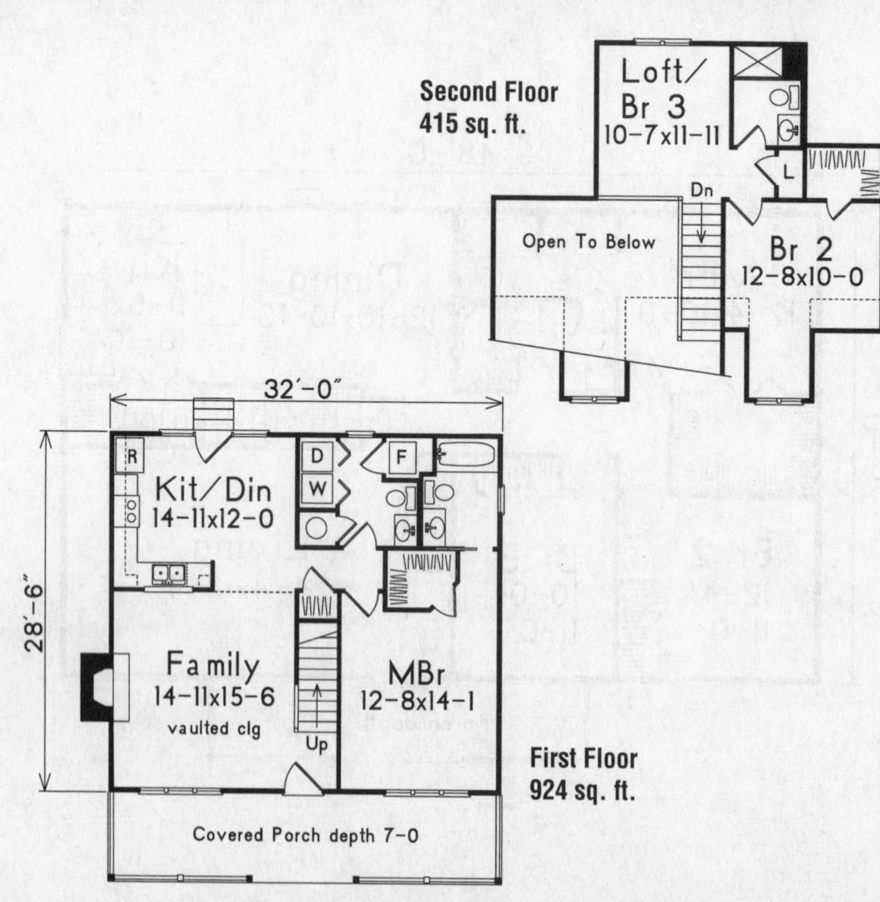
Second Floor
415 sq. ft.
Loft/
Br 3
10-7x11-11
L
Dn
Open To Below
Br 2
12-8x10-0
32'-0"
28'-6"
R
D
W
F
Kit/Din
14-11x12-0
Family
14-11x15-6
vaulted clg
Up
MBr
12-8x14-1
Covered Porch depth 7-0
First Floor
924 sq. ft.

The Family
Handyman

Plan #702-0489

Relax On The Covered Front Porch

1,543 total square feet of living area **Price Code B**

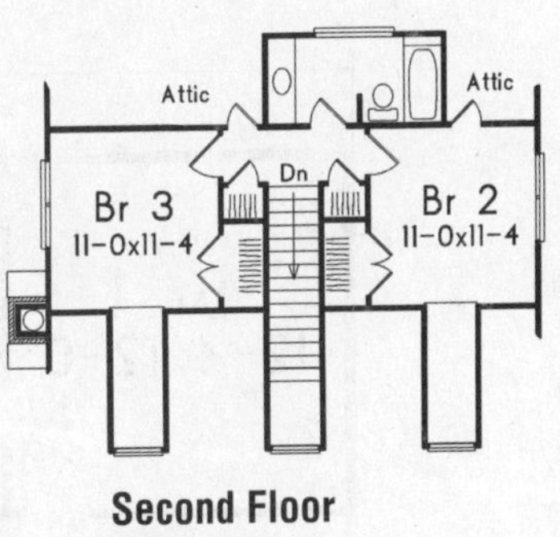
Attic
Attic
Dn
Br 3
11-0x11-4
Br 2
11-0x11-4

Second Floor
503 sq. ft.

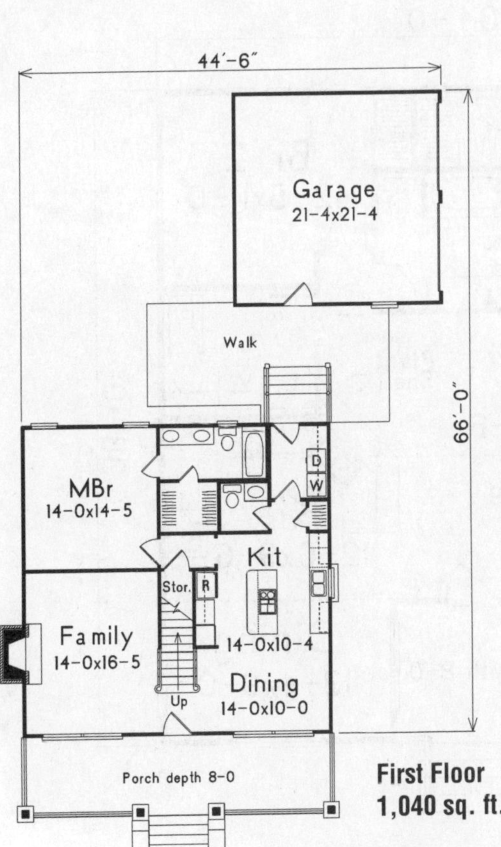
44'-6"
Garage
21-4x21-4
Walk
66'-0"
MBr
14-0x14-5
D
W
Kit
Stor.
R
Family
14-0x16-5
14-0x10-4
Dining
14-0x10-0
Up
Porch depth 8-0

First Floor
1,040 sq. ft.

Special features

- Fireplace serves as the focal point of the large family room
- Efficient floor plan keeps hallways at a minimum
- Laundry room connects the kitchen to the garage
- Private first floor master bedroom has walk-in closet and bath
- 3 bedrooms, 2 1/2 baths, 2-car detached side entry garage
- Slab foundation, drawings also include crawl space foundation

Plan #702-0698

Flexible Layout For Various Uses

1,143 total square feet of living area — **Price Code AA**

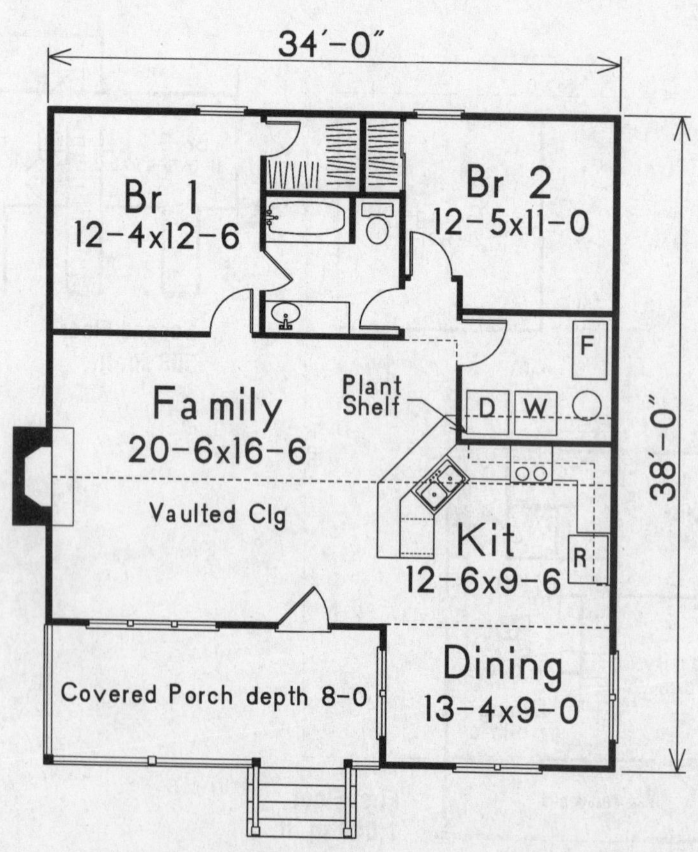

34′-0″
Br 1
12-4x12-6
Br 2
12-5x11-0
F
Plant
Shelf
D
W
Family
20-6x16-6
Vaulted Clg
Kit
12-6x9-6
R
Dining
13-4x9-0
Covered Porch depth 8-0
38′-0″

Special features

- Enormous stone fireplace in family room adds warmth and character
- Spacious kitchen with breakfast bar overlooks family room
- Separate dining area great for entertaining
- Vaulted family room and kitchen create an open atmosphere
- 2 bedrooms, 1 bath
- Crawl space foundation

The Family
Handyman

Plan #702-0678

Pillared Front Porch Generates Charm And Warmth

1,567 total square feet of living area

Price Code B

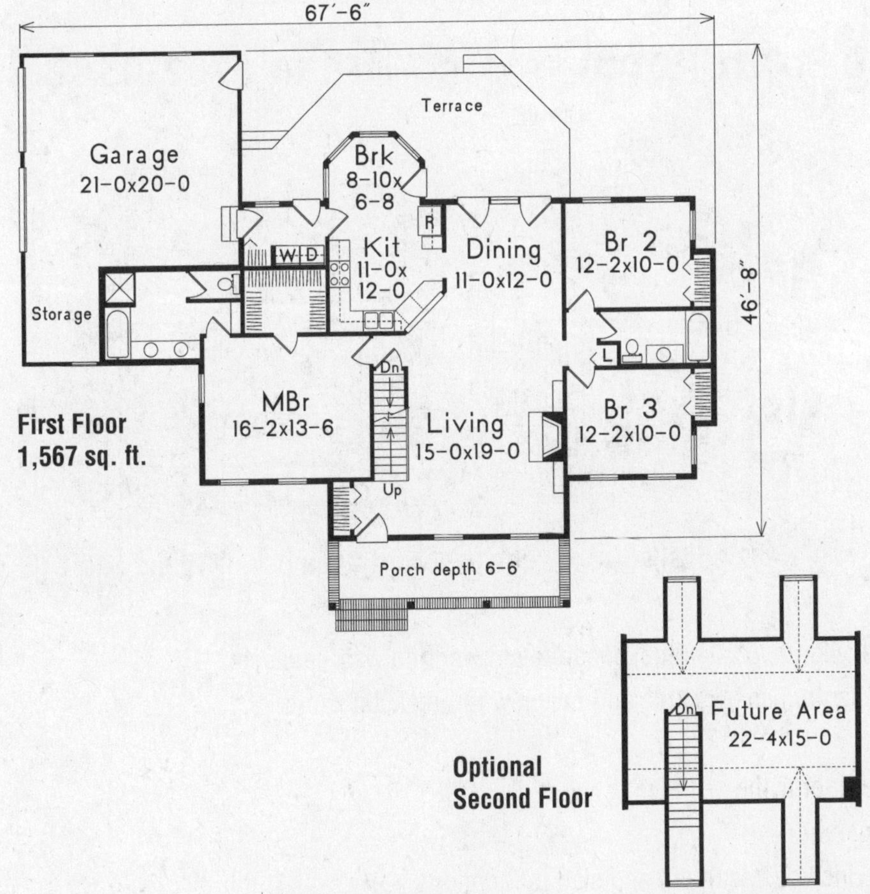
67'-6"
46'-8"
Terrace
Garage
21-0x20-0
Brk
8-10x
6-8
R
W D
Kit
11-0x
12-0
Dining
11-0x12-0
Br 2
12-2x10-0
Storage
L
MBr
16-2x13-6
Dn
Living
15-0x19-0
Br 3
12-2x10-0
Up
Porch depth 6-6
First Floor
1,567 sq. ft.
Dn
Future Area
22-4x15-0
Optional
Second Floor

Special features

- Living room flows into dining room shaped by an angled pass-through into the kitchen
- Cheerful, windowed dining area
- 338 square feet of optional living area is available on the second floor
- Master suite separated from other bedrooms for privacy
- 3 bedrooms, 2 baths, 2-car side entry garage
- Basement foundation, drawings also include slab foundation

Country Cottage Has Vaulted Ceiling — Plan #702-0651

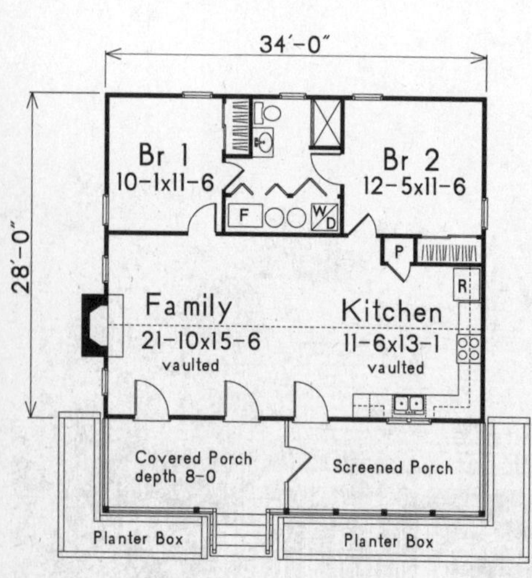
34′-0″
28′-0″
Br 1
10-1x11-6
Br 2
12-5x11-6
F
W/D
P
R
Family
21-10x15-6
vaulted
Kitchen
11-6x13-1
vaulted
Covered Porch
depth 8-0
Screened Porch
Planter Box
Planter Box

962 total square feet of living area — **Price Code AA**

Special features

- Both the kitchen and family room share warmth from the fireplace
- Charming facade features covered porch on one side, screened porch on the other and attractive planter boxes
- L-shaped kitchen boasts convenient pantry
- 2 bedrooms, 1 bath
- Crawl space foundation

Double Gables Frame Front Porch — Plan #702-0542

1,832 total square feet of living area — **Price Code C**

Special features

- Distinctive master suite enhanced by skylights, garden tub, separate shower and walk-in closet
- U-shaped kitchen features convenient pantry, laundry area and full view to breakfast room
- Foyer opens into spacious living room
- Large front porch creates enjoyable outdoor living
- 3 bedrooms, 2 baths, 2-car detached garage
- Crawl space foundation, drawings also include basement and slab foundations

Plan #702-HP-C675

Casual Country Home With Unique Loft

1,673 total square feet of living area | **Price Code B**

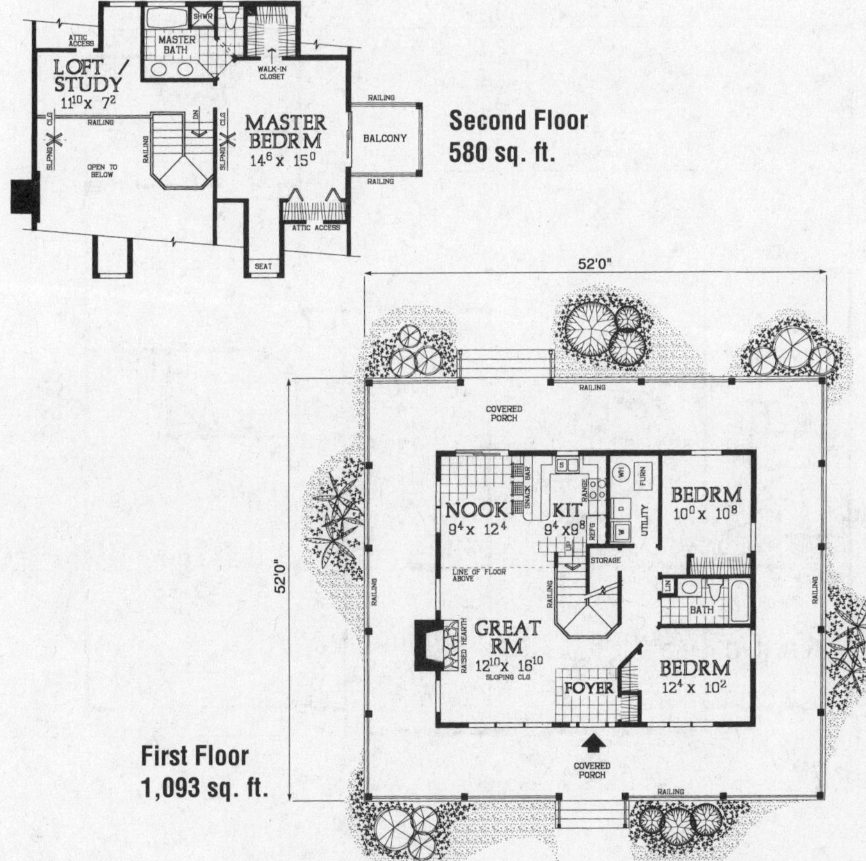
ATTIC ACCESS
MASTER BATH
SHWR
LOFT / STUDY
11^{10} x 7^{2}
WALK-IN CLOSET
MASTER BEDRM
14^{6} x 15^{0}
RAILING
BALCONY
OPEN TO BELOW
SLPNG CLG
DN
ATTIC ACCESS
SEAT
52'0"
52'0"
COVERED PORCH
NOOK
9^{4} x 12^{4}
KIT
9^{4} x 9^{8}
SNACK BAR
RANGE
REFG
UTILITY
FURN
BEDRM
10^{0} x 10^{8}
LINE OF FLOOR ABOVE
STORAGE
UP
LIN
BATH
GREAT RM
12^{10} x 16^{10}
SLOPING CLG
RAISED HEARTH
FOYER
BEDRM
12^{4} x 10^{2}
COVERED PORCH
RAILING

Second Floor
580 sq. ft.

First Floor
1,093 sq. ft.

Special features

- Great room flows into the breakfast nook with outdoor access and beyond to an efficient kitchen
- Master suite on second floor has access to loft/study, private balcony and bath
- Covered porch surrounds the entire home for outdoor living area
- 3 bedrooms, 2 baths
- Crawl space foundation

The Family
Handyman

Plan #702-0724

Upscale Ranch With Formal And Informal Areas

1,969 total square feet of living area

Price Code C

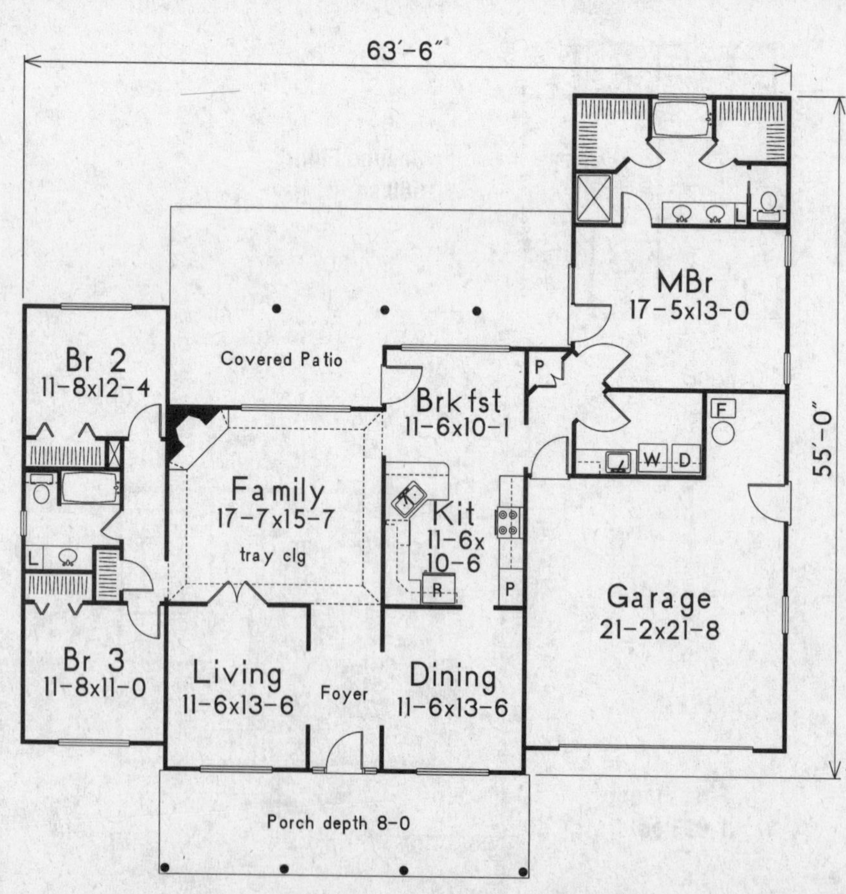
63'-6"
55'-0"
MBr
17-5x13-0
Covered Patio
Br 2
11-8x12-4
Brkfst
11-6x10-1
P
F
W D
Family
17-7x15-7
tray clg
Kit
11-6x
10-6
R
P
L
Garage
21-2x21-8
Br 3
11-8x11-0
Living
11-6x13-6
Foyer
Dining
11-6x13-6
Porch depth 8-0

Special features

- Master suite boasts luxurious bath with double sinks, two walk-in closets and an oversized tub
- Corner fireplace warms a conveniently located family area
- Formal living and dining areas in the front of the home lend a touch of privacy when entertaining
- Spacious utility room has counter space and a sink
- 3 bedrooms, 2 baths, 2-car garage
- Crawl space foundation, drawings also include slab foundation

Practical Layout With Inviting Front Porch

1,883 total square feet of living area **Price Code C**

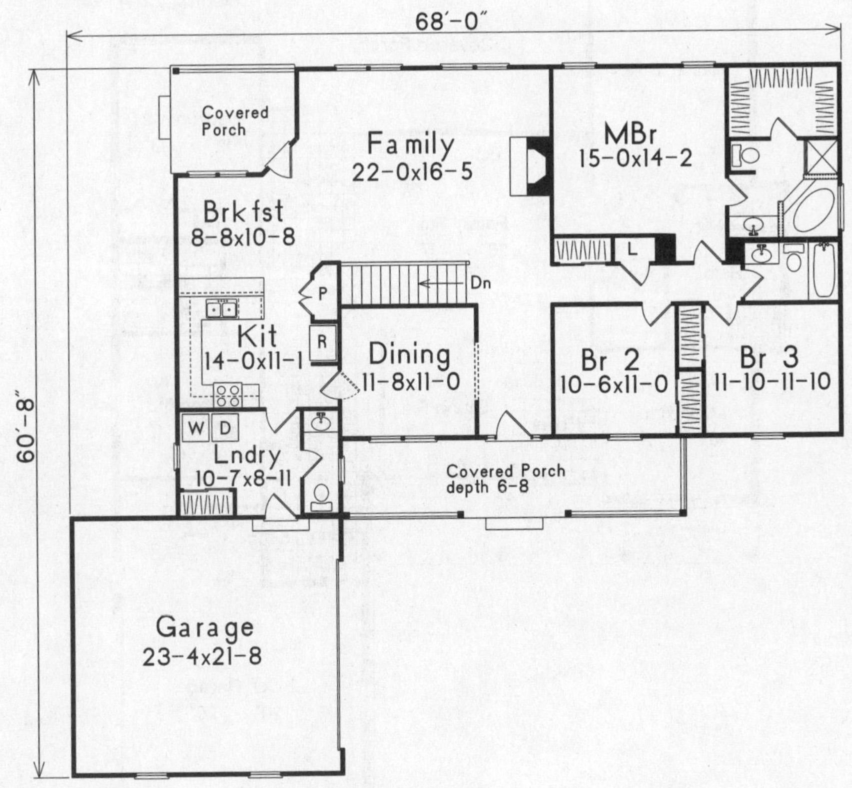
68'-0"
60'-8"
Covered Porch
Family
22-0x16-5
MBr
15-0x14-2
Brk fst
8-8x10-8
L
P
Dn
R
Kit
14-0x11-1
Dining
11-8x11-0
Br 2
10-6x11-0
Br 3
11-10-11-10
W
D
Lndry
10-7x8-11
Covered Porch
depth 6-8
Garage
23-4x21-8

Special features

- Large laundry room located off the garage has coat closet and half bath
- Large family room with fireplace and access to covered porch is a great central gathering room
- U-shaped kitchen has breakfast bar, large pantry and swing door to dining room for convenient serving
- 3 bedrooms, 2 1/2 baths, 2-car side entry garage
- Basement foundation

The Family
Handyman

Plan #702-HDS-1993

Country Living At Its Finest

1,993 total square feet of living area

Price Code C

Special features

- Kitchen and nook share open view to the outdoors
- Ample-sized secondary bedrooms
- Well-designed master bath
- 3 bedrooms, 2 baths, 2-car side entry garage
- Slab foundation

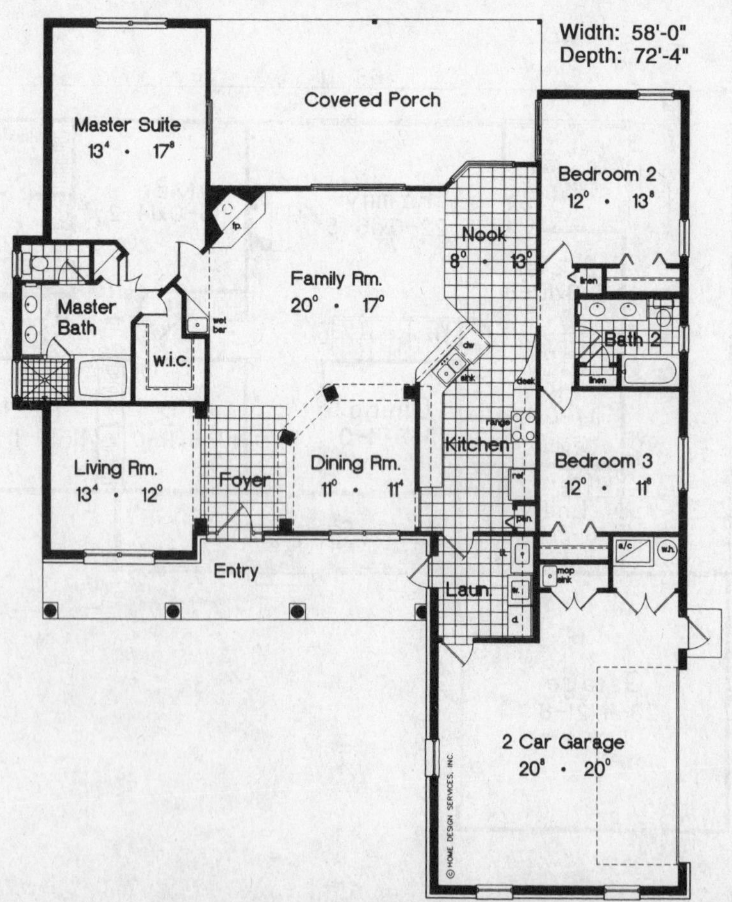
Width: 58'-0"
Depth: 72'-4"
Covered Porch
Master Suite
13⁴ · 17⁸
Bedroom 2
12⁰ · 13⁸
Nook
8⁰ · 13⁰
Family Rm.
20⁰ · 17⁰
Master Bath
w.i.c.
wet bar
Bath 2
Kitchen
Living Rm.
13⁴ · 12⁰
Foyer
Dining Rm.
11⁰ · 11⁴
Bedroom 3
12⁰ · 11⁸
Entry
Laun.
2 Car Garage
20⁸ · 20⁰
© HOME DESIGN SERVICES, INC.

TO ORDER BLUEPRINTS USE THE FORM ON PAGE 19 OR CALL TOLL-FREE 1-877-671-6036

View thousands more home plans online at www.familyhandyman.com/homeplans

The Family
Handyman

Plan #702-0728

Picture Perfect For A Country Setting

2,967 total square feet of living area | **Price Code E**

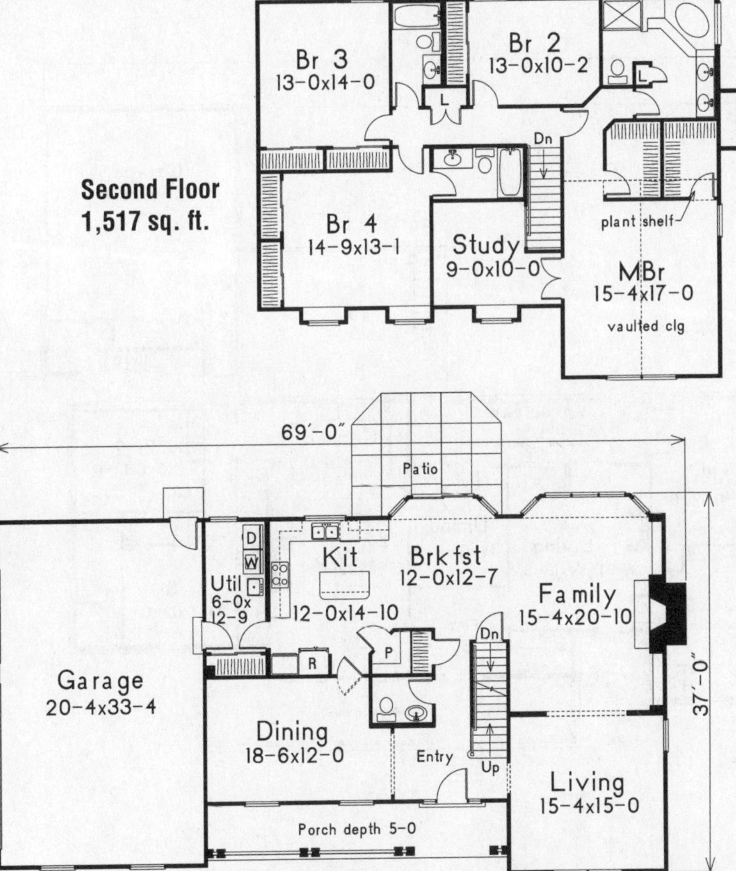

Br 3
13-0x14-0
Br 2
13-0x10-2
L
Dn
Br 4
14-9x13-1
Study
9-0x10-0
plant shelf
MBr
15-4x17-0
vaulted clg
69'-0"
Patio
D
W
Kit
12-0x14-10
Brkfst
12-0x12-7
Util
6-0x
12-9
Family
15-4x20-10
Dn
P
R
Garage
20-4x33-4
37'-0"
Dining
18-6x12-0
Entry
Up
Living
15-4x15-0
Porch depth 5-0

Second Floor
1,517 sq. ft.

First Floor
1,450 sq. ft.

Special features

- An exterior with charm graced with country porch and multiple arched projected box windows
- Dining area is oversized and adjoins a fully equipped kitchen with walk-in pantry
- Two bay windows light up the enormous informal living area to the rear
- 4 bedrooms, 3 1/2 baths, 3-car side entry garage
- Basement foundation

The Family
Handyman

Plan #702-0247

Charming Country Comfort

2,988 total square feet of living area **Price Code E**

Special features

- Bedrooms #2 and #3 share a common bath
- Energy efficient home with 2" x 6" exterior walls
- Rear porch has direct access to master bedroom, living and dining rooms
- Spacious utility room located off garage entrance features a convenient bath with shower
- Large L-shaped kitchen has plenty of work space
- Oversized master suite complete with walk-in closet and master bath
- 3 bedrooms, 3 1/2 baths, 2-car side entry garage
- Partial basement/crawl space foundation

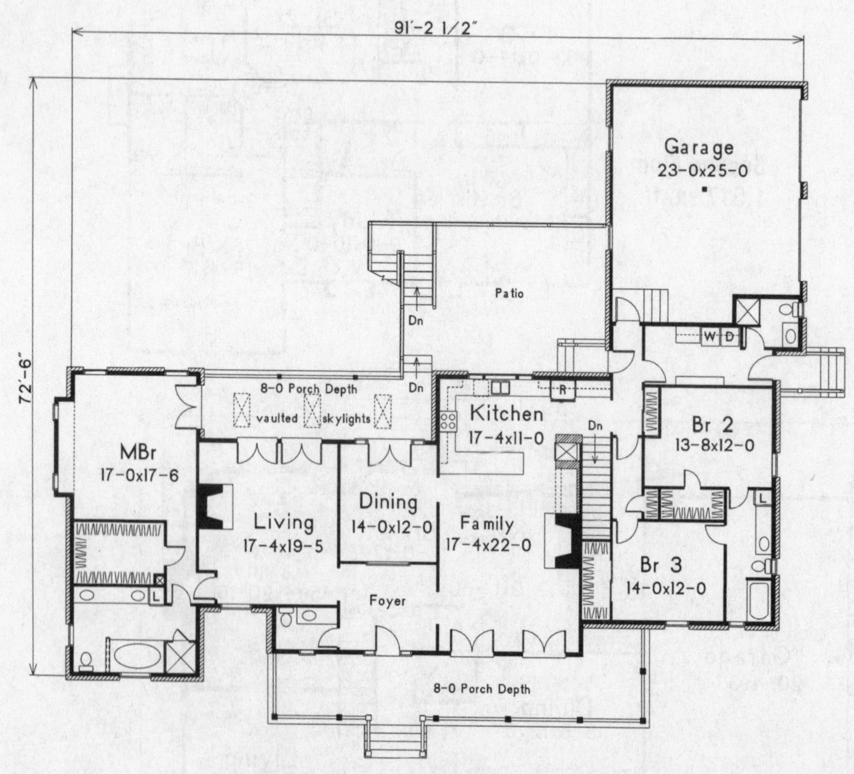
91'-2 1/2"
72'-6"
Garage
23-0x25-0
Patio
Dn
W D
8-0 Porch Depth
vaulted skylights
Kitchen
17-4x11-0
R
Br 2
13-8x12-0
MBr
17-0x17-6
Living
17-4x19-5
Dining
14-0x12-0
Family
17-4x22-0
Br 3
14-0x12-0
Foyer
8-0 Porch Depth

The Family
Handyman

Plan #702-0709

Great Looks Accentuated By Elliptical Brick Arches

2,521 total square feet of living area

Price Code D

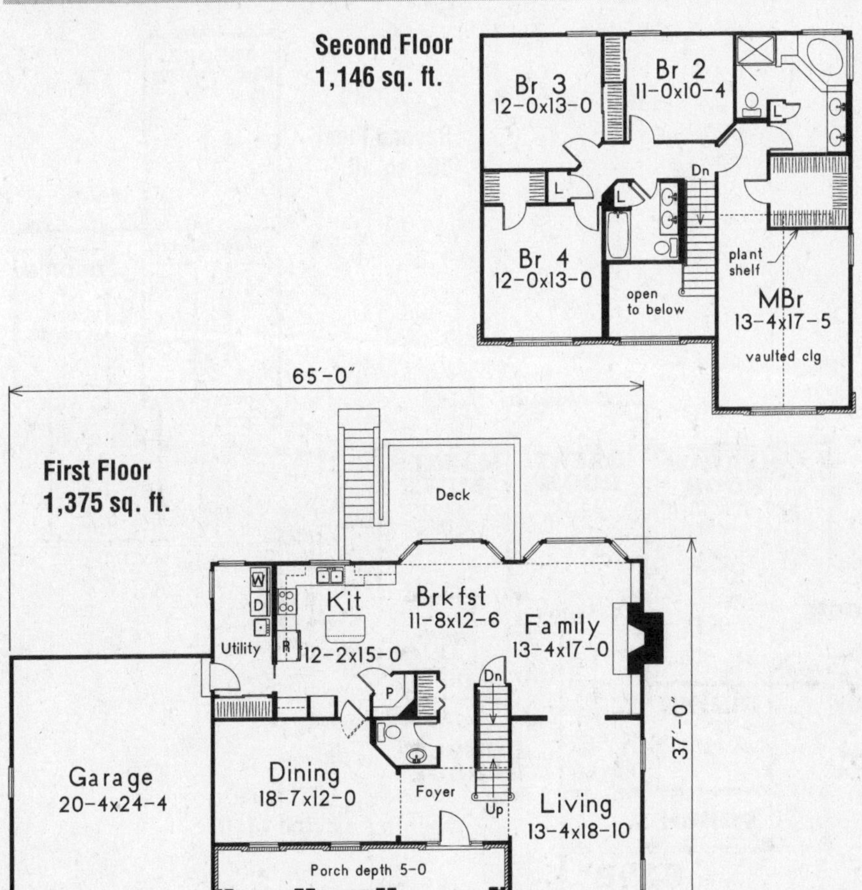
Second Floor
1,146 sq. ft.
Br 3
12-0x13-0
Br 2
11-0x10-4
Dn
L
L
Br 4
12-0x13-0
open
to below
plant
shelf
MBr
13-4x17-5
vaulted clg
65'-0"
First Floor
1,375 sq. ft.
Deck
W
D
Kit
12-2x15-0
Brkfst
11-8x12-6
Family
13-4x17-0
Utility
R
P
Dn
Garage
20-4x24-4
Dining
18-7x12-0
Foyer
Up
Living
13-4x18-10
Porch depth 5-0
37'-0"

Special features

- Large living and dining rooms are a plus for formal entertaining or large family gatherings
- Informal kitchen, breakfast and family rooms feature a 37' vista and double bay windows
- Generous-sized master bedroom and three secondary bedrooms grace the second floor
- 4 bedrooms, 2 1/2 baths, 2-car garage
- Basement foundation

The Family
Handyman

Plan #702-CHD-27-35

A Welcoming Farmhouse Style

2,743 total square feet of living area

Price Code E

Special features

- 9' ceilings on first floor of this home
- Kitchen, breakfast and hearth rooms connect creating one large living space ideal for family living
- Master suite has its own wing with large private bath and walk-in closet
- Wrap-around porch in the front of the home makes a lasting impression
- Future playroom on the second floor has an additional 327 square feet of living area
- 3 bedrooms, 2 1/2 baths, 2-car garage
- Slab foundation

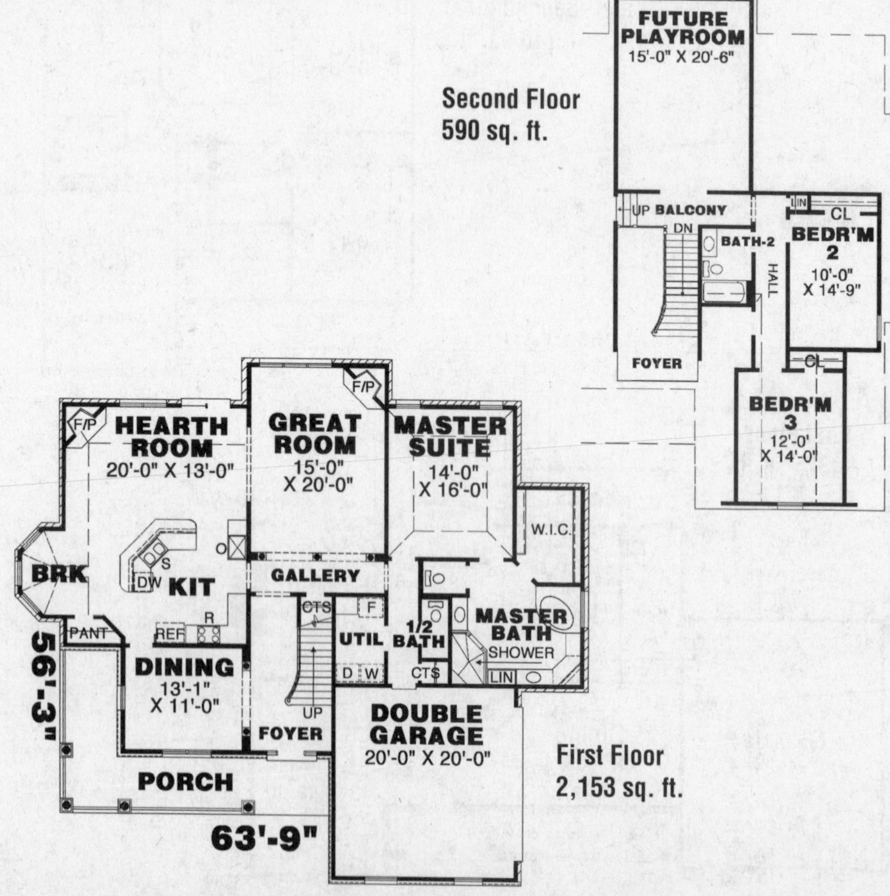
FUTURE PLAYROOM
15'-0" X 20'-6"
UP BALCONY
DN
BATH-2
LIN
CL
BEDR'M 2
10'-0" X 14'-9"
HALL
FOYER
CL
BEDR'M 3
12'-0' X 14'-0'
F/P
HEARTH ROOM
20'-0" X 13'-0"
GREAT ROOM
15'-0" X 20'-0"
MASTER SUITE
14'-0" X 16'-0"
W.I.C.
BRK
S
DW
KIT
GALLERY
R
PANT
REF
CTS
F
UTIL
1/2 BATH
MASTER BATH
SHOWER
DINING
13'-1" X 11'-0"
D W
CTS
LIN
56'-3"
UP
FOYER
DOUBLE GARAGE
20'-0" X 20'-0"
PORCH
63'-9"

Second Floor
590 sq. ft.

First Floor
2,153 sq. ft.

TO ORDER BLUEPRINTS USE THE FORM ON PAGE 19 OR CALL TOLL-FREE 1-877-671-6036

View thousands more home plans online at www.familyhandyman.com/homeplans

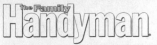

Plan #702-0229

Vaulted Ceilings And Light Add Dimension

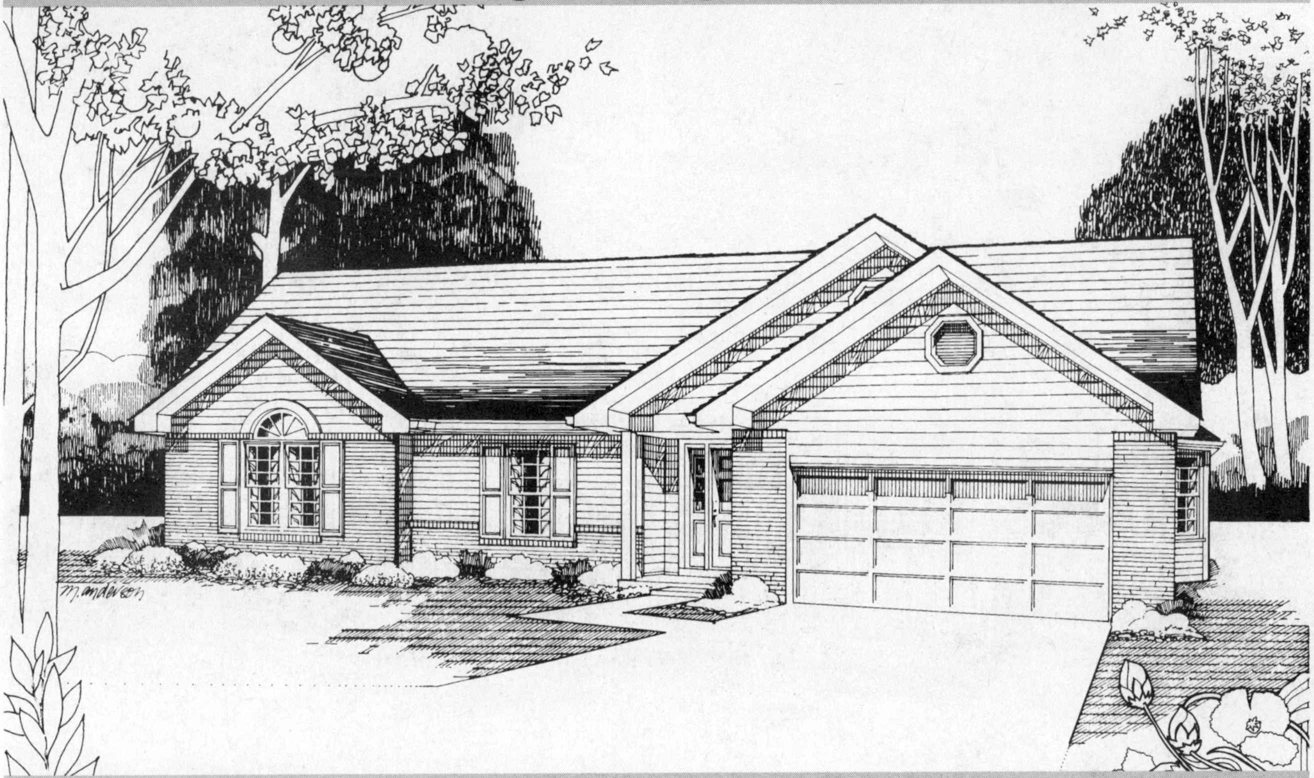

1,676 total square feet of living area

Price Code B

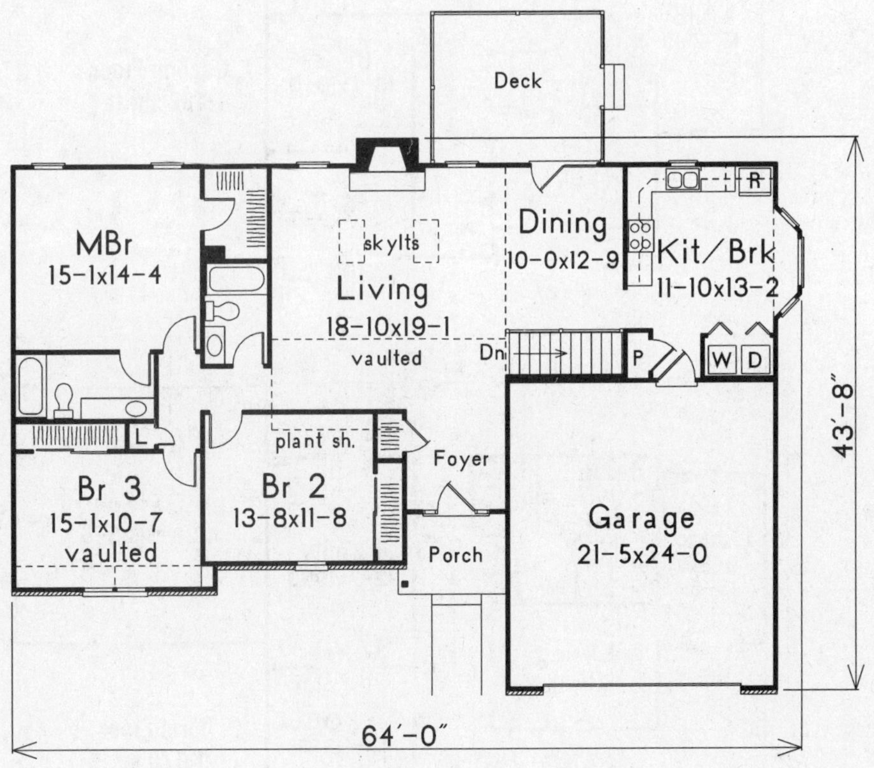
Deck
MBr
15-1x14-4
skylts
Living
18-10x19-1
vaulted
Dining
10-0x12-9
Kit/Brk
11-10x13-2
R
Dn
P
W
D
L
plant sh.
Foyer
Br 3
15-1x10-7
vaulted
Br 2
13-8x11-8
Porch
Garage
21-5x24-0
43'-8"
64'-0"

Special features

- The living area skylights and large breakfast room with bay window provide plenty of sunlight
- The master bedroom has a walk-in closet and both the secondary bedrooms have large closets
- Vaulted ceilings, plant shelving and a fireplace provide a quality living area
- 3 bedrooms, 2 baths, 2-car garage
- Basement foundation, drawings also include crawl space and slab foundations

Plan #702-0540

Large Porch And Balcony Create Impressive Exterior

2,352 total square feet of living area

Price Code D

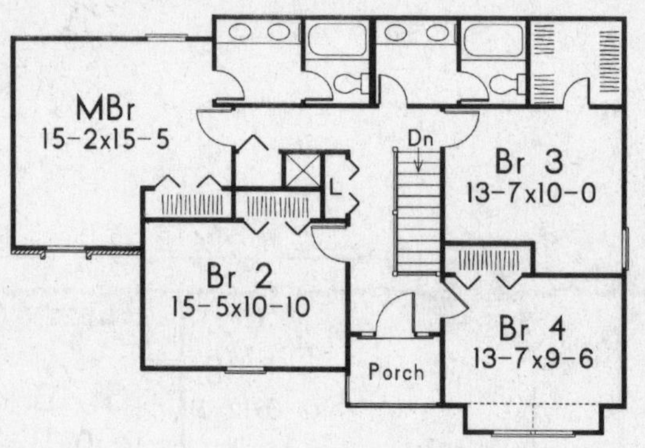
MBr
15-2x15-5
Dn
Br 3
13-7x10-0
L
Br 2
15-5x10-10
Br 4
13-7x9-6
Porch

Second Floor
1,182 sq. ft.

Special features

- Separate family and living rooms for casual and formal entertaining
- Master bedroom with private dressing area and bath
- Bedrooms located on second floor for privacy
- 4 bedrooms, 2 1/2 baths, 2-car rear entry garage
- Crawl space foundation, drawings also include basement and slab foundations

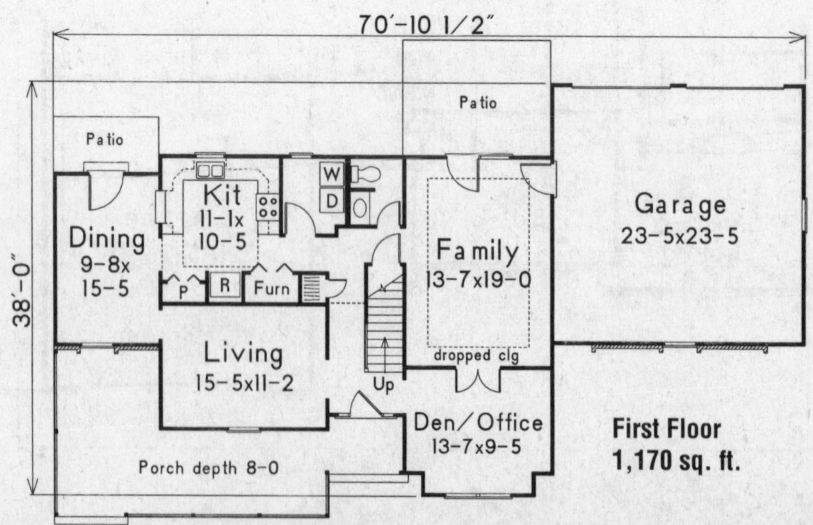
70'-10 1/2"
38'-0"
Patio
Patio
Kit
11-1x
10-5
W
D
Dining
9-8x
15-5
P
R
Furn
Family
13-7x19-0
dropped clg
Garage
23-5x23-5
Living
15-5x11-2
Up
Den/Office
13-7x9-5
Porch depth 8-0

First Floor
1,170 sq. ft.

The Family Handyman

Plan #702-HP-C689

Ranch-Style Home With Many Extras

1,295 total square feet of living area **Price Code A**

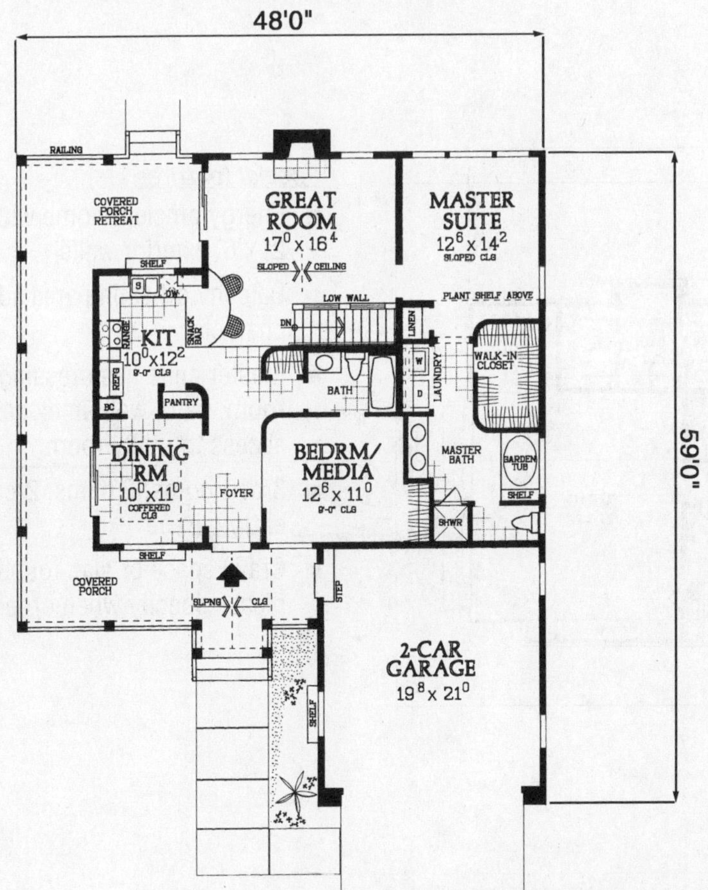
48'0"
RAILING
COVERED PORCH RETREAT
GREAT ROOM
17⁰ x 16⁴
SLOPED CEILING
MASTER SUITE
12⁶ x 14²
SLOPED CLG
LOW WALL
PLANT SHELF ABOVE
SHELF
KIT
10⁰x12²
9'-0" CLG
SNACK BAR
RANGE
REFG
BC
PANTRY
DN
LINEN
BATH
LAUNDRY
WALK-IN CLOSET
DINING RM
10⁰x11⁰
COFFERED CLG
FOYER
BEDRM/ MEDIA
12⁶ x 11⁰
9'-0" CLG
MASTER BATH
GARDEN TUB
SHELF
SHWR
59'0"
COVERED PORCH
SLPNG CLG
STEP
2-CAR GARAGE
19⁸ x 21⁰
SHELF

Special features

- Wrap-around porch is a lovely place for dining
- A fireplace gives a stunning focal point to the great room that is heightened with a sloped ceiling
- The master suite is full of luxurious touches such as a walk-in closet and a lush private bath
- 2 bedrooms, 2 baths, 2-car garage
- Basement foundation

Plan #702-BF-1901

Sunny Eating Area

1,925 total square feet of living area **Price Code C**

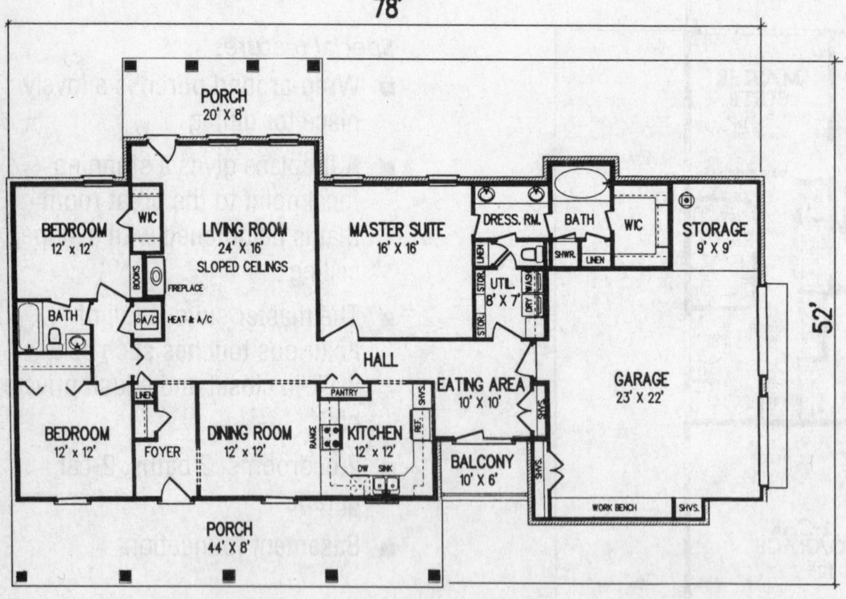
78'
PORCH
20' X 8'
BEDROOM
12' x 12'
WIC
LIVING ROOM
24' X 16'
SLOPED CEILINGS
MASTER SUITE
16' X 16'
DRESS. RM.
BATH
WIC
STORAGE
9' X 9'
BOOKS
FIREPLACE
BATH
HEAT & A/C
LINEN
STOR.
UTIL.
8' X 7'
SHWR.
LINEN
WASH
DRY
HALL
EATING AREA
10' X 10'
GARAGE
23' X 22'
52'
BEDROOM
12' x 12'
LINEN
FOYER
DINING ROOM
12' x 12'
PANTRY
RANGE
KITCHEN
12' x 12'
DW
SINK
REF.
SHVS.
BALCONY
10' X 6'
SHVS.
WORK BENCH
SHVS.
PORCH
44' X 8'

Special features

- Energy efficient home with 2" x 6" exterior walls
- Balcony off eating area adds character
- Master suite has dressing room, bath, walk-in closet and access to utility room
- 3 bedrooms, 2 baths, 2-car side entry garage
- Crawl space or slab foundation, please specify when ordering

Plan #702-DDI-100214

Truly Unique Design

2,104 total square feet of living area

Price Code C

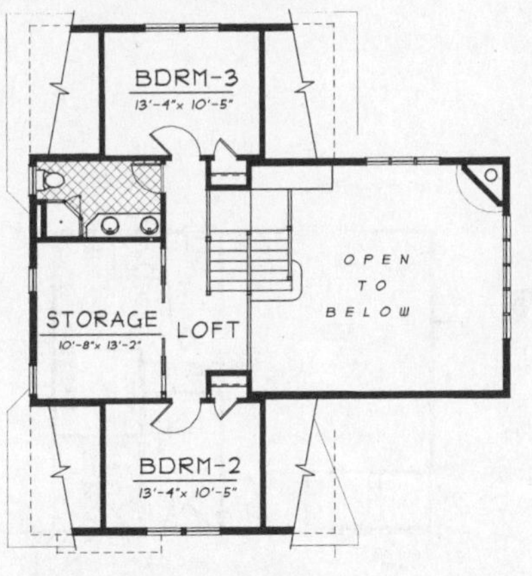
BDRM-3
13'-4" x 10'-5"
OPEN TO BELOW
STORAGE
10'-8" x 13'-2"
LOFT
BDRM-2
13'-4" x 10'-5"

Second Floor
669 sq. ft.

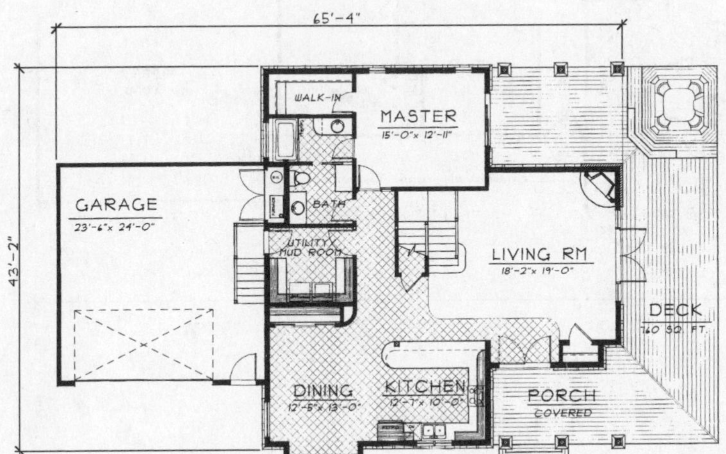
65'-4"
43'-2"
WALK-IN
MASTER
15'-0" x 12'-11"
GARAGE
23'-6" x 24'-0"
BATH
UTILITY/
MUD ROOM
LIVING RM
18'-2" x 19'-0"
DECK
760 SQ. FT.
DINING
12'-6" x 13'-0"
KITCHEN
12'-7" x 10'-0"
PORCH
COVERED

First Floor
1,435 sq. ft.

Special features

- 9' ceilings on the first floor
- Living room opens onto deck through double French doors
- Second floor includes large storage room
- 3 bedrooms, 2 baths, 2-car garage
- Crawl space foundation

TO ORDER BLUEPRINTS USE THE FORM ON PAGE 19 OR CALL TOLL-FREE 1-877-671-6036

View thousands more home plans online at www.familyhandyman.com/homeplans

Plan #702-GH-34043

Handsome Octagon-Shaped Breakfast Room

Rear View

1,583 total square feet of living area **Price Code B**

Special features

- Dining area is open to living room making a terrific gathering place
- Cheerful skylight in private master bath
- Living room has center fireplace creating a cozy atmosphere
- 3 bedrooms, 2 baths, 2-car garage
- Basement, crawl space or slab foundation, please specify when ordering

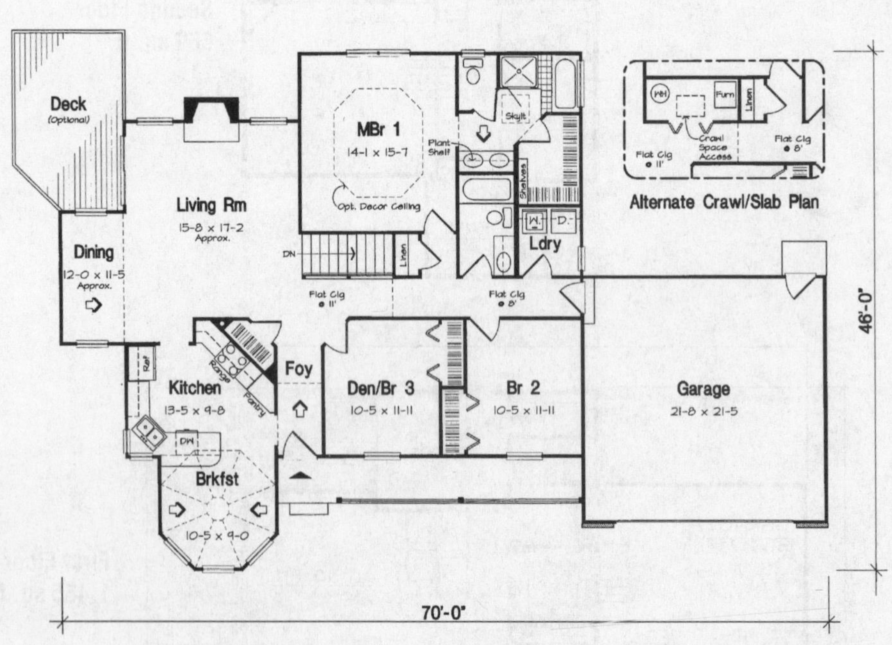
Deck
(Optional)
Living Rm
15-8 x 17-2
Approx.
Dining
12-0 x 11-5
Approx.
MBr 1
14-1 x 15-7
Opt. Decor Ceiling
Plant Shelf
Skylt
Shelves
W
D
Ldry
Linen
DN
Flat Clg 11'
Flat Clg 8'
Ref
Range
Pantry
Kitchen
13-5 x 9-8
DW
Foy
Den/Br 3
10-5 x 11-11
Br 2
10-5 x 11-11
Garage
21-8 x 21-5
Brkfst
10-5 x 9-0
70'-0"
46'-0"
MH
Furn
Linen
Crawl Space Access
Flat Clg 11'
Flat Clg 8'
Alternate Crawl/Slab Plan

Plan #702-0529

Layout Creates Large Open Living Area

1,285 total square feet of living area **Price Code B**

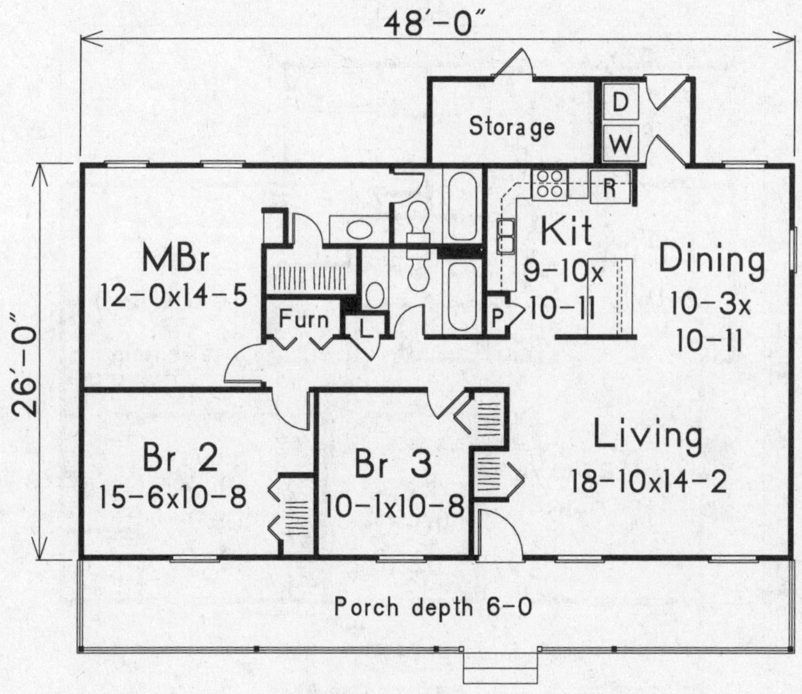

48'-0"
26'-0"
Storage
D
W
R
Kit
9-10x
10-11
Dining
10-3x
10-11
MBr
12-0x14-5
Furn
L
P
Br 2
15-6x10-8
Br 3
10-1x10-8
Living
18-10x14-2
Porch depth 6-0

Special features

- Accommodating home with ranch-style porch
- Large storage area on back of home
- Master bedroom includes dressing area, private bath and built-in bookcase
- Kitchen features pantry, break-fast bar and complete view to dining room
- 3 bedrooms, 2 baths
- Crawl space foundation, drawings also include basement and slab foundations

The Family
Handyman

Plan #702-0239

Front Porch Adds Style To This Ranch

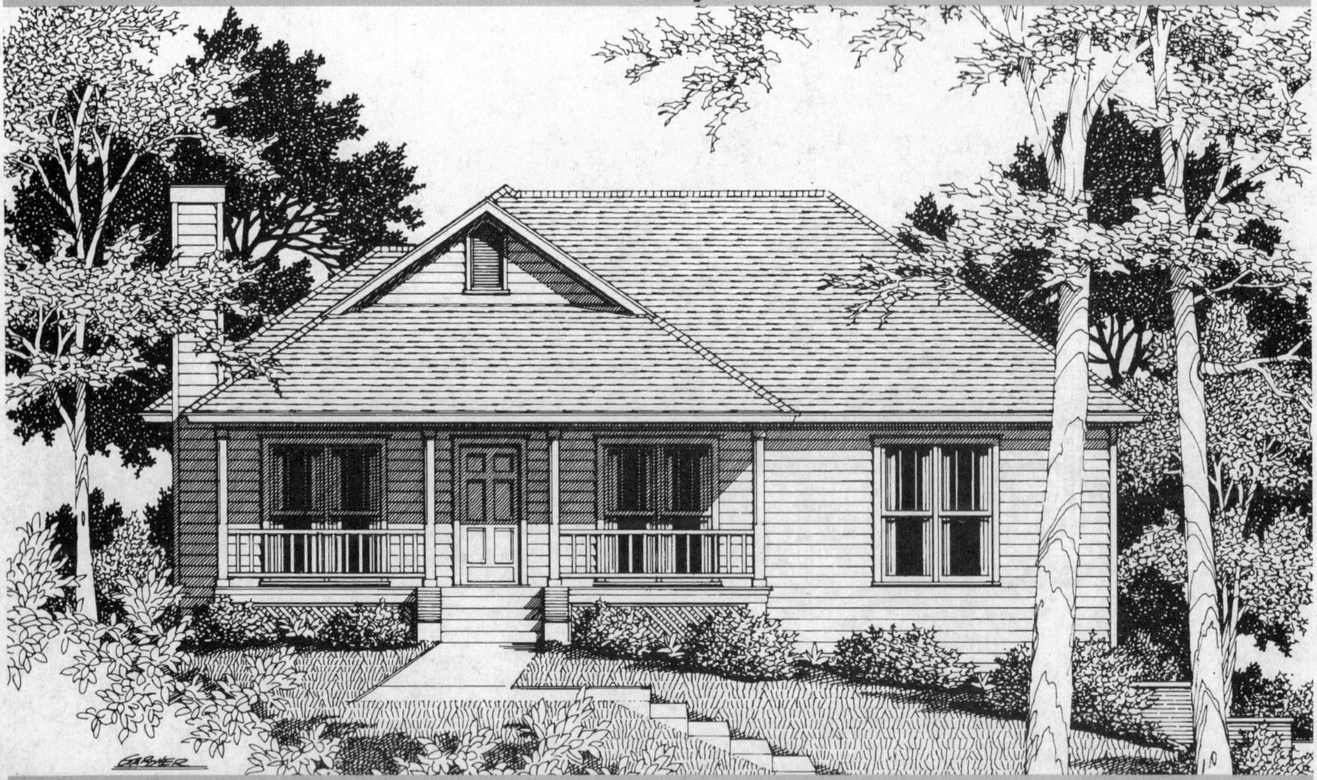

1,496 total square feet of living area **Price Code A**

Special features

- Master bedroom features coffered ceiling, walk-in closet and spacious bath
- Vaulted ceiling and fireplace grace family room
- Dining room is adjacent to kitchen and features access to rear porch
- Convenient access to utility room from kitchen
- 3 bedrooms, 2 baths, 2-car drive under garage
- Basement foundation

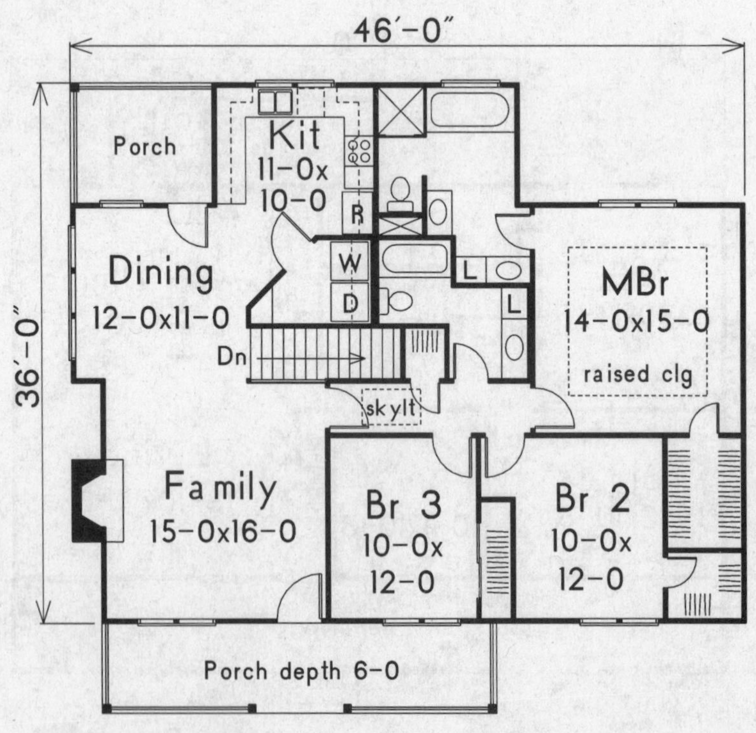
46'-0"
36'-0"
Porch
Kit
11-0x
10-0
R
W
D
Dining
12-0x11-0
Dn
L
L
MBr
14-0x15-0
raised clg
skylt
Family
15-0x16-0
Br 3
10-0x
12-0
Br 2
10-0x
12-0
Porch depth 6-0

Plan #702-0657

Small Home Is Remarkably Spacious

914 total square feet of living area

Price Code AA

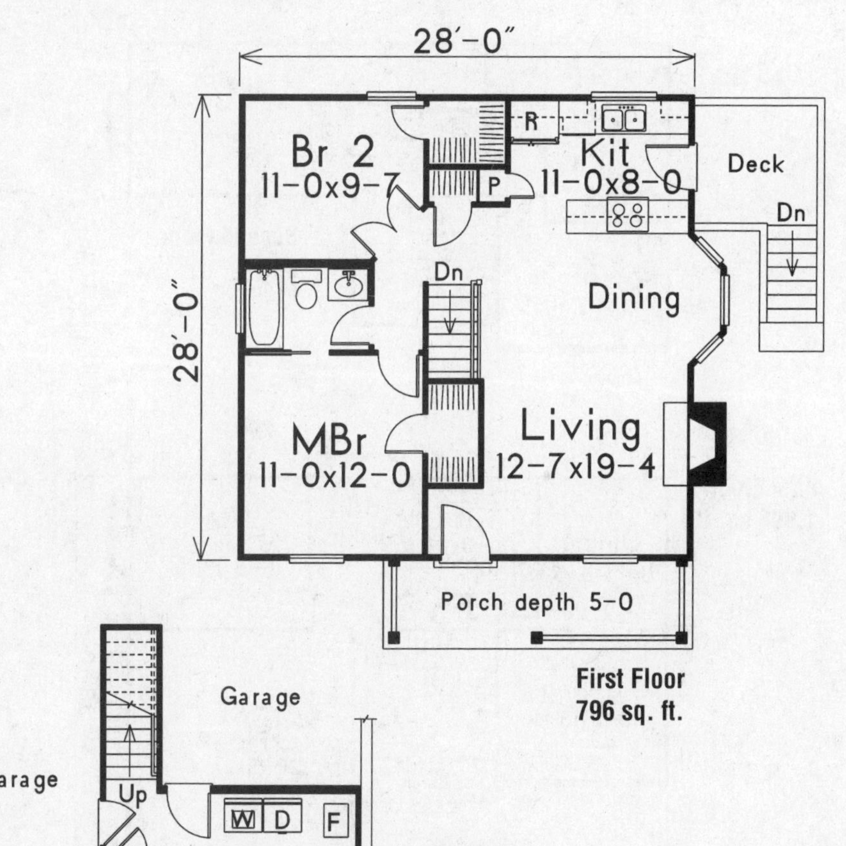

28′-0″
28′-0″
Br 2
11-0x9-7
R
Kit
11-0x8-0
P
Deck
Dn
Dn
Dining
MBr
11-0x12-0
Living
12-7x19-4
Porch depth 5-0
Garage
Garage
Up
W
D
F
Laundry

First Floor
796 sq. ft.

Lower Level
118 sq. ft.

Special features

- Large porch for leisure evenings
- Dining area with bay window, open stair and pass-through kitchen creates openness
- Basement includes generous garage space, storage area, finished laundry and mechanical room
- 2 bedrooms, 1 bath, 2-car drive under garage
- Basement foundation

TO ORDER BLUEPRINTS USE THE FORM ON PAGE 19 OR CALL TOLL-FREE 1-877-671-6036

The Family
Handyman

Plan #702-0171

Practical Two-Story, Full Of Features

2,058 total square feet of living area **Price Code C**

Special features

- Handsome two-story foyer with balcony creates a spacious entrance area
- Vaulted ceiling in the master bedroom with private dressing area and large walk-in closet
- Skylights furnish natural lighting in the hall and master bath
- Conveniently located second floor laundry near bedrooms
- 3 bedrooms, 2 1/2 baths, 2-car garage
- Basement foundation, drawings also include slab and crawl space foundations

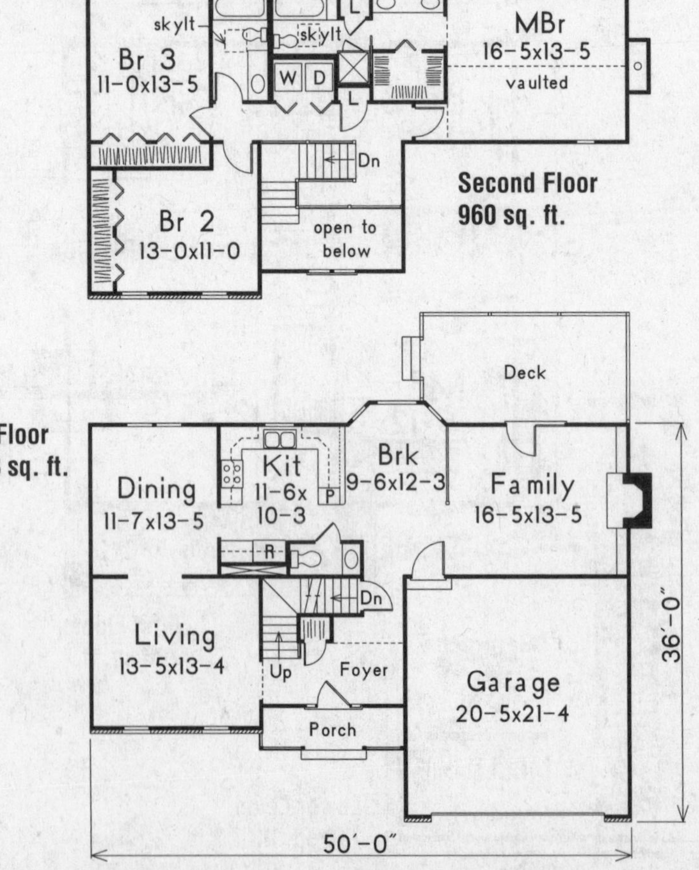

skylt
skylt
L
Br 3
11-0x13-5
W D
L
MBr
16-5x13-5
vaulted
Dn
Br 2
13-0x11-0
open to below
Second Floor
960 sq. ft.
Deck
First Floor
1,098 sq. ft.
Dining
11-7x13-5
Kit
11-6x
10-3
P
Brk
9-6x12-3
Family
16-5x13-5
R
Dn
Living
13-5x13-4
Up
Foyer
Garage
20-5x21-4
Porch
36'-0"
50'-0"

The Family
Handyman

Plan #702-DR-2937

Cathedral Ceiling In Family Room

1,288 total square feet of living area

Price Code A

Second Floor
597 sq. ft.

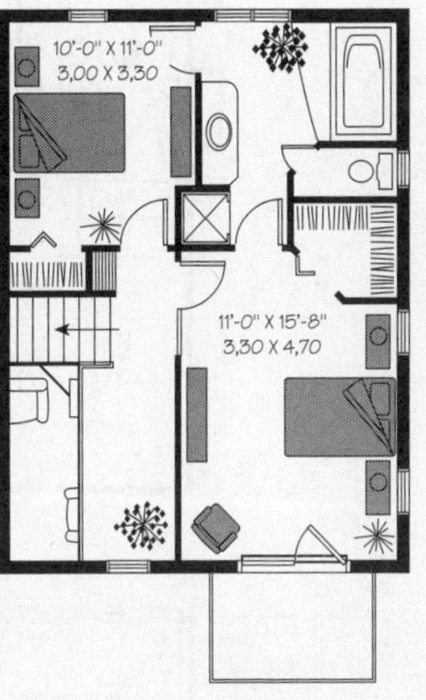
10'-0" X 11'-0"
3,00 X 3,30
11'-0" X 15'-8"
3,30 X 4,70

First Floor
691 sq. ft.

12'-0" X 19'-0"
3,60 X 5,70
14'-0" X 20'-0"
4,20 X 6,00
12'-8" X 15'-8"
3,80 X 4,70
40'-0"
12,0 m
28'-0"
8,4 m

Special features

- Energy efficient home with 2" x 6" exterior walls
- Convenient snack bar in kitchen
- Half bath has laundry facilities on first floor
- Both second floor bedrooms easily access full bath
- 2 bedrooms, 1 1/2 baths, 1-car garage
- Basement foundation

TO ORDER BLUEPRINTS USE THE FORM ON PAGE 19 OR CALL TOLL-FREE 1-877-671-6036

View thousands more home plans online at www.familyhandyman.com/homeplans

Plan #702-0777

Flexible Yet Traditional Two-Story Home

2,458 total square feet of living area

Price Code D

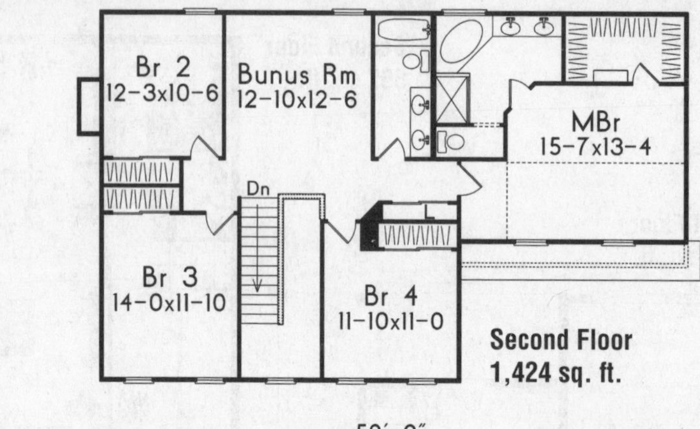
Br 2
12-3x10-6
Bunus Rm
12-10x12-6
MBr
15-7x13-4
Dn
Br 3
14-0x11-10
Br 4
11-10x11-0
Second Floor
1,424 sq. ft.

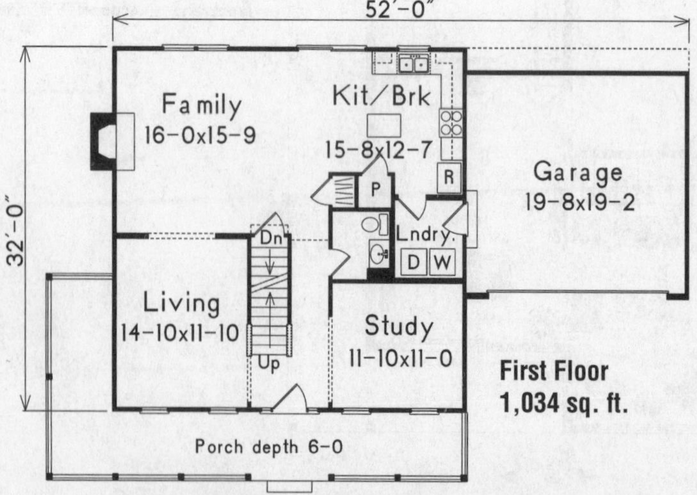
52'-0"
32'-0"
Family
16-0x15-9
Kit/Brk
15-8x12-7
P
R
Garage
19-8x19-2
Dn
Lndry.
D W
Living
14-10x11-10
Up
Study
11-10x11-0
First Floor
1,034 sq. ft.
Porch depth 6-0

Special features

- Study in the front of the home makes an ideal home office
- Second floor has four bedrooms centered around a bonus room that could easily convert to a family room or fifth bedroom
- Private second floor master bedroom is situated above garage
- 4 bedrooms, 2 1/2 baths, 2-car garage
- Basement foundation

Plan #702-1213

Inviting, Cheerful Home

2,554 total square feet of living area **Price Code D**

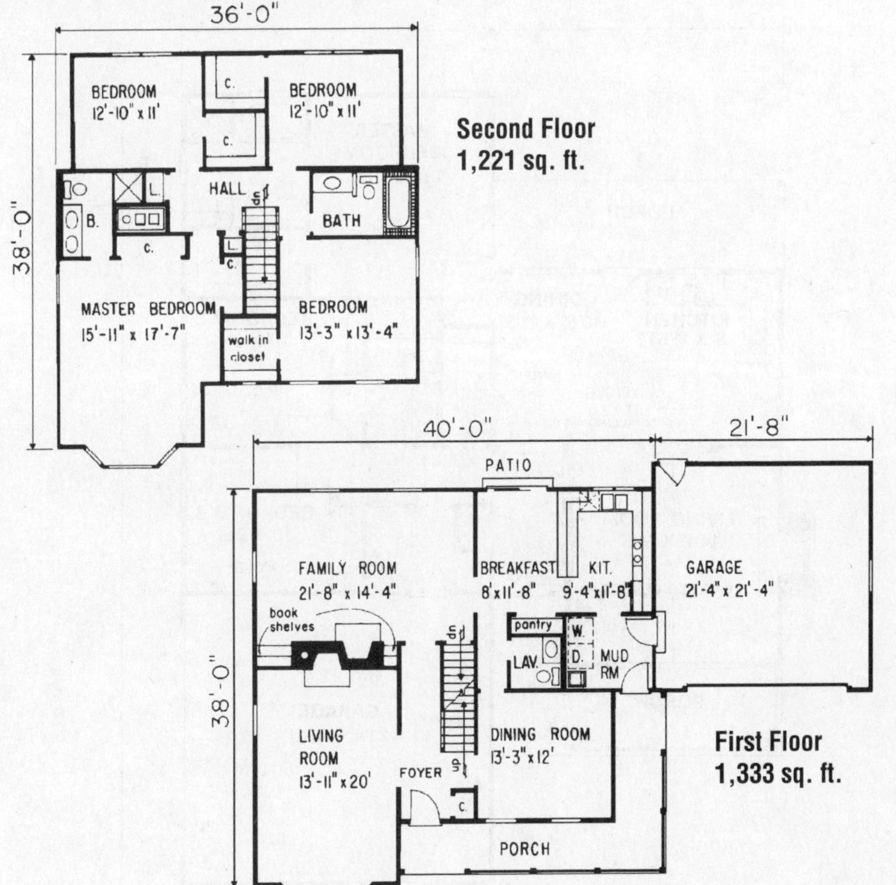
36'-0"
38'-0"
BEDROOM
12'-10" x 11'
BEDROOM
12'-10" x 11'
C.
C.
HALL
B.
C.
BATH
C.
MASTER BEDROOM
15'-11" x 17'-7"
BEDROOM
13'-3" x 13'-4"
walk in closet
40'-0"
21'-8"
PATIO
FAMILY ROOM
21'-8" x 14'-4"
BREAKFAST
8' x 11'-8"
KIT.
9'-4" x 11'-8"
GARAGE
21'-4" x 21'-4"
book shelves
pantry
W.
D.
LAV.
MUD RM
LIVING ROOM
13'-11" x 20'
DINING ROOM
13'-3" x 12'
FOYER
C.
PORCH
38'-0"

Second Floor
1,221 sq. ft.

First Floor
1,333 sq. ft.

Special features

- Dual fireplaces enhance family and living rooms
- All three bedrooms include spacious walk-in closets
- Double-bowl vanity in master bath for convenience
- 4 bedrooms, 2 1/2 baths, 2-car garage
- Basement foundation, drawings also include crawl space and slab foundations

TO ORDER BLUEPRINTS USE THE FORM ON PAGE 19 OR CALL TOLL-FREE 1-877-671-6036

Plan #702-DBI-24045-9P

Arched Entry Adds Appeal

1,263 total square feet of living area **Price Code A**

Special features

- 9' ceilings throughout most of home
- Kitchen features large island eating bar
- 3 bedrooms, 2 baths, 2-car garage
- Basement foundation

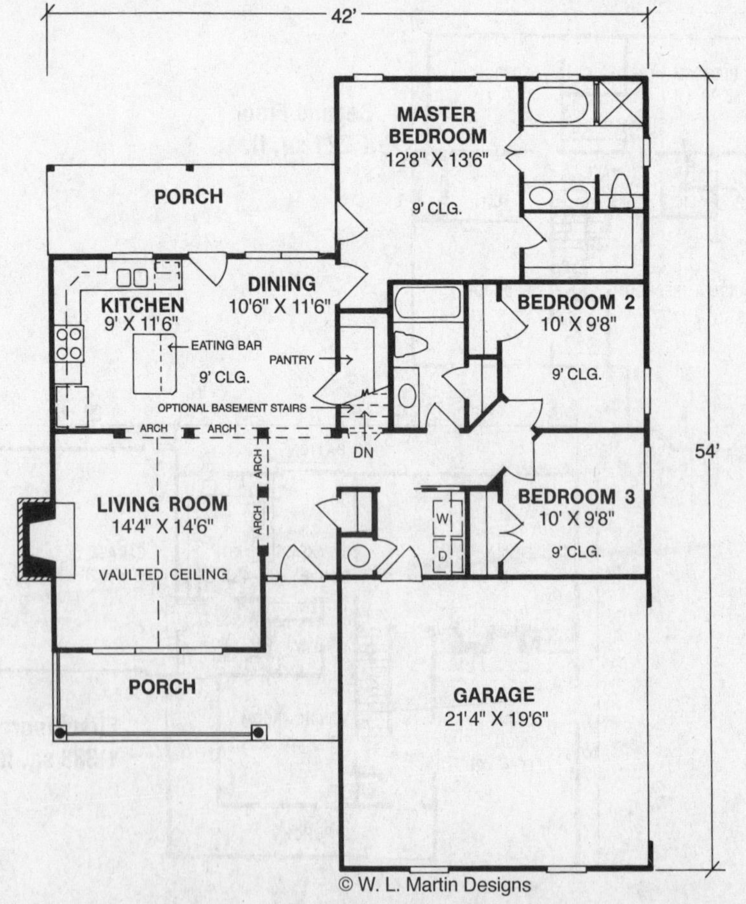
42'
MASTER BEDROOM
12'8" X 13'6"
9' CLG.
PORCH
DINING
10'6" X 11'6"
KITCHEN
9' X 11'6"
EATING BAR
PANTRY
9' CLG.
OPTIONAL BASEMENT STAIRS
ARCH
ARCH
DN
BEDROOM 2
10' X 9'8"
9' CLG.
54'
BEDROOM 3
10' X 9'8"
9' CLG.
LIVING ROOM
14'4" X 14'6"
VAULTED CEILING
W
D
PORCH
GARAGE
21'4" X 19'6"
© W. L. Martin Designs

TO ORDER BLUEPRINTS USE THE FORM ON PAGE 19 OR CALL TOLL-FREE 1-877-671-6036

View thousands more home plans online at www.familyhandyman.com/homeplans

The Family
Handyman

Plan #702-CHP-4156-A-1

Colossal Southern Colonial

ANDREW G. JACKSON

4,187 total square feet of living area

Price Code H

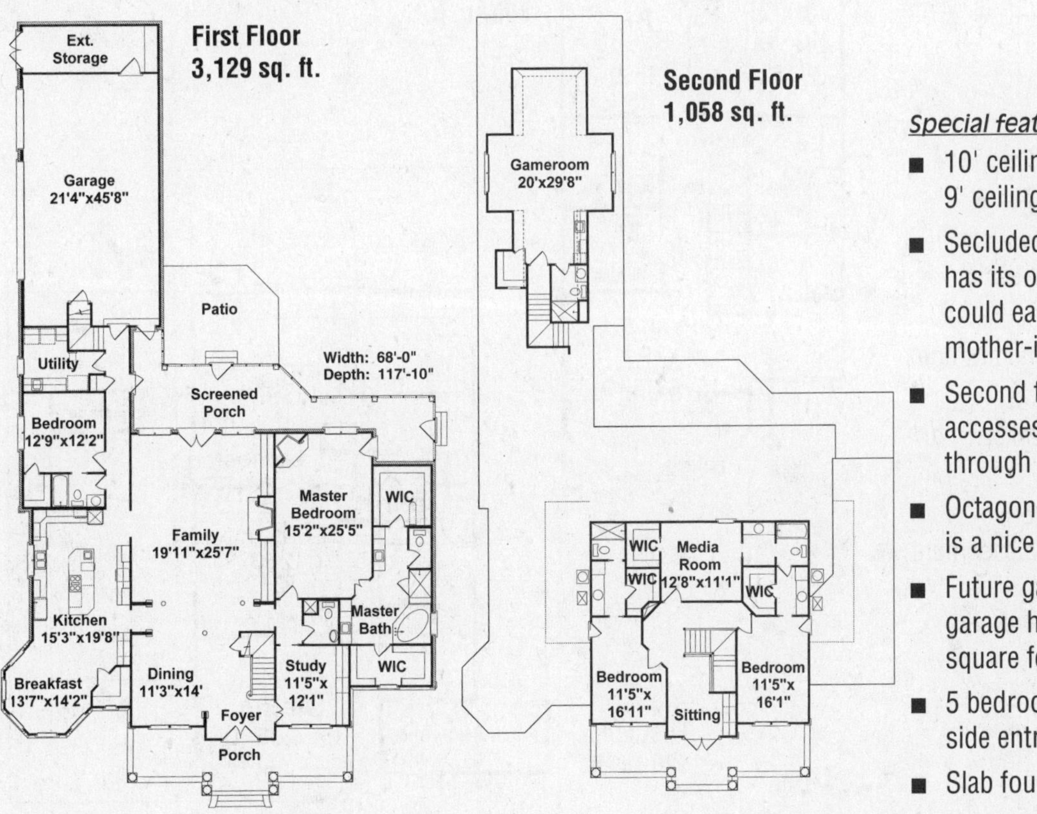

First Floor
3,129 sq. ft.
Ext. Storage
Garage 21'4"x45'8"
Patio
Utility
Width: 68'-0"
Depth: 117'-10"
Screened Porch
Bedroom 12'9"x12'2"
Master Bedroom 15'2"x25'5"
WIC
Family 19'11"x25'7"
Kitchen 15'3"x19'8"
Master Bath
WIC
Breakfast 13'7"x14'2"
Dining 11'3"x14'
Study 11'5"x 12'1"
Foyer
Porch
Second Floor
1,058 sq. ft.
Gameroom 20'x29'8"
WIC
Media Room 12'8"x11'1"
WIC
WIC
Bedroom 11'5"x 16'11"
Sitting
Bedroom 11'5"x 16'1"

Special features

- 10' ceilings on first floor and 9' ceilings on the second floor
- Secluded bedroom on first floor has its own private bath and could easily be converted to a mother-in-law suite
- Second floor sitting area accesses outdoor balcony through lovely French doors
- Octagon-shaped breakfast room is a nice focal point
- Future gameroom above the garage has an additional 551 square feet of living area
- 5 bedrooms, 4 1/2 baths, 3-car side entry garage
- Slab foundation

TO ORDER BLUEPRINTS USE THE FORM ON PAGE 19 OR CALL TOLL-FREE 1-877-671-6036

View thousands more home plans online at www.familyhandyman.com/homeplans

Plan #702-0522

Large Bay Graces Dining And Master Bedroom

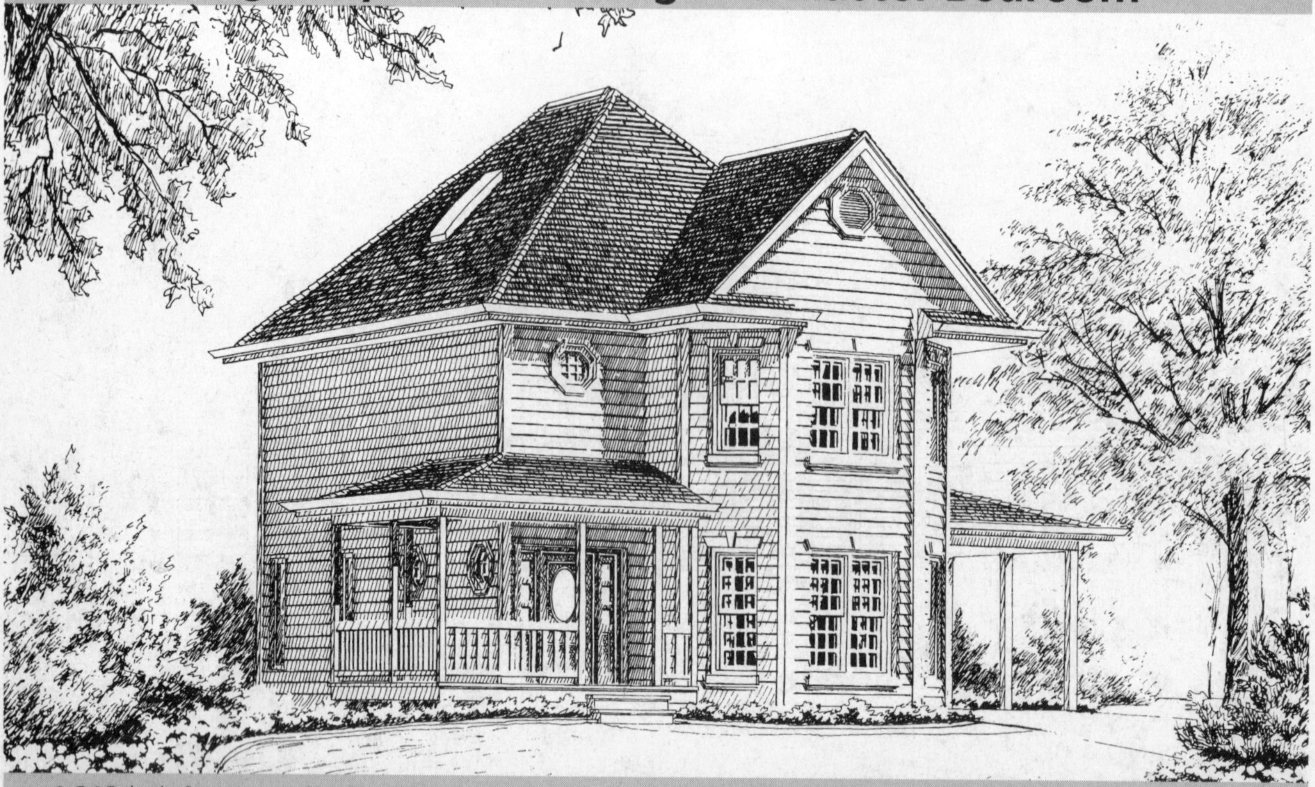

1,818 total square feet of living area — **Price Code C**

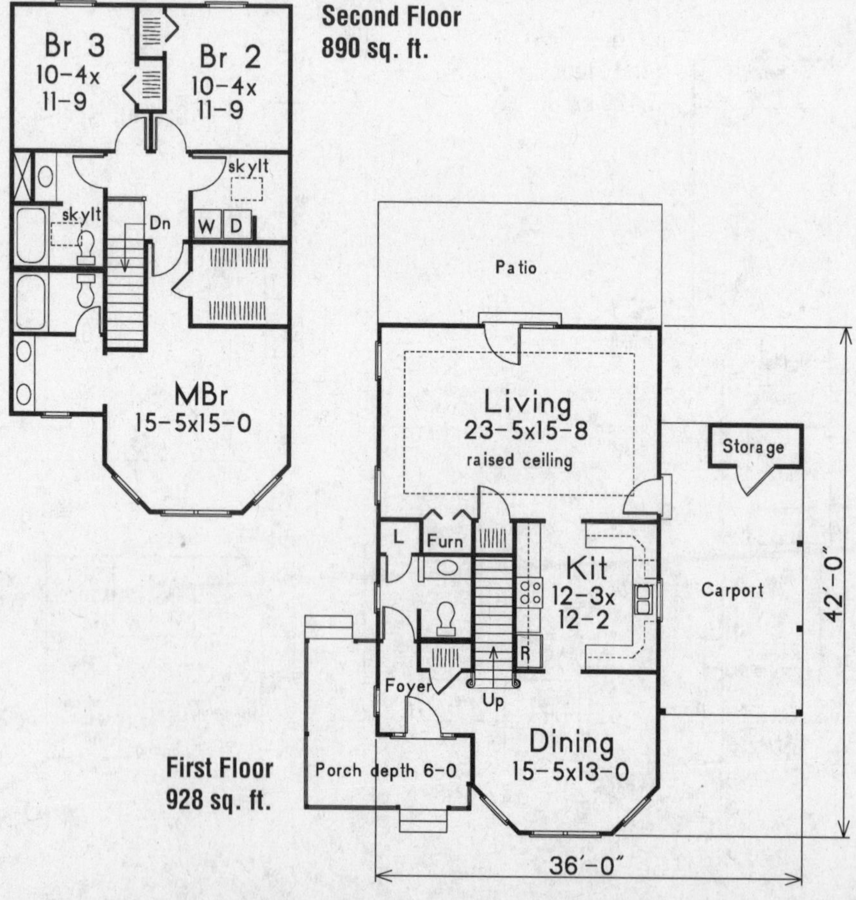
Second Floor
890 sq. ft.
Br 3
10-4x
11-9
Br 2
10-4x
11-9
skylt
skylt
Dn
W
D
MBr
15-5x15-0
Patio
Living
23-5x15-8
raised ceiling
Storage
L
Furn
Kit
12-3x
12-2
R
Carport
42'-0"
Foyer
Up
Dining
15-5x13-0
Porch depth 6-0
First Floor
928 sq. ft.
36'-0"

Special features

- Spacious living and dining rooms
- Master bedroom features large bay, walk-in closet, dressing area and bath
- Convenient carport and storage area
- 3 bedrooms, 2 1/2 baths, 1-car carport
- Crawl space foundation, drawings also include basement and slab foundations

Plan #702-AX-5380

Modest Farmhouse Ranch

1,480 total square feet of living area

Price Code A

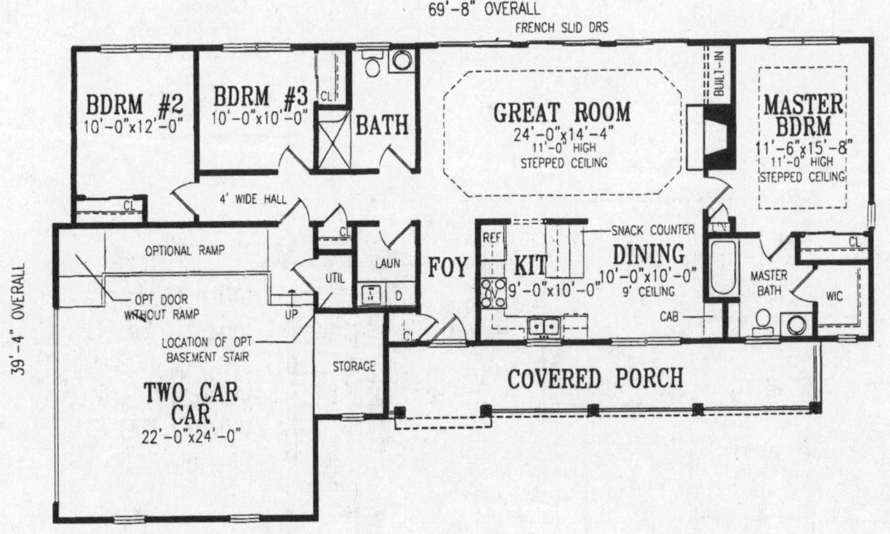
69'-8" OVERALL
FRENCH SLID DRS
BDRM #2
10'-0"x12'-0"
BDRM #3
10'-0"x10'-0"
CL
BATH
GREAT ROOM
24'-0"x14'-4"
11'-0" HIGH
STEPPED CEILING
BUILT-IN
MASTER
BDRM
11'-6"x15'-8"
11'-0" HIGH
STEPPED CEILING
CL
4' WIDE HALL
OPTIONAL RAMP
OPT DOOR
WITHOUT RAMP
UTIL
LAUN
D
FOY
REF
KIT
9'-0"x10'-0"
SNACK COUNTER
DINING
10'-0"x10'-0"
9' CEILING
CAB
MASTER
BATH
WIC
UP
LOCATION OF OPT
BASEMENT STAIR
STORAGE
COVERED PORCH
TWO CAR
CAR
22'-0"x24'-0"
39'-4" OVERALL

Special features

- Split bedroom floor plan with private master suite includes large bath and walk-in closet
- Fabulous great room features 11' high step ceiling, fireplace and media center
- Floor plan designed to be fully accessible for handicapped
- 3 bedrooms, 2 baths, 2-car side entry garage
- Basement, crawl space or slab foundation, please specify when ordering foundation

The Family
Handyman

Plan #702-GM-1550

Private Bedroom Area

1,550 total square feet of living area

Price Code B

Special features

- Wrap-around front porch is an ideal gathering place
- Handy snack bar is positioned so kitchen flows into family room
- Master bedroom has many amenities
- 3 bedrooms, 2 baths, 2-car detached garage
- Slab or crawl space foundation, please specify when ordering

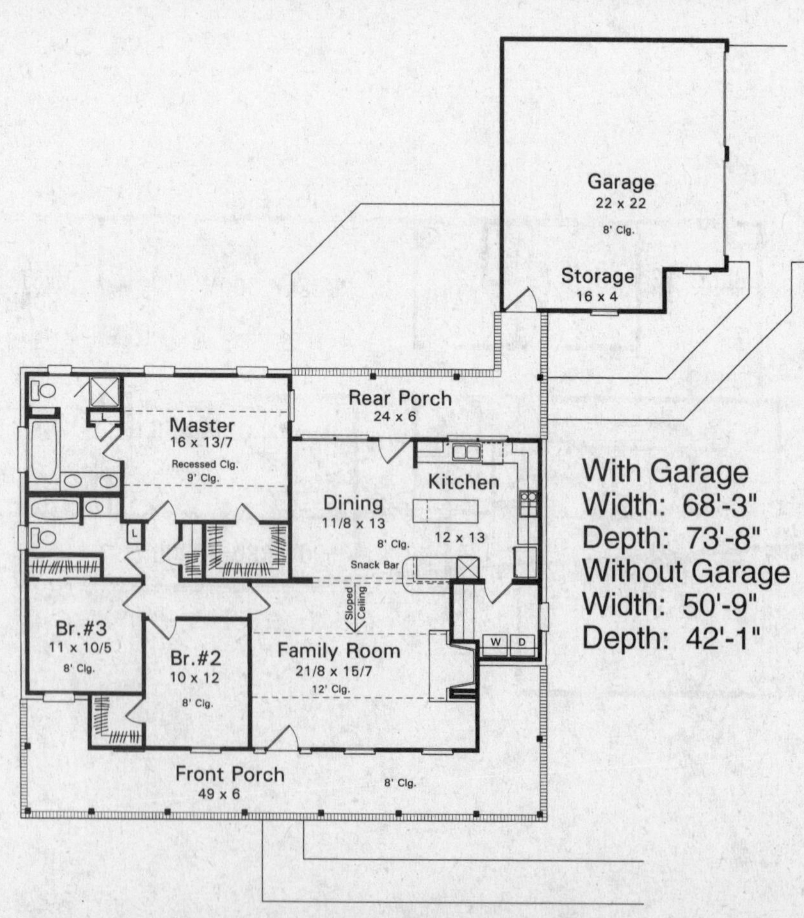

Garage
22 x 22
8' Clg.
Storage
16 x 4
Rear Porch
24 x 6
Master
16 x 13/7
Recessed Clg.
9' Clg.
Dining
11/8 x 13
8' Clg.
Kitchen
12 x 13
Snack Bar
Sloped Ceiling
W
D
Br.#3
11 x 10/5
8' Clg.
Br.#2
10 x 12
8' Clg.
Family Room
21/8 x 15/7
12' Clg.
Front Porch
49 x 6
8' Clg.
With Garage
Width: 68'-3"
Depth: 73'-8"
Without Garage
Width: 50'-9"
Depth: 42'-1"

TO ORDER BLUEPRINTS USE THE FORM ON PAGE 19 OR CALL TOLL-FREE 1-877-671-6036

View thousands more home plans online at www.familyhandyman.com/homeplans

The Family
Handyman

Plan #702-0213

Country Charm Wrapped In A Veranda

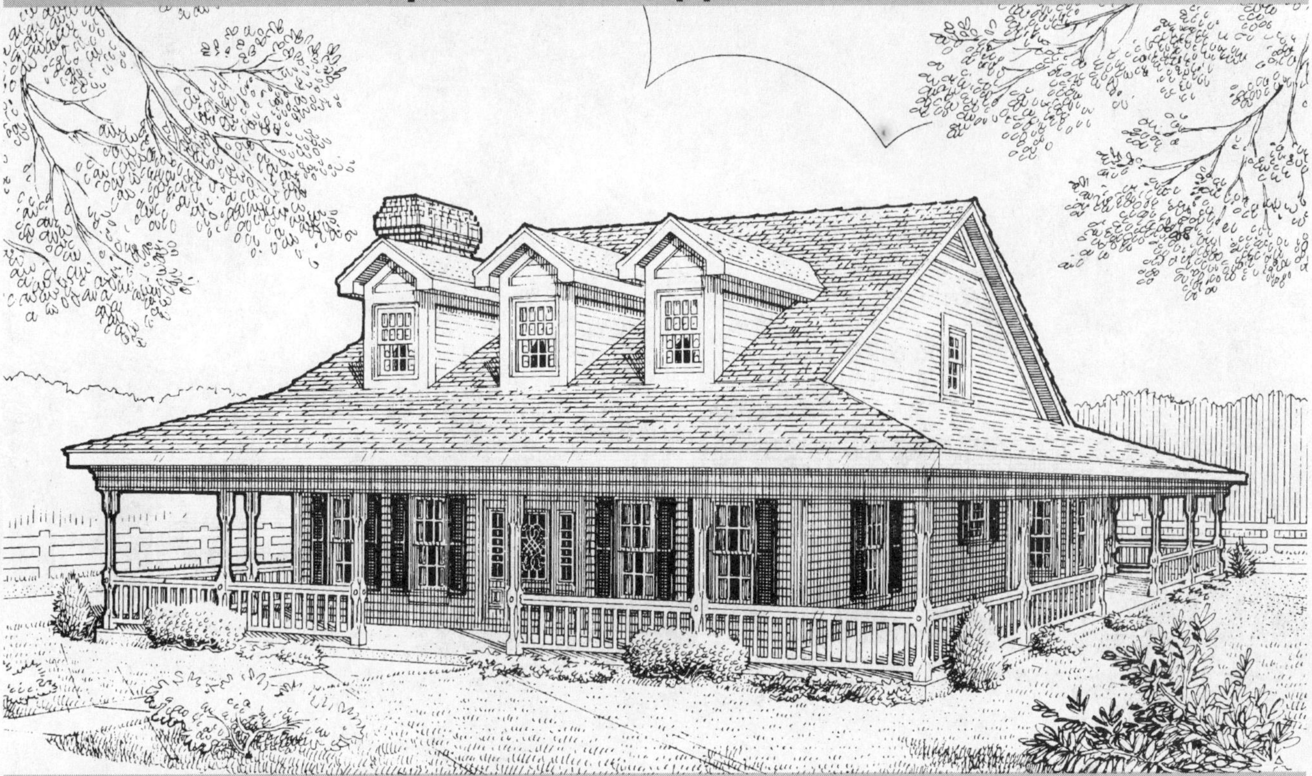

2,059 total square feet of living area **Price Code C**

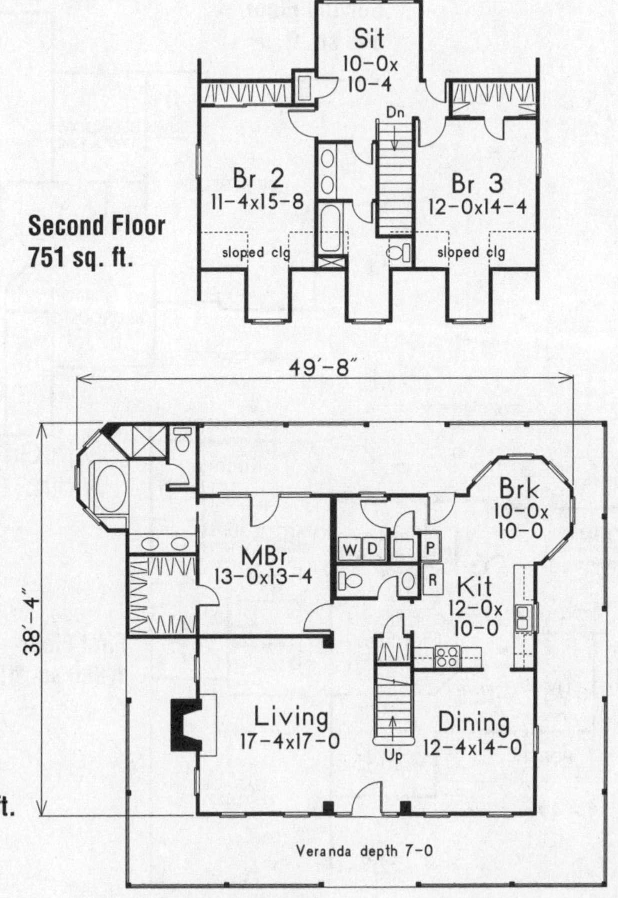
Sit
10-0x
10-4
Dn
Br 2
11-4x15-8
Br 3
12-0x14-4
sloped clg
sloped clg
Second Floor
751 sq. ft.
49'-8"
38'-4"
Brk
10-0x
10-0
W
D
P
R
MBr
13-0x13-4
Kit
12-0x
10-0
Living
17-4x17-0
Up
Dining
12-4x14-0
Veranda depth 7-0
First Floor
1,308 sq. ft.

Special features

- Octagon-shaped breakfast room offers plenty of windows and creates a view to the veranda
- First floor master bedroom has large walk-in closet and deluxe bath
- 9' ceilings throughout the home
- Secondary bedrooms and bath feature dormers and are adjacent to cozy sitting area
- 3 bedrooms, 2 1/2 baths, 2-car detached garage
- Slab foundation, drawings also include basement and crawl space foundations

The Family
Handyman

Plan #702-AP-2416

Irresistible Farmhouse

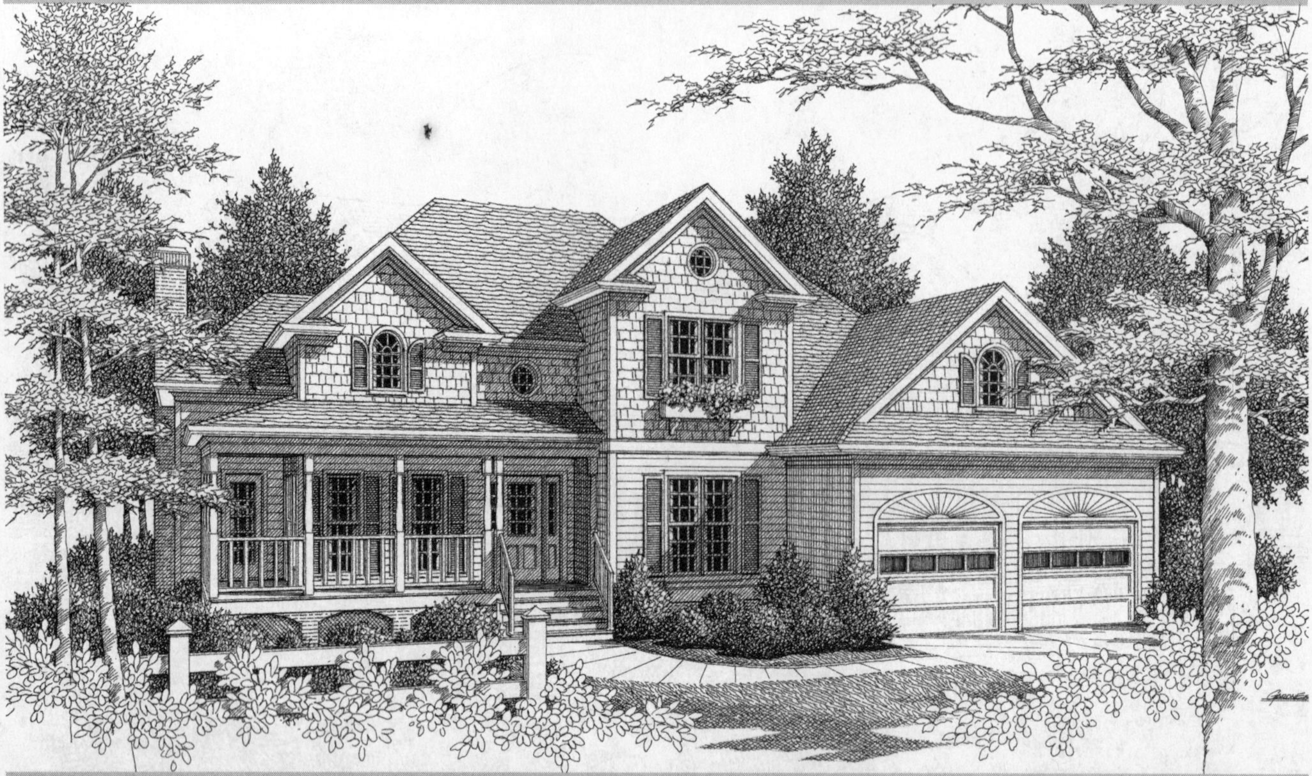

2,484 total square feet of living area **Price Code D**

Special features

- Convenient first floor master suite features his and hers walk-in closets and a dramatic bath with whirlpool and separate vanities
- Living room has 18' ceiling with a radius top window, decorative columns and a plant shelf
- Family room includes built-in bookcases and double French doors leading to outdoor deck
- Bonus room has an additional 262 square feet of living area on the second floor
- 3 bedrooms, 2 1/2 baths, 2-car garage
- Basement or crawl space foundation, please specify when ordering

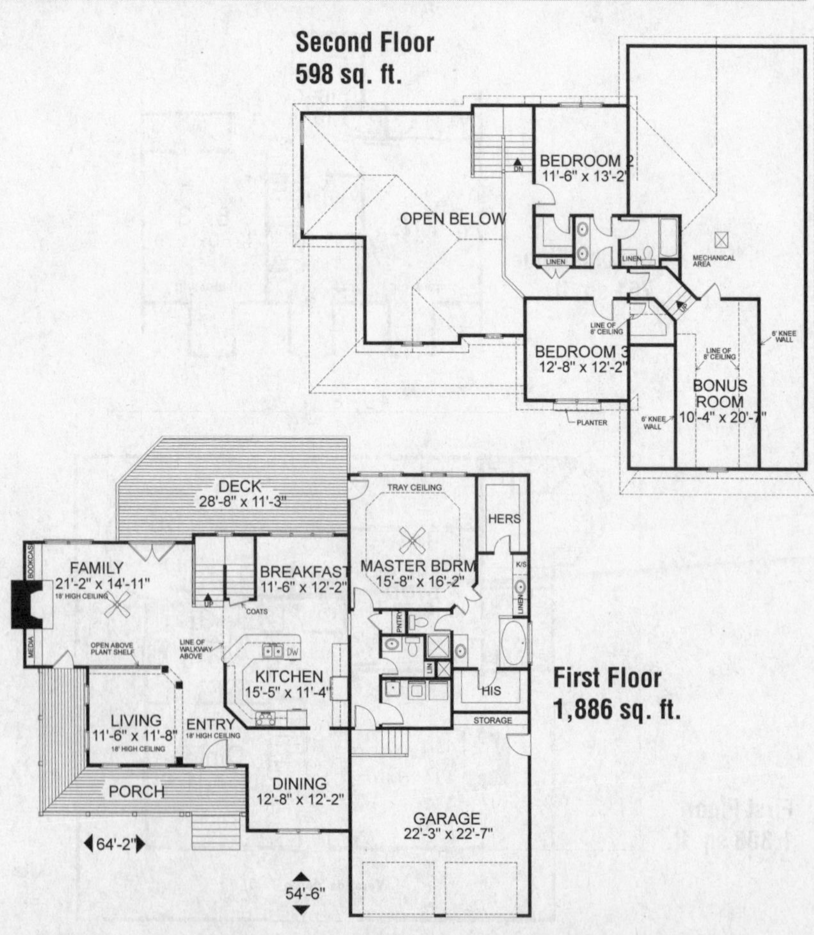
Second Floor
598 sq. ft.
OPEN BELOW
BEDROOM 2
11'-6" x 13'-2"
MECHANICAL AREA
BEDROOM 3
12'-8" x 12'-2"
BONUS ROOM
10'-4" x 20'-7"
PLANTER
DECK
28'-8" x 11'-3"
FAMILY
21'-2" x 14'-11"
BREAKFAST
11'-6" x 12'-2"
MASTER BDRM
15'-8" x 16'-2"
TRAY CEILING
HERS
HIS
KITCHEN
15'-5" x 11'-4"
LIVING
11'-6" x 11'-8"
ENTRY
PORCH
DINING
12'-8" x 12'-2"
STORAGE
GARAGE
22'-3" x 22'-7"
64'-2"
54'-6"
First Floor
1,886 sq. ft.

TO ORDER BLUEPRINTS USE THE FORM ON PAGE 19 OR CALL TOLL-FREE 1-877-671-6036

View thousands more home plans online at www.familyhandyman.com/homeplans

The Family
Handyman

Plan #702-0290

Stucco Finish And Authentic Southern Home Styling

1,700 total square feet of living area

Price Code B

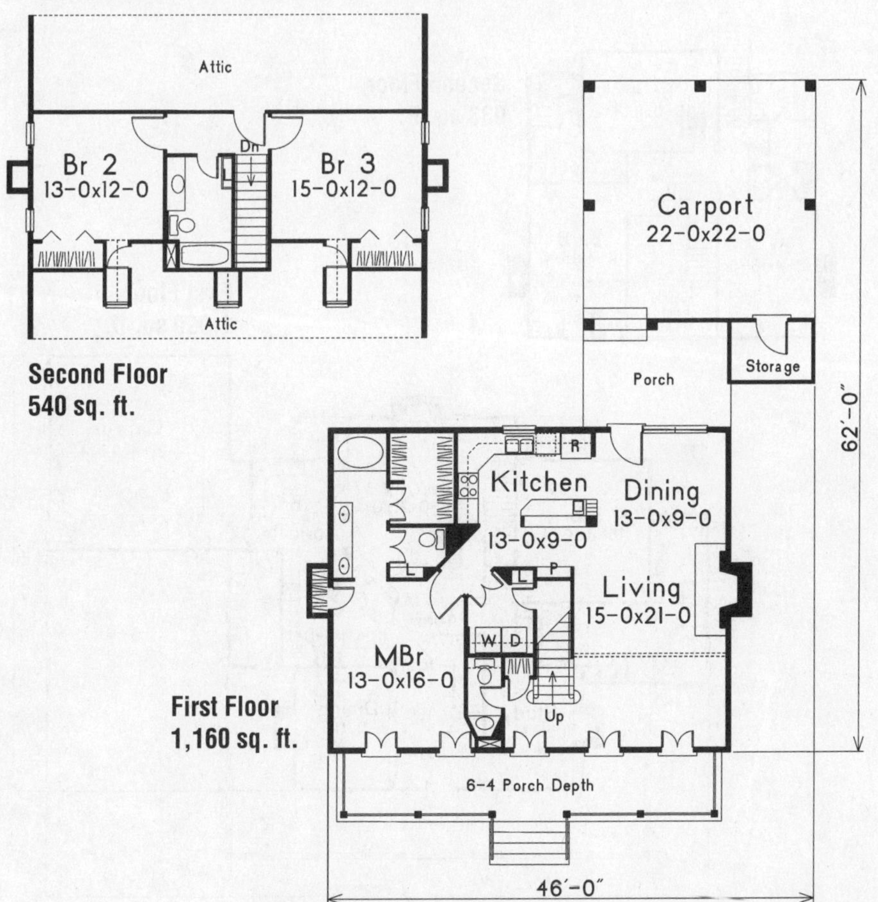
Attic
Br 2
13-0x12-0
Dn
Br 3
15-0x12-0
Attic
Second Floor
540 sq. ft.
Carport
22-0x22-0
Porch
Storage
62'-0"
Kitchen
13-0x9-0
Dining
13-0x9-0
Living
15-0x21-0
MBr
13-0x16-0
W
D
Up
First Floor
1,160 sq. ft.
6-4 Porch Depth
46'-0"

Special features

- Fully appointed kitchen with wet bar
- Energy efficient home with 2" x 6" exterior walls
- Linen drop from the second floor bath to utility room
- Master bath includes raised marble tub and a sloped ceiling
- 3 bedrooms, 2 1/2 baths, 2-car attached carport
- Crawl space foundation, drawings also include basement and slab foundations

The Family Handyman

Plan #702-0232

Fireplaces Add Warm Cozy Feeling

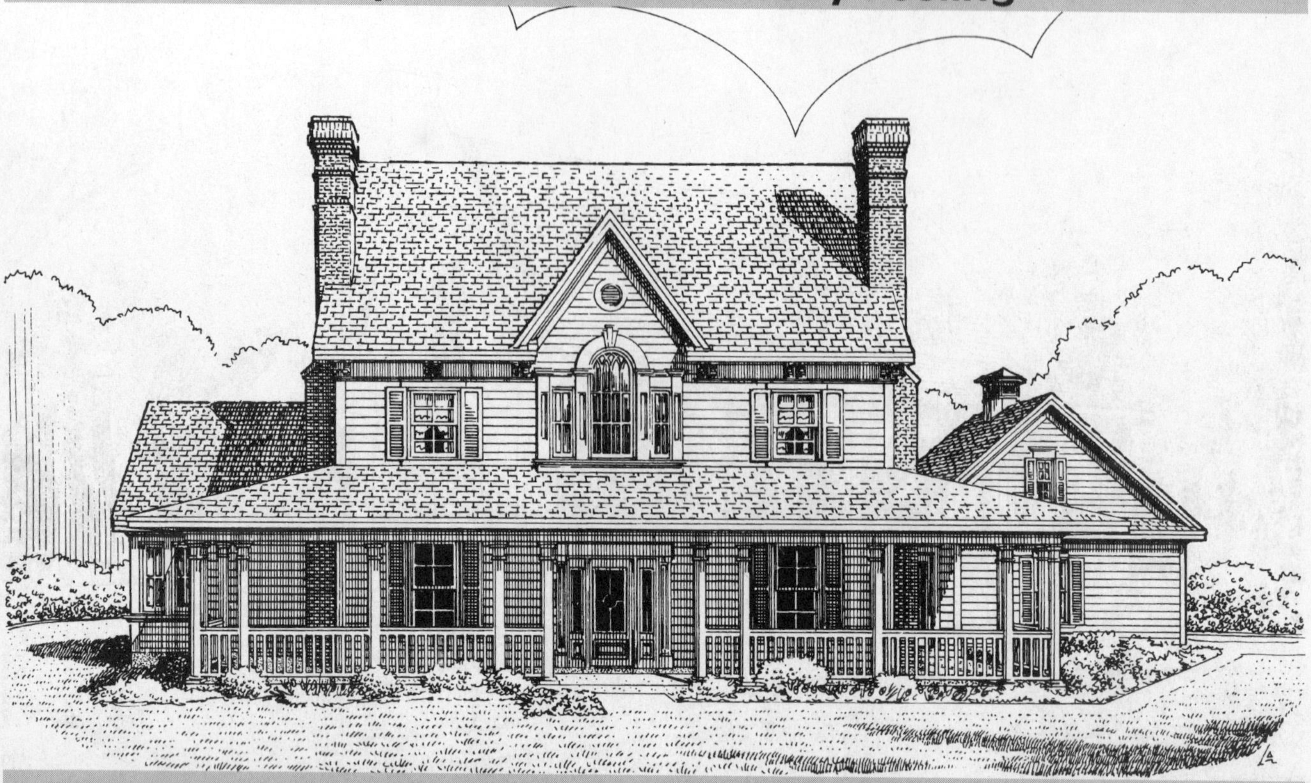

2,932 total square feet of living area **Price Code F**

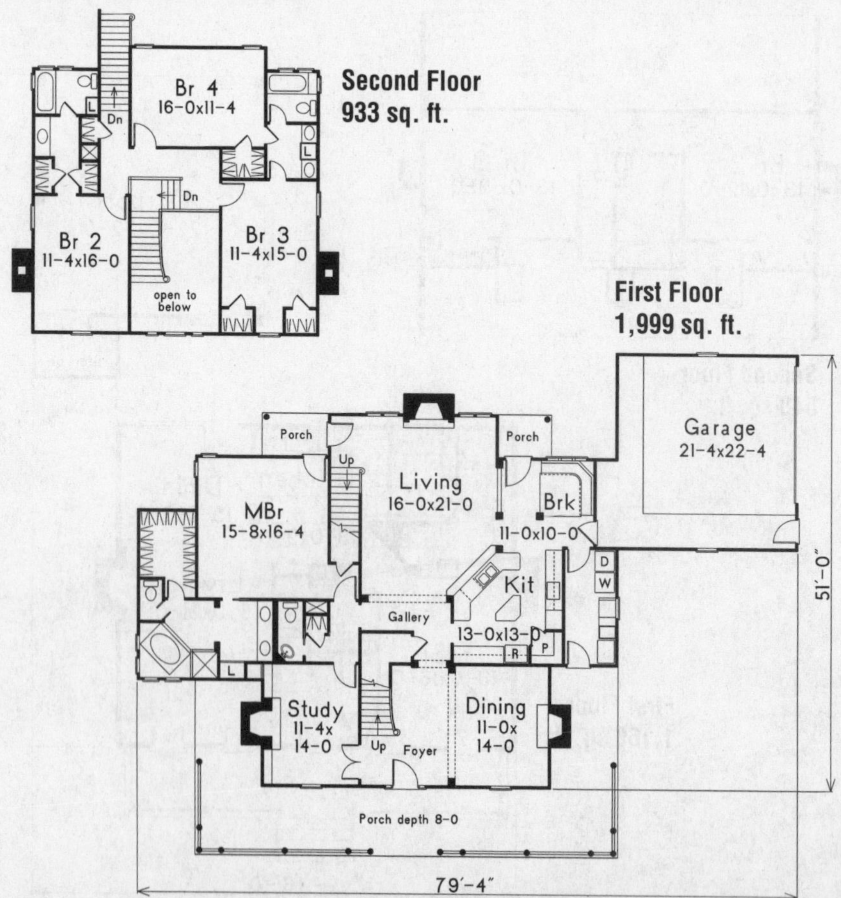
Second Floor
933 sq. ft.
Br 4
16-0x11-4
Dn
Br 2
11-4x16-0
Br 3
11-4x15-0
open to below
First Floor
1,999 sq. ft.
Garage
21-4x22-4
Porch
Porch
Up
Living
16-0x21-0
Brk
11-0x10-0
MBr
15-8x16-4
D
W
Kit
13-0x13-0
Gallery
R
P
L
Study
11-4x
14-0
Up
Foyer
Dining
11-0x
14-0
Porch depth 8-0
51'-0"
79'-4"

Special features

- 9' ceilings throughout home
- Rear stairs create convenient access to second floor from living area
- Spacious kitchen has pass-through to the family room, a convenient island and pantry
- Cozy built-in table in breakfast area
- Secluded master suite with luxurious bath and patio access
- 4 bedrooms, 3 1/2 baths, 2-car side entry garage
- Slab foundation

Plan #702-0168

A Traditional For Lots Of Living

2,940 total square feet of living area **Price Code E**

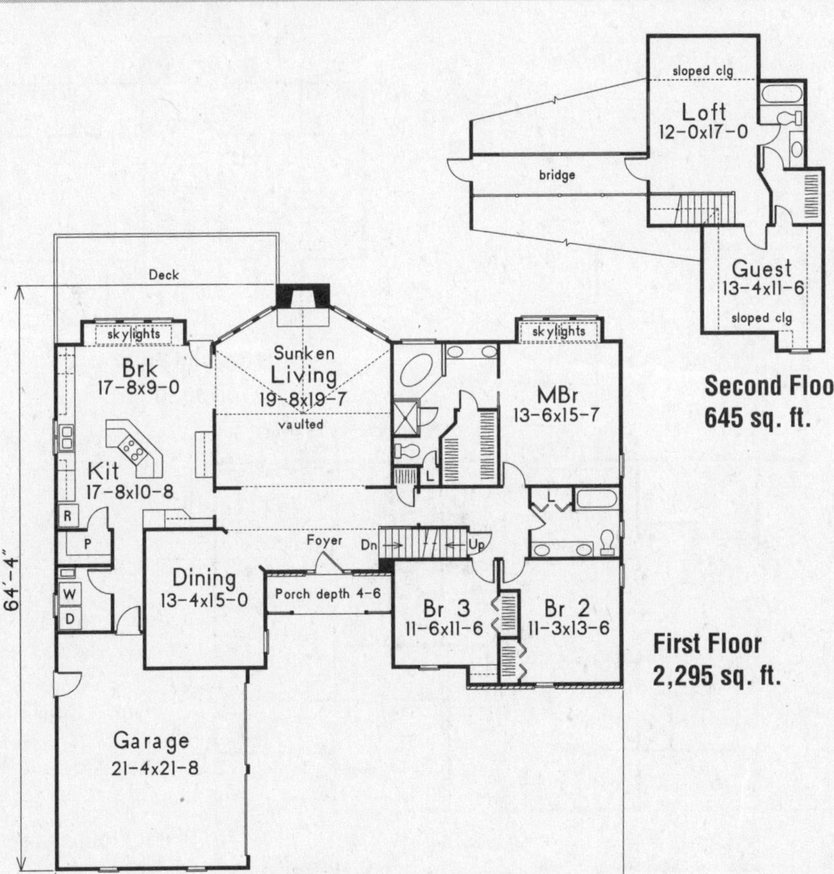
sloped clg
Loft
12-0x17-0
bridge
Guest
13-4x11-6
sloped clg
Deck
skylights
Brk
17-8x9-0
Sunken
Living
19-8x19-7
vaulted
skylights
MBr
13-6x15-7
Kit
17-8x10-8
R
P
W
D
L
L
Foyer
Dn
Up
Dining
13-4x15-0
Porch depth 4-6
Br 3
11-6x11-6
Br 2
11-3x13-6
Garage
21-4x21-8
64'-4"
64'-0"

Second Floor
645 sq. ft.

First Floor
2,295 sq. ft.

Special features

- Two sets of twin dormers add outdoor charm while lighting the indoors
- Massive central foyer leads into sunken living room below and access to second floor attic
- Private master suite, complete with a luxurious corner bathtub and large walk-in closet
- A novel bridge provides view of living room below and access to second floor attic
- 4 bedrooms, 3 baths, 2-car side entry garage
- Basement foundation

Plan #702-0439

Wrap-Around Front Country Porch

2,665 total square feet of living area **Price Code E**

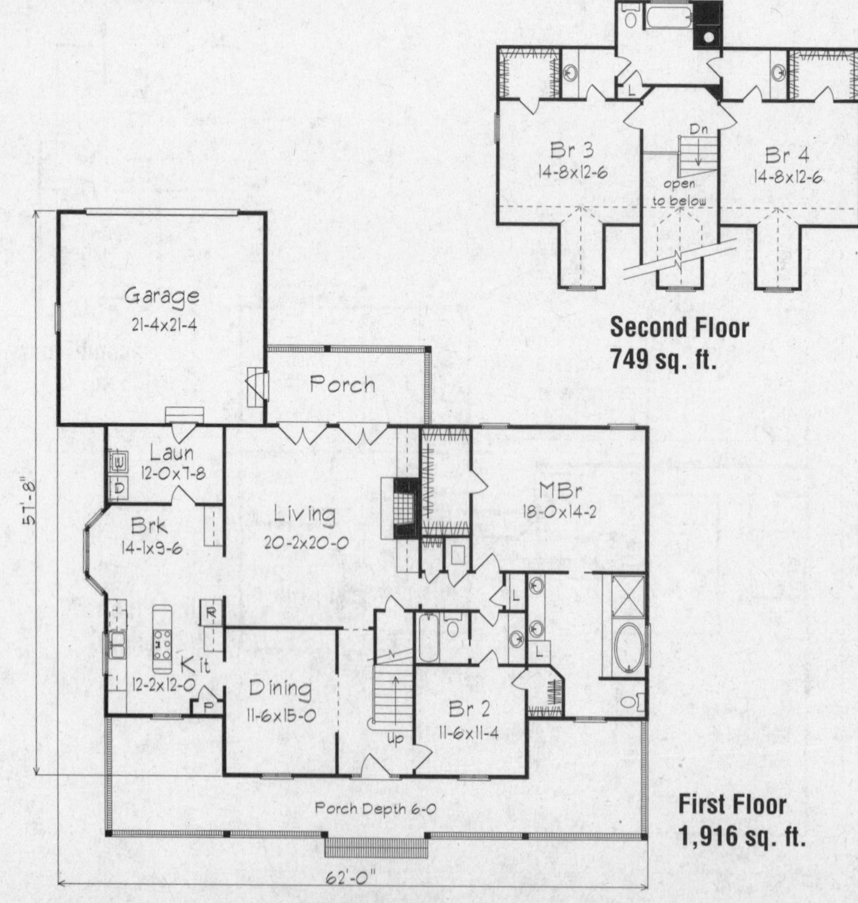
Br 3
14-8x12-6
Dn
open to below
Br 4
14-8x12-6
Garage
21-4x21-4
Porch
Laun
12-0x7-8
Brk
14-1x9-6
Living
20-2x20-0
MBr
18-0x14-2
Kit
12-2x12-0
Dining
11-6x15-0
Br 2
11-6x11-4
Up
Porch Depth 6-0
51'-8"
62'-0"

Second Floor
749 sq. ft.

First Floor
1,916 sq. ft.

Special features

- 9' ceilings on first floor
- Spacious kitchen features many cabinets, center island cooktop and breakfast room with bay window, adjacent to laundry room
- Second floor bedrooms boast walk-in closets, dressing areas and share a bath
- Twin patio doors and fireplace grace living room
- 4 bedrooms, 3 baths, 2-car rear entry garage
- Slab foundation, drawings also include crawl space foundation

TO ORDER BLUEPRINTS USE THE FORM ON PAGE 19 OR CALL TOLL-FREE 1-877-671-6036

View thousands more home plans online at www.familyhandyman.com/homeplans

Plan #702-0523

Wrap-Around Country Porch

1,875 total square feet of living area

Price Code C

Second Floor
820 sq. ft.

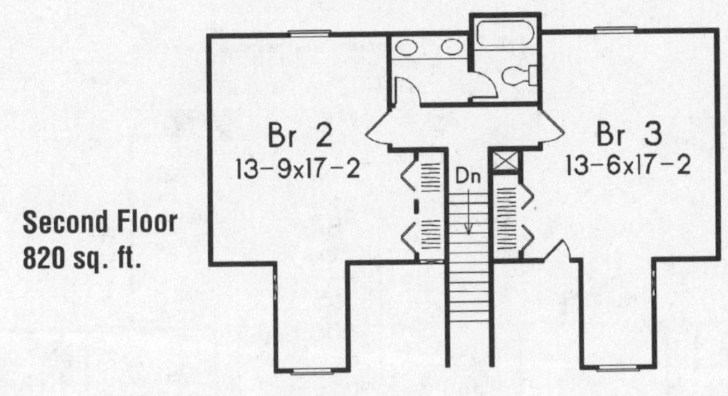
Br 2
13-9x17-2
Dn
Br 3
13-6x17-2

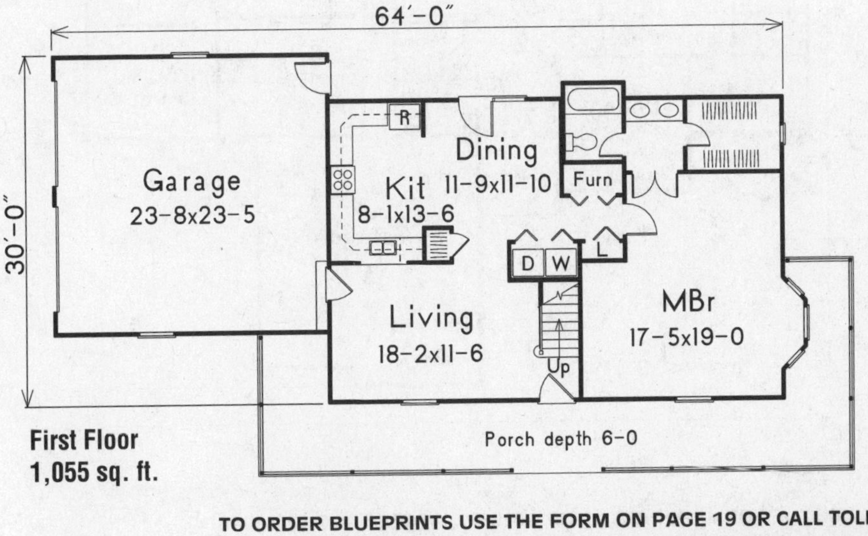

Special features

- Country-style exterior with wrap-around porch and dormers
- Large second floor bedrooms share a dressing area and bath
- Master bedroom suite includes bay window, walk-in closet, dressing area and bath
- 3 bedrooms, 2 baths, 2-car side entry garage
- Crawl space foundation, drawings also include basement and slab foundations

64'-0"
30'-0"
Garage
23-8x23-5
R
Dining
11-9x11-10
Kit
8-1x13-6
Furn
D W
L
Living
18-2x11-6
Up
MBr
17-5x19-0
Porch depth 6-0

First Floor
1,055 sq. ft.

The Family
Handyman

Plan #702-0289

Stylish And Practical Plan

2,513 total square feet of living area **Price Code D**

Special features

- Coffered ceilings in master bedroom, living and dining rooms
- Kitchen features island cooktop and built-in desk
- Dramatic vaulted ceiling in breakfast room is framed by plenty of windows
- Covered entry porch leads into spacious foyer
- Family room features an impressive fireplace and vaulted ceiling that joins the breakfast room creating spacious entertainment area
- 4 bedrooms, 2 full baths, 2 half baths, 2-car side entry garage
- Basement foundation

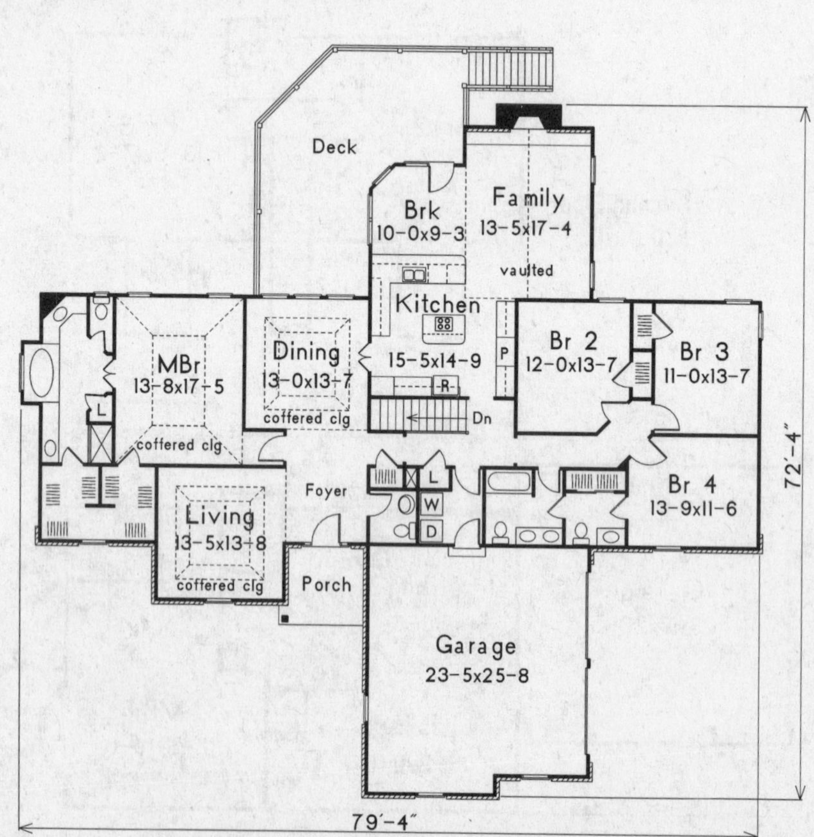
Deck
Brk
10-0x9-3
Family
13-5x17-4
vaulted
Kitchen
15-5x14-9
MBr
13-8x17-5
coffered clg
Dining
13-0x13-7
coffered clg
Br 2
12-0x13-7
Br 3
11-0x13-7
Dn
Foyer
Br 4
13-9x11-6
Living
13-5x13-8
coffered clg
Porch
Garage
23-5x25-8
79'-4"
72'-4"

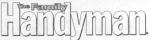

Plan #702-AP-1717

Uncommon Style With This Ranch

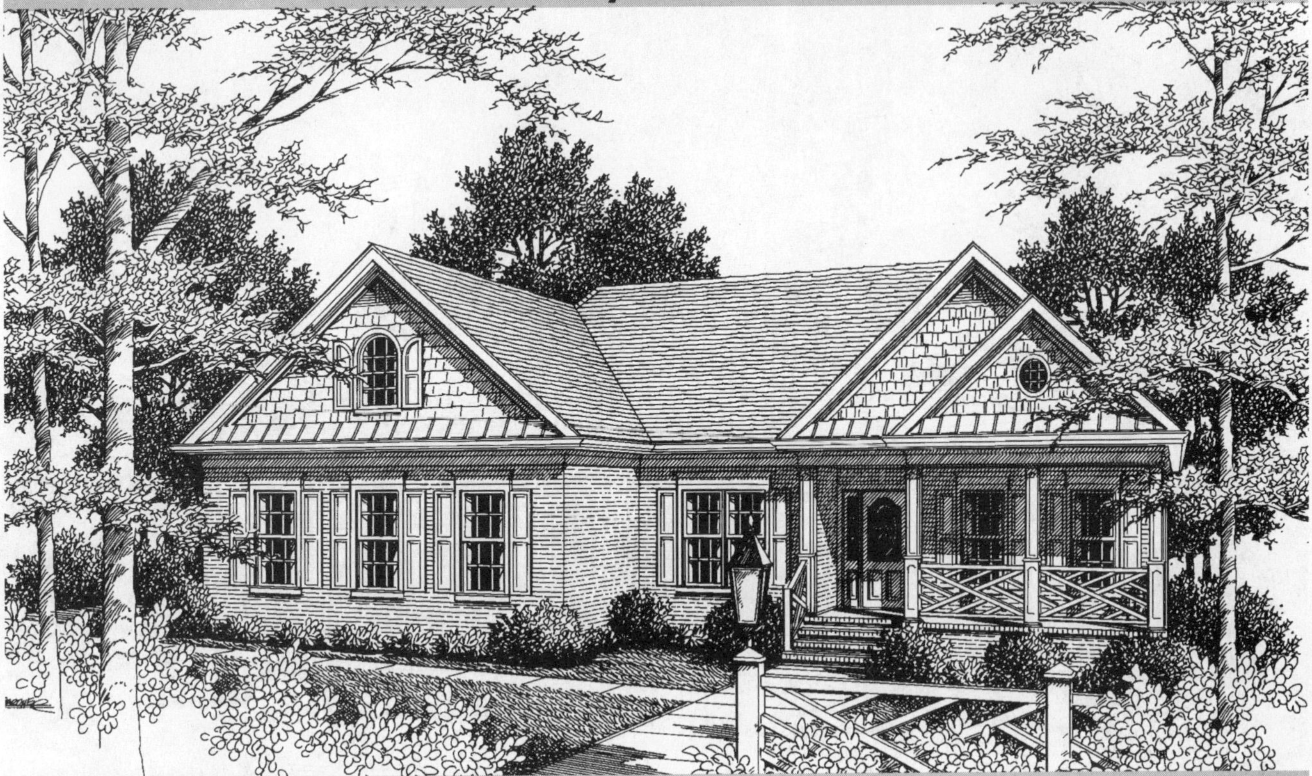

1,787 total square feet of living area

Price Code B

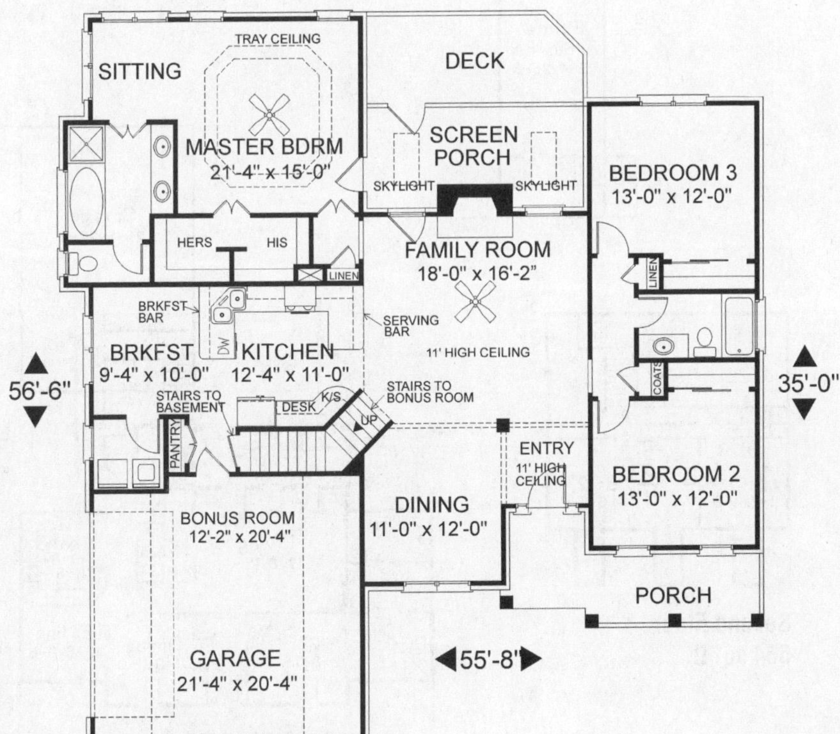
TRAY CEILING
SITTING
DECK
MASTER BDRM
21'-4" x 15'-0"
SCREEN PORCH
SKYLIGHT
SKYLIGHT
BEDROOM 3
13'-0" x 12'-0"
HERS
HIS
LINEN
FAMILY ROOM
18'-0" x 16'-2"
BRKFST BAR
SERVING BAR
BRKFST
9'-4" x 10'-0"
KITCHEN
12'-4" x 11'-0"
11' HIGH CEILING
56'-6"
STAIRS TO BASEMENT
DESK
K/S
STAIRS TO BONUS ROOM
UP
COATS
35'-0"
PANTRY
ENTRY
11' HIGH CEILING
BEDROOM 2
13'-0" x 12'-0"
BONUS ROOM
12'-2" x 20'-4"
DINING
11'-0" x 12'-0"
PORCH
GARAGE
21'-4" x 20'-4"
55'-8"

Special features

- Skylights brighten screened porch which connects to family room and deck outdoors
- Master bedroom features a comfortable sitting area, large private bath and direct access to screened porch
- Kitchen has serving bar which extends dining into family room
- 3 bedrooms, 2 baths, 2-car side entry garage
- Basement, crawl space or slab foundation, please specify when ordering

The Family
Handyman

Plan #702-0303

Distinctive Front Facade With Generous Porch

2,024 total square feet of living area

Price Code C

Special features

- King-size master suite with sitting area
- Living room features corner fireplace, access to covered rear porch, 18' ceiling and a balcony
- Closet for handling recyclables
- Optional bonus room has an additional 475 square feet of living area
- 3 bedrooms, 2 1/2 baths, 2-car side entry garage
- Crawl space foundation, drawings also include slab and basement foundations

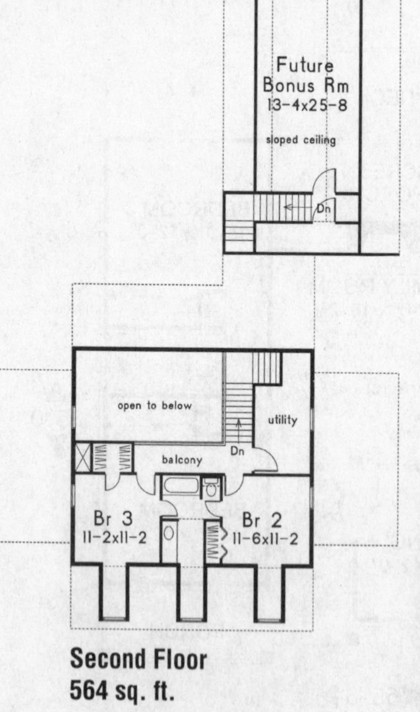
Future
Bonus Rm
13-4x25-8
sloped ceiling
Dn
open to below
utility
Dn
balcony
Br 3
11-2x11-2
Br 2
11-6x11-2

Second Floor
564 sq. ft.

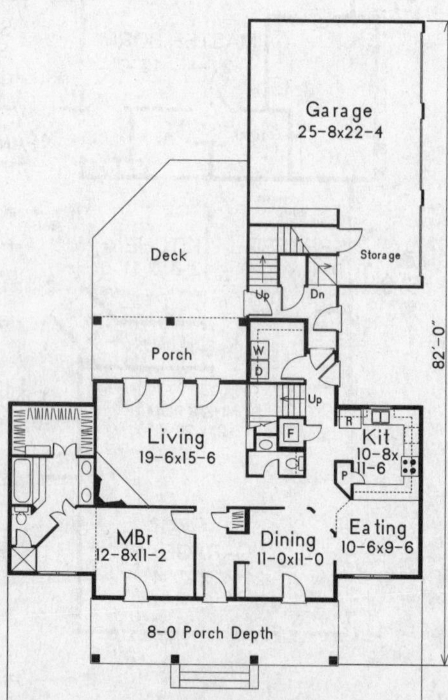
Garage
25-8x22-4
Deck
Storage
Up
Dn
Porch
W
D
Up
Living
19-6x15-6
Kit
10-8x
11-6
Eating
10-6x9-6
MBr
12-8x11-2
Dining
11-0x11-0
8-0 Porch Depth
82'-0"
54'-0"

First Floor
1,460 sq. ft.

The Family
Handyman

Plan #702-GH-24713

Quaint Country Charm

2,269 total square feet of living area

Price Code D

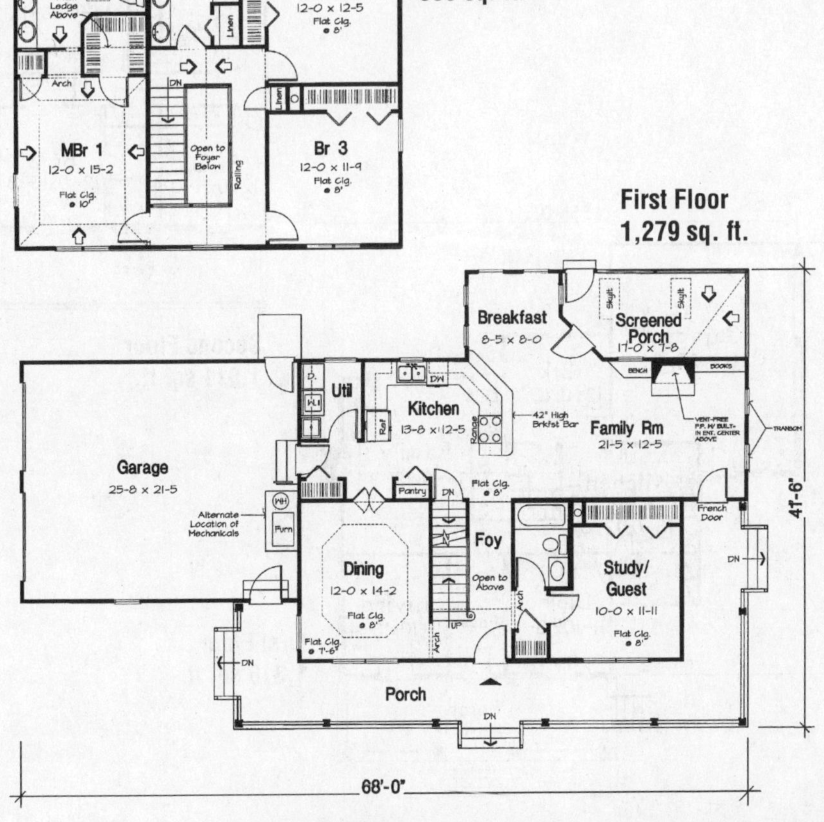
Br 2
12-0 x 12-5
Flat Clg. @ 8'
MBr 1
12-0 x 15-2
Flat Clg. @ 10'
Br 3
12-0 x 11-9
Flat Clg. @ 8'
Plant Ledge Above
Skylt
Linen
Arch
DN
Open to Foyer Below
Railing
Breakfast
8-5 x 8-0
Screened Porch
17-0 x 9-8
Skylt
Bench
Books
Util
Kitchen
13-8 x 12-5
DW
Ref
Range
42" High Brkfst Bar
Family Rm
21-5 x 12-5
Vent-Free F.P. W/ Built-In Ent. Center Above
Transom
Garage
25-8 x 21-5
Alternate Location of Mechanicals
Pantry
Flat Clg. @ 8'
Foy
Open to Above
Dining
12-0 x 14-2
Flat Clg. @ 8'
Flat Clg. @ 7'-6"
Study/Guest
10-0 x 11-11
Flat Clg. @ 8'
French Door
UP
DN
Porch
41'-6"
68'-0"

Second Floor
990 sq. ft.

First Floor
1,279 sq. ft.

Special features

- Master suite offers two closets and a skylight above the whirlpool tub
- Kitchen boasts an angled breakfast bar/extended counter and is open to the family room
- A decorative ceiling treatment adds architectural interest to the elegant dining room
- Centralized foyer gives access to the formal dining room
- 3 bedrooms, 3 baths, 2-car side entry garage
- Basement foundation

The Family
Handyman

Plan #702-0360

Inviting Double French Doors

2,327 total square feet of living area **Price Code D**

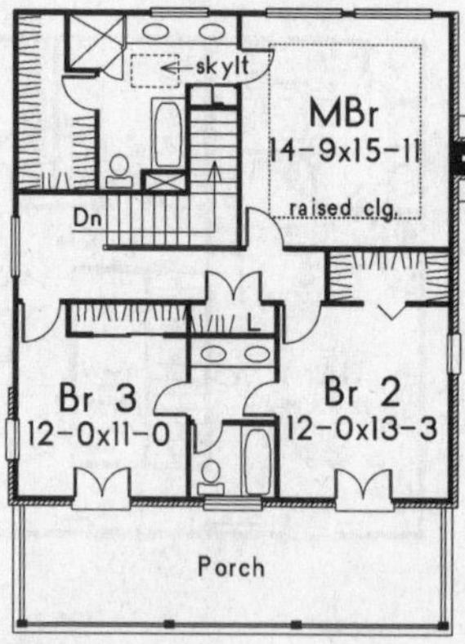

MBr
14-9x15-11
raised clg.
skylt
Dn
Br 3
12-0x11-0
Br 2
12-0x13-3
Porch

Second Floor
1,011 sq. ft.

Special features

- 9' ceilings throughout
- Covered porches on both floors create outside living space
- Secondary bedrooms share full bath
- L-shaped kitchen features island cooktop and convenient laundry room
- 3 bedrooms, 2 1/2 baths, 2-car side entry garage
- Basement foundation

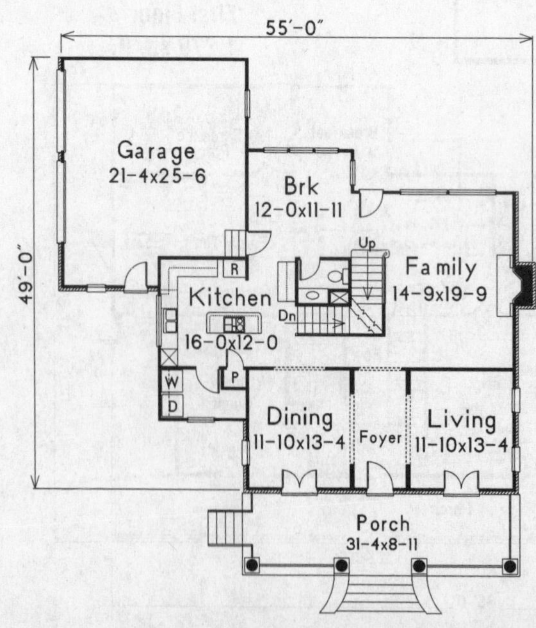
55'-0"
49'-0"
Garage
21-4x25-6
Brk
12-0x11-11
Up
Family
14-9x19-9
R
Kitchen
16-0x12-0
Dn
W
D
P
Dining
11-10x13-4
Foyer
Living
11-10x13-4
Porch
31-4x8-11

First Floor
1,316 sq. ft.

TO ORDER BLUEPRINTS USE THE FORM ON PAGE 19 OR CALL TOLL-FREE 1-877-671-6036

View thousands more home plans online at www.familyhandyman.com/homeplans

Plan #702-0233

Unique Features Create Style And Sophistication

2,772 total square feet of living area | **Price Code E**

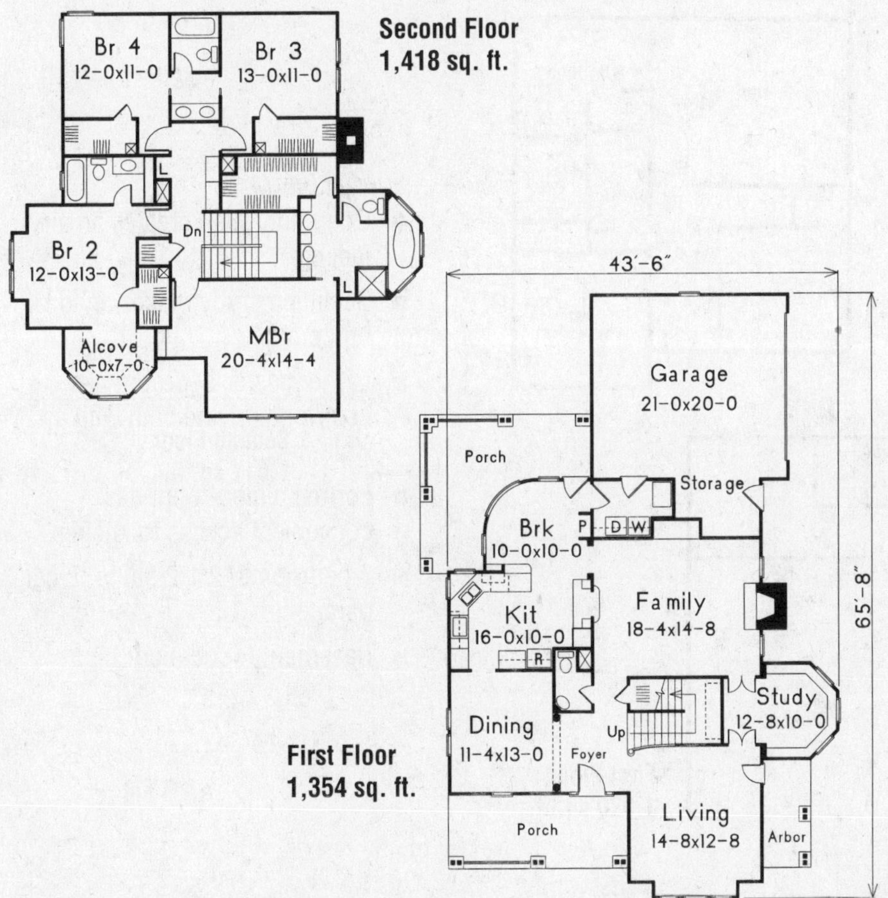
Second Floor
1,418 sq. ft.
Br 4
12-0x11-0
Br 3
13-0x11-0
L
Dn
Br 2
12-0x13-0
L
Alcove
10-0x7-0
MBr
20-4x14-4
43'-6"
Garage
21-0x20-0
Porch
Storage
Brk
10-0x10-0
P
DW
Family
18-4x14-8
Kit
16-0x10-0
R
Study
12-8x10-0
Dining
11-4x13-0
Up
Foyer
65'-8"
First Floor
1,354 sq. ft.
Living
14-8x12-8
Porch
Arbor

Special features

- 10' ceilings on first floor and 9' ceilings on second floor create spacious atmosphere
- Large bay windows accent study and master bath
- Breakfast room features dramatic curved wall with direct view and access onto porch
- 4 bedrooms, 3 1/2 baths, 2-car side entry garage
- Slab foundation

TO ORDER BLUEPRINTS USE THE FORM ON PAGE 19 OR CALL TOLL-FREE 1-877-671-6036

Handyman

Plan #702-JFD-20-1868-1

Plenty Of Closet Space

1,868 total square feet of living area

Price Code C

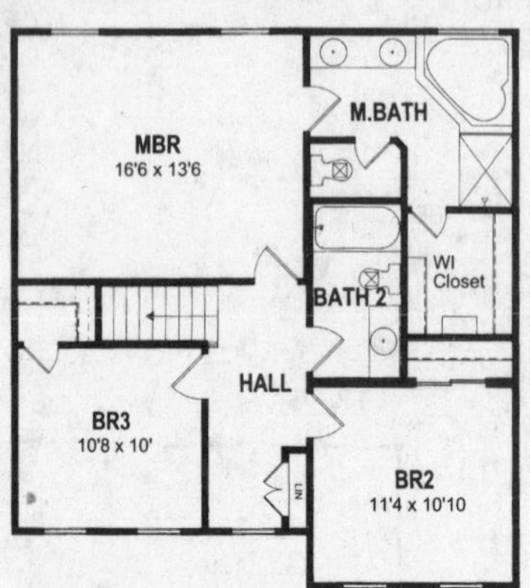

MBR
16'6 x 13'6
M.BATH
WI Closet
BATH 2
HALL
BR3
10'8 x 10'
BR2
11'4 x 10'10

Second Floor
848 sq. ft.

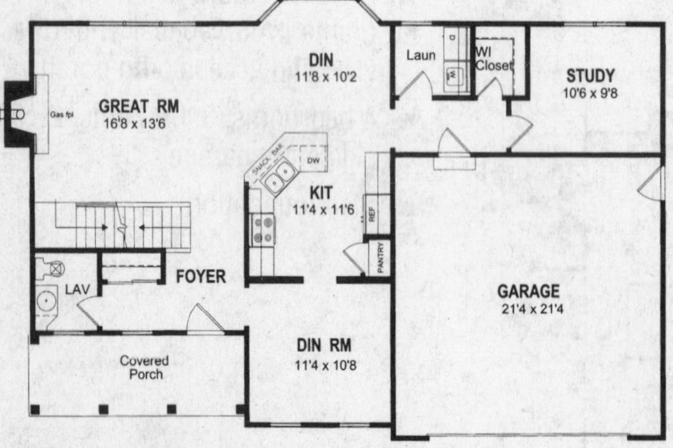

DIN
11'8 x 10'2
Laun
WI Closet
STUDY
10'6 x 9'8
GREAT RM
16'8 x 13'6
Gas fpl
KIT
11'4 x 11'6
DW
REF
PANTRY
LAV
FOYER
GARAGE
21'4 x 21'4
DIN RM
11'4 x 10'8
Covered Porch

First Floor
1,020 sq. ft.

Width: 52'-8"
Depth: 34'-0"

Special features

- Open floor plan creates an airy feeling
- Secluded study makes an ideal home office
- Large master bedroom has luxurious private bath with a walk-in closet
- Formal dining room has convenient access to kitchen
- 3 bedrooms, 2 1/2 baths, 2-car garage
- Basement foundation

Plan #702-FB-1043

Cozy Covered Front Porch

1,692 total square feet of living area **Price Code B**

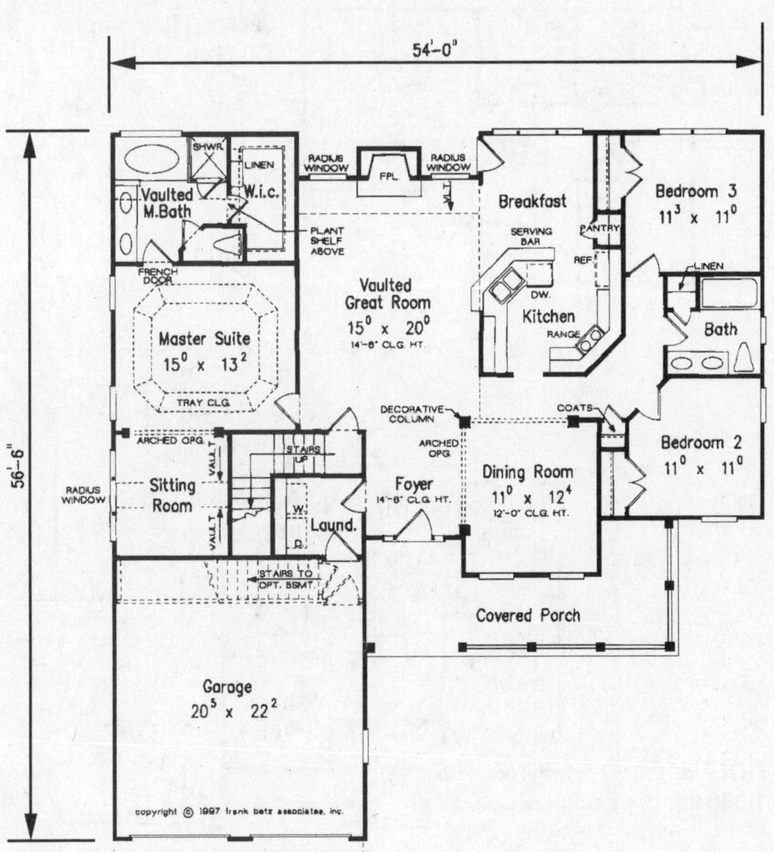

54'-0"
56'-6"
SHWR.
LINEN
Vaulted M.Bath
W.i.c.
RADIUS WINDOW
FPL.
RADIUS WINDOW
Breakfast
Bedroom 3
11³ x 11⁰
PLANT SHELF ABOVE
SERVING BAR
PANTRY
REF.
DW.
LINEN
FRENCH DOOR
Vaulted Great Room
15⁰ x 20⁰
14'-6" CLG. HT.
Kitchen
RANGE
Bath
Master Suite
15⁰ x 13²
TRAY CLG.
DECORATIVE COLUMN
COATS
ARCHED OPG.
STAIRS UP
ARCHED OPG.
Bedroom 2
11⁰ x 11⁰
RADIUS WINDOW
Sitting Room
Foyer
14'-6" CLG. HT.
Dining Room
11⁰ x 12⁴
12'-0" CLG. HT.
Laund.
STAIRS TO OPT. BSMT.
Covered Porch
Garage
20⁵ x 22²
copyright © 1997 frank betz associates, inc.

Special features

- Tray ceiling in master bedroom
- Breakfast bar overlooks vaulted great room
- Additional bedrooms are located away from master bedroom for privacy
- 3 bedrooms, 2 baths, 2-car garage
- Walk-out basement or crawl space foundation, please specify when ordering

TO ORDER BLUEPRINTS USE THE FORM ON PAGE 19 OR CALL TOLL-FREE 1-877-671-6036

View thousands more home plans online at www.familyhandyman.com/homeplans

The Family
Handyman

Plan #702-0390

Three-Season Room Links With Surroundings

2,351 total square feet of living area **Price Code D**

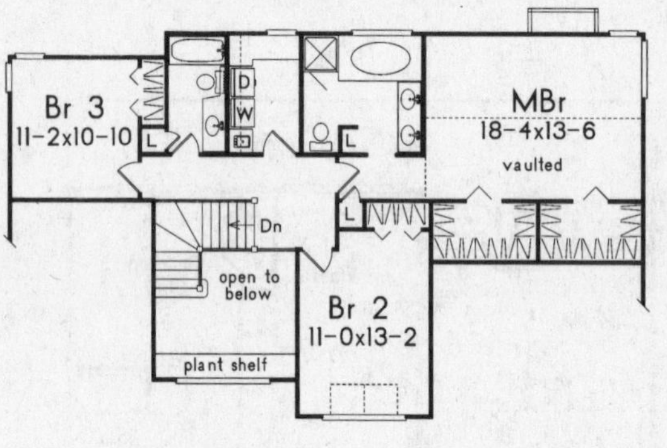

Br 3
11-2x10-10
L
D
W
MBr
18-4x13-6
vaulted
L
L
Dn
open to below
Br 2
11-0x13-2
plant shelf

Second Floor
1,015 sq. ft.

Special features

- Coffered ceiling in dining room adds elegant appeal
- Wrap-around porch creates a pleasant escape
- Cozy study with double-doors and extra storage
- Double walk-in closets balance and organize master suite
- 3 bedrooms, 2 1/2 baths, 2-car garage
- Basement foundation

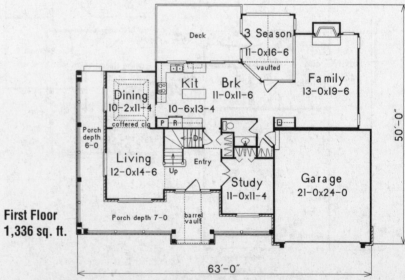

Deck
3 Season
11-0x16-6
vaulted
Family
13-0x19-6
Kit
10-6x13-4
Brk
11-0x11-6
Dining
10-2x11-4
coffered clg
P R
Dn
Porch depth 6-0
Living
12-0x14-6
Up
Entry
Study
11-0x11-4
Garage
21-0x24-0
Porch depth 7-0
barrel vault
50'-0"
63'-0"

First Floor
1,336 sq. ft.

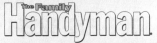

Plan #702-AX-96355

Unusual Three-Sided Porch

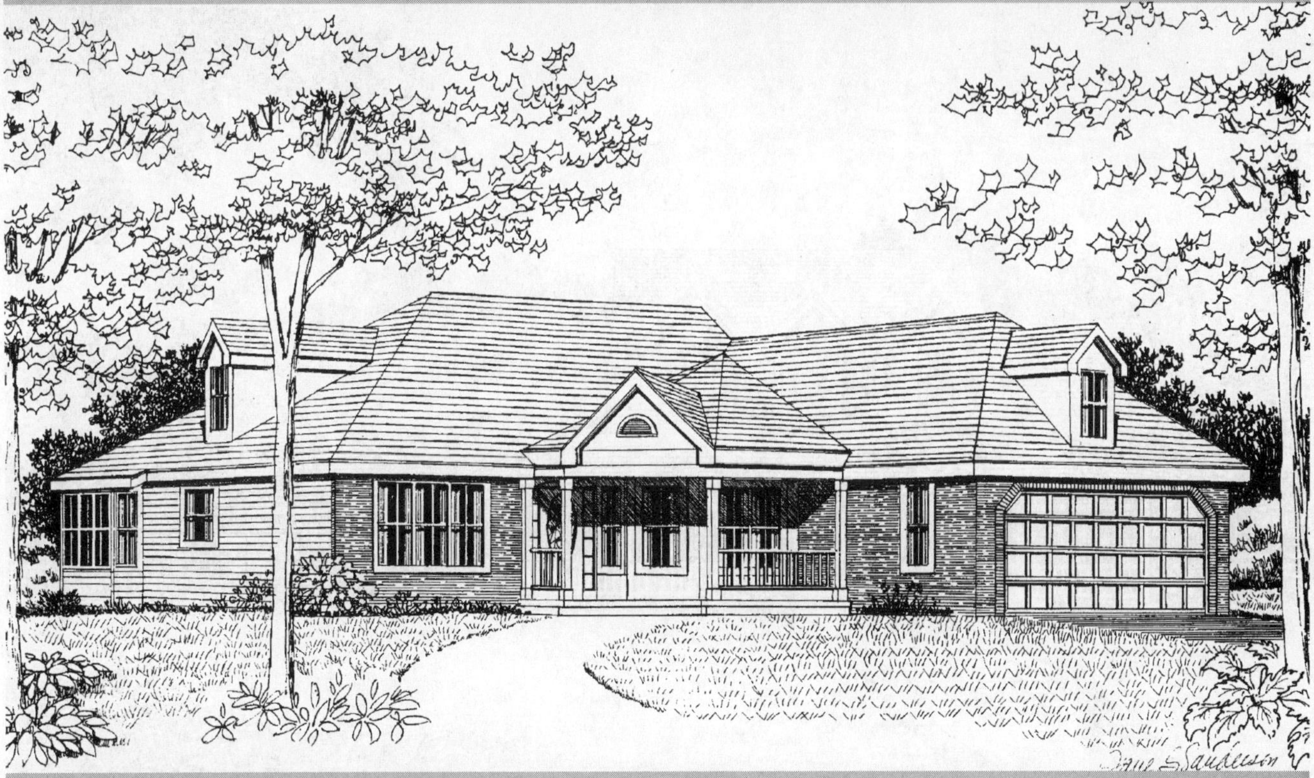

1,699 total square feet of living area **Price Code B**

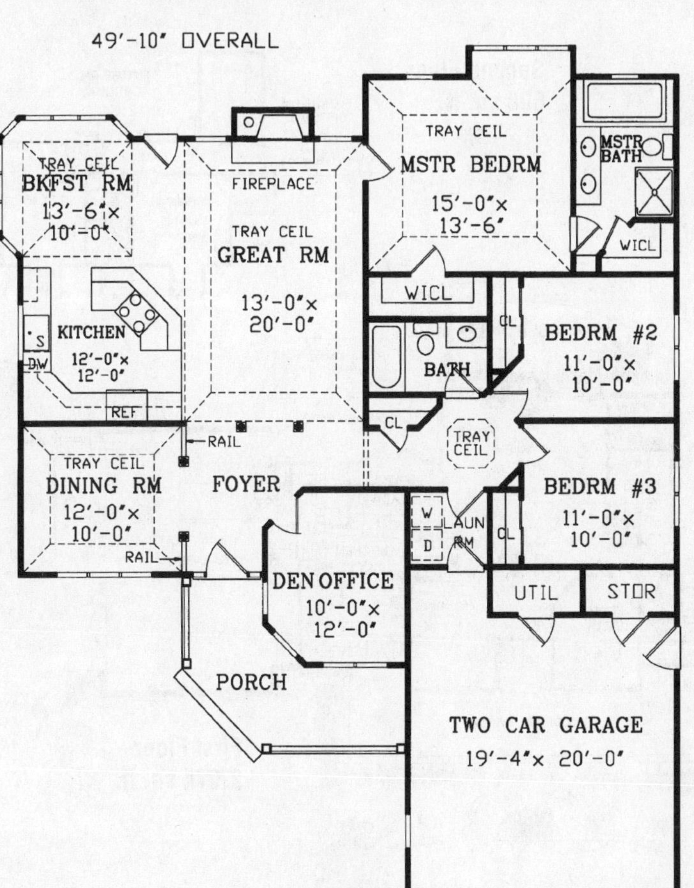
49'-10" OVERALL
TRAY CEIL
BKFST RM
13'-6"x
10'-0"
FIREPLACE
TRAY CEIL
GREAT RM
13'-0"x
20'-0"
TRAY CEIL
MSTR BEDRM
15'-0"x
13'-6"
MSTR BATH
WICL
WICL
KITCHEN
12'-0"x
12'-0"
S
DW
REF
BATH
CL
BEDRM #2
11'-0"x
10'-0"
60'-6" OVERALL
RAIL
TRAY CEIL
DINING RM
12'-0"x
10'-0"
FOYER
CL
TRAY CEIL
BEDRM #3
11'-0"x
10'-0"
W
D
LAUN RM
CL
RAIL
DEN OFFICE
10'-0"x
12'-0"
UTIL
STOR
PORCH
TWO CAR GARAGE
19'-4"x 20'-0"

Special features

- Dramatic wide open interior with angled kitchen and wrap-around counter
- Beautiful corner breakfast area with five-sided angled bay and tray ceiling
- Den office could easily be converted to a fourth bedroom
- 3 bedrooms, 2 baths, 2-car garage
- Basement, crawl space or slab foundation, please specify when ordering

Plan #702-FDG-8753-L

Impressive Gallery

2,674 total square feet of living area

Price Code E

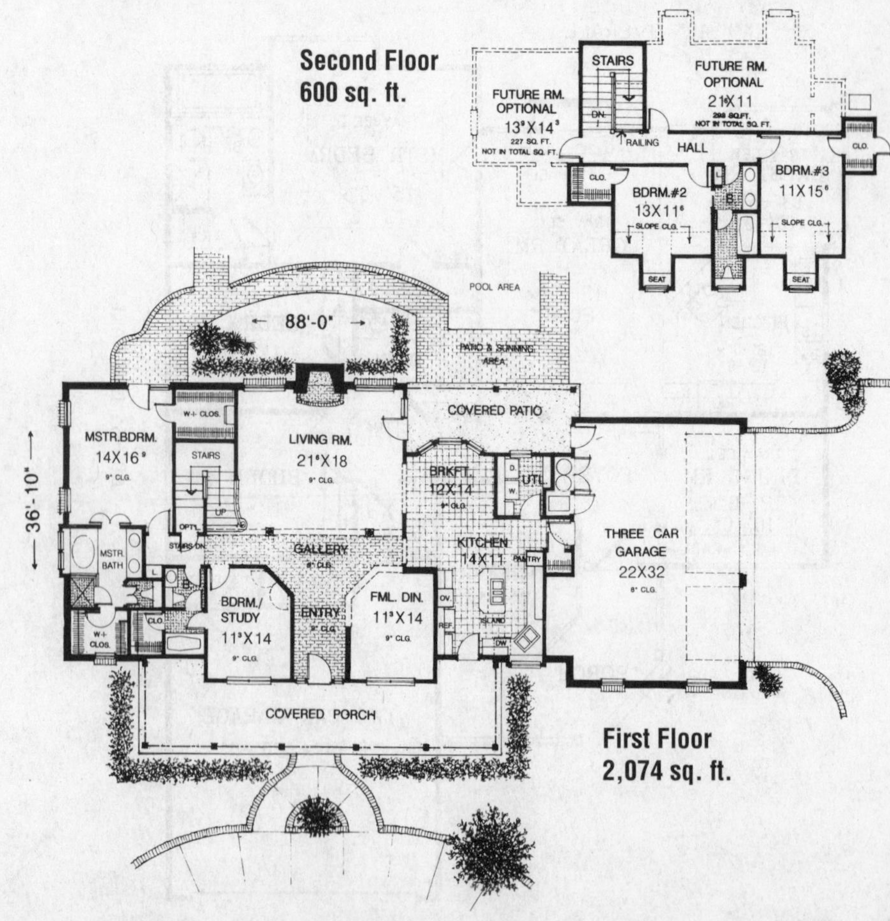

Second Floor
600 sq. ft.
FUTURE RM. OPTIONAL
13⁸X14³
227 SQ. FT. NOT IN TOTAL SQ. FT.
STAIRS
DN
RAILING
FUTURE RM. OPTIONAL
21X11
NOT IN TOTAL SQ. FT.
HALL
CLO.
CLO.
BDRM.#2
13X11⁶
SLOPE CLG.
B
BDRM.#3
11X15⁶
SLOPE CLG.
SEAT
SEAT
POOL AREA
88'-0"
PATIO & SUNNING AREA
COVERED PATIO
W-I- CLOS.
MSTR.BDRM.
14X16⁹
9" CLG.
STAIRS
LIVING RM.
21⁶X18
9" CLG.
BRKFT.
12X14
9" CLG.
UTL
36'-10"
OPT.
STAIRS DN
GALLERY
KITCHEN
14X11
PANTRY
THREE CAR GARAGE
22X32
MSTR. BATH
BDRM./ STUDY
11³X14
9" CLG.
ENTRY
FML. DIN.
11³X14
9" CLG.
W-I- CLOS.
CLO.
ISLAND
DW
REF
COVERED PORCH
First Floor
2,074 sq. ft.

Special features

- First floor master bedroom has convenient location
- Kitchen and breakfast area have island and access to covered front porch
- Second floor bedrooms have dormer window seats for added charm
- Optional future room on second floor has an additional 520 square feet of living area
- 4 bedrooms, 3 baths, 3-car side entry garage
- Basement or slab foundation, please specify when ordering

Plan #702-VL2888

Cheerful And Bright Great Room

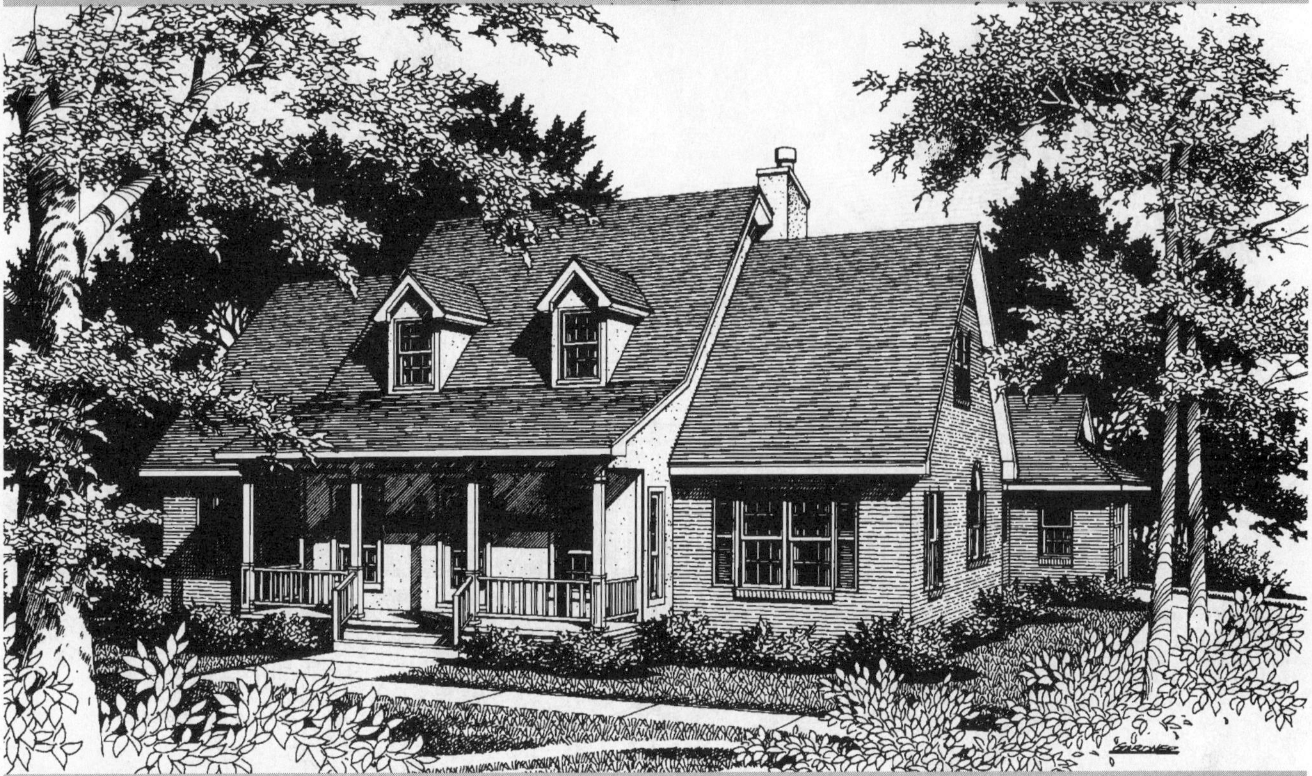

2,888 total square feet of living area **Price Code E**

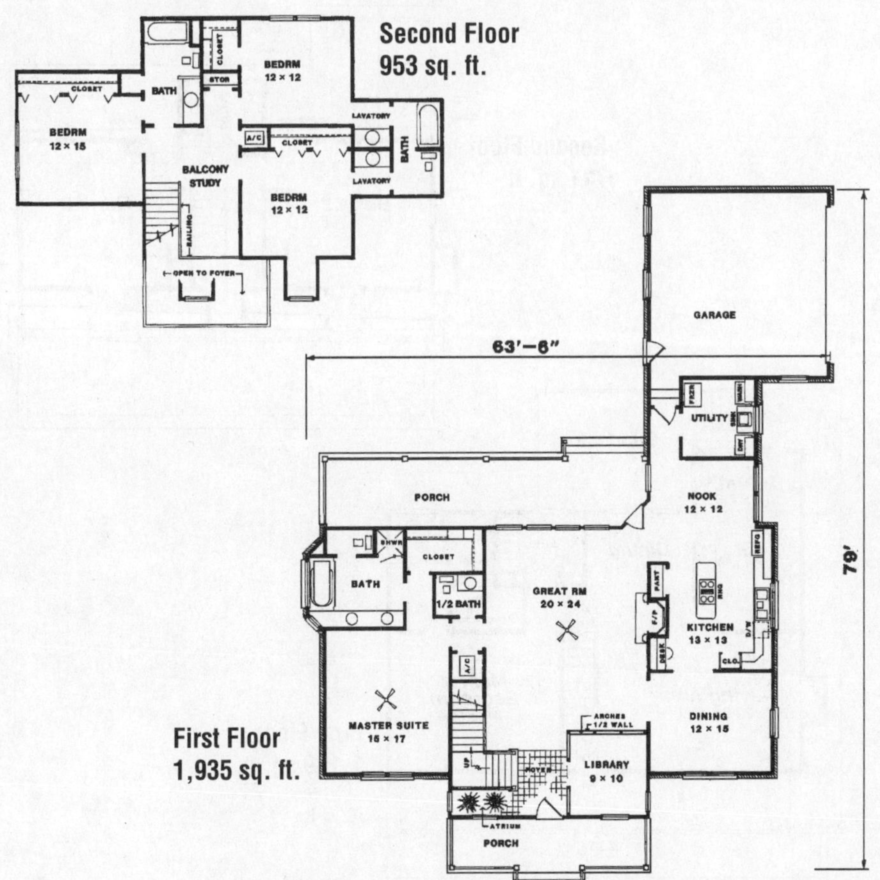
BEDRM 12 × 12
CLOSET
BATH
STOR
BEDRM 12 × 15
LAVATORY
A/C
CLOSET
BATH
BALCONY STUDY
BEDRM 12 × 12
LAVATORY
RAILING
OPEN TO FOYER
GARAGE
63'–6"
UTILITY
PORCH
NOOK 12 × 12
CLOSET
BATH
1/2 BATH
GREAT RM 20 × 24
KITCHEN 13 × 13
79'
MASTER SUITE 15 × 17
ARCHES 1/2 WALL
DINING 12 × 15
FOYER
LIBRARY 9 × 10
ATRIUM
PORCH

Second Floor
953 sq. ft.

First Floor
1,935 sq. ft.

Special features

- An arched half-wall accents secluded library
- First floor master suite has a spacious bath with tub-in-a-bay
- Kitchen has center island with cooktop for convenience
- 9' ceilings on the first floor
- 4 bedrooms, 3 1/2 baths, 2-car side entry garage
- Slab or crawl space foundation, please specify when ordering

TO ORDER BLUEPRINTS USE THE FORM ON PAGE 19 OR CALL TOLL-FREE 1-877-671-6036

Plan #702-JV-1870-A

Ideal For Entertaining

1,870 total square feet of living area

Price Code C

Special features

- Kitchen is open to the living and dining areas
- Breakfast area has cathedral ceiling creating a sunroom effect
- Master suite is spacious with all the amenities
- Second floor bedrooms share hall bath
- 3 bedrooms, 2 1/2 baths, 2-car drive under garage
- Basement foundation

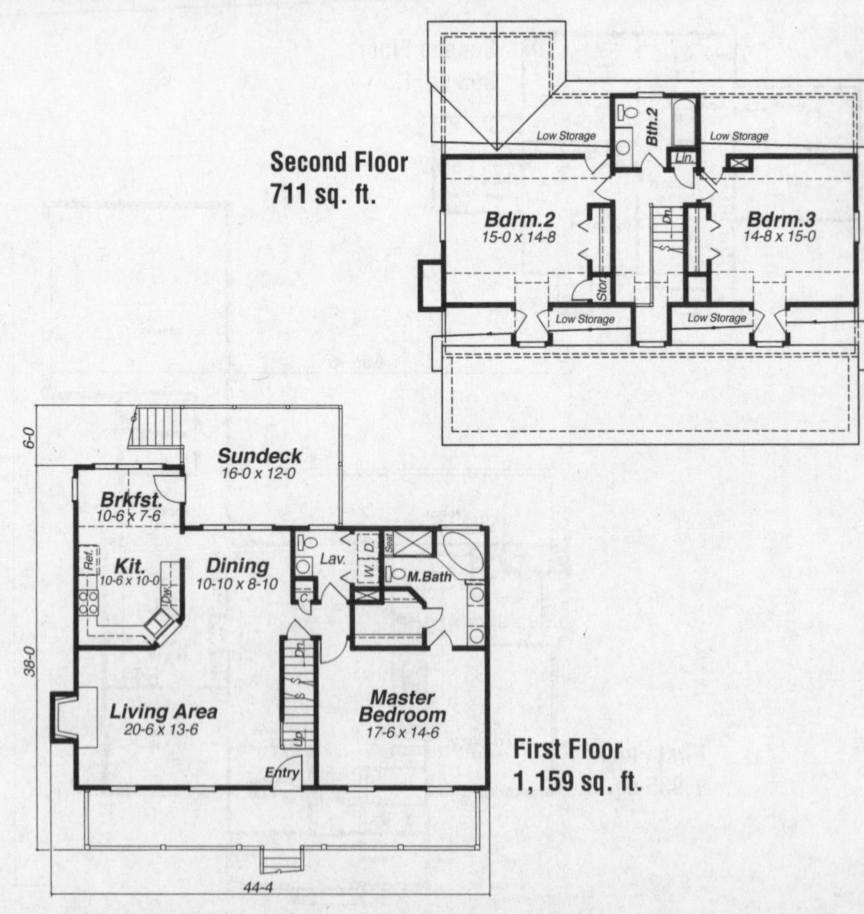

Second Floor
711 sq. ft.
Low Storage
Bth.2
Low Storage
Lin.
Bdrm.2
15-0 x 14-8
Bdrm.3
14-8 x 15-0
Stor.
Low Storage
Low Storage
6-0
Sundeck
16-0 x 12-0
Brkfst.
10-6 x 7-6
Kit.
10-6 x 10-0
Dining
10-10 x 8-10
Lav.
M.Bath
Living Area
20-6 x 13-6
Master
Bedroom
17-6 x 14-6
Entry
38-0
44-4
First Floor
1,159 sq. ft.

TO ORDER BLUEPRINTS USE THE FORM ON PAGE 19 OR CALL TOLL-FREE 1-877-671-6036

View thousands more home plans online at www.familyhandyman.com/homeplans

Vaulted Ceiling Adds Spaciousness

990 total square feet of living area

Price Code AA

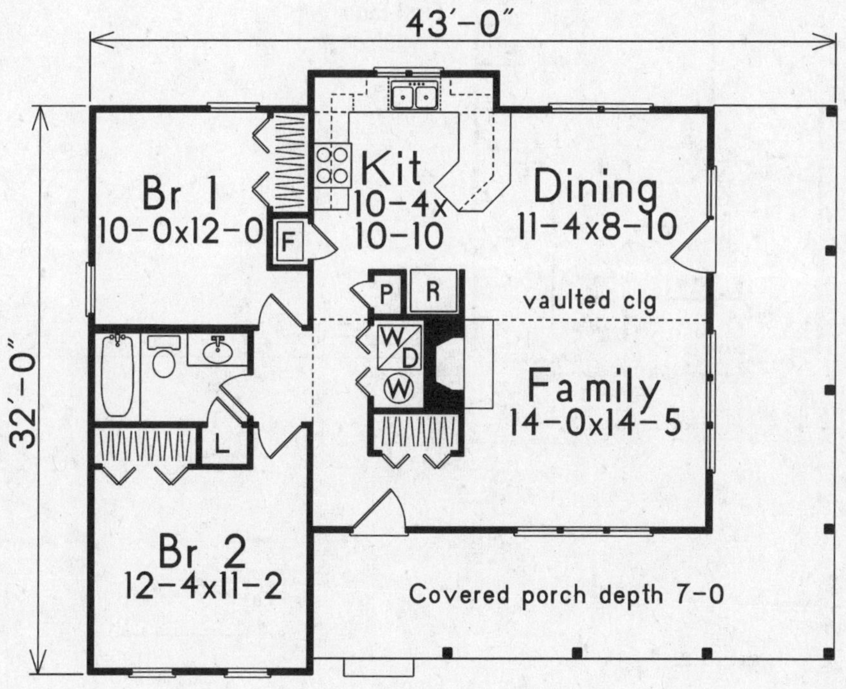
43'-0"
32'-0"
Kit
10-4x
10-10
Br 1
10-0x12-0
F
Dining
11-4x8-10
P
R
vaulted clg
W
D
W
Family
14-0x14-5
L
Br 2
12-4x11-2
Covered porch depth 7-0

Special features

- Wrap-around porch on two sides of this home
- Private and efficiently designed
- Space for efficiency washer and dryer unit for convenience
- 2 bedrooms, 1 bath
- Crawl space foundation

Expansive Counter Space

2,123 total square feet of living area | **Price Code E**

Special features

- Energy efficient home with 2" x 6" exterior walls
- Living room has wood burning fireplace, built-in bookshelves and a wet bar
- Skylights make sun porch bright and comfortable
- 3 bedrooms, 2 1/2 baths, 2-car side entry garage
- Crawl space, slab or basement foundation, please specify when ordering

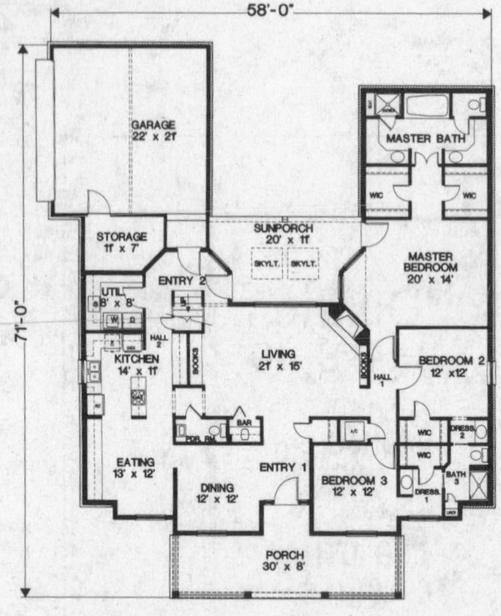
58'-0"
71'-0"
GARAGE
22' x 21'
STORAGE
11' x 7'
SUNPORCH
20' x 11'
SKYLT.
ENTRY 2
UTIL.
MASTER BATH
MASTER BEDROOM
20' x 14'
KITCHEN
14' x 11'
LIVING
21' x 15'
BEDROOM 2
12' x 12'
BAR
EATING
13' x 12'
DINING
12' x 12'
ENTRY 1
BEDROOM 3
12' x 12'
PORCH
30' x 8'

First Floor
2,123 sq. ft.

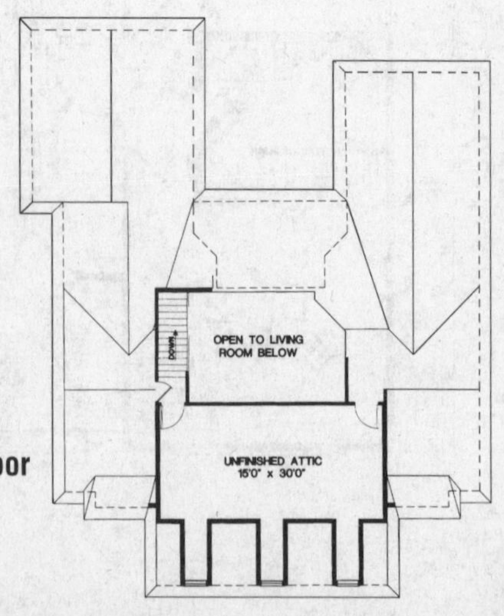
OPEN TO LIVING ROOM BELOW
UNFINISHED ATTIC
15'0" x 30'0"

Second Floor
450 sq. ft.

Plan #702-0224

Great Traffic Flow On Both Floors

2,461 total square feet of living area

Price Code D

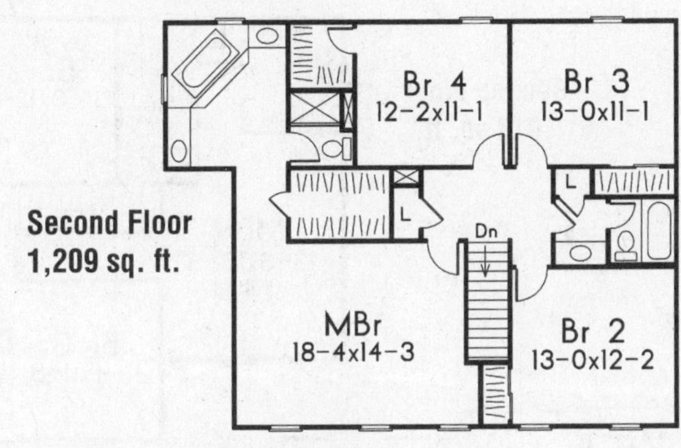

Br 4
12-2x11-1
Br 3
13-0x11-1
L
L
Dn
MBr
18-4x14-3
Br 2
13-0x12-2

Second Floor
1,209 sq. ft.

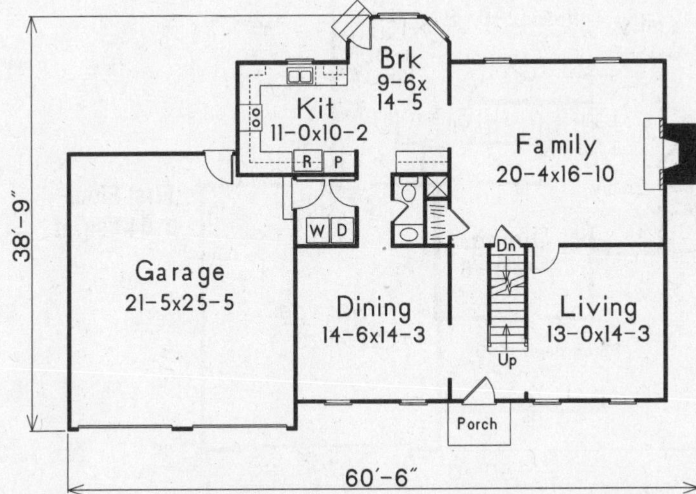

Brk
9-6x
14-5
Kit
11-0x10-2
R
P
Family
20-4x16-10
W
D
Garage
21-5x25-5
Dn
Dining
14-6x14-3
Living
13-0x14-3
Up
Porch
38′-9″
60′-6″

First Floor
1,252 sq. ft.

Special features

- Unique corner tub, double vanities and walk-in closet enhance the large master bedroom
- Fireplace provides focus in spacious family room
- Centrally located half bath for guests
- 4 bedrooms, 2 1/2 baths, 2-car garage
- Basement foundation, drawings also include slab and crawl space foundations

The Family
Handyman

Plan #702-0488

Angled Porch Greets Guests

2,059 total square feet of living area

Price Code C

Special features

- Large desk and pantry add to the breakfast room
- Laundry is located on second floor near bedrooms
- Vaulted ceiling in master suite
- Mud room is conveniently located near garage
- 3 bedrooms, 2 1/2 baths, 2-car garage
- Basement foundation

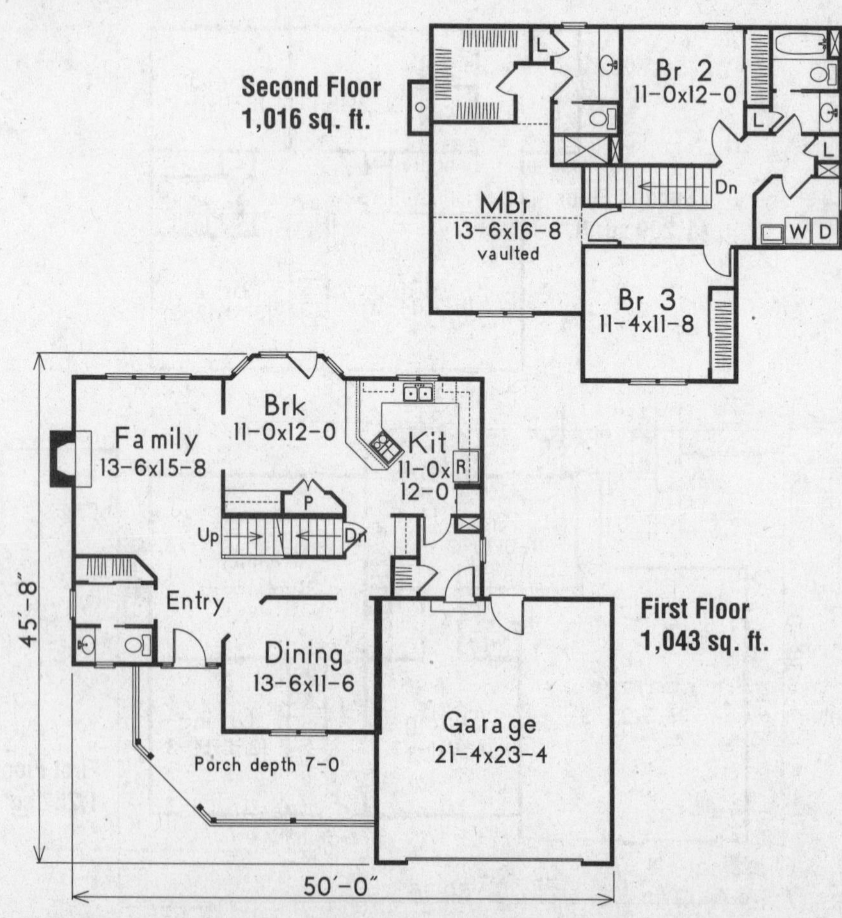

Second Floor
1,016 sq. ft.
Br 2
11-0x12-0
Dn
MBr
13-6x16-8
vaulted
W
D
Br 3
11-4x11-8
Family
13-6x15-8
Brk
11-0x12-0
Kit
11-0x
12-0
R
P
Up
Dn
Entry
Dining
13-6x11-6
Garage
21-4x23-4
Porch depth 7-0
45'-8"
50'-0"
First Floor
1,043 sq. ft.

TO ORDER BLUEPRINTS USE THE FORM ON PAGE 19 OR CALL TOLL-FREE 1-877-671-6036

View thousands more home plans online at www.familyhandyman.com/homeplans

Plan #702-CHP-4355-A-2

Lower Level Designed Perfectly For An In-Law Suite

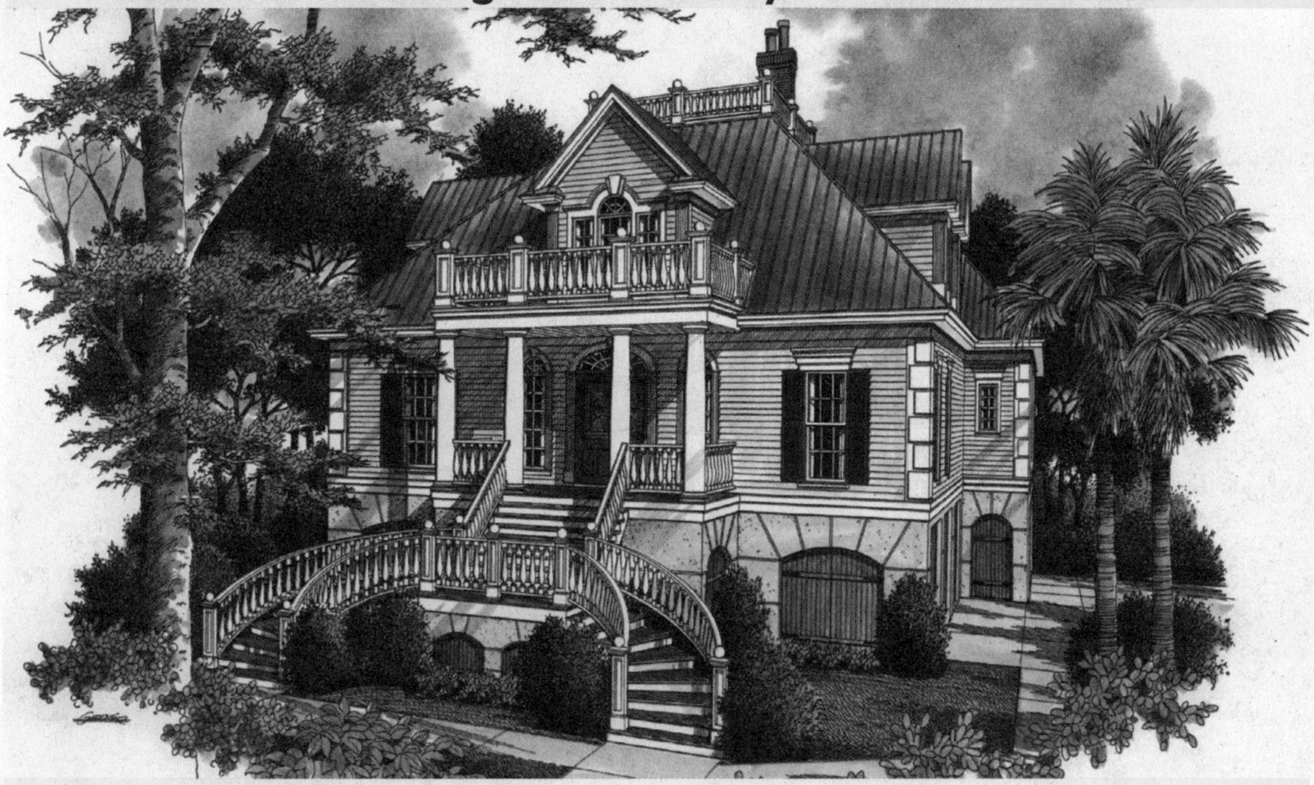

4,380 total square feet of living area **Price Code H**

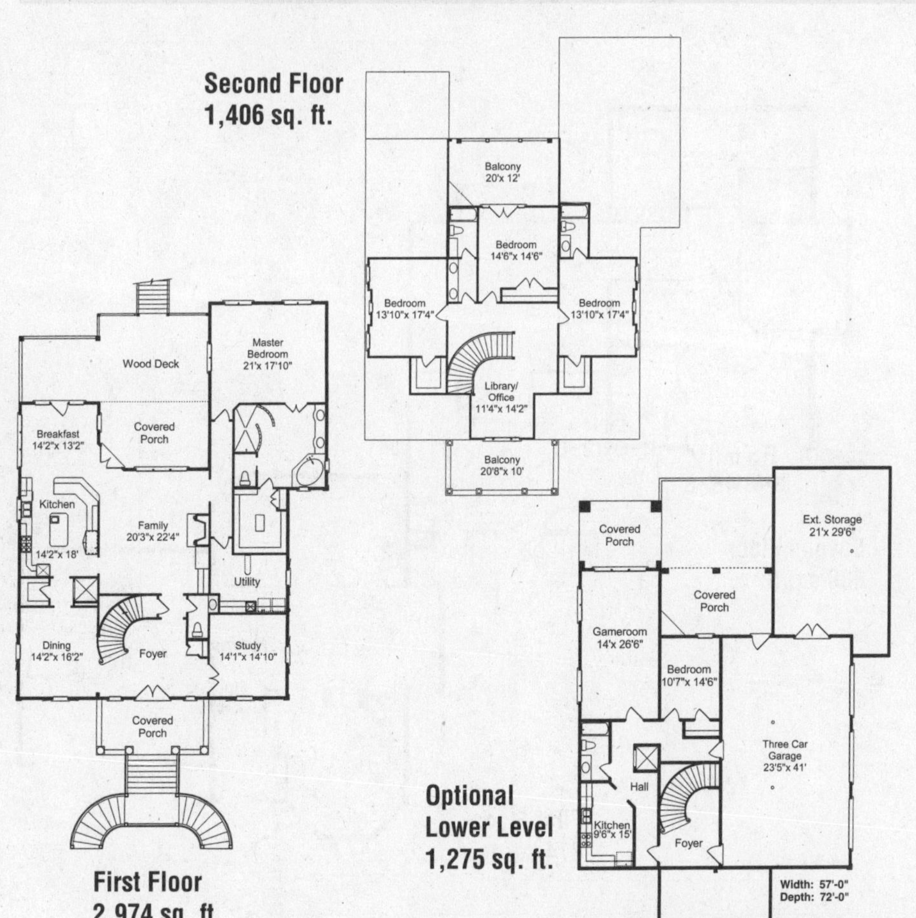
Second Floor
1,406 sq. ft.
Balcony
20'x 12'
Bedroom
14'6"x 14'6"
Bedroom
13'10"x 17'4"
Bedroom
13'10"x 17'4"
Library/
Office
11'4"x 14'2"
Balcony
20'8"x 10'
Wood Deck
Master
Bedroom
21'x 17'10"
Breakfast
14'2"x 13'2"
Covered
Porch
Kitchen
14'2"x 18'
Family
20'3"x 22'4"
Utility
Dining
14'2"x 16'2"
Foyer
Study
14'1"x 14'10"
Covered
Porch
First Floor
2,974 sq. ft.
Covered
Porch
Ext. Storage
21'x 29'6"
Covered
Porch
Gameroom
14'x 26'6"
Bedroom
10'7"x 14'6"
Three Car
Garage
23'5"x 41'
Hall
Kitchen
9'6"x 15'
Foyer
Optional
Lower Level
1,275 sq. ft.
Width: 57'-0"
Depth: 72'-0"

Special features

- 11' ceilings on first floor and 9' ceilings on second floor
- Intricate porch details display one-of-a-kind craftmanship
- Impressive foyer has curved staircase creating a grand entry
- Second floor bedroom accesses private balcony for easy outdoor relaxation
- 4 bedrooms, 3 1/2 baths, 3-car drive under garage
- Walk-out basement foundation

TO ORDER BLUEPRINTS USE THE FORM ON PAGE 19 OR CALL TOLL-FREE 1-877-671-6036

The Family
Handyman

Plan #702-DR-3406

Two-Sided Fireplace Makes An Impression

1,754 total square feet of living area **Price Code B**

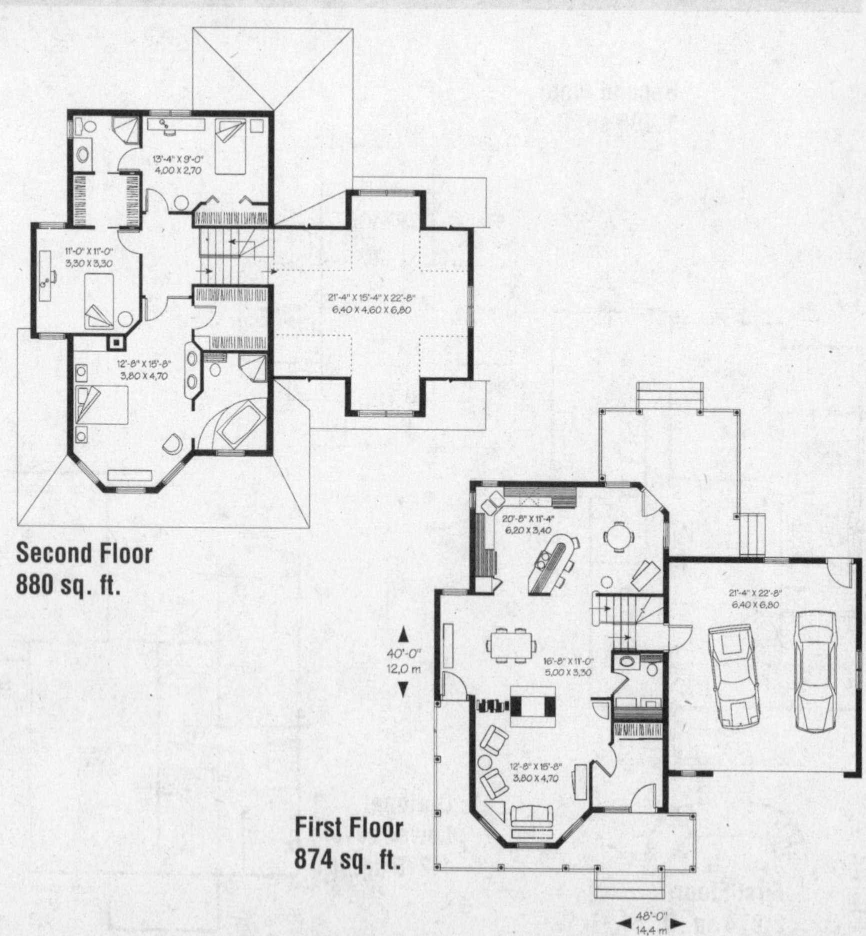
Second Floor
880 sq. ft.
First Floor
874 sq. ft.
40'-0"
12,0 m
48'-0"
14,4 m

Special features

- Energy efficient home with 2" x 6" exterior walls
- Utilities arelocated conveniently in first floor powder room
- U-shaped island in kitchen has stovetop as well as additional dining space
- Bonus room on second floor has 421 square feet of living area
- 3 bedrooms, 2 1/2 bath, 2-car garage
- Basement foundation

Plan #702-CHP-3444-A-16

Stunning Southern Home

3,493 total square feet of living area **Price Code H**

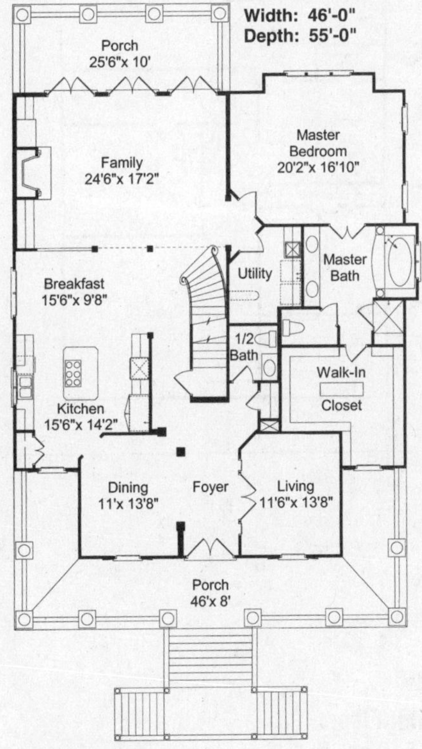
Width: 46'-0"
Depth: 55'-0"
Porch 25'6"x 10'
Family 24'6"x 17'2"
Master Bedroom 20'2"x 16'10"
Breakfast 15'6"x 9'8"
Utility
Master Bath
1/2 Bath
Walk-In Closet
Kitchen 15'6"x 14'2"
Dining 11'x 13'8"
Foyer
Living 11'6"x 13'8"
Porch 46'x 8'

First Floor
2,327 sq. ft.

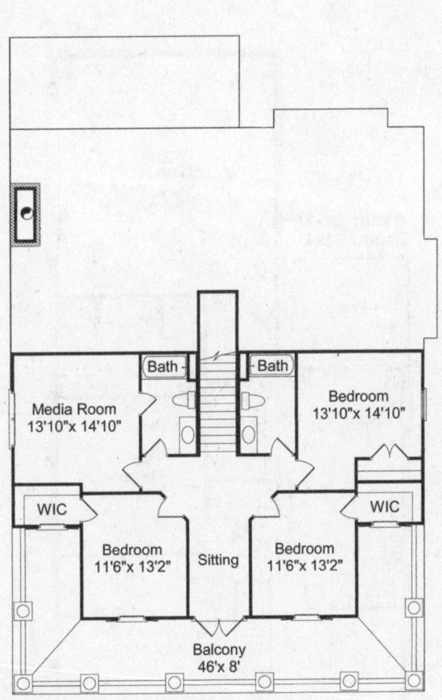
Bath
Bath
Media Room 13'10"x 14'10"
Bedroom 13'10"x 14'10"
WIC
WIC
Bedroom 11'6"x 13'2"
Sitting
Bedroom 11'6"x 13'2"
Balcony 46'x 8'

Second Floor
1,166 sq. ft.

Special features

- First floor master bedroom has enormous walk-in closet and a lavish bath
- Cozy sitting nook on second floor has access onto covered second floor balcony
- Formal living room in the fornt of the home could easily be converted to a study with double-doors for privacy
- 4 bedrooms, 3 1/2 baths, 3-car drive under garage
- Pier foundation

Plan #702-CHP-2343-A-30

Country Charm For A Narrow Lot

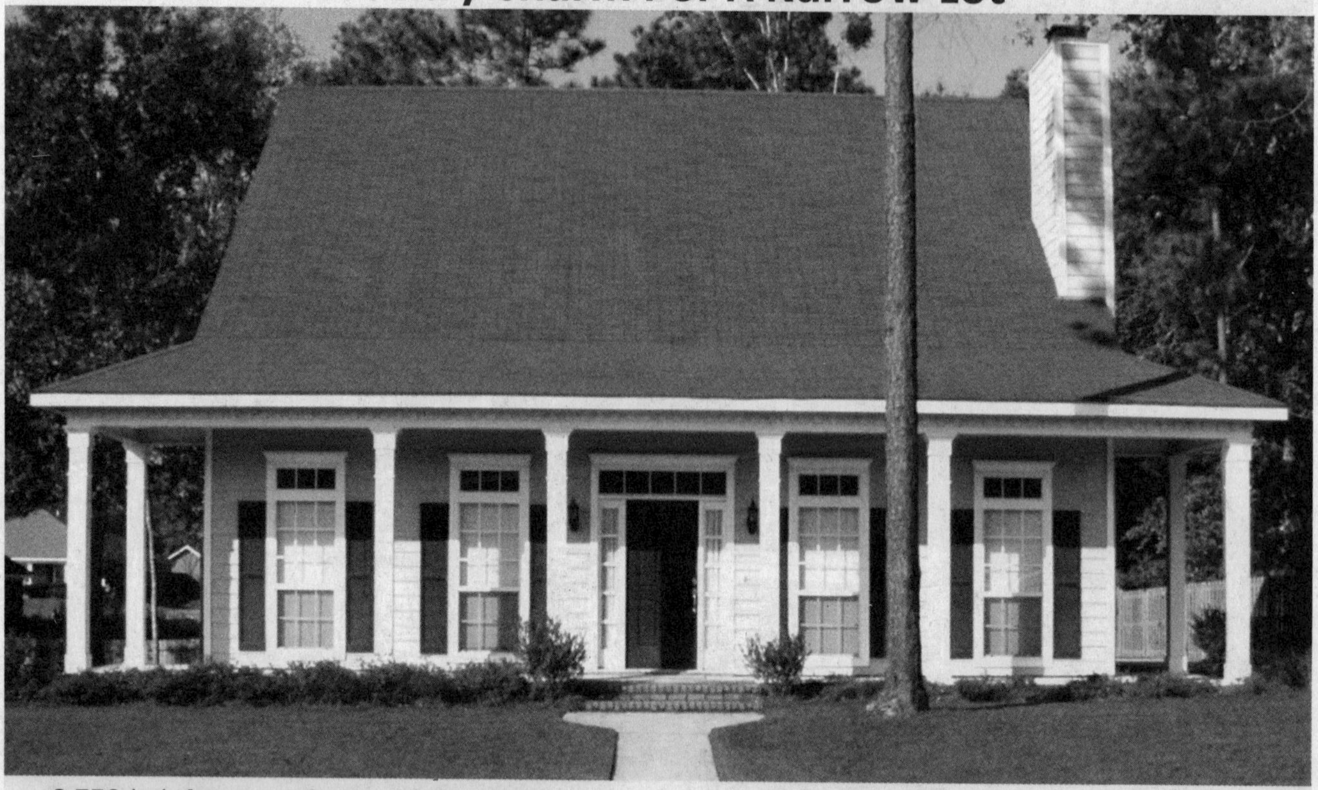

2,356 total square feet of living area

Price Code E

<u>*Special features*</u>

- Transoms above front windows create a custom feel to this design
- Spacious master bath has double vanities, toilet closet, and oversized whirlpool tub
- Covered rear porch off sunny breakfast area ideal for grilling or relaxing
- 4 bedrooms, 2 1/2 baths, 2-car side entry garage
- Slab foundation

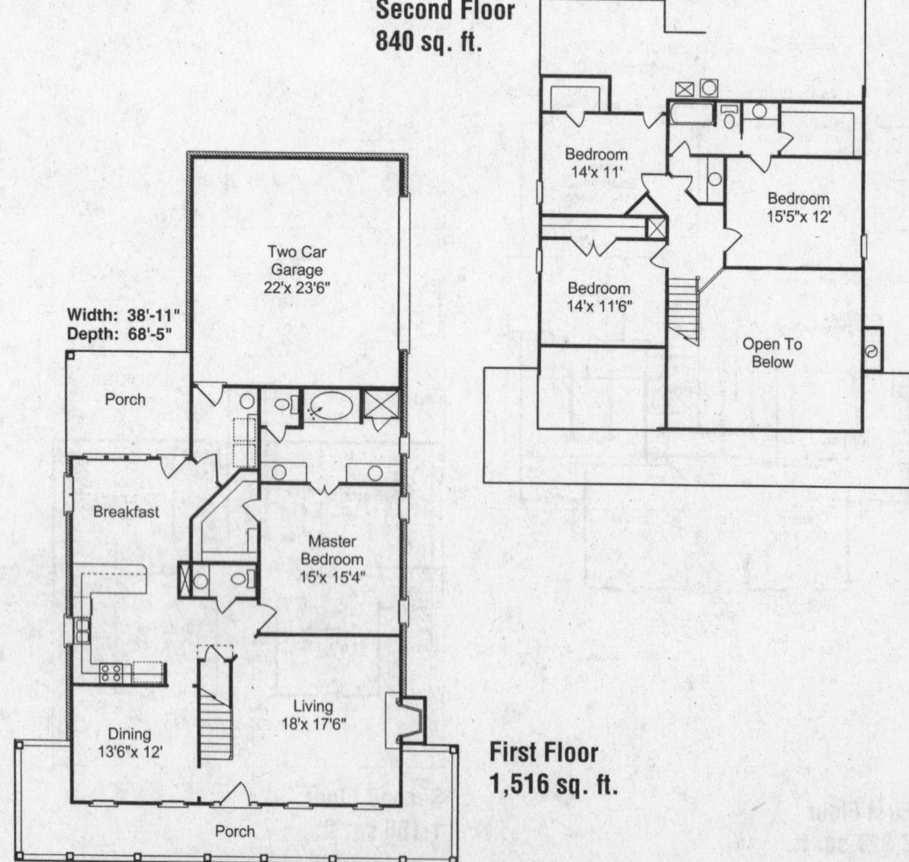
Second Floor
840 sq. ft.
Bedroom
14'x 11'
Bedroom
15'5"x 12'
Bedroom
14'x 11'6"
Open To
Below
Width: 38'-11"
Depth: 68'-5"
Two Car
Garage
22'x 23'6"
Porch
Breakfast
Master
Bedroom
15'x 15'4"
Living
18'x 17'6"
Dining
13'6"x 12'
Porch
First Floor
1,516 sq. ft.

Plan #702-CHP-1833-A-13

Double Dormers Add Curb Appeal

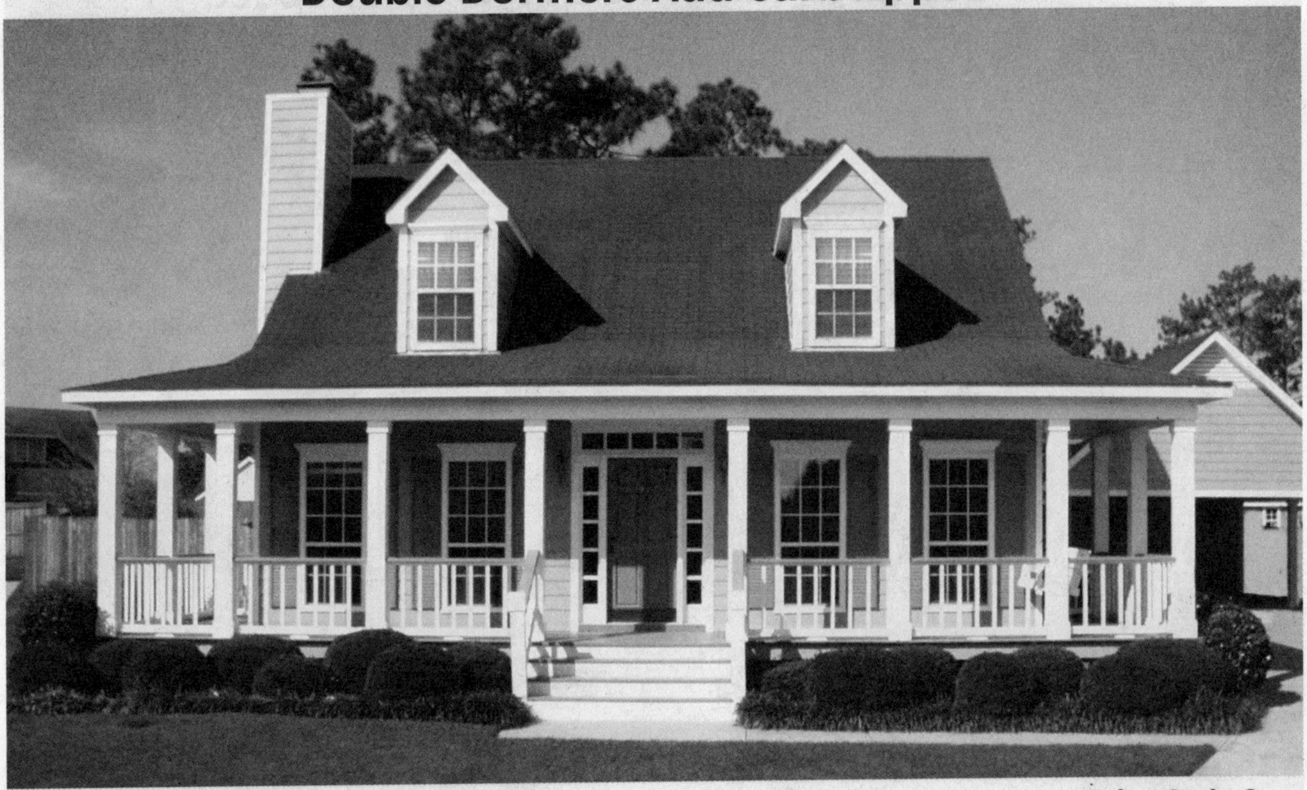

1,819 total square feet of living area **Price Code C**

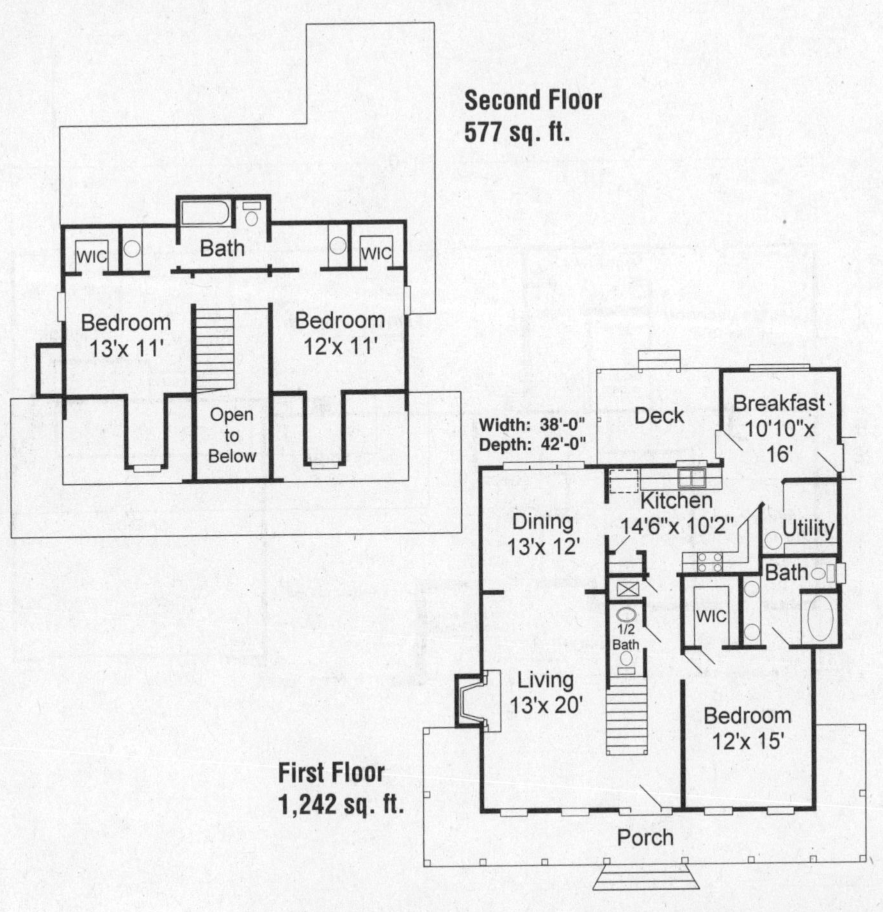
Second Floor
577 sq. ft.
WIC
Bath
WIC
Bedroom
13'x 11'
Bedroom
12'x 11'
Open
to
Below
Width: 38'-0"
Depth: 42'-0"
Deck
Breakfast
10'10"x
16'
Kitchen
14'6"x 10'2"
Dining
13'x 12'
Utility
Bath
WIC
1/2
Bath
Living
13'x 20'
Bedroom
12'x 15'
First Floor
1,242 sq. ft.
Porch

Special features

- Unique bath layout on the second floor allows for both bedrooms to have their own private sink area while connecting to main bath
- Window wall in dining area floods area with sunlight
- Walk-in closets in every bedroom
- 3 bedrooms, 2 1/2 baths
- Crawl space or slab foundation, please specify when ordering

Well-Designed Ranch With Plenty Of Space

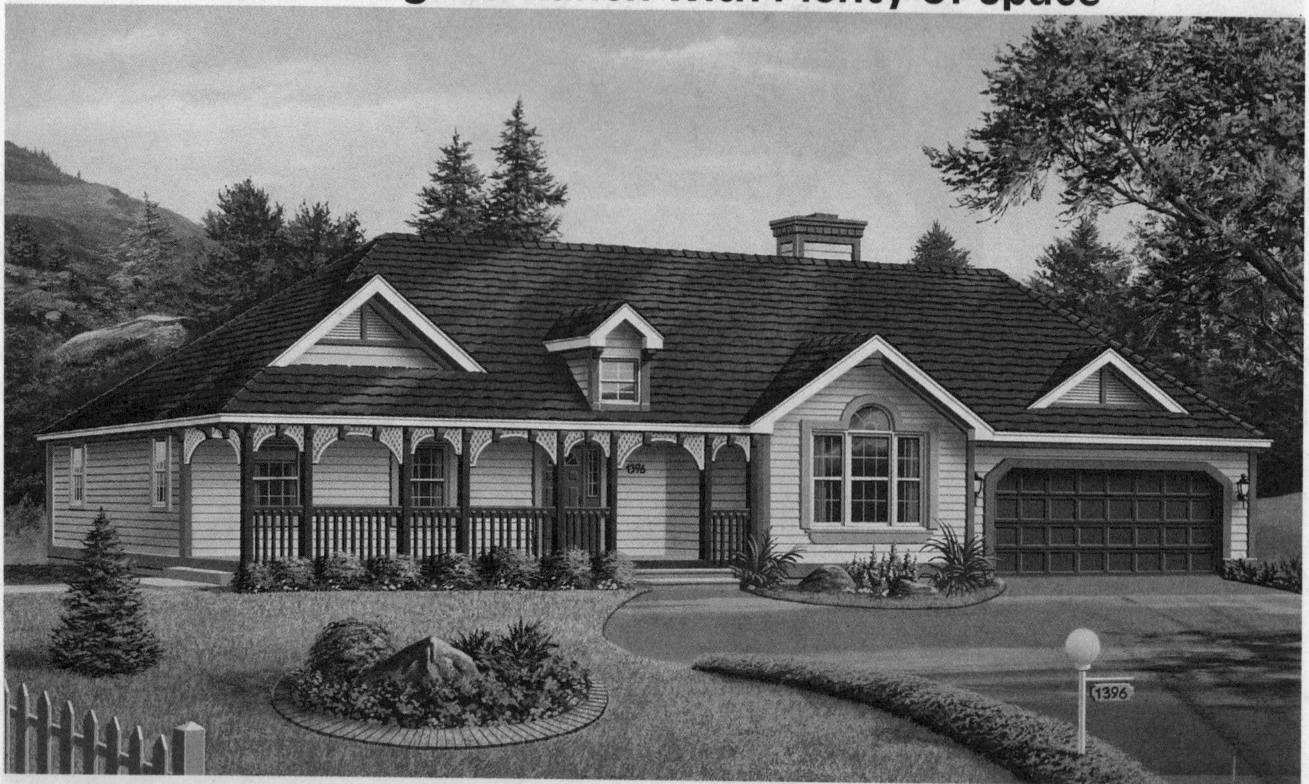

1,820 total square feet of living area

Price Code C

Special features

- Living room has stunning cathedral ceiling
- Spacious laundry room with easy access to kitchen, outdoors and garage
- Plenty of closet space throughout
- Covered front porch enhances outdoor living
- 3 bedrooms, 2 baths, 2-car garage
- Basement foundation

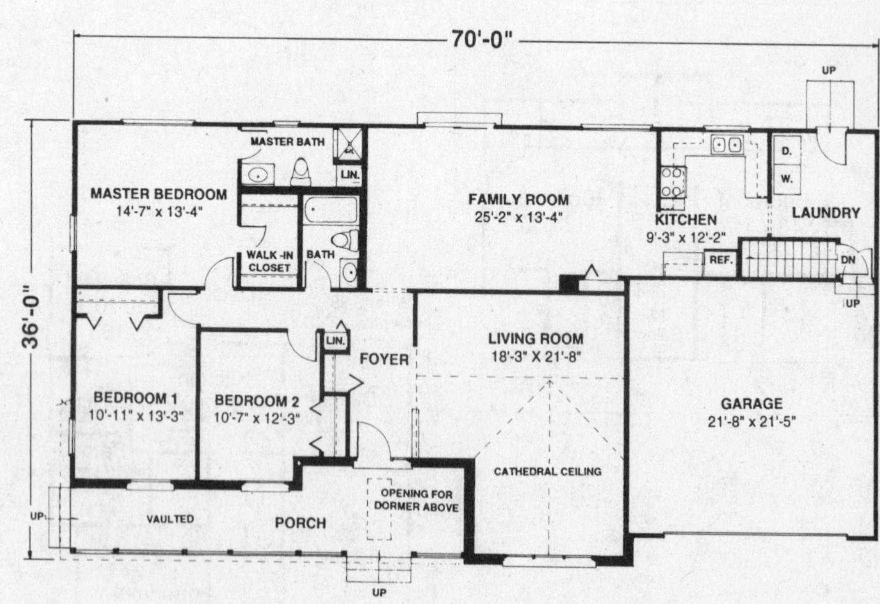
70'-0"
UP
MASTER BATH
LIN.
MASTER BEDROOM
14'-7" x 13'-4"
WALK-IN CLOSET
BATH
FAMILY ROOM
25'-2" x 13'-4"
D.
W.
KITCHEN
9'-3" x 12'-2"
LAUNDRY
REF.
DN
UP
36'-0"
LIN.
FOYER
LIVING ROOM
18'-3" X 21'-8"
BEDROOM 1
10'-11" x 13'-3"
BEDROOM 2
10'-7" x 12'-3"
GARAGE
21'-8" x 21'-5"
CATHEDRAL CEILING
OPENING FOR DORMER ABOVE
UP
VAULTED
PORCH
UP

The Family
Handyman

Plan #702-0714

Sophisticated Ranch With Split Bedrooms

2,808 total square feet of living area

Price Code E

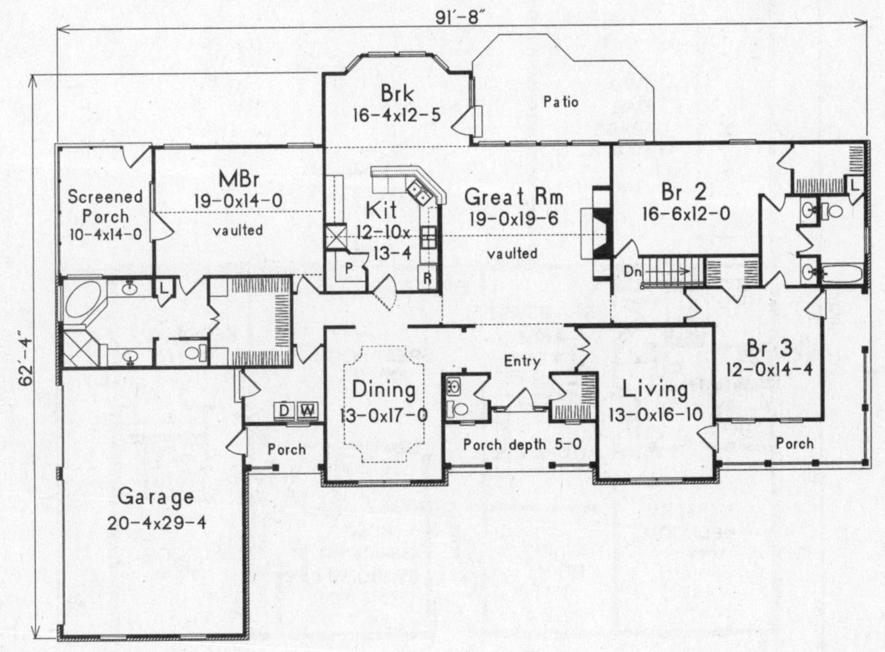
91'-8"
62'-4"
Brk
16-4x12-5
Patio
Screened
Porch
10-4x14-0
MBr
19-0x14-0
vaulted
Kit
12-10x
13-4
P
R
Great Rm
19-0x19-6
vaulted
Br 2
16-6x12-0
L
Dn
Br 3
12-0x14-4
L
D
W
Dining
13-0x17-0
Entry
Living
13-0x16-10
Porch
Porch depth 5-0
Porch
Garage
20-4x29-4

Special features

- An impressive front exterior showcases three porches for quiet times
- Large living and dining rooms flank an elegant entry
- Bedroom #3 shares a porch with the living room and a spacious bath with bedroom #2
- Vaulted master suite enjoys a secluded screened porch and sumptuous bath with corner tub, double vanities and huge walk-in closet
- Living room can easily convert to an optional fourth bedroom
- 3 bedrooms, 2 1/2 baths, 3-car side entry garage
- Basement foundation

Plan #702-DH-1854

An Elegant Southern Home

1,856 total square feet of living area **Price Code C**

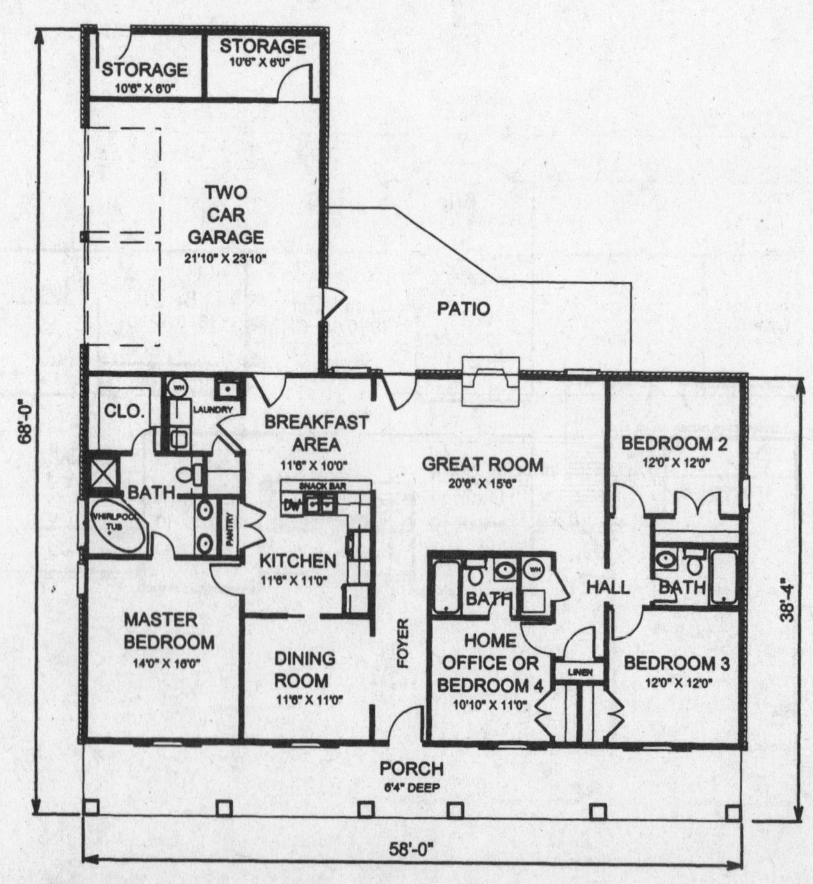

STORAGE
10'6" X 6'0"
STORAGE
10'6" X 6'0"
TWO
CAR
GARAGE
21'10" X 23'10"
PATIO
68'-0"
CLO.
LAUNDRY
BREAKFAST
AREA
11'6" X 10'0"
GREAT ROOM
20'6" X 15'6"
BEDROOM 2
12'0" X 12'0"
SNACK BAR
BATH
WHIRLPOOL TUB
PANTRY
KITCHEN
11'6" X 11'0"
BATH
HALL
BATH
38'-4"
MASTER
BEDROOM
14'0" X 16'0"
DINING
ROOM
11'6" X 11'0"
FOYER
HOME
OFFICE OR
BEDROOM 4
10'10" X 11'0"
LINEN
BEDROOM 3
12'0" X 12'0"
PORCH
6'4" DEEP
58'-0"

Special features

- Kitchen is well-positioned between the formal dining room and the casual breakfast room
- Master bedroom has a luxurious bath with all the amenities
- Home office or bedroom #4 has its own private bath
- 4 bedrooms, 3 baths, 2-car side entry garage
- Crawl space or slab foundation, please specify when ordering

TO ORDER BLUEPRINTS USE THE FORM ON PAGE 19 OR CALL TOLL-FREE 1-877-671-6036

View thousands more home plans online at www.familyhandyman.com/homeplans

Surprisingly Spacious Home

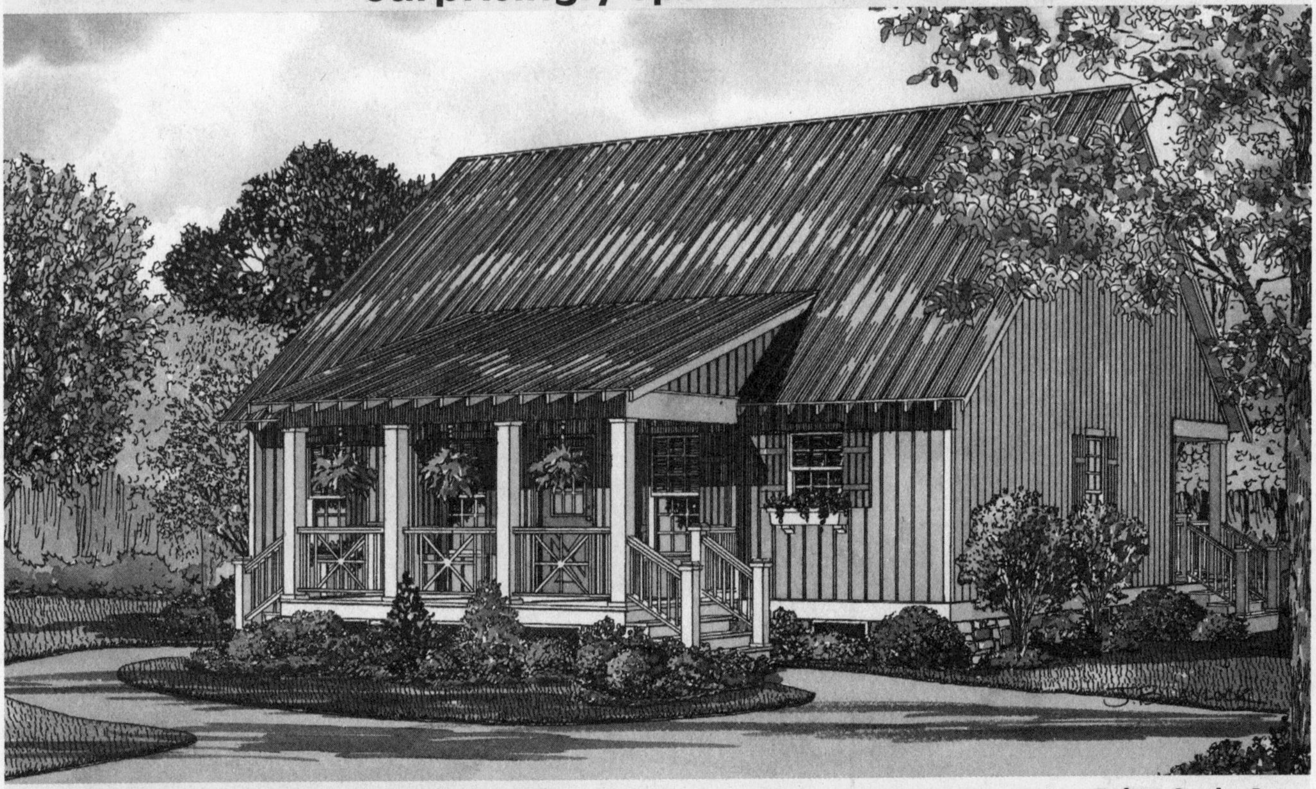

1,458 total square feet of living area

Price Code A

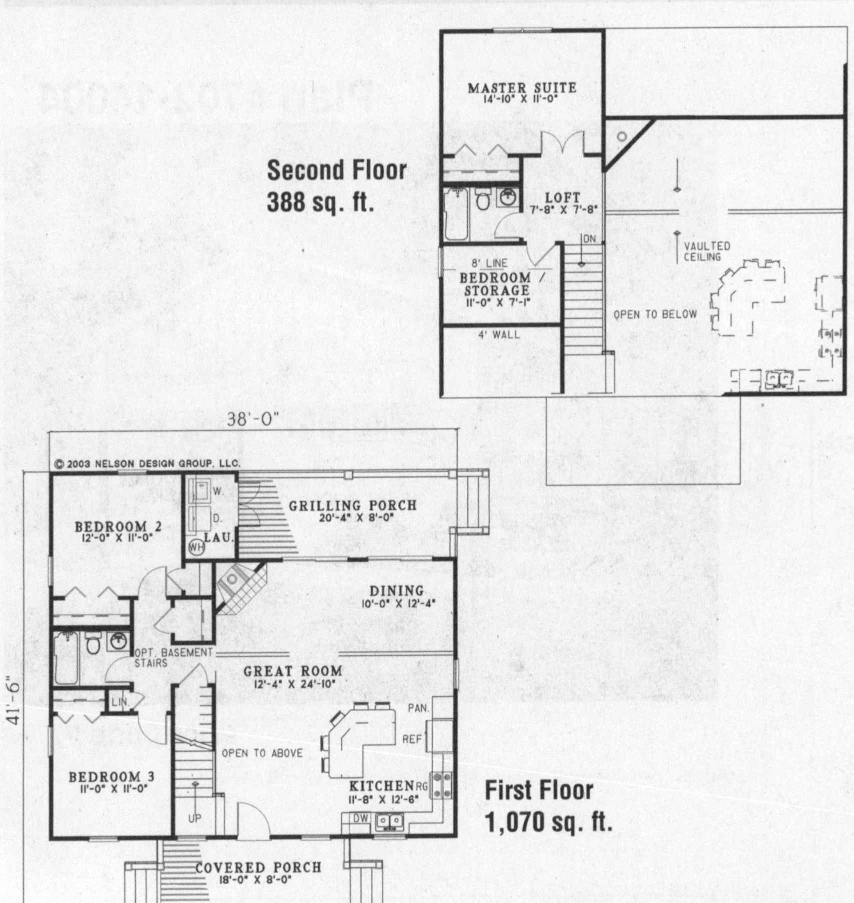
MASTER SUITE
14'-10" X 11'-0"
LOFT
7'-8" X 7'-8"
DN
VAULTED CEILING
8' LINE
BEDROOM / STORAGE
11'-0" X 7'-1"
4' WALL
OPEN TO BELOW
38'-0"
© 2003 NELSON DESIGN GROUP, LLC.
W.
D.
LAU.
WH
GRILLING PORCH
20'-4" X 8'-0"
BEDROOM 2
12'-0" X 11'-0"
DINING
10'-0" X 12'-4"
OPT. BASEMENT STAIRS
GREAT ROOM
12'-4" X 24'-10"
LIN.
PAN.
REF
41'-6"
OPEN TO ABOVE
BEDROOM 3
11'-0" X 11'-0"
KITCHEN
RG
11'-8" X 12'-6"
DW
UP
COVERED PORCH
18'-0" X 8'-0"
8" COLUMNS

Second Floor
388 sq. ft.

First Floor
1,070 sq. ft.

Special features

- Two-story great room makes this home feel open and airy
- Large island in kitchen for dining
- Master suite on second floor for privacy
- 4 bedrooms, 2 baths
- Crawl space or slab foundation, please specify when ordering

2-Car Garage With Loft Plan #702-14002

Special features

- Size - 28' x 24'
- Building height - 21'-0"
- Roof pitch - 12/12
- Ceiling height - 8'-0"
- Loft ceiling height - 7'-6"
- Two 9' x 7' overhead doors
- Complete list of materials
- Step-by-step instructions

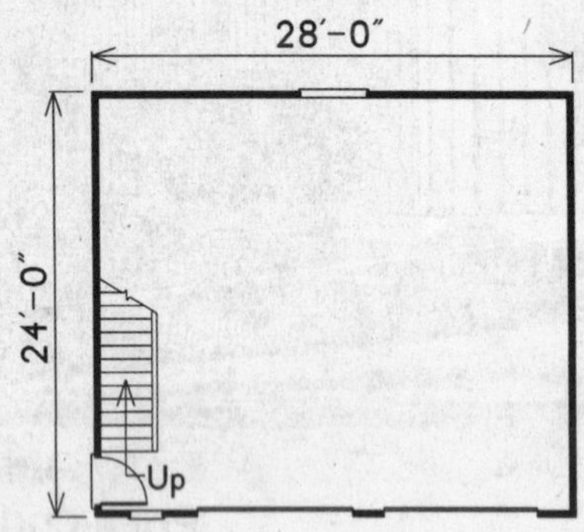

28'-0"
24'-0"
Up

Price Code P8

2-Car Garage Plan #702-14004

Special features

- Size - 24' x 24'
- Building height - 12'-6"
- Roof pitch - 4/12
- Ceiling height - 8'-0"
- Two 9' x 7' overhead doors
- Side-entry is efficient and well-designed
- Complete list of materials
- Step-by-step instructions

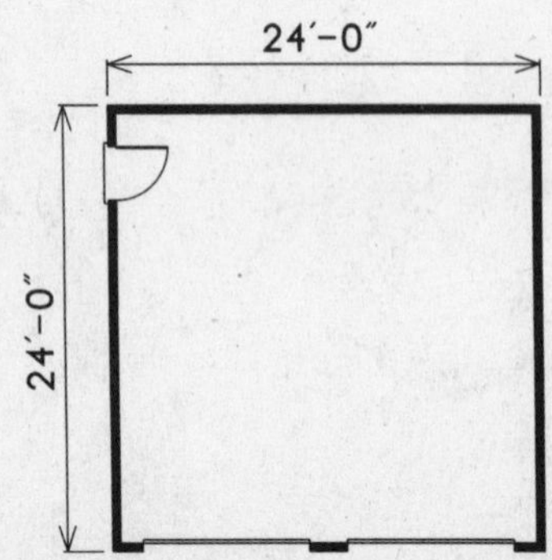

24'-0"
24'-0"

Price Code P7

TO ORDER BLUEPRINTS USE THE FORM ON PAGE 320 OR CALL TOLL-FREE 1-877-671-6036

3-Car Garage With Workshop

Plan #702-14021

Special features

- Size - 32' x 28'
- Building height - 13'-3"
- Roof pitch - 4/12
- Ceiling height - 8'-0"
- 9' x 7' and 16' x 7' overhead doors
- Handy workshop space for hobbies
- Side entry door provides easy access
- Complete list of materials
- Step-by-step instructions

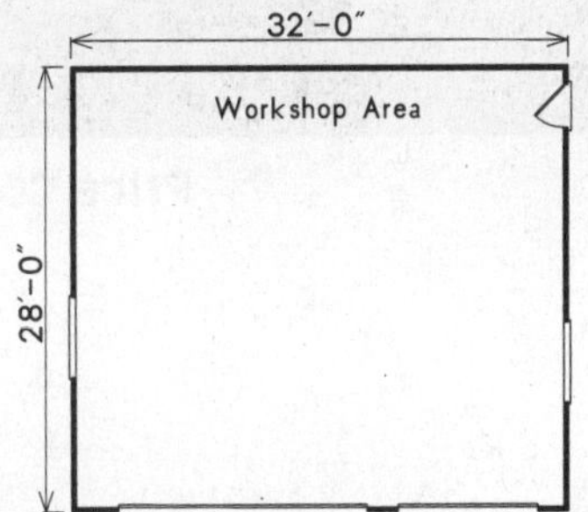
32'-0"
Workshop Area
28'-0"

Price Code P7

3-Car Garage/Workshop

Plan #702-14044

Special features

- Size - 24' x 36'
- Building height - 14'-6"
- Roof pitch - 4/12
- Ceiling height - 10'-0"
- Three 9' x 8' overhead doors
- Oversized for storage
- Ideal size for workshop or maintenance building
- Complete list of materials
- Step-by-step instructions

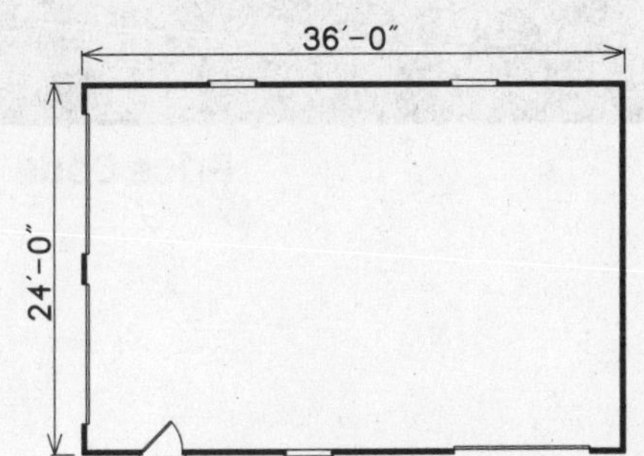
36'-0"
24'-0"

Price Code P7

2-Car Garage With Workshop And Loft   Plan #702-14005

Price Code P8

Special features

- Size - 32' x 24'
- Building height - 21'-0"
- Roof pitch - 12/12
- Ceiling height - 8'-0"
- Loft ceiling height - 7'-6"
- Two 9' x 7' overhead doors
- Plenty of storage space for workshop or hobby center
- Complete list of materials
- Step-by-step instructions

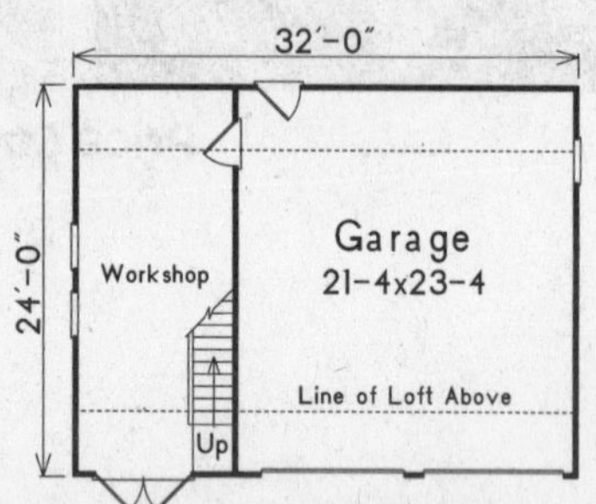
32'-0"
24'-0"
Workshop
Garage
21-4x23-4
Line of Loft Above
Up

1-Car Garage With Four Sizes   Plan #702-14030

Price Code P6

Special features

- Four popular sizes -

  14' x 22'   14' x 24'
  16' x 22'   16' x 24'
- Building height - 11'-2"
- Roof pitch - 4/12
- Ceiling height - 8'-0"
- 9' x 7' overhead door
- Sturdy, attractive design
- Complete list of materials
- Step-by-step instructions

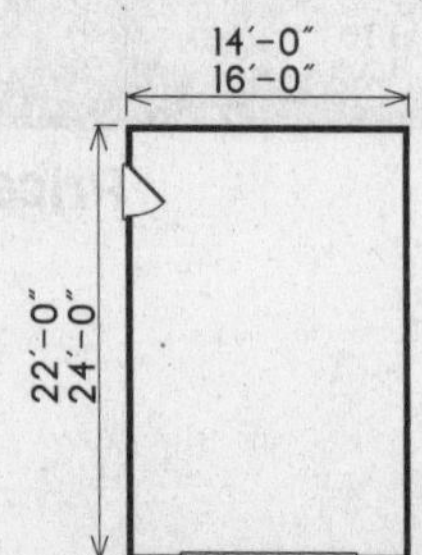
14'-0"
16'-0"
22'-0"
24'-0"

1-Car Garage With Gambrel Roof

Plan #702-14045

Special features

- Size - 16' x 24'
- Building height - 18'-9"
- Roof pitch - 12/6, 6/12
- Ceiling height - 8'-0"
- Loft ceiling height - 6'-7"
- 9' x 7' overhead door
- Ideal loft perfect for workshop or storage area
- Handy side door
- Complete list of materials
- Step-by-step instructions

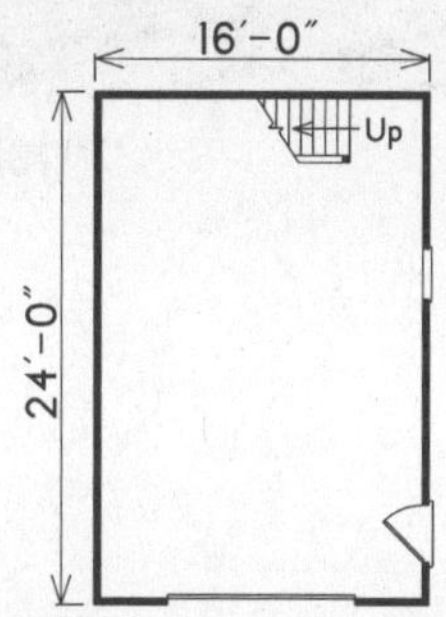
16'-0"
Up
24'-0"

Price Code P8

2-Car Garage With Gambrel Roof

Plan #702-14001

Special features

- Size - 22' x 26'
- Building height - 20'-7"
- Roof pitch - 7/12, 12/7
- Ceiling height - 8'-0"
- Loft ceiling height - 7'-4"
- Two 9' x 7' overhead doors
- Complete list of materials
- Step-by-step instructions

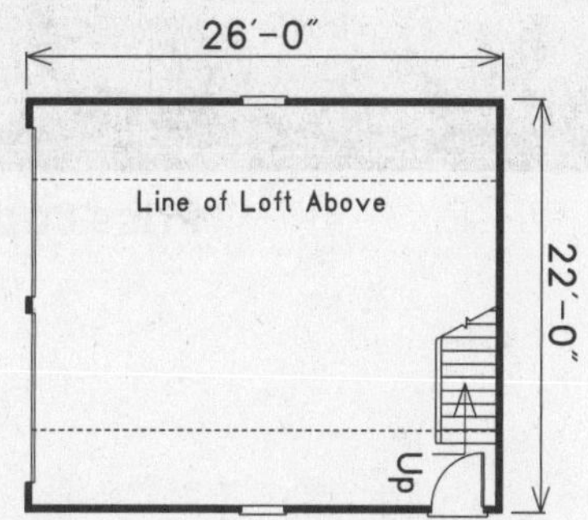
26'-0"
Line of Loft Above
22'-0"
Up

Price Code P8

2-Car Garage With Storage

Plan #702-14018

Special features

- Size - 24' x 26'
- Building height - 12'-8"
- Roof pitch - 4/12
- Ceiling height - 8'-0"
- 16' x 7' overhead door
- Plenty of storage space for yard equipment
- Convenient side entry
- Complete list of materials
- Step-by-step instructions

Price Code P7

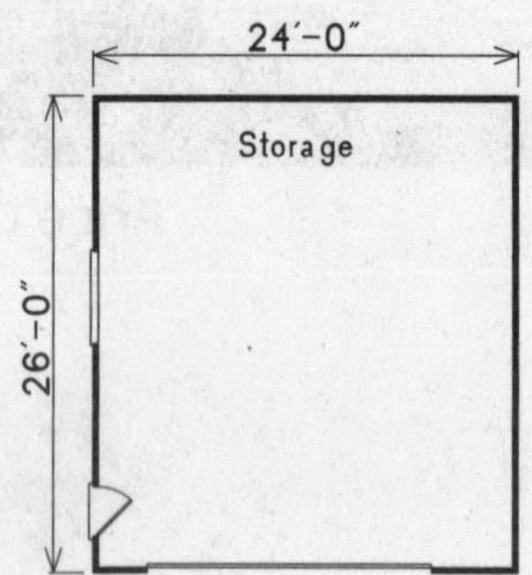
24'-0"
Storage
26'-0"

2-Car Garage With Storage And Loft

Plan #702-14003

Special features

- Size - 32' x 24'
- Building height - 20'-2"
- Roof pitch - 10/12
- Ceiling height - 9'-8"
- Workshop and loft ceiling height - 8'-0"
- 16' x 7' overhead door, 6'-0" x 6'-8" double-door
- Convenient loft above workshop for work space or storage
- Complete list of materials
- Step-by-step instructions

Price Code P8

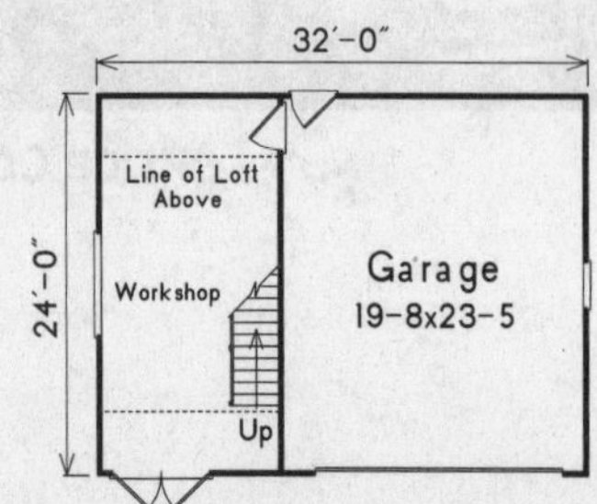
32'-0"
Line of Loft Above
Workshop
Garage
19-8x23-5
24'-0"
Up

2-Car Garage With RV/Boat Storage Plan #702-14506

Special features

- Size - 40' x 40'
- Building height - 21'-0"
- Roof pitch - 6/12
- Ceiling height - 16'-0" @ RV Storage
- Ceiling height - 10'-0" @ Garage
- 12' x 14' and 16' x 8' overhead doors
- Excellent garage for large equipment, RV or boat storage
- Complete list of materials

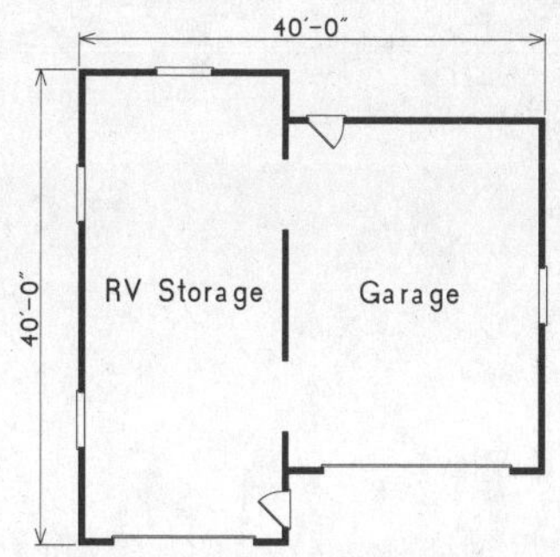
40'-0"
40'-0"
RV Storage
Garage

Price Code P8

3-Car Garage With Storage Plan #702-14510

Special features

- Size - 38' x 30'
- Building height - 22'-0"
- Roof pitch - 10/12
- Ceiling height - 9'-0"
- Three 9' x 8' overhead doors
- Attractive styling fits well with most every home
- Complete list of materials

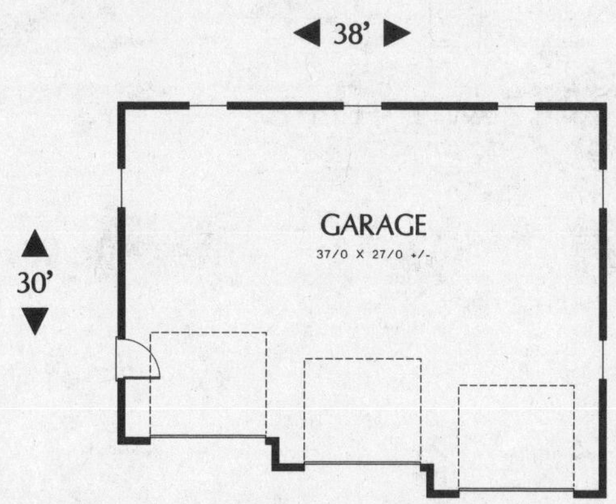
38'
30'
GARAGE
37/0 X 27/0 +/-

Price Code P10

2-Car Garage With Workshop — Plan #702-14529

Special features

- Size - 32' x 20'
- Building height - 13'-0"
- Ceiling height - 8'-0"
- Roof pitch - 5/12
- Workshop ideal for storage, gardening or woodworking hobbies
- Outdoor entrance provides quick access
- Complete list of materials

Price Code P9

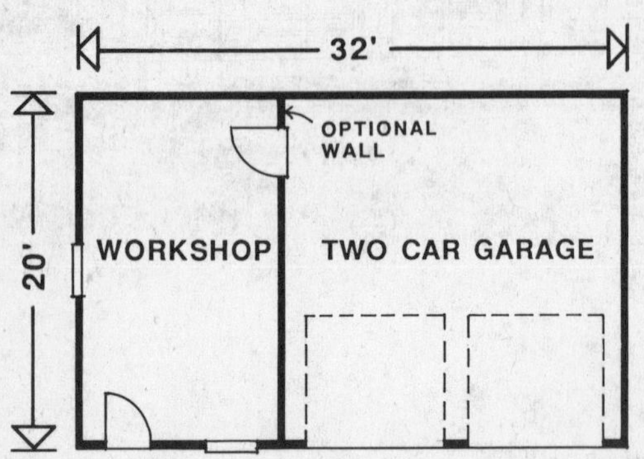
32'
20'
OPTIONAL WALL
WORKSHOP
TWO CAR GARAGE

3-Car Garage — Plan #702-14521

Special features

- Size - 36' x 28'
- Building height - 17'-0"
- Roof pitch - 4/12
- Ceiling height - 9'-0"
- 9' x 8' overhead door
- 16' x 8' overhead door
- Versatile style looks good with many different styles of homes
- Complete list of materials

Price Code P8

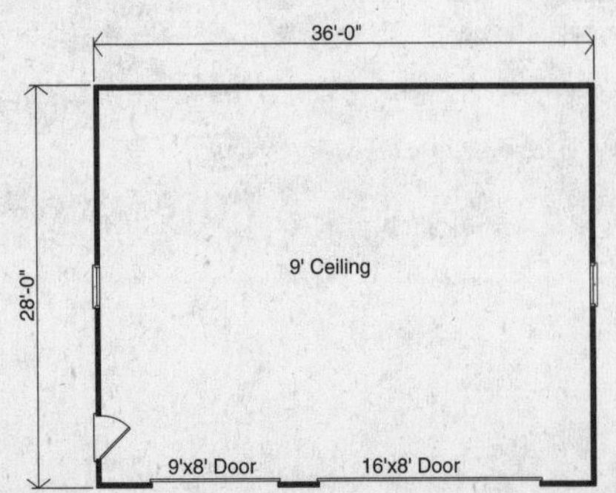
36'-0"
28'-0"
9' Ceiling
9'x8' Door
16'x8' Door

5-Car Garage — Plan #702-14527

Special features

- Size - 58' x 30'
- Building height - 15'-0"
- Roof pitch - 4/12
- Ceiling height - 9'-0"
- Five 9' x 7' overhead doors
- Two convenient side doors allow for easy access
- Complete list of materials

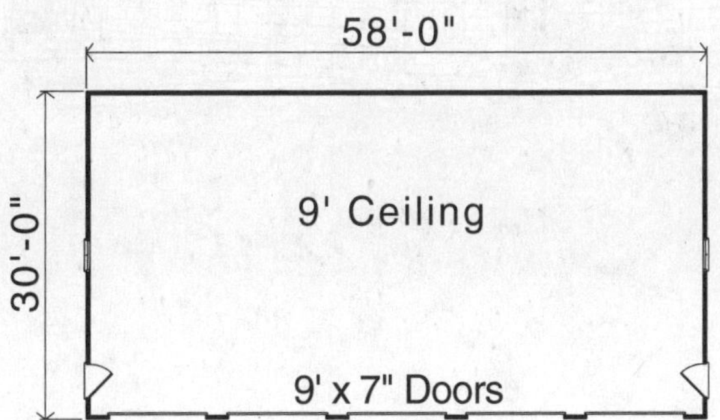
58'-0"
30'-0"
9' Ceiling
9' x 7" Doors

Price Code P9

2-Car Garage With Loft — Plan #702-14016

Special features

- Size - 26' x 24'
- Building height - 20'-0"
- Roof pitch - 6/12
- Ceiling height - 8'-0"
- Two 9' x 7' overhead doors
- Loft provides extra storage area or workshop space
- Clerestory windows brighten inside
- Complete list of materials
- Step-by-step instructions

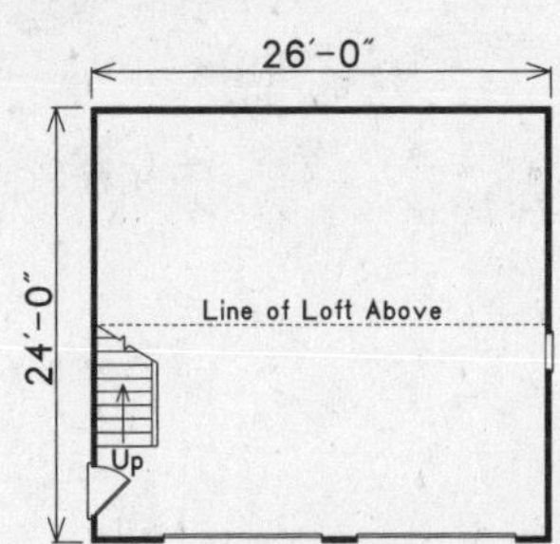
26'-0"
24'-0"
Line of Loft Above
Up

Price Code P8

TO ORDER BLUEPRINTS USE THE FORM ON PAGE 320 OR CALL TOLL-FREE 1-877-671-6036

2-Car Garage with Boat Storage Plan #702-14511

Special features

- Size - 36' x 28'
- Building height - 15'-0"
- Roof pitch - 5/12
- Ceiling height - 8'-0"
- Attractive gable roof style works well with many home styles
- Easily accommodates boat or other recreational vehicles
- Complete list of materials

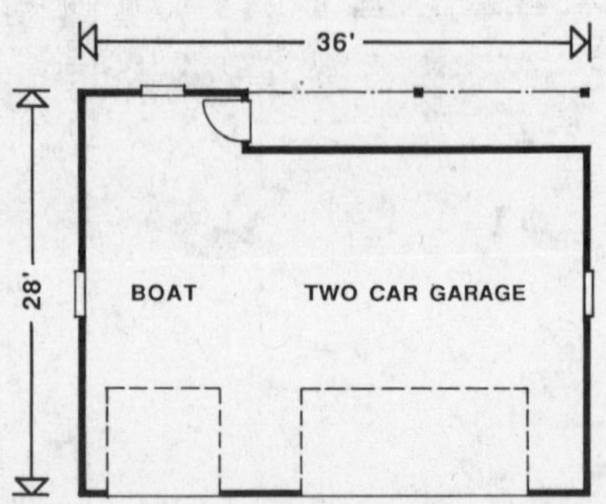
36'
28'
BOAT
TWO CAR GARAGE

Price Code P8

2-Car Garage With Storage Plan #702-14508

Special features

- Size - 25' x 26'
- Building height - 21'-0"
- Roof pitch - 10/12
- Ceiling height - 8'-0"
- Two 9' x 7' overhead doors
- Attractive styling with double gabled front facade and decorative window
- Complete list of materials

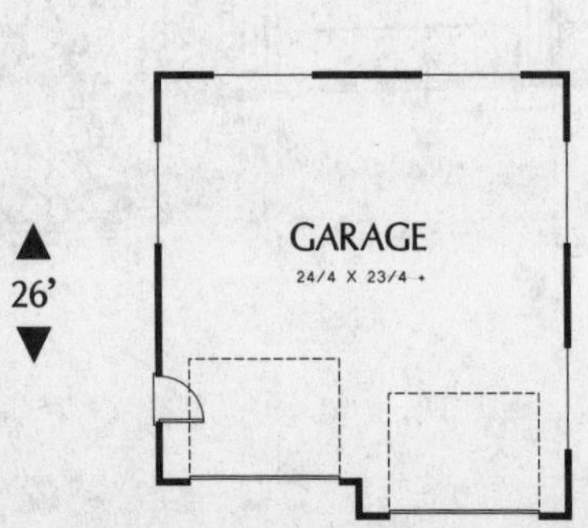
25'
26'
GARAGE
24/4 X 23/4

Price Code P10

The Family
Handyman

3-Car Garage — Plan #702-14520

Special features

- Size - 32' x 22'
- Building height - 13'-6"
- Ceiling height - 8'-0"
- Roof pitch - 5/12
- Three 9' x 7' Overhead doors
- Optional side entry door
- Complete list of windows

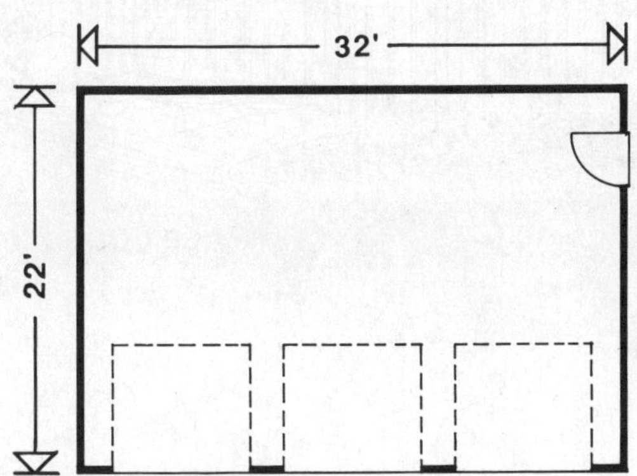
32'
22'

Price Code P8

2-Car Garage — Plan #702-14524

Special features

- Size - 24' x 30'
- Building height - 15'-0"
- Roof pitch - 4/12
- Ceiling height - 9'-0"
- Two 9' x 7' overhead doors
- Side entry and window brighten interior
- Complete list of materials

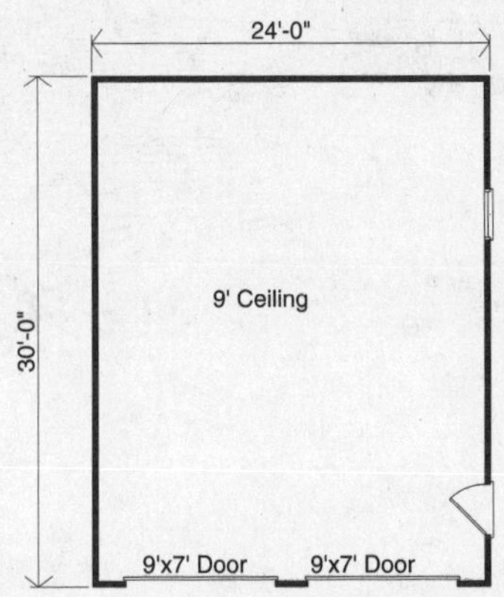
24'-0"
9' Ceiling
30'-0"
9'x7' Door
9'x7' Door

Price Code P8

TO ORDER BLUEPRINTS USE THE FORM ON PAGE 320 OR CALL TOLL-FREE 1-877-671-6036

Yard Barn With Loft Storage

Plan #702-12022

Special features

- Size - 10' wide x 12' deep
- Wood floor on 4x4 runners
- Height floor to peak - 10'-7"
- Ceiling height - 6'-11"
- 6'-0" x 6'-2" double-door for easy access
- Loft provides additional storage area
- Attractive styling suitable for yard
- Complete list of materials
- Step-by-step instructions

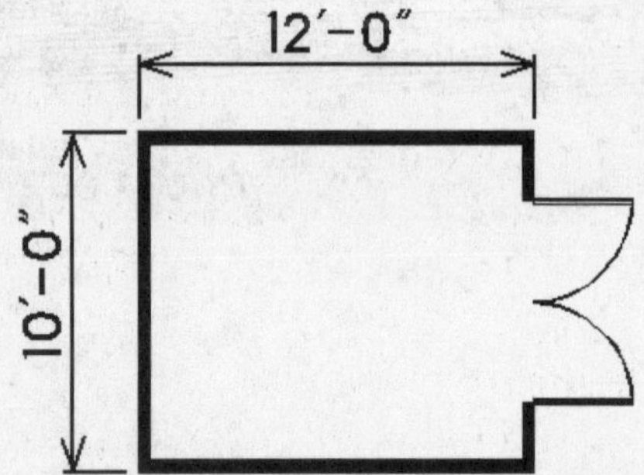
12'-0"
10'-0"

Price Code P5

Garden Shed With Porch

Plan #702-12504

Special features

- Size - 8' x 16'
- Building height -11'-16"
- Ceiling height - 8'-0"
- Roof pitch - 7/12
- Covered front porch
- Handy built-in work bench
- Complete list of materials
- Plans are printed on 8 1/2" x 11" pages

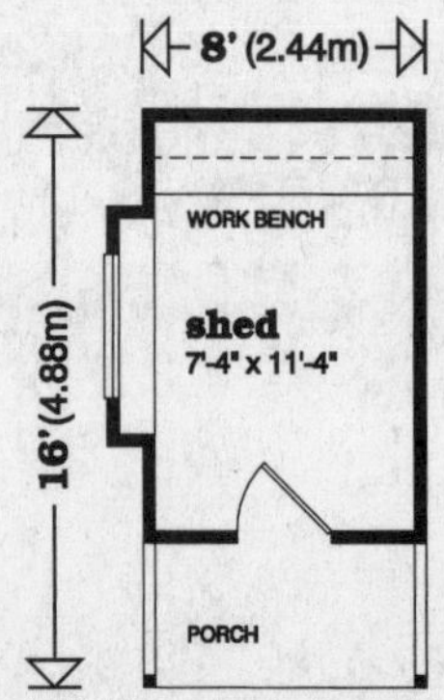
8' (2.44m)
WORK BENCH
shed
7'-4" x 11'-4"
16' (4.88m)
PORCH

Price Code P4

The Family
Handyman

Garden Shed

Plan #702-12025

Special features

- Size - 10' wide x 10' deep
- Wood floor on 4x4 runners
- Height floor to peak - 11'-3 1/2"
- Left wall height - 8'-0"
- Wonderful complement to any backyard
- Perfect space for lawn equipment or plants and flowers
- Plenty of windows for gardening year-round
- Complete list of materials
- Step-by-step instructions

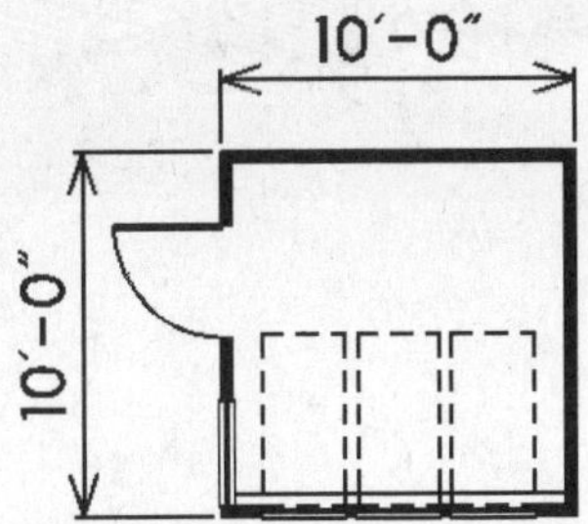
10'-0"
10'-0"

Price Code P5

Barn Storage Sheds With Loft

Plan #702-12002

Special features

- Three popular sizes -
  12' wide x 12' deep
  12' wide x 16' deep
  12' wide x 20' deep
- Wood floor on concrete pier foundation or concrete floor
- Height floor to peak - 12'-10"
- Ceiling height - 7'-4"
- 4'-0" x 6'-8" double-door for easy access
- Complete list of materials
- Step-by-step instructions

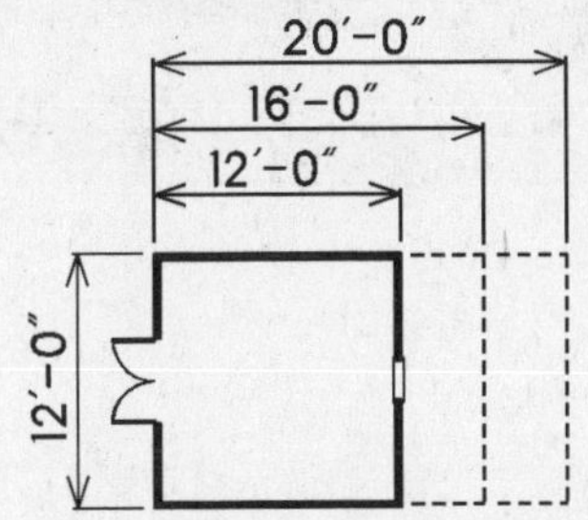
20'-0"
16'-0"
12'-0"
12'-0"

Price Code P5

Yard Barns

Plan #702-12003

Special features

- Three popular sizes -
  10' wide x 12' deep
  10' wide x 16' deep
  10' wide x 20' deep
- Wood floor on 4x4 runners
- Height floor to peak - 8'-4 1/2"
- Ceiling height - 6'-4"
- 4'-0" x 6'-4" double-door for easy access
- Ample storage area for lawn equipment
- Complete list of materials
- Step-by-step instructions

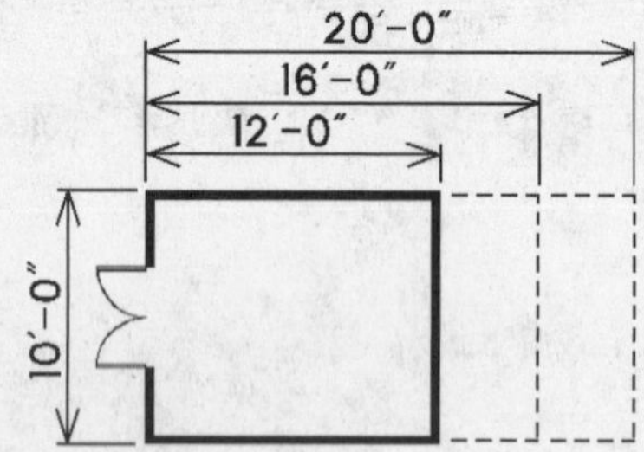
20'-0"
16'-0"
12'-0"
10'-0"

Price Code P5

Gable Storage Sheds

Plan #702-12005

Special features

- Three popular sizes -
  10' wide x 12' deep
  10' wide x 16' deep
  10' wide x 20' deep
- Wood floor on 4 x 4 runners
- Height floor to peak - 8'-8 1/2"
- Ceiling height - 7'-0"
- 4'-0" x 6'-4" double-door for easy access
- Complete list of materials
- Step-by-step instructions

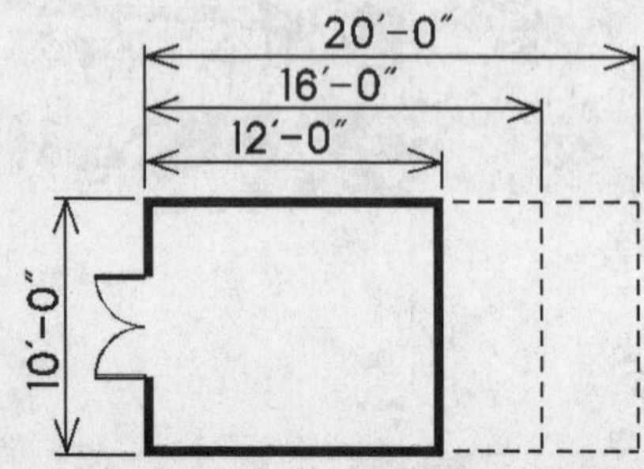
20'-0"
16'-0"
12'-0"
10'-0"

Price Code P5

Convenience Shed

Plan #702-12007

Special features

- Size - 16' wide x 12' deep
- Concrete floor
- Height floor to peak - 12'-4 1/2"
- Ceiling height - 8'-0"
- 8'-0" x 7'-0" overhead door
- Ideal for lawn equipment or small boat storage
- Oversized windows brighten interior
- Complete list of materials
- Step-by-step instructions

Price Code P6

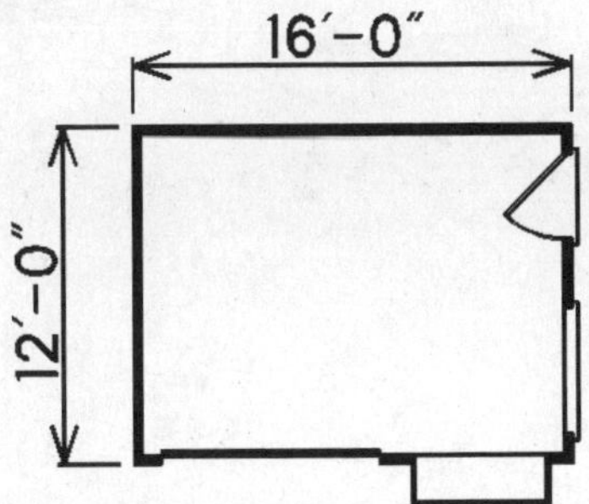
16'-0"
12'-0"

Garden Sheds With Clerestory

Plan #702-12017

Special features

- Three popular sizes -
  10' wide x 10' deep
  12' wide x 10' deep
  14' wide x 10' deep
- Wood floor on 4 x 6 runners
- Height floor to peak - 10'-11"
- Rear wall height - 7'-3"
- 5'-0" x 6'-9" double-door for easy access
- Clerestory windows for added light
- Complete list of materials
- Step-by-step instructions

Price Code P5

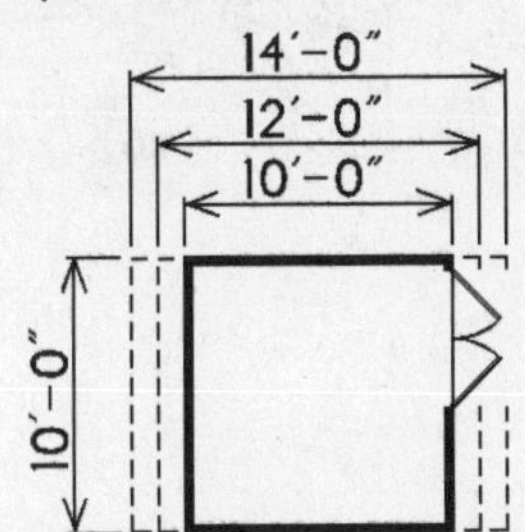
14'-0"
12'-0"
10'-0"
10'-0"

Storage Shed

Plan #702-12518

Price Code P4

Special features

- Size 11'-11" x 8'-0"
- Building height - 8'-6"
- Ceiling height - 6'-6"
- Roof pitch - 4/12
- Wood floor on concrete piers or concrete floor
- Complements traditional home exterior
- Could easily be converted to a children's playhouse
- Complete list of materials
- Plans are printed on 8 1/2" x 11" pages

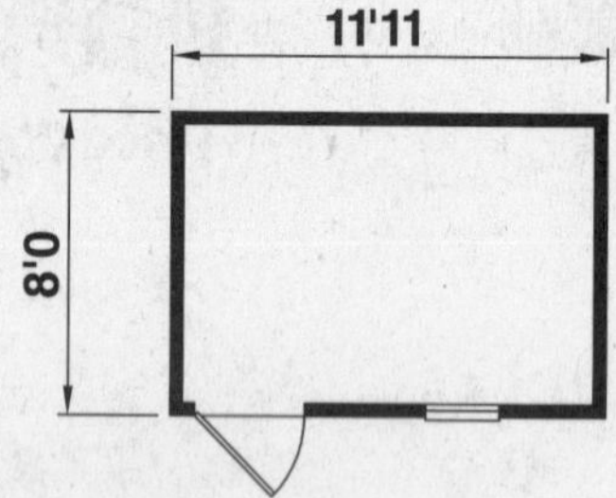
11'11
8'0

Pool Cabana

Plan #702-12507

Price Code P6

Special features

- Size – 12' x 10'
- Building height - 11'-6"
- Ceiling height - 8'-0"
- Roof pitch - 7/12
- Slab foundation
- Charming cottage-style has convenient bath, towel storage and a dressing area
- Complete list of materials
- Plans are printed on 8 1/2" x 11" pages

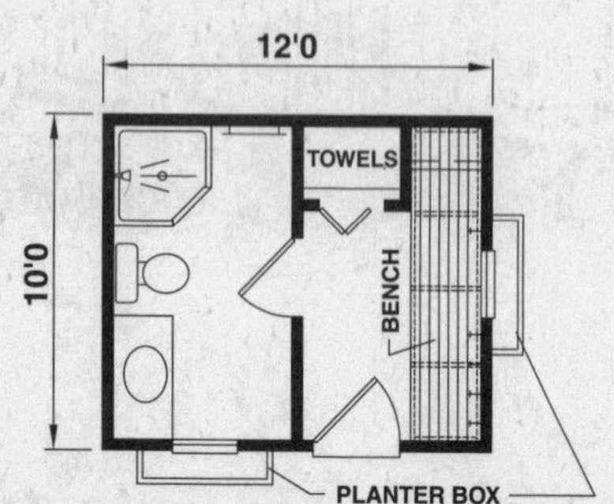
12'0
10'0
TOWELS
BENCH
PLANTER BOX

Barn Storage Sheds

Plan #702-12009

Special features

- Three popular sizes -
  12' wide x 8' deep
  12' wide x 12' deep
  12' wide x 16' deep
- Wood floor on concrete pier foundation or concrete floor
- Height floor to peak - 9'-10"
- Ceiling height - 7'-10"
- 5'-6" x 6'-8" double-door for easy access
- Complete list of materials
- Step-by-step instructions

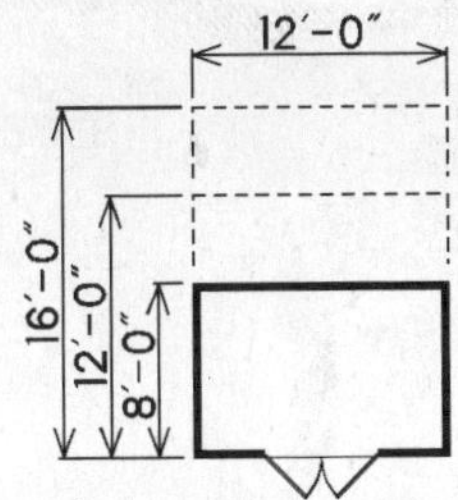
12'-0"
16'-0"
12'-0"
8'-0"

Price Code P5

Salt Box Storage Shed

Plan #702-12021

Special features

- Size - 10' wide x 8' deep
- Wood floor on 4x4 runners
- Height floor to peak - 9'-6"
- Front wall height - 8'-0"
- 4'-0" x 6'-8" double-door for easy access
- Window adds light to space
- Complete list of materials
- Step-by-step instructions

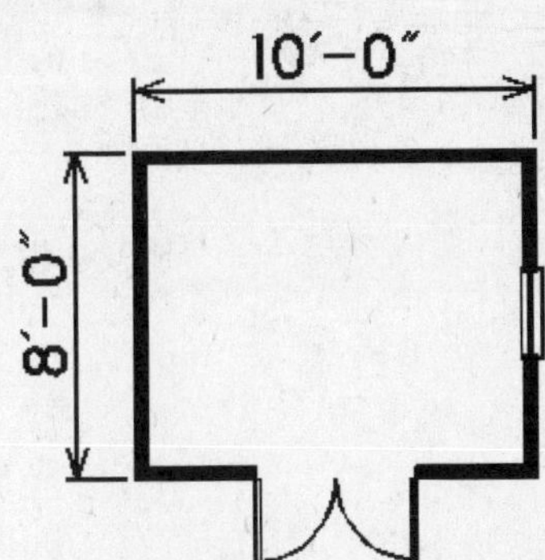
10'-0"
8'-0"

Price Code P5

Storage Shed

Plan #702-12516

Special features

- Size - 7'-11" x 8'-0"
- Building height - 8'-6"
- Ceiling height - 6'-6"
- Roof pitch - 4/12
- Ample storage space for lawn or garden equipment
- Complete list of materials
- Plans are printed on 8 1/2" x 11" pages

Price Code P4

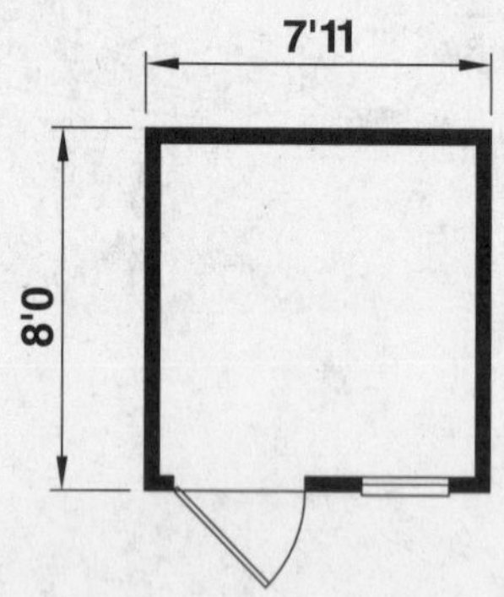
7'11
8'0

Saltbox Storage Shed

Plan #702-12521

Special features

- Size – 19'-11" x 12'-0"
- Building height - 9'-0"
- Ceiling height - 6'-6"
- Wood floor on concrete piers or concrete floor
- Complete list of materials
- Plans are printed on 8 1/2" x 11" pages

Price Code P4

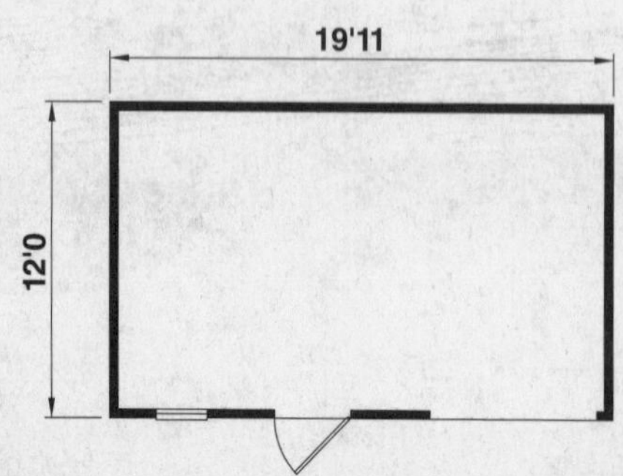
19'11
12'0

TO ORDER BLUEPRINTS USE THE FORM ON PAGE 320 OR CALL TOLL-FREE 1-877-671-6036

View thousands more home plans online at www.familyhandyman.com/homeplans

Slant Roof Shed — Plan #702-12520

Special features

- Size - 7'-11" x 6'-0"
- Building height - 8'-0"
- Front wall height - 7'-6"
- Roof pitch - 4/12
- Wood floor on concrete piers or concrete floor
- Wide double doors allow for easy storage
- Complete list of materials
- Plans are printed on 8 1/2" x 11" pages

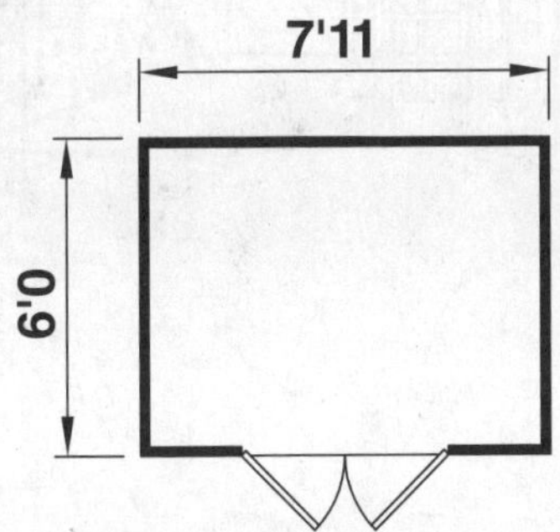
7'11
6'0

Price Code P4

Barn Storage Shed With Overhead Door — Plan #702-12023

Special features

- Size - 12' wide x 16' deep
- Concrete floor
- Height floor to peak - 12'-5"
- Ceiling height - 8'-0"
- 8'-0" x 7'-0" overhead door for easy entry with large equipment
- Side windows adds light to interior
- Complete list of materials
- Step-by-step instructions

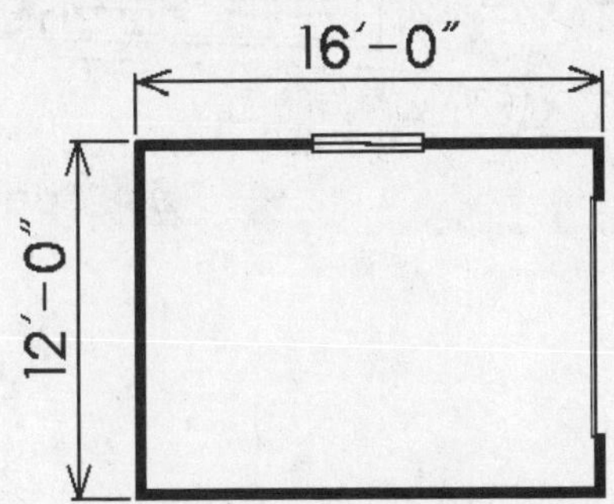
16'-0"
12'-0"

Price Code P5

Storage Shed With Playhouse Loft — Plan #702-12016

Special features

- Size - 12' wide x 12' deep with 2'-8" deep balcony
- Wood floor on concrete piers or concrete floor
- Height floor to peak - 14'-1"
- Ceiling height - 7'-4"
- 4'-0" x 6'-10" door
- Loft above can be used as playhouse for children
- Loft features ladder for easy access
- Complete list of materials
- Step-by-step instructions

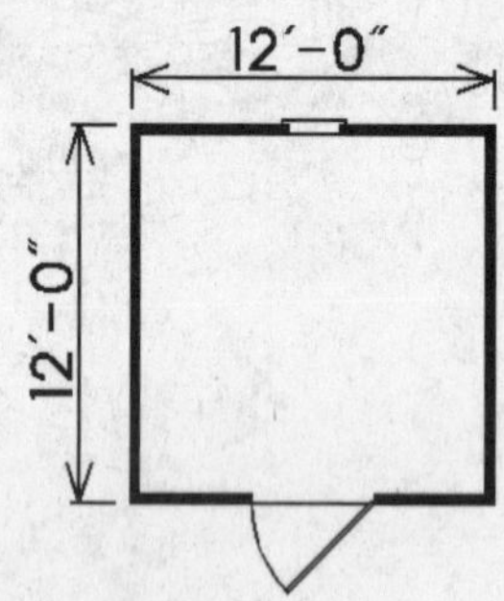
12'-0"
12'-0"

Price Code P5

Storage Shed With Log Bin — Plan #702-12018

Special features

- Size - 10' wide x 6' deep
- Wood floor on gravel base
- Height floor to peak - 9'-7"
- Ceiling height - 6'-7"
- 5'-0" x 6'-9" double-door for easy access
- Log storage area - 2'-6" x 6'-0"
- Complete list of materials
- Step-by-step instructions

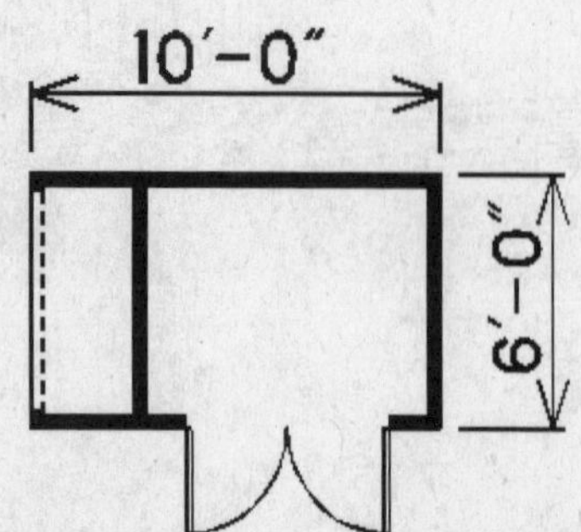
10'-0"
6'-0"

Price Code P5

Mini Barns

Plan #702-12026

Price Code P5

Special features

- Four popular sizes -
  8' wide x 8' deep
  8' wide x 10' deep
  8' wide x 12' deep
  8' wide x 16' deep
- Wood floor on 4 x 4 runners
- Height floor to peak - 7'-6"
- Ceiling height - 6'-0"
- 4'-0" x 6'-0" double-door for easy access
- Storage of lawn and garden equipment
- Attractive styling for any backyard
- Complete list of materials
- Step-by-step instructions

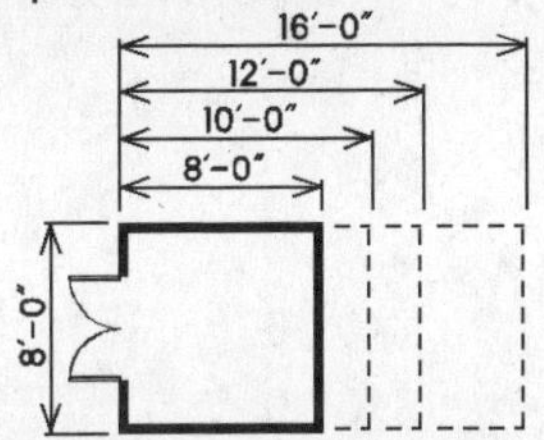
16'-0"
12'-0"
10'-0"
8'-0"
8'-0"

Gable Storage Sheds

Plan #702-12004

Price Code P5

Special features

- Four popular sizes -
  8' wide x 8' deep
  8' wide x 10' deep
  8' wide x 12' deep
  8' wide x 16' deep
- Wood floor on 4 x 4 runners
- Height floor to peak - 8'-4 1/2"
- Ceiling height - 7'-0"
- 4'-0" x 6'-5" double-door for easy access
- Economical and easy to build shed
- Complete list of materials
- Step-by-step instructions

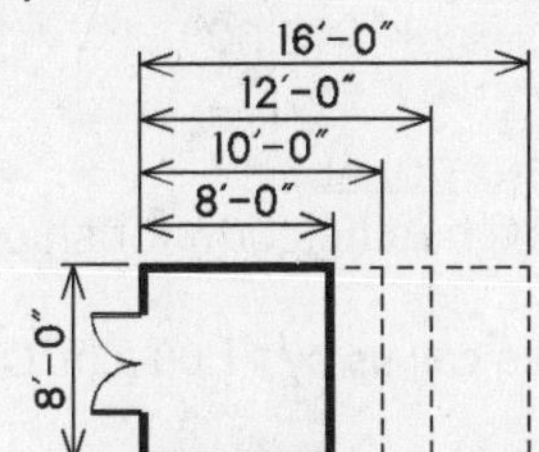
16'-0"
12'-0"
10'-0"
8'-0"
8'-0"

How To Order

For fastest service, Call Toll-Free
1-877-671-6036
24 hours a day

Three Easy Ways To Order

1. CALL toll free 1-877-671-6036 for credit card orders. MasterCard, Visa, Discover and American Express are accepted.
2. FAX your order to 1-314-770-2226.
3. MAIL the Order Form to:

HDA, Inc.
4390 Green Ash Drive
St. Louis, MO 63045

QUESTIONS?
Call Our Customer Service Number
1-877-671-6036

ORDER FORM

Please send me -

PLAN NUMBER **702BT** - ____________

PRICE CODE ______ (see Plan Page)

Reproducible Masters (see chart at right) $ ______
Initial Set of Plans $ ______
Additional Plan Sets (see chart at right)
____ (Qty) at $ ______ each $ ______

SUBTOTAL $ ______
SALES TAX (MO residents add 7%) $ ______
☐ Shipping / Handling (see chart at right) $ ______
(each additional set add $2.00 to shipping charges)

TOTAL ENCLOSED (US funds only) $ ______

☐ Enclosed is my check or money order payable to HDA, Inc. (Sorry, no COD's)

I hereby authorize HDA, Inc. to charge this purchase to my credit card account (check one):

☐ MasterCard ☐ VISA ☐ DISCOVER NOVUS ☐ AMERICAN EXPRESS Cards

Credit Card number ____________________

Expiration date ____________________

Signature ____________________

Name ____________________
(Please print or type)

Street Address ____________________
(Please **do not** use PO Box)

City ____________________

State ________ Zip ____________

Daytime phone number (____) - ____________

Thank you for your order!

IMPORTANT INFORMATION TO KNOW BEFORE YOU ORDER

◆ **Exchange Policies -** Since blueprints are printed in response to your order, we cannot honor requests for refunds. However, if for some reason you find that the plan you have purchased does not meet your requirements, you may exchange that plan for another plan in our collection. At the time of the exchange, you will be charged a processing fee of 25% of your original plan package price, plus the difference in price between the plan packages (if applicable) and the cost to ship the new plans to you.

Please note: Reproducible drawings can only be exchanged if the package is unopened, and exchanges are allowed only within 90 days of purchase.

◆ **Building Codes & Requirements -** At the time the construction drawings were prepared, every effort was made to ensure that these plans and specifications meet nationally recognized codes. Our plans conform to most national building codes. Because building codes vary from area to area, some drawing modifications and/or the assistance of a professional designer or architect may be necessary to comply with your local codes or to accommodate specific building site conditions. We advise you to consult with your local building official for information regarding codes governing your area.

BLUEPRINT PRICE SCHEDULE

Price Code	1-Set	Additional Sets	Reproducible Masters
P4	$20.00	$10.00	$70.00
P5	$25.00	$10.00	$75.00
P6	$30.00	$10.00	$80.00
P7	$50.00	$10.00	$100.00
P8	$75.00	$10.00	$125.00
P9	$125.00	$20.00	$200.00
P10	$150.00	$20.00	$225.00
P11	$175.00	$20.00	$250.00
P12	$200.00	$20.00	$275.00
P13	$225.00	$45.00	$300.00

Plan prices guaranteed through June 30, 2004.
Please note that plans are not refundable.

SHIPPING & HANDLING CHARGES

EACH ADDITIONAL SET ADD $2.00 TO SHIPPING CHARGES

U.S. SHIPPING
Regular *(allow 7-10 business days)* $5.95
Priority *(allow 3-5 business days)* $15.00
Express* *(allow 1-2 business days)* $25.00

CANADA SHIPPING
Standard *(allow 8-12 business days)* $15.00
Express* *(allow 3-5 business days)* $40.00

OVERSEAS SHIPPING/INTERNATIONAL
Call, fax, or e-mail (plans@hdainc.com) for shipping costs.

* For express delivery please call us by 11:00 a.m. CST